Abuse of Platform Power

Leveraging Conduct in Digital Markets Under EU Competition Law and Beyond

Friso Bostoen

Introduction by Catherine Prieto
Foreword by Wouter Devroe

Concurrences, 2023

106 West 32nd Street, Suite 144 New York, NY, 10001, USA
www.concurrences.com
book@concurrences.com

First Printing, July 2023
978-1-954750-11-1 (Paperback)

Library of Congress Control Number: 2023930020

Cover Design : Yves Buliard, www.yvesbuliard.fr
Book Design and Layout implementation: Nord Compo

Concurrences Books

Tributes

Eleanor M. Fox – Antitrust Ambassador to the World, *2021*

Herbert Hovenkamp – The Dean of American Antitrust Law, *2021*

Frédéric Jenny – Standing Up for Convergence and Relevance in Antitrust, (Vol. I & II), *2019 & 2021*

Albert Foer – A Consumer Voice in the Antitrust Arena, *2020*

Richard Whish – Taking Competition Law Outside the Box, *2020*

Douglas H. Ginsburg – An Antitrust Professor on the Bench (Vol. I & II), *2018 & 2020*

Wang Xiaoye – The Pioneer of Competition Law in China, *A. Emch, W. Ng (eds.), 2019*

Ian S. Forrester – A Scot without Borders (Vol. I & II), *A. Komninos (eds.), 2015*

William E. Kovacic – An Antitrust Tribute (Vol. I & II), *2013 & 2014*

Practical Books

Global Dictionary of Competition Law, *D. Healey, W. Kovacic, P. Trevisan, R. Whish, 2023*

Antitrust in Life Sciences, *M. Cowie, G. Gordon M. Thill-Tayara, 2023*

Antitrust and the Digital Economy, *Y. Katsoulacos (ed.), 2023 (in collaboration with Competition & Regulation European Summer School and Conference)*

State Aid & the Energy Transition, *D. Buschle, L. Hancher, M.-T. Richter-Kuhnert (eds.), 2023 (in collaboration with the Energy Community)*

State Aid & National Enforcement, *J. Derenne, D. Jouve, C. Lemaire, F. Martucci (eds.), 2023*

Competition Law Treatment of Joint Ventures, *B. Bleicher, N. Campbell, A. Hamilton, N. Hukkinen, A. Khan, A. Mordaunt (eds.), 2022 (in collaboration with the IBA)*

Information Exchange & Related Risks, *Z. Marosi, M. Soares (eds.), 2022 (in collaboration with the IBA)*

Rulemaking Authority of the US Federal Trade Commission, *D. Crane (ed.), 2022*

The International Competition Network at Twenty, *D. Anderson & P. Lugard (eds.), 2022*

Competition Case Law Digest – 5th Edition, *F. Jenny, N. Charbit (eds.), 2022*

Competition Inspections in 21 Jurisdictions – A Practitioner's Guide, *N. Jalabert-Doury (ed.), 2022*

Perspectives on Antitrust Compliance, *A. Riley, A. Stephan, A. Tubbs (eds.), 2022 (in collaboration with the ICC)*

Turkish Competition Law, *G. Gürkaynak, 2021*

Competition Law – Climate Change & Environmental Sustainability, *S. Holmes, D. Middelschulte, M. Snoep (eds.), 2021*

Merger Control in Latin America – A Jurisdictional Guide, *P. Burnier da Silveira, P. Sittenfeld (eds.), 2020*

Competition Inspections under EU Law – A Practitioner's Guide, *N. Jalabert-Doury, 2020*

Gun Jumping in Merger Control – A Jurisdictional Guide, *C. Hatton, Y. Comtois, A. Hamilton (eds.), 2019 (in collaboration with the IBA)*

Choice – A New Standard for Competition Analysis? *P. Nihoul (ed.), 2016*

PhD Theses

Reform of Chinese State-Owned Enterprises, *X. Bai, 2023*

Bargaining Power, Competition and Innovation, *M. Guignard, 2023*

Competition & Regulation in Network Industries – Essays in Industrial Organization, *J-M. Zogheib, 2021*

The Role of Media Pluralism in the Enforcement of EU Competition Law, *K. Bania, 2019*

Buyer Power, *I. Herrera Anchustegui, 2017*

General Interest

Women and Antitrust – Voices from the Field (Vol I & II), *E. Kurgonaite & K. Nordlander, 2020*

Conference Proceedings

Antitrust in Emerging and Developing Countries – (Vol I & II), *E. Fox, H. First, 2015 & 2016*

Global Antitrust Law – Current Issues in Antitrust Law and Economics, *D. Ginsburg, J. Wright, (eds.) 2015*

Competition Law on the Global Stage – David Gerber's Global Competition Law in Perspective, *D. Gerber, 2014*

e-Book versions available for **Concurrences+** subscribers

DISCLAIMER

This book is based on a Ph.D. thesis I submitted in January 2021 and defended in May 2021 at the University of Leuven (KU Leuven). Wouter Devroe and Peggy Valcke (both KU Leuven) served as supervisors; the supervisory committee was completed by Rupprecht Podszun (HHU Düsseldorf) and Alain Strowel (UCLouvain); the jury consisted of these four professors, joined by Evelyne Terryn (KU Leuven).

The Ph.D. thesis won the Concurrences Ph.D. Award (Law) in 2022. The jury was composed of Catherine Prieto (Université Paris I Panthéon-Sorbonne), Sylvaine Poillot-Peruzzetto (Université Toulouse I Capitole), Jacques Steenbergen (Belgian Competition Authority) and Wouter Wils (European Commission). The award was announced at the New Frontiers of Antitrust *conference in June 2022.*

My Ph.D. scholarship was funded by the KU Leuven Faculty of Law (first two years) and by the Research Foundation – Flanders (thereafter). Of course, the resulting thesis only reflects my personal opinions – not those of any institution to which I am affiliated. In accordance with the ASCOLA Transparency and Disclosure Declaration, I have nothing (else) to disclose.

I revised the thesis for its publication as a book. This revision included cutting certain parts (eg a section on predatory pricing) and adding others (eg the section on 'disruptive discrimination'). The digital economy evolves quickly, as does its antitrust scrutiny. Therefore, I also significantly updated the work (it is current until 28 February 2023). At the same time, I took care to stay close to the original thesis.

Friso Bostoen
Assistant Professor of Competition Law & Digital Regulation, Tilburg University

TABLE OF CONTENTS

INTRODUCTION

Friso Bostoen boldly went straight to the heart of the cyclone that has been blowing through competition law for the last twenty years, undaunted by the flood of controversies that have agitated the sphere of experts, both economists and jurists, until the paroxysm of the last three years. The Ph.D. student studied the economic revolution brought about by platforms with a non-partisan mindset, while emphasizing how this subject has further accentuated the tendency of competition law to polarize.

His thesis entitled 'Abuse Of Platform Power, Leveraging Conduct In Digital Markets Under European Competition Law And Beyond' methodically explores platform economics and strategies that have been so difficult to detect and understand. Based on these analyses of ecosystems, Friso Bostoen has chosen, in a second part, to focus on a particular drift: intra-platform exclusion. The phenomenon is paradoxical in that, at first glance, it is difficult to understand why a platform would want to exclude suppliers and thus reduce the interconnections that fuel its growth. He clearly explains how platforms have chosen to integrate vertically, leading them to be direct competitors of their suppliers and ultimately to drive them out. Then, to understand the diversity of intra-platform exclusion, he considers all the well-known theories of harm for the application of Article 102 TFEU, their weaknesses, their successful adaptations and those that are still necessary. In the third part, Friso Bostoen considers inter-platform competition and compares the envisaged sectoral regulation with the experience of the telecommunications sector. Finally, he examines the role of merger control.

The jury constituted for the Concurrences Ph.D. Award 2022, which I had the honor of chairing, rewarded this thesis for its analytical quality and its high level of views. It quickly became apparent to Jacques Steenbergen (President of the Belgian Competition Authority), Sylvaine Poillot-Peruzzetto (Advisor to the French Supreme Court), Wouter Wils (Legal Advisor in the Legal Service of the European Commission) and me that this thesis deserved to be promoted even though its publication would occur after the adoption of the Digital Market Act. The main reason was that it would allow a better understanding of the DMA's intricacies. In fact, the European legislator has taken advantage of the applications of Article 102 TFEU but has also drawn conclusions from its weaknesses to circumvent them by developing sectoral regulation. Secondly, this thesis remains current insofar as the DMA does not rule out the application of antitrust law purely and simply. In both respects, this work is undoubtedly of great interest. The future still holds many challenges in this complex field and, to face them, it is important to master the experience gained.

Catherine Prieto
Professor, University Paris I Panthéon-Sorbonne

FOREWORD

The subject of Friso's book can be captured in one term: 'intra-platform exclusion'. The term refers to situations in which a digital platform excludes those *within* its ecosystem, in particular the suppliers that use the platform to market their products. An app store could, for example, exclude developers relying on it to reach consumers. In fact, long before any enforcement action, Friso opened his 2016 Ph.D. proposal with the case of *Spotify v. Apple*.

This work is rich in case studies and provides us with tools to sensibly apply Article 102 TFEU to platforms. It does not pluck those tools out of thin air but deeply examines the legal tests of the different leveraging abuses (tying, refusal to supply, margin squeeze and discrimination) before interpreting – or reinterpreting – them in a platform context. As such, it values the wisdom embedded in traditional case law without being afraid to depart from established doctrine where a new approach is called for.

The work does not stop at competition law. Lawmakers have decided that platforms should be subject to *ex ante* regulation, a regulatory evolution that does not surprise those who have long studied network sectors such as telecommunications. Friso exposes the trade-offs inherent in platform regulation including (but not limited to) the Digital Markets Act. While complex regulatory questions are not amenable to easy answers, the work draws on a wide range of sources to provide deeply informed, nuanced views. As such, it can serve as a guide for anyone interested in platform regulation.

This book forms a valuable addition to an already prestigious book series. Friso knows how to captivate an audience, also in writing. He combines thorough legal analysis with an understanding of what is most relevant for consumers and competitors alike at this point in time. It is not a small achievement to add true innovative thinking to an area so much under scrutiny as (abuse of) platform power.

This work also closes Friso's PhD trajectory at KU Leuven's 'Consumer Competition Market' institute, a trajectory which I had the privilege of following closely. Over the past years, Friso rapidly established himself as a true academic, a prolific author, a regular prize winner, a speaker at many a high-level conferences, and an avid blogger – but also as an esteemed and valuable colleague and a true mentor for students. In impeccable English and with an ever-positive and inquisitive mind, Friso has found his place as a respected member of the global competition law community. It is with a feeling of pride and reassurance about the strength of the next generation of competition lawyers that I wholeheartedly recommend you read this book – for once, you might actually *enjoy* reading a PhD thesis!

Wouter Devroe
Professor of Law and Dean of the Law Faculty, KU Leuven

ABBREVIATIONS

General

ACM	Autoriteit Consument & Markt (formerly NMa), ie Dutch Competition Authority
AdC	Autoridade da Concorrência, ie Portuguese Competition Authority
AdlC	Autorité de la concurrence (formerly Conseil de la concurrence), ie French Competition Authority
AG	Advocate General
AGCM	Autorità Garante della Concorrenza e del Mercato, ie Italian Competition Authority
API	Application programming interface
BWB	Bundeswettbewerbsbehörde, ie Austrian Competition Authority
CFI	Court of First Instance (currently General Court)
CMA	Competition and Markets Authority (formerly Office of Fair Trading), ie UK Competition Authority
CSS	Comparison shopping service
DDC	District Court for the District of Columbia (US)
DC Cir	Court of Appeals for the District of Columbia (US)
DMA	Digital Markets Act
DOJ	Department of Justice (US)
EC	European Commission
ECJ	European Court of Justice
EDNY	District Court for the Eastern District of New York (US)
EP	European Parliament

EU	European Union
EUMR	EU Merger Regulation
FAS	Federal Antimonopoly Service of Russia
FBA	Fulfilment by Amazon
FCC	Federal Communications Commission (US)
FRAND	Fair, reasonable and non-discriminatory
FTC	Federal Trade Commission (US)
GAFA(M)	Google, Apple, Facebook, Amazon (and Microsoft)
GC	General Court (formerly Court of First Instance)
GMC	German Monopolies Commission
GMS	Google Mobile Services
IAP	(Apple's) In-App Purchase system
ICN	International Competition Network
IE	Internet Explorer
IPO	Initial public offering
ISP	Internet service provider
MADA	(Google's) Mobile Application Distribution Agreements
MDM	Mobile Device Management
NCA	National competition authority
ND Cal	District Court for the Northern District of California (US)
NFC	Near-field communication
NMa	Nederlandse Mededingingsautoriteit (currently ACM), ie Dutch Competition Authority
NY	Supreme Court of the State of New York (US)
OECD	Organisation for Economic Co-operation and Development
OEM	Original equipment manufacturer
OFT	Office of Fair Trading (currently CMA), ie UK Competition Authority
OS	Operating system
P2B	Platform-to-Business
PSD 2	Payment Services Directive 2
SDK	Software development kit
SEC	Securities and Exchange Commission (US)

SIEC	Significant impediment to effective competition
SMP	Single monopoly profit
TFEU	Treaty on the Functioning of the European Union
US	United States
VC	Venture capital(ist)
WMP	Windows Media Player

Publications

CPI	Competition Policy International
CLSR	Computer Law & Security Review
CoRe	European Competition and Regulatory Law Review
CUP	Cambridge University Press
ECLR	European Competition Law Review
FT	The Financial Times
HBR	Harvard Business Review
HUP	Harvard University Press
JAE	Journal of Antitrust Enforcement
JCLE	Journal of Competition Law & Economics
JECLAP	Journal of European Competition Law & Practice
NYT	The New York Times
OUP	Oxford University Press
WaPo	The Washington Post
WSJ	The Wall Street Journal
YEL	Yearbook of European Law

INTRODUCTION

'The Four'[1] – even the 'Gang of Four'[2] or 'Four Horsemen'[3]. Alternatively, if we don't want to neglect Microsoft (and we don't), the 'Formidable Five'[4], 'Frightful Five'[5] or 'Big Five'[6]. You could bring the number all the way up to nine, but that's overdoing it.[7] And if the quantitative monikers don't ring a bell, the acronyms will: GAFA(M)[8], or FAANG[9] if you kick out Microsoft and let Netflix join the party (even MAGA,[10] but that acronym's tainted). With some minor variations, everyone is talking about a group of tech companies that have so far ruled the 21st century, in particular Google, Apple, Facebook, Amazon and Microsoft. (The acronyms haven't really kept it with reorganizations and name changes: Google has become Alphabet, and Facebook was renamed Meta.)

While these five firms tend to be at the centre of public debate, this is not a book about them. Rather, it is a book about the way in which they – and the many businesses like them – operate, ie as platforms. Platforms play an increasingly important role in today's economy by serving as intermediaries between consumers and suppliers, which is why they are said to operate in multisided markets. The economic literature on multisided markets has grown markedly, from its humble beginnings at the start of the 2000s[11] to full books dedicated to the subject two decades later.[12]

Platform economics helps us understand why a select group of online platforms have grown into the largest – or at least most highly valued – companies in existence today. Indirect network effects, learning from data, and strong economies of scale (due to near-zero marginal costs) have fuelled their growth. These characteristics can be self-reinforcing. Take indirect network effects: more users on one side of the platform attract more users on the other side, which draws still more users on the first side – and

1 Scott Galloway, *The Four: The Hidden DNA of Amazon, Apple, Facebook, and Google* (Portfolio 2017).

2 Erick Schonfeld, 'Eric Schmidt's Gang of Four: Google, Apple, Amazon, and Facebook' (*TechCrunch*, 1 June 2011) <https://techcrunch.com/2011/05/31/schmidt-gang-four-google-apple-amazon-facebook/>.

3 'The *New* Four Horsemen of Tech' (*CNN Money*) <https://money.cnn.com/technology/storysupplement/four-horsemen-of-tech/>.

4 'How to Make Sense of the Latest Tech Surge' (*The Economist*, 20 February 2020) <https://www.economist.com/leaders/2020/02/20/how-to-make-sense-of-the-latest-tech-surge>.

5 Jeremy Philips, 'The "Frightful Five" Aren't So Scary, as Long as They're Competing' (*NYT*, 8 May 2017) <https://www.nytimes.com/2017/05/08/business/dealbook/the-frightful-five-arent-so-scary-as-long-as-theyre-competing.html>.

6 Nigel Walton, 'New Conglomerates and the Ecosystem Advantage' (2011) 13 China–USA Business Review 431.

7 Amy Webb, *The Big Nine: How the Tech Titans and Their Thinking Machines Could Warp Humanity* (PublicAffairs 2019).

8 Google, Apple, Facebook, Amazon and Microsoft.

9 Facebook, Apple, Amazon, Netflix and Google.

10 'The Tech Giants Are Still in Rude Health' (*The Economist*, 4 August 2018) <www.economist.com/business/2018/08/04/the-tech-giants-are-still-in-rude-health> (GAFAM minus Facebook, which is put in a consumer-facing category with Netflix and Twitter).

11 For the paper that started it all, see Jean-Charles Rochet and Jean Tirole, 'Platform Competition in Two-Sided Markets' (2003) 1 Journal of the European Economic Association 990.

12 Paul Belleflamme and Martin Peitz, *The Economics of Platforms* (CUP 2021). See also David Evans and Richard Schmalensee, *Matchmakers: The New Economics of Multi-Sided Platforms* (HBR Press 2016); Geoffrey Parker, Marshall Van Alstyne and Sangeet Choudary, *Platform Revolution* (Norton 2016).

so on. This creates a positive feedback loop that can result in platforms dominating their respective markets.

Many things can go wrong at the 'adoption stage', but if a platform ends up winning most of the market, it may come within the purview of EU competition law's abuse of dominance provision (article 102 TFEU). Dominance in itself is not a problem – only an *abuse* of that dominance is. In this work, I focus on one category of abuse, ie exclusion, and in particular the exclusion of suppliers that rely on the platform – so-called intra-platform exclusion.

One might wonder why a platform would exclude its suppliers in the first place, given that platforms rely on them for growth and monetize their interactions (eg through commission fees on suppliers' transactions with consumers). The short answer to that question is vertical integration. Once platforms have achieved sufficient scale, they tend to integrate vertically, which means they produce their own goods or services and distribute them through their platform. After such vertical integration, the platform competes with certain suppliers, which may create an incentive to exclude them.

An *incentive* to exclude, paired with the *ability* to do so, sets off the alarms at competition authorities. Exclusion can take many forms, from explicit 'delisting' (ie removing a competing supplier from the platform) to more subtle forms of discrimination (eg burying competing products deep down the platform's search results). Suppliers certainly *feel* affected: in a 2016 public consultation, nine out of ten responding businesses voiced their dissatisfaction with the current platform–supplier relationship.[13] In particular, they criticized platforms' application of unbalanced terms and conditions, as well as the promotion of own products to the disadvantage of products provided by suppliers.

Suppliers are the immediate victim, but contemporary competition law's main concern is whether consumers also suffer the consequences. Empirical and theoretical research suggests that this can be the case.[14] The picture that emerges is, however, not black-and-white; rather, there are trade-offs. A certain type of conduct in a certain market setting can, for example, lower prices while hampering innovation, or it may increase quality while decreasing choice. Competition authorities have the difficult task of figuring out which course of action the trade-off advises. They do not have to do so in a vacuum, but within the framework of article 102 TFEU that was developed through case law over the years.

---

13 EC, 'Public Consultation on the Regulatory Environment for Platforms, Online Intermediaries and the Collaborative Economy' (Synopsis Report, 2016) 9.

14 On the empirical side, see eg Feng Zhu and Qihong Liu, 'Competing with Complementors: An Empirical Look at Amazon.com' (2018) 39 Strategic Management Journal 2618; Wen Wen and Feng Zhu, 'Threat of Platform-Owner Entry and Complementor Responses? Evidence from the Mobile App Market' (2019) Strategic Management Journal 1336; Hyunjin Kim and Michael Luca, 'Product Quality and Entering Through Tying: Experimental Evidence' (2019) 65 Management Science 596. On the formal side, see eg Andrei Hagiu, Tat-How Teh and Julian Wright, 'Should Platforms Be Allowed to Sell on Their Own Marketplaces?' (2022) 53 The RAND Journal of Economics 297; Simon Anderson and Özlem Bedre-Defolie, 'Hybrid Platform Model' (2022) CEPR Discussion Paper no DP16243 <https://ssrn.com/abstract=3886686>; Erik Madsen and Nikhil Vellodi, 'Insider Imitation' (2022) <https://fass.nus.edu.sg/ecs/wp-content/uploads/sites/4/2022/05/Insider-Imitation.pdf>.

Applying that framework to platform conduct has proven difficult. The *Google Shopping* case has (perhaps unfairly) become the poster child for that difficulty.[15] Google demoted competing comparison shopping services in its search results while displaying its own service prominently. Did this constitute a quality increase (because consumers searching for a product were served the desired results more quickly) or rather a decrease (because competing services previously did a better job than Google)? Consumer choice certainly decreased as competitors were buried and there might be a long-term effect on innovation (but that is always difficult to establish). Even if we suspect net anticompetitive effects, which form of abuse do we observe? The European Commission (EC) put forward a general leveraging theory, which the General Court (GC) reinterpreted as discrimination, but there were almost as many different opinions as scholars discussing the case. And then there were the issues of timing (the case took almost seven years from opening the investigation to adopting a decision) and of remedies (which, according to critics, have changed little).

The EC has also been pursuing investigations into Apple, Facebook and Amazon. All of these are building on its earlier *Microsoft* cases. Along the way, the perception grew that EU competition law (enforcement) is inadequate in digital markets. When that is the case, the natural step is to adopt sector-specific regulation. The EU has a long tradition of regulating network sectors, the archetypical example being telecommunications. And indeed, EU lawmakers followed this playbook when adopting the Digital Markets Act (DMA). At the same time, governments in Germany, France, the UK and elsewhere took matters into their own hands by either amending their national competition laws or adopting their own platform-specific instruments.

In this book, I clarify the assessment of potentially abusive practices by online platforms, in particular vis-à-vis suppliers (ie the businesses using the platform to market their products). The building blocks of that assessment are, on the one hand, a strong grasp of the economic and technological operation of online platforms and, on the other hand, a deep knowledge of abuse of dominance law. While contemporary platform cases are used to illustrate the issues at hand, the legal principles relied on go back much further. And while the names of the now-prominent platforms pop up throughout this book, the theory applies to any dominant online platform.

The book is structured as follows. Part 1 gives the necessary introduction to the platform economy. In Section 1, the search for a definition offers the opportunity to lay bare the essential characteristics of online platforms. A platform typology helps us understand that not every platform is alike – a diversity that competition law and regulation need to recognize. Section 2 dives into platform economics and business strategy. Business strategy in particular helps us understand how platforms, in the course of their operation, can run into competition law. I illustrate that strategy by reference to the main online platforms that exist today, ie online marketplaces, app stores, search engines and social

15 See Friso Bostoen, 'The General Court's *Google Shopping* Judgment: Finetuning the Legal Qualifications and Tests for Platform Abuse' (2022) 13 JECLAP 75.

networks. Section 3 concludes by categorizing potentially abusive platform conduct. In particular, it distinguishes intra-platform exclusion from inter-platform exclusion, platform exploitation, and platform appropriation.

Part 2 zooms in on intra-platform exclusion – the main topic of this book. Section 4 tackles two preliminary questions. First, as there is no abuse without dominance, it looks at how market power manifests itself in an online platform context. Second, it studies the normative framework, ie the goals and methods of competition law, particularly as they relate to platforms. Next, we move on to the different forms of intra-platform abuse. Importantly, each form of abuse comes with a legal test, which determines under which conditions a certain type of conduct becomes abusive. Those legal tests form the core of every section.

Section 5 starts with the most general intra-platform abuse, leveraging, ie the use of market power in one market, the platform market, to distort competition in an adjacent market, the suppliers' market. Upon closer inspection, however, leveraging is not so much a specific abuse as a container term for other forms of intra-platform exclusion. Nevertheless, examining the mechanism, incentives and effects of platform leveraging helps us understand the dynamic at the heart of intra-platform abuses. The next sections closely examine the more specific forms of intra-platform abuse, ie tying (Section 6), refusal to supply (Section 7) and margin squeeze (Section 8). I show how these traditional forms of abuse should be updated to the online platform context. Even with a modern understanding of the existing forms of abuse, however, there is still potentially abusive platform conduct that escapes article 102 TFEU. To fill that gap, Section 9 suggests relying on a form of non-price discrimination infused with insights from the neglected disruption of supply case law: 'disruptive discrimination'.

Even prima facie abusive conduct can still be justified. Platforms, which need to govern their ecosystems as 'private regulators', have especially good reasons to take exclusionary actions. Section 10 goes over the most important justifications: reducing transactions and search costs, ensuring financial viability, guaranteeing the quality of users on the platform, and safeguarding the security and privacy of users on the platform.

Part 3 concerns platform regulation beyond article 102 TFEU. Section 11 sets out the framework for such regulatory intervention. The next two sections examine the two crucial components of each regulation – its scope (Section 12) and its obligations (Section 13) – with a strong focus on the latter. Platform-specific regulation such as the DMA serves as an illustration, but the goal is to illuminate the trade-offs inherent in *types* of interventions – not specific instruments. The interventions surveyed are merger control (horizontal and vertical), non-discrimination (through behavioural rules and structural separation), portability and interoperability, forced access, and breakup.

PART 1

THE PLATFORM ECONOMY

1

WHAT WE TALK ABOUT WHEN WE TALK ABOUT PLATFORMS

1.1 Online Platform Definition

Unlike traditional businesses, they don't buy inputs, make stuff, and sell it. Instead, they recruit participants, and then sell each group of participants access to the other group of participants.[16]

1.1.1 Introduction

As a part of a 2015 public consultation, the EC proposed the following definition of 'online platform':

> [A]n undertaking operating in two (or multi)-sided markets, which uses the Internet to enable interactions between two or more distinct but interdependent groups of users so as to generate value for at least one of the groups.[17]

The EC then proceeded by giving several examples, including search engines (eg Google, Bing), social networks (eg Facebook, LinkedIn), online marketplaces (eg Amazon, eBay) and app stores (eg Apple's App Store, Google Play). However, it emerged from the replies to the public consultation that 'there is no consensus on a possible legal definition of online platforms' as, depending on the respondent, '[t]he definition appears too broad or narrow'.[18] A debate in the UK House of Lords captured the differing opinions well: 'Broadly interpreted, the proposed definition could

---

16 David Evans and Richard Schmalensee, 'What Platforms Do Differently than Traditional Businesses' (*HBR*, 11 May 2016) <https://hbr.org/2016/05/what-platforms-do-differently-than-traditional-businesses>.

17 EC, 'Regulatory environment for platforms, online intermediaries, data and cloud computing and the collaborative economy' (Public Consultation, 2015) 5.

18 EC, 'Public Consultation on the Regulatory Environment for Platforms, Online Intermediaries and the Collaborative Economy' (Synopsis Report, 2016) 1.

encompass "all of the Internet"; strictly applied, it would only capture specific elements of the businesses with which it is concerned.'[19]

The EC thus concluded that a 'one-size-fits-all' definition may simply not be feasible.[20] While this may be true, such a definition is required for the application of an analytical or regulatory framework to online platforms. At the same time, a definition helps to lay bare the essential characteristics of platforms. Therefore, this section walks you through the essential literature on what distinguishes a platform from other business models, while also shortly discussing what makes a platform 'online'. But first, a note on terminology is in order.

In their seminal 2003 article, Rochet and Tirole coined the term 'two-sided market', using 'multisided market' as a synonym.[21] They identified the businesses operating in such markets as 'platforms'. Shortly after, Evans introduced the term 'multisided platforms',[22] later clarifying that he resisted the 'market'-centred terminology because multisidedness is an attribute of an individual business that may not always be shared by all of its competitors.[23] Moreover, Evans noted that the term 'market' could be confused with the use of that term in antitrust (such as in 'market definition'), which would be a mistake.[24]

Many of the foundational articles that followed stuck to the term 'two-sided markets'.[25] Authors also proposed new terms, such as 'two-sided strategies'[26] or 'two-sided network effects'.[27] But a critical mass has gathered behind the term 'multisided platforms'.[28] This term reflects the fact that many platforms cater not to two but three (or even more) user groups. The producers of operating system software, for example, are said to manage three sides: application developers, hardware providers and users.[29]

---

19 House of Lords Select Committee on European Union, 'Online Platforms and the Digital Single Market' (Report of Session, 2016) 22.

20 EC, 'Public Consultation on the Regulatory Environment for Platforms, Online Intermediaries and the Collaborative Economy' (n 18) 6.

21 Jean-Charles Rochet and Jean Tirole, 'Platform Competition in Two-Sided Markets' (2003) 1 Journal of the European Economic Association 990; Jean-Charles Rochet and Jean Tirole, 'Two-Sided Markets: A Progress Report' (2006) 37 RAND Journal of Economics 645, 645, where they explain: 'We focus on two-sided markets for expositional simplicity. Many markets or platforms … are multi-sided though. The insights obtained for two-sided platforms apply more generally to multi-sided ones.'

22 David Evans, 'The Antitrust Economics of Multi-Sided Platform Markets' (2003) 20 Yale Journal on Regulation 325.

23 David Evans and Richard Schmalensee, 'The Antitrust Analysis of Multi-Sided Platform Businesses' (2012) Coase-Sandor Institute for Law and Economics Working Paper 623, fn 1.

24 David Evans and Richard Schmalensee, 'The Industrial Organization of Markets with Two-Sided Platforms' (2007) 3 CPI 151, 152–53.

25 Eg Julian Wright, 'One-Sided Logic in Two-Sided Markets' (2004) 3 Review of Network Economics 44; Mark Armstrong, 'Competition in Two-Sided Markets' (2006) 37 RAND Journal of Economics 668.

26 Mark Rysman, 'The Economics of Two-Sided Markets' (2009) 23 Journal of Economic Perspectives 125, 126 and 132–33.

27 Geoffrey Parker and Marshall Van Alstyne, 'Two-Sided Network Effects: A Theory of Information Product Design' (2005) 51 Management Science 1494.

28 See eg Glen Weyl, 'A Price Theory of Multi-Sided Platforms' (2010) 100 American Economic Review 1642; Andrei Hagiu and Julian Wright, 'Multi-Sided Platforms' (2015) 43 International Journal of Industrial Organization 162.

29 Evans, 'The Antitrust Economics of Multi-Sided Platform Markets' (n 22) 328; Rysman (n 26) 132 (on Microsoft). Apple manufactures its own hardware, and thus manages only a two-sided platform between consumers and software providers.

In what follows, I will speak of 'multisidedness' rather than 'two-sidedness'. The term 'multisided platform' designates a specific business, while 'multisided market' captures not only this business but also its multisided competitors. For example, Amazon Marketplace is a multisided platform operating in the multisided e-commerce market, where it competes with eBay. It is understood that a multisided market is not necessarily the relevant market for antitrust purposes, as multisided platforms may compete with one-sided businesses, which should in that case be included in the relevant market.

1.1.2 Defining the 'Platform' in 'Online Platforms'

As noted, the economists Rochet and Tirole pioneered multisided market theory in their 2003 article (which started circulating in 2000 already). They described multisided markets as markets with distinct sides that benefit from interacting through a common platform.[30] They thus characterized platforms as intermediaries operating in multisided markets – a characterization that stands largely uncontested today.[31] There is also wide agreement on the fact that platforms solve a transaction problem.[32]

Platforms can thus roughly be defined as intermediaries that reduce transaction costs, but their defining characteristics are contested, to the extent that 'schools of thought' in platform scholarship have been distinguished.[33] The manifold existing definitions are said to 'suffer from excessive specificity, over-inclusiveness, or being too vague to be of use'.[34] Scholars have also derided the 'conceptual proliferation' of platform definitions.[35] Despite their disagreement about an exact definition, authors generally agree that a 'you know it when you see it' approach is not desirable either.[36]

Surveying the authoritative literature on platforms,[37] I will seek to see the forest for the trees. While it is said that chronology is the last refuge of the feeble-minded,[38]

---

30 Rochet and Tirole, 'Platform Competition in Two-Sided Markets' (n 21) 990.

31 See eg the endorsements by Ofcom, the CMA and professors Clemons, Ezrachi, Strowel, Stucke and Vergoute in House of Lords Select Committee on European Union, 'Online Platforms and the Digital Single Market' (n 19) 19. See also the definition offered by GMC, 'Competition Policy: The Challenge of Digital Markets' (Special Report, 2015), 19 ('a platform is usually an intermediary bringing together various groups of users so that they can interact economically or socially').

32 Evans and Schmalensee, 'The Industrial Organization of Markets with Two-Sided Platforms' (n 24) 158 (where they call reducing transaction costs the 'fundamental role' of platforms); Marshall Van Alstyne and Michael Schrage, 'The Best Platforms Are More than Matchmakers' (*HBR*, 2 August 2016) <https://hbr.org/2016/08/the-best-platforms-are-more-than-matchmakers> ('Where traditional business models sell products and/or services, matchmaking models sell reduced transaction costs').

33 Jian Li, 'Is Online Media a Two-Sided Market?' (2015) 31 CLSR 99.

34 Hagiu and Wright, 'Multi-Sided Platforms' (n 28) 163.

35 Dirk Auer and Nicolas Petit, 'Two-Sided Markets and the Challenge of Turning Economic Theory into Antitrust Policy' (2015) 60 The Antitrust Bulletin 426, 432.

36 Rochet and Tirole, 'Two-Sided Markets: A Progress Report' (n 21) 645–46; Auer and Petit (n 35) 433; Li (n 33) 99.

37 For other tentative surveys, see Lapo Filistrucchi, Damien Geradin and Eric van Damme, 'Identifying Two-Sided Markets' (2013) 36 World Competition 33, 33–44; Auer and Petit (n 35) 432–39; Li (n 33) 100–3; Gönenç Gürkaynak, Öznur Inanılır, Sinan Diniz and Ayse Gizem Yasar, 'Multi-Sided Markets and the Challenge of Incorporating Multi-Sided Considerations into Competition Law Analysis' (2017) 5 JAE 100, 101–5; Bertin Martens, 'An Economic Policy Perspective on Online Platforms' (2016) JRC Digital Economy Working Paper 2016/05, 10–18.

38 Joseph Ellis, *Founding Brothers* (Knopf 2003) 18.

describing the evolution of 'platform thinking' is, in my opinion, the most instructive way to present the subject.

1.1.2.1 Defining Characteristic Number One: a 'Non-Neutral' Price Structure

Rochet and Tirole considered that many if not most markets with indirect network effects are multisided.[39] In their view, however, the defining characteristic that makes a market multisided is the fact that platforms can cross-subsidize between the different user groups that are parties to the transaction.[40] This means that the volume of the transactions (and thus the profit of a platform) depends not only on the total price charged to the parties to the transaction, but also on its division between those parties. In other words, platforms must choose not only a price level, but also a price structure.[41] This leads to the following definition:

> A market is two-sided if the platform can affect the volume of transactions by charging more to one side of the market and reducing the price paid by the other side by an equal amount; in other words, the price structure matters, and platforms must design it so as to bring both sides on board.[42]

Consider nightclubs, a popular example of a multisided market thanks to its conceptual simplicity.[43] Women and men constitute the different user groups, and for a nightclub to be successful it needs to attract both in more or less equal measure. To achieve this, the nightclub will choose a particular price structure, which means charging men more and women less. For example, men might be charged a €10 entry fee, while women can enter for free (and might even be offered a complimentary drink). In other words, male partygoers subsidize female partygoers, a formula that increases the volume of transactions and thus the profit of the nightclub.

Rochet and Tirole added that such a 'non-neutral' price structure must be possible,[44] a condition they ground in Coase's article 'The Problem of Social Cost'.[45] Simply put, the Coase theorem states that if outcomes are inefficient and nothing hinders bargaining, people will negotiate their way to efficiency.[46] Rochet and Tirole clarified that it is only

39 Rochet and Tirole, 'Platform Competition in Two-Sided Markets' (n 21) 990 and 1017.

40 ibid 1017–18.

41 ibid 990.

42 Rochet and Tirole, 'Two-Sided Markets: A Progress Report' (n 21) 665.

43 Used in and popularized by early work on platforms, see eg Evans, 'The Antitrust Economics of Multi-Sided Platform Markets' (n 22) 325 and Wright (n 25) 44. However, the conceptual simplicity is deceiving. Firstly, only *heterosexual* nightclubs are multisided. Secondly, these nightclubs are only multisided for *singles*, not for couples, as the latter can renegotiate the price structure between them.

44 Rochet and Tirole, 'Platform Competition in Two-Sided Markets' (n 21) 1018–20.

45 Ronald Coase, 'The Problem of Social Cost' (1960) 3 The Journal of Law & Economics 1. For a more elaborate treatment of the connection between the work of Coase and the platform definition of Rochet and Tirole, see Auer and Petit (n 35) 431–32.

46 Rochet and Tirole, 'Two-Sided Markets: A Progress Report' (n 21) 649; more completely, the Coase theorem states that transaction volume will be efficient when property rights are clearly defined and there are no information asymmetries or transaction costs.

when users cannot bargain their way to an efficient outcome themselves (ie the Coase theorem does not apply) that a platform can maintain a non-neutral price structure.[47] In other words, users must be unable to negotiate away the allocation of the burden chosen by the platform, for example through side payments.[48]

1.1.2.2 Defining Characteristic Number Two: Coordination Problem Solving

While Rochet and Tirole's definition is concerned mainly with the structure of platforms (a formal definition), another early contributor, Evans, focuses on the function of platforms (a more practical definition). Evans opens his 2003 article by stating that '[m]ulti-sided platforms coordinate the demands of distinct groups of customers who need each other in some way.'[49] Together with Schmalensee, he further specified this definition: a multisided platform (which they call an 'economic catalyst') has

> (a) two or more groups of customers; (b) who need each other in some way; (c) but who cannot capture the value from their mutual attraction on their own; and (d) rely on the catalyst to facilitate value-creating interactions between them.[50]

In other words, two groups of customers would benefit from connecting in some way but are unable to coordinate among themselves due to transaction costs (which goes back to the Coase theorem). The platform solves this coordination problem and captures part of the value it creates.[51]

In line with Rochet and Tirole, Evans states that indirect network effects seem to explain empirically why a platform emerges, but are not strictly necessary for the platform to arise.[52] He explains that platforms harness (or internalize) indirect network effects,[53] and that the platform must thus be designed in such a way as to increase positive indirect network effects and limit negative indirect network effects (especially by imposing rules on the platform users).[54]

---

47 Thus, users must be in some way prevented from bargaining. This can be the case (i) when there is no monetary transaction between users to bargain about (eg in the case of telecommunications); (ii) when bargaining directly between user groups about a monetary transaction would involve (significant) transaction costs (eg in the case of a large number of small transactions); or (iii) when the platform prohibits users from bargaining (eg the no-surcharge rule imposed by payment system providers). See Rochet and Tirole, 'Platform Competition in Two-Sided Markets' (n 21), 1018–20. See also Rochet and Tirole, 'Two-Sided Markets: A Progress Report' (n 21) 648–50, where they call the failure of the Coase theorem a necessary but insufficient condition for multisidedness.

48 In the nightclub example, this would mean that men must be unable to 'pass on' part of their higher entry fee on women, which is indeed the case *for singles* (in contrast to couples).

49 Evans, 'The Antitrust Economics of Multi-Sided Platform Markets' (n 22) 325.

50 Evans and Schmalensee, 'The Antitrust Analysis of Multi-Sided Platform Businesses' (n 23) 7.

51 Evans, 'The Antitrust Economics of Multi-Sided Platform Markets' (n 22) 331–33. On the connection with the Coase theorem, see Evans and Schmalensee, 'The Industrial Organization of Markets with Two-Sided Platforms' (n 24) 154.

52 Evans, 'The Antitrust Economics of Multi-Sided Platform Markets' (n 22) 332.

53 ibid 339 and 380.

54 Evans and Schmalensee, 'The Industrial Organization of Markets with Two-Sided Platforms' (n 24) 163 and 177.

1.1.2.3 Defining Characteristic Number Three: Indirect Network Effects

While the above authors consider indirect network effects a feature of multisided platforms, others consider it their defining characteristic.[55] In 2003, Caillaud and Jullien distinguished multisided platforms (or 'intermediation service providers') from resellers because the former operate in the presence of indirect network effects.[56] These indirect network effects give rise to a 'chicken and egg' problem: the platform needs to attract users on both sides, but those users only want to join when there are already users on the other side.[57] For that reason, an emerging platform may find it hard to penetrate the market, especially when established players are already present.

In the same vein, Armstrong describes multisided markets as markets in which two or more groups of agents interact via intermediaries or platforms and 'cross-group externalities' (ie indirect network effects) are present, so that 'the benefit enjoyed by a member of one group depends upon how well the platform does in attracting customers from the other group'.[58] Rysman goes a step further by qualifying multisided market theory as simply a subset of the literature on indirect network effects, distinguished mainly by its emphasis on market intermediaries.[59] In line with the aforementioned authors, he holds that

> a two-sided market is one in which (1) two sets of agents interact through an intermediary or platform, and (2) the decisions of each set of agents affects the outcomes of the other set of agents, typically through an externality.[60]

Under these definitions, every intermediary operating in the presence of indirect network effects may be called a multisided platform. Rysman acknowledges that such a definition may seem very broad, or overly inclusive.[61] He believes this is not a problem, however, as the 'interesting question is often not whether a market can be defined as two-sided – virtually all markets might be two-sided to some extent – but how important two-sided issues are in determining outcomes of interest.'[62] This view that multisidedness is not a binary classification but rather a matter of degree is more widely shared.[63]

---

55 The present discussion sets aside the question whether indirect network effects should be bilateral, or whether unilateral indirect network effects suffice. On this point, see extensively Li (n 33) 99. However, the distinction is largely irrelevant in my opinion, given that the authors that are said to require bilateral network effects – namely, Rochet and Tirole (2003) and Caillaud and Jullien (2003) – use advertising-supported media as an example (while in that case the network effects are unilateral). Moreover, Rochet and Tirole changed their definition in later work (2006). Subsequent authors, most notably Armstrong (2006) and Rysman (2009) require only unilateral indirect network effects. This view is endorsed by Filistrucchi, Geradin and van Damme (n 37) 38.

56 Bernard Caillaud and Bruno Jullien, 'Chicken & Egg: Competition Among Intermediation Service Providers' (2003) 34 RAND Journal of Economics 309, 309–10.

57 ibid.

58 Armstrong (n 25) 668.

59 Rysman (n 26) 127.

60 ibid 125.

61 However, Rochet and Tirole find that a definition based on the existence of indirect network effects is actually underinclusive, see Rochet and Tirole, 'Two-Sided Markets: A Progress Report' (n 21) 657–58.

62 Rysman (n 26) 127.

63 Evans and Schmalensee, 'The Industrial Organization of Markets with Two-Sided Platforms' (n 24) 173; Filistrucchi, Geradin and van Damme (n 37) 42–43; Auer and Petit (n 35) 435.

1.1.2.4 Debated Cases

The foundational economic literature on multisided platforms offers various definitions, focusing either on their skewed price structure, their role as coordination problem solvers, or the presence of indirect network effects. Despite this different focus, there is more that unites these definitions than that divides them. For example, online marketplaces, advertising-supported media and operating systems are multisided under every definition, and thus virtually undebated.[64] Evans and Schmalensee conclude that even though '[e]conomists have proposed several definitions of a multi-sided platform; they will generally agree in specific cases.'[65] Filistrucchi, Geradin and van Damme confirm that 'the different definitions proposed appear consistent enough to allow the practical identification of two-sided markets, that is, of those markets where two-sidedness might matter'.[66]

While there is agreement on a number of 'core' multisided markets, others have sparked considerable disagreement. Authors have primarily taken issue with overly broad definitions, as most of the difficult cases concern the inclusion rather than the exclusion of certain markets. A case in point is offered by Rochet and Tirole, who have asked whether any traditional firm is a multisided platform.[67] They conclude that, under their definition, a firm – which brings together workers and customers – is indeed a multisided platform: workers and customers cannot bargain away the non-neutral price structure of the platform (they do not even meet).[68] However, Rochet and Tirole add that firms are often de facto one-sided platforms given that 'there is little "wriggle room" for them to manipulate the price structure: if they lower wages, workers will leave, and if they raise prices, consumers will seek out other suppliers'.[69]

Supermarkets are another debated example. Armstrong holds that supermarkets (and similar kinds of retailers) constitute a multisided platform connecting suppliers and consumers.[70] After all, consumers will benefit from a greater number of suppliers (and thus a wider choice), while suppliers will benefit from a greater number of consumers.[71] Supermarkets would also be multisided in Rochet and Tirole's sense, as direct bargaining between suppliers and consumers would be inefficient due to high transaction costs. Suppliers and consumers are thus unable to bypass the price structure chosen by the supermarket.[72] Moreover, the pricing decisions on the supplier and the consumer side will have an impact on their sales volume.[73]

---

64 Filistrucchi, Geradin and van Damme (n 37) 36; Auer and Petit (n 35) 437. For a (lone) dissenting opinion when it comes to advertising-supported media, see Li (n 33) 99.

65 Evans and Schmalensee, 'The Antitrust Analysis of Multi-Sided Platform Businesses' (n 23) 6.

66 Filistrucchi, Geradin and van Damme (n 37) 43.

67 Rochet and Tirole, 'Two-Sided Markets: A Progress Report' (n 21) 648–49.

68 ibid.

69 ibid 649.

70 Armstrong (n 25) 678 and 684–86.

71 Especially when those suppliers take on inventory risk, in which case less sales mean not only less profit, but possibly even losses.

72 In the same sense, see Auer and Petit (n 35) 434.

73 Hagiu and Wright, 'Multi-Sided Platforms' (n 28) 163.

1.1.2.5 Closing the Debate

In search of consensus, some authors have combined elements of different definitions.[74] But the most systematic study of the distinction between multisided platform and other business models comes from Hagiu and Wright.[75] They believe that at the most fundamental level, multisided platforms have two key features:[76]

- *They enable direct interactions between two or more distinct sides*. 'Direct interaction' means that the distinct sides retain control over the key terms of the interaction (eg pricing, quality, other terms and conditions, marketing, and delivery), as opposed to the intermediary taking control of those terms.[77]
- *Each side is affiliated with the platform*. 'Affiliation' means that each side consciously makes platform-specific investments that are necessary to interact directly with each other.[78]

Hagiu and Wright clarify that *direct interactions* between the different sides set multisided platforms apart from resellers and vertically integrated firms.[79] A supermarket, for example, may operate as a reseller with regard to branded products, and as a vertically integrated firm with regard to its own private-label products. In neither case, however, will there be direct interaction between the supermarket's suppliers and its customers; therefore, it does not qualify as a platform.

Affiliation by the different sides distinguishes multisided platforms from input suppliers.[80] Microsoft's Windows is an example of such an input supplier structure: any hardware manufacturer can produce Windows-compatible hardware without being formally affiliated with Microsoft.[81] Without this affiliation, hardware manufacturers cannot be said to constitute a side of the Windows platform.[82] But Microsoft's Windows does act as a multisided platform between application developers and PC users, as the first group has to invest in learning the specific programming language, and the second in getting familiar with the system.

74 See eg Weyl (n 28) 1644 (requiring a multiproduct firm, cross-network effects, and bilateral market power). For another sophisticated definitional attempt distinguishing between types of platform markets, see Filistrucchi, Geradin and van Damme (n 37) 33 (in a *non-transaction* market, observing indirect network effects is sufficient to establish its multisided nature; in a *transaction* market, 'one should also identify the presence of transaction costs or, more generally, limits to the bilateral setting of prices among buyers and sellers').

75 Their study was published in a series of articles: Andrei Hagiu and Julian Wright, 'Do You Really Want to Be an eBay?' (*HBR*, March 2013) <https://hbr.org/2013/03/do-you-really-want-to-be-an-ebay>; Andrei Hagiu and Julian Wright, 'Marketplace or Reseller?' (2015) 61 Management Science 184; Hagiu and Wright, 'Multi-Sided Platforms' (n 28) 162.

76 Hagiu and Wright, 'Multi-Sided Platforms' (n 28) 163–64.

77 Hagiu and Wright specify, however, that a multisided platform may contract away some of the control rights of its suppliers, see ibid 170.

78 The investment could be a fixed access fee (eg buying a video game console), expenditure of resources (eg spending time and money on learning how to develop applications for iOS), or an opportunity cost (eg driving to a shopping mall, joining a loyalty programme).

79 Hagiu and Wright, 'Multi-Sided Platforms' (n 28) 164.

80 ibid.

81 Martens (n 37) 17.

82 Hagiu and Wright, 'Multi-Sided Platforms' (n 28) 170.

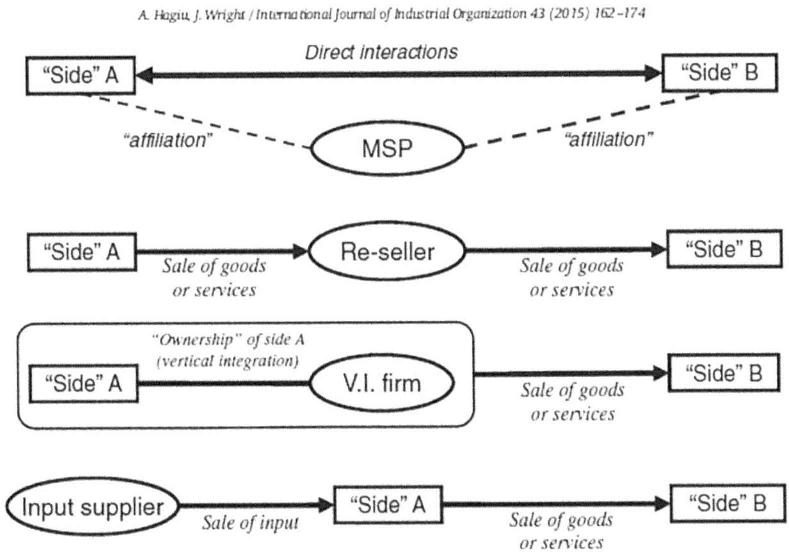

Figure 1 Platforms vs other business models (Hagiu & Wright 2015)

Finally, Hagiu and Wright note that indirect network effects are neither necessary nor sufficient in their definition of multisided platforms while recognizing that most multisided platforms 'do indeed create and capture value through indirect network effects'.[83]

1.1.2.6 Conclusion

The defining characteristics and corresponding typology proposed by Hagiu and Wright are both intuitive and theorized in-depth, which results in a convincing model that is fairly easy to apply. Consider, for example, music streaming services such as Spotify.[84] One may be tempted to conceive them as platforms between artists (or their record labels) and consumers. And indeed, a consumer will benefit from more artists being available on a specific service (and the other way around), so indirect network effects are present. However, one cannot say there is 'direct interaction' in the sense that the different parties remain in control over the key terms of the interaction.[85] It is Spotify, rather than the artists or consumers, that sets the price on each side (a €10 subscription fee on the consumer side, a proportional license fee on the artist side).

83 ibid 164.

84 For an in-depth look at the music streaming business model, see Maria Eriksson, Rasmus Fleischer, Anna Johansson, Pelle Snickars and Patrick Vonderau, *Spotify Teardown: Inside the Black Box of Streaming Music* (MIT Press 2019).

85 Hagiu and Wright's criterion of 'affiliation' can be considered fulfilled, as each streaming service has its own access requirements (on the artist side, fulfilling them is the job of either the record label or – in the case of independent artists – specialized distributors).

However, as every other definition, the approach of Hagiu and Wright can also be questioned. If one requires the platform participants to remain in control over the key terms of the interaction, how should Uber be qualified? After all, the price of rides – perhaps the most important term – is set by the platform rather than its drivers, suggesting it does not constitute a platform. Yet Uber is often considered the quintessential platform business, up to the point where 'uberization' – a term now included in many dictionaries – is broadly synonymous with 'platformization'.[86] At the same time, the rejection of Uber as a platform does fit with the (not uncontroversial) judgment of the European Court of Justice (ECJ) in *Uber Spain*.

In *Uber Spain*, the ECJ was asked to decide whether Uber provided a 'transport service' and/or an 'information society service' (which, in turn, determined the ability of EU Member States to regulate its operations).[87] Without markedly changing the question, one could rephrase it as: Does Uber constitute a platform? The ECJ answered that Uber provided more than just an intermediation service because it exerts 'decisive influence' over the conditions under which the drivers provide their service such as the amount of the fare.[88] Translated to the terminology of Hagiu and Wright, the ECJ essentially holds that the interaction between users on the platform is not *direct* given that drivers do not control the key terms of their offering (ie rides).

The ECJ is not the only institution that appears to agree with Hagiu and Wright. In a clear endorsement, a report by the EC's study service declared that the approach by Hagiu and Wright 'takes us out of the unproductive academic debate' and 'allows us to finally answer the question: What is a platform[?]'[89] Furthermore, the Bundeskartellamt explicitly drew inspiration from Hagiu and Wright's definition, stating that 'businesses are considered a platform in competition law terms if they provide intermediation services which allow for *direct* interaction between two or more distinct groups of users that are connected by *indirect network effects*'.[90] The Bundeskartellamt specified, in line with Hagiu and Wright, that direct interaction 'distinguishes platforms from trade relations and vertical trading or value chains, in which multiple market relations also occur'.[91] In line with these authorities (and rather than adding yet another definition to the list), I therefore endorse the definition put forward by Hagiu and Wright

86 See eg 'uberization' in Collins Dictionary: 'to subject (an industry) to a business model in which services are offered on demand through direct contact between a customer and a supplier, usually via mobile technology' <https://www.collinsdictionary.com/dictionary/english/uberize>.

87 Case C–434/15 *Asociación Profesional Élite Taxi v Uber Systems Spain* EU:C:2017:981, para 33.

88 ibid, para 39: 'Uber exercises decisive influence over the conditions under which that service is provided by those drivers. [I]t appears, inter alia, that Uber determines at least the maximum fare by means of the eponymous application, that the company receives that amount from the client before paying part of it to the non-professional driver of the vehicle, and that it exercises a certain control over the quality of the vehicles, the drivers and their conduct, which can, in some circumstances, result in their exclusion.'

89 Martens (n 37) 17.

90 Bundeskartellamt, 'The Market Power of Platforms and Networks' (Working Paper – English summary, 2016) 2 (emphasis added).

91 ibid 4. The Bundeskartellamt specifies that direct interaction means that the platform 'cannot directly control the specifics of the transaction (prices, conditions, etc) and is not a party to the contract in legal terms'.

1.1.3 Defining the 'Online' in 'Online Platforms'

Platforms are not a new phenomenon.[92] Indeed, they have existed at least since the rise of villages. In such ancient villages, markets already served as a meeting place for sellers and buyers under the supervision of the village chief (the platform operator, who regulates the market and may levy a tax for the use of the physical space).[93] Such platforms then grew in terms of size and organization: think, for instance, of the Grand Bazaar in Istanbul (which is over 500 years old). These marketplaces entered a new era with the advent of the shopping mall, an oft-cited example of a multisided platform,[94] which serves essentially the same function as a village market, ie providing a place for interaction between retailers and customers. In the same village context, the local matchmaker was also operating a multisided platform when he connected the town's eligible men and women. In the 18th and 19th centuries, clergymen were even running marriage agencies in the United Kingdom, and commercial dating agencies emerged strongly after World War II. Nightclubs fulfil the same role of providing a place for interaction between men and women, and thus obey the same economic laws.

In the 18th century, advertisements started appearing in UK newspapers, a practice that then spread to France and the US. This development turned newspapers from a one-sided market (aimed at readers) into a two-sided market (aimed at readers and advertisers). This led to the rise of advertising agencies that bought large amounts of space in various newspapers, which they then resold to advertisers at higher rates – a precursor to the ad exchanges existing today (eg Google's DoubleClick). Stock exchanges, ie marketplaces focused on financial instruments, have also existed for hundreds of years. And in 1950, Frank McNamara introduced the first payment card (Diners Club), offering a payment platform between restaurants and cardholders. Payment cards became general use as competitors, including American Express, Mastercard, and Visa joined the market.

In recent years, the ancient business model has been 'turbocharged' by modern technology – turning platforms into *online* platforms.[95] 'Modern technology' is a broad term including the internet, personal computers and software, the web, mobile broadband, and smartphones.[96]

1. The origins of the *internet* date back to research commissioned by the US government in the 1960s. By the 1980s, its precursor network, the ARPANET, connected regional academic networks. Modern internet arrived in the early 1990s, and its use has grown exponentially ever since.

---

92 On the history of platforms, see David Evans and Richard Schmalensee, *Matchmakers: The New Economics of Multi-Sided Platforms* (*HBR* Press 2016) 7–20.

93 Martens (n 37) 10.

94 See eg Rysman (n 26) 125; Evans and Schmalensee, 'The Antitrust Analysis of Multi-Sided Platform Businesses' (n 23) 13–15.

95 Evans and Schmalensee, *Matchmakers: The New Economics of Multi-Sided Platforms* (n 92) 19–20 and 40–5.

96 On the history of these technologies, see Walter Isaacson, *The Innovators: How a Group of Hackers, Geniuses, and Geeks Created the Digital Revolution* (Simon & Schuster 2014) and Margaret O'Mara, *The Code: Silicon Valley and the Remaking of America* (Penguin 2019).

Put simply, the internet is a 'network of networks' in which every computer can communicate with any other computer.

2. While the first computers were built halfway through the 20th century, the first *personal computers* (then called 'microcomputers') were only developed in the 1970s by companies such as Xerox and Hewlett-Packard. However, personal computers were not successfully mass-marketed until Apple introduced its user-friendly models in the second part of the 1970s. While some firms focused on computer hardware, others (such as Microsoft) focused on *software*.

3. In 1989, Tim Berners-Lee invented the *world wide web* while employed at CERN in Switzerland. The web makes it possible to publish and browse webpages, and is thus a way of accessing information over the medium of the internet. 'Internet' and 'web' are not to be confused: indeed, the web shares the internet with other services such as email, and the two are therefore not synonymous.

4. The 1990s brought the advent of *mobile broadband*, which allowed for wireless access to the internet and thus the web. As such, it was a necessary enabling technology for smartphones.

5. *Smartphones*, ie 'wireless telephones with advanced Internet browsing and app capabilities',[97] were developed in the 2000s. Their current design was pioneered by Apple's iPhone in 2007, and Android – currently the most popular mobile operating system – was released in 2008.

These developments lead multisided platforms to move online, a change that has manifested itself most visibly in the scale of those platforms. While a village market may have served hundreds of customers and a shopping mall thousands, Amazon Marketplace serves millions of customers. The village matchmakers, clergymen, and old-school dating agencies have been replaced by dating sites (such as OkCupid) and apps (such as Tinder). A large part of the advertising market has moved from newspapers to search engines (such as Google), social networks (such as Facebook) and other online media. The financial world, finally, has also experienced a surge of online platform-based models such as crowdfunding and peer-to-peer lending. On top of all this, the digital revolution has given rise to a completely new set of platforms, including Microsoft's Windows, Apple's iOS and App Store, and Google's Android and Play Store.

The developments discussed above made online platforms possible, but what exactly makes a platform *online*? These days, practically every undertaking – and thus platform – has some form of online presence (a website, a social media page) and uses digital tools to carry out its business. That is why the simple qualification 'using the internet' (as in the EC's aforementioned definition) does not suffice to delineate a

97 *Google Android* (Case AT.40099) Commission Decision C(2018)4761, para 75.

specific category. *Online* platforms constitute a narrower subset, best described by reference to their defining features:[98]

1. *Operating (almost) solely over the internet.* Online platforms operate (almost) solely over the internet,[99] which means that any platform that existed before the advent of the internet cannot be an *online* platform. Note that certain businesses operate both a platform and a non-platform business. For example, in addition to its platform Amazon Marketplace, Amazon operates as a traditional retailer both online (eg of books) and offline (eg brick-and-mortar bookstores). The platform Amazon Marketplace, however, operates solely on the internet.
2. *Offering a digital infrastructure.* Online platforms offer a digital infrastructure where their users can meet.[100] The purpose of this meeting can be social (eg Facebook), commercial (eg eBay), informational (eg Google), etc. What matters is the fact that users are embedded digitally; the result of the interaction may be physical (eg a shipment), but is often not (a digital transfer of text, images, video, music – in short: content).[101]
3. *Being part of the network economy.* Online platforms are part of the network economy, which implies the presence of network effects (and the accompanying first-mover advantage and winner-takes-all dynamic), economies of scale, switching costs and lock-in – all of which constitute barriers to entry (for an elaborate discussion of these features, see below).[102]
4. *Displaying a high degree of innovation.* Online platforms display a rapid pace of innovation, which leads to products with short lifecycles.[103] This dynamic is regularly illustrated by reference to 'Moore's law', promulgated by Intel's co-founder Gordon Moore in 1965 and called 'the greatest technological prediction of the century'.[104] Simply put, Moore stated that overall processing power for computers would double every two years.[105] Accordingly, online platforms invest heavily in research and development to keep up (or stay ahead).

98 An approach similar to Miguel Rato and Nicolas Petit, 'Abuse of Dominance in Technology-Enabled Markets: Established Standards Reconsidered' (2013) 9 European Competition Journal 1, 2–6; Massimiliano Kadar, 'European Union Competition Law in the Digital Era' (2015) 4–7 <https://ssrn.com/abstract=2703062> (the article has been published in Zeitschrift für Wettbewerbsrecht, but the publicly available version is relied on); Inge Graef, *EU Competition Law, Data Protection and Online Platforms: Data as Essential Facility* (Kluwer 2016) 9.

99 Graef (n 98) 9.

100 Kadar (n 98) 5.

101 Rato and Petit (n 98) 4.

102 Section 4.1.2.

103 Rato and Petit (n 98) 3–4; Kadar (n 98) 5.

104 Chris Miller, *Chip War: The Fight for the World's Most Critical Technology* (Scribner 2022) 31.

105 More technically, Gordon Moore held that the number of transistors on an integrated circuit would approximately double every two years, see Gordon Moore, 'Cramming More Components onto Integrated Circuits' (1965) 38 Electronics 114.

The following section seeks to categorize the most important businesses that are both multisided as defined in the previous section, and online according to the features set out in this section.

1.2 Platform Typology

Everything should be made as simple as possible, but not simpler.[106]

Previous examples have shown that a wealth of online platforms exists. Einstein's aphorism in mind, not every kind of online platform deserves a separate theory. At the same time, holding that the same principles apply to all online platforms would be an oversimplification. With that guidance in mind, I divide online platforms into two categories, namely, advertising platforms and matching platforms – a distinction that draws inspiration from the work of authors including Evans and Schmalensee,[107] Filistrucchi, Geradin and van Damme,[108] Haucap and Heimeshoff,[109] and Evans and Gawer,[110] but also from competition policy documents.[111]

Before delving into the different types of platforms, a second (and final) note on terminology is in order. The previous remark clarified the use of the term 'multisided platforms', which operate in 'multisided markets'. In the preceding section, I elaborated on what makes a business an 'online' multisided platform. In order to save space, I often refer simply to 'platforms' in what follows.

Additionally, the different sides of the platform merit some specification. The undertaking managing the platform is called the 'platform operator' or 'orchestrator'. The different sides constitute the 'users' of the platform, no matter which side they are on (as they are all using the platform's service, they can also be called its

106 A quote (most likely correctly) attributed to Albert Einstein, see <http://quoteinvestigator.com/2011/05/13/einstein-simple/>. The quote goes back to the scientific premise of parsimony (or Occam's razor), which states (in modern terms): 'Among competing hypotheses, the one that makes the fewest assumptions should be selected.'

107 Evans and Schmalensee, 'The Industrial Organization of Markets with Two-Sided Platforms' (n 24) 154–58, where they distinguish between exchanges, advertiser-supported media, transaction devices and software platforms.

108 Filistrucchi, Geradin and van Damme (n 37) 40–41, where they distinguish between transaction and non-transaction markets.

109 Justus Haucap and Ulrich Heimeshoff, 'Google, Facebook, Amazon, eBay: Is the Internet Driving Competition or Market Monopolization?' (2014) 11 International Economics and Economic Policy 49, 54–61, where they distinguish between search engines, social networks and trading platforms.

110 Peter Evans and Anabelle Gawer, 'The Rise of the Platform Enterprise: A Global Survey' (2016) The Emerging Platform Economy Series 1, where they distinguish between transaction, innovation, integrated and investment platforms.

111 GMC (n 31), where they distinguish search engines, social networks and e-commerce as the most important types of digital platforms, but offer that 'platforms are also found outside the online domain, for instance in payment transactions, mobile telecommunication, financial trading or advertising-funded media'; Bundeskartellamt, 'The Market Power of Platforms and Networks' (n 90), where they distinguish between audience providing and trading platforms; EC, 'Online Platforms' (Staff Working Document) SWD(2016)172, where they distinguish between marketplaces and e-commerce platforms, mobile ecosystems and application distribution platforms, internet search services, social media and content platforms, and online advertising platforms; Martens (n 37), who describes search and matching as 'the core role of platforms'.

'customers'). Users on one side are termed 'consumers', while users on the other side are called 'suppliers'. Figure 2 clarifies the main types of platforms and the users on either side; the following sections zoom in on the two main types of platforms.[112]

	SUPPLIER SIDE	**CONSUMER SIDE**
matching platforms		
> **transaction platforms**	**sellers**	**buyers**
• *e-commerce platforms*	*sellers*	*buyers*
• *innovation platforms*	*app developers/sellers*	*buyers*
advertising platforms	**advertisers**	**eyeballs**
• *ad-supported media*	*advertisers*	*eyeballs*
• *search engines*	*+ indexed websites*	*eyeballs*
• *social networks*	*+ 3rd party content providers (incl. app developers)*	*eyeballs*

Figure 2 Platform typology

1.2.1 Matching Platforms

When a platform connects different user groups for the purpose of direct interaction and the indirect network effects are bilateral (ie each side benefits from a higher number of users on the other side), it is called a *matching platform*. The distinct user groups of a matching platform can be diverse, eg men and women for an online dating site, and employers and employees for an online recruitment agency. When a matching platform brings about not only a direct interaction, but also a transaction, it can be referred to as a *transaction platform*.[113]

When the web became a sales channel, *e-commerce platforms* or online marketplaces arose.[114] eBay was founded in 1995 and enables sellers to offer their goods by organizing a bidding procedure. Bezos established Amazon as an online (one-sided) bookstore in 1994 but turned his business into a platform with the launch of Amazon Marketplace, allowing other sellers to offer their goods at a fixed price.[115] eBay has also moved in the direction of fixed prices, for example with the introduction of the 'buy it now' feature. Amazon, eBay and most other e-commerce platforms offer their services for

112 Weaved into the description of the various types of platforms is a bit of internet history, for which Brian McCullough, *How the Internet Happened: From Netscape to the iPhone* (Liveright 2018) is an excellent resource. See in particular chs 6–7 on e-commerce, 2, 10 and 16–17 on operating systems, 5 and 11 on search engines, and 14–15 on social media.

113 Apart from e-commerce platforms and app stores, the platforms that offer the digital infrastructure for the peer-to-peer economy are also a form of transaction platform. The transaction in this case may concern a taxi ride (Uber), an overnight stay (Airbnb), a new company logo (Upwork) or a leaf-free garden (TaskRabbit).

114 On the e-commerce business model, see especially Evans and Schmalensee, 'The Industrial Organization of Markets with Two-Sided Platforms' (n 24) 154–55; Haucap and Heimeshoff (n 109) 57–58; GMC (n 31) 81–103; Graef (n 98) 16–18; EC, 'Online Platforms' (n 111) 16–21.

115 On Amazon's business (model), see extensively Brad Stone, *The Everything Store* (Corgi 2014).

free on the buyer side while charging the seller side. This charge can be a (monthly) subscription fee, a listing fee, a transaction fee, or a combination of those.

A second, important type of transaction platform is the *innovation platform*, which is built around an operating system (OS).[116] Originally, this category consisted mainly of desktop OSs for PCs (eg Microsoft's Windows and Apple's macOS). With the shift from PCs to smartphones, the focus has moved to mobile OSs (Apple's iOS and Google's Android).[117] These mobile OSs offer the user access to app stores, where the transactions take place (a platform in a platform, really).[118] Apple and Google's de facto duopoly in the mobile OS market translates into two mobile app stores, namely, Apple's App Store and Google's Play Store. Like e-commerce platforms, app stores also connect buyers and sellers, with the difference that the seller is an application developer. Developers have to invest heavily in their affiliation with the OS as they must master its software development kit (SDK) and perhaps even learn a fit-for-purpose programming language. As in e-commerce, app stores charge the sellers/developers, which have to pay a fixed registration fee and a flat fee of 30% on each app purchase or in-app subscription (eg to a music streaming service), with some exceptions. On the other side of the platform, app buyers cannot just 'walk into an app store'. Each app store is embedded in a specific OS, and each OS is embedded in a specific phone (iPhone for iOS and Android for essentially every other phone), which means that the phone in your pocket determines which app store is available to you.

1.2.2 Advertising Platforms

When the platform brings about a direct interaction between user groups but indirect network effects are unilateral (ie only one side benefits from a higher number of users on the other side), it is referred to as an audience providing or *advertising platform*.[119] Such platforms connect advertisers on the one hand with 'eyeballs' on the other. These platforms' business model consists in providing advertisers access to potential customers; they are in the business of grabbing eyeballs (Wu calls them 'attention merchants').[120] Advertising platforms attract their audience's attention either by offering content (eg news websites) or a utility (eg search engines or social networks).

When newspapers and magazines started offering space to advertisers, they became a two-sided market. Later, when radio and broadcast television arrived on the scene, they quickly adopted a similar business model. *Ad-supported media* traditionally derived part of its revenue from advertising, while people also paid for the content. Today,

116 On the innovation platform business model, see especially Evans and Schmalensee, 'The Industrial Organization of Markets with Two-Sided Platforms' (n 24) 157–58.

117 It also includes video game platforms, which connect gamers with video game developers through a console.

118 On the app store business model, see especially; EC, 'Online Platforms' (n 111) 21–26.

119 On the general ad-supported media business model, see especially Evans and Schmalensee, 'The Industrial Organization of Markets with Two-Sided Platforms' (n 24) 155–56; Li (n 33), 105–8; GMC (n 31) 37–49; EC, 'Online Platforms' (n 111) 37–44.

120 Tim Wu, *The Attention Merchants: The Epic Scramble to Get Inside our Heads* (Knopf 2016).

given the ubiquity of 'free'[121] content on the internet, advertising is often the only viable way for businesses to monetize their online activity. However, business models that rely only on attracting and retaining attention are also prone to excess: fake news, for example, is in part a negative consequence of the competition for eyeballs (but not necessarily an antitrust problem).[122]

On the internet, businesses wishing to advertise their product or service ('advertisers') have an abundance of options, which makes it difficult to coordinate a marketing campaign. Businesses that want to host online advertisements ('publishers'), on the other side, may find it burdensome to enter into contracts with several advertisers. Platforms such as Google have sprung up to connect the two sides, which has led to a complicated 'ad tech stack'[123] made up of ad networks such as AdSense,[124] ad servers such as DoubleClick for Publishers (now called Ad Manager) and ad exchanges such as DoubleClick Ad Exchange/AdX (now also called Ad Manager).[125]

Quickly after its arrival, the world wide web became too expansive to be personally navigated, and *search engines* took this task upon themselves.[126] Search engines use web crawlers, which collect information from websites and index it. Early search engines, such as AltaVista, Lycos and Yahoo!, ranked search results according to the number of appearances of the search query on a certain website. In 1998, Brin and Page founded Google, whose success is due to its algorithm PageRank. PageRank did not take a quantitative approach to page ranking, but rather a qualitative approach (relying on a website's reputation, measured in terms of links to that page).[127]

Google, Bing and Yahoo! are examples of general or *horizontal search engines*, meaning they provide search results covering any category of information on the web. Specialized or *vertical search engines*, on the other hand, provide information for specific categories of information, such as Foundem for shopping and TripAdvisor for travel. However, horizontal search engines may integrate vertically, which led Google to be also active in shopping (Google Shopping) and travel (Google Flights), among others. Every search engine facilitates direct interaction between users seeking information, websites

121 At least free *in monetary terms*, given that consumers do 'pay' with their data/attention.

122 See Allen Grunes, 'Is "Fake News" a Competition Problem?' (2017) CPI Antitrust Chronicle December 1.

123 On digital advertising, see especially CMA, 'Online Platforms and Digital Advertising Market Study' (Final Report, 2020).

124 AdSense functions in concert with Google's Display Network (focused on websites) and AdMob (focused on mobile).

125 For an overview, see Daniel Bitton, Maurits Dolmans, Henry Mostyn and David Pearl, 'Competition in Display Ad Technology: A Retrospective Look at Google/DoubleClick and Google/Admob' (2019) CPI Antitrust Chronicle April, 41–43. For a more visual overview, see Keach Hagey and Vivien Ngo, 'How Google Edged Out Rivals and Built the World's Dominant Ad Machine: A Visual Guide' (*WSJ*, 7 November 2019) <https://www.wsj.com/articles/how-google-edged-out-rivals-and-built-the-worlds-dominant-ad-machine-a-visual-guide-11573142071>.

126 On the search engine business model, see especially Haucap and Heimeshoff (n 109) 49; GMC (n 31) 50–69; Graef (n 98) 10–12; EC, 'Online Platforms' (n 111) 26–32.

127 Sergey Brin and Larry Page, 'The PageRank Citation Ranking: Bringing Order to the Web' (1998) Working Paper <http://ilpubs.stanford.edu:8090/422/1/1999-66.pdf>. More generally on Google's business (model), see Eric Schmidt and Jonathan Rosenberg, *How Google Works* (John Murray 2014).

seeking an audience, and advertisers seeking new customers.[128] This intermediation is free for users and websites and financed by advertisers, who generally pay each time a user clicks on the link to their website (a 'pay per click' model).

Social networks, a last form of advertising platform, offer a space for interaction between friends or contacts on the basis of a public or semi-public profile.[129] Social networks like Friendster and MySpace knew temporary success. In 2004, Zuckerberg launched Facebook, initially limiting it to Harvard students – in 2023, the social network boasted about 3 billion users. While Facebook targets the general public, other social networks focus on specific communities (eg LinkedIn for professionals and Academia for academics). Still, other social networks are concerned with specific content (eg YouTube for videos, Snapchat for short disappearing videos, Instagram for images, and Twitter for opinions).

Social networks are primarily financed by advertisers, while users can access them for free. Content providers constitute a third side of many social media platforms. Many businesses are active on social networks, connecting with users while providing the platform with content (eg news articles in the case of a news organization).[130] Additionally, social networks may open up their application programming interfaces (APIs) to developers, allowing them to develop complementary apps – another form of content. While social networks derive the great majority of their revenue from advertisers, a commission on the (in-)app sales may provide additional financing.

While platforms can be categorized as either 'matching' or 'advertising' (and their subdivisions), many platforms combine features of both categories, and can thus be called 'hybrid'. E-commerce platforms like Amazon derive significant revenue from advertising, as do app stores. Facebook opened up its APIs to app developers, thus becoming an innovation platform next to an advertising platform. However, these side activities remain subsidiary, and – in terms of revenue – marginal compared to their main activity. In any case, issues usually relate to a specific function of the platform, whether that is the platform's main function or not.

128 Professor Zimmerman thus describes the search engine market as three-sided, see House of Lords Select Committee on European Union, 'Online Platforms and the Digital Single Market' (n 19) 19.

129 On the social media business model, see especially Haucap and Heimeshoff (n 109), 58–60; GMC (n 31) 70–80; Graef (n 98), 12–16; EC, 'Online Platforms' (n 111) 32–37.

130 This is therefore comparable to the situation of search engines, where businesses/their websites also seek an audience.

2

PLATFORM ECONOMICS AND STRATEGY

[T]here's no economic proposition that can't be stated in clear, accessible language.[131]

The 'rise of the platform enterprise'[132] has led some to declare 'the rise of the platform economy'[133] – and it is true that today, platforms make up an impressive (and increasing) share of the global economy. However, this section is not concerned with the macro perspective, but rather with the microeconomics governing platforms. Combining theoretical economic insights with business strategy literature, it seeks to understand the particularities of the platform business model, in order to prevent mistakes when assessing their behaviour. First, let's take a look at the foundation of platform economics.

In their 2003 article, Rochet and Tirole presented their theory on multisided markets as a crossover between the work on network externalities and the literature on multi-product pricing[134] – a characterization that subsequent authors have repeated.[135] The core idea of each subject matter is the following:

1. *Externalities*. An externality is essentially an effect of an economic action on an unrelated party, be it positive or negative. These externalities are not accounted for in the individual decisions of economic actors – they are not 'internalized'.

---

131 A quote by the economist John Kenneth Galbraith, see <http://www.memorablequotations.com/galbraith.htm>.

132 Evans and Gawer (n 110).

133 Martin Kenney and John Zysman, 'The Rise of the Platform Economy' (2016) 33 Issues in Science and Technology 61.

134 Rochet and Tirole, 'Platform competition in Two-Sided Markets' (n 21) 991; repeated in Rochet and Tirole, 'Two-Sided Markets: A Progress Report' (n 21) 646.

135 Evans, 'The Antitrust Economics of Multi-Sided Platform Markets' (n 22) 331–33; Parker and Van Alstyne, 'Two-Sided Network Effects: A Theory of Information Product Design' (n 27) 1494; Evans and Schmalensee, 'The Industrial Organization of Markets with Two-Sided Platforms' (n 24) 154; Weyl (n 28) 1650; Filistrucchi, Geradin and van Damme (n 37) 38–39.

2. *Multiple products*. The literature on multiproduct pricing is concerned with the price structure of complementary products, eg razors (which are relatively cheap) and the complementary blades (which are relatively expensive). While such products are priced differently, an economic actor will consider the products (and their combined price) together in their purchase decision.

The theory on multisided market builds on the idea that there are non-internalized, positive *externalities*. According to Rochet and Tirole, 'an end-user does not internalize the welfare impact of his use of the platform on other end-users.'[136] For example, the buyer is doing the seller a favour by being active on an e-commerce platform (and vice versa) but does not take this into account.

From the *multiproduct pricing* literature, multisided market theory borrows the focus on price structure. As Parker and Van Alstyne put it: 'The fact that lowering price on one half of a matched pair sells more of the other has precedent in multiproduct pricing.'[137] For example, lowering the price of razors will sell more razor blades. In this case, externalities are internalized, but this process is confined within the same user (group). The difference with platforms can be described as follows:

> [T]he buyer of a razor internalizes in his purchase decision the net surplus that he will derive from buying razor blades. The starting point for the theory of two-sided markets, by contrast, is that an end-user does not internalize the welfare impact of his use of the platform on other end-users.[138]

In conclusion, the novelty with platforms is, firstly, that externalities benefit the user group on the other side of the platform, and secondly, that not the users but the platforms internalize these externalities.[139] Network effects are discussed in the section on the market power of platforms.[140] The particular pricing strategies that these network effects (in combination with a number of other factors) lead to are described in the next section.

136 Rochet and Tirole, 'Two-Sided Markets: A Progress Report' (n 21) 646.

137 Parker and Van Alstyne, 'Two-Sided Network Effects: A Theory of Information Product Design' (n 27) 1496.

138 Rochet and Tirole, 'Two-Sided Markets: A Progress Report' (n 21) 646.

139 This shows, once again, the connection with the Coase theorem. If the different user groups could enter into bilateral transactions, they would be able to internalize the indirect externalities themselves. However, since transaction costs (broadly understood) prevent them from bargaining directly, they need an intermediary. Illustrating this dynamic with the earlier nightclub example, Evans notes that '[m]en could in theory go around a singles bar and pay women to consider them as romantic prospects, but it tends not to happen', see Evans, 'The Antitrust Economics of Multi-Sided Platform Markets' (n 22) 332–33.

140 Section 4.1.2.

2.1 Platform Pricing Strategies

2.1.1 Solving the Chicken and Egg Problem: Picking a Money Side

Platforms are characterized by indirect network effects, which means that users have larger expected gains, the larger the number of users on the other side of the market.[141] On an e-commerce platform, sellers appreciate more buyers (higher demand), and buyers appreciate more sellers (higher chance of finding the right product at the right price). However, a new platform starts with neither buyers nor sellers, and accordingly finds it hard to attract either. Caillaud and Jullien aptly call this conundrum the 'chicken and egg problem'.[142] To solve it, they propose a 'divide-and-conquer' strategy, which consists in 'subsidizing the participation of one side (divide) and recovering the loss on the other side (conquer)'.[143] In other words, to attract users, platforms must figure out how to charge each side appropriately by choosing not only a price level for their service, but also a price structure.[144] Empirical evidence confirms Caillaud and Jullien's proposition that this often means treating 'one side as a profit center and the other as a loss leader, or, at best, financially neutral.'[145] When the platform successfully attracts the required number of users, it is said to achieve 'critical mass'.[146]

While this theory is simple enough, a more difficult question is how to determine the choice of profit centre or 'money side'. Several factors should guide this choice.

Firstly, the platform will choose the side with the lowest *price elasticity* as its profit centre.[147] In other words, the platform will charge the side that is most insensitive to price increases (relative to the other side). Conversely, the platform will court the user group with a high price elasticity (that is sensitive to price increases) by keeping the price low on that side. Rochet and Tirole single out 'captive users', whose extreme loyalty to the platform (eg due to long-term contracts or significant investments) makes them particularly price inelastic; their presence will raise the price on their side and lower it on the other.[148]

141 Caillaud and Jullien (n 56) 309–10.

142 ibid 310, where they describe it as follows (focusing on an e-commerce context): '[T]o attract buyers, an intermediary should have a large base of registered sellers, but these will be willing to register only if they expect many buyers to show up.'

143 ibid 310. Wright warns against terming this a 'cross-subsidy' as 'it ignores the fact that the service that is being provided to each type of user depends on whether the service is also provided to the other type of user', see Wright (n 25) 50.

144 Rochet and Tirole, 'Platform Competition in Two-Sided Markets' (n 21) 990.

145 ibid 991 for the statement, 992 for the empirical evidence, and the remainder of the article for its theoretical foundations; Evans, 'The Antitrust Economics of Multi-Sided Platform Markets' (n 22) 337–38 for empirical evidence, and the remainder of the article for more anecdotal evidence.

146 See David Evans and Richard Schmalensee, 'Failure to Launch: Critical Mass in Platform Businesses' (2010) 9 Review of Network Economics 1.

147 Rochet and Tirole, 'Platform Competition in Two-Sided Markets' (n 21) 996–97; Evans, 'The Antitrust Economics of Multi-Sided Platform Markets' (n 22) 342–43; Rochet and Tirole, 'Two-Sided Markets: A Progress Report' (n 21) 658; Rysman (n 26) 129–30.

148 Rochet and Tirole, 'Platform Competition in Two-Sided Markets' (n 21) 1008 and 1013; Evans, 'The Antitrust Economics of Multi-Sided Platform Markets' (n 22) 353; Rochet and Tirole, 'Two-Sided Markets: A Progress Report' (n 21) 659.

The relative strength of *indirect network effects* also plays a role in determining a platform's price structure. The side exerting greater indirect network effects will receive a lower price, while the side exerting smaller indirect network effects will have to pay a premium.[149] When the indirect network effects from one side are particularly strong,[150] it actually makes sense for a platform to set a negative price on this side because of the benefits from stimulating demand on the other side.[151]

Moreover, a platform's price structure depends on its users' ability to engage in *multihoming*. 'Multihoming' is a technical term appropriated by Rochet and Tirole to mean 'connecting to several platforms'.[152] Multihoming is prevalent, for example, with regard to social networks (many people use both Facebook and Instagram), but not with regard to app stores (as most people have only one phone). Its effects on a platform's price structure are, however, ambiguous.[153] On the one hand, the platform may want to lower the prices on the multihoming side to discourage these users from affiliating with a different platform.[154] On the other hand, multihoming on one side 'intensifies price competition on the other side as platforms use low prices in an attempt to "steer" end users on the latter side toward an exclusive relationship'.[155] In other words, platforms compete on price for exclusive control for the users that do *not* multihome ('single-home'). They do so to create what Armstrong calls a 'competitive bottleneck': when one side can be induced to single-home, the other side will be forced to go through the platform to get access to these users (as the platform has a monopoly over them).[156] In this situation, the multihoming side is charged high prices, while the single-homing side is offered low prices.

---

149 Evans, 'The Antitrust Economics of Multi-Sided Platform Markets' (n 22) 343–45; Wright, (n 25) 47 (speaking of surplus for the other user group rather than indirect network effects); Parker and Van Alstyne, 'Two-Sided Network Effects: A Theory of Information Product Design' (n 27) 1503; Armstrong (n 25) 668–69.

150 Rochet and Tirole call individual users on one side who exert particularly strong network effects 'marquee users'; their presence will reduce the price on their side of the platform and raise it on the other side, see Rochet and Tirole, 'Platform Competition in Two-Sided Markets' (n 21) 1008 and 1013; Evans, 'The Antitrust Economics of Multi-Sided Platform Markets' (n 22) 353; Rochet and Tirole, 'Two-Sided Markets: A Progress Report' (n 21) 659.

151 Evans, 'The Antitrust Economics of Multi-Sided Platform Markets' (n 22) 345; Armstrong (n 25) 682; Rysman (n 26) 130.

152 Defined by Techopedia as 'a mechanism used to configure one computer with more than one network interface and multiple IP addresses', see <https://www.techopedia.com/definition/24984/multihoming>; Rochet and Tirole, 'Platform Competition in Two-Sided Markets' (n 21) 991–93.

153 The effects could offset each other, see Rochet and Tirole, 'Platform Competition in Two-Sided Markets' (n 21) 1025 ('For linear demand on the buyer side, these two effects offset'). However, they could also lead to a drop in the general price level of the platform, see Evans, 'The Antitrust Economics of Multi-Sided Platform Markets' (n 22) 346 (holding that multihoming 'affects both the price level and the pricing structure'). As multihoming means more competition, a drop in the price level is consistent with the Cournot model. It is thus to conclude that 'the impact on relative prices is ambiguous', see Rochet and Tirole, 'Two-Sided Markets: A Progress Report' (n 21) 660.

154 Rochet and Tirole, 'Platform Competition in Two-Sided Markets' (n 21) 1025; Evans, 'The Antitrust Economics of Multi-Sided Platform Markets' (n 22) 346–47.

155 Rochet and Tirole, 'Platform Competition in Two-Sided Markets' (n 21) 993 (quote), 1008 and 1113. See also Evans, 'The Antitrust Economics of Multi-Sided Platform Markets' (n 22) 346, and Rochet and Tirole, 'Two-Sided Markets: A Progress Report' (n 21) 660.

156 Armstrong (n 25) 669–70 and 677–89, where he refers to Caillaud and Jullien (n 56) 319–20 and 323. See also the discussion by Rysman (n 26) 130–31.

These factors play out clearly in *advertising platforms* such as Google, which offer their users a free service while treating the advertisers as the money side.[157] The free users are considered more price sensitive; one can indeed imagine an exodus to alternatives such as DuckDuckGo once Google starts charging users for every search query. The indirect network effects are unilateral: advertisers benefit from the free users' attention, but not the other way around – another argument to let the advertisers bear the costs. Finally, both the free users and the advertisers can multihome, but not without a potential cost (less personalized search results and more crudely targeted advertising, respectively).

2.1.2 Pricing Methods: Membership and Usage Fees

A key finding of the platform literature is the fact that price does not track marginal cost. A different but related question is how platforms implement their particular pricing structure. As noted, a platform facilitates interactions between different user groups. On a matching platform, this interaction consists in finding a suitable counterparty, be it for a date (on a dating platform) or a transaction (on an e-commerce platform or app store); on an advertising platform, the interaction takes place when the potential customers engage with the ad. The question, then, is how a platform monetizes its facilitating role.

First, it is necessary to distinguish between membership (or registration or fixed) and usage (or transaction or variable) fees (see Figure 3). A membership fee is the price owed for getting access to the platform (it is paid *ex ante*), while a usage fee is the price owed when an interaction takes place on the platform (it is paid *ex post*).[158] The pricing method, ie the choice for membership and/or usage fees, will depend on (i) which information the platform possesses and (ii) which behaviour the platform seeks to incentivize.

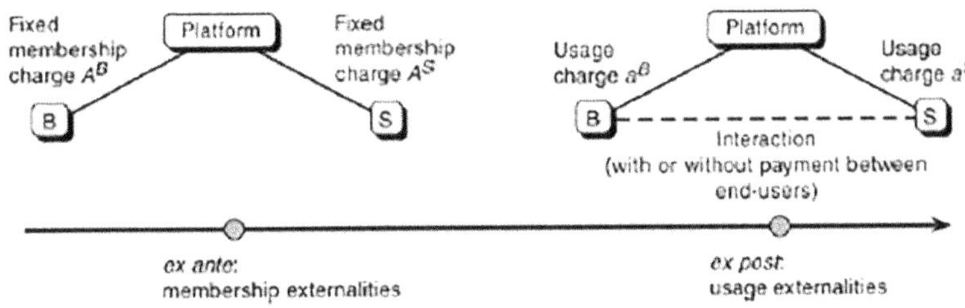

Figure 3 Membership vs usage fees (Rochet & Tirole 2006)

157 This analysis is simplified for illustrative purposes. As set out above, publishers represent another side of Google's advertising platform; including them would greatly complicate the analysis. It is, however, interesting to observe how Google imposed a single-homing obligation on its publishers, see *Google Search (AdSense)* (Case AT.40411) Commission Decision C(2019)2173.

158 Caillaud and Jullien (n 56) 310 and 322.

a. Information. Firstly, a platform's pricing will depend on which information it possesses. Is the platform able to monitor the interactions it facilitates? If so, the platform can charge usage fees for every successful interaction; if not (ie when users can bypass the platform once they find each other), then the platform must resort to membership fees.[159]

Dating platforms, for example, can give different users access to each other, but cannot sufficiently track how many dates actually take place. Thus, they tend to charge users a membership fee, irrespective of the value they end up creating. E-commerce platforms, which usually handle billing, are able to trace transactions and can therefore impose a usage fee on each one they facilitate. For advertising platforms, the billing situation is slightly more complex. They can either keep track of how many potential customers click on an ad ('pay per click') or count the number of times an ad was displayed ('ad impressions').

b. Incentives. Secondly, the platform will want to adjust its price structure so as to induce (potential) users to take the desired course of action, ie incentivize them to either join the platform or use it to interact.[160] Caillaud and Jullien find that *usage fees* 'are a powerful weapon for [platforms] to gain market shares'.[161] With this model, the price paid by the user depends solely on how well the platform does in facilitating interactions, and users cannot 'waste' their money on a useless membership (the infamous business model of gym memberships). Thus, it makes sense for users to join even a small platform: they get access to a number of extra users on the other side, and as long as it does not benefit them (through successful interactions), they are not required to pay. Armstrong holds that with this strategy, 'to attract one side of the market, it is not so important that the platform first gets the other side on board.'[162] Usage fees therefore mitigate the chicken and egg problem.

On the other hand, a successful platform may want to use *membership fees* to induce user loyalty. Amazon Prime, the company's loyalty programme, is a good example. For a fee of around $100, the programme offers US consumers unlimited two-day shipping and a growing number of other benefits (including video streaming, music streaming and e-books). Research shows that Amazon Prime members significantly increase their spending on Amazon's platform and are less likely to buy elsewhere.[163] In the words of one former Amazon employee who worked on the Prime team, it was never about the membership fee, '[i]t was really about changing people's mentality so they wouldn't shop anywhere else'.[164]

159 ibid 310; Rochet and Tirole, 'Two-Sided Markets: A Progress Report' (n 21) 651–52.

160 Caillaud and Jullien (n 56) 310; Rochet and Tirole, 'Two-Sided Markets: A Progress Report' (n 21) 647, speaking of 'usage decisions' and 'membership decisions'.

161 Caillaud and Jullien (n 56) 310; confirmed by Armstrong (n 25) 669.

162 Armstrong (n 25) 669.

163 For an overview, see Lina Khan, 'Amazon's Antitrust Paradox' (2017) 126 Yale Law Journal 710, 750–53.

164 Brad Stone, 'What's in Amazon's Box? Instant Gratification' (*Bloomberg*, 24 November 2010) <https://www.bloomberg.com/news/articles/2010-11-24/whats-in-amazons-box-instant-gratification>.

2.2 Platform Growth Strategies

The previous section examined how platforms must price their services to their various user groups – a fundamental decision for any platform, and one that is strongly underpinned by economic theory. Price is, however, only one component of business strategy. This section broadens the perspective on 'platform strategy'. It seeks to complete the answer to questions such as 'How does a platform successfully enter the market?' and 'How does it grow into one of the behemoths we see today?', or more succinctly, 'How do platforms compete?' These are critical questions of business strategy – as such, they can be put in terms of Porter's seminal five forces model.[165] For platforms, however, these forces behave differently, and new factors come into play.[166] Indeed, 'the scope of strategy for platforms is significantly wider than for normal firms'.[167] Therefore, this section presents the essentials of business strategy in the platform economy. However, the end goal is not to provide an updated five forces analysis; rather, the idea is to show how certain strategies that make good business sense for platforms may conflict with competition law doctrines. This section thus serves as a stepping stone to the next part of this thesis, where platform behaviour is assessed under article 102 TFEU's abuse of dominance provision.

2.2.1 The Importance of Scale: Growth-Over-Profit Strategies

'Competition is for losers.' This provocative statement – at least to antitrust lawyers – comes from Thiel, the author of *From Zero to One*.[168] He argues that every tech startup that wants to turn a profit should aim for monopoly – first in a narrow market, and then in related markets. Of course, building a monopoly is an expensive enterprise, but that is what venture capital (VC) funds are for. While sometimes overstating its thesis, Thiel's book – which is read as a business bible in Silicon Valley – illuminates an important business strategy for tech companies: focus on growth first, profit later.

While Thiel's lessons on business strategy derive mainly from his experience as a startup founder and VC, his intuition is borne out by the economics that guide online platforms. As explained above, platforms need to attract users on both sides of the market in order to be successful: unless they reach a critical mass of users in due time, they disappear. But user acquisition is usually not a linear process. Indeed, network effects imply that the platform's value is determined by the quantity (and quality) of

---

165 These five forces are: (1) threat of new entrants; (2) bargaining power of suppliers; (3) bargaining power of buyers; (4) threat of substitutes; and (5) rivalry among existing competitors, see Michael Porter, 'How Competitive Forces Shape Strategy' (1979) HBR March–April 137.

166 Marshall Van Alstyne, Geoffrey Parker and Sangeet Choudary, 'Pipelines, Platforms, and the New Rules of Strategy' (*HBR*, April 2016) <https://hbr.org/2016/04/pipelines-platforms-and-the-new-rules-of-strategy>.

167 Kevin Boudreau and Andrei Hagiu, 'Platforms Rules: Multi-Sided Platforms as Regulators' in Annabelle Gawer, *Platforms, Markets and Innovation* (Edward Elgar 2009) 187.

168 Peter Thiel, *From Zero to One: Notes on Startups, or How to Build the Future* (Crown Business 2014).

the users on either side, which means that attracting users will attract additional users, which will then attract yet more users – and so on. This 'positive feedback loop'[169] fuels exponential growth and generally leads to concentrated markets. Indeed, in the presence of strong network effects, the market may even 'tip' in favour of one particular platform that comes to dominate the market.[170] Such markets are then qualified as 'winner takes most' or even 'winner takes all'.[171]

Because of the above dynamic, which results in a few or even just one platform dominating the market, platforms are said to compete *for* the market rather than *in* the market.[172] That is why many platforms choose to (or are obliged to) pursue a growth-over-profit strategy.[173] Such a strategy generally implies burning through large amounts of capital. Investors are willing to provide this capital based on the expectation of profits at some point in the future when the platform has captured (a large share of) the market.

Uber offers one of the clearest examples of such a strategy, and the data it filed with the US Securities and Exchange Commission (SEC) for its initial public offering (IPO) even allow us to delve into the numbers.[174] In its filing, Uber states that its strategy is 'to create the largest network in each market so that [it] can have the greatest liquidity network effect'.[175] Creating the largest network, however, is an expensive enterprise: over a period of three years (2016–18), the company reported a loss from operations exceeding $10 billion. A large part of this loss can be ascribed to user acquisition costs, which are central to its strategy:

> We can choose to use incentives, such as promotions for Drivers and consumers, to attract platform users on both sides of our network, which can result in a negative margin until we reach sufficient scale to reduce incentives.[176]

169 Hal Varian, 'Use and Abuse of Network Effects' (2017) 1 and 6 <https://ssrn.com/abstract=3215488>.

170 Michael Katz and Carl Shapiro, 'Systems Competition and Network Effects' (1994) 8 Journal of Economic Perspectives 93, 105–6 (focusing on particular technologies); Joseph Farrell and Paul Klemperer, 'Coordination and Lock-In: Competition with Switching Costs and Network Effects' in Mark Armstrong and Robert Porter, *Handbook of Industrial Organization* (Elsevier 2007) 1975 and 2034–35 (mentioning not only technologies but also products).

171 Geoffrey Parker, Marshall Van Alstyne and Sangeet Choudary, *Platform Revolution* (Norton 2016) 224–27. See also John Hand, 'Evidence on the Winner-Takes-All Business Model: The Profitability Returns-to-Scale of Expenditures on Intangibles Made by U.S. Internet Firms, 1995–2001' (2001) <https://ssrn.com/abstract=292099>.

172 Graef (n 98) ch 3; AdlC and CMA, 'The Economics of Open and Closed Systems' (Report, 2014) 17.

173 See eg Khan, 'Amazon's Antitrust Paradox' (n 163) 746–55 and 803; Nick Srnicek, *Platform Capitalism* (Polity 2017) 119–21 ('there is a complete lack of profitability for most of these businesses. … The "growth before profit" model dictates that taking significant losses is simply part of the strategy, though'); Kenneth Bamberger and Orly Lobel, 'Platform Market Power' (2017) 32 Berkeley Technology Law Journal 1051, 1081–82. Note that firms have long pursued growth over profits, see eg William Baumol, 'On the Theory of Expansion of the Firm' (1962) 52 The American Economic Review 1078. However, largely due to network effects, platforms take this strategy to an extreme.

174 Uber Technologies Inc., Form S-1 Registration Statement to the SEC.

175 ibid.

176 ibid.

This growth strategy appears to be working: while it took Uber five years from launch (2012–16) to complete its first *one* billion trips, it took less than three years (2016–18) to get to a total of *ten* billion trips. However, it remains to be seen when (or even whether) Uber will reach sufficient scale to be profitable, especially as it faces a persistent competitor in its ride-hailing rival, Lyft.

While Uber may offer the clearest example of a growth-over-profit strategy, Amazon offers a subtler (and more mature) example. Amazon suffered losses during the six years following its IPO (1997–2002) but has reported profits for most years since.[177] Still, those profits have remained extremely modest in comparison to the company's revenue – a fact that is clearly illustrated by Figure 4.[178]

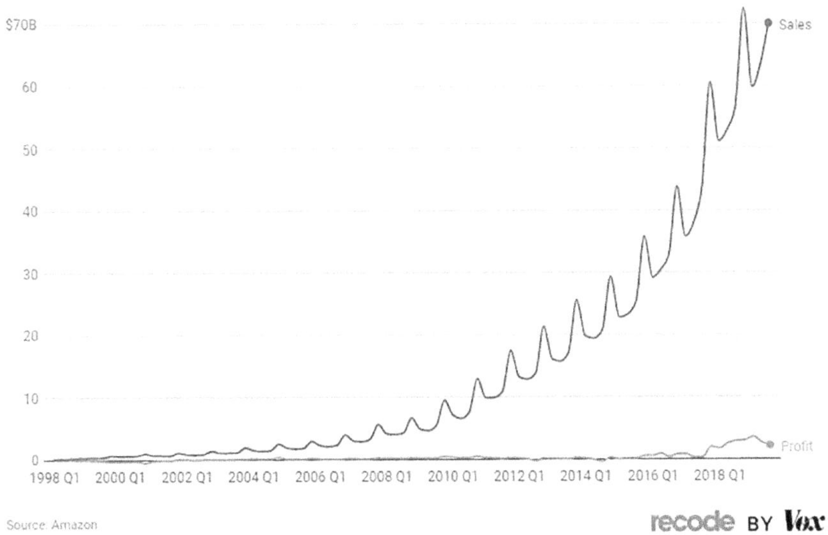

Figure 4 Amazon's revenue vs profit (Recode 2019)

These numbers suggest that Amazon prefers to reinvest rather than distribute profits to shareholders. Such an investment strategy demonstrates a long-term vision, which in itself should be applauded; nevertheless, it has prompted predatory pricing

177 Amazon's first profitable quarter occurred in 2001, see Amazon.com Inc., Form 10-K annual report to the SEC for the fiscal year ended December 31, 2001 ('We have incurred significant losses since we began doing business. As of December 31, 2001, we had an accumulated deficit of $2.86 billion and our stockholders' equity was a deficit of $1.44 billion. We have incurred substantial operating losses since our inception and, notwithstanding our recent performance in the fourth quarter of 2001, we may continue to incur such losses for the foreseeable future.'). Losses still climbed the following year, see Amazon.com Inc., Form 10-K annual report to the SEC for the fiscal year ended December 31, 2002 ('As of December 31, 2002, we had an accumulated deficit of $3.0 billion'). For Amazon, 2003 marked a turning point as it recorded a yearly profit, see Amazon.com Inc., Form 10-K annual report to the SEC for the fiscal year ended December 31, 2003 ('we earned a small amount of net income in 2003', but warning that it 'may incur losses again in the future', which it did during some quarters).

178 Rani Molla, 'Amazon's Tiny Profits, Explained' (*Recode*, 24 October 2019) <https://www.vox.com/recode/2019/8/21/20826405/amazons-profits-revenue-free-cash-flow-explained-charts>. The data that this chart is based on (ie annual reports filed with the SEC) is available via <https://ir.aboutamazon.com/sec-filings>.

allegations. These allegations rest on premises that – even if theoretically valid – are difficult to test, including that Amazon (i) uses loopholes in accounting standards to exclude a significant portion of its expenses;[179] and (ii) cross-subsidizes, ie uses the profits from certain units of its business (eg Amazon Web Services, its lucrative cloud computing service), to make up for losses in other units (eg Amazon Marketplace).[180]

Whether growth is funded with investments (Uber) or via other lines of business (Amazon), the point is to describe a fundamental business strategy of platforms, ie to pursue growth over profits. The growth-over-profit strategy serves as a stepping stone to an even more fundamental platform strategy: ecosystem building. As noted, Thiel advised tech companies to build a monopoly in one market and then branch out. Let's look at how and why platforms expand from their core market into ever more adjacent markets.

2.2.2 The Benefits of Scope: Ecosystem Building

Many platforms thus start their undertaking in a core market: for Google, it was search; for Amazon, online commerce; for Facebook, social networking; for Apple, operating systems.[181] But once a platform has established a strong position in that core market, it rarely stops there; rather, 'successful platform businesses tend to move aggressively into new terrain and into what were once considered separate industries with little warning'.[182] Some even argue that 'leveraging market power to compete in other markets is often at the very core of the platform business model'.[183] What is certain is that once a platform's initial growth strategy has proven successful, it will often start entering different yet related lines of business.[184] This tendency of platforms to enter adjacent markets is driven by a variety of factors. First, platforms control the 'basic building blocks' of the digital economy and can use them as the foundation for related lines of business,[185] which

179 Shaoul Sussman, 'Prime Predator: Amazon and the Rationale of Below Average Variable Cost Pricing Strategies Among Negative-Cash Flow Firms' (2019) 7 JAE 203, 213–18; Slim Shady, 'Understanding How Amazon's Use of Capital Leases Overstates Its Cash Flow Metrics' (*Seeking Alpha*, 9 December 2014) <https://seekingalpha.com/article/2743335-understanding-how-amazons-use-of-capital-leases-overstates-its-cash-flow-metrics>.

180 Khan, 'Amazon's Antitrust Paradox' (n 163) 722–30, 747–53, 756–68 and 791–92.

181 Note that, as explained above, not all these companies started out as platforms (Amazon, for example, started as a book *retailer*); I focus here on their first platform business. Also, the focus on growth over profits has only become stronger over the years, meaning that it applied less to 'older' tech companies such as Apple.

182 Van Alstyne, Parker and Choudary (n 166). See similarly Feng Zhu and Marco Iansiti, 'Why Some Platforms Thrive and Others Don't' (*HBR*, January–February 2019) <https://hbr.org/2019/01/why-some-platforms-thrive-and-others-dont> ('By leveraging [their high number of users and the data on their interactions], firms that have succeeded in one industry vertical often diversify into different lines of business and improve their economics').

183 Orly Lobel and Kenneth Bamberger, 'Platform Market Power' (2017) 32 Berkeley Technology Law Journal 1051, 1088.

184 For general perspectives on this strategy, see Evans and Schmalensee, *Matchmakers: The New Economics of Multi-Sided Platforms* (n 92) 35–37 and 102–18; Parker, Van Alstyne and Choudary (n 171) 213–23; Ariel Ezrachi and Maurice Stucke, *Virtual Competition: The Promise and Perils of the Algorithm-Driven Economy* (HUP 2016) 147–58; Srnicek (n 173) 98–113. More specific literature is referenced below.

185 Alain Strowel and Wouter Vergote, 'Digital Platforms: To Regulate or Not to Regulate?' in Bram Devolder (ed), *The Platform Economy: Unravelling the Legal Status of Online Intermediaries* (Intersentia 2019) 17–18 and Alexandre de Streel, 'Should Digital Antitrust Be Ordoliberal?' Concurrences no 1-2020, art

explains their unique ability to leverage their position from one market to another. Second, platforms' presence across multiple markets generates significant economies of scope (which may benefit consumers, eg through reduced search costs). Third, a multiplicity of services may lock users into the platform, thus ensuring their loyalty. At the same time, existing users can be turned into customers of new products, which can speed up the process of reaching minimum efficient scale or critical mass.

To truly understand the ecosystem-building process, it is useful to start with a categorization of entry into adjacent markets: when it comes to the *method* of entry, the entry can be either organic or artificial; when it comes to the *kind* of entry, the entry can consist in a vertical, horizontal, or conglomerate expansion. Let's look at each of these methods and kinds of entry, and at how platforms engage in them.

First, entry can be organic or artificial. A platform enters an adjacent market *organically* by developing a new product that is closely related to its core market (internal growth). Often, the platform can boost the development and marketing of this product by leveraging the strong (or even dominant) position it maintains in its core market.[186] For one, the platform can use the data it collects as a platform operator to decide which market to expand into.[187] Amazon, for example, is said to use its data on third-party transactions to determine which products to start producing and selling itself.[188] It may also be possible for the platform to leverage its user base from one market to another.[189] When Amazon started a music streaming service, it included access to a basic version (Prime Music) in Prime memberships; when Prime members want to upgrade to the full version (Amazon Music Unlimited), they get a $2 monthly discount.[190] In other words, the platform user base can be enticed to become early adopters of the new service.[191] While the majority of platforms' expansion has been organic, fuelled by their ease of entry in adjacent markets, a considerable part of it has been *artificial*,

no 92610, 2 <www.concurrences.com/92610> ('product development is often based on sharable modules, like Lego blocks, that can be used and reused to develop very different products or services').

186 Howard Shelanski, 'Information, Innovation, and Competition Policy for the Internet' (2013) 161 University of Pennsylvania Law Review 1663, 1676–77; Nigel Walton, 'New Conglomerates and the Ecosystem Advantage' (2014) 13 China-USA Business Review 431, 437 (GAFAM 'can now enter new markets and industries without making high risk acquisitions and taking possession of costly assets by leveraging its core competencies instead'); Kadar (n 98) 5–6 ('market power at the level of the platform may be "amplified" and extended to other markets that are connected to the platform'); Lobel and Bamberger (n 183)1087–89 ('leveraging market power to compete in other markets is often at the very core of the platform business model'); Lina Khan, 'Sources of Tech Platform Power' (2018) 2 Georgetown Law Tech Review 325, 328 (the fact that platforms serve as critical infrastructure 'enables a platform to leverage its platform dominance to establish an advantageous position in a separate or ancillary market').

187 Generally on the ways in which platforms leverage the value of data, see Parker, Van Alstyne and Choudary (n 171) 217–20.

188 Hagiu and Wright, 'Marketplace or Reseller?' (n 75) 196–97; Feng Zhu and Qihong Liu, 'Competing with Complementors: An Empirical Look at Amazon.com' (2018) 39 Strategic Management Journal 2618.

189 See similarly Van Alstyne, Parker and Choudary (n 166) (describing how the primary competitive threat in the platform economy consists in 'an established platform with superior network effects that uses its relationships with customers to enter your industry').

190 Amazon, 'What is Prime Music?' <https://www.amazon.com/primeinsider/music/set-up-music.html>.

191 For another example, see Ashley King, 'Apple Officially Unveils TV+ – Get Ready for Some Serious Bundling' (*Digital Music News*, 1 November 2019) <https://www.digitalmusicnews.com/2019/11/01/apple-tv-plus-launch/> (describing how students with an Apple Music subscription receive a complimentary subscription to Apple's new video streaming service).

realized through the acquisition of competitors or companies offering services related to the platform (external growth).[192] I discuss these acquisitions in more detail below.[193]

Second, platform integration can be vertical, horizontal or conglomerate. The terminology of *vertical* integration is a poor fit for the platform business model: on the one hand, platforms are situated between suppliers and consumers, which invites comparisons to distributors (the downstream level); on the other hand, their control over a digital infrastructure makes them more like the network operators we see in telecommunications (the upstream level). I consider the platform level the upstream level. Platforms thus integrate vertically when they start producing the downstream product, which differs from platform to platform.[194] A search engine, for example, integrates vertically when it starts producing its own output, such as the more specialized services people look for through it – so-called vertical search. Vertical search includes services such as local search (eg Google Local), flight comparison (eg Google Flights) and comparison shopping (eg Google Shopping). An e-commerce platform, by contrast, integrates vertically when it produces its own goods to distribute through its marketplace.

Platforms also expand *horizontally*. Beyond simply growing the platform's flagship product, such expansion can consist in either developing an alternative, competing platform or acquiring such a platform. Horizontal expansion can make strategic sense as it allows the incumbent to 'pack the product space', ie leave no opening in the product space uncovered for potential competitors, thereby raising barriers to entry.[195] At the same time, incumbents have to deal with the risk of cannibalization, ie introducing a new product will draw existing users away from the incumbent's old product instead of increasing its market share.[196] This risk may favour acquisition over development, as the former increases the odds of acquiring new users while the latter is more likely to simply shift users around.[197] However, casual observation shows that even such purely horizontal acquisitions are relatively rare in the platform economy.

---

192 John Newman, 'Antitrust in Digital Markets' (2019) 72 Vanderbilt Law Review 1497, 1511 ('Many digital-focused firms rely heavily on a strategy of acquisitions. But their targets typically compete in separate relevant markets, at least as traditional antitrust analysts employ that concept.').

193 See Section 13.1. An overview of GAFAM acquisitions is appended to US House of Representatives – Judiciary Subcommittee on Antitrust, 'Investigation of Competition in Digital Markets' (Majority Staff Report and Recommendations, 2020) (hereafter, 'House Judiciary Report') 432–51.

194 Hagiu and Wright have explored a number of factors which determine the choice of a platform to vertically integrate, see Hagiu and Wright, 'Multi-sided platforms' (n 28) 164–70.

195 Garth Saloner, Andrea Shepard and Joel Podolny, *Strategic Management* (Wiley 2001) 232–35.

196 Cannibalization occurs every time a firm's new product competes for customers with the firm's older product. The firm will thus – to some extent – attract its own customers instead of capturing additional market share. As there is a cost to developing and marketing the new product, such cannibalization will hurt the firm's profits. For an application to search engines, see Greg Taylor, 'Search Quality and Revenue Cannibalization by Competing Search Engines' (2013) 22 Journal of Economics & Management Strategy 445.

197 This conjecture should be nuanced by the fact that tech giants seem to embrace rather than fear cannibalization. See eg Walter Isaacson, *Steve Jobs* (Abacus 2015) 376 ('If you don't cannibalize yourself, someone else will.'); Antonio García Martínez, *Chaos Monkeys: Obscene Fortune and Random Failure in Silicon Valley* (Harper 2016) 249 (on Zuckerberg's reminder to employees that '[i]f we don't create the thing that kills Facebook, someone else will'); Peter Elstrom and Lulu Chen, 'Alibaba's New Chairman Says He Has to Reinvent Retail Before Someone Else Does' (*Bloomberg*, 9 September 2019) <https://www.bloomberg.com/news/articles/2019-09-09/alibaba-s-new-chair-says-he-ll-find-the-way-to-kill-his-business> ('If we don't kill our existing business, someone else will. So I'd rather see our own new business kill our existing business.').

Conglomerate expansion, finally, may just be the preferred method of expansion for platforms.[198] Such an expansion implies entering into a line of business that is neither a strong substitute for the platform's core product nor vertically related to the platform; nevertheless, the line of business is closely connected to the platform's core market, eg as a *potential* competitor or a complement.[199] Consider, for example, Facebook's acquisition of tbh – an app that let you send prewritten compliments to friends. tbh offered a narrow social networking service and could thus be conceived as both a complement and potential competitor to Facebook. However, we will never be sure of the latter as Facebook shut the app down shortly after acquisition.[200]

The line between vertical, horizontal and conglomerate platform expansions is often a thin one. The fact that platforms provide the digital infrastructure for the distribution of a variety of products means that developing any such product can be qualified as a vertical expansion. Moreover, as platforms have a unique capacity to integrate complementary products into their infrastructure, the distinction between vertical integration and conglomerate expansion can be blurry. Drawing a line between horizontal and conglomerate expansions can also be difficult, as it requires qualifying the undertakings as either actual or potential competitors. In other words, one is asked to make a binary choice while there is, in fact, a whole spectrum between actual and potential competition. For example, at the time of its acquisition, was the photo-sharing app Instagram an actual or potential competitor of Facebook?[201]

Despite the differences between the various kinds and methods of expansion, there is a strategy that unites them: ecosystem building.[202] In one sense, the 'ecosystem' terminology points to the broader environment around platforms: beyond a stable core (eg an OS), there is a wide range of independent third parties adding value by providing complements (eg app developers).[203] Compared to traditional, vertically integrated systems, platform ecosystems are considered a superior way of organizing innovation by those independent third parties.[204] This is explained by platforms' inherent 'generativity', which denotes 'a technology's overall capacity to produce unprompted change driven by large, varied,

198 See eg Marc Bourreau and Alexandre de Streel, 'Digital Conglomerates and EU Competition Policy' (CERRE Report, 2019) 4 ('one of the main and most intriguing characteristics of the digital sector is the resurgence of conglomeralism'). Conglomerate firm structures had fallen out of favour because they were considered difficult for executives to manage and hard for investors to understand, among others. This leads to a 'conglomerate discount', meaning the market value of a conglomerate is lower than the sum value of its parts.

199 See Guidelines on the assessment of non-horizontal mergers under the Council Regulation on the control of concentrations between undertakings [2008] OJ C265/6, paras 5 and 91.

200 Jacob Kastrenakes, 'Facebook is Shutting Down a Teen App It Bought Eight Months Ago' (*The Verge*, 2 July 2018) <https://www.theverge.com/2018/7/2/17528896/>.

201 The OFT, which investigated the transaction, considered both perspectives. See OFT, Case ME/5525/12 *Facebook/Instagram*, 14 August 2012, para 14.

202 The ecosystem terminology was popularized by James Moore, 'Predators and Prey: A New Ecology of Competition' (*HBR*, May–June 1993) <https://hbr.org/1993/05/predators-and-prey-a-new-ecology-of-competition>.

203 Joost Rietveld, Melissa Schilling and Cristiano Bellavitis, 'Platform Strategy: Managing Ecosystem Value Through Selective Promotion of Complements' (2019) 30 Organization Science 1232, 1232.

204 Youngjin Yoo, Richard Boland, Kalle Lyytinen and Ann Majchrzak, 'Organizing for Innovation in the Digital World' (2012) 23 Organization Science 1398; Carmelo Cennamo and Juan Santaló, 'Generativity Tension and Value Creation in Platform Ecosystems' (2019) 30 Organization Science 617, 617.

and uncoordinated audiences'.[205] In other words, innovation within platform ecosystems is both 'distributed' (as it originates with various actors in the ecosystem) and 'permissionless' (as those actors do not need specific authorization to contribute to the platform).

The 'ecosystem' perspective can be broadened to include not only how third parties help build the ecosystem, but also how platforms themselves are constantly adding complements to their core product. Such expansion should proceed with purpose: according to business strategists, '[a] platform business need not own all inimitable resources in its ecosystem, but it should seek to own the resources whose value is greatest'.[206] Consider, for example, how Apple's mobile presence started out with an operating system (iOS), after which it introduced an app marketplace (App Store); later, it added messaging (iMessage), cloud storage (iCloud), payments (Apple Pay), music streaming (Apple Music), video streaming (Apple TV+), gaming (Arcade) and a virtual assistant (Siri). The ecosystem was not only expanded in terms of software; Apple also added hardware with the introduction of a smartwatch (Apple Watch), smart speaker (HomePod), media player (Apple TV), and wireless headphones (AirPods). While this product range is impressive, it still leaves third parties with the opportunity to develop thousands of apps and a variety of Bluetooth-connected devices either to fill the gap left by Apple – or to compete with it. It is thus important to understand that innovation in the ecosystem can originate with the platform (at the core) as well as with third parties (at the edges).

A platform has good reasons to build an ecosystem of interlocking services. One of them is consumer lock-in: as consumers use more and more of the platform's services, their cost of switching to another platform increases (in other words, the barriers to entry or expansion for competitors increase).[207] Consider, for example, switching from an iPhone to an Android phone: getting familiar with the new OS is one thing, but you will also lose the apps you purchased and iMessages you sent, while your phone will have a harder time connecting to your remaining Apple devices – to name just a few drawbacks.[208] Of course, from a firm's perspective, consumer lock-in is a desirable state of affairs: among others, binding consumers to the business leads to recurring revenues and creates cross-selling opportunities.[209] Moreover, increasing its range of services allows the platform to tap into new revenue streams, which can be especially important once the platform's

---

205 Jonathan Zittrain, 'The Generative Internet' (2006) Harvard Law Review 1974, 1980. Elsewhere, Zittrain defines 'generative' as 'designed to accept any contribution that followed a basic set of rules (either coded for a particular operating system, or respecting the protocols of the internet)', see Jonathan Zittrain, *The Future of the Internet – And How to Stop It* (Yale University Press 2008) 3.

206 Parker, Van Alstyne and Choudary (n 171) 216, see also 147–49.

207 Saloner, Shepard and Podolny (n 195) 228; John Newman (n 192) 1509 ('The larger the private ecosystem, the lower the cognitive cost of switching among internally owned portals – but the larger the cost of switching to an externally owned portal.'); Michael Cusumano, Annabelle Gawer and David Yoffie, *The Business of Platforms* (Harper Business 2019) 48 and 98–99. For an application to mobile ecosystems, see *Google Android* (n 97), paras 522–32.

208 Of course, mobile OS developers will try to lower these switching costs to draw customers to their ecosystem. Apple offers an explicit example with its 'Move to iOS' app, which can be downloaded from Google Play – Android's app store. See Apple, 'Move from Android to iPhone, iPad, or iPod touch' <https://support.apple.com/en-us/HT201196>.

209 Markus Eurich and Michael Burtscher, 'The Business-to-Consumer Lock-In Effect' (2014) Cambridge Service Alliance Working Paper 1.

core market is saturated.[210] Analysts consider Apple's extensive range of software and hardware a prime example of such lock-in.[211] Aside from locking in consumers, elaborate ecosystems can also help protect the platform from challenges by competitors, which face difficulty replicating the complete ecosystem rather than just a core service.[212]

In addition to the possibility of consumer lock-in, the addition of services to the ecosystem is driven by economies of scope (or 'synergies').[213] Supply-side economies of scope exist 'where it is less costly to combine two or more product lines in one firm than to produce them separately'.[214] They can derive from every stage in the process of bringing a product to market, including development (drawing on proprietary know-how and shareable assets such as data), advertising (establishing a brand name that boosts all products) and distribution (relying on existing networks). For example, a search engine business that processes billions of search queries may draw on this data to develop an artificially intelligent virtual assistant. Platforms also benefit from demand-side economies of scope, as 'each additional service attracts more users'.[215] Economies of scope, which are said to be particularly significant when it comes to data, help explain why platforms are well-positioned to leverage a strong position from one market to another.[216]

While building and benefitting from an ecosystem is one thing, platforms must also continuously manage its biodiversity. In particular, platforms are faced with the question of how open they want to keep their ecosystem. The ideal of distributed, permissionless innovation in a completely open ecosystem may fit well with the internet's counter-culture roots,[217] but in reality it has proven untenable.[218] After all, if too large a number

---

210 This is said to underlie Apple's move into services, see eg 'Apple's Move to Services' (*Digital Innovation and Transformation*, 22 April 2018) <https://digital.hbs.edu/platform-digit/submission/the-app-store-apples-move-to-services/>.

211 Benedict Evans, 'Apple, Services and Moats' (*Benedict Evans*, 13 September 2019) <https://www.ben-evans.com/benedictevans/2019/9/13/Apple-services-moats> ('everything from the HomePod and Watch to Apple TV, the credit card or iMessage make it more likely that you'll stay on iPhone, and this applies whether they're hardware or software, whether they're paid-for or free, and whether they're high margin or low margin'). When a company started offering a $139 wooden case for Apple's titanium bank card, one technology website even joked: 'Finally, an Apple accessory with no ecosystem lock-in', see Jon Porter, 'You Can Now Waste $139 on a Wooden Case for Your Precious Apple Card' (*The Verge*, 2 September 2019) <https://www.theverge.com/tldr/2019/9/2/20844377/>.

212 *Google Android* (n 97), para 469 (quoting a Google executive on how the hardware and services making up the Android ecosystem 'protect [Google's] position. … These services inherently rely on scale to succeed – no one partner can easily fragment and replicate the complete platform').

213 Bourreau and de Streel (n 198) 9–12.

214 For the paper that coined the term, see John Panzar and Robert Willig, 'Economies of Scale in Multi-Output Production' (1977) 91 The Quarterly Journal of Economics 481. For a follow-up (and the phrase quoted here), see John Panzar and Robert Willig, 'Economies of Scope' (1981) 71 The American Economic Review 268, 268.

215 Nicolai van Gorp and Paul de Bijl, 'Digital Gatekeepers: Assessing Exclusionary Conduct' (Discussion Paper commissioned by the Dutch Ministry of Economic Affairs, 2019) 4.

216 Martens (n 37) 36–37; Jens Prüfer and Christoph Schottmüller, 'Competing with Big Data' (2017) TILEC Discussion Paper 2017-6, 3 (showing that 'a first mover in market A can leverage its dominant position, which comes with an advantage on user information, to let connected market B tip, too, even if market B is already served by traditional incumbent firms').

217 Jonathan Taplin, *Move Fast and Break Things: How Facebook, Google and Amazon Have Cornered Culture and What It Means for All of Us* (Macmillan 2017) 49–65.

218 James Grimmelman and Paul Ohm, 'Dr. Generative, or: How I Learned to Stop Worrying and Love the iPhone' (2010) 69 Maryland Law Review 910, 912 ('generativity is essential but can never be absolute'). See also Hano Kaiser, 'Are "Closed Systems" an Antitrust Problem?' (2011) 7 CPI 91, 97 ('every platform needs rules').

of low-quality or even misbehaving actors are active on the platform, they create 'noise', which may lead users to leave the platform in droves as the positive feedback loop reverses into a death spiral.[219] Platform operators must therefore manage their ecosystem as private regulators, limiting access to new users and interactions between existing users.[220] Again, the analogy with nightclubs is fitting: they, too, need to maintain a door policy; occasionally, they even need to kick drunken or rowdy guests out.[221] However, while every platform needs to exert *some* control over the users in its ecosystem, the degree of control remains a critical question of strategy. This degree of control is one of the factors that determine whether the platform ecosystem is qualified as 'open' or 'closed'.[222]

The difference between open and closed ecosystems is often illustrated by reference to Apple and Google's mobile presence.[223] Apple's iOS is proprietary: it is integrated only in iPhones; Google, by contrast, distributes Android as an open-source OS, licensing it to any phone maker for free and even allowing them to customize it according to their wishes. Thus, Apple manages a closed ecosystem or 'walled garden', while Google embraces openness. This dichotomy is, however, a false one. For one, Apple has given independent app developers access to the iPhone through its App Store, making its ecosystem more open.[224] Google, on the other hand, has chipped away at the open nature of its ecosystem by gradually increasing the number of proprietary apps, which phone makers can only use under strict conditions.[225] In the end, the differences between the two ecosystems are thus subtler than the contrast between 'open' and 'closed' suggests. The main reason is that 'computer systems or stacks consist of various layers – hardware, operating system, software, and content – each of which can be more or less open.'[226]

It is therefore more correct to speak of the 'degree of openness' of an ecosystem, which is reflected in 'the extent of vertical integration and of control of the system components by the system owner, and the compatibility between systems'.[227] The

219 Van Alstyne, Parker and Choudary (n 166).

220 Boudreau and Hagiu (n 167) 163–91. For a broader (political economy) perspective, see Frank Pasquale, 'From Territorial to Functional Sovereignty: The Case of Amazon' (*Law and Political Economy Blog*, 6 December 2017) <https://lpeblog.org/2017/12/06/from-territorial-to-functional-sovereignty-the-case-of-amazon/#more-442>.

221 Kaiser (n 218) 98.

222 For definitions of these terms, see AdlC and CMA (n 172) 12 ('"open" … generally refer[s] to a system that is equipped with an interface that is accessible to component makers or system developers other than the system owner itself and thus can work with a relatively wide variety of other components available on the market; in contrast, in a "closed" system, each component can work only with selected other components').

223 See in particular Zittrain, *The Future of the Internet – And How to Stop It* (n 205). For an inside view, see Isaacson, *Steve Jobs* (n 197) 471–78. See also EC, 'Online Platforms' (n 111) 26.

224 Grimmelman and Ohm (n 218) 911, 921–24 and 934–36.

225 Ron Amadeo, 'Google's Iron Grip on Android: Controlling Open Source by any Means Necessary' (*Ars Technica*, 21 October 2013) <https://arstechnica.com/gadgets/2018/07/googles-iron-grip-on-android-controlling-open-source-by-any-means-necessary/>.

226 Kaiser (n 218) 94.

227 AdlC and CMA (n 172) 12. Offering further guidance, the competition authorities hold that 'an ecosystem may be considered more open than another ecosystem whenever: there are more possible combinations of components within the ecosystem [and] more of those components are not supplied by the system owner'.

more vertically integrated and the less compatible the ecosystem, the more closed it is.[228] Under this test, Apple does present a more closed mobile ecosystem than Google. Further, the day-to-day management of the ecosystem – ie how the platform fulfils its aforementioned regulatory role – should be considered. Comparing app approval processes, it is clear that Apple keeps a closer eye on the apps entering its mobile ecosystem than Google does,[229] which confirms its position as a more closed ecosystem.

In addition to illustrating the spectrum between open and closed systems, the Apple–Google example demonstrates a fundamental strategy rule for platforms, namely, that 'challengers pursue interoperability while incumbents strive for incompatibility'.[230] In other words, while platforms may start up as open, they may start closing off their system once they have won a significant part of the market. Once more, an illustration is found in the mobile OS market: when Google had to challenge the incumbent Apple, it did so through openness;[231] however, when Android overtook iOS as the dominant mobile OS, it gradually became more and more closed.[232]

There are, however, many additional factors that determine the choice between open and closed ecosystems.[233] The compatibility of open systems allows for wide participation, which maximizes network effects and economies of scale; they are therefore seen as a stronger driver of innovation. Closed systems, on the other hand, offer solutions to many of the drawbacks of open systems, namely, security breaches, fragmentation, and free riding. Whether one system is preferable over the other from a competitive point of view is impossible to ascertain in the abstract, as it requires balancing two counteracting forces: open systems spur greater competition *within* the ecosystem ('intra-ecosystem'), while closed systems increase competition *between* ecosystems ('inter-ecosystem').[234]

228 Another useful definition (which puts the bar for openness higher) is found in Parker, Van Alstyne and Choudary (n 171) 130 ('A platform is "open" to the extent that (1) no restrictions are placed on participation in its development, commercialization, or use; or (2) any restrictions – for example, requirements to conform with technical standards or pay licensing fees – are reasonable and non-discriminatory, that is, they are applied uniformly to all potential platform participants.').

229 See CMA, 'Mobile Ecosystems' (Market Study Final Report, 2021), para 6.53.

230 Ben Thompson, 'Apple's Middle Age' (*Stratechery*, 5 February 2018) <https://stratechery.com/2018/apples-middle-age/>. For theoretical support, see Michael Katz and Carl Shapiro, 'Network Externalities, Competition, and Compatibility' (1985) 75 The American Economic Review 424, 425 ('firms with good reputations or large existing networks will tend to be against compatibility[; in] contrast, firms with small networks or weak reputations will tend to favor product compatibility'), confirmed in Katz and Shapiro, 'Systems Competition and Network Effects' (n 170) 107 and 110–11.

231 *Google Android* (n 97), para 1343 (showing an internal Google slide deck stating that that '[t]he marketing arm of "openness" promotes adoption of our services').

232 Closing a system can proceed through technological incompatibility as well as contractual arrangements. In its *Android* decision, the EC took issue with both, see *Google Android* (n 97). See also Parker, Van Alstyne and Choudary (n 171) 153 ('Google, meanwhile, needed to be more open because it entered the market after Apple'; later, 'Google [sought] to restrict access to its platform through a variety of mechanisms').

233 AdlC and CMA (n 172) 25–31.

234 ibid 15–18. See also Kaiser (n 218) 103.

2.3 After Scale and Scope: Profit – and Infringe Competition Law?

The previous section examined two essential tenets of platform strategy: first, prioritize growth over profits; then, build an ecosystem of interlocking products around your platform. As these are matters of *business* strategy, the way in which *consumers* can benefit from these strategies has been left out of focus, but it must be noted that such benefits are real and can be substantial. For example, consumers can benefit from the cost savings associated with economies of scope, from increased complementarity between products, and from lower transaction (including search) costs from having a variety of products at their disposal.

At the same time, the development and management of a platform ecosystem can turn anticompetitive. To illustrate exactly how anticompetitive behaviour can manifest itself, this section introduces four case studies that cover the main types of platforms: two transaction platforms, ie online marketplaces and app stores, and two advertising platforms, ie search engines and social networks.[235] The idea is to illuminate the potentially anticompetitive practices that a certain *type* of platform can engage in. To ground the subsequent analysis in reality, however, the case studies concern *specific* platforms. The ultimate goal is to establish a meaningful categorization of potentially anticompetitive behaviour, which will serve as the metastructure for the remainder of this book.

While the use of existing instead of hypothetical case studies firmly grounds the subsequent analysis in reality, it also requires a number of caveats. Firstly, the description of the practices is based on academic literature where available, but also on technology/business journalism. Evidently, these sources do not meet the evidentiary standards that competition authorities and courts adhere to.[236] Secondly, note that this section simply contains a *description*, not an evaluation. In other words, the case studies by no means establish that any practice *is* anticompetitive – at most, they point to practices that merit further scrutiny. Such scrutiny is carried out in the remainder of this work, but the analysis always focuses on *types* of practices – any discussion of concrete practices is merely illustrative. Thirdly, and as I will discuss later, even those practices that seem anticompetitive at first sight often have a compelling consumer-centred justification. In conclusion, and at the risk of repeating myself, this work merely establishes a framework for analysis; it does not come to any conclusions with regard to concrete practices.

---

235 For a broader background on the platforms discussed here, ie Amazon, Apple, Google and Facebook, see Nicolas Petit, *Big Tech & the Digital Economy: The Moligopoly Scenario* (OUP 2020) 94–102 and 105–10.

236 However, many of the allegations here have been confirmed in the Antitrust Subcommittee investigation of competition in digital markets, which relies on 1,287,997 documents and communications, 38 witness testimonies, a 1,800-page record of hearings of tech executives, and interviews with more than 240 market participants, see House Judiciary Report (n 193).

2.3.1 Online Marketplaces

Amazon's evolution from an online book retailer to the 'everything store' has been extensively chronicled.[237] To offer consumers 'everything', Amazon opened its marketplace to third-party sellers, which were responsible for 58% of sales on the platform in 2018; Amazon's 'first-party' business (its retail operation) made up the other 42%.[238] Even though Bezos has stated that '[t]hird-party sellers are kicking [Amazon's] first party butt', the reality is more complex.[239] Indeed, Amazon is still very busy integrating vertically by developing and then distributing its own private-label products in a variety of product categories, which puts it in competition with third-party sellers. Some of those sellers, like the furniture maker Williams-Sonoma, have accused Amazon of simply copying its products.[240]

In any case, Amazon does not appear to leave the process of vertical integration up to chance: empirical evidence suggests that it uses the vast amount of sales data it gathers on third-party transactions as a guide.[241] Hagiu and Wright find that 'once Amazon reaches information parity with its sellers, it switches [from the marketplace] to the reseller mode in order to exploit its scale advantage'.[242] In particular, Amazon chooses to vertically integrate into short-tail products (with a high sales volume), leaving the long-tail products to the retailers on its platform.[243] Zhu and Liu confirm that Amazon's vertical integration targets products with greater demand, and add that higher prices and lower shipping costs also guide the process.[244] In other words, 'Amazon's entry is motivated by capturing profits from popular products'.[245]

The result of Amazon's vertical integration is that it fulfils a 'dual role': on the one hand, it serves as a platform *distributing* third-party products; on the other hand, it is a retailer *competing* with those products. This dual role can lead to a conflict of

---

237 Stone, *The Everything Store* (n 115). The 'everything store' moniker originates from the company's own communications, see eg Amazon.com Inc., Form 10-K annual report to the SEC for the fiscal year ended December 31, 2001 ('We seek to offer Earth's Biggest Selection and to be Earth's most customer-centric company, where customers can find and discover anything they may want to buy online').

238 Jeff Bezos, '2018 Letter to Shareholders' (*Day One – the Amazon blog*, 11 April 2019) <https://blog.aboutamazon.com/company-news/2018-letter-to-shareholders>.

239 ibid.

240 *Williams-Sonoma v Amazon*, no 18-cv-07548 (ND Cal, 14 December 2018) (Complaint). Williams-Sonoma (WS) accuses Amazon of 'infringing upon a wide spectrum of [WS] intellectual property rights in also setting up competing Amazon brands that sell knockoffs of [WS] products'.

241 In addition to the empirical evidence referenced below, see Brad Stone, *Amazon Unbound* (Simon & Schuster 2021) 200–204 and 367–377; Dana Mattioli, 'Amazon Scooped Up Data from Its Own Sellers to Launch Competing Products' (*WSJ*, 23 April 2020) <https://www.wsj.com/articles/amazon-scooped-up-data-from-its-own-sellers-to-launch-competing-products-11587650015>; Aditya Kalra and Steve Stecklow, 'Amazon Copied Products and Rigged Search Results to Promote Its Own Brands, Documents Show' (*Reuters*, 13 October 2021) <https://www.reuters.com/investigates/special-report/amazon-india-rigging/>.

242 Hagiu and Wright, 'Marketplace or Reseller?' (n 75) 197.

243 ibid 196.

244 Zhu and Liu (n 188).

245 ibid 2627. Moreover, the odds of Amazon entering the product space of a third-party seller that uses Fulfilment by Amazon (FBA) service are slightly lower. This is consistent with Amazon's profit motive: it already profits extra from product orders it fulfils, as sellers pay it to handle shipping and related services.

interest: it may give Amazon an incentive to use its control over its Marketplace to favour its own private-label products over those sold by third parties.[246] Of course, such incentive exists only when the profit margin on sales of its own products is higher than the profit margin on the sales of third-party products (ie its commission fee[247] and any add-on services[248]).

It appears that, in certain cases, Amazon does have an incentive to favour its own products – and acts upon it. The most obvious way to favour those products is to steer shoppers towards them, and there have been a number of reports of Amazon doing so by giving its private-label products more prominent placement within its user interface, including product rankings.[249] Empirical tests confirmed how Amazon regularly populates the 'Buy Box' (the coveted top spot in the product ranking) with its own products – even when they do not constitute the best deal for consumers.[250] Relying on sources from within the company, reporting also describes how Amazon has changed its product ranking algorithm to more prominently feature products that are more profitable for the company.[251]

Beyond search rankings, Amazon has experimented with pushing its products to consumers right before they are about to purchase those of a competitor, either through pop-ups on the mobile app or through a 'similar items to consider' feature on its website.[252] Amazon's smart speaker, Alexa, offers new opportunities for

246 There are a large number of accounts on how Amazon manages its dual role. These accounts usually combine experiences of third-party sellers with information provided by academics and industry consultants, as well as replies from Amazon when offered. For some broad perspectives on the topic, see Jennifer Rankin, 'Third-Party Sellers and Amazon – A Double-Edged Sword in e-Commerce' (*The Guardian*, 23 June 2015) <https://www.theguardian.com/technology/2015/jun/23/amazon-marketplace-third-party-seller-faustian-pact>; Olivia Solon and Julia Carrie Wong, 'Jeff Bezos v the World: Why All Companies Fear "Death by Amazon"' (*The Guardian*, 24 April 2018) <https://www.theguardian.com/technology/2018/apr/24/amazon-jeff-bezos-customer-data-industries>.

247 More specifically, Amazon charges a subscription fee and a referral fee (usually of 15%). Sellers can choose to avoid the subscription fee by paying a per-item fee. Moreover, media items are also subject to a closing fee.

248 Such as logistics, see Amazon, 'Fulfilment by Amazon – benefits' <https://services.amazon.co.uk/services/fulfilment-by-amazon/features-benefits.html>.

249 See eg The Capital Forum, 'Amazon: By Prioritizing Its Own Fashion Label Brands in Product Placement on Its Increasingly Dominant Platform, Amazon Risks Antitrust Enforcement by a Trump Administration' (Brief, 2016); Julia Creswell, 'How Amazon Steers Shoppers to Its Own Products' (*NYT*, 23 June 2018) <https://www.nytimes.com/2018/06/23/business/amazon-the-brand-buster.html>; Noah Smith, 'Amazon's Winner-Take-All Approach to Small Business' (*Bloomberg*, 19 February 2019) <https://www.bloomberg.com/opinion/articles/2019-02-19/amazon-uses-search-to-undercut-small-businesses-on-its-site>.

250 In particular, Amazon's prices can be higher than those of other sellers for the same product. This difference can be particularly significant when the shopper has to pay extra for the shipping of the Amazon product (because they are not a Prime member) but not for that of the competing product (because its seller internalizes the shipping costs). See Julia Angwin and Surya Mattu, 'Amazon Says It Puts Customers First. But Its Pricing Algorithm Doesn't' (*ProPublica*, 20 September 2016) <https://www.propublica.org/article/amazon-says-it-puts-customers-first-but-its-pricing-algorithm-doesnt>.

251 Dana Mattioli, 'Amazon Changed Search Algorithm in Ways That Boost its Own Products' (*WSJ*, 16 September 2019) <https://www.wsj.com/articles/amazon-changed-search-algorithm-in-ways-that-boost-its-own-products-11568645345>.

252 Jay Greene, 'Amazon Tests Pop-Up Feature Touting Its Lower-Priced Products' (*WSJ*, 15 March 2019) <https://www.wsj.com/articles/amazon-tests-pop-up-feature-touting-its-lower-priced-products-11552655614>; Eugene Kim, 'Amazon Quietly Removes Promotional Spots That Gave Special Treatment to its Own Products as Scrutiny of Tech Giants Grows' (*CNBC*, 3 April 2019) <https://www.cnbc.com

steering: whenever consumers do not ask Alexa to order a specific brand, Amazon can ship one of its private-label products.[253] Apart from steering consumers, a platform can favour its own products by exempting from rules that apply to those of other sellers. When various buyers reported that their Amazon charging cable for iPhones melted and started smoking, for example, it remained the number one bestseller while the product listings of third-party sellers get suspended in such situations.[254]

2.3.2 App Stores

'There's an app for that.' Apple's catchy marketing slogan stands for the idea that, whatever you might want to do with your iPhone, you will find a tool for it in its App Store. Most of the apps found there are provided by third-party developers, which are allowed to sell them as long as they comply with Apple's guidelines and pay the company a 30% commission fee on app sales, subscriptions and in-app purchases.[255]

Apple has always developed its own apps too, which are either preinstalled on the iPhone or available in the App Store. When Apple updates its mobile OS, it may include new first-party apps that offer the same functionality as apps that third-party developers have been offering. There is even a term for when Apple introduces an app that competes with yours: you've been 'sherlocked'.[256] In coming up with new apps, Apple is said to be guided by the data it collects from its App Store (eg on the number of downloads) and iOS (eg average time spent on the app).[257] Moreover, Apple's own apps benefit from superior compatibility with its ecosystem.[258]

Not unlike Amazon, Apple thus ends up fulfilling a dual role as both the operator of an app marketplace and as a provider of apps, which can lead to conflicts of interest.

/2019/04/03/amazon-removes-special-promo-spots-for-private-label-products.html>; Jay Greene, 'Aggressive Amazon Tactic Pushes You to Consider Its Own Brand Before You Click "Buy"' (*WaPo*, 28 August 2019) <https://www.washingtonpost.com/technology/2019/08/27/aggressive-amazon-tactic-pushes-you-consider-its-own-brand-before-you-click-buy/>.

253 Maurice Stucke and Ariel Ezrachi, 'How Digital Assistants Can Harm Our Economy, Privacy, and Democracy' (2017) 32 Berkeley Technology Law Journal 1239, 1261–62.

254 Leticia Miranda, 'Amazon Sellers Say the Tech Giant Is Crushing Them with Competitive Pricing' (*BuzzFeed News*, 7 June 2018) <https://www.buzzfeednews.com/article/leticiamiranda/amazon-sellers-say-the-tech-giant-is-crushing-them-with>. Indeed, buying a competitor's product on Amazon, setting it on fire and then posting a review is one of the many dirty business tactics used on the marketplace, see Josh Dzieza, 'Prime and Punishment: Dirty Dealing in the $175 Billion Amazon Marketplace' (*The Verge*, 19 December 2018) <https://www.theverge.com/2018/12/19/18140799/>.

255 See App Store Review Guidelines, section '3.1 Payments' on the various exceptions to the 30% fee.

256 'You've Been Sherlocked' (*The Economist*, 13 July 2012) <https://www.economist.com/babbage/2012/07/13/youve-been-sherlocked>.

257 Reed Albergotti, 'How Apple Uses Its App Store to Copy the Best Ideas' (*WaPo*, 5 September 2019) <https://www.washingtonpost.com/technology/2019/09/05/how-apple-uses-its-app-store-copy-best-ideas/>.

258 For example, Apple's payment app Apple Pay can make use of the iPhone's NFC chip, which facilitates contactless payments; other payment app providers do not have such access to Apple's hardware. This conduct is under investigation, see EC, 'Commission sends Statement of Objections to Apple over practices regarding Apple Pay' (press release, 2 May 2022) IP/22/2764.

For example, Apple has always banned apps that allow users to buy music downloads – a service that Apple's iTunes offers.[259] On the contrary, Apple had for a long time allowed apps that make it possible for iPhone users (and in the case of children, their parents) to control the time they spend on their phones. When Apple introduced its own version of such an app (Screen Time), however, it restricted or removed some of the most popular competing apps.[260] Apple also complicated the process for users to authorize location tracking by apps, while Apple's own apps (such as Find My iPhone) are not subject to the same authorization process.[261] In addition, Apple's app marketplace includes a search function that can be used to steer users towards certain apps. An analysis of six years' worth of App Store data (including the ranking of more than 1,800 specific apps across 13 keywords) shows that, when users search for generic terms (eg 'podcast'), Apple's own apps consistently occupy the top spots.[262]

Spotify, the developer of the world's most popular music streaming app, has filed a complaint against Apple that combines many of the aforementioned allegations.[263] First and foremost, Spotify argues that Apple's 30% 'tax' on its music subscriptions gives Apple Music – Apple's own streaming service – an unfair advantage.[264] Further, the music streaming app takes issue with how Apple restricts the ways in which Spotify can communicate with its users (eg with regard to promotions), how Apple delays app upgrades, and how Apple prevents compatibility between Spotify and various Apple products (Siri, the HomePod and the Apple Watch).

---

259 See eg Stuart Dredge, 'ERA Says Apple's HMV App Ban Raises "Serious Issues of Competition"' (*Musically*, 22 October 2013) <http://musically.com/2013/10/22/era-says-apples-hmv-app-ban-raises-serious-issues-of-competition/>.

260 Jack Nicas, 'Apple Cracks Down on Apps That Fight iPhone Addiction' (*NYT*, 27 April 2019) <https://www.nytimes.com/2019/04/27/technology/apple-screen-time-trackers.html>. One of these apps has submitted a complaint against Apple with Russia's Federal Antimonopoly Service (FAS), see 'Kaspersky's Antitrust Complaint against Apple in Russia' (*Kaspersky Daily*, 19 March 2019) <www.kaspersky.com/blog/apple-fas-complaint/26017/>. Others filed their complaint with the EC, see 'Qustodio & Kidslox File a Complaint against Apple with the European Commission over Abuse of Dominant Position' (*Globenewswire*, 30 April 2019) <https://www.globenewswire.com/news-release/2019/04/30/1812192/0/en/Qustodio-Kidslox-File-a-Complaint-Against-Apple-with-the-European-Commission-over-Abuse-of-Dominant-Position.html>. Afterwards, Apple revised its policy, see Jack Nicas, 'Apple Backs Off Crackdown on Parental-Control Apps' (*NYT*, 3 June 2019) <https://www.nytimes.com/2019/06/03/technology/apple-parental-control-apps.html>.

261 Juli Clover, 'App Developers Claim Apple's iOS 13 Location Tracking Changes Are Anti-Competitive' (*MacRumors*, 16 August 2019) <https://www.macrumors.com/2019/08/16/app-developers-tracking-restrictions-ios-13/>.

262 Jack Nicas and Keith Collins, 'How Apple's Apps Topped Rivals in the App Store It Controls' (*NYT*, 9 September 2019) <https://www.nytimes.com/interactive/2019/09/09/technology/apple-app-store-competition.html>. See also Tripp Mickle, 'Apple Dominates App Store Search Results, Thwarting Competitors' (*WSJ*, 23 July 2019) <https://www.wsj.com/articles/apple-dominates-app-store-search-results-thwarting-competitors-11563897221>.

263 The complaint is set out on a dedicated microsite: Spotify, 'Time to Play Fair' <https://www.timetoplayfair.com/>.

264 To avoid the 30% fee, Spotify has turned off Apple's in-app purchase feature, which means that iPhone users cannot directly subscribe to Spotify. Rather, users have to find their way to Spotify's website to subscribe. Spotify would like to direct users to its website from the app but is prohibited from doing so.

2.3.3 Search Engines

There is clearly no such search engine as 'Bing'.
Or maybe there is – I don't know.
There's really only one way to find out and that's by Googling it.[265]

Google's self-declared mission is 'to organize the world's information and make it universally accessible and useful'.[266] Its *horizontal search engine* – Google Search – has gone a long way in achieving that goal: in response to a search query, it displays links to websites that may contain the information sought after. However, Google does not solely rely on links to websites; basic questions, eg '1 + 1' or 'weather Brussels', are answered directly by the search engine, which obviates the need to click on a website link.

When users do not have a general search query but are looking for more specific information, they often turn to *vertical search engines*. Google has gradually expanded its offering in this area, and now offers video (YouTube), maps (Google Maps), flight comparison (Google Flights), comparison shopping (Google Shopping), jobs (Google for Jobs) and local search (Google Local). Importantly, users do not have to visit the web addresses of these specialized services to enjoy their results. Rather, Google has integrated these services into its main search engine and presents their results in direct response to a general search query.

Two major complaints have arisen regarding the operation of Google's search engine. One relates to how Google sources the information it uses to directly answer more complex search queries. The other relates to the presentation and position of Google's specialized services in its general search results. Let's look at each complaint in turn, starting with the latter.

To understand the issues surrounding the position and presentation of search results, one has to distinguish three categories of search results presented by Google.[267] Firstly, Google presents *generic search results*, ie search results selected and ranked based purely on their relevance (or 'web rank').[268] Secondly, Google shows *advertised search results* drawn from Google's auction-based online search advertising platform Google Ads. While these ads are also selected based on their relevance (or 'ad rank'), they are

265 John Oliver, 'Net Neutrality II' (*Last Week Tonight*, 7 May 2017) <https://www.youtube.com/watch?v=92vuuZt7wak>. For another humorous take on Google's search engine dominance (in Dutch), see Jop Eikelboom and Jos Maalderink, 'Mens gebruikte 20 duizend jaar geleden al geen Yahoo' (*De Speld*, 19 June 2017) <https://speld.nl/2017/06/19/mens-gebruikte-20-duizend-jaar-geleden-al-geen-yahoo/> (this satirical news article describes how researchers discovered that mankind already knew better than to use Yahoo 20,000 years ago). Note that, since 2010, Yahoo no longer powers its own search engine; instead, it uses Microsoft's search engine Bing, see *Microsoft/Yahoo! Search Business* (Case COMP/M.5727) Commission Decision C(2010)1077.

266 Google, 'About Us' <https://www.google.com/about/our-company/>.

267 See *Google Search (Shopping)* (Case AT.39740) Commission Decision C(2017)4444, paras 7–25.

268 Google's Search Quality Evaluator Guidelines give an insight into what it finds important when it comes to (algorithmically) choosing how to rank search results. They are available via <https://static.googleusercontent.com/media/guidelines.raterhub.com/en//searchqualityevaluatorguidelines.pdf>.

placed because advertisers have paid for them. Thirdly, Google presents *specialized search results* from its vertical services. For example, when one searches for 'blue parka', Google shows results from its comparison shopping service (CSS); when one searches for 'call centre jobs', the Google for Jobs tool aggregates postings from many employers; when one searches for an 'Italian restaurant', Google provides local results in the form of a map and a list of nearby restaurants (with their information and reviews).

The presentation and position of each kind of search result differ. Generic search results are displayed as blue links with short excerpts from the website in question ('snippets'). Advertised search results are displayed in the same way, although Google adds a label (eg 'advertisement') to inform users of their paid-for nature. The results from Google's specialized search services, by contrast, are often displayed with attractive graphical features (eg large pictures and dynamic information). Moreover, these specialized results are separated from others by a frame (Google's 'OneBox'). The positioning of various search results varies, but Google's OneBox and advertised search results often take the top spots, while generic search results are featured below them.

In providing specialized search results, Google competes with various other vertical search engines (eg Foundem for comparison shopping, Indeed for jobs, and Yelp for local search). Many of these vertical search providers have complained that Google gives its own vertical services preferential treatment in its horizontal search results, both in terms of positioning (the OneBox on top of the search results) and in terms of presentation (the more attractive format).[269] Such complaints have been grouped under headings such as 'self-preferencing' and 'search bias', although – regrettably – the latter term has been politically co-opted.[270]

Complaints have also arisen with regard to how Google sources the information to directly answer search queries. Indeed, where Google used to answer only the most basic search queries directly (eg the '1 + 1' mentioned above), it is now providing more and more direct answers. For example, when one searches for 'Jay-Z net worth', Google immediately answers that the rapper is worth $1 billion; when one searches for 'Drive Slow lyrics', the song's text appears directly on top of the search results. Apparently, Google's strategy of directly answering search queries is effective: recent

269 With regard to comparison shopping, see *Google Search (Shopping)* (n 267), para 2 ('The Decision establishes that the more favourable positioning and display by Google, in its general search results pages, of its own comparison shopping service compared to competing comparison shopping services … infringes Article 102 of the Treaty'). With regard to local search, see Conor Dougherty, 'Inside Yelp's Six-Year Grudge against Google' (*NYT*, 1 July 2017) <https://www.nytimes.com/2017/07/01/technology/yelp-google-european-union-antitrust.html> and a supporting website 'Focus on the user' set up by Yelp, TripAdvisor and others <http://focusontheuser.eu/>. With regard to job search, see Yun Chee and Paresh Dave, 'Google's Jobs Search Draws Antitrust Complaints from Rivals' (*Reuters*, 13 August 2019) <https://www.reuters.com/article/us-eu-google-antitrust-exclusive/exclusive-googles-jobs-search-draws-antitrust-complaints-from-rivals-idUSKCN1V30IX>. A case number has been assigned to EC cases on local and job search, but no further information is available, see *Google Jobs* (Case AT.40592) and *Google Local* (Case AT.40585).

270 The debate on search bias has shifted from the business/tech world to the political arena, with (mostly conservative) politicians in the US co-opting the term to score points with their base. See eg Sue Halpern, 'The search for anti-conservative bias on Google' (*The New Yorker*, 19 December 2018) <https://www.newyorker.com/tech/annals-of-technology/the-search-for-anti-conservative-bias-on-google>.

data shows that a lot of user searches no longer result in a click on a website link, suggesting many users are satisfied with the immediate answer.[271]

Where does Google get the information to answer such questions?[272] Some information comes from the 'Knowledge Graph', a Google-curated database that draws on Wikipedia, among others.[273] When one searches for 'birthday Jefferson', for example, Google informs you the US President was born on 13 April 1743 without a reference to any source. Other information is algorithmically pulled from the web and displayed in the form of 'Featured Snippets', ie framed excerpts from websites. When one types 'who killed Hamilton' in the search bar, for example, Google pulls information from the Encyclopaedia Britannica and frames it on top of the search results to tell you the culprit was Aaron Burr. When a website's information is displayed as a Featured Snippet, its owner may take a financial hit: as users do not have to click through to the website to get the information they are looking for, the website cannot show them ads, which means they miss out on a major source of financing.

The website Celebrity Net Worth (CNW), for example, compiles information about the wealth of 25,000 celebrities in a database. Google once requested access to CNW data but was turned down. Instead, the search engine scraped the content of the CNW website and displayed it in direct response to search queries.[274] To ascertain that the Google content came from his website, the founder of CNW mixed in a couple of listings for fake celebrities, which subsequently showed up on Google. A year after Google started scraping CNW's content, traffic on the website was down 65%, and it has slipped further since.[275]

Genius.com – a website that provides annotated song lyrics – also noticed that Google was displaying its content in direct response to search queries, on top of the search results and without attribution. Of course, various websites provide lyrics, often with subtle differences. To ascertain that its *specific* content was being scraped, Genius did not mix in fake lyrics but started watermarking the lyrics by alternating the apostrophes between straight and curly quotation marks in the exact same sequence for a number of songs. And indeed, Genius's watermarked lyrics started showing up on Google.

---

271 According to numbers from clickstream data company Jumpshot, over 50% of browser-based searches on Google.com did not result in a click. Part of the explanation must be that Google directly provided the answer, obviating the need to click through. See Rand Fishkin, 'Less Than Half of Google Searches Now Result in a Click' (*SparkToro*, 17 June 2019) <https://sparktoro.com/blog/less-than-half-of-google-searches-now-result-in-a-click/>.

272 For an extensive exposé, see Peter Meyers, 'Google's Walled Garden: Are We Being Pushed Out of Our Own Digital Backyards?' (*Moz Blog*, 27 February 2018) <https://moz.com/blog/googles-walled-garden>.

273 Amit Singhal, 'Introducing the Knowledge Graph: things, not strings' (*Inside Search – Google Blog*, 16 May 2012) <https://search.googleblog.com/2012/05/introducing-knowledge-graph-things-not.html>.

274 Often, these search queries would not even link back to the CNW website, but rather to websites that used CNW as their source.

275 Adrianne Jeffries, 'How Google Eats a Business Whole' (*The Outline*, 17 April 2017) <https://theoutline.com/post/1399/how-google-ate-celebritynetworth-com>. For a more recent version of the Google/CNW story (told by the CNW founder), see Brian Warner, 'How Google Uses Content Theft and Algorithm Updates to Maintain Its Search Monopoly' (*Medium*, 16 October 2019) <https://medium.com/@brian-warner/how-google-uses-content-theft-and-algorithm-updates-to-maintain-its-search-monopoly-a5aeed-4a53e4>.

When the two types of apostrophes were converted to dots and dashes, they spelled out 'red handed' in Morse code.[276] Google replied that it does not scrape lyrics but rather licenses them from lyrics content providers, in particular the firm LyricFind, which thus bears responsibility.[277] Google then removed Genius's watermarks, but – suspecting its lyrics were still being used – the lyrics site devised a second watermark, this time using 'four-per-em' instead of regular spaces. Lyrics with this watermark, too, ended up in Google's OneBox without attribution.[278]

2.3.4 Social Networks

Facebook is a social network with over 2 billion users. In essence, the platform makes money by gathering data on its users, compiling that data into detailed user profiles, and then selling access to those profiles to businesses that want to target their ads. Facebook has expanded from social networking into e-commerce (Facebook Marketplace), online dating (Facebook Dating), and original video content (Facebook Watch), among others. Moreover, it has acquired a number of (potential) competitors, including the photo-sharing app Instagram and the instant-messaging app WhatsApp. Facebook has also bought Onavo, an app that tracks data usage on smartphones, and has used the aggregated data of its millions of users to direct its acquisition strategy.[279]

Of course, not every firm that Facebook takes an interest in is ready to sell – a reality that the social network had to grapple with after Snapchat, a camera-based social media app, refused its acquisition offer. Facebook then went on to copy Snapchat's characteristic 'Stories' feature on its three major platforms (Facebook, Instagram, WhatsApp).[280] Shortly thereafter, Snapchat's user growth slowed considerably.[281]

276 Genius.com filed a case against Google regarding this conduct, see *Genius v Google and LyricFind*, no 526241/2019 (NY, 3 December 2019) (Complaint). See further Robert McMillan, 'Lyrics Site Accuses Google of Lifting Its Content' (*WSJ*, 16 June 2019) <https://www.wsj.com/articles/lyrics-site-genius-com-accuses-google-of-lifting-its-content-11560677400>.

277 Satyageet Salgar, 'How We Help You Find Lyrics in Google Search' (*The Keyword – Google Blog*, 18 June 2019) <https://blog.google/products/search/how-we-help-you-find-lyrics-google-search/>. See also 'LyricFind offers corrections to inaccuracies in Wall Street Journal reporting' (*LyricFind*, 17 June 2019), which has meanwhile been taken down but lives on, eg at <https://celebrityaccess.com/2019/06/18/lyricfind-disputes-genius-lyric-theft-claim-challenges-wsj-reporting/>.

278 This time, when one interprets the four-per-em spaces as dashes (and ignores the song's first fourteen spaces), the sequence spells out 'Genius' in Morse code. See *Genius v Google and LyricFind* (n 276) 26–32.

279 Deepa Seetharaman and Betsy Morris, 'Facebook's Onavo Gives Social-Media Firm Inside Peek at Rivals' Users' (*WSJ*, 13 August 2017) <https://www.wsj.com/articles/facebooks-onavo-gives-social-media-firm-inside-peek-at-rivals-users-1502622003>; Josh Constine, 'Facebook Will Shut Down Its Spyware VPN App Onavo' (*TechCrunch*, 22 February 2019) <https://techcrunch.com/2019/02/21/facebook-removes-onavo/>. See also Margrethe Vestager, 'A digital future that works for Europeans' (Business Forum of the German Ambassadors' Conference, Berlin, 27 August 2019) (discussing Onavo).

280 Farhad Manjoo, 'Why Facebook Keeps Beating Every Rival: It's the Network, of Course' (*NYT*, 19 April 2017) <https://www.nytimes.com/2017/04/19/technology/facebook-snapchat-instagram-innovation.html>; Billy Gallagher, 'Copycat: How Facebook Tried to Squash Snapchat' (*Wired*, 16 February 2018) <https://www.wired.com/story/copycat-how-facebook-tried-to-squash-snapchat/>.

281 Josh Constine, 'Snapchat Growth Slowed 82% After Instagram Stories Launched' (*TechCrunch*, 2 February 2017) <https://techcrunch.com/2017/02/02/slowchat/>; Prachi Bhardwaj, 'As Snapchat Growth Stalls Out, Facebook Stories Hits 150 Million Daily Active Users' (*Business Insider*, 18 May 2018) <https://www.businessinsider.com/facebook-stories-versus-snapchat-users-2018-5>.

The Snapchat story is not an isolated incident; indeed, Facebook is rather notorious for copying the features of promising social media apps and subsequently relying on its established user base to win out against the competitor.[282]

Expanding its reach, whether internally or through acquisition, gives Facebook access to new sources of data. It can then combine the data gathered through its various social media services into more detailed user profiles – which is what Facebook has been doing with the data from its main network ('Facebook Blue'), Instagram, and WhatsApp. Another way to establish more detailed user profiles is to simply increase the extent of user tracking, which is something Facebook gradually did as its position in the market grew stronger.[283] Of course, more detailed user profiles are not the end goal; rather, they allow Facebook to target advertisements more accurately – the higher price those targeted ads command then increases its profitability.

282 For an academic analysis of such conduct, see John Obear, 'Move Last and Take Things: Facebook and Predatory Copying' (2018) 3 Columbia Business Law Review 994. For news reports, see Betsy Morris and Deepa Seetharaman, 'The New Copycats: How Facebook Squashes Competition from Startups' (*WSJ*, 9 August 2017) <https://www.wsj.com/articles/the-new-copycats-how-facebook-squashes-competition-from-startups-1502293444>; Elizabeth Dwoskin, 'Facebook's Willingness to Copy Rivals' Apps Seen as Hurting Innovation' (*WaPo*, 10 August 2017) <https://www.washingtonpost.com/business/economy/facebooks-willingness-to-copy-rivals-apps-seen-as-hurting-innovation/2017/08/10/ea7188ea-7df6-11e7-a669-b400c5c7e1cc_story.html>; Erin Griffith, 'Will Facebook Kill All Future Facebooks?' (*Wired*, 25 October 2017) <https://www.wired.com/story/facebooks-aggressive-moves-on-startups-threaten-innovation/>; Louise Matsakis, 'Facebook Dating Looks a Whole Lot Like Hinge' (*Wired*, 3 May 2018) <https://www.wired.com/story/facebook-dating-hinge-app/>.

283 Dina Srinivasan, 'The Antitrust Case against Facebook' (2019) 16 Berkeley Business Law Journal 39, 46–81.

3

CATEGORIZING POTENTIALLY ANTICOMPETITIVE BEHAVIOUR BY ONLINE PLATFORMS

Section 2.2 reviewed how platforms grow and develop into ecosystems, often by leveraging the strong position they maintain in their core market to adjacent markets. An ecosystem of interlocking services strengthens the platform's position vis-à-vis competitors, through user lock-in, among others. Section 2.3 illustrated how leveraging not only is an effective strategy for ecosystem building, but can also be used to increase the platform's profits (when the profit margin from operating in the adjacent market is higher than simply serving that market as a platform). The dynamic sketched here is in line with the analytical framework presented by Boudreau and Hagiu, which suggests that platform operators follow a two-step approach: first, 'maximize value created for the entire ecosystem', then, 'maximize the value extracted' from that ecosystem.[284] Other authors similarly describe that platforms compete by 'fostering innovation, then capturing its value'.[285] However, while building ecosystems and increasing profits are perfectly legitimate objectives, leveraging – one tool to achieve these objectives – can be anticompetitive. Moreover, while leveraging may constitute the primary strategy for platforms to solidify their competitive position, it is far from the only one.

In other words, while leveraging may be the protagonist in this story, various other forms of platform behaviour feature in supporting roles. To understand the broader narrative, this section offers an overview of the metastructure of this work. This evidently includes the forms of potentially anticompetitive platform behaviour that this work focuses on, but it also includes forms of potentially anticompetitive behaviour that will *not* be discussed as separate issues. This allows the reader to situate this book in the broader literature, but also offers context for those sections

284 Boudreau and Hagiu (n 167) 187.

285 Parker, Van Alstyne and Choudary (n 171) 216–17.

where the discussion does overflow into related topics. Finally, the categorization relied on in this metastructure offers the opportunity to clearly delineate the scope of this work.

The metastructure presented here draws on established categorizations in competition law (eg exclusionary vs exploitative practices under article 102 TFEU) but adds platform-specific distinctions (eg intra-platform vs inter-platform exclusion). In short, it looks as follows:

- platform appropriation
- platform exploitation
- platform exclusion:
    - intra-platform exclusion
    - inter-platform exclusion.

In the next three sections, I discuss each of these potentially anticompetitive types of platform behaviour in turn. The groundwork for assessing platform behaviour has now been laid; the following sections categorize, refine and complement the analysis. Firstly, against a background of platform economics (Section 2.2), the examples of real-world platform behaviour (Section 2.3) are *categorized* according to the metastructure set out above. It should become clear that there is a method to the maddeningly wide range of platform behaviour described earlier. The discussion is *refined* as well: How exactly could these strategies be anticompetitive; how could they conflict with the goal(s) of competition law? Secondly, this mostly economic analysis is *complemented* with the first steps of a legal analysis, guided by two questions: Is this behaviour a matter for competition law's abuse of dominance provision, and if so, which theory of abuse may apply to it? Then, we can move on to Part 2, which offers a detailed analysis of potentially anticompetitive platform behaviour under article 102 TFEU.

3.1 Platform Appropriation

Section 2.3 described a number of instances where platforms allegedly 'copied' the products of the businesses using its platform: Williams-Sonoma accuses Amazon of copying its furniture; various app developers complain they have been 'sherlocked' by Apple; the websites Celebrity Net Worth and Genius argue their content is being scraped by Google; and Facebook is said to have copied the functionality of a number of (potential) competitors in the social media space, including Snapchat. These stories have coalesced into a narrative: first, startups develop innovative products – soon after, established platforms start marketing a copy of those products. In a spin on Facebook's old motto 'move fast and break things', platforms are said to 'move last and take things'.[286] Such behaviour is now starting to attract the attention of policy-makers.[287]

These various instances of alleged copying can be grouped together under the heading 'platform appropriation'. The question remains, however, when – if ever – appropriating a rival's product can be anticompetitive in the sense of competition law. There is no clear answer to this question, as appropriation has featured in investigations by competition authorities but has not yet led to clear decisions. The EC, for example, investigated how Amazon 'relies on non-publicly available data relating to third-party sellers' product listings and transactions to calibrate its retail decisions'.[288] As the investigation ended with a commitment decision, the legal assessment was limited. The EC also examined appropriation in the course of its *Google Shopping* investigation, taking the view that Google engaged in 'copying and use ... without consent of original content from third party websites in its own specialised search services', which 'may infringe Article 102 of the Treaty'.[289] While this statement featured in the EC's preliminary assessment, however, it was absent from the final decision.[290] On the other side of the Atlantic, the FTC did further investigate allegations 'that Google had unfairly "scraped," or misappropriated, the content of certain competing websites, passed this content off as its own, and then threatened to delist these rivals entirely from Google's search results when they protested the misappropriation of their content'.[291] The scraped content included user reviews and star ratings (eg from Yelp), which were then used to improve Google's vertical search offerings such as Google Local.[292] While various commissioners 'found the record evidence to support strong concerns about Google's conduct', the investigation was closed when Google committed to 'refrain[ing] from misappropriating online content' from vertical competitors in the future.[293]

A complicating factor in resolving the issue of platform appropriation is the fact that it concerns not only competition law but also intellectual property law. Indeed, when a platform copies a rival's product, one would expect the rival to rely on its intellectual

286 Josh Constine, 'Instagram Stories Hits 200M Users, Surpassing Snapchat as It Copies Its AR Stickers' (*TechCrunch*, 13 April 2017) <https://techcrunch.com/2017/04/13/instagram-stories-bigger-than-snapchat/>.

287 Elizabeth Warren, 'Here's How We Can Break Up Big Tech' (*Medium*, 8 March 2019) <https://medium.com/@teamwarren/heres-how-we-can-break-up-big-tech-9ad9e0da324c> ('Amazon crushes small companies by copying the goods they sell on the Amazon Marketplace and then selling its own branded version').

288 *Amazon Marketplace* and *Amazon Buy Box* (Cases AT.40462 and AT.40703) Commission Decision C(2022)9442, para 113.

289 *Google Search (Shopping)* (n 267), para 63.

290 Scraping does surface again in the decision, but without specific legal consequences. See ibid, para 381 for complaints of competing CSSs on how 'Google published consumer reviews on Google Shopping that had been taken ... from our ... websites'.

291 FTC, File no 111-0163, *In the Matter of Google* (Statement regarding Google's search practices, 3 January 2013) 3.

292 FTC, 'Google agrees to change its business practices to resolve FTC competition concerns in the markets for devices like smart phones, games and tablets, and in online search' (press release, 3 January 2013) <https://www.ftc.gov/news-events/press-releases/2013/01/google-agrees-change-its-business-practices-resolve-ftc>.

293 ibid and *In the Matter of Google* (n 291) 3. The specific commitments are described in a letter from Google, available at <https://www.ftc.gov/system/files/documents/closing_letters/google-inc./130103googleletterchairmanleibowitz.pdf>.

property rights (eg a copyright for content) to halt such copying. However, intellectual property rights may not be 'strong' enough to do so. The reach of a copyright over user-generated content such as Yelp reviews, for example, is not yet entirely clear.[294] And in other instances, the rival whose content has been appropriated does not even own the copyright. The aforementioned lyrics database Genius, for example, does not hold the rights to the lyrics they have transcribed on their website (music publishers do).[295] Copyright is thus an ineffective tool to prevent those lyrics from showing up on Google.[296]

Given the (perceived) insufficient reach of intellectual property laws, firms whose content has been appropriated may want to resort to competition law. A credible theory of anticompetitive harm could be construed around innovation as well as quality. Firstly, when platforms (systematically) appropriate the investments of rivals, the rivals' incentive to come up with new products decreases, as does their incentive to improve the quality of existing products. Moreover, appropriation may also reduce the platform's own incentive to innovate by (further) developing its own product in that market.[297]

There are, however, counterarguments to applying competition law in appropriation cases. For one, 'weak' intellectual property rights in certain areas may reflect the view of the legislator that innovation in this area does not require or merit legal protection from copying. Intervention is thought to be counterproductive given that the benefits of copycat behaviour (often in the form of lower prices) outweigh the costs (in terms of innovation).[298] Competition law should not be too quick to frustrate such (deliberate) choices by the legislator. Additionally, there is the issue of enforcement. On this point, a dissenting FTC commissioner in the *Google* case opined that qualifying scraping as a violation of competition law would 'put the FTC in the position of becoming the enforcer of the copyright laws on the Internet – a task for which it has neither the resources nor expertise, and was surely not envisioned by Congress.'[299]

The challenge is thus to find a balance between intellectual property and competition law in addressing appropriation (which, in many cases, comes down to a balance between price and innovation). I do not seek to determine this balance here, but offer some initial

294 To some extent, this is a contractual question: Did the user agreement confer a license to the firm/platform for certain user-generated content? However, the scope of intellectual property rights also matters. See Michael Carrier, 'Only "Scraping" the Surface: The Copyright Hole in the FTC's Google Settlement' (2013) 46 UBC Law Review 759.

295 This is (in part) why Genius's complaint was dismissed, see *Genius v Google and LyricFind*, no 19-cv-7279 (EDNY, 20 August 2020).

296 See also Spencer Soper, 'Got a Hot Seller on Amazon? Prepare for E-Tailer to Make One Too' (*Bloomberg*, 20 April 2016) <https://www.bloomberg.com/news/articles/2016-04-20/got-a-hot-seller-on-amazon-prepare-for-e-tailer-to-make-one-too> (the seller of a popular laptop stand that was allegedly copied by Amazon declared that 'there's nothing [it] can do because they didn't violate the patent').

297 *In the Matter of Google* (n 291) 3 ('The Commission considered whether this conduct could have diminished the incentive of Google's rivals to invest in bringing new and innovative content and services to the Internet in the future or reduced Google's own incentive to innovate in the relevant markets'). For an overview of both empirical and anecdotal evidence pointing towards a decrease in innovation resulting from Facebook's alleged copying practices, see Newman (n 192) 1516–17.

298 Ramsi Woodcock, 'The Time's Elastic Concept of Monopoly' (*What Am I Missing?*, 16 December 2019) <https://zephyranth.pw/2019/12/16/the-times-elastic-conception-of-monopoly/>.

299 FTC, File no 111-0163, *In the Matter of Google* (Concurring and Dissenting Statement of Commissioner Thomas Rosch, 3 January 2012) 4.

thoughts.[300] When one firm simply copies a rival's product (conduct that is widespread in a variety of industries), that rival can rely on intellectual property rights, but – in the absence of such rights – there appears to be little room for intervention under competition law.[301] When a platform copies a business using its platform by relying on its position as the dominant platform operator, there *may* be a competition law concern. In that case, the copying conduct could qualify as a form of anticompetitive leveraging because there is a connection between the platform's dominant position and its potentially harmful conduct.[302] In line with this distinction, Shelanski limits his theory of anticompetitive copying (which he terms 'forced free riding') to situations where 'a platform appropriates innovation by other firms that depend on the platform for access to consumers'.[303]

Accordingly, when Amazon copies a shoe sold by a business that is not using its platform, there appears to be little room for an intervention under competition law.[304] When Amazon copies products on the basis of third-party transaction data it has access to as a marketplace operator, there may be cause for concern. Even in that case, however, the merits of a competition law case are uncertain. Instead, competition authorities have focused on conduct that follows such vertical integration (from marketplace to retailer in the above example), ie favouring the platform's downstream products over those of third parties. This book focuses on instances of such potentially anticompetitive leveraging. However, since leveraging often follows vertical integration, the supporting role of appropriation must be recognized.

3.2 Platform Exploitation

Most allegations of exploitation by platforms focus on the 'collaborative' economy and Uber in particular.[305] The basis of such allegations consists of various studies on the hourly wages of Uber drivers, which generally conclude that those wages are low

300 See also Friso Bostoen, '"We Have Reached 'Peak Cloning' in Silicon Valley": When Does Copying Your Competitor's Product Become Anticompetitive?' (*CoRe Blog*, 26 September 2019) <https://core-blog.lexxion.eu/anticompetitive-copying/>.

301 For a different perspective, see Obear (n 282) (construing a theory of 'predatory copying' that may apply to Facebook even when it is copying rivals that are not active on its platform).

302 The required 'connection' between the firm's dominant position and its abusive conduct remains unclear. The ECJ did not require a causal connection in Case 6–72 *Continental Can v Commission* EU:C:1973:22, para 27 ('the question of the link of causality raised by the applicants which in their opinion has to exist between the dominant position and its abuse, is of no consequence, for the strengthening of the position of an undertaking may be an abuse and prohibited under Article [102] of the treaty, regardless of the means and procedure by which it is achieved, if it has [anticompetitive] effects'). The ECJ did require a 'link' in Case C–333/94 P *Tetra Pak v Commission* EU:C:1996:436, para 27 ('It is true that application of Article [102] presupposes a link between the dominant position and the alleged abusive conduct').

303 Shelanski (n 186) 1699–1701 ('Viewed through a conventional antitrust lens, the practice of content scraping appears to present more of an intellectual property issue than a competitive concern. But when viewed from the perspective of innovation, such conduct is damaging, even absent any intellectual property violation.'). For a discussion, see OECD, 'Implications of e-Commerce for Competition Policy' (Background Note) DAF/COMP(2018)3, 36–37.

304 See Nick Statt, 'Facebook May Copy Your App, but Amazon Will Copy Your Shoe' (*The Verge*, 19 September 2019) <https://www.theverge.com/tldr/2019/9/19/20874818/>.

305 See Bostoen, 'Competition Law in the Peer-to-Peer Economy' (n 185) 162–63.

(often below minimum wage).[306] One of the reasons for such behaviour is said to be the high commission fees charged by Uber.[307] As explained in the introduction, however, this work focuses on the platform economy but shies away from the specific subset of the collaborative economy.

Disregarding the collaborative economy does not eliminate concerns of exploitation by platforms. App Store commission fees, for example, are set at 30% – a number approximating the estimates of Uber's commission fee. Amazon pockets more than 50% of its third-party sellers' revenue, although that is explained not only by commission fees but also by fulfilment and advertising services.[308] And some argue that Facebook's increasingly extensive data collection and processing practices amount to a form of exploitation.[309] In contrast to exclusionary practices, the harm from such exploitative practices is direct: the platform's trading partners (eg app developers) are subject to high fees; consumers using the platform (eg Facebook users) are subject to more invasive data collection, which could be considered their payment for the service.

At least in theory, a remedy against exploitation is found in article 102(a) TFEU, which prohibits 'directly or indirectly imposing unfair ... selling prices or other unfair trading conditions'. An excessively high commission fee could, for example, qualify as such an 'unfair trading condition'. However, competition authorities show great reservation in taking up such cases. One reason is that markets are presumed to self-correct for excessive prices because such prices attract new entrants that will bring the price down (in theory, to marginal cost).[310] Moreover, in relation to platforms, it has been argued that '[t]he two-sided nature of intermediation markets may legitimate a higher price for providers where this balances demand between both sides of the platform'.[311]

306 See eg Lawrence Mishel, 'Uber and the Labor Market: Uber Drivers' Compensation, Wages, and the Scale of Uber and the Gig Economy' (2018) Economic Policy Institute Working Paper, (finding that Uber driver 'compensation' averages $11.77/hour, 'discretionary compensation' averages $10.87/hour, and 'wage' averages $9.21/hour); Stephen Zoepf, Stella Chen, Paa Adu and Gonzalo Pozo, 'The Economics of Ride-Hailing: Driver Revenue, Expenses and Taxes' (2018) MIT CEEPR Working Paper 2018-5, and the head author's correction: Stephen Zoepf, 'The Economics of Ride Hailing, Revisited' (Statement, 2018) (finding that Uber drivers' median profit amounts to $8.55/hour).

307 In its filings with the SEC, Uber states its commission fee (or 'take rate') amounted to 18–19% for the first half of 2019, see Uber Technologies, Inc., Form 10-Q Quarterly Report to the SEC for the quarterly period ended June 30, 2019. Independent studies put the number significantly higher. See Aaron Gordon and Dhruv Mehrotra, 'Uber and Lyft Take a Lot More from Drivers than They Say' (*Jalopnik*, 26 August 2019) <https://jalopnik.com/uber-and-lyft-take-a-lot-more-from-drivers-than-they-sa-1837450373> (estimating the commission fee to be 35% based on 15,000 fare receipts provided by drivers – a sample that may involve some selection bias, as the authors acknowledge); Mishel (n 306) (estimating the commission fee to be about a third of what passengers pay).

308 Juozas Kaziukėnas, 'Amazon Takes a 50% Cut of Seller's Revenue' (*Marketplace Pulse*, 23 February 2023) <https://www.marketplacepulse.com/articles/amazon-takes-a-50-cut-of-sellers-revenue>.

309 Srinivasan (n 283).

310 See eg Case C–177/16 *AKKA/LAA v Konkurences padome* EU:C:2017:286, Opinion of AG Wahl, para 48 ('the market should, in principle, be able to self-correct in the short to medium term: high prices should normally attract new entrants or encourage existing competitors to expand'). This theoretical argument does presuppose the absence of significant barriers to entry.

311 Niamh Dunne, 'Competition Law (and Its Limits) in the Sharing Economy' in Nestor Davidson, Michèle Finck and John Infranca (eds), *Cambridge Handbook on Law and Regulation of the Sharing Economy* (CUP 2018) 97. See also Stephen King, 'Sharing Economy: What Challenges for Competition Law?' (2015) 6 JECLAP 729, 731–32.

The focus of this work is on exclusionary conduct by online platforms and in particular leveraging – not on exploitative conduct. But sometimes – and increasingly so – the two forms of abuse intersect. In its *Facebook* decision, the Bundeskartellamt held that Facebook is subjecting users to excessive data collection and processing, which not only amounts to an exploitative abuse (an unfair trading condition) but also has an exclusionary component (increasing entry barriers for competitors).[312] An even better illustration of the interaction between exploitative and exclusionary abuses is offered by a French case concerning Amazon.[313]

The case, brought by the French Ministry of Economic Affairs, concerned various contractual clauses between Amazon and third-party sellers regarding the use of its online marketplace (eg regarding amendments, suspensions, terminations and performance indicators).[314] The court found these clauses to constitute an abusive exploitation of the sellers by Amazon, but referred not to article 102 TFEU but rather to France's provision on abuse of *relative* dominance (or economic dependence).[315] While the court's judgment focused on abusive *exploitation*, the court also hinted at an *exclusionary* aspect. In the judgment's introduction, for example, the court mentions the risk of having a platform operator decide on the ranking of third-party sellers while at the same time competing with those sellers by offering its own products.[316] In its conclusion, the court further discusses how Amazon – inspired by third-party sellers – can start selling similar products, which it can then algorithmically preference over the products of those third-party sellers, eg through placement in the Buy Box.[317]

The *Facebook* and *Amazon* cases show that exploitative and exclusionary practices may overlap. For that reason, and as is the case with appropriation, exploitation will not be discussed separately but only to the extent it intersects with exclusionary behaviour and leveraging in particular.

312 Bundeskartellamt, Case B6-22/16, *Facebook*, 7 February 2019.

313 A similar example is offered by the Bundeskartellamt's *Amazon* case, which was closed when Amazon amended the general terms of business for sellers on its marketplace. See Bundeskartellamt, Case B2-88/18, *Amazon*, 17 July 2019 (while the case mainly concerned allegations of exploitative abuse, '[a]llegations regarding the cancellation and blocking of seller accounts, rights of use and parity requirements, product reviews and seller ratings or European delivery schemes were i.a. reviewed under exclusionary abuse considerations').

314 Tribunal de commerce de Paris, case 2017050625, *Ministre de l'Économie et des Finances v Amazon*, 2 September 2019. The judgment is only available in French; for a discussion in English, see Friso Bostoen, 'Abuse of Relative Dominance in the Platform Economy: A French Court Finds Amazon's Contracts with Third-Party Sellers Significantly Imbalanced' (*CoRe Blog*, 12 November 2019) <https://coreblog.lexxion.eu/amazon-case-france/>.

315 The legal basis of the case is art L420-2 of the French Commercial Code (free translation: 'The abusive exploitation by one (or more) undertakings of the state of economic dependence in which its suppliers or customers find themselves is prohibited insofar as it can affect the functioning or structure of the market.'). That article refers to the practices listed in art L442–6, of which sub I, 2° prohibits 'subjecting of trying to subject trading partners to obligations that create a significant imbalance between the rights and obligations of the contracting parties'.

316 *Ministre de l'Économie et des Finances v Amazon* (n 314) 2.

317 ibid 41. The court does not dive deeper into these exclusionary aspects. The chosen legal basis of the case offers one reason; the ongoing EC case on such exclusionary practices another, see EC, 'Commission sends Statement of Objections to Amazon for the use of non-public independent seller data and opens second investigation into its e-commerce business practices' (press release, 10 November 2020) IP/20/2077.

3.3 Platform Exclusion

The most controversial area in competition policy is that of exclusionary practices[.][318]

Exclusionary conduct by online platforms forms the core subject of this work, but even this subject exceeds the scope of a book (that people might actually read). Given the focus on the platform economy, a useful further distinction is between *intra*-platform competition and *inter*-platform competition.[319]

Inter-platform competition refers to competition *between* platforms, not only to attract consumers, but also for the affiliation of suppliers. As explained above, platforms must attract a sufficient number of users from both sides of the platform ('critical mass') in order to be successful.[320] Due to indirect network effects, markets are prone to 'tipping' in favour of a few platforms (or even just one), which pushes platforms to compete aggressively *for* that market, eg through growth-over-profit strategies. Inter-platform competition (ie between platforms, for the market) is thus usually fierce – at least until one platform dominates the market.

Intra-platform competition refers to competition *on* the platform, which takes place between the various suppliers on the platform, but – increasingly – also between suppliers and the platform itself. The reason for the latter form of intra-platform competition is vertical integration by platforms, which takes place when platforms develop their own products and distribute them through their platform. In that case, the platform does offer not only the digital infrastructure for the distribution of products or services (upstream), but also some of those products or services themselves (downstream).[321] As explained above, platforms are exceptionally well placed to enter markets that are vertically related to their core market.[322] Once platforms have integrated vertically, they fulfil a 'dual role' vis-à-vis suppliers, namely, *distributing* their products as well as *competing* with them.

As this book is concerned with platform–supplier relations, its focus is on intra-platform competition rather than inter-platform competition. The two forms of competition are, however, related: as a platform becomes more significant compared to the other platforms in its market, its suppliers become more dependent on it, given that switching to other platforms becomes less of an option. For that reason, I discuss intra-platform

318 Chiara Fumagalli, Massimo Motta and Claudio Calcagno, *Exclusionary Practices: The Economics of Monopolization and Abuse of Dominance* (CUP 2018) foreword.

319 See Kaiser (n 218) 96–97 (distinguishing competition *among* ecosystems and competition *within* a given ecosystem). See also Jacques Crémer, Yves-Alexandre de Montjoye and Heike Schweitzer, 'Competition Policy for the Digital Era' (Special Advisers' Report, 2019) (hereafter, 'Crémer Report'), ch 4 (distinguishing between platform competition *for* the market and competition *on* platforms), and Ezrachi and Stucke (n 184) 148–51 (distinguishing competition *between* and *within* super-platforms).

320 See Section 2.2.1.

321 See Section 2.2.2, on how two-sided markets do not fit easily with the terminology of vertical integration.

322 ibid.

competition extensively (Part 2) but later broaden the perspective to inter-platform competition (Part 3). Before moving on to the next Part, the next two sections introduce what a legal perspective on these different forms of platform competition entails.

3.3.1 Intra-Platform Exclusion

Increasingly, online platforms provide not only an online infrastructure for interaction and commerce in particular (eg an app store, online marketplace or search engine), but also the products distributed through that infrastructure (eg apps, goods or vertical search services). Following such vertical integration, platform operators find themselves in a dual role: *distributor* of their suppliers' products on the one hand, *competitor* to those products on the other. This dual role can lead to a conflict of interest: it may give the operator an incentive to use its control over the platform to favour its own products over those sold by independent suppliers.

Favouring one's own downstream operations (or 'self-preferencing') implies the exclusion (or 'discrimination') of those of others. Such exclusion can be carried out explicitly by banning certain suppliers from the platform ('delisting'). Often, however, this exclusion proceeds more subtly, eg by imposing restrictive conditions on suppliers (which do not apply to its own products) or pushing the suppliers' products down the ranking of results presented to the consumer (while promoting its own products). Under certain circumstances, exclusionary behaviour can constitute an abuse under article 102 TFEU. In particular, it can constitute an instance of leveraging, ie using one's market power in one market (the platform market) to distort competition in a related market (the suppliers' market).

Given its prevalence in platform–supplier relations, anticompetitive leveraging is at the heart of this thesis. The strategic value of leveraging has been described in the economic literature on platforms, but not every supplier should fear it:

> If you are a platform manager, you don't want to let an outside firm control a primary source of user value on your platform. When this happens, you need to move to take control of the value-creating app .... On the other hand, when an extension app adds a modest amount of additional value, then it's perfectly safe and generally very efficient to allow the outside developer to retain control of it.[323]

Platforms thus want to avoid certain suppliers becoming key players in their ecosystem, which may allow them to become platforms in their own right at some point.[324] In fact, such a concern was at the basis of the *Microsoft* cases: Microsoft feared that browsers (so-called middleware) could become a full-fledged platform hosting other applications, thereby replacing Windows OS. Microsoft thus engaged in *defensive* leveraging, using

323 Parker, Van Alstyne and Choudary (n 171) 147, see also 216–17.

324 ibid 148.

its dominant position in desktop OS to favour its own browser, Internet Explorer (IE), over those of competitors. Attaining a strong position in the vertically related browser market then shielded Microsoft's dominance in the OS market.[325]

However, most instances of platform leveraging do not seek to safeguard the platform's position in the upstream market, but are rather *offensive*, ie aimed at extracting additional profit from being active in the downstream product market. Of course, an incentive to do so only exists when the profit margin on the platform's products exceeds the profit margin from facilitating the distribution of its suppliers' products (ie the fees or other form of payment from users minus the costs of that facilitation).[326] Thus, when a platform is looking for additional profit, vertical integration constitutes an alternative to simply raising user fees (eg commissions on sales).[327]

To summarize: the relationship between platforms and suppliers can evolve. Generally, they are in a relation of mutually beneficial dependency: platforms need suppliers and vice versa, while both parties benefit (through increased user fees and distribution, respectively). However, this relationship changes when the platform achieves (relative) market power, in which the dependency becomes more one-sided to the disadvantage of suppliers. In that case, platforms may increase user fees, or – more relevant for the purpose of this book – seek additional profit through vertical integration. In the latter case, the platforms start fulfilling a dual role and, as Kaiser puts it, 'problems arise when [platforms] wear multiple hats'.[328] In that case, the platform may be incentivized to leverage its market power in the platform market to the detriment of suppliers it competes with at the downstream level.

Given this dynamic, platforms and suppliers have been termed 'frenemies': they collaborate as friends but may also compete as enemies – a competition that can lead the platform to favour its own downstream operations over those of suppliers.[329] A final question, though, is whether such favouring (or self-preferencing) is particularly effective. After all, supermarkets have long given their private-label products favourable shelf space.[330] Of course, the exclusionary effects of self-preferencing depend on the firm's market power – any difference with supermarkets on that point is a factual question. However, there are additional factors suggesting that platforms could be more effective than supermarkets at favouring their own products.

325 Extensively on the *Microsoft* cases, see Section 6. This defensive leveraging theory was particularly prevalent in the US *Microsoft* case, see *United States v Microsoft* 253 F3d 34 (DC Cir 2001).

326 See Section 2.3.1, for an application of this principle to Amazon.

327 For economic modelling, see Joseph Farrell and Michael Katz, 'Innovation, Rent Extraction, and Integration in Systems Markets' (2000) 48 The Journal of Industrial Economics 413. The authors write about two different complements rather than a platform and a complement. Their reference to Windows OS and independent application developers (fn 2), however, shows that they had platform–supplier relations in mind – the platform terminology simply had not yet (fully) developed at that point. Note that the authors' model incorporates the single monopoly profit theory.

328 Kaiser (n 218) 96–97.

329 Ezrachi and Stucke (n 184) 147–58. See also Ron Adner, Jianqing Chen and Feng Zhu, 'Frenemies in Platform Markets: Heterogeneous Profit Foci as Drivers of Compatibility Decisions' (2019) 66 Management Science 2432.

330 Further on the supermarket analogy, see Section 5.2.1.

For one, curation is a central aspect of the role of platforms; they are essentially algorithmic recommender systems that bring order to the chaos of the web. As Newman puts it, users turn to platforms 'as a means of cutting through the fog of information overload, which is felt most acutely in digital contexts. It is this unique backdrop that makes users particularly vulnerable to steering – and makes steering strategies more attractive – in digital markets.'[331] In other words, since the alternative is finding needles in the digital haystack, users are quick to accept the platform's ranking of recommendations, whether the platform's own products are at the top of it or not.[332] To safeguard the centrality of their intermediary recommendation system (ie to avoid 'disintermediation'), platforms make sure to keep suppliers and consumers separated.[333]

While steering users constitutes a soft form of self-preferencing, a platform can also engage in harder forms, such as suspending users or terminating relations with them. This power is vested in platforms by virtue of their role as private regulators of their ecosystem.[334] Platforms have policies on the removal of low-quality or misbehaving users, but those self-imposed rules are often vague enough to justify removing any user on the platform (cf the *Amazon* case discussed above).[335] Therefore, platforms in a dual role could call upon these policies to remove competing rather than low-quality/misbehaving users.

In conclusion, intra-platform exclusion generally proceeds by leveraging (defensively or offensively) upstream market power. Such leveraging usually takes the form of self-preferencing, which can – in turn – take many forms: one high-level division is between steering users and removing users, but there is a broad spectrum between (and beyond) these practices.[336] The billion-euro question (given the current fining practice of the EC) is how to qualify these practices, given that leveraging is not an independent form of abuse. Rather, leveraging is an umbrella term covering various forms of abuse, including refusal to supply, margin squeeze and tying. As this question of qualification (and corresponding legal tests) is at the heart of this book, the extensive Part 2 is dedicated to it.

Before moving on, I must once more dispel the notion that practices that may, at first sight, support leveraging are necessarily anticompetitive. Rather, they often find a compelling justification in the need for platform governance. The point is not that platforms should

331 Newman (n 192) 1530.

332 See eg *Google Search (Shopping)* (n 267), paras 454–61 ('the ten highest-ranking generic search results on the first Google general search results page together generally receive approximately 95% of all clicks on generic search results'; this division of clicks largely remained the same when the positioning of search results was changed, which demonstrates that the positioning rather than the relevance of the results matters).

333 Zhu and Iansiti (n 182) ('Platforms have used various mechanisms to deter disintermediation, such as creating terms of service that prohibit users from conducting transactions off the platform, and blocking users from exchanging contact information'); Khan, 'Sources of Tech Platform Power' (n 186) 328 (platforms 'limit … the ability of third-party merchants to reach users independently – and thereby cultivat[e] deeper business dependence on their infrastructure').

334 See Section 2.2.2 and further Section 10.

335 Section 2.3.1.

336 For illustrations, see Section 2.3.

not use their soft and hard powers over their ecosystem; if they refrain from doing so, their success will be short-lived. *Under certain circumstances*, however, these powers can be abused. It is a challenge to filter out those cases. The first step is to carefully spell out theories of abuse that work in the platform economy; the second step is to consider the justification of platform governance separately, which is done in the final section of Part 2.

3.3.2 Inter-Platform Exclusion

Inter-platform competition, ie competition between platforms, is not the central concern of this book. But it is related to intra-platform competition: as a platform becomes more significant compared to the other platforms in its market (upstream), its suppliers (downstream) become more dependent on it, given that switching to other platforms becomes less of an option. For that reason, Part 3 of this book zooms out from intra-platform to inter-platform competition – and exclusion in particular. The scope is also extended in another way: while Part 2 presents a competition law assessment, Part 3 examines the broader regulatory environment, which includes *ex ante* platform regulation.

Broadening the perspective in this way leads to a list of regulatory measures that can be organized along different lines:

- Some measures promote competition in the *upstream*/platform market (horizontal merger control, portability), while others primarily safeguard competition in the *downstream* market (vertical merger control, non-discrimination) – certain measures can have effects on both upstream and downstream competition (interoperability, forced access, breakup).
- Some measures fit better under the *competition law* umbrella (merger control, breakup), while others better qualify as *ex ante* regulation (structural non-discrimination, portability), but many can be imposed through both regimes (behavioural non-discrimination, interoperability, forced access).
- Some measures are rather *structural* (merger control, structural non-discrimination, breakup), while others are rather *behavioural* (portability, interoperability, behavioural non-discrimination, forced access).

Including a discussion of these regulatory interventions is necessary to present a complete analysis. However, these interventions are not examined to the same extent as the abusive practices in Part 2. By way of context, their regulatory precedents in the telecom sphere are discussed. Next, I introduce the current (proposals for) platform regulation. The analysis ends with a demonstration of the trade-offs in each (proposed) regulation, and a cautious indication of which direction these trade-offs point – in other words, which kind of regulation shows promise.

PART 2

INTRA-PLATFORM EXCLUSION UNDER ARTICLE 102 TFEU

4

INTRA-PLATFORM EXCLUSION PRELIMINARIES

An article 102 TFEU analysis requires establishing a dominant position before assessing whether any conduct is abusive. This goes back to the 'special responsibility' imposed on dominant firms,[337] the essence of which 'is to prohibit some practices when exerted by a dominant firm while considering them lawful if practiced by smaller competitors'.[338] In other words, dominance is a *sine qua non* for abuse. For this reason, I summarily survey dominance in the platform economy in Section 4.1.

Once a dominant position has been established, the abuse itself must be assessed. For this assessment, a normative framework is essential. In particular, it is necessary to understand the goals of competition law (which kind of harms are we concerned about?) and the methods of competition law (what is the best way to assess these harms – and to adapt the rules accordingly?). Therefore, I discuss the goals and methods of competition law in Section 4.2.

4.1 The Prerequisite of Platform Power

The ECJ defines a dominant position as 'a position of economic strength enjoyed by an undertaking which enables it to prevent effective competition being maintained on the relevant market by giving it the power to behave to an appreciable extent independently of its competitors, customers and ultimately of its consumers'.[339] This

337 Case 322/81 *Michelin v Commission* EU:C:1983:313, para 10 ('A finding that an undertaking has a dominant position is not in itself a recrimination but simply means that, irrespective of the reasons for which it has such a position, the undertaking concerned has a special responsibility not to allow its conduct to impair genuine undistorted competition on the common market').

338 Rafael Allendesalazar Corcho, 'Can We Finally Say Farewell to the "Special Responsibility" of Dominant Companies?' (2007) EUI Robert Schuman Centre EU Competition Law and Policy Workshop/ Proceedings 3.

339 Case 27/76 *United Brands v Commission* EU:C:1978:22, para 65 (quote); Case 85/76 *Hoffmann-La Roche v Commission* EU:C:1979:36, para 38; Case T–201/04 *Microsoft v Commission* EU:T:2007:289, para 229.

'position of economic strength' is not assessed in a vacuum, but rather by reference to the relevant product market the undertaking is operating in.[340] Therefore, in order to establish dominance, first, one needs to correctly define that market.[341] In the platform economy, however, this preliminary exercise becomes slightly more complicated.[342]

4.1.1 Defining Platform Markets

The relevant product market comprises all products that are sufficiently interchangeable, based on the idea that those products exert a competitive constraint on each other.[343] This competitive constraint can emanate from the demand side (consumers shifting their purchases) or the supply side (suppliers, both current and potential, adapting their production). From an economic point of view, demand substitution forms the most effective competitive constraint on suppliers of a particular product, which is why it is given outsize importance when defining markets.[344] In practice, demand substitution is determined by testing whether consumers would switch to substitute products in response to a small but significant, non-transitory increase in price (the so-called SSNIP test). If such substitution makes the price increase unprofitable because of the resulting loss of sales, additional substitute products are added to the relevant market until the price increase is profitable.[345]

However, many platforms (including Google and Facebook) offer their services for 'free', at least to the consumer side of the platform. Can a market for free services even exist? While it has been argued that free services cannot constitute a market,[346] the EC has repeatedly defined such a market, eg for free consumer communications services[347] and general search services.[348] In Germany, lawmakers left no room for doubt when they

340 The relevant *geographic* market is also pertinent but will not be discussed, apart from noting this market can be relatively wide in case of (purely) digital products.

341 This modus operandi has been criticized, see eg Louis Kaplow, 'Why (Ever) Define Markets?' (2010) 124 Harvard Law Review 437.

342 For an excellent work on market definition in digital markets, see Viktoria Robertson, *Competition Law's Innovation Factor: The Relevant Market in Dynamic Contexts in the EU and the US* (Hart 2020).

343 *Hoffmann-La Roche v Commission* (n 339), para 28 ('The concept of the relevant market in fact implies that there can be effective competition between the products which form part of it and this presupposes that there is a sufficient degree of interchangeability between all the products forming part of the same market in so far as a specific use of such products is concerned'). See also 'Commission Notice on the definition of relevant market for the purposes of Community competition law' [1997] OJ C372/5, para 7.

344 Commission Notice on the definition of relevant market for the purposes of Community competition law (n 343), para 13.

345 ibid, para 17.

346 Miguel Sousa Ferro, 'De Gratis Non Curat Lex: Abuse of Dominance in Online Free Services' (2017) 12 Competition Law Review 153, 155–58. For the opposing view, see eg John Newman, 'Antitrust in Zero-Price Markets: Applications' (2016) 94 Washington University Law Review 49, 60–71.

347 *Microsoft/Skype* (Case COMP/M.6281) Commission Decision C(2011)7279, paras 18–63, confirmed in Case T–79/12 *Cisco v Commission* EU:T:2013:635, paras 65–74. The same market has been defined in subsequent cases: *Microsoft/Nokia* (Case COMP/M.7047) Commission Decision C(2013)8873, paras 43–45; *Facebook/WhatsApp* (Case M.7217) Commission Decision C(2014)7239, paras 20–34; *Microsoft/LinkedIn* (Case M.8124) Commission Decision C(2016)8404, paras 77–83.

348 *Google Search (Shopping)* (Case AT.39740) Commission Decision C(2017)4444, paras 145–263 and in particular para 152.

amended their Competition Act to state that free services can constitute a market.[349] This approach is logical, as supposedly free services are often provided in return for a non-monetary consideration, which does not mean there is no market exchange.

A more persistent issue is how to determine *the extent of* a market for free services. Obviously, an SSNIP test is not workable when the price of the product in question is zero: a 5% increase would not change the price and thus demand.[350] Yet, while suppliers of zero-priced services do not compete on price, they do compete on other dimensions such as quality.[351] Based on this idea, competition authorities and scholars have put forward the alternative small but significant non-transitory decrease in quality (SSNDQ) test, which seeks to measure shifts in customer demand in response to a quality degradation rather than a price increase.[352] In *Google Android*, for example, the EC asked whether original equipment manufacturers (OEMS) (and app developers) would switch to a different licensable mobile OS in case of 'a small but significant, non-transitory deterioration of the quality' of Google Play.[353] Recognizing that precise quantitative measurements are all the more difficult in case of quality degradations, however, authorities have mostly relied on more qualitative evidence of substitutability such as consumer surveys, internal business documents and views from the industry.[354]

Adapting to zero-priced services is not the only challenge when defining platform markets. Another question is *how many* markets to define in case of a multisided market. Is a platform active in one 'platform' market or in two markets – one for each 'side'?

---

349 Competition Act in the version published on 26 June 2013 (Federal Law Gazette I, p 1750), as last amended by art 2 of the Act of 19 July 2022 (Federal Law Gazette I, p 1214) (hereafter, 'German Competition Act'), s 18(2a), which states: 'The assumption of a market shall not be invalidated by the fact that a good or service is provided free of charge.'

350 Even when there is a price in multisided markets, the SSNIP test should be modified to take account of the indirect network effects between different sides of the platform market, see Lapo Filistrucchi, Damien Geradin, Eric van Damme and Pauline Affeldt, 'Market Definition in Two-Sided Markets: Theory and Practice' (2014) 10 JCLE 293, 329–38.

351 *Google Search (Shopping)* (n 348), para 160.

352 *Google Android* (Case AT.40099) Commission Decision C(2018)4761, paras 284–322 and 483–566. For a critical appraisal, see Daniel Mândrescu, 'Lessons and Questions from *Google Android* – Part 1: The Market Definition' (*CoRe Blog*, 29 October 2019) <https://coreblog.lexxion.eu/lessons-and-questions-from-google-android-part-1-the-market-definition/>. The Chinese Supreme People's Court also carried out an SSNDQ-test in *Qihoo 360 v Tencent*, which concerned the market for free internet messaging services, see David Stallibrass and Sharon Pang, 'Clash of Titans: How China Disciplines Internet Markets' (2015) 6 JECLAP 418.

353 *Google Android* (n 352), para 286. The GC confirmed that the EC carried out the test correctly, see Case T–604/18 *Google v Commission* EU:T:2022:541, paras 174–181.

354 On this difficulty, see Jacques Crémer, Yves-Alexandre de Montjoye and Heike Schweitzer, 'Competition Policy for the Digital Era' (Special Advisers' Report, 2019) (hereafter, 'Crémer Report') 45 ('it is unclear how this test could be made operational in practice without a precise measurement of quality … and without a way to quantify the effects of the quality degradation on the firm's revenues in order to determine whether such a degradation would be profitable'). In *Google Android* (n 352), the EC accorded a lot of importance to the views of intervening OEMs/app developers and consumer surveys. A similar approach was followed in *Qihoo 360 v Tencent*, see Vanessa Zhang's contribution to 'The First Antitrust Decision by the Chinese Supreme People's Court: Qihoo 360 vs. Tencent' (transcript of CPI webinar, 16 December 2014) ('Being aware that quality decrease could not be easily assessed and the quality data is not available, the court suggested qualitative but not quantitative hypothetical monopoly test with decrease of quality'). See also Competition Bureau of Canada, 'Big Data and Innovation: Implications for Competition Policy in Canada' (Draft Discussion Paper, 2017) 12–14 ('Faced with such difficulties [measuring changes in consumption in response to a small but significant change in quality], the Bureau may rely on other evidence of substitutability, such as views expressed in consumer surveys, business documents, or evidence of switching').

Take, for example, Amazon: is the online marketplace part of the 'e-commerce intermediation' market, or the consumer-facing 'online retail' and supplier-facing 'online distribution' markets? Or consider Facebook: is the company active in the 'advertising-funded social networking market' or in the consumer-facing 'social network' and supplier-facing 'online advertising' markets? The answers to these questions tend to tie in with the platform typology established above.[355] In 2014 already, Filistrucchi et al put forward a promising theory: 'In two-sided non-transaction markets, two (interrelated) markets need to be defined. In two-sided transaction markets, only one market should be defined.'[356] However, the authors stressed that – even when two markets are defined – authorities should pay due attention to their interrelation (through indirect network effects), which implies that one side of the market may still be competitively constrained by the other side.[357]

The US Supreme Court fully endorsed Filistrucchi's theory in its *American Express* Opinion, writing (or rather quoting) that '[i]n two-sided transaction markets, only one market should be defined', and accordingly defining a single market for credit-card transactions.[358] However, this theory – especially when it comes to the number of markets to be defined – should not be elevated to a legal rule but rather be used as a rule of thumb. Indeed, scholars have argued that defining only one market can have negative implications.[359] As a consequence of the single market definition in *American Express*, for example, the Supreme Court appears to require proof that *all* participants in this market (merchants *and cardholders*) were harmed – a high burden of proof that could 'immunize' transaction platforms.[360] Scholars have also criticized defining a single market for multisided transaction platforms because it may unduly exclude one-sided substitutes.[361] While this is a valid concern, it must be noted that defining a

355 See Section 1.2.

356 Filistrucchi, Geradin, van Damme and Affeldt (n 350) 302, drawing on earlier case law including *Travelport/Worldspan* (Case COMP/M.4523) Commission Decision C(2007)3938; *Google/DoubleClick* (Case COMP/M.4731) Commission Decision C(2008)927; *GIMD/Socpresse* (Case COMP/M.3420) Commission Decision [2004] OJ C265/3; NMa, Case 5901 *Bloemenveiling Aalsmeer/FloraHolland*, 21 August 2007.

357 Filistrucchi, Geradin, van Damme and Affeldt (n 350) 322. There is one exception: 'It is only in a two-sided non-transaction market with only one externality that one could safely perform a market definition exercise on the side of the market that exerts no externality on the other without considering the other side.' See further GMC, 'Competition Policy: The Challenge of Digital Markets' (Special Report, 2015), 24–26.

358 *Ohio v American Express* 585 US ____ (2018) 14–15. The majority opinion refers to 'Filistrucchi' no less than ten times, and many more times through the use of 'ibid' and 'id'.

359 Some scholars have even argued that multiple markets should *always* be defined, see Michael Katz and Jonathan Sallet, 'Multisided Platforms and Antitrust Enforcement' (2018) 127 The Yale Law Journal 2142, 2153–58 ('the fundamental principle of market definition, legal precedent, and sound economics all counsel against use of the single-market approach').

360 While the market definition plays an important role in this regard, the wrong application of the rule of reason is considered at least equally problematic. The transaction platforms most likely to be 'immunized' are thought to be Uber/Lyft and perhaps Amazon. See Tim Wu, 'The *American Express* Opinion, the Rule of Reason, and Tech Platforms' (2019) 7 JAE 117; Herbert Hovenkamp, 'Platforms and the Rule of Reason: The *American Express* Case' (2019) Columbia Business Law Review 35, 57–64 (calling the market definition 'irrational' and an 'abandonment of sensible economics'); Ina Fried and David McCabe, 'DOJ Antitrust Official: Supreme Court Ruling Won't Shield Big Tech' (*Axios*, 26 June 2018) <https://www.axios.com/makan-delrahim-in-aspen-1530038874-a289ad1a-012b-4ccb-9cb7-69658ee78c33.html> ('Delrahim did say he thought that the ruling could limit antitrust enforcers' ability to take on Uber, Lyft, and Airbnb').

361 Sebastian Wismer and Arno Rasek, 'Market Definition in Multi-Sided Markets' in OECD (ed), 'Rethinking Antitrust Tools for Multi-Sided Platforms' (Report, 2018) 56–60; Daniel Mândrescu, 'Applying (EU) Competition Law to Online Platforms, Reflections on the Definition of the Relevant Market(s)' (2018) 41

market is only the first step in determining a firm's market power – additional competitive constraints can always be taken into account at a later stage.[362]

The Bundeskartellamt has explicitly addressed the 'one vs two markets' question in a working paper.[363] Put simply, the authority assumes that (i) in case of 'matching platforms', one should define a single intermediation market; and (ii) in case of 'audience providing platforms', one should define multiple markets. Given that these types of platforms are largely equivalent to transaction and non-transaction platforms, respectively, the Bundeskartellamt essentially agrees with Filistrucchi et al. However, the authority incorporates the above criticism on substitutability and nuances its theory accordingly:

> The Bundeskartellamt, applying the concept of demand-side substitutability, considers it possible to regard a platform as a single market if the platform is understood as a provider of an intermediary service and both user groups are understood as consumers of this service with essentially the same needs. The market definition needs to take into account that bilateral positive indirect network effects occur between the user groups. ... To the extent that user groups have obvious different possibilities of substitution, market sides have to be considered separately with a view to the function of the market definition, which is to describe existing competition relations.[364]

Given that this theory is somewhat abstract, it helps to look at the case law for both illustration and evaluation. Returning to the examples introduced earlier, Amazon – a matching/transaction platform – should be operating in a single intermediation market; by contrast, Facebook – an audience-providing/non-transaction platform – should be operating in multiple markets. The case law bears out this conclusion. The Bundeskartellamt considers Amazon's platform business to operate in the single market for 'B2C online platform services for the sale of a general product range'[365] or simply 'online marketplace services'.[366] In the case of Facebook, on the other hand, the authority defined a market for private users of social networks, while holding that advertisers had to be attributed to another market.[367] Also in line with the theory above, the EC has defined a single market for transaction platforms such

---

World Competition 453; Jens-Uwe Franck and Martin Peitz, 'Market Definition and Market Power in the Platform Economy' (CERRE Report, 2019) 23–27.

362 In its *Android* decision, for example, the EC defined a market for 'licensable mobile OSs' but then considered the competitive constraint from Apple's (non-licensable) mobile OS, see *Google Android* (n 352), paras 497–559.

363 Bundeskartellamt, 'The Market Power of Platforms and Networks' (Working Paper, 2016) 25–32.

364 ibid 28–29.

365 Bundeskartellamt, Case B6-46/12, *Amazon removes price parity obligation for retailers on its Marketplace platform* (Case Report) 9 December 2013, 2 (excluding auction platforms and price comparison engines from the definition).

366 Bundeskartellamt, Case B2-88/18, *Amazon* (Case Summary), 17 July 2019 (the Bundeskartellamt did not adopt a decision in this case but stated it 'inclined to assume a product market for online marketplace services').

367 Bundeskartellamt, Case B6-22/16, *Facebook* (Case Summary), 15 February 2019, 3–5.

as app stores.[368] In contrast to the Bundeskartellamt, however, it preliminarily defined two markets in case of Amazon: one for the provision of online marketplace services *to third-party sellers* and another for the provision of online marketplace services *to consumers*.[369] More in line with the theory above, the EC suggested at least two markets for advertising platforms such as search engines.[370] Given that the market definition exercise is tied to the suspected anticompetitive practices, however, competition authorities zoom in on the market where the abuse takes place.[371]

A final challenge in defining markets in the presence of platforms is found in the ecosystems of interrelated products and services some of them present.[372] The Crémer Report argued that when platforms are able to nudge users toward the other products and services within their ecosystem, 'a "classical" definition of markets … may fail to capture a firm's strategy, as firms essentially compete for "access points" to consumers'.[373] It suggests that 'where the firms' lock-in strategies are successful, and consumers are drawn into ecosystems which they find difficult to leave, ecosystem-specific aftermarkets may need to be defined'.[374] Given that the Crémer Report refers to mobile devices as an example of such ecosystems, it appears to support the *Google Android* decision, where the EC defined the ecosystem-specific aftermarket of 'app stores *for Android devices*'.[375] However, when such narrow markets are defined, this should be compensated by duly weighing the competitive constraints that emanate from inter-platform competition in the primary market (eg between Android and iOS devices).[376]

As may be clear from this short survey, platforms are not making the market definition exercise any easier. At the same time, various scholars have argued that in multisided markets, less importance should be given to the exercise of market definition.[377] The Crémer Report, for example, holds that 'in digital markets, less emphasis should

368 *Google Android* (n 352), where the EC acknowledges the market for Android app stores is multisided (para 638), serving both OEMs and developers – as well as consumers, but since the abuse was not consumer-facing, this side was largely left out of focus. The EC considered substitutability from these different perspectives (in particular paras 284–94) but ended up defining a single market for 'Android app stores'. This was confirmed in *Google v Commission* (n 353), paras 243–254.

369 *Amazon Marketplace* and *Amazon Buy Box* (Cases AT.40462 and AT.40703) Commission Decision C(2022)9442, para 64.

370 *Google Search (Shopping)* (n 348), para 159, where the EC acknowledges that '[g]eneral search services and online search advertising constitute the two sides of a general search engine platform' (para 159).

371 In ibid, the EC focuses only on the market for general search services. In *Amazon Marketplace* and *Amazon Buy Box* (n 369), the EC focused on the market for marketplace services for retailers to reach consumers.

372 See Section 2.2.2.

373 Crémer Report (n 354) 47–48.

374 ibid 48.

375 *Google Android* (n 352), para 281 (emphasis added). For the EC's earlier views on aftermarkets, see EC, 'The Application of Article 82 of the Treaty to Exclusionary Abuses' (Discussion Paper, 2005) 69–70.

376 See similarly Alfonso Lamadrid de Pablo, 'Shortcuts and Courts in the Era of Digitization' (2019) CPI Antitrust Chronicle October 7. For earlier criticism on the definition of ecosystem-specific aftermarkets, see Hano Kaiser, 'Are "Closed Systems" an Antitrust Problem?' (2011) 7 CPI 91, 104–6. For a non-*Android* example of considering inter-platform competition, see *Microsoft/Skype* (n 347), para 70, where the GC nuances Microsoft/Skype's strong position on Windows-based devices by referring to 'other platforms' such as Apple and Google.

377 Wismer and Rasek (n 361) 15 ('There might be little value in carrying out a market definition exercise in markets involving multi-sided platforms'); Francesco Ducci, 'Procedural Implications of Market Definition in Platform Cases' (2019) 7 JAE 419.

be put on the market definition part of the analysis, and more importance attributed to the theories of harm and identification of anti-competitive strategies' (a recommendation I take to heart in this book).[378] Still, Commissioner Vestager has announced that the EC will be updating its Market Definition Notice (dating from 1997) to provide further guidance.[379] But defining the relevant market is only the first step towards determining whether a firm is in a dominant position. The final step of establishing market power has also been complicated by the particularities of platforms.

4.1.2 Establishing Platform Power

According to established case law, the existence of a dominant position (or 'position of economic strength') 'derives from a combination of several factors which, taken separately, are not necessarily determinative'.[380] The assessment of these factors needs to happen on a case-by-case basis, but – in the case of platforms – some of these factors may have to be interpreted differently, while others may need to be added.

A 'highly important' factor in establishing dominance is the firm's *market share*, which is why correctly defining the market is such a crucial exercise. While the exact importance of market shares depends on the market in question, the ECJ has held that a dominant position may be presumed in case of market shares exceeding 50%.[381] In 2011, however, the EC approved Microsoft's acquisition of Skype, which would give the entity an 80–90% market share in the markets for messaging and calling on (Windows-based) PCs.[382] On appeal, the GC affirmed the EC's decision, inter alia, because 'the consumer communications sector is a recent and fast-growing sector which is characterised by short innovation cycles in which large market shares may turn out to be ephemeral'.[383] In dynamic contexts, high markets shares are thus 'not necessarily indicative of market power'.[384]

---

378 Crémer Report (n 354) 46.

379 Margrethe Vestager, 'Defining Markets in a New Age' (Chillin' Competition Conference, Brussels, 9 December 2019). A German expert committee has even recommended that a separate notice on market definition and the definition of market power with respect to digital platforms be published, see Commission 'Competition Law 4.0', 'A New Competition Framework for the Digital Economy' (Report for the Federal Ministry for Economic Affairs and Energy, 2019) 3.

380 *United Brands v Commission* (n 339), para 66; *Hoffmann-La Roche v Commission* (n 339), para 39.

381 *Hoffmann-La Roche v Commission* (n 339), para 41 ('very large shares [held for some time] are in themselves, and save in exceptional circumstances, evidence of the existence of a dominant position'), refined in Case C–62/86 *AKZO Chemie v Commission* EU:C:1991:286, para 60 ('the Court has held that very large shares are in themselves, and save in exceptional circumstances, evidence of the existence of a dominant position, [which] is the situation where there is a market share of 50% such as that found to exist in this case'). In case of a market share between 40 and 50%, additional factors (such as the strength of competitors) are required to establish a dominant position, see *United Brands v Commission* (n 339), paras 108–10 ('UBC's share of the relevant market is always more than 40% and nearly 45%. This percentage does not however permit the conclusion that UBC automatically controls the market. It must be determined having regard to the strength and number of the competitors.'). See also 'Guidelines on the assessment of horizontal mergers under the Council Regulation on the control of concentrations between undertakings' [2004] OJ C31/5, para 17.

382 *Microsoft/Skype* (n 347). Mergers should be blocked when they create or strengthen a dominant position, see Council Regulation (EC) 139/2004 on the control of concentrations between undertakings [2004] OJ L24/1, art 2(2).

383 *Cisco v Commission* (n 347), para 69. See similarly *Facebook/WhatsApp* (n 347), para 99 ('the consumer communications sector … is characterised by frequent market entry and short innovation cycles in which large market shares may turn out to be ephemeral').

384 *Cisco v Commission* (n 347), para 69.

This idea of *short innovation cycles*, at the turn of which one monopoly is displaced by the next, is an old one. In 1942 already, Schumpeter put forward his idea of 'creative destruction', according to which entrenched monopolists are regularly replaced by technologically progressive entrants, which will, in time, suffer the same faith.[385] More recently, Christensen popularized the idea of 'disruptive innovation' – 'a process by which a product or service takes root initially in simple applications at the bottom of a market and then relentlessly moves up market, eventually displacing established competitors'.[386] New Schumpeterians continue to claim that invention that will dethrone the current platform incumbents is already being developed in some garage.[387] The risk of destruction or disruption is supposed to keep the monopolist on its toes, so that it keeps innovating rather than enjoying the economic rents its position allows it to reap. While this nuance of high market shares is welcome, it should not be taken to mean – as some appear to do – that online dominance is virtually impossible.[388] As with every indicator of market power, the stability of market shares is a factual question. In many platform markets, market shares did indeed seem to shift radically between parties in the 'early days' but appear to be more stable now.[389]

A firm's market share should not (only) be considered in the abstract but should be viewed in the light of the shares of *competitors, actual and potential*: both competing firms with a strong market position and the threat of entry by other competitors can put the high market share of the incumbent in perspective. In digital markets, it has been argued that the major online ecosystems are competitively disciplined by each other. In this sense, Varian argues that 'we see intense competition among the [major tech] firms' – 'they are all competing against each other in many different industries'.[390] While such multimarket competition is undeniable, online platforms have been slow to enter each other's core market. According to Petit, however, this focus on the market shares of tech giants in their core markets is mistaken; rather, 'the tech giants are conglomerates that compete three-dimensionally as oligopolists across industries, and not within itemized relevant markets where they (inevitably) are monopolists'.[391]

---

385 Joseph Schumpeter, *Capitalism, Socialism and Democracy* (Harper & Brothers 1942).

386 See Clayton Christensen, *The Innovator's Dilemma: When New Technologies Cause Great Firms to Fail* (HBR Press 1997). The quoted definition is taken from <http://claytonchristensen.com/key-concepts/>. However, this idea does not always hold up well to (historical) scrutiny, see Jill Lepore, 'The Disruption Machine: What the Gospel of Innovation Gets Wrong' (*The New Yorker*, 16 June 2014) <https://www.newyorker.com/magazine/2014/06/23/the-disruption-machine#>.

387 Alexandre de Streel, 'Should Digital Antitrust Be Ordoliberal?' Concurrences no 1-2020, art no 92610, 2 <www.concurrences.com/92610> ('the neo-Schumpeterians claim that the digital economy is very competitive, with rival products just "one click away" and new invention one garage away, hence markets should be left alone').

388 See eg David Evans, 'Why the Dynamics of Competition for Online Platforms Leads to Sleepless Nights but not Sleepy Monopolies' (2017) 18–34 <https://ssrn.com/abstract=3009438>.

389 For a review of the two most commonly cited examples of digital disruption, namely, Facebook (which succeeded Friendster and MySpace) and Google (which succeeded AltaVista, Lycos and Yahoo!), see John Newman, 'Antitrust in Digital Markets' (2019) 72 Vanderbilt Law Review 1497, 1520–23. When it comes to search engines, the EC has tried to clarify this new-found stability, see *Google Search (Shopping)* (n 348), para 290 ('in the late 1990s, Google was able to overtake the former market leaders, AltaVista and Lycos [because at] that time, scale was less of a critical factor because the indexing technology of general search engines was not yet able to assess user behaviour'). More generally, see Ben Thompson, 'The End of the Beginning' (*Stratechery*, 7 January 2020) <https://stratechery.com/2020/the-end-of-the-beginning/>.

390 Hal Varian, 'Use and Abuse of Network Effects' (2017) 14 <https://ssrn.com/abstract=3215488>.

391 Nicolas Petit, 'Technology Giants, the "Moligopoly" Hypothesis and Holistic Competition: A Primer' (2016) 3 <https://ssrn.com/abstract=2856502>.

In *Microsoft/Skype*, the GC clarified how a number of additional characteristics of online platforms – beyond potentially high market shares – should factor into a market power analysis. With regard to the *'free' nature of many services*, it noted that 'the fact that the services are offered free of charge is a relevant factor in assessing the market power of the new entity. In so far as users expect to receive consumer communications services free of charge, the potential for the new entity to set its pricing policy freely is significantly restricted.'[392] In other words, the GC held that market power should be less prevalent with regard to free services.

While the prevalence of free services may be relatively new, the more traditional 'barriers to entry' remain as relevant when assessing market power in the platform economy. For one, online platforms enjoy considerable *economies of scale*:[393] given that they generally incur high fixed costs[394] but low variable costs, increasing output significantly reduces per-unit costs. Indeed, after the technological development of an online platform, the cost of accepting more users to the platform is extremely low.[395] This dynamic is widespread in telecommunications: once a telephone network is in place, for example, the cost of connecting extra users is relatively limited. However, given that a new platform 'can only be successful if a specific sales volume is achieved within a short period of time ("minimum scale of entry")',[396] it may have to invest heavily in attracting users on both sides of the platform.[397]

Online platforms also benefit from *network effects*[398] (also termed 'demand-side economies of scale'), meaning that '[t]he value of adopting a service to an incremental user is larger when more users have already adopted'.[399] Joining Facebook, for example, is more

392 *Cisco v Commission* (n 347), para 73. See also *Google Search (Shopping)* (n 348), para 152 ('The fact that a product or service is provided free of charge … is simply a factor to be taken into account in assessing dominance'). For additional guidance on the relation between free services and market power, see Newman, 'Antitrust in Zero-Price Markets: Applications' (n 346) 71–73.

393 On their role in (online) platforms, see David Evans and Richard Schmalensee, 'The Industrial Organization of Markets with Two-Sided Platforms' (2007) 3 CPI 151, 165; Justus Haucap and Ulrich Heimeshoff, 'Google, Facebook, Amazon, eBay: Is the Internet Driving Competition or Market Monopolization?' (2014) 11 International Economics and Economic Policy 49; Bundeskartellamt, 'The Market Power of Platforms and Networks' (n 363) 54–56.

394 See eg, with regard to search engines, *Google Search (Shopping)* (n 348), para 286 ('the establishment of a fully-fledged general search engine requires significant investments in terms of time and resources').

395 The variable costs will consist of (i) data centres, which can now essentially be leased due to cloud computing, making the cost variable; and (ii) platform governance, such as policing hate speech on social networks. The customer acquisition cost can also be steep.

396 Bundeskartellamt, 'The Market Power of Platforms and Networks' (Working Paper – English summary, 2016) 14.

397 Platforms need to attract users on both sides, but those users will only be attracted when there are users on the 'other side' of the platform, which are themselves only attracted by users on the first side – the chicken and egg problem, see Bernard Caillaud and Bruno Jullien, 'Chicken & Egg: Competition Among Intermediation Service Providers' (2003) 34 RAND Journal of Economics 309.

398 As in much of the literature, 'network effects' is understood here to mean '*positive* network effects'. Network effects can also turn negative, in particular in case of congestion of the platform, but given the low marginal cost of accepting extra users and the data-based possibility to guide them to their right counterparts, such congestion is rather rare.

399 Varian (n 390) 3. On the role of network effects in platform markets, see Evans and Schmalensee, 'The Industrial Organization of Markets with Two-Sided Platforms' (n 393) 164; Haucap and Heimeshoff (n 393); Bundeskartellamt, 'The Market Power of Platforms and Networks' (n 363) 45–54 (indirect network effects) and 92–101 (direct network effects). For an application, see *Google/DoubleClick* (n 356), para 304.

attractive when more of your acquaintances are on the platform.[400] Again, there are apt analogies in telecommunications, as a connection to the phone network becomes more valuable as more people own phones. These kinds of network effects are considered *direct*, as the relevant users are homogeneous. Platforms also benefit from *indirect* network effects: they facilitate interaction between two different user groups, and the value of the platform to users on one side will often depend on the number of users on the other side. Buyers on Amazon.com, for example, will value its Marketplace higher when it hosts more sellers – and the other way around. As a growing number of users make the platform more valuable, which in turn attracts more users, platforms can benefit from a 'positive feedback loop', which leads to a concentrated or even 'winner takes all' market.[401]

The extent to which network effects form a barrier to entry depends – again – on the facts of the case. On the one hand, network effects can cement a platform's dominant position. Indeed, when another platform enters the market, users (eg of Facebook or Amazon) will not easily make the switch because all other users (friends or sellers) are on the incumbent platform. Users could, in theory, all make the switch at the same time, but a collective action problem prevents them from doing so.[402] This holds true even when users consider the entrant platform superior (eg in terms of privacy standards or commission fees). Note also how, apart from network effects, the platform's ecosystem of interrelated products and services can form a barrier to entry by increasing users' switching costs.[403]

On the other hand, there are phenomena counteracting the lock-in brought about by network effects. One such phenomenon is multihoming, 'where users make parallel use of several platforms with comparable offers' (eg using both Uber and Lyft).[404] In *Microsoft/Skype*, for example, the GC pointed out that 'the existence of network effects does not necessarily procure a competitive advantage' because 'there is no economic or technical obstacle to switching by small group[s] and to users continuing to use several communications programs at the same time'.[405] While this is true for messaging apps, it appears less true for platforms where users have built up a valuable profile (eg pictures on Facebook or reputation scores on Uber). Secondly, competing operators can seek to sufficiently differentiate their platform so that it appeals to either a different kind of user or a different need of the same kind of user.

Further, while every firm benefits from learning by doing (as workers become more efficient as they repeat a similar task),[406] *learning effects* operate in a particular way in the platform economy. Rather than learning from labour, platforms learn from data.

400 In particular, Metcalfe's law states that the value of a network grows as the square of the number of its users, see Bob Metcalfe, 'Metcalfe's Law After 40 Years of Ethernet' (2013) 46 Computer Society 26.

401 See Section 2.2.1. See GMC (n 357) 23–24 and 88 for an application to marketplaces, and EC, 'Online Platforms' (Staff Working Document) SWD(2016)172, 4–5 and 24 for an application to mobile ecosystems.

402 Garth Saloner, Andrea Shepard and Joel Podolny, *Strategic Management* (Wiley 2001) 313.

403 See Section 2.2.2.

404 Bundeskartellamt, 'The Market Power of Platforms and Networks' (n 363) 56–66.

405 *Cisco v Commission* (n 347), paras 76 and 80.

406 The landmark paper on learning by doing is Kenneth Arrow, 'The Economic Implications of Learning by Doing' (1962) 29 The Review of Economic Studies 155.

For example, '[t]he more queries a search engine receives from users, the better it is able to fine-tune its algorithm, which in turn affects the quality of search hits', which in turn attracts even more search queries.[407] Entrants, which do not yet process as many search queries, may therefore find it difficult to compete.[408] Varian holds that economies of scale and network effects 'pale in significance compared to learning by doing, which, in [his] view, is the major source of competitive advantage in technology industries'.[409]

The presence and strength of each market power indicator/barrier to entry need to be established on a case-by-case basis. However, based on these indicators, various academics and policymakers have concluded that the dominant platforms – with their expansive ecosystems – constitute *gatekeepers* in the digital economy.[410] The idea is that platforms essentially offer the infrastructure for digital markets and are vital intermediaries for sellers, app developers, content providers and advertisers looking to reach consumers, given that they control access to their users as gatekeepers. While it is not always clear whether this gatekeeper role is considered a contributor *to* or a consequence *of* dominant positions in the platform economy, it is viewed as an additional factor justifying regulatory intervention. As with more supposedly platform-specific phenomena, however, the concern is not entirely new: regulatory interventions in telecom markets have also been premised on the view that operators served as gatekeepers (or bottlenecks).[411]

While all of the above factors can be integrated into market power analyses by competition authorities (without deviating too radically from established precedent), lawmakers in Germany have opted for a more direct approach. Based on an apparent fear that traditional market power indicators would not sufficiently capture the economic strength of online platforms, they have amended their Competition Act so that it explicitly includes the economic characteristics of platforms:

> In particular in the case of multi-sided markets and networks, in assessing the market position of an undertaking account shall also be taken of: 1. direct and indirect network effects, 2. the parallel use of services from different providers and the switching costs for users [ie multihoming], 3. the undertaking's economies of scale arising in connection with network effects, 4. the undertaking's access to data relevant for competition, 5. innovation-driven competitive pressure.[412]

407 Bundeskartellamt, 'The Market Power of Platforms and Networks' (n 363) 84. See also *Google Search (Shopping)* (n 348), para 287–88 ('because a general search service uses search data to refine the relevance of its general search results pages, it needs to receive a certain volume of queries in order to compete viably').

408 Having processed a certain amount of data, however, the returns from learning effects start to diminish. See *Google Search (Shopping)* (n 348), para 289 ('there may be diminishing returns to scale in terms of improvements in relevance once the volume of queries a general search service receives exceeds a certain volume').

409 Varian (n 390) 4.

410 See eg Lina Khan, 'Sources of Tech Platform Power' (2018) 2 Georgetown Law Technology Review 325, 326–28; Nicolai van Gorp and Paul de Bijl, 'Digital Gatekeepers: Assessing Exclusionary Conduct' (Discussion Paper commissioned by the Dutch Ministry of Economic Affairs, 2019) 6–9. For a policy perspective, see EC, 'Mid-Term Review on the implementation of the Digital Single Market Strategy' (Communication) SWD(2017)155, 8; EP, 'Online Platforms and the Digital Single Market' (Report) A8-0204/2017, 15–16.

411 See Part 3.

412 German Competition Act, s 18(3a). For an application of these new factors, see *Facebook* (n 367) 5–7.

In a further amendment, the German legislature even added a reference to gatekeeper power by inserting a provision stating: 'In assessing the market position of an undertaking acting as an intermediary on multi-sided markets, account shall be taken in particular of the importance of the intermediary services provided by the undertaking for accessing supply and sales markets.'[413] This amendment was prompted by a report on the modernization of Germany's abuse of dominance law, which proposed anchoring 'intermediation power' as an independent, third form of power in German competition law (next to supply side/seller and demand side/buyer power).[414] The proposal was aimed specifically at vertically integrated platforms that seek to distort competition in neighbouring markets.

The above description of the *indicators of dominance* in the platform economy is, of course, just that: a description. Insofar as it is possible to draw sweeping conclusions about platform dominance, I do not seek to do so here. Having given the reader an idea of the components of a market power assessment, I thus limit my conclusion to the truism that – as in other industries – 'a case-by-case analysis is needed'. This work is concerned mainly with the *consequences of dominance*, in particular the leveraging of market power at the level of the platform. Therefore, please keep in mind that the sections that follow – which seek to clarify the tools, rules and standards of abusive conduct in the platform economy – apply only insofar as a platform is found dominant. To judge platform conduct, however, a normative framework is indispensable. Ideally, one also has at their disposal the means to implement that framework. That is why the next section discusses the goals and methods of competition law.

4.2 The Normative Framework: Goals and Methods of Competition Law

Antitrust policy cannot be made rational until we are able to give a firm answer to one question: what is the point of the law – what are its goals?[415]

4.2.1 The Goals of Competition Law

Unearthing the fundamental goal of competition law has long been a Sisyphean task for scholars, policymakers, enforcers and courts: every time the goal appears firmly and finally established, a new movement comes along to put into question the complete normative framework.[416] In 2005, for example, Hovenkamp wrote on the dust jacket

413 German Competition Act, s 18(3b).

414 Heike Schweitzer et al, 'Modernising the Law on Abuse of Market Power – Summary of the Report's Recommendations' (Report for the Federal Ministry for Economic Affairs, 2018), para 6.

415 Robert Bork, *The Antitrust Paradox* (Basic Books 1978) 50.

416 This section is indebted to John Newman, 'Reactionary Antitrust' Concurrences no 4-2019, art no 92005, 66 <www.concurrences.com/92005>.

of his classical handbook: 'After thirty years, the debate over antitrust's ideology has quieted. Most now agree that the protection of consumer welfare should be the only goal of antitrust laws.'[417] Only a decade later, antitrust's fundamental goal was once more heavily disputed by the New Brandeis Movement. The 'battle for the soul of antitrust' thus rages on with renewed vigour.[418]

The *raison d'être* of this section on the elusive goal(s) of antitrust is twofold. Firstly, understanding the goal(s) of antitrust law is a prerequisite for making normative statements, at least *within* the current framework. Secondly, the latest movement puts into question the current state of antitrust law and advocates a shift towards a *new* framework. Importantly, the rise of powerful online platforms is an important driver of this movement, up to the point where it is 'popularly known as a movement to "break up big tech"'.[419] Therefore, this section summarily surveys the evolution of the debate on antitrust's goals before zooming in on its most recent iteration. Of course, based on the same sources, widely differing accounts may emerge – I do not pretend to be the first one to give an objective account (if that is even possible).

While laws with antitrust tendencies have existed for centuries, the substantive debate on antitrust's goals really took off with the adoption of the Sherman Act in the US. The Sherman Act was enacted in 1890, in the middle of the Second Industrial Revolution, in response 'to growing public demands to address the influence of large businesses on the economy, then known as the "trust problem"' (hence the name 'anti-trust').[420] Even though this context is fairly clear, Congress did not clearly articulate a legislative goal when it adopted the act, thus leaving courts with ample room for interpretation of its broad statutes.[421]

After some initial neglect, antitrust went through its 'formative era'[422] in the first decades of the 20th century with a number of breakups (eg of Standard Oil) pursued by 'the trustbuster', President Roosevelt,[423] and mandated by the Supreme Court.[424]

---

417 Herbert Hovenkamp, *The Antitrust Enterprise: Principle and Execution* (HUP 2005).

418 This phrase was coined in an article against the Chicago School, see Eleanor Fox, 'The Battle for the Soul of Antitrust' (1987) 75 California Law Review 917, and has started to resurface, see Ariel Ezrachi and Maurice Stucke, 'The Fight over Antitrust's Soul' (2018) 9 JECLAP 1.

419 Tim Wu, 'The Utah Statement: Reviving Antimonopoly Traditions for the Era of Big Tech' (*Medium*, 18 November 2019) <https://onezero.medium.com/the-utah-statement-reviving-antimonopoly-traditions-for-the-era-of-big-tech-e6be198012d7>. See further Tim Wu, *The Curse of Bigness* (Columbia Global Reports 2018) 119–26 (on 'the rise of the tech trusts').

420 Barak Orbach, 'The Present New Antitrust Era' (2019) 60 William & Mary Law Review 1439, 1445.

421 John Flynn, 'The Reagan Administration's Antitrust Policy, "Original Intent" and the Legislative History of the Sherman Act' (1988) 33 The Antitrust Bulletin 259, 260 ('Today, there is no general consensus on the question of the legislative goals of antitrust policy; instead there are many conflicting views concerning the goals Congress had in mind when it enacted the Sherman Act.'). Some even argue that the Sherman Act was motivated by a grudge of its spiritual father, John Sherman, against Russell Alger, a political rival, see Patrick Newman, 'Revenge: John Sherman, Russell Alger and the Origins of the Sherman Act' (2018) 174 Public Choice 257.

422 Orbach (n 420) 1444–48; Marc Winerman, 'The Origins of the FTC: Concentration, Cooperation, Control, and Competition' (2003) 71 Antitrust Law Journal 1.

423 Wu, *The Curse of Bigness* (n 419) 45–77.

424 *Northern Securities v United States* 193 US 197 (1904); *The Standard Oil Company of New Jersey v United States* 221 US 1 (1911); *United States v American Tobacco* 221 US 106 (1911).

During this time, the Court adopted a number of cardinal rules (eg against resale price maintenance) and legal tests (in particular, the rule of reason) that shape antitrust law until today. Lawmakers added further substance to the antitrust regime by adopting the Clayton Act in 1914, which was meant 'to cope with monopolistic tendencies in their incipiency' by prohibiting certain mergers.[425] In the same year, antitrust was also strengthened institutionally through the establishment of an administrative agency responsible for its enforcement: the Federal Trade Commission (FTC).[426]

The Clayton and FTC Acts were adopted under Roosevelt's successor, President Wilson, who was advised on antitrust matters by Brandeis – the lawyer and soon-to-be Supreme Court justice who lent his name to the current antitrust movement.[427] Brandeis was concerned with 'the curse of bigness'.[428] His issue with big business was twofold: on the one hand, he argued that economic power came with political power, which distorts democracy;[429] on the other hand, he believed that small businesses were actually more efficient than (very) big ones.[430] Based on the latter belief, he defended the view that both consumers *and small businesses* should be protected from the monopolistic practices of big business. According to Brandeis, the protection of small business implied allowing resale price maintenance, which 'stimulate[s] … the little man as against the department store, and as against the large unit which may otherwise monopolize [retail] trade'.[431] Also with a view to protecting small businesses, Brandeis was in favour of cooperation between them, eg through trade associations.[432]

Antitrust thus made a promising start during the first two decades of the 20th century. In the next two decades, however, 'associationalism' (also known as the 'fair trade movement') narrowed its scope. During this period, 'the federal government actively encouraged collaborations among competitors and courts developed the rule of reason in a pursuit of an elusive distinction between constructive and destructive collaborations

---

425 Derek Bok, 'Section 7 of the Clayton Act and the Merging of Law and Economics' (1960) 74 Harvard Law Review 226, 255 (citing legislative sessions).

426 For background on the FTC's establishment, see extensively Winerman (n 422).

427 ibid 32–38.

428 On Brandeis' views, see ibid; 'Mr. Justice Brandeis, Competition and Smallness: A Dilemma Re-Examined' (1956) 66 The Yale Law Journal 69; Wu, *The Curse of Bigness* (n 419) 33–44.

429 In addition to adverse *political* consequences, Brandeis was worried that big business came with adverse *social* consequences, see eg 'Mr. Justice Brandeis, Competition and Smallness: A Dilemma Re-Examined' (n 428) 73 ('The business unit to Brandeis was more than an economic organization; it was also an instrument of social growth. As the owners of individual enterprises and their helpers became the dependent servants of big business, Brandeis warned that society was being transformed into a nation of robots, unfit to perform the duties which a democratic government demanded of its citizens.').

430 See eg US Senate (62nd Congress), Hearing before the Committee on Interstate Commerce S Res 98, vol 1, 1174 ('I think we are in a position, after the experience of the last 20 years, to state two things: In the first place, that a corporation may well be too large to be the most efficient instrument of production and of distribution, and, in the second place, whether it has exceeded the point of greatest economic efficiency or not, it may be too large to be tolerated among the people who desire to be free.').

431 Cited in 'Mr. Justice Brandeis, Competition and Smallness: A Dilemma Re-Examined' (n 428) 88.

432 See *American Column & Lumber v United States* 257 US 37 (1921) (Brandeis L, dissenting), where Brandeis defended the 'Open Competition Plan' under which lumber producers sent sales data to a central clearing house which then disseminated it in digested form, including suggestions on future prices and output.

among competitors.'[433] An illustrative (but short-lived) instrument from this era is the National Industry Recovery Act, which sought to combat the Great Depression by supporting the adoption of 'codes of fair competition' in various industries.[434]

After World War II, antitrust entered its 'golden era'.[435] The Supreme Court described the Sherman Act in lofty, constitutional terms as 'a comprehensive charter of economic liberty' and 'the Magna Charta of free enterprise'.[436] These weighty phrases were matched by aggressive enforcement, which was facilitated by plaintiff-friendly premises (which were translated into burdens and standards of proof), including that 'vertical arrangements tend to exclude competition, that horizontal market arrangements tend to be collusive' and can be proven with circumstantial evidence, and 'that horizontal mergers that increase concentration harm competition'.[437] Especially in the 1960s, however, enforcement may have crossed the line between aggressive and excessive. Illustrative of this evolution are judgments such as *Brown Shoe*[438] and *Von's Grocery*[439], in which the Supreme Court blocked very small horizontal and vertical mergers.

These kinds of judgments were met by strong counterreaction, which found its first forceful formulation in a 1965 article by Bork and Bowman titled *The Crisis in Antitrust*.[440] While the authors supported the antitrust rule against price fixing, they found the notion of exclusionary practices 'theoretically weak' and 'remarkably lacking in factual support'.[441] In addition, they faulted courts for not recognizing that a trend towards more concentration 'is prima facie evidence that greater concentration is socially desirable' – in other words, efficiencies should be presumed in merger cases (and actually, with regard to every restrictive practice).[442] Bork and Bowman, together with other scholars that would make up the Chicago School, thus took it upon themselves to change the status quo.[443] They started from the strong presumption that markets are self-correcting and accordingly defended a policy of non-enforcement in many areas. They sought to convince others of their position by inserting (more) economics into antitrust analysis. Moreover, they alleged to have 'discovered' the overarching goal

433 Orbach (n 420) 1448–50.

434 National Industrial Recovery Act of 1933 (NIRA), 48 Stat 195. The Act was declared unconstitutional in *ALA Schechter Poultry v United States* 295 US 495 (1935).

435 Maurice Stucke and Ariel Ezrachi, 'The Rise, Fall and Rebirth of the U.S. Antitrust Movement' (*HBR*, 15 December 2017) <https://hbr.org/2017/12/the-rise-fall-and-rebirth-of-the-u-s-antitrust-movement>.

436 See respectively *Northern Pacific Railway v United States* 356 US 1, 4 (1958) and *United States v Topco Associates* 405 US 596, 610 (1972).

437 Orbach (n 420) 1452–53 and the case law referenced there.

438 *Brown Shoe v United States* 370 US 294 (1962), blocking a primarily vertical merger between a shoe manufacturer with a 4% market share and a shoe retailer with a 1.2% market share.

439 *United States v Von's Grocery* 384 US 270 (1966), blocking a horizontal merger between the third- and sixth-largest grocery chain, which held a combined market share of 8.9%.

440 Robert Bork and Ward Bowman, 'The Crisis in Antitrust' (1965) 65 Columbia Law Review 363.

441 ibid 367.

442 ibid 368.

443 Other scholars commonly associated with the Chicago School include Aaron Director, Frank Easterbrook, Richard Posner, and George Stigler. The Chicago School theories are distilled in Bork, *The Antitrust Paradox* (n 415).

of antitrust law – namely, consumer welfare[444] – which they wrongly defined as the sum of consumer *and producer* welfare and measured primarily in terms of output.[445]

These ideas came at the right time: given recently (excessively) interventionist decisions based on poor economics, 'the Chicago School call to use economics in antitrust analysis would generate less enforcement – and have the handy side effect of being correct.'[446] However, it has also been argued that the Chicagoans 'embraced economics when it would achieve their anti-enforcement ends, but largely ignored its advances in theory and empirical technique after 1970 because those tools sometimes proved that anticompetitive conduct had occurred, and that enforcement was needed'.[447] In that sense, the Chicago School's anti-enforcement stance turned out to be more of an ideology than an economic inevitability.[448]

Whether the Chicago School was completely accurate and sincere in its use of economics or not, it certainly had an impact:[449] from the 1970s 'through 1990 the Supreme Court deviated rightward from a path in which the government won nearly all of its antitrust cases and private plaintiffs won many, to one that was far more favorable to defendants.'[450] Moreover, the Court quoted Bork in declaring that 'Congress designed the Sherman Act as a "consumer welfare prescription"'.[451] And the influence of the Chicago School continues until this day. For example, when the Supreme Court abolished the per se rule against resale price maintenance in favour of rule of reason analysis in its 2009 *Leegin* judgment, it cited Bork in support of the change.[452] Ironically, allowing resale price maintenance in certain cases is one instance where the often diametrically opposite views of Brandeis and Bork converge (albeit for different reasons).

To unearth the goals of antitrust and understand its direction today, a look at the US antitrust regime – probably the most influential in the world – is indispensable. However,

444 Robert Bork, 'Legislative Intent and the Policy of the Sherman Act' (1966) 9 The Journal of Law & Economics 7.

445 Fox (n 418) 918–19.

446 Herbert Hovenkamp and Fiona Scott Morton, 'Framing the Chicago School of Antitrust Analysis' (2019) 168 University of Pennsylvania Law Review 1843, 1848.

447 ibid 1853.

448 See also Orbach (n 420) 1457 (the Chicago School 'offered economics as the only legitimate methodology for antitrust analysis and promoted a false equivalence between economics and laissez faire').

449 At the same time, the Chicago School's influence should not be overstated either; the more moderate Harvard School had perhaps less of an ideological influence on antitrust law, but probably more of a concrete influence on rulemaking, see ibid 598 and 601–2, and William Kovacic, 'The Intellectual DNA of Modern U.S. Competition Law for Dominant Firm Conduct: The Chicago/Harvard Double Helix (2007) Columbia Business Law Review 1.

450 Herbert Hovenkamp, 'Whatever *Did* Happen to the Antitrust Movement?' (2019) 94 Notre Dame Law Review 583, 599–600 and cases referenced there. See similarly Chris Sagers, *United States v Apple: Competition in America* (HUP 2019) 71 ('Since about the mid-1970s, the courts have fashioned a long series of prodefendant substantive and procedural rules. [...] Fundamentally, these trends reflect a shift away from a presumption in favor of enforcement, which was in place from World War II until the late 1960s or 1970s.').

451 *Reiter v Sonotone* 442 US 330, 343 (1979), citing Bork, *The Antitrust Paradox* (n 415). On the Supreme Court's consumer welfare conception, see Hovenkamp, 'Whatever *Did* Happen to the Antitrust Movement?' (n 450) 590–91 ('The Supreme Court has never categorically embraced any particular definition of consumer welfare, even though it has used the term several times.').

452 *Leegin Creative Leather Products v PSKS* 551 US 877 (2007).

while the EU antitrust regime is of more recent vintage, it also deserves discussion, not only because it is the focus of this book, but also because it is now more influential on the global stage than its transatlantic counterpart.[453]

The European project took its start after World War II, when a number of nations agreed 'to substitute for age-old rivalries the merging of their essential interests' by creating 'an economic community'.[454] From the start, the Treaty establishing this community included provisions on restrictive agreements, abuse of dominance and mergers, as well as State aid – a peculiarity of EU competition law.[455] As in the US, the overarching goal of the law was to protect competition;[456] however, there was an additional objective, namely, the integration of various national markets into one European economy.[457] Some argue that, in addition, 'the Ordoliberal concept of competition, namely achieving effective competition through the realisation of individual economic freedom, has been a relevant standard for interpreting [EU] competition rules'.[458] However, it does not appear that the protection of the economic freedom of market actors has ever been a distinct goal.[459]

As EU competition policy matured, a benchmark for its primary goal of protecting competition developed: consumer welfare.[460] At times, it even seems that competition (as well as market integration) is but a means of achieving consumer welfare.[461] In that sense, the GC has held that 'the ultimate purpose of the rules that seek to ensure that competition is not distorted in the internal market is to increase the well-being of consumers'.[462] The ECJ, however, appears to consider these different objectives on the same level, stating

---

453 Anu Bradford, *The Brussels Effect: How the European Union Rules the World* (OUP 2020) chs 4–5.

454 Treaty establishing the European Coal and Steel Community (1951) preamble.

455 ibid, arts 65–67. Interestingly, the merger provision was omitted in the subsequent EC Treaty. It was later added again through a separate regulation.

456 ibid, see the various references to 'distort[ions of] normal competition' and 'hinder[ing] effective competition'. For a recent confirmation, see Consolidated version of the Treaty on European Union – Protocol (no 27) on the internal market and competition [2008] OJ C115/309 ('the internal market as set out in Article 3 [TFEU] includes a system ensuring that competition is not distorted').

457 See Information Service High Authority of the European Community for Coal and Steel, 'The General Common Market' (Spaak Report, 1956); David Gerber, 'The Transformation of European Community Competition Law?' (1994) 35 Harvard International Law Journal 97, 98 ('the Community's competition law system … has been understood primarily as part of a program designed to achieve the specific goal of unifying the European market').

458 Kati Cseres, 'The Controversies of the Consumer Welfare Standard' (2007) 3 The Competition Law Review 121, 151.

459 Pinar Akman, 'Searching for the Long-Lost Soul of Article 82 EC' (2009) 29 Oxford Journal of Legal Studies 267 (studying the drafting process in detail).

460 The insertion of art 81(3) in the Treaty establishing the European Community [2002] OJ C325/33 is an important sign of this evolution. See also 'Guidelines on the application of Article 81(3) of the Treaty' [2004] OJ C101/97, para 13 ('The objective of Article 81 is to protect competition on the market as a means of enhancing consumer welfare and of ensuring an efficient allocation of resources.').

461 'Guidelines on the application of Article 81(3) of the Treaty' (n 460), para 13 ('Competition and market integration serve these ends [ie consumer welfare and an efficient allocation of resources] since the creation and preservation of an open single market promotes an efficient allocation of resources throughout the Community for the benefit of consumers.'); 'Guidance on the Commission's enforcement priorities in applying Article 82 of the EC Treaty to abusive exclusionary conduct by dominant undertakings' [2009] OJ C45/7 (hereafter, 'Exclusionary Conduct Guidance Paper'), para 19 ('The aim of the Commission's enforcement activity in relation to exclusionary conduct is to ensure that dominant undertakings do not impair effective competition by foreclosing their competitors in an anti-competitive way, thus having an adverse impact on consumer welfare').

462 Joined Cases T–213/01 and T–214/01 *Österreichische Postsparkasse v Commission* EU:T:2006:151, para 115.

that the competition rules aim 'to protect not only the interests of competitors or of consumers, but also the structure of the market and, in so doing, competition as such'.[463] In the end, there is no more than a semantic conflict between those statements, given that protecting competition prevents harm to consumers. Indeed, an anticompetitive practice can harm consumers *directly*, or *indirectly* through its impact on competition.[464]

As in the US, competition policy in the EU has become a more economic enterprise over the years – a process that the EC started in the late 1990s.[465] By now, the so-called more economic approach has transformed the assessment framework of every branch of EU competition law.[466] In the area of abuse of dominance, this has meant a shift from more form-based assessments towards assessments focusing on the *efficiency* of the conduct in question.[467] 'Anticompetitive effects' are those that harm consumers, and they have to be measured rather than presumed.

Taking a bird's-eye view, one can thus argue that the US and EU antitrust regimes went through a similar evolution and arrived at more or less the same destination, at least substantively.[468] Still, differences remain. Most importantly, the US and the EU have diverged with regard to (certain forms of) unilateral conduct.[469] Even more so than with regard to substantive legal differences, the US and EU regimes differ when it comes to the level of enforcement, again in particular when it comes to unilateral conduct, but also when it comes to mergers.[470] US antitrust is said to be 'failing and losing whatever effectiveness it once had'.[471] Baker notes that decisions on unilateral

463 Case C–501/06 P *GlaxoSmithKline* EU:C:2009:610, para 63 (continuing: 'Consequently, for a finding that an agreement has an anti-competitive object, it is not necessary that final consumers be deprived of the advantages of effective competition in terms of supply or price.').

464 Case C–209/10 *Post Danmark v Konkurrencerådet* EU:C:2012:172, para 20 (art 102 TFEU 'covers not only those practices that directly cause harm to consumers but also practices that cause consumers harm through their impact on competition') and Case C–377/20 *Servizio Elettrico Nazionale* EU:C:2022:379, para 44 (art 102 TFEU 'seeks to sanction not only practices likely to cause direct harm to consumers but also those which cause them harm indirectly by undermining an effective structure of competition').

465 See extensively Anne Witt, *The More Economic Approach to EU Antitrust Law* (Hart 2016).

466 The EC's Guidance Paper offers a clear illustration of how contemporary economic thinking shaped the (proposed) assessment of exclusionary practices, see Exclusionary Conduct Guidance Paper (n 461).

467 See ibid, paras 5 (the EC 'will direct its enforcement to ensuring that markets function properly and that consumers benefit from the efficiency and productivity which result from effective competition') and 28 (a dominant undertaking may claim that its conduct is justified 'by demonstrating that its conduct produces substantial efficiencies which outweigh any anti-competitive effects on consumers'). Case C–413/14 P *Intel v Commission* EU:C:2017:632 is emblematic of this shift.

468 Institutional differences remain, of course. In particular, the EU has a stronger administrative system and a corresponding focus on public enforcement. In the US, by contrast, antitrust is more of a judicial matter, with stronger private enforcement.

469 Heike Schweitzer, 'Parallels and Differences in the Attitudes Towards Single-Firm Conduct: What Are the Reasons? The History, Interpretation and Underlying Principles of Sec. 2 Sherman Act and Art. 82 EC' (2007) EUI Working Paper Law 2007/32; Pierre Larouche and Maarten Pieter Schinkel, 'Continental Drift in the Treatment of Dominant Firms: Article 102 TFEU in Contrast to § 2 Sherman Act' (2013) TILEC Discussion Paper 2013-20; William Kovacic, 'Two Views of Exclusion: Why the European Union and the United States Diverged on Google' in Guy Rolnik (ed), *Digital Platforms and Concentration* (ProMarket e-book 2018).

470 Substantive differences in assessments and enforcement levels are, of course, related: if the legal test to prove an anticompetitive practice becomes more stringent, the level of enforcement will likely be lower. However, even taking the differing legal frameworks (and institutional setups) as a starting point, it appears that enforcement activity is lower in the US.

471 Sagers, *United States v Apple: Competition in America* (n 450) 70.

conduct 'likely went too far towards relaxation, at times conferring de facto legality on exclusionary conduct'.[472] Along those lines, Picker remarks that 'Section 2 enforcement has in some ways shut down since the 1990s'.[473] Ezrachi and Stucke agree that the US turns 'a blind eye to abuse', while also condemning how it maintains 'a "light-if-any-touch" antitrust review of mergers'.[474] Similarly, Sagers argues that courts now uphold 'a general presumption against merger enforcement so strong that only the most massive horizontal mergers are now typically challenged'.[475] In line with the above, Marco Colino concludes that US antitrust has been 'relegated to little more than pursuing the most blatant forms of collusion'.[476] The bluntest assessment actually comes from the famous Chicago School scholar Posner, who declared that 'antitrust is dead'.[477] Baker observes, finally, that '[i]n comparison to their U.S. counterparts, EU enforcers have struck a better … balance.'[478]

One can debate the merits of these assessments. A counterargument goes that the EU is actually mistaken in more aggressively enforcing its law against unilateral anticompetitive conduct, in particular in the tech sector. Still, the (perceived) lack of enforcement in the US, combined with 'the extreme and growing concentration in most sectors of the American economy' (ie a market power problem),[479] has served as the fertile soil for the growth of a new antitrust movement.[480] The New Brandeis Movement traces its intellectual roots to the Justice who was nominated to the Supreme Court more than 100 years ago (given its connection to the past, the movement is also – with some derision – called 'Hipster Antitrust').[481] In particular, New Brandeisians advocate for a break with the Chicago School, whose focus on consumer welfare and thus efficiency 'has largely blinded enforcers to many of the harms caused by undue market power, including on workers, suppliers, innovators, and independent entrepreneurs – all harms that Congress intended for the antitrust laws to prevent.'[482] Like Brandeis, they are also concerned with the undue political

---

472 Jonathan Baker, *The Antitrust Paradigm: Restoring a Competitive Economy* (HUP 2019) 16.

473 Randal Picker, 'The Arc of Monopoly: A Case Study in Computing' (2020) 87 The University of Chicago Law Review 523, 526.

474 Stucke and Ezrachi (n 435).

475 Chris Sagers, 'The Worst Opinion in Living Memory: AT&T/Time Warner and America's Broken Merger Law' (2019) 2 <https://ssrn.com/abstract=3346431>.

476 Sandra Marco Colino, 'The Antitrust F Word: Fairness Considerations in Competition Law' (2019) The Chinese University of Hong Kong Faculty of Law Research Paper 2018–19, 7.

477 Asher Schechter, 'Richard Posner: "The Real Corruption Is the Ownership of Congress by the Rich"' (*ProMarket*, 28 March 2017) <https://promarket.org/richard-posner-real-corruption-ownership-congress-rich/>.

478 Baker, *The Antitrust Paradigm: Restoring a Competitive Economy* (n 472) 72.

479 Lina Khan, 'The New Brandeis Movement: America's Antimonopoly Debate' (2018) 9 JECLAP 131, 131. Taking a closer look at evidence on concentration, see Thomas Philippon, *The Great Reversal: How America Gave Up on Free Markets* (HUP 2019); Carl Shapiro, 'Antitrust in a Time of Populism' (2018) 61 Journal of Industrial Organization 714; Gustavo Grullon, Yelena Larkin and Roni Michaely, 'Are US Industries Becoming More Concentrated?' (2019) 23 Review of Finance 697.

480 To get an idea of the scholars associated with the New Brandeis Movement, see the overview of books, articles, studies and symposia listed by Tim Wu, 'Antitrust Revival, a Reading List' (*Medium*, 18 November 2019) <https://medium.com/@superwuster/antitrust-revival-a-reading-list-8ff8bcca0d67>.

481 This term was coined by Konstantin Medvedovsky, who has edited a journal issue on the topic, see Konstantin Medvedovsky (ed), 'Hipster Antitrust' (2018) CPI Antitrust Chronicle April.

482 Khan, 'The New Brandeis Movement: America's Antimonopoly Debate' (n 479) 132. On the connection between the consumer welfare standard and market power, see Sandeep Vaheesan, 'How Robert Bork

influence that comes with market power. To combat these various harms, New Brandeisians propose 'refocusing antitrust analysis on a structural inquiry about process and power'.[483] Consumer welfare would thus be replaced by a more structural standard, eg that of 'effective competition' or 'protection of competition'.[484] The normative underpinnings of the movement have been translated into concrete proposals to reform antitrust law as it relates to:

- Labour: barring non-compete clauses and broadening the exemption for collective bargaining;
- Horizontal mergers: restoring structural presumptions;
- Vertical mergers and restraints: abandoning the presumption of benefit to the public;
- Unilateral conduct: reforming the legal test for predatory pricing, reinvigorating the essential facilities doctrine, recognizing margin squeeze as a form of monopolization, and restoring a less stringent standard for monopoly leveraging.[485]

The movement has been successful in reaching stakeholders beyond academia, as shown by its coverage in the popular press[486] and the incorporation of its ideas into political platforms.[487] Unsurprisingly for a movement with bold proposals, it has also been intensely critiqued, eg for being 'populist' and 'pseudo-economic', and for chasing a set of incoherent, vague and overly broad goals that will turn antitrust enforcement into a discretionary (or even arbitrary) exercise.[488] These critics, which have already been categorized into their own 'Reactionary Antitrust' movement, have in turn been criticized for demeaning New Brandeisians 'as "populists" while apparently remaining blind to [their] own populist arguments and inherently ideological and political positions'.[489] One thing is for certain: 'Antitrust is sexy again.'[490]

Fathered the New Gilded Age' (*ProMarket*, 5 September 2019) <https://promarket.org/how-robert-bork-fathered-the-new-gilded-age/>.

483 Lina Khan, 'The Ideological Roots of America's Market Power Problem' (2018) The Yale Law Journal Forum 960, 979. For a New Brandeisian critique on the consumer welfare standard, see Sandeep Vaheesan, 'The Profound Nonsense of Consumer Welfare Antitrust' (2019) 64 The Antitrust Bulletin 479.

484 Marshall Steinbaum and Maurice Stucke, 'The Effective Competition Standard: A New Standard for Antitrust' (2018) Roosevelt Institute Issue Brief; Tim Wu, 'After Consumer Welfare, Now What? The "Protection of Competition" Standard in Practice' (2018) CPI Antitrust Chronicle April.

485 Wu, 'The Utah Statement: Reviving Antimonopoly Traditions for the Era of Big Tech' (n 419) (the statement was published by Wu but drafted by a group of participants at the conference *A New Future for Antitrust*).

486 See eg the NYT profile of Lina Khan, one of the most productive and vocal proponents of the New Brandeis Movement: David Streitfeld, 'Amazon's Antitrust Antagonist Has a Breakthrough Idea' (*NYT*, 7 September 2018) <https://www.nytimes.com/2018/09/07/technology/monopoly-antitrust-lina-khan-amazon.html>.

487 House Democrats, 'Crack Down on Corporate Monopolies & the Abuse of Economic and Political Power' (A Better Deal) <https://abetterdeal.democraticleader.gov/the-proposals/crack-down-on-abuse-of-power/>; Elizabeth Warren, 'Here's How We Can Break Up Big Tech' (*Medium*, 8 March 2019) <https://medium.com/@teamwarren/heres-how-we-can-break-up-big-tech-9ad9e0da324c>.

488 See eg Joshua Wright, Elyse Dorsey, Jonathan Klick and Jan Rybnicek, 'Requiem for a Paradox: The Dubious Rise and Inevitable Fall of Hipster Antitrust' (2019) 51 Arizona State Law Journal 293. Politicians have also come out against the movement, see Nitasha Tiku, 'Do Not Mistake Orrin Hatch for #HipsterAntitrust' (*Wired*, 3 August 2017) <https://www.wired.com/story/orrin-hatch-antitrust-hipster-antitrust/>.

489 Newman, 'Reactionary Antitrust' (n 416) 66. On that same movement, see Ezrachi and Stucke (n 418) 1 ('In arguing for a "pure" antitrust, they endorse, outside of cartels, a "light" touch enforcement, if any.').

490 Shapiro, 'Antitrust in a Time of Populism' (n 479) 714.

The calls for antitrust reform thus appear to be inversely correlated with the (perceived) effectiveness of enforcement and are compounded by high levels of economic concentration.[491] According to this hypothesis, the higher level of enforcement and lower level of economic concentration in the EU should lead to a more muted call for reform.[492] This does appear to be the case: the EU has not really seen radical proposals regarding the goals and legal tests shaping antitrust enforcement. Instead, there has been a relatively modest push to instil more 'fairness' into (or in addition to) the consumer welfare standard.[493] As in the US, some critics argue that 'antitrust law is taken away from the rule of law'.[494]

However, such critique starts from a misunderstanding of the concept of fairness and its impact on EU antitrust enforcement. First of all, fairness is not a new value for competition; it has long been in the preamble and the specific antitrust provisions of the TFEU.[495] Secondly, while Commissioner Vestager regularly refers to fairness in public remarks,[496] she has clarified that fairness is the natural result of guaranteeing competition on the merits, not a separate benchmark against which conduct is assessed.[497] Similarly, Director-General Laitenberger has clarified that fairness 'is not meant as a self-sufficient, generic legal test to be applied in cases'; indeed, 'the very concept of "fairness" excludes that it substitutes rigorous, fact-based analysis'.[498] Thus, while the concept of fairness underpins competition law and its specific legal tests, references to 'fairness' do not divorce the discipline from economics; rather, they are 'a way to express the overall goals and benefits of EU competition policy in a more tangible manner'.[499] Expressing the benefits from economically rigorous antitrust

491 See similarly Baker, *The Antitrust Paradigm: Restoring a Competitive Economy* (n 472) 3 ('The more our antitrust institutions fall short, the more politically difficult it will become to fix them. Instead, the public will favor more draconian responses, such as treating businesses in more sectors of the economy as public utilities while effective competition would have been possible.') and ch 1 on market power.

492 Philippon (n 479) 'Part one. The rise of market power in the United States' vs 'Part two. The European experience'.

493 Alfonso Lamadrid de Pablo, 'Competition Law as Fairness' (2017) 8 JECLAP 147; Ezrachi and Stucke (n 418); Damien Gerard, 'Fairness in EU Competition Policy: Significance and Implications' (2018) 9 JECLAP 211.

494 Thibault Schrepel, 'Antitrust Without Romance' (2019) 3 <https://ssrn.com/abstract=3395001>.

495 TFEU, preamble ('fair competition'), art 101 (to be justified on account of redeeming efficiencies, an agreement between competitors must allow 'consumers a fair share of the resulting benefit'), art 102 (prohibiting, as a form of exploitative abuse, 'directly or indirectly imposing unfair purchase or selling prices or other unfair trading conditions'). Further on 'fairness' as a goal of EU competition law, see Ariel Ezrachi, 'EU Competition Law Goals and the Digital Economy' (BEUC Discussion Paper 2019) 12–15.

496 Gerard (n 493) 211 ('fairness has been mentioned in one way or another in more than half of the Commissioner's public remarks since 2014').

497 Margrethe Vestager, 'Fairness and Competition' (GCLC Annual Conference, Brussels, 25 January 2018) ('It doesn't mean that just because something is unfair, it's automatically also against the competition rules. All it means is that simply by doing our job – simply by enforcing the competition rules in our Treaty – we do our bit to make Europe a fairer place to live.').

498 Johannes Laitenberger, 'Fairness in Unilateral Practice Cases' (GCLC Conference, Brussels, 26 January 2018). See also Johannes Laitenberger, 'Fairness in EU Competition Law Enforcement' (British Chambers of Commerce EU & Belgium, Brussels, 20 June 2018).

499 Laitenberger, 'Fairness in Unilateral Practice Cases' (n 498). See also Lamadrid de Pablo, 'Competition Law as Fairness' (n 493) 148 ('Connecting "fairness" to competition law is therefore not a way to divorce the discipline from economics but to reconcile it with society, showing the wider public that it can contribute to their well-being.').

enforcement in intelligible terms may help to boost European citizens' trust in business and public institutions, and proponents of change do not find much support when such trust is high. Therefore, a focus on fairness may actually provide *an antidote to* calls for radical reform.

That is not to say that EU competition policy has remained static beyond a change in rhetoric. Upon closer inspection, one can discern a shift *within* rather than *away from* consumer welfare. The main parameters of consumer welfare are output, price, quality, choice and innovation.[500] Output and price can be considered the most basic parameters,[501] which may have to do with the fact that they are the most easily measurable.[502] In digital markets, however, output and price do not play a decisive role, given that marginal costs are often near-zero and services are provided to consumers for free, at least in monetary terms. Accordingly, the focus of assessments shifts to the other three parameters of competition (quality, choice and innovation), but not without difficulties.[503]

In particular in non-monetary-price markets, the first reflex is to shift the focus of assessments towards competition on quality.[504] At first sight, this should not pose any problems since 'from an economic perspective, higher quality and lower cost are two sides of the same coin' (a 'quality-adjusted price' captures both parameters in one metric).[505] However, quality is more difficult to measure, which is illustrated by the issues with the SSNDQ test described above.[506] Moreover, one can argue over what counts as quality: for example, can a decrease in privacy be equated to a quality degradation (and therefore a price increase)?

Consumer choice implies that 'the consumer has the power to define his or her own wants and the ability to satisfy these wants at competitive prices' and has even been called 'the ultimate goal of antitrust'.[507] In digital ecosystems, platform operators have a strong ability to influence consumer choice, eg by hiding certain options and promoting others. The case studies described above indicate that platform operators make use of this ability, in particular when they also provide their own products

---

500 *Intel v Commission* (n 467), para 136; Case C–413/06 P *Bertelsmann and Sony v Independent Music Publishers and Labels Association (Impala)* EU:C:2008:392, para 121; Case T–168/01 *GlaxoSmithKline Services Unlimited v Commission* EU:T:2006:265, para 106 (particularly with regard to innovation).

501 See eg *GlaxoSmithKline* (n 463), para 62 (referring only to supply and price).

502 Kevin Caves and Hal Singer, 'When the Econometrician Shrugged: Identifying and Plugging Gaps in the Consumer Welfare Standard' (2018) 26 George Mason Law Review 395.

503 Johannes Laitenberger, 'EU Competition Law in Innovation and Digital Markets: Fairness and the Consumer Welfare Perspective' (MLex/Hogan Lovells event, Brussels, 10 October 2017). A similar shift is discernible on the other side of the Atlantic, see Makan Delrahim, 'All Roads Lead to Rome: Enforcing the Consumer Welfare Standard in Digital Media Markets' (Jevons Institute Colloquium, Rome, 22 May 2018).

504 ibid. See also Dina Srinivasan, 'The Antitrust Case against Facebook' (2019) 16 Berkeley Business Law Journal 39, 46 ('In digital markets where consumers do not pay a price, antitrust enforcement must become comfortable with a paradigm that focuses on quality'). For an application, see *Google Search (Shopping)* (n 348), para 596 ('the Conduct is likely to reduce the incentives of Google to improve the quality of its comparison shopping service as it does not currently need to compete on the merits').

505 Philippon (n 479) 20, see 41–42 on the measurement of quality-adjusted prices.

506 See Section 1.1.1.

507 Robert Lande, 'Consumer Choice as the Ultimate Goal of Antitrust' (2001) 62 University of Pittsburgh Law Review 503, 503.

through their platform.[508] Based on such observations, there have been calls to attach more importance to consumer choice (or, more fundamentally: autonomy) in cases regarding online platforms.[509]

Finally, innovation is a crucial objective of competition policy.[510] From an economic perspective, the relation between the two has been disputed. On one side of the debate, Schumpeter holds that larger firms have greater incentives to invest and that the prospect of market power spurs innovation; on the other, Arrow argues that monopoly power disincentivizes innovation while competition spurs it.[511] This debate becomes all the more relevant when intervening in a relatively concentrated tech sector: if one takes a Schumpeterian view, the case for intervention becomes weaker. In any case, 'the promotion of innovation needs more consideration in constellations where companies compete in dynamic sectors and engage in "competition *for* the markets".'[512]

These various parameters of competition differ in important respects. For one, output, price and quality are considered *static* efficiencies, while innovation is considered a *dynamic* efficiency.[513] Assessing these different efficiencies thus requires an appropriate time horizon: changes in output, price and quality can manifest themselves in the short run, while innovation requires a long-term perspective. In a way, the time horizon for consumer choice is also longer: competition authorities seek to safeguard consumer choice *now* because it leads to efficiencies (in terms of output, price or quality) *later*. Such reasoning comes to the fore in the ECJ's margin squeeze case law,[514] and is more implicitly present in the EC's *Google Shopping* decision.[515] Finally, and perhaps most importantly, even when the effects of a practice on the various parameters of consumer welfare are measured correctly, a fundamental issue presents itself when these effects have to be balanced against each other to determine the 'net' result: since the parameters are qualitatively different, trading them off against each other necessarily implies a

508 See Section 2.3.

509 Rupprecht Podszun, 'Digital Ecosystems, Decision-Making, Competition and Consumers – On the Value of Autonomy for Competition' (2019) <https://ssrn.com/abstract=3420692>; Alain Strowel and Wouter Vergote, 'Digital Platforms: To Regulate or Not to Regulate?' in Bram Devolder (ed), *The Platform Economy: Unravelling the Legal Status of Online Intermediaries* (Intersentia 2019) 17.

510 See generally Bundeskartellamt, 'Innovations – Challenges for Competition Law Practice' (Series of papers on 'Competition and Consumer Protection in the Digital Economy', 2017).

511 Carl Shapiro, 'Competition and Innovation: Did Arrow Hit the Bull's Eye?' in Josh Lerner and Scott Stern (eds), *The Rate and Direction of Inventive Activity Revisited* (University of Chicago Press 2012), 362–63.

512 Rupprecht Podszun and Stephan Kreifels, 'Digital Platforms and Competition Law' (2016) 5 Journal of European Consumer and Market Law 33, 34.

513 See Melissa Schilling, 'Towards Dynamic Efficiency: Innovation and Its Implications for Antitrust' (2015) 60 The Antitrust Bulletin 191.

514 Case C–280/08 P *Deutsche Telekom v Commission* EU:C:2010:603, para 182 ('the margin squeeze also has the effect that consumers suffer detriment as a result of the limitation of the *choices* available to them and, therefore, of the prospect of a longer-term reduction of retail *prices* as a result of competition exerted by competitors who are at least as efficient in that market' (emphasis added)).

515 *Google Search (Shopping)* (n 348), para 180 ('the Conduct is capable of leading competing comparison shopping services to cease providing their services [ie less *choice*]. This would allow Google to impose and maintain higher fees on merchants for participation in its own comparison shopping service. These higher costs for merchants are capable of leading to higher product *prices* for consumers' (emphasis added)).

value judgment.[516] For example, is a choice of two additional product providers worth a short-term 5% price increase? There is no neutral way to answer this question.

These difficulties are on display in recent cases concerning online platforms. In *Google Android*, for example, the EC determined that Google's tying practices harmed consumers by decreasing their *choice* of search engines and web browsers, and by limiting *innovation* in those markets.[517] However, Google argued that tying was a financial necessity: given that OEMs could use Android for free, Google could only generate sufficient revenue from its web browser and search engine – to safeguard that revenue, it tied these services to its OS's 'must-have' app store. After the EC's tying prohibition, Google threatened to start charging OEMs for using Android,[518] which would likely increase the final *price* of mobile devices. Which conversion rate does one use to balance the value of an increase in choice/innovation against one in price?

It is fair to conclude that online platforms are in no small part responsible for reopening the age-old debate on the goals of antitrust law. In the US, this has led to the emergence of the New Brandeis Movement, which seeks to replace the consumer welfare standard with a more structural one. In the EU, due to the greater (perceived) effectiveness of antitrust enforcement and lower levels of concentration, progressive voices do not amount to a movement, but the digital economy has led to an increased (rhetorical) focus on fairness and a shift within the consumer welfare standard, from the parameters of output and price to those of quality, choice and innovation (parameters that are, however, more difficult to assess).

The consumer welfare standard constitutes the normative framework of this book. However, this standard leaves ample room: both US and EU competition policy are guided by consumer welfare, but enforcement (in particular with regard to unilateral conduct) differs markedly between these two jurisdictions. What matters more for enforcement are the specific legal tests that guide the assessment of potentially anticompetitive conduct. These tests, in particular as they apply to leveraging conduct, are at the heart of this thesis. The design of those tests proceeds according to a specific method, which is set out in the next section.

4.2.2 The Methods of Competition Law

Competition policy is a form of market regulation – one that is exceedingly economics-based now that noneconomic values are largely left out of the equation. As market regulation, its concrete shape should generally be determined through a cost-benefit

516 Rebecca Allensworth, 'The Commensurability Myth in Antitrust' (2016) 69 Vanderbilt Law Review 1.

517 *Google Android* (n 352), ss 11.3.4.2 and 11.4.4.2.

518 Hiroshi Lockheimer, 'Complying with the EC's Android Decision' (*The Keyword – Google Blog*, 16 October 2018) <https://www.blog.google/around-the-globe/google-europe/complying-ecs-android-decision/> ('Since the pre-installation of Google Search and Chrome together with our other apps helped us fund the development and free distribution of Android, we will introduce a new paid licensing agreement for smartphones and tablets shipped into the EEA.').

analysis.[519] When it comes to shaping competition policy, however, cost-benefit analysis takes the more sophisticated form of error cost analysis (also called 'decision theory').[520] In the words of Baker:[521]

> The error-cost perspective evaluates antitrust rules – individually and as a whole – on the basis of whether they minimize total social costs. The relevant costs include those of false positives (finding violations when conduct did not in fact harm competition) [and] false negatives (failure to find violations when conduct harmed competition)[.][522]

When designing rules governing anticompetitive conduct, the one that minimizes the social cost from errors – ie false positives ('type I errors') and false negatives ('type II errors') – should thus be chosen over alternatives. By minimizing error costs, one prevents the rule from either under-deterring anticompetitive conduct or over-deterring procompetitive conduct.[523] Striking the correct balance between these two poles should maximize consumer welfare.

Errors and the associated costs are unavoidable, but their incidence can be reduced by making rules more nuanced so as to better capture anticompetitive conduct. However, as Lambert points out, '[n]uance isn't free':

> It's costly for regulators to anticipate and properly express exceptions, and the more complicated they make the rule in an effort to reduce errors, the harder it is for those being regulated ... to learn what's allowed and to plan their conduct accordingly. It's also harder for adjudicators to assess whether a violation has occurred.[524]

These costs incurred by the drafters, subjects and adjudicators of the rules are termed 'decision costs'.[525] It is thus easy to see how error and decision costs are in tension: when making a rule more nuanced, one decreases error costs while increasing decision costs; by contrast, doing away with nuance may decrease decision costs but leads to more errors. In designing antitrust rules, the ultimate goal is to minimize *the sum of* error and decision costs.[526] However, while this method appears to be neutral,

---

519 See generally Cass Sunstein, *The Cost-Benefit Revolution* (MIT Press 2018).

520 Thomas Lambert, *How to Regulate: A Guide for Policymakers* (CUP 2017) 13 (describing how error cost analysis 'is really just a form of cost–benefit analysis' but improves upon it by 'ensur[ing] that we are taking account of the opportunity costs of selecting one regulatory approach over its alternative').

521 Error cost analysis entered (mainstream) antitrust scholarship through the seminal article: Paul Joskow and Alvin Klevorick, 'A Framework for Analyzing Predatory Pricing Policy' (1979) 89 The Yale Law Journal 213.

522 Baker, *The Antitrust Paradigm: Restoring a Competitive Economy* (n 472) 73.

523 See ibid for a caveat on how 'false positives and false negatives may not neatly map to over- and under-deterrence'.

524 Lambert (n 520) 11.

525 Baker, *The Antitrust Paradigm: Restoring a Competitive Economy* (n 472) 73 (categorizing these costs under the heading 'transaction costs').

526 Lambert (n 520) 13 and ch 7 on applying error cost analysis to the market failure of market power. For a critique of Lambert's regulatory theory, see Lisa Heinzerling, 'How Not to Regulate' (2018) 85 The University of Chicago Law Review 2015.

its application is often infused with assumptions. One influential example is Easterbrook, who – in his seminal article 'The Limits of Antitrust' – posited:

> If the court errs by condemning a beneficial practice, the benefits may be lost for good. Any other firm that uses the condemned practice faces sanctions in the name of stare decisis, no matter the benefits. If the court errs by permitting a deleterious practice, though, the welfare loss decreases over time. Monopoly is self-destructive.[527]

In other words, Easterbrook assumed that 'judicial errors that tolerate baleful practices are self-correcting, while erroneous condemnations are not'.[528] When designing rules, he thus put more weight on false positives than false negatives, given that the latter are supposedly self-correcting.[529] Such an assumption counsels against vigorous antitrust enforcement.[530] Others argue that, at least when it comes to online platforms, the assumption should be reversed: '[T]he costs of [false negatives] may be higher in the digital economy because of the possible irreversibility of market tipping while the risks of [false positives] may be lower in the digital economy because of the high market concentration.'[531] Rather than choosing a side in this debate, it appears wise to limit the assumptions one starts from.

The following sections apply error cost analysis to exclusionary – and in particular leveraging – conduct by online platforms. The basic question is: 'For the type of conduct at issue, which *legal test* likely maximizes consumer welfare over the long run?'[532] Framing the question in this way accords with the Crémer Report recommendation that 'competition law should not try to work with the error cost framework case by case, but rather should try to translate general insights in error costs into legal tests'.[533] In addition to using error cost analysis to shape legal tests, I rely on it to formulate guidelines for applying those tests.

Answering the above question proceeds by a (deceivingly simple) two-step approach. First, it is necessary to consider the likely consumer harms and benefits from the type of conduct, as well as its prevalence. Second, one must design a legal test that minimizes the cost of false positives and false negatives as well as decision costs. Before continuing, however, it is worth clarifying how legal tests compare to related concepts such as the burden of proof, the standard of proof, and presumptions.

---

527 Frank Easterbrook, 'The Limits of Antitrust' (1984) 63 Texas Law Review 1, 2.

528 ibid 3.

529 This was an important element of the Chicago School's ideology. It goes back to the fundamental belief that markets are self-correcting. See Hovenkamp and Scott Morton (n 446) 1870–71.

530 Others assume that decision (in particular compliance and legal process) costs are high, which similarly counsels against vigorous antitrust enforcement.

531 De Streel (n 387) 4. For other rebukes of Easterbrook's central point, see Salil Mehra, 'Paradise Is a Walled Garden? Trust, Antitrust, and User Dynamism' (2011) 18 George Mason Law Review 889, 914–21 (explicitly reassessing Easterbrook's assumptions in a platform context); Jonathan Baker, 'Taking the Error Out of "Error Cost" Analysis: What's Wrong with Antitrust's Right' (2015) 80 Antitrust Law Journal 1.

532 Mark Popofsky, 'Defining Exclusionary Conduct' (2006) 73 Antitrust Law Journal 435, 437.

533 Crémer Report (n 354) 51. Among others, the report argues that 'in the context of highly concentrated markets characterised by strong network effects and subsequently high barriers to entry … one may want to err on the side of disallowing types of conduct that are potentially anticompetitive, and to impose the burden of proof for showing pro-competitiveness on the incumbent'.

The starting point is the *burden of proof*. Regulation 1/2003 states that 'the burden of proving an infringement of [article 102 TFEU] shall rest on the party or the authority alleging the infringement'.[534] When it comes to public enforcement, it is thus for the EC or national competition authority (NCA) to prove the existence of a violation of article 102 TFEU. Once they prove each of the conditions under which the conduct at issue constitutes an abuse (the legal test), the burden of proof shifts to the dominant undertaking, which can then justify its conduct by proving countervailing efficiencies. However, while the foregoing applies to the overall legal burden, 'the "evidential burden" of proving the facts in issue may shift to and fro' during proceedings.[535]

Thus, the party that carries the burden of proof needs to establish that the *legal test* of the abuse in question (which depends on the type of conduct at issue) is fulfilled. For a refusal to supply to be abusive, for example, the EC has to prove that (i) the undertaking in question is dominant; (ii) the refusal relates to a facility that is objectively necessary to be able to compete in a downstream market; (iii) and the refusal is likely to lead to the elimination of effective competition in the downstream market.[536] The test is stringent as the refusal must be 'likely' to result in anticompetitive effects; other tests only require a 'capability', 'potential' or 'probability' of anticompetitive effects. While it is easy to conflate these various levels of harm with the *standard of proof*, that would be a mistake.[537]

In proving certain conditions of the legal test, the party that bears the burden of proof can rely on *presumptions* to discharge that burden.[538] A presumption is 'an inference that a showing of Fact A implies Fact B, or a sufficient likelihood of Fact B to satisfy the burden of production'.[539] The inference that Fact A implies Fact B is based on economic theory and/or practical experience. Depending on the clarity of this theory/ experience, the presumption can be weaker (easy to rebut) or stronger (difficult to rebut) – in extreme cases, it may even be conclusive. Presumptions are thus a useful tool to recalibrate the burden of proof between parties, thus decreasing decision costs (but at the risk of increasing error costs).[540]

---

534 Council Regulation (EC) 1/2003 of 16 December 2002 on the implementation of the rules on competition laid down in Articles 81 and 82 of the Treaty [2003] OJ L1/1, art 2. Further on the burden of proof (in art 102 TFEU cases), see Adriani Kalintiri, *Evidence Standards in EU Competition Enforcement* (Hart 2019) 32–60.

535 David Bailey, 'Presumptions in EU Competition Law' (2010) 31 ECLR 20, 20. Under US antitrust law, various types of conduct are assessed by application of a 'burden-shifting framework', where the allocated burden of proof shifts between the parties more readily, see eg Andrew Gavil, 'Burden of Proof in U.S. Antitrust Law' in *Issues in Competition Law and Policy* (ABA Section of Antitrust Law 2008) 125–57.

536 Case C–7/97 *Oscar Bronner v Mediaprint* EU:C:1998:569 and Exclusionary Conduct Guidance Paper (n 461), paras 81 and 83–89.

537 Kalintiri (n 534) 78–81. The standard of proof in EU competition law enforcement is elusive. Kalintiri maintains that the standard for the EC is/should be one of 'firm conviction' and that undertakings 'entertain no real prospect of having their "defence" upheld unless they establish an *at least equally strong* level of confidence'. However, Bailey suggests that the standard of proof is rather one of balance of probabilities, Bailey (n 535) 21.

538 On presumptions, see Kalintiri (n 534) 142–72.

539 Steven Salop, 'An Enquiry Meet for the Case: Decision Theory, Presumptions, and Evidentiary Burdens in Formulating Antitrust Legal Standards' (2017) 2 <https://ssrn.com/abstract=3068157>.

540 Calling for the increased use of presumptions in antitrust law, see ibid 4 ('presumptions deserve an even more central role') and Baker, *The Antitrust Paradigm: Restoring a Competitive Economy* (n 472) 80 ('antitrust's rules and presumptions need to be strengthened').

In *Akzo Chemie*, for example, the ECJ held that a market share of 50% is evidence of a dominant position; in other words, from that threshold onwards, dominance is presumed.[541] The presumption is, however, rebuttable.[542] Exclusivity rebates used to constitute a per se abuse, which meant that once the EC had proven the existence of such rebates, their anticompetitive effect was irrefutably presumed.[543] The burden of proof then shifted to the undertaking, which could – at least in theory – establish countervailing efficiencies.[544] In *Intel*, however, the ECJ 'clarified' the case law. An undertaking that maintains exclusivity rebates can now prove that its conduct is not capable of restricting competition.[545] The EC then has to analyse 'the intrinsic capacity of that practice to foreclose competitors which are at least as efficient as the dominant undertaking' – only once it proves such a capacity, does the burden of proof shift back to the dominant undertaking, which can then still justify its conduct.[546] The legal test for exclusivity rebates has thus been recalibrated (but not without criticism).[547]

In conclusion, I take the view that an error cost analysis, applied without (baseless) assumptions, is the preferred way to design legal tests. However, a legal test only comes into play once a type of conduct has been qualified as a certain form of abuse. This initial qualification can easily determine whether an abuse is established or not. In the appeal proceedings of the *Google Shopping* decision, for example, the debate centred around whether Google's conduct should be qualified as an independent form of leveraging or rather as a refusal to supply.[548] Given that the legal test for refusal to supply is significantly more stringent, the qualification question can easily decide the outcome of a case.[549]

Given that leveraging is at the heart of intra-platform exclusion, the next section examines this overarching figure, the specifics of *platform* leveraging, and how those challenge existing qualifications and tests.

---

541 *AKZO Chemie v Commission* (n 381), para 60.

542 The EC even appears to reject the presumption, holding that market shares are only 'a useful first indication', see Exclusionary Conduct Guidance Paper (n 461), para 13.

543 *Hoffmann-La Roche v Commission* (n 339), para 86 ('An undertaking which is in a dominant position on a market and ties purchasers – even if it does so at their request – by an obligation or promise on their part to obtain all or most of their requirements exclusively from the said undertaking abuses its dominant position').

544 Although it seems very unlikely that those would be accepted. However, at the time of *Hoffmann-La Roche* (ibid), the possibility to justify prima facie abusive conduct was still unclear.

545 *Intel v Commission* (n 467), paras 137–39. This analysis requires analysing the extent of the undertaking's dominant position, the share of the market covered by the exclusivity rebate, as well as the conditions of the rebate. In addition, the EC must assess 'the possible existence of a strategy aiming to exclude competitors that are at least as efficient as the dominant undertaking from the market'.

546 ibid, para 140.

547 Defending the previous legal test from a decision-theoretic standpoint, see Wouter Wils, 'The Judgment of the EU General Court in *Intel* and the So-Called More Economic Approach to Abuse of Dominance' (2014) 37 World Competition 405.

548 Case T–612/17 *Google v Commission* (Hearing Report), paras 307–44.

549 In *Google Search (Shopping)*, the General Court rejected refusal to supply as the correct qualification, see Section 9.

5

LEVERAGING

This work focuses on intra-platform exclusion.[550] Such exclusion proceeds primarily through platforms treating their own downstream services differently (ie preferentially) from those of competitors, making it easier for those services to outcompete the alternatives from independent suppliers. One example is Apple treating Spotify differently from its own Apple Music.[551] Although the term is a bit more loaded, such 'differentiated treatment' can be described in one word as 'discrimination'.[552] While the 'discrimination' terminology focuses on the object of the action (the supplier, eg Spotify), 'self-preferencing' puts the spotlight on the subject (the platform, eg Apple, in particular its App Store). The question is whether such self-preferencing can be abusive in the sense of article 102 TFEU, and if so, under which conditions. Given that instances of self-preferencing almost invariably fit the label of 'leveraging',[553] that is where our inquiry starts.

5.1 The Law and Economics of Leveraging

According to the US Supreme Court, leveraging occurs when 'a seller exploits his dominant position in one market to expand his empire into the next'.[554] Others have similarly defined leveraging as an undertaking 'with a substantial degree of market power in one market engaging in anticompetitive practices with the aim of extending

550 See Section 3.3.

551 For more examples, see Section 2.3.

552 One could argue that the 'discrimination' terminology presupposes that the services treated differently are equivalent, which is the case in *Spotify v Apple*. Using both the 'discrimination' and 'self-preferencing' terminology, see AGCM, 'Amazon: investigation launched on possible abuse of a dominant position in online marketplaces and logistic services' (press release, 16 April 2019) <https://en.agcm.it/en/media/press-releases/2019/4/A528> and AdlC, 'Targeted advertising/Apple's implementation of the ATT framework' (press release, 17 March 2021) <https://www.autoritedelaconcurrence.fr/en/press-release/targeted-advertising-apples-implementation-att-framework-autorite-does-not-issue>.

553 See similarly Pablo Ibáñez Colomo, 'Exclusionary Discrimination Under Article 102 TFEU' (2014) 51 Common Market Law Review 141, 141–42 ('discrimination by a vertically-integrated firm to favour its activities may lead to the leveraging of a dominant position from one market to another').

554 *Times-Picayune v United States* 345 US 594, 611 (1953).

its market power into another market'.[555] In line with these definitions, the idea of self-preferencing is that a platform uses its control over its upstream platform to give its downstream operations a leg up over competitors. However, tagging the 'leveraging' label on self-preferencing only shifts the question to whether and when (under which conditions) leveraging is abusive.

5.1.1 Leveraging under EU Competition Law

Under EU competition law, leveraging is generally not considered an independent *form* of abuse, but rather a *category* of abuse.[556] In other words, leveraging is not considered an abuse in itself, but rather an umbrella term for a number of other forms of prohibited conduct – namely, refusal to supply, margin squeeze, tying, and certain instances of (price) discrimination.[557] While each of these forms of abusive conduct can serve the *objective* of extending a dominant position from one market to the next, the *method* differs.

First, in tying scenarios, customers that purchase one product (the tying product) must also purchase another product from the dominant undertaking (the tied product). The firm thus uses its dominance in one product market to give itself a (distributional) advantage in a second product market.[558] Customers may want to purchase the second product elsewhere but are hindered from doing so because they need the dominant firm's primary product. Second, with refusals to supply, a vertically integrated firm generally uses its dominance upstream to distort competition downstream. Specifically, refusing access to their upstream input can drive downstream competitors that rely on that input from the market.[559] A third form of leveraging, related to refusal to supply, is margin squeeze. This abuse occurs when a dominant firm charges a price for the upstream input which, compared to the price it charges on the downstream market, does not allow competitors to continue trading profitably in that market. Rather than simply refusing access, margin squeezes distort competition by manipulating the spread between upstream and downstream prices.[560] Fourth and finally, discrimination can constitute leveraging. Again, however, it only does when discrimination occurs in one

555 Pietro Crocioni, 'Leveraging of Market Power in Emerging Markets: A Review of Cases, Literature, and a Suggested Framework' (2007) 4 JCLE 449, 449.

556 See Robert O'Donoghue and Jorge Padilla, *The Law and Economics of Article 102 TFEU* (Hart 2020) 307 ('leveraging is simply a label for various types of conduct'); Giorgio Monti, *EC Competition Law* (CUP 2007) 186–95; Crocioni (n 555) 454 ('The term leveraging of market power refers to a wide range of anticompetitive behaviors or activities undertaken by a firm aiming at protecting or expanding its market power'); Patrick Todd, 'Digital Platforms and the Leverage Problem' (2019) 98 Nebraska Law Review 486, 489 ('Importantly, leverage is not a standalone theory of abuse in antitrust law. It is better thought of as a *category* that encompasses numerous legal theories of harm'); Magali Eben, 'Fining Google: A Missed Opportunity for Legal Certainty?' (2018) 14 European Competition Journal 129, 147–48 ('"leveraging" is the common denominator for different types of abuses').

557 Predatory pricing based on cross-subsidization (see Section 2.2.1, on Amazon) constitutes another form of leveraging. It is, however, the odd one out: first, the method is not one of self-preferencing or discrimination; second, the raising rivals' costs theory does not apply to it. I therefore do not discuss it.

558 See eg Case C–333/94 P *Tetra Pak v Commission* EU:C:1996:436.

559 See eg Case 311/84 *CBEM v CLT and IPB ('Télémarketing')* EU:C:1985:394.

560 See eg *Deutsche Telekom v Commission* (n 514).

market so as to distort competition in another market. For example, a firm dominant upstream may charge discriminatory prices – either directly or via rebates – to competitors of its downstream division.[561]

Thus, in the EU, leveraging is not necessarily anticompetitive but may refer to a more specific type of conduct that is. This view is shared across the Atlantic. In *Trinko*, a telecom provider was refused access to the incumbent's upstream network (despite a regulatory access obligation) and sought to rectify the situation with a claim of 'monopoly leveraging'. In a footnote, the US Supreme Court summarily rejected this claim, as 'leveraging presupposes anticompetitive conduct' (in that case, the refusal to supply, which the Court did not find).[562] Much earlier, the Court already described 'the wielding of monopolistic leverage' as 'the essence of illegality in tying agreements'.[563] However, then too, it tested the conduct in question against the conditions of the abuse in question, ie tying, thus confirming that leveraging is a category rather than a form of abuse.

However, the Supreme Court has been criticized for being overly hostile to leveraging claims. Reviewing the aforementioned case, Economides argues that '[f]rom an economist's point of view, *Trinko* is a poor decision' as the Court 'missed the leveraging of monopoly power'.[564] The Court's hostility to leveraging theories of anticompetitive conduct was inspired by Chicago School scholars who sought to disprove the anticompetitive effects of leveraging. Given the influence that their economic theories wield to this day (in the US and, albeit to a lesser extent, the EU), it is worth going over the economics of leveraging.

5.1.2 Economics of Leveraging

The economics of leveraging have been – and continue to be – hotly debated. The main disagreement is that between Chicago School scholars and those refuting their arguments (the 'post-Chicago School'). Sketching their debate is an effective way to understand the economics of leveraging. The centre of gravity of the debate has historically been tying. For one, focusing on a specific form of leveraging allows for more pointed arguments. Moreover, tying was subject to a rule of (quasi-)per se illegality under US antitrust law at the time. The distance between that rule and the Chicagoan preference for one of (quasi-)per se legality made for a logical focal point.

A first substantial critique of tying theory was formulated by Bowman in the 1950s. In his seminal article on 'the leverage problem', he posited that tying was not – or indeed could not be – anticompetitive in certain scenarios. First, this is the case when

561 See eg Case T-228/97 *Irish Sugar v Commission* EU:T:1999:246.

562 *Verizon Communications v Law Offices of Curtis V Trinko* 540 US 398 (2004), fn 4.

563 *Times-Picayune v United States* (n 554) 611.

564 Nicholas Economides, 'Vertical Leverage and the Sacrifice Principle: Why the Supreme Court Got *Trinko* Wrong' (2005) 61 New York University Annual Survey of American Law 379, 412.

fixed proportions are involved (static ties).[565] Second, this is the case when variable proportions are involved (dynamic ties) and different buyers use different quantities of the tied product, which 'serves as a counting device to measure how intensively the first product is being used'.[566] While the tying product (eg a copy machine) is sold at the same price irrespective of its usage, a second product (eg ink cartridges) is tied to it so as to 'meter' usage and indirectly charge more intensive users a higher price for the tying product.[567] In both cases, the firm does not create a new monopoly; 'tying is used simply as a means of insuring the full monopoly return on the tying product, where a monopoly already existed'.[568] In other words, the tie does not lead to *additional* monopoly profits, hence the name 'single monopoly profit' (SMP) theory.[569]

In *The Antitrust Paradox*, Bork generalized Bowman's critique in two ways. Firstly, he expanded the critique from tying to all abuses based on leveraging (or, in his words, 'transfer-of-power theory'), although he did stick to tying as a *pars pro toto*.[570] Secondly, Bork believed that the SMP theory was not limited to specific circumstances but had general validity. Tying, he held, 'is obviously not a means of gaining two monopoly profits from a single monopoly': if the firm can already charge a monopoly price for the tying product, supplying a competitive tied product in addition does not yield additional profit.[571] Given that tying cannot be explained by a profit motive, Bork reasoned that the practice must reflect efficiencies such as economies of scale and scope.[572] Where Bowman sought a modification of the per se rule against tying, Bork suggested repealing it altogether in favour of per se legality.

However, the SMP theory – as an argument against the potentially anticompetitive nature of leveraging and tying in particular – has been largely disproven. Chicagoans argued that, as a result of the SMP theory, tying can only be anticompetitive in very specific scenarios (or even never). In fact, the opposite is true: the SMP theory only holds under very restrictive assumptions.[573] One such assumption is that the tying and

565 Ward Bowman, 'Tying Arrangements and the Leverage Problem' (1957) 67 The Yale Law Journal 19, 23.

566 ibid 23–24.

567 *Vaessen/Moris* (Case IV/C-29.290) Commission Decision 79/86/EEC [1979] OJ L19/32 provides an example of this scenario: the maker of a sausage-making machine gave sausage producers free use of the machine on the condition that they bought sausage casings from the firm. The EC decided that this practice restricted competition as it 'deprives the [sausage maker] of its business freedom to obtain supplies from other undertakings, perhaps on more favourable terms' (para 15), even though Bowman would argue that tying just serves as a 'metering' device to correctly charge more intensive users.

568 Bowman (n 565) 24.

569 Bowman did accept that tying can create a new monopoly when variable proportions of complementary products are involved. When demand for two products is interrelated, 'a seller can realize more aggregate profit from setting the two prices together than by setting the two prices independently.' See ibid, fn 18.

570 In characteristic hyperbole, he did declare that 'no other variety of that theory [than tying] has been so thoroughly and repeatedly demolished in the legal and economic literature', see Bork, *The Antitrust Paradox* (n 415) 372.

571 ibid 372–75.

572 ibid 375–79. Bork also considers price discrimination an efficiency, but that is only the case because Bork – despite his consumer welfare rhetoric – considered total welfare the goal of antitrust law (and even then, price discrimination does not always increase total welfare).

573 Steven Salop, 'Economic Analysis of Exclusionary Vertical Conduct: Where Chicago Has Overshot the Mark' in Robert Pitofsky (ed), *How the Chicago School Overshot the Mark: The Effect of Conservative*

tied products are used in fixed proportions. This assumption holds in textbook tying scenarios (eg nuts and bolts) but not in many real-life scenarios. Once the assumption is relaxed, the SMP theory breaks down and tying can have anticompetitive effects.[574] The same goes for 'metering' ties, which under realistic market conditions often harm consumer welfare.[575]

More generally, the SMP critique of leveraging focused on the short-term effect on consumer prices, ie *exploitation*.[576] But leveraging can also be implemented with a view to *exclusion* – the focus of this work. Exploitation and exclusion differ mainly as to their time horizon: the market power resulting from successful exclusion can *later* be exploited.[577] However, Chicagoans assumed that markets were (and would remain) perfectly competitive, ignoring the reality of markets that are imperfectly competitive (eg due to entry barriers).[578] Economic evidence has since shown that tying can affect the structure of the market. When the *tied* market is not perfectly competitive, as is often the case, tying can deter the entry and lead to the exit of equally efficient competitors.[579] Moreover, Chicagoans assumed that the degree of market power in the *tying* market was fixed. This is another unrealistic assumption, which led them to miss the fact that tying can be used defensively, ie by pre-empting competition in the tied market so as to maintain or increase market power in the tying market.[580] Whether the goal of tying is to gain market power in a new market or protect it in an established market, the resulting foreclosure gives the tying firm (additional) power over price.

Economic Analysis on U.S. Antitrust (OUP 2008) 145 (the validity of the SMP theory 'requires a number of restrictive assumptions', including that '(1) the monopolist has a durable and unregulated monopoly in the one product; (2) the products are consumed in fixed proportions; (3) all consumers have identical preferences'). See similarly Einer Elhauge, 'Tying, Bundled Discounts, and the Death of the Single Monopoly Profit Theory' (2009) 123 Harvard Law Review 397, 400 (the assumptions are '(1) Buyers do not use varying amounts of the tied product with the tying product. (2) Buyer demand for the two products has a strong positive correlation. (3) Buyers do not use varying amounts of the tying product. (4) The competitiveness of the tied market is fixed. (5) The competitiveness of the tying market is fixed.'). Note that some authors continue to argue that it is not the Chicago School but rather its critics that rely on strict assumptions, see eg Roger Van den Bergh, *Comparative Competition Law and Economics* (Edward Elgar 2017) 317–18 (commenting on the 'strict assumptions of the new theories' but recognizing that '[t]he Chicago critique applies only if the tied market is perfectly competitive').

574 Tying can even have anticompetitive effects in case of fixed proportions if buyer demand for two products does not have a strong positive correlation, see Einer Elhauge and Damien Geradin, *Global Antitrust Law and Economics* (Foundation Press 2018) 605–6.

575 Einer Elhauge and Barry Nalebuff, 'The Welfare Effects of Metering Ties' (2017) 33 The Journal of Law, Economics, and Organization 68, showing such ties *always* harm consumer welfare under realistic market conditions. However, such ties could be justified when they effectively shift financing or risk-bearing costs to the firm that can minimize them, see ibid 612.

576 The focus of the critique is explained by the fact that the leverage theory responsible for the per se rule against tying was one of extraction rather than foreclosure, see Hovenkamp and Scott Morton (n 446) 1867.

577 See Louis Kaplow, 'Extension of Monopoly Power through Leverage' (1985) 85 Columbia Law Review 515, 523–25 and 527–31.

578 ibid 536–39.

579 Michael Whinston, 'Tying, Foreclosure, and Exclusion' (1990) 80 The American Economic Review 837 (also finding that the SMP theory does not hold when the tying product is not essential for all uses of the tied product, ie when the tied product has a separate utility); Barry Nalebuff, 'Bundling as an Entry Barrier' (2004) 119 The Quarterly Journal of Economics 159.

580 Robin Feldman, 'Defensive Leveraging in Antitrust' (1999) 87 The Georgetown Law Journal 2079, 2081 ('the Chicago school is wrong because it fails to consider changes in the structure of the primary market').

Starting with work by Salop and Scheffman in the 1980s, the economics of leveraging have crystallized in an overarching paradigm, namely, that of 'raising rivals' costs foreclosure'.[581] This paradigm applies to most exclusionary abuses, but in particular leveraging.[582] The focus is on how partial or total foreclosure from access to either critical inputs or customers increases the costs and prices of rivals, which in turn allows the excluding firm to charge supra-competitive prices, thus harming consumers.[583]

Vertically integrated firms may have both the ability and incentive to distort competition in this way. The *ability* to distort competition derives from market power, generally located upstream but potentially also downstream. The *incentive* to leverage that market power exists when the leveraging scenario comes with increased profits compared to the 'do nothing' scenario (ie continuing to only provide the upstream input, potentially increasing its price further). Given that market power has been discussed above,[584] the next section pays special attention to platforms' incentives to leverage.

5.2 Platform Leveraging: Mechanism, Incentives and Effects

Leveraging by platforms is not fundamentally different from leveraging by traditional, analogue firms. However, it is different enough to merit specific treatment – not a wholesale new theory, but a reinterpretation of key parts of the current theory. For example, platform leveraging – or self-preferencing – is often not price-based. This is not a fundamental problem, given that 'price' has always served as a shorthand for other competitive parameters, including innovation.[585] In addition, the incentives to engage in anticompetitive conduct invariably feature in the analysis. In platform leveraging cases, however, the incentives for leveraging deserve a more pre-eminent role in the analysis. Finally, anticompetitive effects, while substantively similar, emerge in different forms. To illustrate key similarities and differences between traditional and platform leveraging, this section starts with an often-made analogy between the conduct of supermarkets and platforms.

581 Steven Salop and David Scheffman, 'Raising Rivals' Costs' (1983) 73 American Economic Review 267.

582 ibid, 267–68, offering discrimination and price squeezes as examples. See also Thomas Krattenmaker and Steven Salop, 'Anticompetitive Exclusion: Raising Rivals' Costs to Achieve Power over Price' (1986) 92 The Yale Law Journal 209, 248–49 on 'the leverage debate', and Willard Tom and Gregory Wells, 'Raising Rivals' Costs: The Problem of Remedies' (2003) 12 George Mason Law Review 389 describing Microsoft as a prominent raising rivals' costs case.

583 Steven Salop, 'The Raising Rivals' Cost Foreclosure Paradigm, Conditional Pricing Practices, and the Flawed Incremental Price-Cost Test' (2017) 81 Antitrust Law Journal 371, 376.

584 See Section 4.1.2.

585 One important difference is that price is a static parameter of competition, while innovation is a dynamic one, see Section 4.2.1.

5.2.1 The Supermarket Analogy

Self-preferencing conduct by online platforms generally – and Amazon in particular – has often been likened to practices engaged in by supermarkets. The major premise of the syllogism generally goes: 'Supermarkets have always produced their own private-label products, and have been promoting those to consumers in their stores.'[586] The (often implicit) minor premise is that this has not been a problem, so the conclusion is that it cannot be problematic either when Amazon preferences the sales of its own private-label products.[587] Even Amazon itself has used this defence when it was called out for prompting customers to consider Amazon's version of the product they were about to buy, stating: '*Like any retailer* we promote our own brands in our stores, which provide high-quality products and great value to customers.'[588]

The supermarket analogy is thus generally used as a defence against allegations of anticompetitive self-preferencing by platforms. This section takes the analogy seriously by exploring it in depth, finding that it does not hold up as a defence. It does, however, help illuminate the mechanism, incentives and potential effects of platform leveraging.

The fact that a dominant supermarket promoting its own private-label products can distort competition has long been known. The academic writing on this topic is rich,[589] and it has been accepted by competition authorities[590] and courts. The High Court of Justice, for example, has noted that

> if a supermarket was dominant in a discrete market for supermarket grocery retailing but also produced its own-label brands of tea, sugar and biscuits which competed with those of third party manufacturers, it could be an abuse if the supermarket reserved the preferential display positions for its own brands, notwithstanding that customers who wanted other brands could still find them elsewhere in the store.[591]

---

586 See eg Randal Picker, 'Breaking up Amazon? Platforms, Private Labels and Entry' (*Truth on the Market*, 17 July 2019) <https://truthonthemarket.com/2019/07/17/breaking-up-amazon-platforms-private-labels-and-entry/>; Alec Stapp, 'Amazon, Antitrust, and Private Label Goods' (*Progressive Policy Institute*, 24 April 2020) <https://www.progressivepolicy.org/pressrelease/amazon-antitrust-and-private-label-goods/>.

587 Alternatively, the analogy is used as a slippery-slope argument, the idea being that if one prohibits self-preferencing by online platforms, one would also have to go after supermarkets for similar conduct, which is considered either infeasible or unjustified.

588 Jay Greene, 'Aggressive Amazon Tactic Pushes You to Consider Its Own Brand Before You Click "Buy"' (*WaPo*, 28 August 2019) <https://www.washingtonpost.com/technology/2019/08/27/aggressive-amazon-tactic-pushes-you-consider-its-own-brand-before-you-click-buy/> (emphasis added). Supermarket analogies have also moved beyond online marketplaces, see eg *Google Android* (n 352), para 1212 ('Just as supermarkets sell (premium) shelf space to suppliers, so, too, do OEMs and MNOs seek to generate additional revenue by monetizing the "real estate" of the smartphone's screen.')

589 See eg the various contributions in Ariel Ezrachi and Ulf Bernitz (eds), *Private Labels, Brands and Competition Policy* (OUP 2009). See also Chloé Binet, 'Buyer Power in EU Competition Law: A Boon or Impediment to Consumer Welfare?' (2015) unpublished PhD thesis, available at <https://dial.uclouvain.be/pr/boreal/object/boreal:156352>.

590 Belgische Mededingingsautoriteit, 'Prijsniveau in supermarkten' (Study, 2012).

591 *Streetmap.eu v Google* [2016] EWHC 253 (Ch) [60].

The concerns – and even the terminology – regarding supermarkets and private labels are virtually identical to those regarding platforms.[592] Supermarkets have various *incentives* to start producing and selling private-label products, including increased profits and the strengthening of their bargaining power.[593] In certain cases, supermarkets can achieve a 'gatekeeper' position between consumers and suppliers of branded goods.[594] To increase sales of their private-label products, they can also copy the packaging of the most popular brands, thus free riding on their reputation.[595] Once well established, supermarkets can use their strengthened bargaining power to extract more favourable contract terms from suppliers in the upstream market; in the downstream market, they can prioritize the sale of their private-label goods to consumers, to the detriment of independent suppliers.[596]

The *effects* of private label entry and preferencing are ambiguous.[597] Private labels generally have a positive effect on prices, both directly (they are priced lower) and indirectly (they put competitive pressure on brands). The effects on innovation are less straightforward. On the one hand, private-label goods offer supermarkets the possibility to innovate (eg by filling gaps in the market), while also pressuring suppliers of branded goods to innovate. On the other hand, when supermarkets quickly follow up on the innovation of branded goods, the resulting inability to profit from said innovation may reduce suppliers' incentive to invest. This effect is compounded because supermarkets have access to inside information on suppliers' products, which can be used to launch similar products. Promotion of the supermarket's private label, or even the delisting of a competing brand, further reduces incentives to invest, while also limiting consumer choice. In the long term, as brands are foreclosed from the market, average consumer prices can even increase.[598]

It should be clear that the promotion by a supermarket of its private-label goods can have negative economic effects. Why have we not seen any article 102 TFEU cases? This is

---

592 Remember though that supermarkets do not qualify as platforms, see Section 1.1.

593 Hila Nevo and Roger Van den Bergh, 'Private Labels: Challenges for Competition Law and Economics' (2017) 40 World Competition 271, 271 ('Private labels increase retailers' power by strengthening their gatekeeper's role.').

594 UNCTAD, 'Enforcement of Competition Policy in the Retail Sector: Competition Issues in the Food Retail Chain' (Note by the Secretariat) TD/B/C.I/CLP/38, 3 ('the increasing size of supermarket chains and increasingly important role of supermarkets as market gatekeepers may present risks to competition that can lead to a decrease in social welfare'); Ariel Ezrachi, 'Unchallenged Market Power? The Tale of Supermarkets, Private Labels, and Competition Law' (2010) 33 World Competition 257, 266 ('The dependence of the producer on the supermarket as a gatekeeper should not be underestimated.').

595 Ezrachi, 'Unchallenged Market Power? The Tale of Supermarkets, Private Labels, and Competition Law' (n 594) 264 (on 'copycat packaging').

596 Nevo and Van den Bergh (n 593) 272. See also David George, 'Trends in Retail Competition: Private Labels, Brands and Competition Policy' (Report on the Eleventh Annual Symposium on Competition Amongst Retailers and Suppliers, 2015) 18 ('The large retailers' position as gatekeepers to the market could lead to "rent appropriation" and "hold up"').

597 The remainder of the paragraph is mostly based on Ezrachi, 'Unchallenged Market Power? The Tale of Supermarkets, Private Labels, and Competition Law' (n 594) 258–64. See also Nevo and Van den Bergh (n 593) 277–84.

598 Nevo and Van den Bergh (n 593) 283–84, referencing Alessandro Bonanno and Rigoberto Lopez, 'Private Label Expansion and Supermarket Milk Prices' (2005) 3 Journal of Agricultural & Food Industrial Organization 1; Christophe Bontemps, Valerie Orozco, Vincent Réquillart and Audrey Trévisiol, 'Price Effects of Private Label Development (2005) 3 Journal of Agricultural & Food Industrial Organization 1; Rainer Olbrich and Gundula Grewe, 'Consequences of Competition Between National Brands and Private Labels: Empirical Results from Different German Outlet Formats' (2009) 37 International Journal of Retail & Distribution Management 933.

due to the limiting principles of EU competition law, which may not always apply in the case of platforms. First, dominance is an issue: given that most countries have at least a couple of large supermarket chains, 'most actors are in a strong but not dominant position'.[599] This does not mean that the conduct cannot have any negative economic effects, but supermarkets' *ability* to distort competition in the sense of article 102 TFEU is generally limited. For that reason, the practices of supermarkets are mostly addressed in sector inquiries[600] and as unfair trade practices.[601] By contrast, some online platforms are dominant in their respective product and geographic markets. Such dominance exacerbates the negative effects of self-preferencing. A second difference is that Amazon has access to more granular data on brands (gathered through its marketplace, fulfilment and advertising services) than supermarkets. As Amazon also has access to such data earlier in a product's lifecycle, the suppliers have a shorter opportunity to profit from it, which means incentives to invest are further reduced.[602] A third difference concerns the promotional capacities of supermarkets versus online platforms. Foreclosure – and thus negative economic effects – depend on the promotion's effect on consumer behaviour.[603] Of course, both a supermarket and a platform can simply delist a supplier's product. Shy of doing so, however, a platform's promotional capacity is greater. It would be impossible – or at least impractical – for a supermarket to send out an army of store clerks to tell every customer buying a branded good to also consider the private label competitor right before they buy it. But this is exactly what Amazon can do – and does.[604] Similarly, a supermarket putting its own product at eye level and brands at the bottom will not be as effective as a platform burying competitors on page 4 of the search results.

In conclusion, given the differences between supermarkets and platforms, the analogy does not hold up as a defence. However, it is informative as to the mechanism, incentives and potential effects of self-preferencing by platforms. As two of those components – incentives and effects – merit specific analysis in a platform context, they are addressed in the next two sections.

5.2.2 Platform Leveraging Incentives

Incentives to engage in anticompetitive conduct regularly come up in abuse of dominance cases, although often only shortly, especially when compared to the other two components of a strong case, ie the *ability* to engage in anticompetitive conduct and its *effects*. There are good reasons to start paying more attention to incentives in assessments of platform leveraging.

599 UNCTAD (n 594) 3. See similarly Ezrachi, 'Unchallenged Market Power? The Tale of Supermarkets, Private Labels, and Competition Law' (n 594) 267–69.

600 See eg Hellenic Competition Commission, 'Basic Consumer Goods' (Sector Inquiry, 2020) <https://www.epant.gr/en/enimerosi/sector-inquiry-into-basic-consumer-goods.html>.

601 See Directive (EU) 2019/633 of the European Parliament and of the Council on unfair trading practices in business-to-business relationships in the agricultural and food supply chain [2019] OJ L111/59.

602 Hal Singer and Shaoul Sussman, 'Can It. Amazon Is *Not* Your Typical Grocery Store' (*Wired*, 4 May 2020) <https://www.wired.com/story/opinion-can-it-amazon-is-not-your-typical-grocery-store/>.

603 *Streetmap.eu v Google* (n 591) [60].

604 Greene (n 588).

Easterbrook already argued that it is better 'to start the inquiry with questions about power and incentives than with questions that are essentially definitional' (eg whether a practice qualifies as this or that form of abuse).[605] This holds especially true in platform leveraging scenarios for two reasons. Firstly, qualification questions are particularly challenging when it comes to the conduct of platforms.[606] Secondly, leveraging cases – especially in digital markets – come with significant uncertainty, which complicates the effects analysis. As Crocioni explains, the incentives analysis thus becomes relatively more important:

> Furthermore, in leveraging [cases, it] may be particularly complex to provide actual evidence of harm and this is compounded if the case is in an emerging market. However, it may be possible to provide some evidence or provide a coherent story of why a firm may or may not have the incentive to engage in an allegedly abusive practice.[607]

Importantly, the economics of platforms limit their incentives to engage in anticompetitive conduct to some extent. The basic idea is that because a platform's value to consumers is determined largely by its suppliers, excluding suppliers hurts the platform and is therefore irrational. More academically, this idea finds expression in the 'internalizing complementary efficiencies' (ICE) argument, which holds that platforms generally benefit from the presence of third-party suppliers ('complementors') as they internalize their efficiencies (amongst others through commission fees). Accordingly, 'even a monopolist has incentives to provide access to its platform when it is efficient to do so, and to deny such access only when access is inefficient'.[608]

In response to allegations or investigations of exclusionary conduct, platforms themselves have advanced the incentives argument. Apple, for example, has held that 'it would not be rational to discriminate unfairly against third-party apps. If the third-party app offers better quality, Apple has no incentive to hinder the app in any way.'[609] Similarly, Amazon has claimed that it has no incentive to abuse sellers' trust by accessing their data because third-party sales make up nearly 60% of its sales.[610] Google, finally, holds that its demotion is aimed at low-quality sites, implying that excluding high-quality sites would not serve consumers and thus be irrational.[611]

605 Easterbrook (n 527) 19.

606 See Section 5.3.

607 Crocioni (n 555) 531.

608 For versions of this argument, see Barbara van Schewick, *Internet Architecture and Innovation* (MIT Press 2010) 223, and Joseph Farrell and Philip Weiser, 'Modularity, Vertical Integration, and Open Access Policies: Towards a Convergence of Antitrust and Regulation in the Internet Age' (2003) 17 Harvard Journal of Law & Technology 85, 89 (quote). See also van Gorp and de Bijl (n 410) 6 on how platforms seek to maximize value creation because they subsequently skim part of that value.

609 ACM, 'Market Study into Mobile App Stores' (Report, 2019) ACM/18/032693, 83–84.

610 US House of Representatives – Judiciary Subcommittee on Antitrust, 'Investigation of Competition in Digital Markets' (Majority Staff Report and Recommendations, 2020) (hereafter, 'House Judiciary Report') 276–77.

611 *Google Search (Shopping)* (n 348), para 655.

However, excluding suppliers is not *always* inefficient. At some point, a platform may find it efficient (ie profitable) to start favouring its own downstream products over those of suppliers. I described above how platforms *only* have such an incentive to self-preference when the gains from supplying their own products exceed the losses from not facilitating the distribution of competing products (eg foregone commission fees).[612] In this sense, vertical integration and subsequent self-preferencing constitute an alternative to simply increasing the price of the platform service (which is not always possible).

Importantly, the aforementioned 'gains' and 'losses' from exclusion (via self-preferencing) must be interpreted broadly. Firstly, gains do not only manifest themselves as *monetary* profits from the platform's downstream product. As explained, a platform's exclusion of downstream firms can also have *strategic* benefits, in particular (further) locking in consumers and erecting barriers to entry to safeguard upstream market power (defensive leveraging).[613] The benefits of cementing one's dominance in this way can be considerable.

Secondly, the conception of 'losses' as foregone fees is too narrow as well, given that it does not consider ripple effects on the ecosystem. If the exclusionary conduct of a platform concerns a supplier whose product (some) consumers value more than the platform's own substitute, it may decrease the quality of the platform *as a whole*, and consumers may turn to competing platforms. Moreover, suppliers – both those directly affected by self-preferencing and those who now fear it – may be discouraged from expending their efforts on a platform where they are or could be expropriated.[614] This is true not only in case of exclusion of suppliers but also in case of exploitation.[615] Jobs already knew that 'Apple lives in an ecosystem' and therefore 'needs help from other partners'.[616] And when Amazon allegedly copied a partner's video intercom, its founders viewed this as 'putting their whole ecosystem at risk and letting people know that they're not necessarily a trusted partner'.[617] The ripple effects of exclusionary conduct

612 See Section 3.3.1 (generally) and Section 2.3.1 (for an application to Amazon). For economic modelling, see Joseph Farrell and Michael Katz, 'Innovation, Rent Extraction, and Integration in Systems Markets' (2000) 48 The Journal of Industrial Economics 413. In addition to relative profit margins, diversion ratios are required to assess when this is the case.

613 See Section 2.2.2 (on ecosystem consumer lock-in) and Section 6.2.1 (on defensive leveraging).

614 Michael Cusumano, Annabelle Gawer and David Yoffie, *The Business of Platforms* (Harper Business 2019) 86–87 ('Innovation platform owners need to be careful not to hurt complementors' incentives to innovate by carelessly trampling over their businesses.'); Hye Kang, 'Intra-Platform Envelopment: The Coopetitive Dynamics Between the Platform Owner and Complementors' (2017) 4 <https://doi.org/10.5465/AMBPP.2017.11205abstract>.

615 AdlC and CMA, 'The Economics of Open and Closed Systems' (Report, 2014) 17 ('if the system owner's reputation is likely to suffer due to the exploitation of its installed base, it may refrain from raising its prices on lock-in users, in order to keep attracting new users'); Mehra (n 531) 893 ('users will lack incentives to adopt a network and may change their conduct if they believe that the network will exploit them without redress after adopting that network').

616 Walter Isaacson, *Steve Jobs* (Abacus 2015) 296–97 (continuing: 'Relationships that are destructive don't help anybody in this industry').

617 Ben Rubin, 'Amazon "Probably Copied Us" on Echo Show, Startup CEO Says' (*CNET*, 10 May 2017) <https://www.cnet.com/news/amazon-echo-show-alexa-probably-copied-us-nucleus-intercom-startup-ceo-says/> (the company in question, Nucleus, worked closely with Amazon, which was also its biggest investor).

can even extend further, namely, to the platform's activities in other layers of the ecosystem, which may be more profitable.[618]

While this preliminary calculus of (dis)incentives to exclude is complex and fact-specific, the principle that platform conduct is generally irrational stands. The long-term health of the ecosystem provides a significant, multilayered disincentive. The immediate monetary benefits from exclusion are meagre (especially when accounting for the fact that intermediation is a more profitable and scalable business than first-party supply);[619] the longer-term strategic benefits from exclusion (lock-in and as a barrier to entry) are larger but will generally not win out. That is, until market power enters the picture.

Market power provides the ability to distort competition, but it also strengthens the incentive to do so. Definitionally, market power implies a lack of alternatives for the platform's users, both businesses and consumers. Thus, when a platform with market power engages in exclusionary conduct, users' lack of outside options will often make them stick with the platform. Amazon sellers, for example, have complained that they cannot turn to alternative marketplaces, regardless of how much Amazon increases their costs of doing business.[620] Under such circumstances, the platform's disincentive to exclude is evidently smaller than in a competitive market; correspondingly, the incentive to exclude is more likely to win out.[621] In other words, a platform making its ecosystem less attractive is 'one of the luxuries that it is afforded by the weakness of the competitive constraints that it faces'.[622] Economic modelling of particular relevance to Apple, for example, shows that 'a gatekeeper device-seller facing potentially saturated demand for its device has the incentive and the ability to exclude from the market third-party suppliers of a service that consumers buy via its devices', ie apps.[623]

In conclusion, and not unlike the SMP theory to which it relates, the ICE argument does not have general validity. It cannot be assumed a priori that a platform has no incentive to exclude suppliers. In particular when it holds market power, it may have good business reasons to do so. The exact strength of the incentive is a factual matter that depends on a complex calculus of the gains and losses (interpreted broadly) of vertical integration and subsequent self-preferencing.

618 For example, if an app store operator is vertically integrated into OSs and/or devices, it has to worry about the chilling effects of self-preferencing not only in its store but also on the sale of devices, which may be more profitable (although this requires informed and rational consumers), see ACM, 'Market Study into Mobile App Stores' (n 609) 83–84 for Apple's explanation of this dynamic.

619 See eg Brad Stone, *Amazon Unbound* (Simon & Schuster 2021) 183 on how Amazon's third-party marketplace is higher-margin than its own retail efforts.

620 House Judiciary Report (n 610) 258–59.

621 Similarly, see van Gorp and de Bijl (n 410) 34–36 where they assess platform incentives in antitrust cases (*Microsoft*, *Google*, *Amazon*) *in the absence of dominance*, finding most forms of exclusionary conduct would no longer make sense.

622 OECD, 'Line of Business Restrictions' (Background Note) DAF/COMP/WP2(2020)1, 21. See also Lina Khan, 'The Separation of Platforms and Commerce' (2019) 119 Columbia Law Review 973, 1092–98, developing the exceptions to the ICE argument already recognized by van Schewick (n 608), and Farrell and Weiser (n 608).

623 Jorge Padilla, Joe Perkins and Salvatore Piccolo, 'Self-Preferencing in Markets with Vertically-Integrated Gatekeeper Platforms' (2020) 1 <https://ssrn.com/abstract=3701250>.

5.2.3 Platform Leveraging Effects

Like the effects of supermarkets' conduct explored above, the effects of platform leveraging are ambiguous. The relevant theory, which goes back at least two decades, focuses on two effects – each going in a different direction.[624] On the one hand, a platform's entry into the downstream market can improve *ex post* efficiency as competitive pressure from the platform reduces suppliers' price–cost margins. Such pressure, in the form of lower prices, can derive from the traditional efficiencies associated with vertical integration, such as the elimination of double marginalization. On the other hand, downstream entry by the platform may worsen *ex ante* efficiency by discouraging investment by suppliers. As already touched upon in the previous section, platform entry – and a fortiori subsequent self-preferencing – frustrates the expectations of ecosystem members. In such a situation of uncertainty, suppliers – both those affected by self-preferencing and those fearing it – may be discouraged from investing in a platform where they are or could be expropriated.[625]

Thus, there is a primary trade-off between short-term (price) effects and long-term (innovation) effects. This theoretical trade-off has been confirmed by empirical research on Amazon's marketplace: Zhu and Liu have found that 'Amazon's entry discourages affected third-party sellers from subsequently pursuing growth on the platform, [but] increases product demand and reduces shipping costs for consumers.'[626] Similarly, Wen and Zhu observed that Google's entry into app markets reduces innovation and increases prices from independent suppliers of the affected apps. However, incentives to innovate are not completely suppressed: affected developers tend to shift innovation to unaffected and new apps.[627] Other empirical research is largely consistent with these findings.[628]

While the above effects are in line with those of leveraging conduct generally, there are reasons to think leveraging is *more* harmful in platform markets. Firstly, this has to do with the network effects platform markets are subject to. Given that leveraging can help tip an adjacent market in favour of the dominant platform, such conduct may result in harm not only more quickly than in other cases, but also of greater magnitude.[629] The problem is not that the market ultimately tips (which can be efficient), but rather that the platform that wins the race is not determined by competition but is the result

624 See in particular Farrell and Katz (n 612). More recently, see van Gorp and de Bijl (n 410).

625 For an illustration involving app developers, see Manton Reece, 'Micro.blog Moving iOS App to React Native' (*Michael Tsai Blog*, 10 February 2020) <https://mjtsai.com/blog/2022/02/10/micro-blog-moving-ios-app-to-react-native/> ('[W]hy invest so much time in Apple-only frameworks when Apple could upend our business with a new App Store tax or other disruptions?').

626 Feng Zhu and Qihong Liu, 'Competing with Complementors: An Empirical Look at Amazon.com' (2018) 39 Strategic Management Journal 2618, 2630.

627 Wen Wen and Feng Zhu, 'Threat of Platform-Owner Entry and Complementor Responses? Evidence from the Mobile App Market' (2019) Strategic Management Journal 1336.

628 For an overview, see Feng Zhu, 'Friends or Foes? Examining Platform Owners' Entry into Complementors' Spaces' (2019) 28 Journal of Economics & Management Strategy 23. More recently, and providing inconsistent results (suppliers *increasing* their price), see Yiting Deng et al, 'Friend or Foe: When a Platform Enters the Market to Compete with its Third-Party Sellers' (2021) <https://ssrn.com/abstract=3979173>.

629 Crocioni (n 555) 450.

of anticompetitive conduct.[630] This has implications not only for the need for intervention, but also for its timing. Given that it is difficult, if not impossible, to reverse tipping after the fact, intervention need not wait until the exclusion of most or all competition, as the EC recognized in *Microsoft I*:

> [T]hat a company might survive in the face of anti-competitive conduct on the part of a dominant company does not prove the absence of a foreclosure effect … If it were otherwise, antitrust scrutiny in certain software markets would come too late as evidence of market impact would likely be concomitant to the 'tipping' of the market, that is to say, a technology would gain enough momentum so that the attendant network effects themselves would propel the technology to dominance.[631]

Further, particular vigilance is warranted when one can expect substantial innovation to take place in the adjacent market in question (both in terms of total amount of investment and value added to consumers) and when entry into the adjacent market could facilitate future entry into the platform's core market.[632]

In the first scenario (substantial innovation potential in the adjacent market), attention to digital innovation cycles is important. Think of how mainframe computers, dominated by IBM, gave way to personal computers, dominated by Microsoft, which in turn gave way to the web, dominated by Google, but also to mobile, dominated by Google and Apple.[633] The EC (and its colleagues in the US) intervened at the crucial shifts from one cycle to the next when incumbents sought to maintain or extend their market power through leveraging. Deterrence of innovation in 'technologies which Microsoft could conceivably take an interest in' was a specific concern in *Microsoft I*.[634] To prevent this, the EC served as a 'policeman at the elbow', which afforded entrants enough space to compete for dominance in the next wave of technology.[635] One of those next waves was mobile, where Google and others were given room to grow. Indeed, Gates has stated that, without the distraction of antitrust cases, 'instead of using Android today you would be using Windows Mobile'.[636] Now Apple, which – next to Google – rode the last cycle to success, is under scrutiny for trying to cement its App Store market power

630 ibid 469–70.

631 *Microsoft* (Case COMP/C-3/37.792) Commission Decision C(2004)900, para 946. See also Case C–52/09 *Konkurrensverket v TeliaSonera Sverige* EU:C:2011:83, para 108 ('Particularly in a rapidly growing market, Article 102 TFEU requires action as quickly as possible').

632 Crocioni (n 555) 489.

633 The incumbents of yore do not disappear: mainframe and PCs are still big business, and IBM and Microsoft still enjoy dominant (and profitable) positions; the focal point has simply shifted away from those segments.

634 *Microsoft* (n 631), para 983; confirmed in *Microsoft v Commission* (n 339), para 1088.

635 See Tim Wu, 'Tech Dominance and the Policeman at the Elbow' (2019) Columbia Public Law Research Paper 14-623 (focusing on IBM).

636 Tom Warren, 'Bill Gates Thinks Windows Mobile Would Have Beaten Android Without Microsoft's Antitrust Woes' (*The Verge*, 6 November 2019) <https://www.theverge.com/2019/11/6/20952370/>. For an analysis of Windows Mobile's failure, see Cusumano, Gawer and Yoffie (n 614) 129–37. For a contrasting perspective, see Benedict Evans, 'How to Lose a Monopoly' (*Benedict Evans*, 1 January 2020) <https://www.ben-evans.com/benedictevans/2020/01/01/microsoft-monopoly-and-dominance>.

at the expense of innovation such as web apps, cloud gaming and the metaverse.[637] In short, when a platform impedes not just a particular innovation but potentially a complete cycle, intervention is particularly justified.

In the second scenario (adjacent entry facilitating future entry into the platform's core market), the notion of disruptive innovation is important. When innovation is disruptive in the sense of Christensen, entrants start with a niche product and then continue to expand, perhaps one day challenging the platform through which they supply it.[638] As Tirole notes, the incumbent platform may want to block the entrant from gaining even a partial foothold in an adjacent market so as to pre-empt future competition in its core market.[639] Such defensive tying whereby the incumbent seeks to protect its legacy position can significantly hamper innovation.

Finally, note that impeding competition in platform-adjacent markets has ripple effects. For one, reduced competitive pressures in those markets will reduce not only third-party suppliers' but also the platform's incentives to innovate, both in the adjacent market *and* the core platform market.[640] In addition, exclusionary conduct in *specific* adjacent markets could give the platform a reputation for exclusion in adjacent markets.[641] Such a reputation could deter third-party innovation *more generally*, which could manifest itself in reduced venture capital investment, for example.[642]

5.3 Platform Leveraging: a Gap in the EU Legal Framework?

Market power gives platforms an *ability* to distort competition; in certain scenarios, platforms may also have an *incentive* to leverage that market power in adjacent markets. And the *effects* of such leveraging conduct can be significant, especially when it comes to innovation. Of course, none of that is a problem if EU competition law – as currently interpreted – effectively captures and deters platform leveraging. Therefore, this section checks whether the EU leveraging doctrine covers anticompetitive instances of platform leveraging. To the extent that is not the case, it puts forward a method to fill any gaps.

637 CMA, 'Mobile Ecosystems' (Market Study Interim Report, 2021), paras 5.130–142 on Apple's web app restrictions and paras 6.305–361 on Apple's cloud gaming restrictions, and *Epic Games v Apple*, no 4:20-cv-05640-YGR (ND Cal, 10 September 2021) on metaverse development impediments.

638 See Section 4.1.2.

639 Jean Tirole, 'Regulating the Disruptors' (*Project Syndicate*, 9 January 2019) <https://www.project-yndicate.org/onpoint/regulating-the-disrupters-by-jean-tirole-2019-01>.

640 *Microsoft* (n 631), para 725.

641 ibid, para 983.

642 See further Friso Bostoen, 'Venture Capital and Antitrust: On Exit Strategies, Killer Acquisitions, and Innovation Harms' (*CoRe Blog*, 23 April 2000) <https://www.lexxion.eu/coreblogpost/venture-capital-and-antitrust/>.

5.3.1 The Platform Leveraging Gap Hypothesis

Leveraging comprises various, more specific forms of abuse, including refusal to supply, margin squeeze, tying, and certain instances of (price) discrimination. Therefore, to check whether platform leveraging creates a gap, the question is: are there forms of anticompetitive self-preferencing conduct that are *not* captured by the *existing* leveraging abuses? To answer that question, *Google Shopping* provides a useful case study.

In its *Google Shopping* decision, the EC fined Google for 'leverag[ing] its market dominance in general internet search into a separate market, comparison shopping'.[643] Given that leveraging is a category rather than a form of abuse, the EC had to further qualify the abuse in question. Remember that this qualification question is not (just) theoretical, given that legal *qualifications* come with corresponding legal *tests*, and those tests determine the burden of proof that the plaintiff or authority has to fulfil when establishing an abuse of dominance.

Various aspects of Google's conduct complicated the qualification question. For one, Google *reserved* prominent display and positioning (at the top of the search results) to its own CSS, but it also actively *demoted* competing services. Moreover, Google's conduct was not price-based but could affect other competition parameters such as quality (of search display and positioning 'supply' to competing services, and of its entire engine to consumers), choice (of consumers), and long-run innovation in the comparison shopping space. In addition, given the operation of Google's search engine (crawling, indexing and ranking webpages), it had no contractual relations with the services it was said to foreclose.

Mindful of these complications, scholars sought to fit Google's conduct within one of the established qualifications – with widely varying results. Some leaned on refusal to supply.[644] But, while this could perhaps apply to reservation of prominent display and positioning, does it effectively capture the demotion? Scholars barely considered margin squeeze as an option. When mentioned, it was concluded swiftly that 'there is neither an upstream nor a downstream price, so there can be no margin squeeze'.[645] Tying received more support,[646] but what exactly are the two products being tied – general search and the shopping unit? And are consumers really forced to take both – can they not scroll down to alternatives? Discrimination also surfaced as a

643 EC, 'Commission fines Google €2.42 billion for abusing dominance as search engine by giving illegal advantage to own comparison shopping service' (Factsheet, 27 June 2017) MEMO/17/1785.

644 *Pro*, see eg Lisa Mays, 'The Consequences of Search Bias: How Application of the Essential Facilities Doctrine Remedies Google's Unrestricted Monopoly on Search in the United States and Europe' (2015) 83 George Washington Law Review 721; *contra*, see eg Anca Chirita, 'Google's Anti-Competitive and Unfair Practices in Digital Leisure Markets' (2015) 11 The Competition Law Review 109.

645 Renato Nazzini, '*Google* and the (Ever-stretching) Boundaries of Article 102 TFEU' (2015) 6 JECLAP 301, 307.

646 *Pro*, see eg Benjamin Edelman, 'Does Google Leverage Market Power Through Tying and Bundling?' (2015) 11 JCLE 365 and Yi Sng, 'Tying Conduct Under Article 102 TFEU: Can Intervention against Google Be Justified?' (2016) 37 ECLR 406.

candidate, though with few proponents.[647] Precedent on vertically integrated firms discriminating against downstream competitors is scarce and, where available, concerns discrimination based on *price*, which is absent here.

Google argued that, given that the EC essentially imposes on Google 'a duty to promote competition by allowing competing comparison shopping services to have access to a significant proportion of its general search results pages', it should prove a refusal to supply in line with *Bronner*.[648] This line of argument is not surprising given that *Bronner* sets a high bar to find conduct abusive. It is not illogical that Google qualified its conduct – if abusive at all – as the abuse with the most stringent legal test.

In the decision's section on the applicable legal test, the EC held that 'conduct consisting in the use of a dominant position on one market to extend that dominant position to one or more adjacent markets ... constitutes a well-established, independent, form of abuse falling outside the scope of competition on the merits'.[649] The EC thus qualified Google's conduct as an *independent* leveraging abuse rather than a refusal to supply.[650] The choice for this new abuse, with a standard effects test, implies that while the EC found Google's conduct anticompetitive, it found none of the existing leveraging qualifications fitting.

At the same time, the EC recognized the umbrella nature of leveraging, albeit implicitly. When setting out the legal principles of the case, it corroborated article 102 TFEU's prohibition of leveraging by referencing a variety of judgments.[651] However, while those judgments contain statements to the effect that leveraging can be abusive, every one of them concerns conduct that is qualified as a specific form of abuse, in particular refusal to supply (*Télémarketing*, *Microsoft I*), margin squeeze (*TeliaSonera*), tying (*Tetra Pak II*, *Microsoft I*), and discriminatory rebates (*Irish Sugar*).[652]

In short, what the EC did was elevate leveraging from a category to a specific form of abuse. It drew on precedent regarding the forms of abuse within that category to pass off the independent leveraging abuse as 'well-established'. Commentators disagreed with the EC's framing, instead calling the decision 'unprecedented'.[653]

---

647 *Contra*, see eg Chirita (n 644) and Nazzini (n 645).

648 ibid, para 645, referencing *Oscar Bronner v Mediaprint* (n 536).

649 *Google Search (Shopping)* (n 348), para 649.

650 The EC concretized the leveraging abuse as 'favouring': Google's conduct falls outside the scope of competition on the merits as it more favourably positions and displays its own CSS in its search results compared to those of competitors – a diversion of traffic that is capable of having, or likely to have, anti-competitive effects, see ibid, para 341. However, that concretization did not change the legal qualification; rather, it was meant to show how the legal test of leveraging is fulfilled.

651 *Google Search (Shopping)* (n 348), para 334 (fn 349).

652 *CBEM v CLT and IPB ('Télémarketing')* (n 559), para 27; *Tetra Pak v Commission* (n 558), para 25; *Irish Sugar v Commission* (n 561), para 166; *Konkurrensverket v TeliaSonera* (n 631), para 85; *Microsoft v Commission* (n 339), para 1344.

653 See eg Alfonso Lamadrid de Pablo, 'Google Shopping Decision – First Urgent Comments' (*Chillin'Competition*, 27 June 2017) <https://chillingcompetition.com/2017/06/27/> and Bo Vesterdorf and Kyriakos Fountoukakos,

5.3.2 Ascertaining and – if Need Be – Filling the Platform Leveraging Gap

Both 'well-established' and 'unprecedented' are hyperboles to describe the EC's decision and in particular its conceptualization of the abuse, ie as 'leveraging' (further concretized as 'favouring'). At the same time, the EC unquestionably came up with a new form of abuse. This is not a problem in itself: if the type of anticompetitive conduct is novel and existing qualifications are thus unsuitable, the EC may add new forms of abuse to article 102 TFEU's non-exhaustive list.[654] The EC's fault lies mainly in the way it failed to engage with that novelty.[655] Apart from some references to leveraging cases, it did not fit its decision within the existing legal framework. Insofar as the EC tried to square Google's conduct with established forms of abuse, that exercise did not make it into the decision. Indeed, the decision even confused the existing framework, given that it made leveraging both a category of abuse *and* an independent form of abuse within that category.

If the conduct at issue in *Google Shopping* were unique, this would not be a larger problem. However, many cases concern self-preferencing conduct that similarly escapes simple classification. Investigations into Google's treatment of other downstream competitors are already underway.[656] Investigations into Apple's App Store concern, in part, how it treats competing apps differently from its own apps.[657] An investigation into Amazon, which ended with commitments, explicitly concerned 'the possible preferential treatment of Amazon's own retail offers' on its Marketplace.[658] The EC appears determined to continue pursuing these cases. As Commissioner Vestager stated:

> [M]any platform businesses act as both player and referee – they run a platform, and also compete with other companies that rely on that platform. There's an obvious conflict of interest here, an obvious temptation to adjust the way the platform works, to favour their own services ahead of others.[659]

In addition to the EC, NCAs are pursuing similar cases, sometimes explicitly referencing *Google Shopping*.[660] A framework is thus necessary to solve such cases. As mentioned above, such a framework should consist of legal qualifications – more specifically,

---

'An Appraisal of the Remedy in the Commission's *Google Search (Shopping)* Decision and a Guide to its Interpretation in Light of an Analytical Reading of the Case Law' (2018) 9 JECLAP 3, 3. Note that all authors have advised Google, either in the *Shopping* case or in a different case.

654 Case 6–72 *Continental Can v Commission* EU:C:1973:22, para 26; *Tetra Pak v Commission* (n 558), para 37.

655 See similarly Alison Jones, Brenda Sufrin and Niamh Dunne, *EU Competition Law: Text, Cases, and Materials* (OUP 2019) 533.

656 *Google Jobs* (Case AT.40592) and *Google Local* (Case AT.40585).

657 *Apple – App Store Practices (music streaming)* (Case AT.40437), *Apple – App Store Practices (e-books/audiobooks)* (Case AT.40652) and *Apple – App Store Practices* (Case AT.40716).

658 EC, 'Commission sends Statement of Objections to Amazon for the use of non-public independent seller data and opens second investigation into its e-commerce business practices' (press release, 10 November 2020) IP/20/2077 (quote); *Amazon Marketplace* and *Amazon Buy Box* (n 369).

659 Margrethe Vestager, 'A Digital Future That Works for Europeans' (Business Forum of the German Ambassadors' Conference, Berlin, 27 August 2019).

660 See Section 9.1.3.1.

a taxonomy of such qualifications – and corresponding legal tests. The way to arrive at those is through error cost analysis.[661] It must be acknowledged, however, that this theory offers no exact science – indeed, it is perhaps more art than science. Let's think through each component.

The first step is to *identify* the potential abuse, ie to legally *qualify* the conduct in question. Legal qualifications can be thought of as Platonic ideals: conduct observed in the real world may reflect those ideals, but never perfectly. The task is to find the legal qualification that the conduct corresponds to *most* closely. If it corresponds closely *enough* to the legal qualification, one can start assessing the conduct against the applicable legal test. If it does not correspond closely enough to an existing legal qualification, there are two options: if the conduct truly is anticompetitive, then the taxonomy of qualifications is incomplete and needs to be adapted; otherwise, the conduct is simply not abusive. Thus, in order to know whether self-preferencing exposes a gap in the current taxonomy, one first needs to go over the existing leveraging abuses to determine the exact scope of those qualifications.

Once the abuse has been identified, the next step is to *test* the conduct in line with its qualification. Legal tests serve to structure the assessment. The more structured the test, the clearer – and thus more legally certain – the assessment. That same structure makes the test more administrable for authorities and judges. With its four separate conditions, for example, the legal test for tying is on the more structured end of the spectrum.[662] Less defined is the EC's two-tiered leveraging test, holding that the use of a dominant position on one market to extend that dominant position to an adjacent market is abusive when it is likely to have anticompetitive effects.

However, the differences between the forms of abuse and corresponding legal tests must be put into perspective. Firstly, while some forms of abuse find specific support in one of the limbs of article 102 TFEU (eg discrimination in limb (c) and tying in limb (d)), the EC often relies on article 102 TFEU *generally* in addition to a specific limb to avoid semantic discussions.[663] The GC has similarly downplayed the importance of specific legal bases, holding that 'bundling by an undertaking in a dominant position may also infringe Article [102 TFEU] where it does not correspond to the example given in Article [102(d) TFEU]'.[664]

Secondly, while a more defined legal test helps structure the analysis, the most important aspect of any test is the 'anticompetitiveness threshold', which can be broken down into two components.[665] First, which *probability* of harm must be shown? That

661 See Section 4.2.2.

662 See Section 6.

663 See eg *Microsoft v Commission* (n 339), para 849.

664 ibid, para 861.

665 On anticompetitive effects, see Pablo Ibáñez Colomo, 'Anticompetitive Effects in EU Competition Law' (2021) 17 JCLE 309.

anticompetitive effects are 'plausible', 'likely' or even 'certain'? These various degrees of probability can be assessed prospectively (at that point, the effects are 'potential') or retrospectively (in which case not only potential but also 'actual' effects can be established).[666] Second, which *severity* of harm must be shown? Does a 'competitive disadvantage' suffice, or can there be no abuse without the 'elimination of all competition', for example?[667] The more likely it is that a form of conduct is anticompetitive (based on economic evidence and practical experience), the lower the threshold (in other words, the milder the burden of proof).[668]

While various forms of abuse continue to exist, a rift has emerged between them. There can be no abuse without a restriction of competition, but – as will be further explored in the following sections – two different anticompetitiveness thresholds have become dominant.[669] On the one hand, refusal to supply is subject to an enhanced effects test: the plaintiff or authority needs to prove the elimination of all competition/indispensability – a high bar.[670] By contrast, other leveraging abuses (margin squeeze, tying, discrimination) are subject to a standard effects test: the plaintiff or authority only needs to prove they are likely to have anticompetitive effects – a lower bar.[671]

The relative importance of the qualification vs the legal test depends on how much those tests diverge. Given that most leveraging abuses require the same anticompetitiveness threshold, the choice between margin squeeze/discrimination/tying – while not a free one – may not be determinative for the outcome of a case. But refusal to supply sets a higher bar, which is why defendants tend to prefer that qualification and authorities/plaintiffs tend to avoid it. This also shows that qualifying and testing are not as independent as the theory would suggest: as in *Google Shopping*, parties on opposing sides may strategically qualify the abuse with the test in mind.[672]

The above does not mean that one should simplify the leveraging category into refusal to supply and 'other forms of leveraging'. Economists may favour a broad

666 ibid 313. See also Case C–549/10 P *Tomra Systems v Commission* EU:C:2012:221, para 79 and Case C–413/14 P *Intel v Commission* EU:C:2016:788, Opinion of AG Wahl, para 114, contrasting conduct with 'actual' effects and conduct 'capable' of such effects (and thus aligning 'potential' effects and conduct 'capable' of such effects), which shows how the probability of harm and the temporal perspective are related (or perhaps conflated). Note that 'potential' effects can be situated on a spectrum between 'hypothetical' and 'concrete', see Case C–23/14 *Post Danmark v Konkurrencerådet* EU:C:2015:651, paras 65–66.

667 One could rephrase 'competitive disadvantage' and 'elimination of competition' in terms of anticompetitive effects with varying probability, which shows their interrelation. That is why authorities and courts often discuss the probability and severity of harm in the same breath.

668 This is only logical: if theoretical evidence/practical experience shows that a practice is *almost always* anticompetitive, it does not make sense to burden the EC with proving *with absolute certainty* that it is also anticompetitive *in every specific instance*.

669 See Pablo Ibáñez Colomo, 'Legal Tests in EU Competition Law: Taxonomy and Operation' (2019) 10 JECLAP 424, 426–28.

670 *Oscar Bronner v Mediaprint* (n 536), para 41.

671 On margin squeeze, see *Konkurrensverket v TeliaSonera* (n 631), para 64; on tying, see *Microsoft v Commission* (n 339), para 1035; on discrimination, see Case C–525/16 *MEO v Autoridade da Concorrência* EU:C:2018:270, paras 26, 28 and 37.

672 This is true not only when arguing existing qualifications but also when coming up with new qualifications.

leveraging abuse as it affords them leeway to show anticompetitive effects as opposed to being boxed into a narrower form of abuse that the anticompetitive effects must accord with.[673] However, the structured analysis offered by specific forms of abuse (or rather their legal tests) still offers benefits in terms of legal certainty (from the firms' perspective) and administrability (from the enforcers' and courts' perspective).

5.4 Conclusion

Self-preferencing conduct by online platforms can be anticompetitive. However, growing the ecosystem by integrating vertically is also a fundamental business strategy of platforms.[674] Even when a platform does so by relying on its upstream market power, such conduct can generate significant efficiencies and thus be procompetitive. That is why we need a sophisticated rule – or set of rules – to distinguish between anti- and procompetitive instances of leveraging. In the EU competition law framework, this translates to a clear taxonomy of abuse qualifications and corresponding legal tests. That taxonomy includes, of course, the various rules targeting leveraging already in existence (in particular, the doctrines of tying, refusal to supply and margin squeeze). However, those rules need to be updated given the particular (economic) features of online platforms. Therefore, Sections 6–8 cover the main forms of leveraging, shortly going over their fundamentals but focusing on the extent to which they capture anticompetitive instances of platform leveraging. Borrowing from AG Kokott, this exercise is not 'influenced so much by current thinking ("Zeitgeist") or ephemeral trends, but [has] regard rather to the legal foundations on which the prohibition of abuse of a dominant position rests in EU law'.[675] For that reason, a balance is sought between the existing framework (and its interpretation by the European courts) and the new challenges posed by platforms.

A detailed analysis of the existing rules as they apply to platforms will confirm or reject the hypothesis that platform leveraging creates a gap in the EU legal framework. Should that gap be confirmed, it can be filled either by (further) reinterpreting existing forms of abuse or by adding a new form of abuse to article 102 TFEU's non-exhaustive list. That new form can be either a more open leveraging norm (à la *Google Shopping*) or a more targeted form of abuse but should, in either case, be consistent with the legal framework of article 102 TFEU.[676] Designing the corresponding legal test – and in

673 At a 2021 conference, an economist at DG COMP suggested this helps explain (or at the very least is in line with) the EC's choice for a broad, independent leveraging abuse in *Google Shopping*.

674 See Section 2.2.2.

675 Case C–23/14 *Post Danmark v Konkurrencerådet* EU:C:2015:343, Opinion of AG Kokott, para 4.

676 The EC shares the concern that new forms of abuse are 'consistent with the legal framework of Article 102 TFEU' (and that 'the rules must be knowable in advance'), see *Google Search (Shopping)* (n 348), para 646 (internal quotation marks omitted).

particular setting the anticompetitiveness threshold – is a central part of this exercise. Ideally, the final test finds the right balance between the competing risks of false negatives and positives, all the while providing legal certainty and remaining administrable. Section 9 finds that the platform leveraging gap, which does indeed exist, is best filled by the abuse of 'disruptive discrimination'. However, enforcers and plaintiffs should only have recourse to that abuse under specific conditions and taking account of certain limiting principles.

6
TYING

Tying is the most traditional form of leveraging, which has led much of the leveraging debate to centre around this abuse. As discussed above, the Chicago School focused its criticism of leveraging conduct on tying.[677] This form of abuse has not lost relevance in the digital economy, as many (potential) leveraging abuses have been examined through the lens of tying. This goes for competition authorities: the EC's *Microsoft* cases of the 2000s were both based on tying behaviour (as was the DOJ's in the US); in the more recent *Android* case, the EC also qualified one of Google's abuses as tying. It also goes for academia: in *Google Shopping*, for example, many commentators supported a theory of harm based on tying,[678] even though the EC ended up relying on a more general theory of leveraging. Tying is therefore both an established and a controversial form of leveraging in digital markets.

This section starts by going over tying's different varieties and positioning the concept within the leveraging context (6.1) before looking at the specificities of tie-ins in platform markets (6.2). Next, the section examines the legal status of tying, with particular attention to its evolving legal test (6.3). Given that said legal test requires the existence of distinct products and anticompetitive foreclosure, the following two sections are dedicated to those conditions (6.4–5). Before concluding (6.7), the penultimate section deals with procompetitive justifications, which are available for every abuse but deserve particular analysis in a tying context (6.6).

6.1 Tying Theory

Tying refers to situations where customers that purchase one product (the tying product) must also purchase another product from the dominant undertaking (the tied product).[679] A distinction can be made between 'static ties', in which the quantity of the tied product

---

677 See Section 5.1.2.

678 See eg Edward Iacobucci and Francesco Ducci, 'The Google Search Case in Europe: Tying and the Single Monopoly Profit Theorem in Two-Sided Markets' (2019) 47 European Journal of Law and Economics 15.

679 Exclusionary Conduct Guidance Paper (n 461), para 48.

is fixed, and 'dynamic ties', in which the quantity of the tied product is variable.[680] A related practice is '(pure) bundling', in which case products are only sold jointly in fixed proportions.[681]

Tying is the prototypical leveraging abuse. Even before the EU competition regime had matured, leveraging concerns informed a hostile approach to tying. In *Times-Picayune*, the US Supreme Court described 'the wielding of monopolistic leverage' as 'the essence of illegality in tying agreements'.[682] From a consumer (welfare) perspective, the issue is one of choice: as the Court held in *Jefferson Parish*, a consumer's 'freedom to select the best bargain in the second market is impaired by his need to purchase the tying product'.[683] Zooming out to the broader market, the risk is that 'a potentially inferior product may be insulated from competitive pressures'.[684] But it is competition itself – not power in an adjacent market – that should serve as the process to decide which product the market (ie the amalgamation of consumers) prefers. Tying thus decidedly conflicts with competition on the merits.

In the EU, tying received an explicit basis in article 102(d) TFEU (and its predecessors), which prohibits 'making the conclusion of contracts subject to acceptance by the other parties of supplementary obligations which, by their nature or according to commercial usage, have no connection with the subject of such contracts'. The explicit legal basis is remarkable, especially given that most other exclusionary (and a fortiori leveraging) abuses are categorized under the more general-purpose article 102(b) TFEU, which prohibits 'limiting production, markets or technical development to the prejudice of consumers'.

6.2 Tying in Platform Markets

Tying cases, while generally rare, have been relatively prevalent in platform markets. The reason is that the economic infrastructure offered by platforms uniquely lends itself to tying (Section 6.2.1). Because of the incidence of tying in digital markets, its potential anticompetitive effects in that context have received outsized academic attention, which has led to clear theories of harm (Section 6.2.2).

6.2.1 Methods of Tying in Platform Markets

Digital markets are a particularly attractive target for tying strategies.[685] This goes back to the business strategy of platforms, which tend to initially pursue growth over profits

680 Van den Bergh (n 573) 316–17.

681 In 'mixed bundling' scenarios, products are also sold separately, but the price of the bundle is lower than the sum of the prices of the separate products. The EC assesses such conduct under the predatory pricing rather than the raising rivals' costs paradigm, see Exclusionary Conduct Guidance Paper (n 461), paras 59–61.

682 *Times-Picayune v United States* (n 554) 611.

683 *Jefferson Parish Hosp v Hyde* 466 US 2, 15 (1984).

684 ibid 14.

685 See similarly OECD, 'Abuse of Dominance in Digital Markets' (Background Note, 2020), 41–43.

and – after having achieved critical mass – build an ecosystem of interrelated products around their core offering.[686] The core platform serves as a foundation or 'building block' for complements, which is why expansion often benefits from economies of scope. A distinction can be made between on-platform and cross-platform expansion.[687] On-platform expansion entails adding matching functionality to the platform interface (eg a hotel booking platform adding car rentals). Cross-platform expansion implies developing an additional platform, but with a potential link between the two (eg universal sign-in account of a social media conglomerate with different networks).[688] Both strategies can be successful, but the platform will be able to transfer their user base more effectively to the new product through on-platform expansions, which do not disrupt the built-up indirect network effects.

Platform markets are prone to tying behaviour not only because of expansionist tendencies, but also because of the methods their digital infrastructure allows for. Traditional ties are contractual, meaning that customers who purchase the tying product undertake to also purchase the tied product (eg an obligation to purchase/use the manufacturer's capsules with its coffee machine). In digital markets, ties are often technical, meaning the dominant firm integrates the tying and tied products, or makes the tying product incompatible with competing complements.[689]

First, *integration* is prevalent in digital markets thanks to products' plasticity and modularity. Embedding new products in the core platform is thus particularly feasible – all the more so given the near-zero marginal cost of many digital products. In software settings, *preinstallation* can be conceived as a soft form of integration: consumers can still use other products, but – given consumers' status quo bias (a tendency to stick with the default)[690] – are less likely to do so.[691]

Second, platforms can work with the compatibility of their ecosystem's different components. In an analogue world, *incompatibility* can be achieved through product design (eg designing a coffeemaker so that it only works with certain capsules). However, it is often possible for competitors to replicate a compatible tied product.[692] In digital markets, by contrast, technical ties may be more challenging to circumvent,

686 See Section 2.2.

687 Daniel Mândrescu, 'Tying and Bundling by Online Platforms: Distinguishing Between Lawful Expansion Strategies and Anti-Competitive Practices' (2021) 40 CLSR 1, 8.

688 The Bundeskartellamt investigated a potential tie between the Oculus virtual reality headset and Facebook platform. Meta responded by no longer requiring a Facebook account to use the Oculus headset. See Bundeskartellamt, Case B6–55/20, *Linkage of Meta Quest (formerly Oculus) with the Facebook network*, 23 November 2022 (Case Summary).

689 Exclusionary Conduct Guidance Paper (n 461), fn 33. Note that technical ties – especially those achieved through integration – are more difficult to reverse. Apart from complicating the remedy, the difficult-to-reverse nature also signals commitment, which many theories of harm rely on, see Chiara Fumagalli, Massimo Motta and Claudio Calcagno, *Exclusionary Practices: The Economics of Monopolization and Abuse of Dominance* (CUP 2018) 428.

690 Daniel Kahneman, Jack Knetsch and Richard Thaler, 'Anomalies: The Endowment Effect, Loss Aversion, and Status Quo Bias' (1991) 5 Journal of Economic Perspectives 193, 197–99.

691 See *Google Android* (n 352), paras 791–93 for an illustration.

692 Intellectual property laws may limit such replication.

as the competitor in the tied market then has to reverse engineer code for software to be compatible. This is a more difficult undertaking, especially when the tying firm intentionally designs its code so as to exclude compatibility rather than simply not facilitating it (through APIs). Compatibility comes in various forms. Some approximate integration, ie when the platform is only compatible with its own components.[693] Others leave more room for third parties, ie when the platform's components just work better together.

Finally, given that platforms function as recommendation engines, platforms can *nudge* users to take an additional product from them, eg via the ranking of search results. Consumers often accept the platform's ranking without much thought given that they trust platforms to have their best interests at heart and thus highlight the 'best' options.[694] For suppliers, the ranking of their products determines their commercial success. Thus, suppliers may be induced to take additional services from the platform if their product ranking depends on it.[695]

The problem, from a legal perspective, is that the above scenarios do not fit neatly with the traditional idea of tying. Firstly, the plasticity of digital products and their subsequent integration puts into question whether there are (or were) two separate products in the first place. Secondly, consumers and suppliers may not be forced to use the second product but may simply be induced to do so by the platform's digital architecture. Of course, these questions do not even arise if the conduct does not appear anticompetitive in the first place, which is why the next section surveys the economic research on digital tie-ins.

6.2.2 Anticompetitive Effects of Tying in Platform Markets

As recounted above, the Chicago School made tying the focal point of its economic critique of leveraging.[696] The SMP theory on which it relied was subsequently restricted to a set of assumptions by the post-Chicago School starting in the 1980s (eg fixed proportions, perfectly competitive tying and tied markets). From the end of the 1990s onwards, this line of scholarship got another boost, with authors focusing on the effects of tying in digital markets specifically. Triggering renewed interest was the US antitrust case against Microsoft, which focused on an apparent tie between Windows OS and its web browser Internet Explorer, to the detriment of other web browsers, ie a scenario of intra-platform exclusion.[697]

693 For example, only Apple's own payment services can make use of the iOS platform's NFC functionality – a restriction that is being investigated, see EC, 'Commission sends Statement of Objections to Apple over practices regarding Apple Pay' (press release, 2 May 2022) IP/22/2764.

694 See *Google Search (Shopping)* (n 348), paras 454–61 for an illustration.

695 See AGCM, Case A528, *Amazon*, 9 December 2021 for an illustration.

696 See Section 5.1.2.

697 This section leaves to the side exploitative theories of tying, which rely on inter-product price discrimination, intra-product price discrimination or the extraction of individual consumer surplus.

A first theory relies on foreclosure in the tied market. This theory was developed significantly by Eisenmann, Parker and Van Alstyne, who introduced the concept of 'platform envelopment'.[698] Platform envelopment entails 'entry by one platform provider in another's market by bundling its own platform's functionality with that of the target's so as to leverage shared user relationships and common components.'[699] The authors find that platforms routinely violate the Chicago assumption of perfect competition in the tied market, in particular due to economies of scale and network effects, which means that bundling becomes a profitable strategy.[700] They find that bundling is particularly likely to succeed when it involves complementary products with significant user overlap.[701] Bundling can also succeed in case of weak substitutes or unrelated platforms when bundling offers significant economies of scope or when users overlap significantly and economies of scope are high, respectively.[702] Condorelli and Padilla have built on the work of Eisenmann et al, showing that bundling unrelated platforms can be profitable even in the absence of direct economies of scope.[703]

A second theory focuses on foreclosure not in the tied but in the tying market. Carlton and Waldman showed 'how a firm that is currently a monopolist in its primary market can use tying of a complementary product to preserve its monopoly position by deterring future entry into the primary market'.[704] This strategy is of particular importance in innovative industries, and its success depends on there being economies of scale or network effects in the tied market – realistic assumptions in the platform economy.[705] Fumagalli and Motta have extended this work, showing that incumbents may even have an incentive to engage in exclusionary tying even when entry into the primary market cannot be deterred because it puts them in a favourable position when such entry does occur.[706] Choi and Stefanadis have also shown that in markets where entry requires a risky upfront R&D investment, tying makes a successful entry in the primary market dependent on success in the complementary market (and vice versa).[707] The risk of entry thus increases, which reduces entrants' incentive to invest and innovate.

698 Thomas Eisenmann, Geoffrey Parker and Marshall Van Alstyne, 'Platform Envelopment' (2011) 32 Strategic Management Journal 1270. See also Geoffrey Parker, Marshall Van Alstyne and Sangeet Choudary, *Platform Revolution* (Norton 2016) 222–23.

699 Eisenmann, Parker and Van Alstyne (n 698) 1271.

700 ibid 1280, building on Whinston's seminal article referenced above (n 579) as well as newer work of his, see Michael Whinston, 'Exclusivity and Tying in U.S. v. Microsoft: What We Know, and Don't Know' (2001) 15 Journal of Economic Perspectives 2001.

701 Eisenmann, Parker and Van Alstyne (n 698) 1279–80.

702 ibid 1280–82. Multihoming can counteract the anticompetitive effects of tying to some extent, see Jay Pil Choi, 'Tying in Two-Sided Markets with Multi-Homing' (2010) 58 The Journal of Industrial Economics 607.

703 They focus on the specific case of 'privacy policy tying', see Daniele Condorelli and Jorge Padilla, 'Harnessing Platform Envelopment in the Digital World' (2020) 16 JCLE 143. Taking an explicit intra-platform perspective, see also Kang (n 614).

704 Dennis Carlton and Michael Waldman, 'The Strategic Use of Tying to Preserve and Create Market Power in Evolving Industries' (2002) 33 The RAND Journal of Economics 194, 194.

705 ibid 195–96.

706 Chiara Fumagalli and Massimo Motta, 'Tying in Evolving Industries, when Future Entry Cannot Be Deterred' (2020) 73 International Journal of Industrial Organization 1. They find that tying is a profitable strategy if the entrant's advantage in the primary market is large enough.

707 Jay Pil Choi and Christodoulos Stefanadis, 'Tying, Investment, and the Dynamic Leverage Theory' (2001) 32 The RAND Journal of Economics 52, 53 (explaining: 'If only one entrant succeeds, the incumbent can

Salop captures a related idea when describing how, through tying, 'the monopolist forces entrants to enter both markets simultaneously'.[708]

In short, the assumptions of the SMP theory are unlikely to be fulfilled in case of online platforms, which can give them an incentive to engage in tying. Whether such conduct is illegal depends on the legal test for tying, which has evolved over the years, in line with economic insight and the particulars of digital markets. However, it is important to stress that any legal test – especially in case of tying, which often generates efficiencies – should be accompanied by an economically rigorous theory of harm, which is why the literature described in this section is so crucial.

6.3 Tying's Evolving Legal Status

As appropriate in competition law, the legal status of tying evolved in tandem with the understanding of its economics. The initial scepticism was most apparent in the US. In 1949 still, the Supreme Court held that: 'Tying agreements serve hardly any purpose beyond the suppression of competition.'[709] As touched upon above,[710] this scepticism was rooted in a concern for leveraging of market power: tying 'den[ies] competitors free access to the market for the tied product not because the party imposing the tying requirements has a better product or a lower price, but because of his power or leverage in another market'.[711] Such a distortion of competition – and the corresponding restriction of consumer choice – justified a per se illegality rule under US antitrust law.[712] However, while often described as per se, the rule was only ever 'quasi' per se: before declaring a tying arrangement illegal, the court would determine whether (i) the firm has market power in the tying product market; (ii) the tying and tied products are separate; (iii) the tying product cannot be bought without the tied product; (iv) the amount of sales in the tied product is non-trivial; and (v) there are no offsetting efficiencies.[713] Given these various conditions, the quasi-per se rule has been called a misnomer; rather, US tying doctrine provides a structured rule of reason test.[714]

---

use its monopoly position in the other component to practice a "price squeeze," capturing a share in the value of the entrant's innovation').

708 Salop, 'Economic Analysis of Exclusionary Vertical Conduct: Where Chicago Has Overshot the Mark' (n 573) 147.

709 *Standard Oil v United States* 337 US 293, 305 (1949).

710 See Section 6.1.

711 *Northern Pacific Railway v United States* 356 US 1, 6 (1958) (continuing: 'At the same time, buyers are forced to forego their free choice between competing products.').

712 *Eastman Kodak v Image Technical Servs* 504 US 451, 487 (1992) (Scalia, Dissenting) ('[T]he stated rationale for our *per se* rule has varied little over the years. When the defendant has genuine "market power" in the tying product – the power to raise price by reducing output – the tie potentially enables him to extend that power into a second distinct market, enhancing barriers to entry in each.').

713 *Jefferson Parish Hosp v Hyde* (n 683). If these conditions are not met, 'an antitrust violation can be established only by evidence of an unreasonable restraint on competition in the relevant market.'

714 Elhauge and Geradin (n 574) 613–14.

US tying doctrine has influenced its EU counterpart. The TFEU's tying provision, article 102(d), developed into a doctrine mostly through the *Hilti* and *Tetra Pak II* cases. In the former case, Hilti, a manufacturer of nail guns, explosive cartridge strips and nails, refused to sell distributors cartridges without a corresponding quantity of nails.[715] In the latter case, Tetra Pak obliged customers of its filling machines to also purchase the cartons used with those machines.[716] The focus of the EC (and the European courts confirming its decisions) was similar in both cases. Firstly, it attached considerable importance to the firms' market power in the tying product, ie cartridges (a market share of 70–80%) and filling machines (a market share of 90%), respectively. Tying firms tend to argue that their products form 'an indivisible whole', which is why, secondly, the EC took care to ascertain that the products at issue were separate. It did so by examining commercial usage, in particular the independent supply of the tied product, ie nails and cartons, respectively.[717] Thirdly, the EC noted how suppliers of the tying product were excluded from the market, but it did not economically establish such effects. Rather, it presumed them based on the tying firms' high market shares in the tying market,[718] while focusing on how the conduct deprived consumers of a choice of suppliers. Finally, in both cases the EC assessed whether the tie was justified based on quality or safety considerations but ended up rejecting those arguments.[719]

The EU case law thus suggests a legal test for tying requiring that (i) the firm is dominant in the tying market; (ii) customers cannot obtain the tying product without the tied product ('coercion'); (iii) the tying and tied products are separate; (iv) the tie forecloses competition; and (v) the tie is not objectively justified. The conditions of this legal test remain unchanged, but their interpretation has further evolved over the years. The views of the Chicago School, ie that tying was generally not anticompetitive but reflected efficiencies,[720] demanded that the foreclosure and justification limbs of the legal test be taken more seriously. However, this did not happen until enforcers were faced with tying cases in the digital economy.

Tying conduct was front and centre in the *Microsoft* cases pursued on both sides of the Atlantic. Preinstallation agreements between Microsoft and OEMs obliged the latter to install not only the Windows OS but also additional applications, in particular

---

715 *Eurofix-Bauco v Hilti* (Cases IV/30.787 and 31.488) Commission Decision 88/138/EEC [1988] OJ L65/19; Case T–30/89 *Hilti v Commission* EU:T:1991:70. Various other strategies supported this exclusionary conduct, including reducing discounts for orders of cartridges without nails, not supplying cartridges to independent nail manufacturers, and delaying or frustrating the grant of patent licences for cartridges by fixing high royalty rates.

716 *Tetra Pak II* (IV/31043) Commission Decision [1992] OJ L72/1; Case T–83/91 *Tetra Pak v Commission* EU:T:1994:246; Case C–333/94 P *Tetra Pak v Commission* (n 558).

717 *Eurofix-Bauco v Hilti* (n 715), para 57; *Hilti v Commission* (n 715), para 68. *Tetra Pak II* (n 716), para 119; Case T–83/91 *Tetra Pak v Commission* (n 716), para 82.

718 This approach closely resembles the quasi-per se rule governing tying in the US, although the latter includes an additional condition of non-trivial sales in the tied product – a sort of anticompetitive effects *de minimis*.

719 *Eurofix-Bauco v Hilti* (n 715), paras 87–96; *Hilti v Commission* (n 715), paras 115–19; *Tetra Pak II* (n 716), para 119; Case T–83/91 *Tetra Pak v Commission* (n 716), paras 83–84.

720 See Sections 5.1.2 and 6.2.2.

Internet Explorer (IE) and Windows Media Player (WMP).[721] The primary concern was that Microsoft was foreclosing developers of competing browsers and media players, which could pose future threats to its OS monopoly.

In the US, the case centred around the tie between Windows and IE. The district court found Microsoft's conduct to amount to monopolization under a (quasi-)per se analysis,[722] but its judgment was reversed in part on appeal. In its appeal judgment, the circuit court 'carv[ed out] an exception to the per se rule when the tying product is platform software'.[723] This 'platform software exception', and its deviation from precedent, was justified for two reasons.[724] First, integration is common in platform software markets, and the 'separate products' test fails to screen out those cases where such integration is efficient. Second, platform software markets are pervasively innovative, and tying may thus produce efficiencies that were not factored in when the per se rule was adopted.

In the EU, the EC focused on the tie between Windows and WMP in its first Microsoft case, but it too reconsidered its doctrine. The EC described how foreclosure used to be presumed from the fact that a product was tied to a dominant product, but noted there are good reasons not to presume that the tie in question is by its very nature liable to foreclose competition.[725] The EC thus distanced itself from the (quasi-)per se approach to tying in *Hilti* and *Tetra Pak II*. The GC also picked up on this, repeating that the EC 'examined the actual effects which the bundling had already had on the market and the way in which that market was likely to evolve, rather than merely considering – as it normally does in cases of abusive tying – that the tying has by its nature a foreclosure effect.'[726] The case did not make it up to the EU's highest court, but the absence of an ECJ judgment does not matter much, given that the EC bound *itself* to carry out an effects analysis in tying cases. It did so first in technology markets, through its *Microsoft* decisions,[727] but later also more generally, in its Guidance Paper[728] and subsequent case law.[729] The GC is bound to hold the EC to the standard it set for itself. In *Google Android*, for example, it commented on how the EC 'correctly found ... that close examination of the actual effects ... was required before it could be concluded

721 Despite these agreements, the tie was enforced largely technically. Not only could IE not be uninstalled, sometimes it even overrode the user's choice of another default browser. And to be completely sure that IE could not be uninstalled, Microsoft placed code specific to web browsing in the same files as code that provided OS functions so that deleting IE would cripple Windows.

722 *United States v Microsoft* 87 F Supp 2d 30 (DDC 2000) (on remedies, see *United States v Microsoft* 97 F Supp 2d 59 (DDC 2000)).

723 *United States v Microsoft* 253 F3d 34, 85 (DC Cir 2001).

724 ibid 93–95.

725 *Microsoft* (n 631), para 841.

726 *Microsoft v Commission* (n 339), para 1035.

727 See *Microsoft (tying)* (Case COMP/C-3/39.530) Commission Decision, paras 34 and 39–58, in which the EC once again examined foreclosure effects more closely, while maintaining that according to the case law, it can normally presume tying to have such effects by its nature.

728 Exclusionary Conduct Guidance Paper (n 461), paras 50 and 52–58 (referencing *Microsoft v Commission* (n 339) setting the threshold at 'likely anticompetitive foreclosure' and listing factors of particular importance for identifying cases involving such foreclosure), which was preceded by EC, 'The Application of Article 82 of the Treaty to Exclusionary Abuses' (n 375), in which the EC already committed itself to assess foreclosure and efficiencies.

729 *Rio Tinto Alcan* (Case AT.39230) Commission Decision C(2012)9439.

that the tying in question was harmful to competition'.[730] Even without confirmation by the ECJ, legal certainty and the protection of legitimate expectations thus require the EC to act consistent with the effects-based approach it put forward.

The reorientation of the legal test for tying is sensible and perhaps even inevitable, given the more economic approach and the need for a certain consistency between different forms of exclusionary abuse. However, several questions remain. Firstly, how should we interpret the 'separate products' condition in digital markets? This condition is supposed to operate as a screen to filter out tying cases that are not anticompetitive or are even procompetitive but may – in its current interpretation – lose that function in the digital economy. Secondly, while tying now shares 'likelihood of anticompetitive effects' as a threshold with most other leveraging abuses, the robustness of the analysis may still diverge. Relatedly, it is necessary to figure out what 'coercion' means where ties are not contractual but rather rely on platform architecture (from recommendations to integration). Thirdly, there is the question of justifications, given that tying – more so than other forms of abuse – can generate substantial efficiencies. The following sections provide answers to those questions, organized around the limbs of the legal test for tying, ie the 'separate products' condition (6.4), the foreclosure analysis (6.5) and procompetitive justifications (6.6).[731] The answers draw on a relatively rich set of cases, which involve innovation platforms (such as OSs) but also advertising platforms (search engines); they include tying (of an OS to apps) but also bundling (of various apps); some ties are technical (as in *Microsoft*), while others are contractual (as in *Android*). An overview of those cases with a short description of their key features can be found in Figure 5.

	Products/ services	**Type of tie/ bundle**	**Offensive/ defensive**	**Fore-closure**	**Justification**
Microsoft (US)	Windows & IE	technical tie	mainly def.	protecting OS monopoly vs middleware	no | software copyright, quality
Microsoft I	Windows & WMP	technical tie	mainly off. (*gaining* tied mkt power)	artificial comp. advantage from ubiquity, denying crucial scale	no | 'out of the box', standardization
Microsoft II	Windows & IE	technical tie	mainly off. (*maintaining* tied mkt power), def.	artificial comp. advantage, protecting OS monopoly	no | not in decision but similar to *I* and *US*

730 *Google v Commission* (n 353), para 295.

731 Thus leaving to the side the dominance requirement (see Section 4.1.2) and the definition of tying (customers are forced to obtain the tied product with the tying product). The coercion component of the definition is, however, discussed under the section on foreclosure.

	Products/ services	Type of tie/ bundle	Offensive/ defensive	Fore-closure	Justification
Google Shopping	Search & Comparison Shopping	technical bundle	off. (*gaining* tied mkt power)	artificial comp. advantage, denying crucial traffic	no | quality of results/user experience (↔ US)
Google Android	Play Store & Search; Play Store/ Search & Chrome	contractual tie	off. (*maintaining* tied mkt power); off. (*gaining* tied mkt power)	artificial comp. advantage, denying crucial usage	no | incentives to invest, 'out of the box', 'free' app store

Figure 5 Tying case law overview

6.4 Existence of Separate Products

What exactly is the use of the 'separate products' condition in the legal test for tying? The condition has been criticized as formalistic – or even as 'a back-door way of introducing considerations of efficiency' at the wrong stage of the analysis.[732] It is true that, historically, the 'separate products' test was forged to screen out false positives when there was no possibility to argue efficiencies under the per se rule.[733] But it can still play a role in testing for efficiencies from integration today. The idea is that, if the products are not separate, either (i) suppliers of the inexistent tied product cannot be foreclosed, or there is no harm in doing so; and/or (ii) the alleged tie presents an efficient integration. Testing for separate products at the start of the analysis can be an effective way to avoid costly investigations or procedures – in other words, it reduces decision costs. As such, the 'separate products' condition can function as an efficient first screen in tying cases.

Of course, the effectiveness of that screen depends on how error-prone and easy-to-administer the 'separate products' condition is. So how do you ascertain whether products are separate? In earlier cases, the EC (with approval from the European courts) focused on commercial usage: if the tied product is supplied separately *in a competitive market*, it is separate from the tying product. In *Tetra Pak II*, for example, the EC and GC pointed to the previous existence of independent suppliers of aseptic cartons and to the contemporary existence of independent suppliers in the related, more competitive market for non-aseptic cartons.[734] More recently, the EC shifted its

732 Andrew Gavil and Harry First, *The Microsoft Antitrust Cases: Competition Policy for the Twenty-First Century* (MIT Press 2014) 223.

733 *United States v Microsoft* (n 723) 85–87, referencing *Jefferson Parish Hosp v Hyde* (n 683).

734 *Tetra Pak II* (n 716), para 119 and Case T–83/91 *Tetra Pak v Commission* (n 716), para 82.

focus from supply to demand. According to its Guidance Paper, there is *direct* evidence of separate products when, given a choice, customers purchase the tied products from different sources of supply.[735] This can still be proven *indirectly* by showing the presence in the market of undertakings specialized in the supply of the tied product without the tying product.[736]

Applying the 'separate products' test in a platform context comes with difficulties. But easy cases continue to exist. As in an analogue world, *contractual* ties generally involve separate products. The reasoning is simple: if two seemingly separate products were actually one, there would be no need for a contractual obligation to use the two together. Moreover, contractual platform tying is generally used for *cross-platform* (inter-platform) rather than on-platform expansion, which makes the separate products still easier to detect. Take, for example, *Google Android*. Google concluded Mobile Application Distribution Agreements (MADAs) with OEMs providing that 'once a hardware manufacturer decides to pre-install one or more Google proprietary apps on its devices, it must pre-install all mandatory apps'.[737] The EC saw two problematic ties: one between the Play Store and Google Search; another between the Play Store *plus Google Search* and Google Chrome. The EC had no trouble showing the separate nature of these products; indeed, Google did not even contest it.[738] Such contractual and/or cross-platform ties do not complicate the separateness assessment. Of course, these cases are only easy at the screening stage: the fact that the products *are* separate invites a more in-depth analysis of foreclosure and efficiencies.

The difficult cases concern *technical* tying, generally of the *on-platform* (intra-platform) variety. In digital markets, such ties manifest themselves as the integration of two products.[739] These are instances where the platform expands its ecosystem with complements that either are completely new or were previously provided by independent complementors. In the former scenario, there is unlikely to be an issue; in the latter, leveraging concerns may arise. The *Microsoft I* case involved a tie of this nature.[740] At issue were not ties between different apps, but rather the integration of a media player in the OS. In that case, it is more convincing to take a systems perspective: the OS expands by providing a new functionality that was previously offered separately.[741] Nevertheless, the EC disagreed, holding that distinctness has to be assessed with a view to consumer demand for the tied product, which it proved *indirectly*: the fact that there are developers who supply media players on a stand-alone basis, in particular

735 Exclusionary Conduct Guidance Paper (n 461), para 51.

736 Commercial usage can still play a role: to prove separate products, one can rely on 'evidence indicating that undertakings with little market power, particularly in competitive markets, tend not to tie or not to bundle such products' (ibid).

737 *Google Android* (n 352), para 180.

738 ibid, paras 756–62 and 879–85.

739 Or, alternatively, as decreased incompatibility with competing complements, see Section 6.2.1.

740 *Microsoft II* also involved a technical integration (of a web browser in the OS), but its predecessor is more informative as there is an infringement decision and an appeal decision, as opposed to a commitment decision.

741 By contrast, it is less convincing to argue that one app (eg an app store) swallows the functionality of another app (eg a search engine).

RealNetworks (as well as Microsoft itself and Apple), evidences separate consumer demand.[742] The EC did not accept Microsoft's argument that the tie constitutes a normal commercial practice.[743]

Two criticisms can be levelled against the EC's 'separate products' test in *Microsoft I*. They should inform the application of such tests in platform markets more generally.

First, testing demand for just the tied product is insufficient. The EC should also ascertain that there is demand for the tying product *without* the tied product. The EC actually did note, albeit summarily and not entirely convincingly, that there is separate consumer demand for OSs without media players (eg for workplaces, which can do without the distraction of media).[744] The issue came up on appeal, where the GC blessed the EC's test of ascertaining separate demand for the tied product, rejecting Microsoft's argument that it should be tested whether there is demand for the tied product without the tying product.[745] The reasoning goes that it may be true that most (but not all) consumers want to obtain both products, but they might want to do so from different sources. The GC pointed to the role of OEMs, which combine hardware with Microsoft's software: without the tie, they could preinstall alternative media players, which may better satisfy consumer demand. This is more convincing: consumers want OSs to come with a media player, but that does not mean the media player must be chosen by Microsoft.

Second, the consumer demand test is backwards-looking and may thus punish the innovative integration of *previously* separate products.[746] The EC did acknowledge that a direct consumer demand test 'focuses on historic consumer behaviour, likely before integration and therefore risks ignoring efficiency benefits deriving from new product integration'.[747] Still, it concluded that 'non-insignificant' separate consumer demand continues to exist years after the start of the tie. This point too came up on appeal, where the GC acknowledged that the notion of separate products evolves rapidly in digital markets. However, it agreed with the EC that OSs and media players were separate products *at the time* of the (first) tie.[748] This position can be defended only if enough attention is given to innovative integration at the justification stage; if not, a tie could be found between smartphones and cameras (after all, 'non-insignificant' consumer demand for cameras continues to exist).[749]

---

742 *Microsoft* (n 631), paras 804–5. The EC also discusses other factors, including separate promotional activities (para 810) and functionality (para 811).

743 ibid, paras 821–24. Given Microsoft's 90+% market share, it is difficult to ascertain which commercial practices would be prevalent in a competitive market.

744 ibid, para 807.

745 *Microsoft v Commission* (n 339), paras 917–24.

746 See similarly *United States v Microsoft* (n 723) 89.

747 *Microsoft* (n 631), para 808.

748 *Microsoft v Commission* (n 339), paras 913–14.

749 Pablo Ibáñez Colomo, 'Is It an Abuse for Apple to Embed a Camera in Its iPhones? What Is Special and Different about Digital Cases' (*Chillin' Competition*, 21 July 2020) <https://chillingcompetition.com/2020/07/21/>.

Antitrust decisions are too rarely evaluated *ex post*, but the *Microsoft* decisions are, due to their notoriety, an exception.[750] Such an evaluation does not cast the EC's theory of harm in the best light but does not invalidate its 'separate products' finding either.

As a remedy, the EC ordered Microsoft to offer a version of Windows without WMP.[751] That remedy cannot be called successful. There was simply no demand for the WMP-free version, called 'Windows XP N': in April 2006, Microsoft reported that XP N sales represented 0.005 of all Windows XP sales in Europe, which meant that fewer than 2,000 copies had been sold.[752] OEMs did not integrate it into their hardware, reportedly due to a lack of consumer demand.[753] There are different explanations for the remedy's failure. For one, Microsoft's leveraging had made WMP the dominant media player, which meant most files were encoded specifically for it, which spurred consumer demand. Given that this was its theory of harm, the EC should have foreseen the resulting ineffectiveness of the remedy. Windows was also allowed to sell Windows including WMP at the same price as Windows without WMP, further reducing the incentive for customers to replace WMP.

Whatever the exact explanation may be, the failure did support Microsoft's initial contention that there was no demand for Windows without WMP. The GC addressed the remedy's failure, albeit cursorily, noting that 'any doubts as to the effectiveness of the remedy ordered by the Commission do not in themselves prove that its finding as to the existence of two separate products is wrong'.[754] While this is technically true, it may still mean that the EC's limited resources could have been expended more productively elsewhere. The EC translated this lesson into institutional knowledge. In its Guidance Paper, it writes that '[t]wo products are distinct if, in the absence of tying or bundling, a substantial number of customers would purchase or would have purchased the tying product without also buying the tied product from the same supplier'.[755] When it comes to separate consumer demand for the tied product, 'substantial' seems a more appropriate benchmark than 'non-insignificant', although how this translates into a more quantitative measurement is anyone's guess.

Despite improvements in previous practice, the 'separate products' test remains backwards-looking, which is problematic in fast-moving markets. Here, the slow pace of antitrust enforcement may actually provide a benefit. Given its *ex post* nature, it should be possible – by the time of the decision – to determine whether previously

750 See in particular Daniel Gore and Ashwin van Rooijen, '*Ex Post* Assessment of European Competition Policy: The *Microsoft* Cases' in Assimakis Komninos and Nicolas Petit (eds), *Ex Post Evaluation of Competition Cases* (Kluwer 2021) 17–44.

751 *Microsoft* (n 631), para 1011. Microsoft was also barred from preferencing WMP in any other way, including through privileged interoperability (in the form of selective API access) or promotion of WMP within Windows (see para 1013).

752 'Fact Sheet: Windows XP N Sales' (*Microsoft*, April 2006) <https://regmedia.co.uk/2009/06/12/microsoft_windows_xp_n_fact_sheet.pdf>.

753 ibid and Ingrid Marson, 'Still "No Demand" for Media-Player-Free Windows' (*CNET*, 18 November 2005) <https://www.cnet.com/news/still-no-demand-for-media-player-free-windows/>.

754 *Microsoft v Commission* (n 339), para 943.

755 Exclusionary Conduct Guidance Paper (n 461), para 51.

separate products have actually become one, or at the very least to discern whether the trend is going in that direction. Then again, there is a risk that the sunk cost fallacy may prevent competition authorities from ending an investigation at an advanced stage. At the end of the day, though, the *Microsoft I* decision did not exactly misjudge the trend: media players did not develop into an integrated-only OS functionality. Rather, OEMs started installing more media players,[756] and usage of other media players – in particular Apple's iTunes – grew considerably.

In conclusion, while *Microsoft I* can be criticized, the 'separate products' conclusion was not necessarily mistaken. The problem is more fundamental: in platform markets, the 'separate products' condition is not effective at fulfilling its function as an efficiency screen. Two solutions present themselves. Firstly, the 'separate products' condition should be relieved from (some) responsibility. Instead, the objective justification stage should be taken more seriously, generally but especially in tying cases. Secondly, there is another way to think about the utility of having the tied product provided separately. The question to ask is not 'Are these two products separate?' (the answer will generally be positive) but rather 'Is the tied product commoditized?' A product is commoditized, for this purpose, when there is no significant (demand for) innovation in the product market in question, which has rendered it static. For example, consider horizontal and vertical search services. When Google starts answering queries such as 'weather Leuven today' directly, this should not be considered a tie. Weather information is already provided for free by national meteorological institutes and repackaged without much additional analysis. It is, in a word, commoditized.[757] And indeed, when an association of (online) weather services sued Google for integrating weather information in its search results to their detriment, a court in Hamburg dismissed the case because the abuse of dominance provision is not meant 'to safeguard traditional business models that can no longer withstand change'.[758] In other words, legacy providers have no protected right to offer their services profitably in perpetuity. However, the situation is different in the case of, say, local information. Providers of such information do not rely on public sources, but rather on properly gathered data as well as the reviews written by an army of enthusiasts. There are clear differences between services (eg TripAdvisor and Yelp), and consumers may thus be harmed when they are buried in the search results – especially when their integrated replacement (Google Local) first scrapes their data for its own use.

756 The number of *additional* media players installed by OEMs climbed from an average of 1.4 in 2004 to 3.2 in 2006, see 'Fact Sheet: Windows XP N Sales' (n 752).

757 The same can perhaps not be said with regard to hyperlocal weather information. If such information were commoditized, Apple would not have to buy the weather app Dark Sky for an undisclosed amount (and the app would not have been selling for $3.99 in the App Store before that), see Jay Peters, 'Apple Acquires Popular Weather App Dark Sky and Will Shut Down the Android Version' (*The Verge*, 31 March 2020) <https://www.theverge.com/2020/3/31/21201666/>.

758 Court of Hamburg, Case 408 HKO 36/13 *Verband Deutscher Wetterdienstleister v Google*, 11 April 2013; for reporting in English, see Greg Sterling, 'Google Wins Vertical Search Antitrust Case in Germany' (*Search Engine Land*, 7 May 2013) <https://searchengineland.com/google-wins-vertical-search-antitrust-case-in-germany-158544> (quote).

6.5 Foreclosure Analysis

Given tying's current legal status, a foreclosure analysis is an essential step in establishing the illegal nature of a tie. First, the tying scenario in question must fit a theory of harm, which I discussed several above.[759] These theories have evolved from their Chicago School days. Today, post-Chicagoan economics is the norm, all the more so in digital markets. In a deeply symbolic reflection of this shift, Bork himself ended up defending Netscape against Microsoft's browser tying practices, decrying how Microsoft 'imposes conditions on those with whom it deals that exclude rivals without any apparent justification on the grounds of efficiency'.[760] Competition authorities too are well aware of the assumptions of the SMP theory, and in particular when they do not apply.[761]

While a theory of harm indicates when tying can be anticompetitive, competition authorities need to go one step further and prove that foreclosure is likely in the case at hand. A first question is which market to focus on when proving foreclosure: the adjacent market (offensive leveraging) or the primary market (defensive leveraging)? A second question is how to prove such foreclosure, especially when the tie in question is a nudge rather than a hard obligation. Let's address each question in turn.

6.5.1 Offensive vs Defensive Tying

Offensive tying, which transfers market power from a primary to an adjacent market, is the default. When this is done to pre-empt future competition in the primary market, the tying is (also) defensive. In either case, anticompetitive effects (say, the marginalization of equally or more efficient competitors) occur first in the adjacent market. Arguing an offensive or defensive ratio is thus more about telling a plausible and coherent story about the case being brought. It also says something about the potential magnitude of the competitive distortion. As Tirole warned, protecting an existing monopoly from disruption can significantly hamper innovation.[762]

An important question is: *when* is a defensive tying strategy credible? Such a strategy is generally alleged in addition to rather than instead of its offensive counterpart but seems to hold up less well before courts and in *ex post* analyses. To answer the question, let's examine two cases where it did not hold up and one where it did.

In *Microsoft I*, while the tying strategy was mainly considered offensive, the EC also discussed a potential defensive ratio.[763] It argued that middleware (eg Java or a browser)

759 See Section 6.2.2; see also Section 5.2.3.

760 Robert Bork, 'What Antitrust Is All About' (*NYT*, 4 May 1998) <https://www.nytimes.com/1998/05/04/opinion/what-antitrust-is-all-about.html> (referencing the tying case *Lorain Journal v United States* 342 US 143 (1951) – one of the few monopolization cases he previously described as correctly decided).

761 See Exclusionary Conduct Guidance Paper (n 461), paras 52–58 on how the EC builds its foreclosure analysis around the Chicagoan SMP assumptions, referring inter alia to variable proportions, separate utility of the tied product, price regulation in the tying market and complementary nature of products.

762 Tirole (n 639).

763 *Microsoft v Commission* (n 339), paras 971–77.

in combination with a media player could be a substitute for a general-purpose platform. A widely used media player was, in any case, a necessary component of a full-fledged platform threat. An entrant in the OS market would *also* have to provide such application, which makes such entry riskier and thus less likely. Microsoft was said to be strengthening its 'applications barrier to entry'.

Similarly, in *Google Shopping*, the EC considered Google's leveraging conduct offensive and, very secondarily, defensive. Notwithstanding the qualification as an independent form of leveraging,[764] the EC also noted that Google's conduct 'has similar effects to the tying practice' in *Microsoft I*.[765] To support its defensive leveraging/tying theory, the EC had to prove potential anticompetitive effects in the primary market, general search. To do so, it argued that Google was channelling traffic to its CSS to protect its ad revenue, which was, in turn, used to finance its general search service.[766]

Neither of these defensive theories held up well. With regard to the theory in *Microsoft I*, Adobe's Flash Player went on to become the media player of choice for web browsers, thus contributing to the platform threat posed by web browsers. As the EC recognized but not fully, however, media players never constituted more than a small part of an already hypothetical threat. The defensive prong of the *Google Search* decision fared even worse, as it was annulled on appeal. The GC held that the EC's capital-related considerations were so imprecise as to be 'purely speculative'.[767]

Contrast these two cases with *Microsoft II* and its Windows–IE tie.[768] The EC examined Microsoft's defensive motives to a comparatively greater extent than in *Microsoft I*.[769] On the other side of the Atlantic, defensive tying was at the heart of the *Microsoft* case.[770] The idea is that browsers constitute 'middleware', ie software that provides independent capabilities to apps ('web apps'). As such, browsers have the potential to replace PC OSs as the main platform to access and run apps. By depriving competing browsers (Netscape Navigator in the US, Mozilla's Firefox in the EU) of users, and thus making them a less attractive platform for developers, Microsoft pre-empted the platform threat presented by middleware.

---

764 See Section 5.2.1.

765 *Google Search (Shopping)* (n 348), para 600 and fn 715, referencing *Microsoft v Commission* (n 339), paras 982 and 1088.

766 *Google Search (Shopping)* (n 348), paras 642–43 (regrettably, the statements from internal Google documents supporting this theory are redacted). The EC argued it thus becomes more difficult for competing CSSs 'to reach a critical mass of users that would allow them to compete against Google', although the connection with the foregoing is not entirely clear.

767 Case T–612/17 *Google v Commission* EU:T:2021:763, para 457.

768 The tie was contractual in nature (based on preinstallation agreements with OEMs) but was enforced largely technically. Not only could IE not be uninstalled, but sometimes it even overrode the user's choice of another default browser. And to be completely sure that IE could not be uninstalled, Microsoft placed code specific to web browsing in the same files as code that provided OS functions, so that deleting IE would cripple Windows.

769 *Microsoft (tying)* (n 727), paras 55–58.

770 See *United States v Microsoft* (n 723).

In this case, the middleware theory was vindicated: Google later developed Chrome OS, a browser-based laptop OS that primarily runs web apps – a development US courts and the EC predicted. How do we distinguish such cases a priori, ie before the benefit of hindsight (and thus in an administrable way)? The key is that the tie in *Microsoft II* concerned two platforms of the same type, and in particular innovation platforms, with a close substitution link. Put simply, a defensive strategy was credible because both OSs and browsers serve as the technical foundation for other apps.

This was not the case in *Google Shopping*. The two platforms at issue were of the same type, ie advertising platforms and in particular search engines, but not innovation platforms. And the risk of substitution was very indirect, as it came via access to capital (ad revenue) – not similar functionality. In *Microsoft I*, the substitution link was a bit closer. And media players constituted something of an innovation platform, given that files had to be encoded specifically for it (this has become much less important over time, among others, thanks to the rise of media players such as VLC that play virtually all file formats). But the link was still quite tenuous because media players were a small part of an OS threat at best.

Defensive tying theories are inherently forward-looking, which means we should not expect them to be proven to the same standard as offensive tying theories. At the same time, they cannot be purely speculative either. To determine whether a defensive tying theory is credible, it helps to ask whether (i) there are two platforms of the same type, and in particular two innovation platforms, which – as the stable core of ecosystems – are particularly worth defending; and (ii) whether the substitution link is close enough, which is not the case when it is purely a matter of capital (something efficient markets should solve in any case).

6.5.2 Competitive Advantage

The anticompetitive effects of tying start from choice: through coercion, a dominant firm deprives customers of free choice.[771] While exploitative theories of tying exist, we are concerned with exclusion (foreclosure). This means that price takes a backseat, all the more so in digital markets where the tied good is often free.[772] Therefore, the anticompetitive effects that follow a lack of choice tend to concern quality and innovation, which are more difficult to measure than price.[773]

In the past, competition authorities scarcely sought to measure the effects of tying on those competition parameters. Even after tying doctrine started including an effects analysis, the focus has been on the foreclosure of competition itself. Given that protecting a competitive market structure is a goal of EU competition law,[774] this is

771 See Section 6.1.

772 On the tying of free goods, see Andrea Amelio and Bruno Jullien, 'Tying and Freebies in Two-Sided Markets' (2012) 30 International Journal of Industrial Organization 436.

773 See Section 4.2.1.

774 ibid.

not necessarily problematic but raises two questions. Firstly, to which degree must competition be distorted? In digital tying cases, a competitive advantage appears to be the norm, although authorities have sought to connect such an advantage to wider anticompetitive effects. Secondly, and relatedly, what kind of coercion suffices to provide such a competitive advantage (and corresponding distortion)? In digital markets, authorities have shifted from asking '*Can* users go around the tie?' (eg by installing an additional application) to '*Do* users go around the tie?' Let's track these evolutions in the case law, starting with the two *Microsoft* cases.

In *Microsoft I*, OEMs were the direct 'addressees' of the coercion, as they could only license Windows with WMP preinstalled.[775] End users, to which OEMs sold Windows PCs with WMP, were indirectly coerced. Neither OEMs nor consumers could uninstall WMP (making the tie technical).[776] Of course, consumers were not forced to use WMP, but due to inertia and technical unsophistication, they were likely to use WMP over alternatives – a dynamic known as 'status quo bias' in behavioural economics.[777] The GC agreed with the EC that there was an inability to acquire Windows without WMP – in other words, coercion.[778]

The more difficult question is whether this coercion leads to foreclosure. In that respect, the EC argued that tying WMP to Windows affords Microsoft 'unmatched ubiquity' on PCs worldwide.[779] The status quo bias of unsophisticated consumers means that alternative media players are rarely downloaded. Moreover, competing media player developers cannot overcome this bias through preinstallation agreements with OEMs.[780] Given that WMP cannot be uninstalled, OEMs have little incentive to fill up the hard drive with a similar product. Moreover, additional programs lead to additional support calls to OEMs – a major cost for a business operating on thin margins.

It is worth repeating that media players are (or at least *were*) themselves platforms. Given that they worked with proprietary file formats, indirect network effects played a role: increased users of a media player motivate suppliers to offer their content in that specific format. Therefore, the ubiquity guaranteed by Microsoft's tying draws developers to WMP while denying rivals the necessary scale.[781] The platform envelopment strategy gives WMP a 'significant competitive advantage, which is liable to have a harmful effect on the structure of competition in that market'.[782] The EC's

775 *Microsoft* (n 631), para 827.

776 ibid, para 829.

777 ibid, paras 832–33, 845–46 and 866–70. Further on this behavioural economics approach, see Nicolas Petit and Norman Neyrinck, 'Behavioral Economics and Abuse of Dominance: A Fresh Look at the Article 102 TFEU Case-Law' (2010) 6 ÖZK 203, 207.

778 *Microsoft v Commission* (n 339), paras 960–75.

779 *Microsoft* (n 631), paras 843–48.

780 ibid, paras 849–57.

781 ibid, paras 863 and 879–96. Encoding a file in multiple formats is expensive and time-consuming for suppliers, and confusing for end users.

782 ibid, para 878. In addition to effects in the market for media players, the EC held that the conduct would also have spillover effects in related markets (eg mobile media players, online music players, and digital rights management), see ibid, paras 897–99.

theory was borne out by the numbers: while usage of WMP was declining before the tie, it started climbing quickly thereafter – to the detriment of competing media players.[783] Importantly, this happened despite the fact that users and trade journals rated the competing media player of RealNetworks more highly.[784]

The GC confirmed this analysis of anticompetitive effects: competition on the merits was indeed harmed because WMP was at a 'significant competitive advantage' compared to inherently better products, and innovation was impeded or deterred in the media player market.[785]

In *Microsoft II*, the EC's analysis was very similar. It found foreclosure in the artificial distributional advantage that competing browsers were unable to match through preinstallation agreements with OEMs and direct downloads by end users. The EC did note that the penetration of broadband internet made direct downloads more feasible, but not enough to offset IE's advantage. This time, the EC also brought empirical evidence to demonstrate status quo bias: more than half of Windows users and about two thirds of Windows users having IE as their main web browser do not download web browsers from the internet or are reluctant to do so.[786] Most users either found no need for an additional browser given the presence of a preinstalled one or did not know how to install software.

Again, the status quo bias could not be explained by the tied product's superior quality: Microsoft did not release a new version of IE 6 over a period of over five years (2001–2006), and then not for another three years (2006–2009).[787] Reviews by trade journals were devastating. One contended that in terms of speed, other browsers 'beat IE by a country mile', while another declared that IE 'might be the least secure software on the planet', before adding it to its list of worst tech products of all time.[788] Firefox offered a far superior browser. However, IE was a platform for which suppliers developed apps and content, which meant that the ubiquity – not the quality – of IE helped draw them away from competing web browsers.[789]

There are clear trends in these foundational cases on tying in platform markets. First, the EC shows coercion of the direct addressees of the tie, ie OEMs, but also of the end users, ie consumers. The link between the two is end users' status quo bias, for which the EC increasingly brings data: indeed, it appears consumers stick to preinstalled apps.

---

783 ibid, paras 905–26. The EC also looked at relative format usage, website content and installed base.

784 ibid, paras 947–51. In fifteen reviews by trade journals, RealNetworks' media player came out on top eight times; WMP only twice.

785 *Microsoft v Commission* (n 339), para 1088.

786 *Microsoft (tying)* (n 727), paras 50–51.

787 ibid, para 54.

788 Eric Lai, 'IE Still Top Dog Over Firefox in Corporate Browser Kennel' (*Computerworld*, 11 January 2008) <https://www.computerworld.com/article/2538552/>; Dan Tynan, 'The 25 Worst Tech Products of All Time' (*PCWorld*, 26 May 2006) <https://www.pcworld.com/article/125772/>. See Cusumano, Gawer and Yoffie (n 614) 125–27 for a more in-depth discussion.

789 *Microsoft (tying)* (n 727), paras 55–56.

As apps become ever easier to download, however, that may change. Second, the EC consistently makes the point that the tied product is inferior. In a way, this is superfluous: the point of undoing ties is to free up choice so that consumers can decide which product is superior – there is no need to take a position on that in advance. From a prioritization perspective, however, it makes sense to focus on those ties where the foreclosed products appear more qualitative. This also helps corroborate the anticompetitive effects: in a competitive market, consumers would obviously not choose the inferior product. When there is less of a quality difference between the tied product and alternatives, however, this analysis may become trickier. Finally, the tied products often have platform characteristics. Tying may thus halt indirect network effects and prevent competing products from achieving critical mass.[790]

Let's now look at how tying's foreclosure analysis evolved post-Microsoft *I* and *II*. Tying theories of harm continued to haunt Microsoft, but the real follow-up was *Google Android* (and, to a lesser extent, the tying-adjacent *Google Shopping*).

In subsequent merger investigations involving Microsoft, the EC regularly assessed potential tying scenarios, though sometimes with different conclusions. In *Microsoft/Skype*, the EC examined whether Microsoft could integrate Skype and Windows 'in order to increase Skype's footprint in the consumer communications market and make it a "must-have" product, creating or reinforcing its dominant position (i.e., tying)'.[791] The EC concluded, however, that the effects of such a tie would be 'non-existent or at most limited'.[792] Skype was already preinstalled on every second Windows PC, but such preinstallation was only a small driver of usage. Moreover, consumer communications had shifted in part to smartphones, where there were strong players with competing services (Google and Apple). In *Microsoft/LinkedIn*, the EC was more concerned about the potential integration of LinkedIn and Windows.[793] Given the network effects governing professional social networks (PSNs), such integration could tip the market. This was addressed by a commitment from Microsoft not to preinstall LinkedIn in Windows (or at least allow OEMs not to preinstall it).[794] In a non-merger context, Microsoft also continues to walk a fine line – and crosses it at times. In 2020, for example, it forced its Edge browser on users in an update.[795] And the workplace communications platform Slack has filed a formal complaint with the EC against Microsoft for tying its competing product, Teams, to its enterprise suite Microsoft 365.[796]

790 This ties in well with the theories of harm described above, Section 6.2.2.

791 *Microsoft/Skype* (n 347), paras 137–38. Microsoft could also degrade interoperability between Windows and competing communications services (para 136).

792 ibid, para 159–69, confirmed in *Cisco v Commission* (n 347).

793 *Microsoft/LinkedIn* (n 347).

794 ibid, paras 418–21. Microsoft also committed not to discriminate against other PSNs by degrading interoperability with Outlook (paras 413–17).

795 Sean Hollister, 'With Edge, Microsoft's Forced Windows Updates Just Sank to a New Low' (*The Verge*, 2 July 2020) <https://www.theverge.com/21310611/>.

796 For a preliminary analysis, see Daniel Mândrescu, '*Slack v. Microsoft* – More Than Just Another Tying Case' (*CoRe Blog*, 27 August 2020) <https://www.lexxion.eu/coreblogpost/slack-v-microsoft-more-than-just-another-tying-case/>.

In *Google Shopping*, the EC held that the preferential ranking and display of Google's CSS confer a competitive advantage on it. Given that traffic from Google accounts for a large portion of traffic to CSSs, which cannot be effectively replaced, competitors are foreclosed.[797] The prominence of Google Shopping cannot be explained by its quality.[798] The conclusions are essentially those of *Microsoft*: a competitive advantage not based on quality; the exclusion of rivals from the most important means of distribution, thereby denying them critical mass. But Google challenged the story of coercion and foreclosure by arguing that competition is just 'one click away' (more precisely, a click to page 4 of the search results, to which competitors were relegated)[799]. Again, the argument is reminiscent of Microsoft stating that users can simply install a second media player or browser. It is, however, much easier to navigate to an alternative shopping service than it is (and especially *was*) to install a second app. But do users *actually* carry out those easier actions more often? Given 'saliency bias', the tendency of users to decide based on what is most prominent to them, behavioural economics predicts that they do not.[800] The EC confirmed this in testing, which found that (i) users are most likely to click on the first generic search result (more than twice as likely than on the second); (ii) the first three results generate more than half of the clicks on desktop (and 70% on mobile); and (iii) the top ten account for 95% of clicks.[801] Quality plays no decisive role: moving the first result to the third place means a 50% reduction in clicks; moving it to the tenth place leads to an 85% reduction. Considering the impact on traffic of Google's conduct, as well as other potential sources of traffic, the GC confirmed the EC's analysis.[802]

In *Google Android*, the EC did explicitly rely on tying.[803] The presence of coercion was uncontested: under the MADAs, OEMs could only preinstall the Play Store if they also preinstalled the Google Mobile Services (GMS) bundle, which included Google Search and Google Chrome.[804] Therefore, the devil was in the foreclosure analysis.[805] Google's strategic rationale differed for each tied product, so let's take

797 *Google Search (Shopping)* (n 348), paras 341–643.

798 ibid, paras 381–82 (on how Google was aware that its own service would not rank highly organically, ie based on quality, inter alia because it scraped content from other websites) and 490–91 (on how Google executives wrote that Google Shopping 'isn't really a serious contender' and 'simply doesn't work').

799 See EC, 'Commission fines Google €2.42 billion for abusing dominance as search engine by giving illegal advantage to own comparison shopping service' (press release, 27 June 2017) IP/17/1784 (describing that the most highly ranked competing services appeared on average only on page 4).

800 CMA, 'Online Choice Architecture: How Digital Design Can Harm Competition and Consumers' (Discussion Paper, 2022), paras 4.35–4.41. In addition, users tend to assume that the most highly ranked results are also the most qualitative ones.

801 *Google Search (Shopping)* (n 348), paras 454–61.

802 *Google v Commission* (n 767), paras 518–43. The 'advantage' terminology was less prominent, although the GC does note differentiated treatment necessarily comes with a competitive advantage (para 294).

803 *Google Android* (n 352), confirmed – at least with regard to the ties discussed here – in *Google v Commission* (n 353).

804 In addition, OEMs were obliged to place on the device's home screen the Google Search and Play Store icons, as well as the 'Google folder' containing other mandatory apps. Finally, OEMs were required to set Google Search as the default search engine for all web access points.

805 *Google Android* (n 352), paras 773–876 and 896–992. On the economics of foreclosure in this case, see in particular Jay Pil Choi and Doh-Shin Jeon, 'A Leverage Theory of Tying in Two-Sided Markets' (2016) TSE Working Paper 16–689, and Federico Etro and Cristina Caffarra, 'On the Economics of the Android

them separately. First, with regard to Google Search, the leveraging was aimed at foreclosure in the tied market of search engines. Google was already dominant in that market, so the idea was not to gain market power but to *maintain* it. Indeed, Google's entered the mobile OS market at least in part as a way to safeguard its position as a gateway to the web while the web was moving from desktop to mobile.[806] Mobile searches now account for more than half of all searches, and through preinstallation, Google Search can capture a disproportionate share of those searches. This competitive advantage derives from users' status quo bias, as Google itself knows: 'People rarely change defaults.'[807] This is not (fully) explained by quality. Consider users of Windows Mobile devices that have Bing preinstalled. Given that competition is 'one click away' and Google provides the superior search engine, owners of such devices have swapped Bing for Google Search in droves, right? Wrong. In 2017, only 10–20% of search queries on Windows Mobile happened on Google Search.[808] Google pointed to its high share of queries on desktop to show how its high share on mobile was not explained by the MADAs, but that argument failed, given that Google Search is also set as the default on all major PC web browsers except IE/Edge.[809] And Google is the default search engine not only of major PC web browsers but also of most mobile web browsers,[810] while OEMs – of which only a minority was even allowed to install a second search engine – have little incentive to do so.[811] Google's conduct thus increases barriers to entry in the search market: competing engines cannot gain the critical amount of queries, revenue and user data needed to improve their services. As a result, consumers suffer from a lack of choice and innovation in search.

Second, with regard to Google Chrome, the tie was also offensive but – given how Chrome's market share on mobile was initially modest – aimed at *gaining* market power. Again, it was shown that the great majority of users rely on the preinstalled mobile web browser. Competing browsers could not offset this advantage through alternative distribution channels, ie user downloads or preinstallation by OEMs (as second browser). In the relevant market for non-OS-specific mobile web browsers, Chrome's usage grew markedly in the period covered by MADAs (2012–17), from 4.7%

Case' (2017) 13 European Competition Journal 282, extending Choi and Jeon's model to more closely reflect the facts of the *Android* case (note that Etro and Caffarra represented parties adverse to Google).

806 *Google Android* (n 352), paras 112–54. That is also why Google pays Apple an estimated $8–12 billion per year to be the default search engine in its web browser Safari and other search tools. These agreements are part of the DOJ's *Google* case, see *United States and 11 States v Google*, no 1:20-cv-03010 (DDC, 20 October 2020) (Complaint).

807 *Google Android* (n 352), para 787.

808 ibid, para 793. The share was higher in previous years. In addition, it must be acknowledged that a lower share of Google Android search queries happened on Bing. Google Search's stronger 'retention rate' suggests it may be more qualitative than Bing. Reviews of various search engines in the Play Store also point toward a very slight quality difference with Bing (but not with Yandex, for example).

809 ibid, paras 795–96.

810 On top of Google's preinstallation agreements directly with mobile web browsers (eg Apple's Safari), several OEMs understood that the MADAs required them to set Google Search as the default search engine on mobile web browsers.

811 OEMs would incur transaction costs while expected revenues were low. Moreover, duplication would hurt the user experience and take up storage space. In addition, Google had revenue-sharing agreements with OEMs based on the exclusive preinstallation of Google Search (the third limb of the *Google Android* case, on top of the MADAs and anti-fragmentation agreements).

to 74.9%. At least a significant part of that growth must be ascribed to preinstallation given that (i) Chrome's usage grew much slower on PCs where it did not benefit from preinstallation to the same extent, namely, from 32.1% to 53.4% over the same period;[812] and (ii) there are no quality differences with other browsers.[813] Again, the increased barriers to entry resulted in less choice and innovation.

To conclude, let's return to the trends observed in the *Microsoft* cases. First, the coercion question has been settled. Coercion of the direct addressee of the tie, generally OEMs, suffices. Due to status quo bias, such coercion tends to transfer to the end-user level, although that bias now mainly comes in when assessing anticompetitive effects. When it comes to such anticompetitive effects, the analysis starts from the competitive advantage that the conduct confers on the tied product. A competitive advantage, however, does not necessarily amount to foreclosure. This issue came to the fore in the *Google Android* appeal, where Google contended that the EC conflated competitive advantage and foreclosure. The GC blessed the EC's analysis as it established not only a competitive advantage that competitors cannot offset, but also the anticompetitive effects of that advantage.[814] Considering the collection of tying cases, the EC generally does go through two steps. In a first step, the EC establishes a competitive advantage, in particular by examining the coverage of the tie and whether users *actually* go around the tie. Even though the users' increased technical sophistication, combined with more user-friendly download flows, has made it easier to go around ties, it seems appropriate to consider actual user behaviour. In a second step, the EC shows how the competitive advantage results in anticompetitive effects. This is the difficult part. Dominant firms tend to argue that the ubiquity of their tied product is simply explained by its quality. Logically, this argument is unconvincing: if the tied product is superior, there is no need to force it upon customers, who would recognize that quality anyway.[815] More concretely, the EC has taken care to show that the tied product is inferior, initially based on trade journal reviews and more recently based on app store ratings. This achieves two things. First, showing that an inferior product comes out on top demonstrates that the competitive process is distorted. There is no competition on the merits when equally or more efficient competitors are excluded. Second, it shows that the conduct directly harms consumers, who would otherwise use a more qualitative product. In more recent cases, however, the quality difference between the tied product and its competitors has not been as stark as in the *Microsoft* era, or has even been non-existent, which complicates this line of reasoning. Other arguments hold up better, in particular that the conduct increases barriers to entry in the tied product market (especially if the product is subject to network or learning effects), which in turn limits consumer choice and innovation.

812 Moreover, superior quality would result in users of iOS devices (where Chrome is not preinstalled) flocking to Chrome, which did not happen.

813 Other mobile browsers actually received equally good *or better* reviews than Chrome.

814 *Google v Commission* (n 353), para 564.

815 Unless there is an information issue, and consumers can somehow not properly estimate the quality of the tied product. Alternatively, the quality difference may be so small as to make consumers ambivalent, in which case tying can make a difference.

6.6 Procompetitive Justifications

While procompetitive justifications are given due treatment below,[816] they deserve a separate discussion within the tying context for several reasons. First, as the GC recognized in *Google Android*, tying 'is a common practice in the course of trade which is normally intended to provide customers with better products or offerings in more cost-effective ways'.[817] As enforcers and courts on both sides of the Atlantic recognized in their *Microsoft* cases, such benefits are especially prevalent in case of technological integration.[818] Second, the 'separate products' test has lost some of its ability to filter out cases of procompetitive integration.[819] Added to that is the fact that the EC and European courts tend not to accept justifications (although they likely play an important role at the case selection stage).

The insight that tying is often procompetitive, in that it produces efficiencies that benefit consumers, must be credited to the Chicago School, although many of the efficiencies they put forward benefit the dominant firm rather than consumers.[820] Of the efficiencies that can credibly benefit consumers, four are discussed here. First, tying can produce economies of scope, and the associated cost savings can be passed onto consumers. Second, tying may be necessary to appropriate the benefits of an investment, and thus to safeguard incentives to invest. Third, tying may reduce transaction and search costs for consumers. Fourth, tied products can make an ecosystem more attractive because of the superior compatibility afforded by having the platform complements developed in-house. Let's take these one by one, drawing on case law for legal grounding and illustration. Bear in mind that efficiencies must be conduct-specific and proportional (meaning there is no less restrictive way to realize the efficiencies).[821]

First, a tie may produce economies of scope.[822] Such economies of scope must derive from joint distribution rather than joint production, as the efficiencies from joint production can be achieved without distributing the products together. When it comes to software, it may be efficient to bundle, say, an OS with apps, rather than setting up a separate distribution channel for each.[823] This is primarily the case when distribution costs are significant (eg in a world of packaged software sales rather than downloads) *and* the firm in question sells directly to consumers. When it sells on an intermediate market (say, to OEMs), a tie is generally not necessary to realize efficiencies. Moreover,

816 See Section 10.

817 *Google v Commission* (n 353), para 283.

818 See Section 6.3.

819 See Section 6.4.

820 Bork, *The Antitrust Paradox* (n 415) 376–78. Bork puts forward the evasion of price regulation in the tying market, price discrimination, and metering as justifications, but as we have seen, those do not benefit the consumer in most cases under realistic market conditions.

821 See further Section 10.1.

822 Bowman (n 565) 29; Bork, *The Antitrust Paradox* (n 415) 379 (referring to economies of scale but describing economies of scope).

823 *Microsoft* (n 631), para 958.

there is often a less restrictive way to realize efficiencies from joint distribution, namely, introducing a discounted multiproduct bundle next to the regularly priced separate products, thus safeguarding consumer choice.[824] This becomes difficult, however, when the tied good is provided for free. The remedy in *Microsoft I* is a testament to the futility of selling the separate tying product and the bundle at the same price.

Second, tying may be necessary for reasons of appropriability. Appropriability is 'the extent to which an innovator can capture the social benefits of its innovation'.[825] When appropriability is weak, such as in the case of open-source software, a platform may want to introduce a tie to increase appropriability. If profits from the tied good, for example specific apps, safeguard the firm's incentives to invest, the strategy may be justified as promoting innovation. Appropriability played a key role in *Google Android*.[826] Google claimed that tying is a legitimate way to monetize its investments in Android and its non-revenue-generating apps. The EC was not convinced, given that Google benefits from significant revenue from the Play Store (from commission fees and advertising).[827] Although the EC does not go as far as stating so, this suggests that tying Android with Google Play may be legitimate.[828] By contrast, tying Google Search and Chrome to the Play Store was not considered necessary to maintain incentives to invest. In announcing its compliance with the unbundling remedy, however, Google made clear that it did consider the tie a financial necessity:

> [D]evice manufacturers will be able to license the Google mobile application suite separately from the Google Search App or the Chrome browser. Since the pre-installation of Google Search and Chrome together with our other apps helped us fund the development and free distribution of Android, we will introduce a new paid licensing agreement for smartphones and tablets shipped into the EEA.[829]

Google thus makes it out that the EC decision means it *has* to start charging licensing fees for the GMS suite to finance Android but leaves out any reference to Play Store revenue.[830] At a minimum, it shows that Google *can* start charging for the GMS suite.

---

824 Renato Nazzini, 'The Evolution of the Law and Policy on Tying: A European Perspective from Classic Leveraging to the Challenges of Online Platforms' (2017) 27 Journal of Transnational Law and Policy 1, 52–53.

825 Dirk Auer, 'Appropriability and the European Commission's Android Investigation' (2017) 23 Columbia Journal of European Law 647, 648.

826 *Google Android* (n 352), paras 993–99.

827 In addition, Google benefits from search advertising revenue as well as valuable user data gathered through Android. Finally, Google had a strategic motive for Android's purchase and development, ie countering risks to its search-advertising business model. This in itself may already have provided enough of an incentive.

828 Indeed, the EC did not bring a case against that tie. In any case, OEMs need no tying obligation to make them license the Play Store, given the importance of indirect network effects for app stores and the Play Store's dominance (meaning far fewer apps are developed for competing app stores).

829 Lockheimer (n 518).

830 In confirming the EC's analysis, the GC held that 'revenues generated by the Play Store … are now sufficient on their own to enable Google to recoup its investment in the development and maintenance of

Third, tying can reduce transaction and search costs.[831] Software providers in particular have argued the need to provide an 'out of the box' experience, meaning consumers are immediately able to use their device without having to shop around for apps.[832] Microsoft relied on this argument when justifying its Windows–WMP tie,[833] and Google did so to justify its GMS bundle.[834] It is certainly true that consumers want to be able to watch videos and browse the web when acquiring a device. The argument becomes difficult, however, when made by sellers in an intermediate market. When software providers sell their product to OEMs, which package it and sell it to consumers (as in the *Microsoft* and *Google Android* cases), those OEMs can guarantee the 'out of the box' experience. Indeed, they may even do so better than the OS provider, given that OEMs are incentivized to include the best apps rather than their own. A tie simply constrains the OEMs' choice of how to satisfy consumer demand. To convincingly argue an 'out of the box' justification, the software provider needs to show that it can bundle software more qualitatively or at a lower cost.

Fourth, there may be 'technological interdependence' between the tying and tied product, so that the tying product does not work well – or at least *as* well – with the complementary products of competing suppliers.[835] The lack of interoperability may lead not only to less qualitative results, but in the worst case even to safety or health hazards. When it does, users may blame the manufacturer of the primary product rather than those of inferior complements, which harms the manufacturer's reputation. Tying can thus protect goodwill. This is the basis of the arguments of Hilti and Tetra Pak, which considered their conduct justified based on technical grounds, quality, product safety or public health.[836] Again, the crucial question is whether there is a less restrictive alternative to achieve the same result. In this case, the production and use of inferior complements can be prevented by carefully specifying the interoperability requirements.[837] Along those lines, the EC noted that 'there are less restrictive means available to Google in order to compete with the "look-and-feel" of vertically integrated competitors, such as design and interface guidelines'.[838]

When the conduct in question is suitable to realize the claimed efficiencies *and* is the least restrictive way to do so, there is a justification case to be made. Many justification

the Android platform during the corresponding year', and Google also has other sources of revenue. See *Google v Commission* (n 353), para 609.

831 This is essentially the demand-side consequence of the supply-side economies of scope discussed above.

832 On this justification, see Patrick Todd, 'Out of the Box: Illegal Tying and Google's Suite of Apps for the Android OS' (2017) 13 European Competition Journal 62.

833 *Microsoft* (n 631), paras 956–61, confirmed in *Microsoft v Commission* (n 339), para 1155.

834 *Google Android* (n 352), paras 1000–1002.

835 Bowman (n 565) 27–28; Bork, *The Antitrust Paradox* (n 415) 379–80; Nazzini, 'The Evolution of the Law and Policy on Tying: A European Perspective from Classic Leveraging to the Challenges of Online Platforms' (n 824) 55–57.

836 *Hilti v Commission* (n 715), paras 20, 108–11 (EC) and 115–19 (GC); Case T–83/91 *Tetra Pak v Commission* (n 716), paras 83–84 and 138–40.

837 Bowman (n 565) 28 ('In many cases of technological interdependence, a careful description of the specifications necessary for successful performance might overcome the objections of the manufacturer.').

838 *Google Android* (n 352), para 1003. Google provides such guidelines, see eg 'Design for Android' Quality Guidelines <https://developer.android.com/design>.

claims stumble over proportionality, particularly when the dominant firm is active in an intermediate rather than a retail market. If the conduct is proportional, the balancing exercise starts: Do the procompetitive effects outweigh the anticompetitive effects (say, the reduction in choice or innovation) in a way that benefits consumers? Very few justification claims have made it up to that point, which either shows how careful prioritization filtered out those cases from the start, or how authorities have given such claims short shrift.

6.7 Conclusion

When it comes to competition law enforcement in platform markets, tying has led the way. On a theoretical level, *Microsoft I* was commendable in how it updated the legal test for tying for the digital age. But *Microsoft I* and *II* were, in many ways, 'easy' cases. Microsoft was a clear monopolist, and the products it forced upon OEMs and consumers were widely seen as inferior. Moreover, Microsoft was not able to come up even with a prima facie plausible justification for its conduct. This was especially apparent in the US case, where the judge noted: 'Microsoft proffers no justification for two of the three challenged actions that it took in integrating IE into Windows – excluding IE from the Add/Remove Programs utility and commingling browser and operating system code.'[839] In other words, Microsoft integrated IE unnecessarily deeply into Windows.[840] The case was essentially one of 'naked exclusion', ie 'conduct unabashedly meant to exclude rivals, for which no one offers any efficiency justification' – at least no *credible* justification.[841] Bork voiced a similar message when condemning how Microsoft 'imposes conditions on those with whom it deals that exclude rivals without any apparent justification on the grounds of efficiency'.[842]

In the absence of a credible justification, there is no harm in summarily condemning such tying cases.[843] As cases became harder, however, the enforcement engine started to sputter. It became clear that the promised effects analysis ended up focusing in large part on the existence of a competitive advantage – a lower bar than foreclosure. When the product is *not* clearly inferior, or the proffered justifications *are* credible, a theory of harm based simply on the 'ubiquity' afforded by the tie does not suffice. Such cases can still be saved when the tied market is imperfectly competitive, eg due to the presence of network effects. In that case, denying competing providers of the tied product minimum efficient scale (critical mass) can – but does not necessarily – result in anticompetitive effects.

839 *United States v Microsoft* (n 723) 66.

840 Focusing on the level of integration, see William Page and John Lopatka, *The Microsoft Case: Antitrust, High Technology, and Consumer Welfare* (The University of Chicago Press 2007).

841 Eric Rasmussen, Mark Ramseyer and John Wiley, 'Naked Exclusion' (1991) 81 The American Economic Review 1137.

842 Bork, 'What Antitrust Is All About' (n 760).

843 For a similar logic, see O'Donoghue and Padilla (n 556) 285 ('a good case can be made for saying that conduct harming an equally efficient firm should be presumed abusive, absent compelling efficiencies').

While this work does not focus on remedies, they are a crucial coda to the tying story. Two points are important. First, the effectiveness of technological ties generally means that competition is already foreclosed by the time remedies are imposed. Nevertheless, remedies can still (re)open the market for the next wave of disruptors. Even then, remedies have to fight the familiarity that the tie has bred. That is why choice screens, while helpful, are no panacea: it is easy for consumers to return to the preinstalled option they are familiar with ('better the devil you know'). Second, technological ties may be costly to reverse. As far as software is concerned, however, incompatibility can often be replaced by interoperability through APIs, which – when implemented correctly – can result in the (re)launch of competition. Especially given the prior suppression of competition and the continued benefits that come with it, I find it difficult to understand how some consider remedies that (re)introduce consumer choice radical. Spurring choice and the innovation that comes with it should be the goal of tying remedies. Let me shortly illustrate these comments with a little browser market case study.

The US *Microsoft* case ended in a settlement with remedies that had relatively little bite (especially considering that the district court judgment had initially imposed a breakup). Netscape Navigator was essentially wiped from the market by Microsoft's tying of IE. In an act of defiance, however, Netscape made the source code of Navigator freely available via Mozilla.org.[844] Out of the Mozilla Foundation then grew a new browser, Firefox (initially named 'Phoenix', as it rose from the ashes of Navigator – a casualty of what is now known as the first browser war). Given IE's lacklustre performance, Firefox quickly gained market share, so that in 2009, it was a viable competitor to IE.[845] The EC's *Microsoft II* case was thus aimed at not letting this second browser war play out as the first. Under the commitment decision, Microsoft would give OEMs the option to disable IE, and to present end users with a choice screen prompting them to install one of the five main web browsers.[846] The commitments were a significant improvement on *Microsoft I*. Regrettably, Microsoft did not comply with the remedy from May 2011 until July 2012, for which the EC fined it €560 million.[847] In the end, however, the second browser war would not be won by Firefox but by Google Chrome. Chrome was released in 2008 with glowing coverage. *Wired* repeated the claim that in benchmark tests, Chrome was 56 times faster than IE.[848] It would quickly become the browser of recommendation by trade journals.[849] While estimates vary, Chrome

844 Janet Kornblum, 'Netscape Sets Source Code Free' (*CNET*, 31 March 1998) <https://www.cnet.com/news/netscape-sets-source-code-free/>.

845 In *Microsoft (tying)* (n 727), fn 34, the EC writes that for 'the period running from November 2007 to October 2009, according to NetApplications data, the gap between Internet Explorer's and Firefox's market shares on the Windows platform was on average 34.41% (and consistently over 21.91%) in Europe'. One can deduce a rough split of 60% market share for IE and 30% for Firefox, which is in line with other estimates.

846 ibid, para 60.

847 *Microsoft (tying)* (Case AT.39530) Commission Decision C(2013)1210 on the imposition of a fine for failure to comply with a commitment.

848 Steven Levy, 'Inside Chrome: The Secret Project to Crush Internet Explorer and Remake the Web' (*Wired*, 2 September 2008) <https://www.wired.com/2008/09/mf-chrome/>. Chrome also ran a multiprocess architecture limiting crashes and a sandboxed model improving security.

849 See eg Megan Geuss, 'Which Browser Should You Use?' (*PCWorld*, 26 February 2012) <https://www.pcworld.com/article/250566/which_browser_should_you_use_.html>.

usage surpassed that of Firefox somewhere around 2012 and that of IE not much later.[850] Almost a decade later, in a final act of irony, Microsoft based its new Edge browser on Chromium – Google's open-source project on which Chrome is based.[851] There is a debate on whether the choice screen was effective in spurring browser competition.[852] Apart from the effects specifically attributable to it, one idea gaining traction is that antitrust enforcement put Microsoft on notice, which made it more cautious when making product design choices that anticompetitively leveraged its market power.[853] In any case, there is little to disagree with in remedies that prevent a dominant firm from pushing its clearly inferior product in an adjacent market, thus foreclosing firms that may one day challenge its monopoly. It was no surprise then that the *Google Android* decision also led to a browser choice screen.[854]

With its structured legal test, tying is an administrable form of abuse. It has been transformed for application in the digital economy and can, given some tweaks, continue to fulfil an important role. There is, however, a risk that – perhaps due to the familiarity of the abuse – competition authorities conceive every potential abuse as a tie. When announcing its App Store investigation, for example, the EC hinted at a tie between the App Store and IAP, Apple's in-app purchase system.[855] While a tying theory (in particular one based on extraction rather than foreclosure) is not entirely out of place,[856] the core of the issue appears to be one of exploitation.[857]

850 Cusumano, Gawer and Yoffie (n 614) 127–29. Interestingly, while Firefox and IE were declining, Firefox's usage still surpassed IE given that it declined more slowly.

851 Tom Warren, 'Microsoft's New Edge Chromium Browser Launches on Windows and MacOS' (*The Verge*, 15 January 2020) <https://www.theverge.com/2020/1/15/21066767/>.

852 Compare Gore and van Rooijen (n 750) 17–44 with Omar Vásquez Duque, 'Active Choice vs. Inertia? An Exploratory Analysis of Choice Screens Applied in the European Microsoft Antitrust Case' (2021) <https://ssrn.com/abstract=3766468>. The EC touted its success, see EC, 'Commission fines Microsoft for non-compliance with browser choice commitments' (press release, 6 March 2013) IP/13/196 ('the choice screen was very successful with users: for example, until November 2010, 84 million browsers were downloaded through it').

853 There are signs of this in annual reports, see eg Microsoft Corporation, Form 10-K annual report to the SEC for the fiscal year ended June 30, 2008, 15–16 ('The European Commission closely scrutinizes the design of high-volume Microsoft products and the terms on which we make certain technologies used in these products, such as file formats, programming interfaces, and protocols, available to other companies.'). For statements corroborating this theory, see David Dayen, *Monopolized: Life in the Age of Corporate Power* (The New Press 2020) 282.

854 Paul Gennai, 'Presenting Search App and Browser Options to Android Users in Europe' (*The Keyword – Google Blog*, 18 April 2019) <https://www.blog.google/around-the-globe/google-europe/presenting-search-app-and-browser-options-android-users-europe/>. While the remedy can be criticized, the main issues related not to the browser but the search engine choice screen.

855 EC, 'Commission opens investigations into Apple's App Store rules' (press release, 16 June 2020) IP/20/1073 (focusing on 'the mandatory use of Apple's own proprietary in-app purchase system'). In the end, the EC dropped the objection. For an analysis of Apple's conduct as tying, see Bapu Kotapati, Simon Mutungi, Melissa Newham, Jeff Schroeder, Shili Shao and Melody Wang, 'The Antitrust Case against Apple' (2020) Digital Platform Theories of Harm Paper Series: Paper 2, 9–14.

856 See Friso Bostoen and Daniel Mândrescu, 'Assessing Abuse of Dominance in the Platform Economy: A Case Study of App Stores' (2020) 16 European Competition Journal 431, 470–73. The main problem is that the App Store setup may be one of the cases where the conditions of the SMP theory are fulfilled. The tying perspective may thus not provide a fitting theory of harm.

857 The Dutch competition authority framed Apple's IAP obligation as exploitation, see ACM, Case ACM/19/035630, *Apple*, 24 August 2021 (Summary of Decision). Still, it could not help hinting at a tie (eg by going to some lengths to show that the App Store and IAP are separate products).

7

REFUSAL TO SUPPLY

The legal status of unilateral refusals to deal and related practices (such as a decision to stop supplying a rival) has always been a complex and controversial issue in (EU) competition law.[858]

The idea is growing that certain online platforms constitute essential digital infrastructure that users – who often compete with the platform's own offering – should be guaranteed access to. The refusal to supply doctrine is the obvious legal basis for such access. It appears from an ICN survey that the conduct raising most concerns in digital markets is refusal to supply.[859] At the same time, competition authorities have faced relatively few refusal to supply decisions, which may have to do with its uncertain legal status.

Section 7.1 takes a closer look at the idea behind, conditions of, and trade-offs inherent in the refusal to supply doctrine. Section 7.2 then examines how this doctrine may be applied to online platforms, because while not *every* instance of leveraging should be qualified as a refusal to supply, *some* situations in which a platform extends its dominance from one market to another are properly characterized as such. The challenge is to uncover more generally applicable principles to help us determine when that is the case.

7.1 Refusal to Supply Doctrine

Refusals to supply come in different varieties. Firstly, a dominant firm that never before gave access to its input may refuse to do so. This is the traditional scenario, often simply referred to as 'refusal to supply' but better designated as '*de novo* refusal'. Secondly, a dominant firm that had been supplying its input may stop doing so. In that

858 Pablo Ibáñez Colomo, *The Shaping of Competition Law* (CUP 2018) 198.

859 ICN, 'Survey on Dominance/Substantial Market Power in Digital Markets' (Report on the Results, 2020) 4 (out of 30 competition authorities, 12 have been/are investigating refusals to supply in digital markets). Few refusal to supply decisions have been adopted.

case, there is no *de novo* refusal but rather a *disruption* of supply. Thirdly, in both scenarios, the refusal can be outright or *constructive*. In the latter case, there is no explicit refusal, but the same result is attained by demanding unreasonable conditions (eg an absurdly high price) for the input. Given that the refusal to supply doctrine has taken shape mostly through *de novo* refusals (whether recognized as such or not), this section starts by looking at the traditional doctrine but only summarily, given that the subject is well trodden (Section 7.1.1). It then examines disruptions of supply, with a focus on the question of whether such disruptions merit a different legal test (Section 7.1.2). Given that platforms often disrupt rather than *de novo* refuse access, the distinction is crucial.

7.1.1 *De Novo* Refusals of Supply

In exceptional cases, a firm may operate facilities that are essential for rivals to be able to compete in a neighbouring market but for which there are neither actual nor potential substitutes. Under the refusal to supply doctrine, such a firm can be forced to grant access to its facilities to competitors. This abuse of dominance is grounded in article 102(b) TFEU, which prohibits 'limiting production, markets or technical development to the prejudice of consumers'. The denial of access to an essential facility or – more broadly – 'input' is a classic form of leveraging: without such upstream access, competition on a downstream market may be eliminated. The EC recognizes this, noting that 'typically competition problems arise when the dominant undertaking competes on the "downstream" market with the buyer whom it refuses to supply'.[860] Like other forms of leveraging, this abuse thus originates from a platform's vertical integration, which may give it the incentive to use its upstream market power to exclude downstream competitors.

The refusal to supply or essential facilities doctrine was developed through a series of cases before the EU courts.[861] According to this case law, a refusal is abusive only if it concerns an input that is indispensable for carrying out business in an adjacent market and eliminates all (effective) competition in that market.[862] In addition, when the refusal concerns intellectual property, it must prevent the appearance of a new product[863] or at least limit technical development.[864] This legal test is particularly strict in comparison to those of other (leveraging) abuses. This is explained by the fact the remedy for a *de novo* refusal – ie forcing the dominant firm to deal with a (downstream)

860 Exclusionary Conduct Guidance Paper (n 461), para 75. See also Richard Whish and David Bailey, *Competition Law* (OUP 2018) 715.

861 While 'refusal to supply' and 'essential facilities' have a different meaning (and legal test) under US antitrust law, they are interchangeable in EU competition law, even though the 'facility' terminology is more natural in reference to physical infrastructure. 'Essential', 'objectively necessary' and 'indispensable' are also used interchangeably.

862 Joined Cases 6 and 7–73 *Commercial Solvents v Commission* EU:C:1974:18, para 25; *CBEM v CLT and IPB ('Télémarketing')* (n 559), paras 25–27; *Oscar Bronner v Mediaprint* (n 536), paras 41–47. Similar conditions are described in the Exclusionary Conduct Guidance Paper (n 461), para 81.

863 Joined Cases C–241/91 P and C–242/91 P *RTE and ITP v Commission* ('*Magill*') EU:C:1995:98, paras 49–58; C–418/01 *IMS Health v NDC Health* EU:C:2004:257, para 38.

864 *Microsoft v Commission* (n 339), para 647.

competitor – is especially detrimental to the freedom of contract.[865] To interfere with this fundamental right, the ECJ set a high bar.[866]

The crux of this legal test is the condition of 'indispensability' for competition in an adjacent market. According to the ECJ in *Bronner*, 'indispensability' means that there is no actual substitute for the facility in question and it is impossible to duplicate such a facility due to technical, legal or economic reasons under current market conditions.[867] Importantly, the possibility of duplication is assessed not subjectively (could the firm requesting access duplicate the facility?) but objectively (could a firm operating at equivalent scale to the dominant firm duplicate the facility?).[868] In that sense, the indispensability condition has been qualified as 'a variation on the "as efficient competitor" standard, requiring it to be demonstrated that duplication is objectively unfeasible … and not merely because the party requesting access is small and lacks the required financial resources'.[869]

For a refusal to supply to be abusive, not only must the input be indispensable, but the refusal must also eliminate all competition. The 'elimination of all competition' is the mirror image of 'indispensability': if a refusal to supply an input leads to the elimination of all competition, that input is indispensable for those firms seeking access to it.[870] However, the probability with which the refusal must eliminate all competition has shifted over the years. Initially, the refusal needed to come with the 'risk'[871] or the 'possibility'[872] of eliminating all competition. The ECJ also noted that the elimination of *one* competitor of a vertically integrated undertaking could suffice if it had repercussions on the competitive structure of the market.[873] In *Bronner*, however, the ECJ held that the elimination of all competition must be 'likely' – a seemingly stricter test.[874] In *Microsoft*, the GC opined that the difference between 'risk', 'possibility' or 'likelihood' is purely one of terminology; they reflect the same idea,

865 Case C-165/19 P *Slovak Telekom v Commission* EU:C:2021:239, para 46; Exclusionary Conduct Guidance Paper (n 461), para 75. In addition to freedom of contract, the right to property is also interfered with.

866 Of course, every remedy interferes to some extent with an undertaking's right to dispose freely of its property. In refusal to supply cases, however, the interference is greater because remedies are generally (but not necessarily) proactive rather than reactive.

867 *Oscar Bronner v Mediaprint* (n 536), paras 42–46.

868 ibid, paras 46–47. It is not entirely clear whether this 'scale' must be equivalent only in the downstream market or in general. In *Bronner*, the ECJ refers to the smaller circulation of the newspaper requesting access to a distribution network, implying that scale on the downstream market is the relevant benchmark.

869 Niamh Dunne, 'Dispensing with Indispensability' (2019) LSE Law, Society and Economy Working Paper 15/2019, 7.

870 See Ibáñez Colomo, 'Exclusionary Discrimination Under Article 102 TFEU' (n 553) 156–57 (noting that the opposite is not necessarily true).

871 *Commercial Solvents v Commission* (n 862), para 25 ('risks eliminating all competition on the part of this customer').

872 *CBEM v CLT and IPB ('Télémarketing')* (n 559), para 26 ('the possibility of eliminating all competition from another undertaking').

873 *Commercial Solvents v Commission* (n 862), para 33.

874 *Oscar Bronner v Mediaprint* (n 536), para 38–41, in which the ECJ references *Commercial Solvents*, *Télémarketing* and *Magill* (see previous footnotes) even though these judgments did not put forward a 'likelihood' threshold. In *IMS Health v NDC Health* (n 863), paras 40–47, the ECJ also puts forward 'likelihood' (and 'capability') as the relevant threshold.

namely, that the EC can apply article 102 TFEU *before* all competition is eliminated, especially in markets characterized by significant network effects, because the elimination of competition would be more difficult to reverse.[875] In addition, the GC held that the refusal must not be likely to eliminate *all* competition, but rather all *effective* competition.[876]

Finally, a refusal to supply can be objectively justified.[877] While this is the case for every form of abuse, objective justifications play a prominent role in case of refusals. It was in a refusal to supply case that AG Jacobs criticized 'the two-stage analysis suggested by the distinction between an abuse and its objective justification' as being 'artificial': it would be more accurate to say that dominant firm conduct, when justified, does not fall in the category of abuse at all.[878] In ECJ judgments, too, objective justification is often mentioned in the same breath as the legal test – or even as part of it, rather than as an afterthought.[879] In order to successfully plead an objective justification, the dominant firm must show that 'it pursues a legitimate interest other than its own commercial advantage, and that it has behaved in a proportionate way'.[880]

The legal test for finding a refusal to supply – and in particular the indispensability condition – must guide competition authorities in making a difficult trade-off. On the one hand, mandating access to a facility can lower prices/expand output (allocative efficiency) while also spurring innovation (dynamic efficiency) as entrants make use of the facility to provide competing or alternative products downstream. On the other hand, forced access can decrease incentives to innovate upstream, both for the incumbent (which profits less from its innovation when it has to be shared) and the entrants (which are not motivated to develop their own facilities).[881] This effect may be wider than the market in question: the threat of forced access may discourage investment in high-risk, high-reward ventures more generally, given that the financial reward from successful ventures may be curtailed.[882] To prevent entrants from simply free riding on the investment of incumbents, a fair price for access has to be determined, but competition authorities do not always have the expertise and/or willingness to engage in this exercise (and courts even less so).

---

875 *Microsoft v Commission* (n 339), paras 561–62.

876 ibid, para 653.

877 *CBEM v CLT and IPB ('Télémarketing')* (n 559), para 26; *RTE and ITP v Commission* ('*Magill*') (n 863), para 55; *Microsoft v Commission* (n 339), paras 668–712; Joined Cases C–468/06 to C–478/06 *Sot. Lélos v GlaxoSmithKline* EU:C:2008:504, para 34.

878 Case C–53/03 *Syfait v GlaxoSmithKline* EU:C:2004:673, Opinion of AG Jacobs, para 72. Notably, the AG found that an objective justification was present here (paras 73–104), but the ECJ did not subsequently rule on the substance. For a discussion, see Albertina Albors-Llorens, 'Refusal to Deal and Objective Justification in EC Competition Law' (2006) 65 The Cambridge Law Journal 24.

879 See eg *Sot. Lélos v GlaxoSmithKline* (n 877), para 34.

880 Whish and Bailey (n 860) 724. Possible justifications include that the customer is a bad debtor, that the dominant firm is facing capacity constraints, or that the dominant firm needs to realize an adequate return on investment.

881 Exclusionary Conduct Guidance Paper (n 461), para 75.

882 Fumagalli, Motta and Calcagno (n 689) 547.

7.1.2 Disruptions of Supply

The refusal to supply (or *Bronner*) conditions have provided the dominant paradigm for assessing situations in which a dominant firm declines to deal with competitors. There is, however, an often disregarded but distinct strain of this case law. Refusals to supply within established commercial relations – ie *disruptions* of supply – have at times been treated differently. This section traces the case law on disruptions of supply, asking whether such cases merit separate standards.[883]

The *Commercial Solvents* judgment, which marked the start of the refusal to supply case law, concerned a disruption of supply. Commercial Solvents (CS) had been supplying Zoja with aminobutanol – a raw material required to manufacture the medicine ethambutol – for five years. After CS started manufacturing ethambutol itself, it stopped supplying Zoja with aminobutanol. In confirming the EC's finding of abuse, the ECJ underlined the underlying leveraging strategy:

> [A]n undertaking which has a dominant position in the market in raw materials and which, with the object of reserving such raw material for manufacturing its own derivatives, refuses to supply a customer, which is itself a manufacturer of these derivatives, and therefore risks eliminating all competition on the part of this customer, is abusing its dominant position[.][884]

Télémarketing concerned a similar leveraging scenario. Centre Belge had been conducting telemarketing operations on the Belgian television station RTL (which held a legal monopoly) via Information Publicité – RTL's exclusive agent for television advertising. After two years, Information Publicité notified advertisers it would no longer accept any telemarketing except its own. In its preliminary ruling, the ECJ cited *Commercial Solvents* in holding that:

> [A]n abuse within the meaning of article [102] is committed where, without any objective necessity, an undertaking holding a dominant position on a particular market reserves to itself or to an undertaking belonging to the same group an ancillary activity which might be carried out by another undertaking as part of its activities on a neighbouring but separate market[.][885]

These two cases thus put forward the refusal to supply test including indispensability and the elimination of all competition.[886] However, in its *United Brands* judgment – adopted between *Commercial Solvents* and *Télémarketing* – the ECJ

883 This section is adapted from Friso Bostoen, 'Disruptions vs Refusals of Supply: A Guide to the Case Law' (*CoRe Blog*, 4 May 2022) <https://www.lexxion.eu/coreblogpost/disruptions-vs-refusals-of-supply/>.

884 *Commercial Solvents v Commission* (n 862), para 25.

885 *CBEM v CLT and IPB ('Télémarketing')* (n 559), para 27.

886 *Télémarketing* did so more clearly than *Commercial Solvents*; the indispensability condition is rather implicit in the latter.

took a different approach. United Brands (UB) had stopped providing Chiquita bananas to Olesen – one of its most important long-standing customers in Denmark. In a section dedicated to the 'refusal to continue supplies', the ECJ asserted positively that 'an undertaking in a dominant position for the purpose of marketing a product ... cannot stop supplying a long-standing customer who abides by regular commercial practice'.[887] The ECJ found such conduct inconsistent with article 102(b) TFEU in that it limits markets to the prejudice of consumers and with article 102(c) as it amounts to discrimination liable to eliminate a trading partner from the market.[888]

When the ECJ crystallized its refusal to supply doctrine in the *Magill* and *Bronner*, two cases of *de novo* refusal, the distinction between disruptions and refusals seemed headed for extinction. But then came *Microsoft I*, in which the EC assessed Microsoft's refusal to provide interoperability information to Sun Microsystems and other developers of work group server operating systems. This refusal actually constituted a disruption: disclosures that Microsoft undertook with respect to Windows NT had been discontinued with the development of Windows 2000.[889] The EC argued that the list of circumstances to be taken into account when assessing a refusal to supply should not be exhaustive.[890] It pointed out – not entirely convincingly – how, in *Commercial Solvents* and *Télémarketing*, 'the European Courts have given weight to circumstances where a refusal to supply constituted a disruption of previous levels of supply'.[891] Nevertheless, the EC went on to prove that Microsoft's conduct fulfilled the more stringent test for *de novo* refusals. On appeal, the EC clarified that it treated the disruption of supply 'not as an abuse in itself but as one factor relevant to the assessment of Microsoft's refusal to supply', elaborating at the hearing that the disruption was one of three factors allowing Microsoft's conduct to be characterized as abusive.[892] The GC too ended up applying the *Bronner* test.[893]

In between its *Microsoft* decision and the appeal judgment, the EC took the opportunity to reflect on the standards guiding the application of article 102 TFEU, which resulted in a Discussion Paper. The paper is remarkable for its clear distinction between 'termination of an existing supply relationship' and 'refusal to start supplying an input',

887 *United Brands v Commission* (n 339), para 182.

888 In this case, however, the firm halting supplies was not entering the downstream market. Rather, UB referred to the fact that Olesen had participated in an advertising campaign for competing Dole bananas. While the ECJ recognized a firm may protect its commercial interests, it considered UB's action disproportionate.

889 *Microsoft* (n 631), paras 578–84.

890 ibid, para 555.

891 ibid, paras 556 *juncto* 578.

892 *Microsoft v Commission* (n 339), paras 308 and 317. The other two factors are 'the fact that the information which Microsoft refuses to disclose to its competitors relates to interoperability in the software industry, a matter to which the Community legislature attaches particular importance' and 'the fact that Microsoft uses its extraordinary power on the client PC operating systems market to eliminate competition on the adjacent work group server operating systems market'.

893 Or perhaps a slightly less stringent version, given that it did not require the refusal to prevent the appearance of a new product – a limitation of technological development sufficed.

arguing the former should be subject to less stringent standards than the latter.[894] The three main reasons to uphold stringent standards for *de novo* refusals do not apply (to the same extent) in case of disruptions. Firstly, duties to deal decrease the dominant firm's incentives to invest in building essential facilities: if they are forced to share them, they may not get an adequate return on investment. This is different for disruptions of supply:

> That the dominant company in the past has found it in its interest to supply an input to one or more customers shows that the dominant company at a certain point in time considered it efficient to engage in such supply relationships. This and the fact that its customers are likely to have made investments connected to these supply relationships create a rebuttable presumption that continuing these relationships is pro-competitive.[895]

Secondly, duties to deal interfere with the dominant firm's fundamental freedom of contract, but that freedom is not equally imperilled in cases where the dominant firm has already chosen to contract. Thirdly, it is challenging to design duty-to-deal remedies, but previous dealing facilitates the exercise by serving as a benchmark – the competition authority or court does not have to start from scratch when setting access conditions. For these reasons, the EC proposed a less stringent standard for disruptions, namely, a 'likely market distorting effect'. The impact on the level of competition in the market depends mainly on the preexisting level of competition in the downstream market and whether the dominant upstream firm is active in that market. For instance, 'if the input owner is itself active in the downstream market and terminates supplies to one of its few competitors, it will normally be presumed that there is a negative effect on competition on the downstream market'.[896]

In the EC's subsequent Guidance Paper, however, little remained of the distinction. On the contrary, the EC held that the *Bronner* conditions apply to both disruptions of supply and *de novo* refusals. It did note that the termination of an existing supply arrangement is more likely to be found abusive than a *de novo* refusal to supply, especially in view of relation-specific investments made by co-contractors and the fact that previous supply indicates the dominant firm was receiving adequate compensation for its investment. Therefore, a light reversal of the burden of proof remains justified: the EC states that, in such cases of disruption, '[i]t would therefore be up to the dominant company to demonstrate why circumstances have actually changed in such a way that the continuation of its existing supply relationship would put in danger its adequate compensation'.[897]

894 EC, 'The Application of Article 82 of the Treaty to Exclusionary Abuses' (n 375), ss 9.2.1–9.2.2.

895 ibid, para 217.

896 ibid, para 222. In addition, the identity of the excluded competitor may be important for the assessment: 'The exclusion of a particular competitor may have a special effect on competition, for instance if it follows a different business model than the established competitors on the market' (para 223).

897 Exclusionary Conduct Guidance Paper (n 461), para 84.

Just before the publication of the Guidance Paper, the ECJ got another opportunity to rule on disruptions of supply. In *Sot. Lélos*, it was asked for guidance in proceedings brought by pharmaceutical wholesalers against GlaxoSmithKline's Greek subsidiary (GSK). After years of fulfilling orders, GSK had halted supplies, which wholesalers distributed on the Greek market and in other Member States (sometimes in competition with GSK). Referencing *Commercial Solvents* and *United Brands*, the ECJ held:

> The established case-law of the Court shows that the refusal by an undertaking occupying a dominant position on the market of a given product to meet the orders of an existing customer constitutes abuse of that dominant position under Article [102] where, without any objective justification, that conduct is liable to eliminate a trading party as a competitor[.][898]

It is important to ascertain whether the orders are not out of the ordinary,[899] but if not, a lower standard of anticompetitiveness (liable to eliminate a trading party as competitor) applies. However, it must be noted that GSK's disruption of supply was aimed at impeding parallel trade by wholesalers. Given EU competition law's unique market integration goal, parallel trade enjoys special protection, which may explain the lower standard applied in this case.[900]

Finally, the refusal to supply question came to the fore in the recent *Slovak Telekom* case. It concerned a telecom incumbent subject to a regulatory (*ex ante*) duty to deal that impeded access to its network by withholding information and setting unfair terms, including high prices.[901] In a careful opinion, the AG started from the logic of *Bronner*. Its strict conditions are justified for reasons touched upon earlier. First, penalizing refusals to supply – ie requiring an undertaking to conclude an agreement – is especially detrimental to the freedom of contract.[902] Second, the *Bronner* criteria must balance the short- and long-term benefits of competition.[903] But that logic only applies to what he terms 'refusals to make available' – not to unfair contract terms.[904] In its judgment, the ECJ did not use the term 'refusals to make available' but, leaning on the rationale put forward by the AG, conceived *Bronner* as being about 'a refusal by a dominant undertaking to give a competitor access to infrastructure *that it had developed for the needs of its own business*'.[905] This phrasing, even more clearly than the AG's, restricts the scope of *Bronner* to *de novo* refusals. Where access has previously been granted,

---

898 *Sot. Lélos v GlaxoSmithKline* (n 877), para 34.

899 ibid, para 70. See similarly *United Brands v Commission* (n 339), para 182.

900 Dunne (n 869) 28.

901 *Slovak Telekom v Commission* (n 865).

902 Cases C–152/19 P and C–165/19 P *Slovak Telekom v Commission* EU:C:2020:678, Opinion of AG Saugmandsgaard Øe, paras 66–74 (referencing Case C–7/97 *Oscar Bronner v Mediaprint* EU:C:1998:264, Opinion of AG Jacobs).

903 ibid, paras 75–78.

904 The AG rejects as spurious another distinction put forward by Slovak Telekom, namely, that between implicit and explicit/outright refusals to supply.

905 *Slovak Telekom v Commission* (n 865), para 45–47 (emphasis added).

the dominant undertaking's freedom to conduct business and its incentives to invest are not equally imperilled.[906]

In conclusion, when assessing disruptions of supply, enforcers are also faced with a difficult trade-off. That trade-off, however, is generally less indeterminate than in cases of *de novo* refusal. First of all, the history of prior dealing shows that supplying a competitor is – or at least *was* – efficient for the dominant firm, meaning it was receiving adequate compensation for its investment. Secondly and relatedly, an authority or court ordering a dominant firm to continue supplying a competitor does not have to make up a fair price out of thin air; rather, it can use the conditions of prior dealing as a benchmark. Barring a significant change in market conditions, the concern for efficiency (primarily the dominant firm's incentives to invest) is thus mitigated in case of prior dealing.[907] In addition, the dominant undertaking's freedom of contract is not interfered with to the same degree. For all these reasons, disruptions of supply merit separate standards from *de novo* refusals. More specifically, they should be subject to a standard effects test, meaning a likelihood of anticompetitive effects must be established. The case law and policy documents discussed above already contain the seeds of the distinction discussed here, although it has regrettably suffered from neglect.[908]

7.1.3 *Bronner*'s Expansionist Tendencies

Ever since the Big Bang, the universe has been expanding. After the short inflationary epoch right after the Big Bang, that growth slowed, but about 10 billion years later (4 billion years ago), it started accelerating again. Scientists theorize this accelerating expansion is due to dark energy – a form of energy of which little is known. By contrast, dark matter – of which equally little is known – works in the opposite direction, slowing down the expansion of the universe.

The refusal to supply case law is also subject to two counteracting forces, although we luckily understand them better than their cosmic counterparts. The expansionist force is provided by the defendants. In courtrooms and other fora of antitrust enforcement, they have a strong interest in conceiving any practice as – if any form of abuse – a refusal to supply, for the simple reason that *Bronner*'s legal test is the strictest one.[909] By contrast, complainants and competition authorities are incentivized to keep cases out of *Bronner* territory, in favour of abuses with a less stringent test.

The judicial wrangling of parties is, of course, only secondary – what is at stake is the effectiveness of article 102 TFEU. On the exact scope of *Bronner*, the case law of the European courts has proven less immutable than the laws of physics. Upon

906 ibid, para 51.

907 More easily finding a refusal to supply in cases of prior dealing may have an unintended side effect, namely, that upstream firms may not even *start* dealing with downstream competitors.

908 Even in *Slovak Telekom v Commission* (n 865), the ECJ references the not particularly helpful Case 238/87 *Volvo v Veng* EU:C:1988:477 rather than previous cases on disruptions of supply.

909 See eg Case T–612/17 *Google v Commission* (Hearing Report), paras 328–29.

publication of the judgment, as noted, many took it to be the standard for refusals to supply. As shown above, however, disruptions of supply should be distinguished – and have been, both before and after *Bronner*. What about other forms of abuse? The problem is that – with a little creativity – any abuse can be made to resemble a refusal to supply.

Consider tying. Determining whether a potentially abusive practice is a tie or a refusal to supply is not always straightforward.[910] Arguing *ad absurdum*, one could say that every tie implies a refusal to supply (and should be assessed as such) – namely, a refusal to provide the tying without the tied product. Of course, doing so would make tying as a separate form of abuse superfluous, which goes against the wording of article 102 TFEU. The ECJ has also suggested that, if a tie is present, its legal test takes precedence over that of the implied refusal to supply.[911] Alternatively, one could focus on the remedy imposed: if one can simply break the tie, the conduct should be assessed as tying; if one imposes an access remedy, then a refusal to supply must be established. Following this reasoning, the choice screen remedy in *Microsoft II*, which gave competing browsers access to the Microsoft OS, shows that it was actually a disguised refusal to supply case.[912] However, while the remedy did promote access, one cannot reverse engineer the abuse from the remedy. Apart from practical difficulties (enforcers would need to come up with the remedy *before* starting their investigation), there are additional arguments against doing so. Tying, by definition, constricts the freedom of choice of consumers (or other trading partners subject to the tie). In software markets, breaking the tie is future-oriented, which already limits its effectiveness ('Fine, your app has been preinstalled on millions of PCs, but please refrain from doing so *from now on*'). Such a remedy does nothing to restore consumer choice and means that competing app developers will be foreclosed for years to come (given the lifecycle of devices such as PCs and mobile phones). It only makes sense to fully consider the present situation and impose, for example, a choice screen to restore choice and competition (and innovation) *in addition to* prohibiting similar ties in the future. Competition law enforcement already takes years; there is no reason to add another couple of years for the remedy to meaningfully kick in.

---

910 On this point, see Ibáñez Colomo, *The Shaping of Competition Law* (n 858) 211–12 and Pablo Ibáñez Colomo, 'How to Distinguish Between Tying and Refusal to Deal Cases (Hint: It's Not Just Words)' (*Chillin' Competition*, 24 April 2015) <https://chillingcompetition.com/2015/04/24/>. See also Whish and Bailey (n 860) 705 (describing refusal to supply as a form of tying).

911 The ECJ did so in *Konkurrensverket v TeliaSonera* (n 631), para 57, although the paragraph is not crystal clear:

> Moreover, it must be observed that since the Court was, in the said paragraphs of Bronner, called upon, in essence, only to interpret [article 102 TFEU] with regard to the conditions under which a refusal to supply may be abusive, the Court did not make any ruling on whether the fact that an undertaking refuses access to its home-delivery scheme to the publisher of a rival newspaper where the latter does not at the same time entrust to it the carrying out of other services, such as sales in kiosks or printing, constitutes some other form of abuse of a dominant position, such as tied sales.

The EC agrees, see Exclusionary Conduct Guidance Paper (n 461), para 77:

> Other types of possibly unlawful refusal to supply, in which the supply is made conditional upon the purchaser accepting limitations on its conduct, are not dealt with in this section. For instance, halting supplies in order to punish customers for dealing with competitors or refusing to supply customers that do not agree to tying arrangements, will be examined by the Commission in line with the principles set out in the sections on exclusive dealing and tying and bundling.

912 Making this argument, see Nicolas Petit and Norman Neyrinck, 'Back to Microsoft I and II: Tying and the Art of Secret Magic' (2011) 2 JECLAP 117.

The relation between margin squeeze and refusal to supply has also been heavily debated. While the debate is treated in more depth later,[913] a short review of the most consequential ruling is called for here. In *TeliaSonera*, the eponymous firm argued that undertakings should be free to fix their terms of trade unless they amount to a refusal in the sense of *Bronner*.[914] The ECJ retorted that it cannot be inferred from that judgment that 'the conditions to be met in order to establish that a refusal to supply is abusive must necessarily also apply when assessing the abusive nature of conduct which consists in supplying services or selling goods on conditions which are disadvantageous'.[915] Such conduct may constitute an independent form of abuse – in this case, margin squeeze.[916] The ECJ also made a broader statement on *Bronner*'s expansionist tendencies:

> [I]f *Bronner* were to be interpreted otherwise, in the way advocated by TeliaSonera, that would ... amount to a requirement that before any conduct of a dominant undertaking in relation to its terms of trade could be regarded as abusive the conditions to be met to establish that there was a refusal to supply would in every case have to be satisfied, and that would unduly reduce the effectiveness of Article 102 TFEU.[917]

This statement already refers to 'terms of trade' generally. In *Slovak Telekom*, the ECJ confirmed that it was not just referring to margin squeezes when distinguishing the practices to which *Bronner* does not apply.[918] Indeed, in any scenario where access is given but made subject to unfair conditions (including excessive prices), the indispensability of the input may be relevant to but not required for a finding of abuse.[919]

In contrast to the universe, the scope of *Bronner* is not expanding but contracting.[920] While it was an AG who wrote that 'the judgment in *Bronner* is and must remain a special case within the regulatory landscape of Article 102 TFEU',[921] the statement could just as well describe the ECJ's philosophy. Disruptions of supply, tying, margin squeeze and other unfair terms (including excessive prices) are *not* subject to *Bronner*. As discussed below (Section 9), discrimination is not either. The indispensability condition is thus only relevant in cases of *de novo* refusal – a state of affairs for which there are good arguments, as set out in the previous section.

---

913 See Section 8.2.2.

914 *Konkurrensverket v TeliaSonera* (n 631), para 54.

915 ibid, para 55.

916 ibid, para 56.

917 ibid, para 58.

918 *Slovak Telekom v Commission* (n 865), para 53.

919 ibid, para 50.

920 From a more originalist perspective, which is not misplaced here, one could argue that *Bronner* always had a narrow scope and subsequent judgments simply made that more explicit.

921 Opinion of AG Saugmandsgaard Øe (n 902) para 3.

7.2 Platforms as Essential Facilities

Abusive refusals to supply have mostly been found in network sectors such as telecommunications, energy and transport.[922] These sectors rely on extensive physical infrastructure (eg telecom cables, gas pipelines and railway tracks) subject to significant economies of scale and network effects. Indeed, scale economies and network effects may be so strong that the incumbent qualifies as a 'natural monopoly', which exists when 'the entire demand within a relevant market can be satisfied at lowest cost by one firm rather than by two or more'.[923] Thus, while monopolies generally entail inefficiency,[924] *natural* monopolies exceptionally constitute the most efficient market structure. In case of natural monopoly, it is not economically viable – nor desirable – for competitors to duplicate the infrastructure. Along those lines, the EC recognizes that 'an input is likely to be impossible to replicate when it involves a natural monopoly due to scale or scope economies [or] where there are strong network effects'.[925] Given that the indispensability condition is likely to be fulfilled, natural monopolies are a natural fit for the essential facilities doctrine.[926]

As discussed above, online platforms also benefit from scale economies and network effects.[927] Platform markets are prone to 'tipping' in favour of one firm (a 'winner takes all' dynamic), which is why platforms are said to compete *for* the market. Platforms thus have a lot in common with natural monopolies, and some may even qualify as such.[928] Aside from the 'natural monopoly' terminology, the market power of certain platforms goes by names such as 'strategic bottleneck power'[929] and 'gatekeeper power'.[930] However, these different terms try to capture the same idea: given the lack of actual substitutes and unviability of duplication, access to these platforms is objectively necessary to compete in the downstream market – in other words, the essential facilities doctrine should apply. But how are we to decide which platforms should be mandated to provide access to downstream firms (that they compete with)?

It is useful to make a distinction between two kinds of platform access. Firstly, one could mandate access to the *platform* infrastructure itself, determining, for example,

922 Whish and Bailey (n 860) 720–23.

923 Richard Posner, 'Natural Monopoly and Its Regulation' (1968) 21 Stanford Law Review 548, 548.

924 Monopolies entail allocative inefficiency (deadweight loss), x-inefficiency (see Section 11.2.1) and potentially dynamic inefficiency (see Kenneth Arrow, 'Economic Welfare and the Allocation of Resources for Invention' in *The Rate and Direction of Inventive Activity: Economic and Social Factors* (Princeton University Press, 1962) 609–22).

925 Exclusionary Conduct Guidance Paper (n 461), fn 58.

926 Some argue that the essential facilities doctrine should be limited to cases of natural monopoly, see Gregory Werden, 'The Law and Economics of the Essential Facility Doctrine' (1987) 32 Saint Louis University Law Journal 433, 476.

927 See Sections 2.2.1 and 4.1.2.

928 See Francesco Ducci, *Natural Monopolies in Digital Platform Markets* (CUP 2020) and further Section 11.2.1.

929 See eg Jason Furman, Diane Coyle, Amelia Fletcher, Derek McAuley and Philip Marsden, 'Unlocking Digital Competition' (Digital Competition Expert Panel's Report, 2019) (hereafter, 'Furman Report') (discussing 'enduring market power over a strategic bottleneck market').

930 See eg van Gorp and de Bijl (n 410) 6–9.

that app developers should have access to the two dominant app stores.[931] Note that such access would address self-preferencing concerns as it would imply that the app store operators cannot exclude the apps of independent app developers once they start competing with their own apps. Secondly, one could oblige platforms to give third parties access to their *data*, which would primarily promote competition in the platform market. An important reason for Google's superior search engine is that it has processed billions of search queries and learned from those; if an entrant in the search market had access to this data, it could more easily develop into a viable competitor.[932] In other words, access to platform infrastructure tends to be a matter of *intra*-platform competition, while access to data is more likely to affect *inter*-platform competition.[933] In line with the subject of this work, this section focuses on the former.[934]

7.2.1 Matchmakers vs Market Makers

How should one assess refusals of access to platform infrastructure? One particularly helpful difference is that between 'matchmakers' and 'market makers'. Consider two platforms: Amazon Marketplace and Apple's App Store. Being delisted by any of these platforms would be a significant blow for a supplier. However, are (the effects of) these removals quantitively and qualitatively the same? They are not.

- A seller removed by Amazon may *largely* lose access to its customer base. In the US, for example, over 50% of e-commerce is facilitated by Amazon Marketplace.[935] In certain product categories, this market share is higher; in others, lower. Moreover, for some sellers, Amazon Marketplace is their primary (or even only) distribution channel; for others, it is simply an additional outlet. Whatever the specific situation, however, a seller has other options, including other platforms, an online storefront (powered by Shopify, for example), comparison shopping engines (including Google Shopping), and perhaps even brick-and-mortar stores.
- A developer whose app is delisted from the App Store *completely* loses its ability to reach its customer base, ie iPhone users.[936] Apple controls the OS of iPhones and makes it impossible to install alternative app stores. Nor can users download individual apps outside of the app store ('sideloading'). The only alternative is 'web apps', but their technical inferiority means they are not a *viable* alternative. A developer cannot simply distribute its app on phones running Android, either.

931 'Access' should be interpreted broadly here; it does not only cover being present on the app store, but also more subtle forms of access, eg to essential APIs that facilitate communication between the various parts of the mobile ecosystem.

932 See Cédric Argenton and Jens Prüfer, 'Search Engine Competition with Network Externalities' (2012) 8 JCLE 73.

933 Access to data, in particular to which extent suppliers have access to data on the transactions they conclude and to which extent the platform has access to that data, can certainly be a matter of intra-platform competition as well.

934 Access to data is touched upon in Section 13.4.

935 'Amazon's Share of US eCommerce Sales Hits All-Time High of 56.7% in 2021' (*PYMNTS*, 14 March 2022) <https://www.pymnts.com/news/retail/2022/amazons-share-of-us-ecommerce-sales-hits-all-time-high-of-56-7-in-2021/>.

936 See Bostoen and Mândrescu (n 856) 437–46 and 459–62.

> They would have to 'port' their app from one OS to the other – a demanding process that can even take longer than the initial development of the app.[937]

Being delisted from an online marketplace is thus different from being removed from an app store. The underlying reason is that online marketplaces and app stores are different *kinds* of platforms. According to the platform typology set out above, online marketplaces and app stores can be qualified as 'matching' and even 'transaction' platforms, given that they facilitate the sale of products – those products being 'everything' and 'apps', respectively.[938] Within this category, online marketplaces constitute e-commerce platforms, while app stores constitute innovation platforms. This distinction between *innovation* platforms and other transaction platforms – in fact, the distinction between innovation platforms and *all other* platforms – is crucial.

Cusumano, Gawer and Yoffie define innovation platforms as 'offer[ing] technological building blocks that third-party innovators use to develop new complementary products or services'.[939] By contrast, other platforms (which they group under the 'transaction platform' heading) simply 'enable the exchange of goods, services, and information'.[940] Thompson goes one step further and believes only innovation platforms are worthy of the name 'platform', defining it as 'the foundation on which entire ecosystems are built'.[941] He relabels other platforms as 'aggregators', which do not offer a technological foundation, but rather 'collect a critical mass of users and leverage access to those users to extract value from suppliers'.[942] To (over)simplify matters: innovation platforms are about *technology* (in the form of APIs), while other platforms are about *scale*; innovation platforms are *market* makers, while other platforms are *match*makers.

How does this distinction relate to the refusal to supply doctrine? As Thompson notes, innovation platforms are 'essential for the ecosystem to function'.[943] The operators of platforms completely control access to the ecosystem: when Apple delists a developer from its App Store, there is no viable way to reach users – the app becomes useless because it can no longer be distributed.[944] Suppliers do not rely on other platforms in the same way: when Amazon removes a seller from its Marketplace, it has other ways to reach consumers – its product does not become worthless.

---

937 See CMA, 'Mobile Ecosystems Market Study' (Final Report) June 2022, ss 4.154–4.161. See also Aaron Smith, 'How to Port Your iOS App to Android' (*Marino Software*, 30 January 2018) <https://www.marinosoftware.com/insights/so-you-want-to-port-to-android> ('porting [is] not necessarily faster [than initial development]').

938 See Section 1.2.

939 Cusumano, Gawer and Yoffie (n 614) 68 (emphasis omitted). In other words, '[t]he platform serves as a technological foundation upon which other firms develop complementary innovations' (p 19).

940 ibid. Thus, their value 'come[s] mainly from allowing different sides of a market to interact' (p 66).

941 Ben Thompson, 'A Framework for Regulating Competition on the Internet' (*Stratechery*, 9 December 2019) <https://stratechery.com/2019/a-framework-for-regulating-competition-on-the-internet/>.

942 ibid. Warning against placing too much importance on Thompson's theories, see Tim Wu, 'Ben Thompson's "Stratechery": Smart, but a Little Too Much Kool-Aid' (*Medium*, 29 October 2020) <https://superwuster.medium.com/reviewing-ben-thompsons-stratechery-45b545dd959>.

943 Thompson, 'A Framework for Regulating Competition on the Internet' (n 941).

944 ibid. Cusumano, Gawer and Yoffie (n 614) are not entirely clear on the App Store's status in their typology. They first qualify the App Store as a transaction platform (p 50) but later as an innovation platform (p 218). They do note that 'Apple … tightly connected its main innovation platform (the iOS operating system …) with its transaction platform (the App Store)', making Apple an 'integrated platform' – a view I endorse.

Innovation platforms are thus significantly more likely to be essential for suppliers in the downstream market. This goes not only for iOS (App Store), but also for Google's Android OS (Play Store) as well as for Windows OS (Microsoft Store).[945] Other platforms, including Amazon Marketplace but also Google Search and Facebook, are less likely to be essential.[946]

This distinction is derived mainly from business strategy/technology literature and thus needs to be tested against the case law. The only EC prohibition decision concerning a refusal to supply in platform markets is *Microsoft I*.[947] In its 2004 decision, the EC was already attuned to the platform terminology, writing that '"platform" … not only refers to operating systems, but to any software product that exposes an API for use by applications'.[948] It thus used the term 'platform' restrictively, referring only to innovation platforms (in line with Thompson). The EC found Microsoft to be dominant in the PC OS market due to its market share of over 90%, but also because of its 'applications barrier to entry': because Microsoft's market is so large, developers continue to write apps for it, which guarantees that Microsoft remains dominant.[949] Switching to another OS comes with a huge cost, as one Microsoft manager noted: 'The Windows API is so broad [and] so deeply embedded in the source code of many Windows apps that there is a huge switching cost to using a different operating system instead.'[950] Thus, according to the manager, 'it would be so much work to move over that they hope we just improve Windows rather than force them to move.'[951] In addition to PC OSs, Microsoft also developed work group server OSs, which deliver work group server services to a network of PCs (eg at a workplace). Those services include the sharing of files and printers as well as central administration by the IT department. Microsoft's share of the work group server OS market was also high: in the 60–75% range for most measures.[952] Interestingly, the EC took a broader view of Microsoft's market power given that the PC OS and workgroup server OS markets 'are closely

945 While the question of indispensability asks for a yes or no answer, some innovation platforms may still be *more* indispensable than others. For example, while the App Store is the only way to distribute apps within iOS, there are more (but still restricted) options than the Play Store in Android, see Bostoen and Mândrescu (n 856) 437–46 and 459–62.

946 On Google Search, see eg Thompson, 'A Framework for Regulating Competition on the Internet' (n 941) ('There is no "Google API" that makes 3rd party websites functional, and there are alternative search engines or simply the URL bar for users to go directly to 3rd party websites.'). However, there is still an important difference between the potentially indispensable nature of Google (with its 90+% market share) and Amazon Marketplace (with its much lower market share).

947 An earlier case involving IBM was settled, see EC, 'Competition Policy' (XIVth Report, 1985) 77–79 (the statement of objections is also discussed in an appeal judgment against the statement, see Case 60/81 *IBM v Commission* EU:C:1981:264). The alleged abuse in this case involved, among others, 'failing to supply other manufacturers in sufficient time with the technical information needed to permit competitive products to be used with System/370' (IBM's range of computers). IBM undertook 'to disclose, in a timely manner, sufficient interface information to enable competing companies in the EEC to attach both hardware and software products of their design to System/370'. For a national prohibition decision, see AGCM, Case A529, *Google (Android Auto)*, 13 May 2021. The refusal concerned access to an OS (Android Auto) but was *de novo* rather than a disruption.

948 *Microsoft* (n 631), para 39.

949 ibid, paras 448–60.

950 ibid, para 463.

951 ibid.

952 ibid, para 514.

associated through commercial and technical links'.[953] Without too much imagination, one can read into these words a budding ecosystem perspective.[954]

While Microsoft had a quasi-monopoly in the PC OS market, the work group server OS market still counted a number of competitors, including Sun Microsystems. According to the EC, however, Microsoft was exploiting the link between these two markets by 'leveraging its quasi-monopoly from the client PC operating system market to the work group server operating system market'.[955] In particular, Microsoft abused its dominant position by refusing to supply Sun and others with interface information, namely, 'the full specification of the protocols underlying the Windows domain architecture, which organises the way through which Windows work group servers deliver work group server services to Windows ... PCs.'[956] The EC found that there were no substitutes for Microsoft's disclosure of the interface information, and the non-disclosure risked eliminating competition in the work group server OS market.[957] Microsoft tried arguing that the forced licensing of its interface information would eliminate its future incentives to invest, but was unsuccessful.[958]

To remedy the abuse, the EC ordered Microsoft 'to disclose complete and accurate specifications for the protocols used by Windows work group servers in order to provide file, print and group and user administration services to Windows work group networks'.[959] To Microsoft's benefit, it did not have to do so freely; to the benefit of Sun Microsystems and other work group server OS developers, it had to do so on reasonable and non-discriminatory terms.[960] The GC upheld the EC's decision,[961] but it did take another two EC decisions (and over a billion euros in penalty payments) to get Microsoft to fully comply with the remedy.[962]

Microsoft I provides an early yet effective example of applying the refusal to supply doctrine to platforms. The EC and GC recognized that OSs, through their APIs, offer the technological foundation for an entire ecosystem of complementary products. For providers of such complements, access to this technological foundation can be – and often is – indispensable. The notion of 'innovation platform' is thus useful to help identify those cases of indispensability. The reverse is also true: other (transaction)

953 ibid, para 526, relying on *Tetra Pak v Commission* (n 558).

954 See eg *Microsoft* (n 631), para 588 (on a 'Windows environment').

955 ibid, para 533. Such leveraging is considered primarily offensive, but secondarily also offensive, see paras 770–71.

956 ibid, para 546 and 566 (quote).

957 *Microsoft* (n 631), paras 585–692. See paras 693–708 on how Microsoft's refusal to supply limits technical development to the prejudice of consumers.

958 ibid, paras 709–78. Under this section, the EC also discusses the IBM settlement described in EC, 'Competition Policy' (n 947) 77–79.

959 *Microsoft* (n 631), para 999.

960 ibid, paras 1005–1009.

961 *Microsoft v Commission* (n 339). The GC only annulled art 7 of the EC decision, which concerned the remedy monitoring mechanism (including a trustee).

962 *Microsoft* (Case COMP/C-3/37.792) Commission Decision C(2005)4420 setting the penalty payment and the decisions of 12 July 2006 and 27 February 2008 fixing the definitive amounts.

platforms are less likely to be indispensable for competition in an adjacent market given that they do not create that market but simply facilitate transactions (or interactions) within it. In line with this theory, the Luxembourgish competition authority rejected a complaint alleging a refusal to supply on Amazon's part.[963]

To constitute an abuse, a refusal to supply must not only concern an indispensable facility or input, but also eliminate effective competition in an adjacent market. The two limbs of this legal test are closely linked but do not overlap fully,[964] so we must consider the second limb separately. Of course, whether a refusal eliminates effective competition *in an adjacent market* depends on how this adjacent market is defined. In the case of innovation platforms, a central role is played by so-called aftermarkets.[965] Aftermarkets (or 'secondary markets') are markets for products to be used in connection with a durable good that has already been acquired (the 'primary market').[966] The aftermarket product 'is generally a consumable product (e.g., toner for printers or spare parts for car[s]), but can also simply consist of a complementary product for associated use with a primary product (a DVD with respect to a DVD player, or a game with respect to a game console)'.[967] Hardware and software offer a more modern – and relevant – example of aftermarkets. Taking a closer look at aftermarkets can tell us something about the control of platforms over adjacent markets – and thus their ability to eliminate effective competition in them.

Most ECJ judgments concern the archetypical aftermarket of spare (car) parts.[968] In *Hugin*, a case involving a supplier of cash registers, the ECJ found a separate market for 'Hugin spare parts required by independent undertakings'.[969] The secondary market was thus considered not only distinct from the primary market but also brand-specific. The definition of such narrow aftermarkets also characterizes the EC's decisional practice.[970] This approach is crystallized in the Market Definition Notice, where the EC writes: 'A narrow definition of market for secondary products, for instance, spare parts, may result when *compatibility* with the primary product is important.'[971] In its Discussion Paper, the EC further explained:

> Aftermarkets typically appear in competition cases when they are 'proprietary', that is, when they are brand-specific in that secondary products that can be used with one brand of primary product cannot be

963 Conseil de la concurrence, Decision 2017-C-02, *Amazon Services Europe*, 21 June 2017 (noting how the complainant could – and did – continue its business via its own websites and other platforms).

964 As noted above, Section 7.1.1, the 'elimination of all competition' is the mirror image of 'indispensability'.

965 See already Section 4.1.1.

966 OECD, 'Competition Issues in Aftermarkets' (Background Note) DAF/COMP(2017)2, 5.

967 ibid.

968 *Volvo* (n 908) and Case 53/87 *Renault* EU:C:1988:472. On spare computer parts (and technical information), there has been a commitment decision, see *IBM Maintenance Services* (Case COMP/C-3/39692) Commission Decision C(2011)9245.

969 Case 22/78 *Hugin v Commission* EU:C:1979:138.

970 For an overview, see OECD, 'Competition Issues in Aftermarkets' (Note from the European Union) DAF/COMP/WD(2017)3, 4 ('in all cases decided so far by the Commission, distinct markets were found').

971 Commission Notice on the definition of relevant market for the purposes of Community competition law (n 343), para 56 (emphasis added).

> used with another brand of primary product although the primary products themselves are substitutes. The contentious issue is often that the supplier of a primary product attempts to reserve the secondary market for itself.[972]

In defining secondary markets, just like primary markets, what matters is substitution. The particularity of aftermarkets is that substitution must be tested in both the secondary *and* primary markets. The GC confirmed this test in the *Luxury Watches* case, which concerned spare parts for watches:

> [T]he spare parts market for primary products of a particular brand may not be a separate relevant market in two situations: first, if it is possible for a consumer to switch to spare parts manufactured by another producer; second, if it is possible for the consumer to switch to another primary product in order to avoid a price increase on the market for spare parts.[973]

How does the case law on aftermarkets relate to digital ecosystems? These ecosystems often consist of various layers, in particular hardware and software. Firstly, software can constitute an aftermarket of that hardware.[974] In *Microsoft I* already, the EC considered defining a hardware-specific aftermarket of 'OSs for Intel-compatible PCs' – in contrast to OSs for non-Intel-compatible PCs (such as Apple Macintosh).[975] It explained that porting a non-Intel-compatible OS to run on Intel-compatible hardware would be a long and costly process (cf the earlier discussion on porting apps), but ultimately left the question open. Secondly, software itself often consists of various layers (eg an OS, an app store, and apps), and one software layer can constitute an aftermarket of another layer. In *Google Android*, for example, the EC determined that the two main mobile ecosystems – namely, the Android OS and iOS – operate in different markets.[976] It then defined an ecosystem-specific aftermarket for 'app stores *for Android devices*'.[977]

The innovation platforms at the heart of these ecosystems, ie Google and Apple, have almost complete control over competition in these aftermarkets.[978] Apple's iOS is not

972 EC, 'The Application of Article 82 of the Treaty to Exclusionary Abuses' (n 375), para 244.

973 Case T–427/08 *Confédération européenne des associations d'horlogers-réparateurs v Commission* EU:T:2010:517, para 79. Applying this test, the EC found 'the existence of multiple separate markets for spare parts, each associated, in principle, with a particular watch brand', see *Watch Repair* (Case AT.39097) Commission Decision C(2014)5462, para 96. The GC also stressed that 'if certain economic operators are specialised and are active solely on the after market of a primary market, that constitutes in itself a strong indication of the existence of a [separate aftermarket]' (para 108).

974 OECD, 'Competition Issues in Aftermarkets' (n 966) 5.

975 *Microsoft* (n 631), para 326.

976 *Google Android* (n 352), where the EC defined a relevant market for 'licensable smart mobile OSs', which includes Android but excludes iOS.

977 ibid, para 281 (emphasis added). The EC did consider the competitive constraint emanating from inter-platform competition (between Android and iOS).

978 See extensively ACM, 'Market Study into Mobile App Stores' (n 609).

compatible with third-party app stores, and makes it impossible to sideload apps, so the App Store is the only place to get apps – in other words, Apple has reserved the app distribution aftermarket for itself.[979] Google's ecosystem is slightly less proprietary: it does allow for third-party app stores and sideloading but discourages them within Android,[980] which leads to a near-monopoly of Google Play.[981] Going back to the *Luxury Watches* test, it is thus impossible to switch in secondary markets (eg between app stores). Switching in the primary market – between mobile phones, ie Android devices and iPhones – is difficult because the phones' initial purchase price is high, and consumers are locked into not only the device but also the broader ecosystem.[982]

This section has sought to inform the two limbs of the refusal to supply test as applied to platforms by reference to the notions of 'innovation platforms' and 'aftermarkets'. Firstly, *innovation platforms* offer the technological foundations for suppliers, in particular developers, which makes it more likely for the *indispensability* condition to be fulfilled (in contrast to eg transaction platforms). Secondly, this technological foundation itself often consists of layers of hardware and software, up to the point that innovation platforms are at the heart of complete ecosystems. Within this ecosystem, software may constitute an *aftermarket* for hardware – or other software. A (vertically integrated) innovation platform controls the compatibility between various layers and thus has the ability to *eliminate competition*. Vertical integration – and the resulting competition with suppliers within the ecosystem (app developers) – may give it the incentive to do so. In those cases, neither developers nor consumers can easily switch between ecosystems.

7.2.2 Installed Base Opportunism

The previous section discussed how the type of *platform* in question helps inform the application of the refusal to supply doctrine. This section examines which kind of platform *conduct* should be considered particularly likely to constitute an abusive refusal to supply. Remember that the case law has, albeit inconsistently, distinguished *de novo* refusals to supply from refusals in the context of established commercial relations.[983] There are good reasons to subject disruptions of supply to a less stringent test: the history of prior dealing shows that such dealing was efficient for the dominant firm (ie it was receiving adequate compensation for its investment) and

979 Note an important difference between the aftermarket for spare parts and app stores: app stores constitute platforms facilitating the distribution of apps, while spare parts are not a gateway to another market.

980 On third-party app stores, see Natasha Lomas, 'Aptoide, a Play Store Rival, Cries Antitrust Foul over Google Hiding Its App' (*TechCrunch*, 4 June 2019) <https://techcrunch.com/2019/06/04/aptoide-a-playstore-rival-cries-antitrust-foul-over-google-hiding-its-app/> (Aptoide alleges that 'Google Play Protect flags Aptoide as a harmful app, hiding it in users' Android devices and requesting them to uninstall it'); on sideloading, see 'Fortnite Reluctantly Comes to Google Play Store' (*BBC*, 22 April 2020) <www.bbc.com/news/technology-52383286> (Epic alleges that 'new efforts such as Google Play Protect outright block software obtained outside the Google Play store').

981 *Google Android* (n 352), paras 590–600.

982 See similarly Crémer Report (n 354), 47–48 ('where the firms' lock-in strategies are successful, and consumers are drawn into ecosystems which they find difficult to leave, ecosystem-specific aftermarkets may need to be defined', using the example of mobile ecosystems).

983 See Section 7.1.2.

an order to *continue* rather than *start* dealing does not equally imperil the dominant firm's freedom of contract. In case of (innovation) platforms, there is an additional reason.

According to Shapiro, '[t]he most troublesome cases arise when the dominant firm appears to be following a strategy of "open early, closed late."'[984]

> For example, in a network industry, a firm might obtain a dominant position based in part on certain 'open' policies that induce reliance by complementary firms, and then later exploit that position by offering less favorable interconnection terms or by refusing to interconnect with them altogether.[985]

Using the examples of iOS and Android, I have already examined how (innovation) platforms can evolve from more open to more closed systems as they become more established.[986] One commentator summarized this dynamic simply as 'challengers pursue interoperability while incumbents strive for incompatibility'.[987] The dynamic is driven by necessity: challengers generally do not have the resources to both run the platform *and* develop a wide variety of complements for it; by contrast, incumbents may. Developing complements, ie entering the downstream market, may increase the value the platform operator can extract, which can give it an incentive for doing so.

From a (dynamic) efficiency perspective, however, installed base opportunism is more harmful than *de novo* refusals to supply. For one, according to Shapiro, 'the return to opportunistic behavior is above and beyond the return to innovation and risk taking that would arise in a well-functioning, competitive market'.[988] The perspective of suppliers of complements/downstream firms is equally if not more important. They have already invested significantly in the relationship, in particular by developing their product for a *specific* innovation platform. Often, their investment devaluates significantly or becomes worthless when no longer permitted on the platform; insofar as alternative platforms are available, the product will have to be redeveloped. Moreover, acts of opportunism have ripple effects: the *fear of* opportunism can dull complementors' incentives to invest in the wider market.

---

984 Carl Shapiro, 'Exclusionary Conduct' (Testimony before the Antitrust Modernization Commission, 2005) 15. See also Michael Katz and Carl Shapiro, 'Antitrust in Software Markets' in Jeffrey Eisenach and Thomas Lenard (eds), *Competition, Innovation and the Microsoft Monopoly: Antitrust in the Digital Marketplace* (Springer 1999) 65–66.

985 Shapiro, 'Exclusionary Conduct' (n 984) 15.

986 Section 2.2.2.

987 Ben Thompson, 'Apple's Middle Age' (*Stratechery*, 5 February 2018) <https://stratechery.com/2018/apples-middle-age/>. For theoretical support, see Michael Katz and Carl Shapiro, 'Network Externalities, Competition, and Compatibility' (1985) 75 The American Economic Review 424, 425 ('firms with good reputations or large existing networks will tend to be against compatibility[; in] contrast, firms with small networks or weak reputations will tend to favor product compatibility'), confirmed in Michael Katz and Carl Shapiro, 'Systems Competition and Network Effects' (1994) 8 Journal of Economic Perspectives 93, 107 and 110–11.

988 Shapiro, 'Exclusionary Conduct' (n 984) 9.

Interestingly, the EC identified an 'open early, closed late' strategy behind Microsoft's practice of reducing interoperability:

> The value that [complementors'] products brought to the network also augmented the client PC operating systems' value in the customers' eyes and therefore Microsoft – as long as it did not have a credible work group server operating system alternative – had incentives to have its client PC operating system interoperate with non-Microsoft work group server operating systems. While entering the work group server operating system market, pledging support for already established technologies was important in gaining a foothold and the confidence of the customers. Once Microsoft's work group server operating system gained acceptance in the market, however, Microsoft's incentives changed and holding back access to information relating to interoperability with the Windows environment started to make sense.[989]

In sum, enforcers should be particularly sensitive to situations of installed base opportunism. When a platform closes its system to complementors (most flagrantly, by simply booting them off the platform) after first having grown thanks to those complementors, innovation is threatened. The platform may increase its profit but without discernibly contributing to innovation, while suppliers' expectations are severely frustrated as their investment is appropriated, which may chill innovation in the market for complements more generally.

7.3 Case Study

In the parental control app saga, many of the factors that should guide the application of the refusal to supply test to platforms are at play.[990] Apple is, of course, a prime example of an innovation platform, which – through its SDK – offers developers tools and access to a variety of APIs.[991] It has thus opened up its ecosystem to suppliers of complements, which have added significant value to the platform. Apple does reserve the aftermarket for app distribution to itself, which means it is in complete control of which apps are available on the iPhone/iOS. At some point, Apple used this control to remove parental control apps, while also introducing its own version of such an app, Screen Time. To justify the removal, Apple referred to the use of invasive technologies such as mobile device management (MDM), which allows parents to control their children's phones (eg to block certain apps).[992] But parental control apps had been

989 *Microsoft* (n 631), paras 587–88.

990 Introducing the saga, see Section 2.3.2.

991 See <https://developer.apple.com/ios/>.

992 Apple, 'The facts about parental control apps' (press release, 28 April 2019) <www.apple.com/mg/newsroom/2019/04/the-facts-about-parental-control-apps/>.

making use of those technologies for years with Apple's approval, and argued they are ineffective without it (it is hard to develop a parental *control* app without implementing control). Moreover, they noted that Apple's app makes use of the same or similar technologies.

After widespread criticism and allegations of anticompetitive conduct, Apple partially reversed course by adopting a separate approval mechanism for the use of MDM.[993] Still, the Russian Federal Antimonopoly Service (FAS) ruled on a complaint it received from one of the parental control app developers.[994] While it is unclear on which theory of harm the FAS relied, its assessment at least incorporates some of the above considerations. For one, it referred to how Apple had monopolized the aftermarket of its innovation platform iOS: 'Apple occupies a dominant position with a 100% share of the market for mobile apps based on the iOS operating system because it is only legally possible to install such apps from the App Store.'[995] The ruling focuses on how Apple has made competing apps ineffective by denying access to key iOS capabilities. In this sense, the ruling resembles the *Microsoft I* decision, which also concerned a limitation of interoperability. The FAS also noted that Apple's new policy coincided with the introduction of its competing app – a chronology that hints at installed base opportunism. Finally, the FAS took issue with how Apple reserves the right to refuse or remove apps even when they comply with all of Apple's conditions and guidelines.

In short, Apple's removal of apps by established developers ticks all the boxes that make an abuse of dominance likely: (i) a disruption of supply, (ii) by an innovation platform, (iii) with complete control over its aftermarket, (iv) reflecting installed base opportunism. If such a case were to surface in an EU enforcement forum, there would be no need to rely on *Bronner* (given the disruption rather than refusal), and its legal test would be more likely to be fulfilled (given the other three characteristics of the case). This does not mean, however, that *Bronner* is dead. Consider a related case revolving around how Apple has denied mobile wallet developers access to its near field communication (NFC) technology, which makes tap-and-go payments possible.[996] Since Apple never opened up this technology to complementors in the first place (ie the refusal is *de novo*), access can only be mandated if it is indispensable.

993 See App Store Review Guidelines, s '5.5 Mobile Device Management'.

994 See FAS, 'FAS recognized Apple as abusing its dominant position in the application distribution market' [translation] (press release, 10 August 2020) <https://fas.gov.ru/news/30275>. For reporting, see 'Russian Regulator Says Apple in Breach of Mobile Apps Market Regulations' (*Interfax*, 10 August 2020) <https://interfax.com/newsroom/top-stories/69512/> and 'Kaspersky Statement on the FAS ruling in the Antimonopoly Investigation against Apple' (*Kaspersky*, 10 August 2020) <https://www.kaspersky.com/about/press-releases/2020_kaspersky-statement-on-the-fas-ruling-in-the-antimonopoly-investigation-against-apple>.

995 FAS (n 994).

996 EC, 'Commission sends Statement of Objections to Apple over practices regarding Apple Pay' (n 693). The language (eg 'access to key technology necessary to develop rival mobile wallet solutions on Apple's devices') suggests reliance on the refusal to supply doctrine.

7.4 Conclusion

Even more so than other forms of abuse, refusals to supply in the platform economy give rise to two distinct questions: *when* to rely on this theory of harm and *how* to apply it.

As to the first question, it has been rightly noted that refusals to supply are 'not easy to distinguish from several other categories of conduct in antitrust law'.[997] Correct identification is, however, crucial, given that the *Bronner* conditions surpass those of any other abuse in terms of strictness. A first important distinction is that between *de novo* refusals and disruptions of supply. While that distinction comes to the fore only inconsistently in the ECJ's jurisprudence, there are good decision-theoretic reasons for restricting *Bronner* to situations of *de novo* refusal. While *Bronner* has an expansionist tendency, the effectiveness of article 102 TFEU (and the Treaty text) requires that other forms of abuse (eg tying and unfair terms) are not subject to its stringent conditions.

This brings us to the second question: In cases of *de novo* refusal, how should *Bronner* be applied? This section clarified when the most crucial condition, ie indispensability, may be fulfilled. Importantly, this is more likely to be the case for *innovation platforms* than for other platforms. Innovation platforms offer the foundation for complementary innovation, which can lead to expansive ecosystems. Given that they control the heart of the ecosystem (the OS), they can eliminate competition from developers in *after-markets* (eg apps). Such elimination can proceed via technical compatibility (APIs) but also through simple delisting (often due to alleged infringement of developer guidelines). Once removed from the ecosystem, developers often have no effective way of reaching the ecosystem's consumers. While perhaps somewhat hidden, these principles were already present in *Microsoft I*, the original EC decision on platform refusals. There is an even stronger case for intervention in case of *installed base opportunism*, ie cases where a platform first welcomes developers to complement its platform but later removes them. Such actions often coincide with the platform's introduction of its own complement and thus constitute a classic instance of leveraging.

997 Shapiro, 'Exclusionary Conduct' (n 984) 9. On the relation with other types of conduct, see Section 7.1.3 and Section 9.3.

8
MARGIN SQUEEZE

In discussions of leveraging conduct, one form of abuse often remains underdiscussed – or even undiscussed: margin squeeze.[998] One can only speculate as to the reasons for its obscurity. The fact that the US judiciary does not accept margin squeeze as an independent form of abuse probably has something to do with it. As does the fact that in Europe, margin squeeze is generally perceived as specific – or even limited – to the telecom sector. More often, the limelight is occupied by the related but distinct abuse of refusal to supply. However, the tendency towards vertical integration and the subsequent (price-related) conduct of online platforms could renew the relevance of margin squeeze as an analytical tool. To test this relevance, this section first introduces margin squeeze (Section 8.1) and then examines its foundations while also addressing possible misconceptions (Section 8.2). It then investigates whether and how this theory of harm could apply to online platforms with the help of case studies involving app stores, search engines and online marketplaces (Section 8.3), and concludes (Section 8.4).

8.1 Introduction

Margin squeeze is defined as a situation where a vertically integrated, dominant undertaking charges 'a price for the product on the upstream market which, compared to the price it charges on the downstream market, does not allow even an equally efficient competitor to trade profitably in the downstream market on a lasting basis'.[999] In other words, an upstream operator forces its downstream competitor, which is just as efficient, off the market by squeezing its profit margins.

998 This section is an adapted and updated version of the author's article 'Online Platforms and Vertical Integration: The Return of Margin Squeeze?' (2018) 6 JAE 355 (published as a working paper on SSRN mid-2017, see <https://ssrn.com/abstract=3075237>).

999 Exclusionary Conduct Guidance Paper (n 461), para 80.

Margin squeeze knew a period of active enforcement in the 2000s. These antitrust actions followed or even complemented[1000] the liberalization of the telecom sector under the direction of the EC, which started in the 1990s.[1001] Many telecom incumbents were legally obliged to grant competitors access to their network for a fee (upstream market). If this fee was too high, or the retail price charged by the incumbent too low, entrants' margins would be squeezed, and they could not compete effectively in providing end users with services (downstream market). In that case, the EC would intervene.[1002]

Fast forward to the present, when the most important network is not the telephone network, but rather the internet and the online platforms populating it. Then Director-General of DG COMP Alexander Italianer acknowledged this in a 2014 speech, stating: 'Indeed, the Internet is essentially a network. There are many types of networks, and all of them have been subject to competition enforcement: whether electricity and telephone networks, TV cable companies, railways, roads or airline industries.'[1003] Italianer spoke of both the internet *and* online platforms when he warned against incumbents that block or throttle competing operators.[1004] Referring to Italianer's speech, a DG COMP colleague made the analogy between telecom and digital markets more explicit:

> It is normally not disputed amongst commentators that the Commission can and should intervene when, say, a telecom network operator abuses its market position at the level of the provision of wholesale access to local fixed networks in order to gain market share in the downstream market for retail access to local fixed networks. It is not clear why the Commission should not intervene when a similar conduct takes place in a digital market.[1005]

The analogy between telecom operators and online platforms is a recurring theme in this work. Not only is their market power explained by many of the same factors as that of telecom operators,[1006] but their functions also show commonality: both offer a network or infrastructure that others use to provide their services.[1007] Moreover, just like telecom

1000 Erkki Liikanen, 'The European Union Telecommunications Policy' (Telecommunications Seminar, Sarajevo, 16 July 2001). See also Commission Directive 2002/77/EC on competition in the markets for electronic communications, networks and services [2002] OJ L249/21, art 3.

1001 For an overview, see EC, 'Telecommunications' (overview, 18 December 2019) <https://ec.europa.eu/competition/sectors/telecommunications/overview_en.html>.

1002 Also discussing this dynamic, see Zoltan Biro, George Houpis and Matt Hunt, 'Applying Margin Squeeze in Telecommunications: Some Economic Insights' (2011) 2 JECLAP 588, 589–90; Damien Geradin and Robert O'Donoghue, 'The Concurrent Application of Competition Law and Regulation: The Cases of Margin Squeeze Abuses in the Telecommunications Sector' (2005) 1 JCLE 355, 360.

1003 Alexander Italianer, 'Competition Policy in the Digital Age' (47th Innsbruck Symposium, Innsbruck, 7 March 2014).

1004 ibid.

1005 Massimiliano Kadar, 'European Union Competition Law in the Digital Era' (2015) 9 <https://ssrn.com/abstract=2703062> (the article has been published in Zeitschrift für Wettbewerbsrecht, but the publicly available version is relied on).

1006 On market power, see Section 4.1.2; on a potential qualification as natural monopoly, see Section 7.2.

1007 Although it must be noted that the business users of platforms provide complements, while the business users of telephone networks (the local loop) provide a service similar to the network operator.

operators, platforms are often vertically integrated, which means they provide services in competition with those of their users.[1008] This may give them an incentive to exclude those competing users. The basic ingredients for a leveraging abuse are thus present, and there is good reason to examine the leveraging abuse that defined telecom operators, ie margin squeeze. In addition, while rather anecdotical, it is worth mentioning that many commentators use the 'squeeze' terminology, sometimes even referring specifically to margins, when discussing the conduct of platforms vis-à-vis suppliers.[1009] Those commentators do not place such conduct within the margin squeeze framework (many are presumably unaware of it), but the next section does, starting with its foundations.[1010]

8.2 Margin Squeeze: Foundations

8.2.1 Traditional Theory

While margin squeeze was at its peak in the 2000s, the theory of harm dates back to 1975. In the *National Carbonising* case (an application for interim measures in the coal industry), the EC identified margin squeeze for the first time.[1011] A dominant producer of coking coal (the upstream input) not only sold its product to coke manufacturers (the downstream product), but also manufactured coke itself in competition with those customers. The EC argued that the dominant undertaking 'may abuse its dominant position if it acts in such a way as to eliminate the competition from its customers in the [downstream] market'.[1012] In that case, the dominant undertaking 'may have an obligation to arrange its prices so as to allow a *reasonably efficient* [downstream competitor] a margin sufficient to enable it to survive in the long term'.[1013] This is the so-called reasonably-efficient-competitor test.

This initial test was modified in subsequent cases. In the 1988 *British Sugar* case, the EC reproached British Sugar (BS), a wholesaler and retailer of sugar, for engaging 'in

1008 See Section 2.2.2 on this tendency towards vertical integration.

1009 Ariel Ezrachi and Maurice Stucke, *Virtual Competition: The Promise and Perils of the Algorithm-Driven Economy* (HUP 2016) 141 ('the sellers, whose margins are squeezed') and 189 ('the independent app developer is squeezed out of the market'); Martin Kenney and John Zysman, 'The Rise of the Platform Economy' (2016) 33 Issues in Science and Technology 61, 68 ('the platform owner can squeeze the platform community'); Margrethe Vestager, 'Clearing the Path for Innovation' (Web Summit, Lisbon, 7 November 2017) (on Google using its dominance in search to 'squeeze out innovation'); Zhu and Liu (n 626) (various references to Amazon 'squeezing complementors'); Ben Thompson, 'Day Two to One Day' (*Stratechery*, 17 September 2019) <https://stratechery.com/2019/day-two-to-one-day/> (including a section on Amazon 'squeezing suppliers'); Karen Weise, 'Prime Power: How Amazon Squeezes the Businesses Behind Its Store' (*NYT*, 19 December 2019) <https://www.nytimes.com/2019/12/19/technology/amazon-sellers.html>; 'How to Make Sense of the Latest Tech Surge' (*The Economist*, 20 February 2020) <https://www.economist.com/leaders/2020/02/20/how-to-make-sense-of-the-latest-tech-surge> (on how tech giants 'squeeze suppliers').

1010 For an extensive overview, see Friso Bostoen, 'Margin Squeeze: Where Competition Law and Sector Regulation Compete' (2017) 53 Jura Falconis 3.

1011 Case 109/75 R *National Carbonising v Commission* EU:C:1975:133.

1012 ibid 1197.

1013 ibid 1197–98 (emphasis added).

a price cutting campaign leaving an insufficient margin for a packager and seller of retail sugar, *as efficient* as BS itself in its packaging and selling operations, to survive in the long term'.[1014] Thus, the EC exchanged the reasonably efficient competitor for the as-efficient competitor.

After an aberration by the GC in the *IPS* case,[1015] margin squeeze theory was rationalized throughout the 2000s in a series of judgments originating in the telecom sector (*Deutsche Telekom*,[1016] *TeliaSonera*[1017] and *Telefónica*[1018]). As explained in the introduction, these cases arose in the context of the EC-led liberalization of the European telecom sector. Thus, they have in common that they sought to safeguard the access of (downstream) providers of telecom services to the (upstream) telecom network. Safeguarding the market access of competitors is traditionally seen as a task for *ex ante* regulation rather than for *ex post* competition law, which is why the EC's approach in this area has been called 'activist'.[1019] However, while margin squeeze indeed intersects with telecom regulation,[1020] the EC and the European courts have firmly grounded the theory in general competition law through reliance on two important principles. Firstly, margin squeeze was conditioned on the capacity to exclude as-efficient competitors from the market – a legal standard not only used in previous margin squeeze cases, but also central to other theories of harm under article 102 TFEU, including discrimination,[1021] refusal to supply,[1022] predatory pricing[1023] and rebates[1024]. Secondly, an anticompetitive effect on the downstream market must be shown – another contrast with *ex ante* regulation, of which the adoption assumes a lack of competition. These two principles are explained in more detail below, while additional requirements (or the absence thereof) are addressed in the next section.

1014 *Napier Brown – British Sugar* (Case IV/30.178) Commission Decision 88/518/EEC [1988] OJ L284/41, para 65 (emphasis added).

1015 Case T–5/97 *IPS v Commission* EU:T:2000:278, para 179 where the GC required either abusive pricing in the upstream market or predatory pricing in the downstream market.

1016 *Deutsche Telekom* (Cases COMP/C-1/37.451, 37.578, 37.579) Commission Decision 2003/707/EC [2003] OJ L263/9; Case T–271/03 *Deutsche Telekom v Commission* EU:T:2008:101; *Deutsche Telekom v Commission* (n 511).

1017 *Konkurrensverket v TeliaSonera* (n 631).

1018 *Wanadoo España v Telefónica* (Case COMP/38.784) Commission Decision; Case T–336/07 *Telefónica v Commission* EU:T:2012:172; Case C–295/12 P *Telefónica v Commission* EU:C:2014:2062.

1019 See eg Alexandre de Streel, 'The Antitrust Activism of the European Commission in the Telecommunications Sector' in Philip Lowe and Mel Marquis (eds), *European Competition Law Annual 2012* (Hart 2014) 189–208.

1020 See Hendrik Auf'mkolk, 'The "Feedback Effect" of Applying EU Competition Law to Regulated Industries: Doctrinal Contamination in the Case of Margin Squeeze' (2012) 3 JECLAP 149; Margherita Colangelo, 'The Interface Between Competition Rules and Sector-Specific Regulation in the Telecommunications Sector: Evidence from Recent EU Margin Squeeze Cases' (2013) 14 Competition and Regulation in Network Industries 214.

1021 See Section 9.

1022 See Section 7.1.1.

1023 See eg *AKZO Chemie v Commission* (n 381), para 72 (on how predatory prices 'can drive from the market undertakings which are … as efficient as the dominant undertaking').

1024 See eg *Post Danmark v Konkurrencerådet* (n 666), para 66 ('it is sufficient to demonstrate that there is an anticompetitive effect which may potentially exclude competitors who are at least as efficient as the dominant undertaking') and *Intel v Commission* (n 467), para 139 ('it is also required to assess the possible existence of a strategy aiming to exclude competitors that are at least as efficient as the dominant undertaking from the market').

In the first place, the presence of a margin squeeze must be established through the *as-efficient-competitor test*:[1025]

> [T]he appropriate test for establishing the margin squeeze consist[s] in determining whether a competitor having the same cost structure as that of the downstream activity of the vertically integrated undertaking would be in a position to offer downstream services without incurring a loss if that vertically integrated undertaking had to pay the upstream access price charged to its competitors.[1026]

In other words, this test establishes whether the vertically integrated dominant undertaking would have been able to offer its retail services to end users profitably if it had first been obliged to pay its own wholesale prices.[1027] If the answer is negative, that undertaking may be engaging in a margin squeeze. Note that, as the test only refers to the undertaking's own prices and costs, any dominant undertaking can assess the lawfulness of its conduct in the light of its 'special responsibility'. Thus, it conforms to the principle of legal certainty.[1028]

Secondly, it must be shown that the conduct is capable of having, or likely to have, *anticompetitive effects* on the downstream market.[1029] However, this effect does not necessarily have to be concrete; it is 'sufficient to demonstrate that there is a potential anti-competitive effect which may exclude competitors who are at least as efficient as the dominant undertaking'.[1030] This exclusionary effect is presumed when the wholesale price the undertaking charges to competitors is higher than the retail price it charges to end users.[1031] If this is not the case, it must be demonstrated that the application of that pricing practice was (due, for example, to reduced profitability) likely to have the consequence that it would be at least more difficult for the operators concerned to trade in the market.[1032]

8.2.2 Possible Misconceptions

While the as-efficient-competitor test and the anticompetitive effect requirement make margin squeeze a generally administrable theory, margin squeeze assessments have

1025 *Deutsche Telekom v Commission* (n 514), paras 196–202; *Konkurrensverket v TeliaSonera* (n 631), paras 31–33; Case T-336/07 *Telefónica v Commission* (n 1018), para 194.

1026 Case T-336/07 *Telefónica v Commission* (n 1018), para 194.

1027 *Deutsche Telekom v Commission* (n 514), para 201; Case T-336/07 *Telefónica v Commission* (n 1018), para 194.

1028 *Deutsche Telekom v Commission* (n 514), para 202; *Konkurrensverket v TeliaSonera* (n 631), para 44; Case T-336/07 *Telefónica v Commission* (n 1018), para 192.

1029 *Deutsche Telekom v Commission* (n 514), paras 252–54 ('capable of making market entry more difficult' for competitors); *Konkurrensverket v TeliaSonera* (n 631), paras 60–74 ('likely to hinder' competitors/'capable of having anti-competitive effects'); Case T-336/07 *Telefónica v Commission* (n 1018), paras 267–76 ('capable of having, or likely to have [anticompetitive] effects').

1030 *Konkurrensverket v TeliaSonera* (n 631), para 64; Case T-336/07 *Telefónica v Commission* (n 1018), para 268.

1031 *Konkurrensverket v TeliaSonera* (n 631), para 73.

1032 ibid, para 74.

been restricted, for the most part, to utility sectors. Every judgment at the EU level after 2000 concerned telecom providers.[1033] In addition to the telecom sector, NCAs have looked at margin squeeze in the gas, water, railways and postal services sectors, among others.[1034] But one should not read conditions into this correlation: margin squeeze does not have to involve industries that require extensive physical infrastructure. To address the factually justified but legally inaccurate perceptions of this utility-centred abuse, three clarifications with regard to the infringing undertaking are in order.

First, while telecom and other utility sector providers often enjoy(ed) a natural monopoly, a super-dominant position is not required to be found guilty of engaging in a margin squeeze. There must evidently be a dominant position to be abused, but the ECJ has stated that 'the degree of dominance in the market concerned is not relevant'.[1035] Potential infringers can thus be assessed according to the established standards of dominance.

Second, the ECJ has clarified that dominance in the downstream market is not a condition to establish a margin squeeze.[1036] Rather, condemning margin squeeze seeks to prevent an operator dominant in the upstream market from acquiring or strengthening a dominant position in the downstream market by using means other than reliance on its own merits.[1037] Margin squeeze is, in other words, a typical leveraging abuse.

Third, the relation between margin squeeze and refusal to supply has been heavily contested within the EU and beyond. The issue first came up in the *Telefónica* case, where the telecom operator argued that the EC was essentially accusing it of a refusal to supply, which meant the *Bronner* criteria would have to be fulfilled (ie the telecom network would have to qualify as essential facility).[1038] Telefónica contended that it was under no such obligation to supply, and its pricing policy could thus not infringe article 102 TFEU.[1039] The EC accepted the argument but added two exceptions: the *Bronner* criteria do not need to be fulfilled to find a margin squeeze when (i) there is a sector-specific (as opposed to an antitrust) obligation to supply, or (ii) the incumbent has developed its infrastructure while special or exclusive rights shielded it from competition.[1040] This theory was then crystallized in the EC's Guidance Paper.[1041]

1033 The aforementioned *Deutsche Telekom*, *TeliaSonera* and *Telefónica* judgments and Case T–851/14 *Slovak Telekom v Commission* EU:T:2018:929 (under appeal). One case in the railway transport sector was also investigated, but eventually settled with commitments: *Deutsche Bahn I and II* (Cases AT.39678 and AT.39731) Commission Decision.

1034 OECD, 'Margin Squeeze' (Roundtable) DAF/COMP(2009)36.

1035 *Konkurrensverket v TeliaSonera* (n 631), para 82.

1036 ibid, paras 83–89; Case T–336/07 *Telefónica v Commission* (n 1018), paras 146 and 185.

1037 *Konkurrensverket v TeliaSonera* (n 631), para 88.

1038 *Wanadoo España v Telefónica* (n 1018), para 299–300.

1039 ibid, para 301.

1040 These are the so-called Telefónica exceptions established in ibid, paras 302–9. For a critical assessment, see Damien Geradin, 'Refusal to Supply and Margin Squeeze: A Discussion of Why the "Telefónica Exceptions" Are Wrong' (2011) TILEC Discussion Paper Series 2011–51.

1041 Exclusionary Conduct Guidance Paper (n 461), para 81 for the principle and para 82 for the exceptions.

However, the whole exercise proved futile when the issue made it up to the ECJ, which decided – against the Opinion of the AG – that an obligation to supply competitors is not required for a finding of margin squeeze.[1042] Nuancing this position slightly, the ECJ noted that without indispensable input, it will be more difficult to establish anticompetitive effects.[1043] In its next margin squeeze case, the EC adopted the ECJ's position, repeating its statement that '[m]argin squeeze constitutes an independent form of abuse distinct from that of refusal to supply.'[1044]

On the other side of the Atlantic, the US Supreme Court took a markedly different position. In *linkLine*, it refused to accept margin squeeze as a form of unlawful monopolization under section 2 of the Sherman Act, holding that 'if a firm has no antitrust duty to deal with its competitors at wholesale, it certainly has no duty to deal under terms and conditions that the rivals find commercially advantageous'.[1045] In an OECD roundtable, a number of authorities expressed a concurring opinion.[1046] The US Supreme Court's argument has intuitive appeal: if an undertaking can lawfully refuse to provide its products, how can it be reproached for providing them at disadvantageous conditions? In fact, a similar argument was made in the *TeliaSonera* proceedings before the ECJ.[1047] As mentioned above, the ECJ rejected such reasoning, holding that it cannot be inferred from the case law 'that the conditions to be met in order to establish that a refusal to supply is abusive must necessarily also apply when assessing the abusive nature of conduct which consists in supplying services … on conditions which are disadvantageous'.[1048] The underlying idea is that this would unduly reduce the effectiveness of article 102 TFEU. Additionally, several authors have argued that a stand-alone margin squeeze abuse addresses the negative consequences of vertical leveraging in a way that other theories of abuse cannot.[1049] Dunne, for example, argues that '[g]iven the potential for consumer harm and the difficulties in addressing price-squeezing behaviour through established competition abuses, there is a strong argument for recognising margin squeeze as a standalone offence'.[1050]

1042 *Konkurrensverket v TeliaSonera* (n 631), paras 54–59 (where the AG disagreed, see Case C–52/09 *Konkurrensverket v TeliaSonera* EU:C:2010:483, Opinion of AG Mazák, paras 8–33). See also Case T–336/07 *Telefónica v Commission* (n 1018), paras 180–84.

1043 *Konkurrensverket v TeliaSonera* (n 631), paras 69–72.

1044 *Slovak Telekom* (Case AT.39523) Commission Decision C(2014)7465, para 822.

1045 *Pacific Bell Telephone v linkLine Communications* 555 US 438, 446 (2009). The Court referred to *Verizon Communications v Law Offices of Curtis V Trinko* (n 562) for precedent and stressed that it has to be an *antitrust* duty to deal (a duty to deal imposed by the regulator does not qualify).

1046 OECD, 'Margin Squeeze' (n 1034) 8 ('it does not make sense to impose potential liability for engaging in a margin squeeze when the integrated firm has no duty to deal, since, in this case, the firm could avoid liability simply by refusing to sell the essential input at all').

1047 *Konkurrensverket v TeliaSonera* (n 631), para 54.

1048 ibid, para 55. See Section 7.1.3.

1049 Economides (n 564) 412 ('From an economist's point of view, *Trinko* is a poor decision' as 'the Supreme Court … missed the leveraging of monopoly power'); Gianluca Faella and Roberto Pardolesi, 'Squeezing Price Squeeze Under EC Antitrust Law' (2010) 6 European Competition Journal 255, 266 ('a properly defined analytical framework for the assessment of price squeeze allows for detection of potentially anti-competitive conduct of a discriminatory or predatory nature that is not directly observable due to the vertical integration of the dominant firm').

1050 Niamh Dunne, 'Margin Squeeze: Theory, Practice, Policy – Part 1' (2012) 33 ECLR 29, 32. See also Niamh Dunne, 'Margin Squeeze: Theory, Practice, Policy – Part 2' (2012) 33 ECLR 61, 61 ('a standalone

8.3 Case Studies

Equipped with a clearer understanding of the margin squeeze theory, and an idea about the business model of online platforms and the factors determining their market power, let's turn to a number of case studies. The first one involves app stores, a type of innovation platform that – in line with its economic importance – plays a central role in this work.[1051] Two other case studies concerning different platforms, search engines and marketplaces, follow.

8.3.1 Apple Music: in Tune with Competition Law?

Depending on how one defines the market, Apple is a monopolist or duopolist in app distribution.[1052] Apple also distributes its own apps, including music streaming service Apple Music. Those first-party apps compete with apps from independent developers such as Spotify. That competition is complicated, however, by the policies governing the App Store. Through its mandatory IAP billing system, the App Store charges a 30% commission fee on each (in-)app purchase of digital content, including subscriptions.[1053] There is a limited exception for so-called reader apps (including book, music and video services), which can allow users to access content/subscriptions purchased elsewhere (via the web).[1054] But while this option to purchase/subscribe elsewhere exists, reader app developers were, until recently, not allowed to inform users of its existence by including 'buttons, external links, or other calls to action that direct customers to purchasing mechanisms other than in-app purchase' (the anti-steering obligation).[1055]

Spotify, as a music streaming provider, must abide by Apple's IAP obligation if it wishes to offer subscriptions within its iOS app.[1056] It initially did so but found it necessary to increase its price to account for the 30% commission fee, offering its subscription at €13 per month – a less attractive proposition compared to Apple's €10 service. After a while, Spotify simply disabled IAP, thus making it impossible to subscribe within its app. Following a complaint by Spotify, the EC started investigating this conduct, issuing

---

margin-squeeze offence addresses the impact of vertical integration of the dominant firm in a way that assessing wholesale or retail prices separately for evidence of discrete abuses cannot').

1051 This section draws on Bostoen and Mândrescu (n 856) 462–66.

1052 See Sections 4.1, 7.2.1 and 7.3.

1053 App Store Review Guidelines, s '3.1.1 In-App Purchase' ('If you want to unlock features or functionality within your app (by way of example: subscriptions, in-game currencies, game levels, access to premium content, or unlocking a full version), you must use in-app purchase.'). The fee is lowered to 15% once the subscription exceeds one year.

1054 ibid, s '3.1.3(a) "Reader" Apps'.

1055 ibid, s '3.1.1 In-App Purchase'. In response to an investigation by the Japanese Fair Trade Commission, Apple started allowing reader app developers to link out, but those developers cannot advertise the (lower) price charged elsewhere. See Apple, 'Japan Fair Trade Commission closes App Store investigation' (press release, 1 September 2021) <https://www.apple.com/newsroom/2021/09/japan-fair-trade-commission-closes-app-store-investigation/>.

1056 Spotify's account of the facts is set out in the 'Timeline' and 'Fast Facts' sections of Spotify's 'Time to Play Fair' website <https://www.timetoplayfair.com/>. Spotify's complaint goes beyond the 30% commission fee, but that is the most salient fact for the purpose of a margin squeeze assessment.

objections against both the IAP and the anti-steering obligation[1057] but later dropping the former.[1058] While it is not clear why the EC dropped its objection relating to the 30% fee, the lack of a suitable form of abuse and corresponding theory of harm may have played a role.[1059] One wonders, however, whether margin squeeze does not fit the bill. To ascertain whether this is the case, let's go over its constituent elements, ie the as-efficient-competitor test and the related requirement of anticompetitive effects.

The pivotal question is whether Spotify is an 'as efficient competitor' to Apple Music; if not, it does not deserve protection under competition law (at least its prohibition of margin squeeze). To answer this question, it must be tested whether the vertically integrated dominant undertaking could offer its retail services to end users profitably if it were obliged to pay its own wholesale prices. In other words, would Apple Music's €10 subscription model be profitable if it had to pay its own 30% fee? If the answer is negative, Apple may be engaging in a margin squeeze. There is, however, some difficulty in applying this profitability-based test to music streaming as the industry is not (very) profitable. Spotify has been making losses for years but is slowly moving towards profitability.[1060] Apple does not report the financial results of Apple Music separately, but – certainly in comparison with Apple's other products and services – it has definitely not been a profit booster. One way to ascertain the firms' relative efficiency is to compare gross margins. Estimates of Apple Music's gross margin put it at 15%,[1061] while Spotify's gross margin is around 25%.[1062] Thus, while a more in-depth assessment based on non-public data is needed, it seems probable that Spotify is at least as efficient as Apple.

In addition, the EC must demonstrate that the conduct is capable of having anticompetitive effects in the downstream market. It can do so by showing that the pricing policy makes it more difficult for as-efficient competitors to trade in the downstream market, eg through 'delayed prospect[s] of becoming profitable'[1063] This might apply. Spotify's high marginal costs (royalty payments to rights holders) mean it is left with low margins (certainly for a tech company). This means another 30% fee can push it towards unprofitability, at least

1057 EC, 'Commission sends Statement of Objections to Apple on App Store rules for music streaming providers' (press release, 30 April 2021) IP/21/2061.

1058 EC, 'Commission sends Statement of Objections to Apple clarifying concerns over App Store rules for music streaming providers' (press release, 28 February 2023) IP/23/1217.

1059 Friso Bostoen, 'Requiem for an Objection: The Commission Drops Half of Its App Store Case' (*CoRe Blog*, 8 March 2023) <https://www.lexxion.eu/coreblogpost/requiem-for-an-objection/>.

1060 See Spotify Technology SA, Form 20-F Annual Report to the SEC for the fiscal year ended 31 December 2019, 5 (showing significant operating losses in the years 2015–2019) and Spotify Technology SA, Form 20-F Annual Report to the SEC for the fiscal year ended 31 December 2022 (showing a better but still delicate financial outlook after 2020).

1061 Anne Steele and Tripp Mickle, 'Apple Music Overtakes Spotify in Paid U.S. Subscribers' (*WSJ*, 5 April 2019) <https://www.wsj.com/articles/apple-music-overtakes-spotify-in-u-s-subscribers-11554475924> (Apple Music 'has a gross margin of roughly 15%, the lowest of any of Apple's services, according to RBC Capital Markets') and Evan Niu, 'Apple Music Is Boosting Services Revenue, but Not Profits' (*The Motley Fool*, 17 April 2018) <https://www.fool.com/investing/2018/04/17/apple-music-is-boosting-services-revenue-but-not-p.aspx> (reporting on the model of Macquarie Research analyst Ben Schachter, which puts Apple's gross margin at 15%).

1062 Spotify Technology SA, Form 20-F Annual Report to the SEC for the fiscal year ended 31 December 2022, 49.

1063 Case T–336/07 *Telefónica v Commission* (n 1018), para 279. See also *Slovak Telekom v Commission* (n 1033), para 254.

when it comes to subscriptions subject to the fee. Before Spotify disabled IAP, mobile subscriptions were responsible for a significant part of total revenue.[1064] At the same time, Spotify has continued to grow (although it may have grown more in the counterfactual scenario with a lower fee). Again, an in-depth assessment is called for.

Finally, margin squeeze theory is interesting because it offers a clear remedy: the dominant firm has to adjust its upstream prices up to the point where its downstream division would be profitable if it were charged those prices. Apple would thus have to lower its commission fee for music streaming services until Apple Music could pay it without making a loss.[1065] If one credits the above estimate of Apple Music's gross margins, this adapted commission fee would be closer to 15% than the current 30%.[1066]

8.3.2 Google Shopping: Browsing for a Fitting Theory of Abuse

Before the EC handed down its *Google Shopping* decision, scholars heavily debated which form of abuse – if any – fitted Google's conduct.[1067] A lone suggestion of margin squeeze was followed by the conclusion that 'there is neither an upstream nor a downstream price, so there can be no margin squeeze'.[1068] This is not entirely correct. As long as the CSS does not pay Google for preferential placement, there is no upstream price. However, merchants do have to pay CSSs – a downstream price that can consist in a flat fee for inclusion in the service and/or a fee owed each time a user clicks through to the merchant's website. Google Shopping demands a fee for being listed, and ranks results based on both their relevance and the amount paid by the merchant.[1069] The second group of downstream customers, the consumers browsing the web for a product, do get to enjoy a free service.

Applying the as-efficient-competitor test is certainly not straightforward. It means asking: Could Google offer its comparison shopping to end users profitably if it had to pay its own upstream prices? But what is this upstream price that other comparison shopping websites have to pay to Google? These websites are generally found through Google for free. There is, however, an upstream price if they pay Google to be featured on top of the search results, alongside Google's own CSS.[1070] So perhaps this is the

1064 See Mark Sweney, 'Spotify UK Revenues Surge to Almost £190M as Mobile Subscriptions Take Off' (*The Guardian*, 14 October 2016) <https://www.theguardian.com/media/2016/oct/14/spotify-uk-revenues-surge-to-almost-190m-as-mobile-subscriptions-take-off> (according to Spotify, 'the majority of new users signing up for Spotify are mobile').

1065 Alternatively, the vertically integrated undertaking can opt to increase its upstream prices. However, in the music streaming market – where the €10/month standard is ingrained in consumers' minds – this option seems competitively unfeasible.

1066 A 15% commission fee already applies from the first year onwards, but – under a margin squeeze remedy – would have to apply from day one.

1067 See Section 5.3.1.

1068 Nazzini, '*Google* and the (Ever-stretching) Boundaries of Article 102 TFEU' (n 645) 307.

1069 Sameer Samat, 'Building a Better Shopping Experience' (*Google Commerce Blog*, 31 May 2012) <https://commerce.googleblog.com/2012/05/building-better-shopping-experience.html>.

1070 In *Google Search (Shopping)* (n 348), the EC notes how comparison shopping websites tried to make up for lost traffic by buying search ads.

closest we get to a workable test: Would Google Shopping be profitable if it had to pay Google Search to be listed in its current position, ie on top of the search results?[1071] A direct discrimination theory may fit better than these testing acrobatics.

In its decision, the EC ordered Google to ensure that it 'treats competing comparison shopping services no less favourably than its own comparison shopping service within its general search results pages', leaving Google significant leeway to decide what that meant exactly.[1072] Google announced it would comply by creating a stand-alone unit for Google Shopping. Where Google Search's coveted top spots (the 'Shopping Box') were previously reserved for Google Shopping, it would now have to bid for those spots in competition with other CSSs.[1073] According to a spokesperson, this means that 'Google Shopping will compete on equal terms ..., participating in the auction in the same way as everyone else'.[1074] Interestingly, this behavioural vertical separation means that – at least in theory – other CSSs should be able to compete with Google on its own platform when they are as efficient as its independent comparison shopping unit.[1075] In this sense, the outcome would have been similar after a margin squeeze infringement.

Google's auction mechanism has been criticized.[1076] Shortly after its implementation, complainants started claiming that Google's mechanism is non-compliant with the EC's decision and 'has terrible consequences for consumers'.[1077] They argue that Google is the only winner. Having competing services bid against each other – and Google – raises the cost of being featured on top of the search results. And whichever service is featured, Google cannot lose out: either Google Shopping wins the auction and is paid by the company it is promoting, or rival CSSs win the auction with the proceeds flowing to Google Search. Meanwhile, traffic to competing CSSs has not meaningfully increased.[1078] Complainants conclude that 'without full ownership unbundling (structural separation), Google Shopping's participation in the auction is essentially meaningless'.[1079]

1071 Making this test even harder to apply is the fact that, pre-*Google Shopping*, Google reserved the top spots for its own CSS, not allowing other services to bid for them.

1072 *Google Search (Shopping)* (n 348), para 699.

1073 Olivier Heckmann, 'Changes to Google Shopping in Europe' (*Ads & Commerce – Google Blog*, 27 September 2017) <https://www.blog.google/products/ads/changes-to-google-shopping-in-europe>.

1074 James Kanter, 'Google Offers Concessions to Europe After Record Antitrust Fine' (*NYT*, 27 September 2017) <https://www.nytimes.com/2017/09/27/business/google-eu-antitrust.html>.

1075 At least when Google does not cross-subsidize its CSS or preferences it in other ways.

1076 In defence of the auction-based remedy, see Vesterdorf and Fountoukakos (n 653) (note that the authors represent the defendant in *Google Shopping*).

1077 See eg <http://www.foundem.co.uk/Open_Letter_Commissioner_Vestager_Feb_2018.pdf> (quote) and <https://www.shopalike.nl/downloads/Joint_Letter_of_41_CSSs_to_Ms_Vestager_on_Google_Shopping-Non-Compliance_28.11.2019.pdf>.

1078 See in particular Thomas Höppner, 'Google's (Non-)Compliance with the EU Shopping Decision: A Study Based upon Empirical Data of 25 Comparison Shopping Services' (2020) <https://ssrn.com/abstract=3700748> (note that the author represents complainants in *Google Shopping*).

1079 See <http://www.foundem.co.uk/Open_Letter_Commissioner_Vestager_Feb_2018.pdf>. This objection was echoed by the EP, which noted in its 2018 report on competition policy that 'without a full-blown structural separation between the company's general and specialised search services, an auction-based approach might not deliver equal treatment', see EP, 'On the Annual Report on Competition Policy' (Report) A8-0049/2018, para 42.

8.3.3 Amazon Marketplace: a Prime Example?

Amazon operates an e-commerce platform, facilitating third-party sales in exchange for a referral fee of 15% on most items.[1080] Moreover, if sellers choose the 'Fulfilment by Amazon' (FBA) option, Amazon also takes care of shipping and customer service.[1081] The price of this service depends on a number of factors but tends to range from 20 to 35%.[1082] Finally, sellers can advertise their wares on Amazon, which may add another 15%. All in all, Amazon takes a 50% cut of sellers' revenue.[1083] While FBA and advertising fees may appear optional, that is not entirely the case. First, as the EC found in its preliminary assessment, using FBA increases a seller's odds of winning the Buy Box, which is responsible for 90% of sales.[1084] And, as analysts argue: 'Advertising on Amazon is not optional. Most of the best-converting screen space is allocated to advertising; thus, sellers inevitably have to advertise to have a chance to be discovered.'[1085]

Amazon also sells products on its Marketplace. One of the keys to its success is the paid loyalty programme Amazon Prime, which offers consumers free shipping on Amazon and other Prime-eligible products, together with a number of other benefits (including video streaming, audio streaming and cloud storage).[1086] Prime not only offers free shipping but is also a factor in product rankings. The simplest way to be eligible for Prime is to use FBA – another way in which sellers are pushed towards the service. Even when sellers pay for FBA, however, they do not compete on an equal footing. All else being equal (eg price, seller rating), Amazon still tends to win the Buy Box.[1087] Consumers may thus be steered towards an inferior product offering, while third-party sellers are discouraged from continuing to offer their competing products.[1088] As a result, various authors refer to Amazon as 'squeezing its suppliers'.[1089] Might it be engaging in a margin squeeze? The question is: Would Amazon be able to offer its products to end users profitably if it were obliged to pay its own wholesale prices (at a minimum, the referral and FBA fees)?

1080 For an overview of fees in Germany, see <https://sell.amazon.de/en/preisgestaltung>.

1081 Amazon, 'Fulfilment by Amazon – benefits' <https://sell.amazon.de/en/versand-durch-amazon>.

1082 Juozas Kaziukėnas, 'Amazon Takes a 50% Cut of Seller's Revenue' (*Marketplace Pulse*, 13 February 2023) <https://www.marketplacepulse.com/articles/amazon-takes-a-50-cut-of-sellers-revenue>. A storage fee is also factored in.

1083 ibid.

1084 *Amazon Marketplace* and *Amazon Buy Box* (n 369).

1085 Kaziukėnas (n 1082).

1086 The benefits and prices vary per country. For Germany, see <https://www.amazon.de/amazonprime>.

1087 *Amazon Marketplace* and *Amazon Buy Box* (n 369), para 205. For earlier research on this, see Julia Angwin and Surya Mattu, 'Amazon Says It Puts Customers First. But Its Pricing Algorithm Doesn't' (*ProPublica*, 20 September 2016) <https://www.propublica.org/article/amazon-says-it-puts-customers-first-but-its-pricing-algorithm-doesnt>.

1088 Zhu and Liu (n 626).

1089 From a legal perspective: Lina Khan, 'Amazon's Antitrust Paradox' (2017) 126 Yale Law Journal 710; from an economic perspective: Zhu and Liu (n 626); from a technology perspective: Thompson, 'Day Two to One Day' (n 1009).

8.4 Conclusion

Could – and *should* – there be such a thing as a 'platform squeeze'? The main argument for applying margin squeeze as a theory of abuse is its clear analytical framework, which provides a helpful tool to competition authorities on the one hand and legal certainty to undertakings on the other. Competition authorities simply have to test whether the vertically integrated dominant undertaking would have been able to offer its retail services to end users profitably if it had first been obliged to pay its own wholesale prices. For dominant undertakings, this as-efficient-competitor test offers legal certainty: as it only refers to prices and costs that are known by these undertakings, they can self-assess the lawfulness of their conduct. In addition, margin squeeze is an established form of abuse, so its application could hardly be called 'unprecedented' – a criticism that novel applications of more general theories of harm (such as leveraging in *Google Shopping*) are particularly subject to.[1090] Moreover, the case studies examined above confirm that the margin squeeze theory can be applied to online platforms, although it must be noted that the theory appears better suited when there is a clearly identifiable upstream price (eg the commission rates of app stores and online market-places) as opposed to when the upstream price is more difficult to observe and possibly absent (eg search engines).

Further, it is worth reflecting on how margin squeeze relates to other (potential) forms of abuse. The distinction between margin squeeze and *refusal to supply* has already been addressed above.[1091] An even closer relation exists between margin squeeze and *self-preferencing*. One form of margin squeeze consists in the vertically integrated dominant undertaking charging its downstream subsidiary different – ie more favourable – rates than competitors.[1092] This differentiated treatment or *discrimination* raises the cost of downstream competitors, thus putting them at a disadvantage vis-à-vis the vertically integrated firm's downstream division, which may lead to foreclosure. This margin squeeze mechanism has been termed 'undercover *raising rivals' costs*'.[1093] Given that Apple's App Store does not appear to be charging Apple Music the same commission fee as competing music streaming services, its conduct may fall into this category.

While margin squeeze may involve such discrimination, it does not have to. The vertically integrated firm can, for example, choose to charge its downstream subsidiary and competitors an equal price – more specifically, an equally high price. This method of squeezing downstream competitors' margins avoids discrimination, but generally also means the vertically integrated firm's subsidiary is not making any profits. Indeed,

1090 See Section 5.3.1.

1091 See Sections 7.1.3 and 8.2.2.

1092 In two cases, the EC homed in on discriminatory rebates (granted to the own downstream division but not to downstream competitors) as the mechanism for margin squeeze, see *RWE Gas Foreclosure* (Case COMP/39.402) Commission Decision and *Deutsche Bahn I and II* (n 1033).

1093 OECD, 'Line of Business Restrictions' (n 622) 9.

given the high price of the upstream input, it may be selling the downstream product below cost.[1094] This is not necessarily a problem for the vertically integrated firm: it simply means that profits are shifted from the downstream to the upstream level, and the firm can cross-subsidize between the different divisions to make up for downstream losses. For obvious reasons, this margin squeeze mechanism has been termed 'undercover *predatory pricing*'.[1095]

Competition authorities could thus examine whether there is either upstream discrimination or downstream predation in order to establish – or instead of establishing – a firm is engaging in a margin squeeze.[1096] Actually, as Petzold argues, it is possible to further boil down margin squeeze to just predatory pricing if you incorporate opportunity costs in the assessment.[1097] When examining the upstream level, this means asking not (only) whether the vertically integrated firm sold its input below production cost, but whether it *could have* sold that upstream input at a higher price to a downstream firm.[1098] If so, the vertically integrated firm is transferring its input from its upstream to its downstream division below opportunity cost. In fact, in the *Google Shopping* case study above, the most workable margin squeeze test implied opportunity costs. The test asked: 'Would Google Shopping be profitable if it had to pay Google Search to be listed in its current position, ie on top of the search results?' Given that Google used to reserve the top spots for its own shopping service, this hypothetical payment is in fact the opportunity cost of awarding those spots to itself.[1099] As Petzold acknowledges, however, authorities and courts, when assessing potentially predatory conduct, do not use economic costs (which include opportunity costs), but rely on costs originating from the dominant firm's accounting.[1100] An (adapted) predatory pricing theory is thus less practical – and has been rejected by the ECJ.[1101]

In the end, an independent margin squeeze theory is preferable to combinations and adaptations of other forms of abuse. The main reason is that the margin squeeze framework allows for the most effective identification of the abuse. Other tests – in particular those of discrimination and predatory pricing – require a clear view of the internal transfer price, ie the price that the downstream division pays for the upstream

1094 To some extent, this appeared to be the case in *RWE Gas Foreclosure* (n 1092), where the EC noted that 'RWE constantly had negative results in its downstream gas supply business' (para 31). This gap could be 'solved' by relying on price discrimination and predatory pricing in tandem, but there are other arguments against relying (solely) on other forms of abuse, see Bostoen, 'Margin Squeeze: Where Competition Law and Sector Regulation Compete' (n 1010) 25–26.

1095 OECD, 'Line of Business Restrictions' (n 622) 9.

1096 See Faella and Pardolesi (n 1049) 259 ('If there is neither downstream predation nor upstream discrimination, there is no risk of exclusion of equally efficient competitors.').

1097 Daniel Petzold, 'It Is All Predatory Pricing: Margin Squeeze Abuse and the Concept of Opportunity Costs in EU Competition Law' (2015) 6 JECLAP 346.

1098 One would also have to account for diversion ratios, see ibid 349.

1099 In a case of academic inception, this was pointed out in a discussion of my own research, see OECD, 'Line of Business Restrictions' (n 622) 10, referencing Bostoen, 'Online Platforms and Vertical Integration: The Return of Margin Squeeze?' (n 998).

1100 Petzold (n 1097) 349.

1101 *Deutsche Telekom v Commission* (n 514), para 183 ('The General Court was not, therefore, obliged to establish, additionally, that the wholesale prices for local loop access services or retail prices for end-user access services were in themselves abusive on account of their excessive or predatory nature, as the case may be.').

input. However, such a price can only be readily identified when the accounting of the upstream and downstream divisions is separated, which is often not the case. For example, it is not entirely clear whether the App Store charges Apple Music a 30% commission fee on music streaming subscriptions (although it does not appear so), so both discrimination and predatory pricing are more difficult to establish. A margin squeeze test, which checks whether Apple Music would be profitable given a 30% commission, is significantly simpler. And note that this case, where the platform charge is very homogeneous – the 30% fee applies to most (in-)app purchases – already presents a simpler scenario than most cases, where fees are more differentiated. Moreover, a clear legal test offers legal certainty to dominant firms, which do not, for example, have to start calculating the opportunity cost of certain business decisions.

Margin squeeze presents a promising framework to assess the leveraging and in particular self-preferencing conduct of online platforms. Since I first presented this idea,[1102] it has garnered some support in academic[1103] and policy[1104] circles. If anything, there is room to expand – or perhaps better: generalize – the theory. As for other forms of leveraging (except predatory pricing), the anticompetitive mechanism underlying margin squeeze is to raise rivals' costs.[1105] More directly than other forms of leveraging, however, margin squeeze addresses self-preferencing – the primary exclusionary concern in digital markets.[1106] One approach would be to assess how self-preferencing affects rivals' costs and then calculate the resulting upward pricing pressure on both those rivals and the dominant firm.[1107] Of course, while this would reduce the number of false negatives, it would increase false positives. Moreover, such a (purely) economic exercise increases decision costs compared to the current margin squeeze test, which is more administrable.

1102 Bostoen, 'Online Platforms and Vertical Integration: The Return of Margin Squeeze?' (n 998).

1103 See eg Inge Graef, 'Differentiated Treatment in Platform-to-Business Relations' (2019) 38 YEL 448, 477–79 ('It is particularly promising to analyse self-preferencing as a form of margin squeeze'); Adrian Kuenzler, 'Advancing Quality Competition in Big Data Markets' (2020) 15 JCLE 500, 520–21; Eleni Tzoulia, 'Competition Law Issues' in Ioannis Iglezakis (ed), *Legal Issues of Mobile Apps: A Practical Guide* (Kluwer 2020); Damien Geradin and Dimitrios Katsifis, 'The Antitrust Case against the Apple App Store' (2020) 17 JCLE 503. See also Peter Alexiadis and Alexandre de Streel, 'Designing an EU Intervention Standard for Digital Platforms' (2020) EUI Working Paper RSCAS 2020/14, 48 ('The rationale for self-preferencing being treated as a self-standing theory of harm can be derived inter alia from the Commission's practice in relation to margin squeeze cases under Article 102 TFEU.').

1104 OECD, 'Implications of e-Commerce for Competition Policy' (Background Note) DAF/COMP(2018)3, 35–36; OECD, 'Line of Business Restrictions' (n 622) 9–10, 20 and 22 (although this note focuses on the *Google Shopping* case study, which – as acknowledged – presents the 'undercover predatory pricing' variety of margin squeeze).

1105 Extensively and incisively on this mechanism, see Krattenmaker and Salop (n 582).

1106 In OECD, 'Line of Business Restrictions' (n 622), self-preferencing and margin squeeze are essentially presented as synonyms, see eg 'self-preferencing (margin squeeze)' (p 4) and '"self-preferencing" that raises rivals' costs and squeezes their margins' (pp 5–6).

1107 ibid.

9

DISRUPTIVE DISCRIMINATION

I previously identified a 'leveraging gap': there are instances of leveraging that do not, prima facie, fit the existing forms of abuse.[1108] When faced with this gap in *Google Shopping*, the EC plugged the gap in perhaps the most obvious way, ie by putting forward a general leveraging abuse. But the obvious solution is not necessarily the best one. That is why I asked whether retrofitting existing forms of abuse for the platform economy could not fill the gap. The previous sections have shown that the typical leveraging abuses – tying, refusal to supply, and margin squeeze – can be updated to account for the economic and technical specificities of platforms.[1109] At the same time, there are limitations that cannot be overcome without denaturing the form of abuse in question. Tying may be an administrable abuse that has served relatively well in the digital economy, but not every potential platform abuse can or should be conceived as tying. Despite its expansionist tendencies, the well-known refusal to supply doctrine must be limited to cases of *de novo* refusal. Conceptually, margin squeeze is well aligned with conduct taking place in platform markets, but jerry-rigging it to fit non-price (or not explicitly price-based) conduct reduces its administrability – one of its greatest strengths.

There is one form of leveraging abuse that I did not yet discuss in depth: discrimination. Discrimination, as such, has not taken the spotlight in the leveraging debate. There are different potential reasons. It may be that the focus on its popular price-based variety – *price* discrimination – led to neglect in a digital economy that is often not price-based. Or perhaps its absence in the leveraging debate is explained by the fact

1108 See Section 5.3.

1109 See Sections 6–8.

that many types of price discrimination do not constitute leveraging (think, for example, of the rebates that have kept the EC and European courts busy). This section starts by taking a closer look at discrimination as a leveraging abuse, finding it a good fit for certain conduct in platform markets (Section 9.1).[1110] It then dives deeper into a theory that surfaced earlier, namely, that the refusal to supply test should govern most if not all self-preferencing conduct (Section 9.2). The section ends by laying out the now-completed leveraging puzzle (Section 9.3).

9.1 Abusive Discrimination

Article 102(c) TFEU offers as an example of abuse: 'applying dissimilar conditions to equivalent transactions with other trading parties, thereby placing them at a competitive disadvantage' in other words, anticompetitive discrimination. Let's examine, in turn, the conduct in question (Section 9.1.1), and the threshold at which said conduct becomes anticompetitive and thus illegal (Section 9.1.2).

9.1.1 Conduct

Intra-platform exclusion often comes down to discrimination (or differentiated treatment, or self-preferencing).[1111] In pursuing cases of intra-platform exclusion, however, the EC never unambiguously opted for a theory based on discrimination. The reason cannot be a lack of precedent: in non-platform markets, the EC and European courts have regularly found that discrimination by a vertically integrated undertaking in favour of its own downstream operations/at the expense of downstream competitors is abusive.[1112] Such cases often involve network industries (eg railways,

1110 This section is adapted from Friso Bostoen, 'The General Court's *Google Shopping* Judgment: Finetuning the Legal Qualifications and Tests for Platform Abuse' (2022) 13 JECLAP 75.

1111 See Section 5.

1112 On such (price) discrimination, see Case T–229/94 *Deutsche Bahn v Commission* EU:T:1997:155 (on Deutsche Bahn using its dominant position in the German rail transport market to impose discriminatory tariffs on seaborne container transport via Belgium and the Netherlands in favour of Transfracht, its maritime transport subsidiary); Case C–242/95 *GT-Link v De Danske Statsbaner* EU:C:1997:376 (on a port company favouring its own ferry services by exempting them from duties); the *ITT Promedia* case, which did not lead to a decision, see EC, 'Competition Policy' (XXVIIth Report, 1997) 67 and EC, 'Settlement reached with Belgacom on the publication of telephone directories – ITT withdraws complaint' (press release, 11 April 1997) IP/97/292 (on a telecom provider charging discriminatory prices for directory information in favour of its own directory services); *Irish Sugar v Commission* (n 561) (on a wholesale sugar company withholding rebates to those distributors it competed with in the retail market); *British Post/Deutsche Post* (Case COMP/C-1/36.915) Commission Decision [2001] OJ L331/40 (on Deutsche Post discriminating against the British Post Office in favour of its own UK operations for outgoing cross-border mail); the *E.ON* commitment decision, see *German Electricity Wholesale Market and German Electricity Balancing Market* (Case COMP/39.388-389) Commission Decision C(2008)7367 (on an electricity company dominant in the electricity balancing market favouring its production affiliate); Case T–301/04 *Clearstream v Commission* EU:T:2009:317 (on a dominant primary clearing and settlement services provider discriminating against a secondary clearing and settlement provider in favour of its sister company active in that market). Moreover, most margin squeeze cases also imply discrimination between the vertically integrated undertaking's own downstream operations and competitors, see Bostoen, 'Margin Squeeze: Where Competition Law and Sector Regulation Compete' (n 1010) 25–26. This is particularly apparent in *Deutsche Bahn I and II* (n 1033), which concern a margin squeeze implemented through discriminatory rebates.

ports, telecommunications, postal services), but have also concerned goods such as sugar and services such as banking. Given these precedents, article 102(c) TFEU has been called a 'straightforward legal basis for a theory of abusive self-preferencing'.[1113] Still, it is worth dissecting the wording of the provision as it relates to conduct ('applying dissimilar conditions to equivalent transactions with other trading parties').

First, while article 102(c) cases have mainly concerned discrimination *based on price*, this is simply a reflection of the economic reality, which has been heavily price-centred – a reality that is now being challenged by platforms, which often do not even charge a price (at least to one side). Article 102(c) TFEU, however, does not refer to different prices but to 'dissimilar *conditions*' more generally. Similarly, the reference to 'equivalent *transactions*' should be interpreted in a modern fashion. In a case such as *Google Shopping*, there are no transactions, at least in the strict sense of the word: Google crawls the web, indexes webpages and algorithmically ranks them, which does not require the active participation of the owners of those digital properties. (Other cases of self-preferencing, eg involving marketplaces and app stores, do involve transactions between the platform and the downstream competitor being excluded.) While the wording of the article should not be disregarded, it must be noted that exclusionary conduct under article 102 TFEU does not generally presuppose a contractual relationship between parties. The EC has also interpreted article 102(c) TFEU in this sense, holding that 'business contacts' are considered sufficient for its application.[1114] One could then still question whether there are 'business contacts' between Google and (comparison shopping) websites, but the broad wording certainly leaves room for this.[1115]

The most recurring objection against using article 102(c) TFEU as a legal basis for intra-platform exclusion cases is that the equivalence of transactions is considered by reference to 'other trading parties', which are not believed to cover a dominant firm's own downstream business. Graef, for example, holds that the article 'is not the most suitable to address cases of self-preferencing' as 'transactions with a dominant undertaking's downstream business are difficult to regard as equivalent to a transaction with a third party'.[1116] Similarly, Akman holds that, given the reference to 'other' trading parties, 'it appears difficult to argue that the prohibition can be applied to discrimination

1113 Nicolas Petit, 'Theories of Self-Preferencing Under Article 102 TFEU: A Reply to Bo Vesterdorf' (2015) 3 <https://ssrn.com/abstract=2592253>. The article has been published in Competition Law & Policy Debate, but the publicly available version is relied on (note that the paper was commissioned by ICOMP, a complainant against Google).

1114 *BdKEP/Deutsche Post* (Case COMP/38.745) Commission Decision, para 92 ('there is no Commission or Court precedent … to support [the] view that "*trading partners*" should be construed in a narrow way as "contracting parties". Mere business contacts between the dominant undertaking and its "*trading partners*" are generally considered to be sufficient').

1115 As it is possible to prevent crawling/indexing by Google, website owners could be said to 'allow' Google to crawl/index their webpages, which may qualify as 'business contact'. Indeed, the competitive advantage of its search engine is explained in part by the fact that more websites allow Google to crawl/index them, CMA, 'Online Platforms and Digital Advertising Market Study' (Final Report, 2020) paras 3.52–63.

1116 Graef (n 1103) 474.

between one's self and others'.[1117] The case law referenced above is less formalistic on this point, and does qualify the downstream business of vertically integrated undertakings (whether organized as a subsidiary or not) as 'other trading parties' for the purpose of establishing discrimination in the sense of article 102(c) TFEU. The EC has been more explicit on this point, noting that the provision covers discrimination whereby 'the customer of the dominant firm is placed at a competitive disadvantage vis-à-vis the dominant firm itself'.[1118]

9.1.2 Anticompetitiveness Threshold

The anticompetitiveness threshold relates to the probability and severity of harm that must be shown to find a certain conduct anticompetitive and thus illegal.[1119] Article 102(c) TFEU sets an anticompetitiveness threshold of 'competitive disadvantage'. In its plain meaning, this is not a high threshold: when a vertically integrated undertaking treats its own downstream operation more favourably than its competitors, those competitors are at a competitive disadvantage. In a number of decisions, the EC interpreted the threshold liberally, seemingly inferring competitive disadvantage from the existence of discrimination.[1120] This led scholars to characterize the condition of competitive disadvantage as 'not very demanding' and even occasionally 'ignored'.[1121]

Over the years, the European courts refined the threshold. In *British Airways*, the ECJ held that, in order for the conditions of article 102(c) TFEU to be met,

> there must be a finding not only that the behaviour of an undertaking in a dominant market position is discriminatory, but also that it tends to distort that competitive relationship, in other words to hinder the competitive position of some of the business partners of that undertaking in relation to the others[.][1122]

For a competitive disadvantage to exist, it thus suffices that the discrimination 'tends' to lead to a distortion of competition between business partners, without it being required 'that proof be adduced of an actual quantifiable deterioration in the competitive position of the business partners taken individually'.[1123]

1117 Pinar Akman, 'The Theory of Abuse in *Google Search*: A Positive and Normative Assessment Under EU Competition Law' (2017) Journal of Law, Technology & Policy 302, 330–31 (note that the paper was commissioned by Google). See also 334–36 arguing that transactions within a vertically integrated undertaking cannot be considered equivalent to those with a non-integrated third party.

1118 *BdKEP/Deutsche Post* (n 1114), para 93.

1119 See Section 5.3.2.

1120 Whish and Bailey (n 860) 781.

1121 Damien Geradin and Nicolas Petit, 'Price Discrimination Under EC Competition Law: The Need for a Case-by-Case Approach' (2005) GCLC Working Paper 07/05, 10.

1122 Case C–95/04 P *British Airways v Commission* EU:C:2007:166, para 144; reaffirmed in *Clearstream v Commission* (n 1112), para 193.

1123 *British Airways v Commission* (n 1122), para 145.

In 2018, the ECJ further clarified the notion of 'competitive disadvantage' in *MEO*.[1124] It held that discriminatory conduct must be 'capable' of distorting competition to fall under the prohibition of article 102(c) TFEU.[1125] On the one hand, the mere presence of an immediate disadvantage does not prove such a capability.[1126] On the other hand, there is no 'appreciability (*de minimis*) threshold for the purposes of determining whether there is an abuse of a dominant position'.[1127] The ECJ repeated it is not required that 'proof be adduced of an actual, quantifiable deterioration in the competitive position of the business partners taken individually'.[1128] Rather, the capability to distort competition must be established with regard to all circumstances, which may include 'the possible existence of a strategy aiming to exclude from the downstream market one of its trade partners which is at least as efficient as its competitors'.[1129] In particular, it may be relevant to examine the effect of the discrimination on the profitability of the undertaking concerned.[1130]

9.1.3 Intra-Platform Discrimination

Discrimination as a form of leveraging by a vertically integrated, dominant firm is, if not a well-established, certainly a recognized form of abuse. Compared to the theory put forward by the EC in *Google Shopping*,[1131] it has distinct advantages in terms of legal certainty and administrability. In contrast to leveraging as a form of abuse, it fits *under* the leveraging umbrella rather than overlapping with it. In contrast to favouring under specific circumstances, discrimination is more widely useful. In other words, it is neither too broad nor too narrow. Discrimination also comes with a developed legal test. There may be a concern that the test sets the bar too low, leading to false positives. However, the current interpretation of the anticompetitiveness threshold of 'competitive disadvantage' should prevent this. Moreover, two case studies at the national level show that discrimination theories do not necessarily lead to condemnation of unequal treatment by platforms (Section 9.1.3.1). And in confirming *Google Shopping*, the GC took an important step towards recognizing intra-platform discrimination as an abuse at the EU level (9.1.3.2).

9.1.3.1 National Application

National authorities and courts have led the way in conceiving allegations of intra-platform exclusion as cases of abusive discrimination, with reference to article 102(c) TFEU. Two cases stand out.

1124 *MEO v Autoridade da Concorrência* (n 671).

1125 ibid, paras 26, 28 and 37. The ECJ also repeats the '*tends* to distort competition' threshold, but mainly rephrases it as the '*capable* of distorting competition' threshold.

1126 ibid, para 26.

1127 ibid, para 29, referencing Case C-23/14 *Post Danmark v Konkurrencerådet* (n 666), para 73.

1128 *MEO v Autoridade da Concorrência* (n 671), para 27, referencing *British Airways v Commission* (n 1122), para 145.

1129 ibid, para 31, referencing *Intel v Commission* (n 467), para 139.

1130 ibid, para 34 ('where the effect of a tariff differentiation on the costs borne by the operator which considers itself to be wronged, or on the profitability and profits of that operator, is not significant, it may, in some circumstances, be deduced that that tariff differentiation is not capable of having any effect on the competitive position of that operator').

1131 See Section 5.3.1.

In the *Streetmap* case before the UK's High Court of Justice, a provider of online mapping claimed that Google abused its dominant position in search 'by the prominent and preferential display given to [its] own related online map product, thereby restricting competition from competing suppliers of online maps'.[1132] While Streetmap initially framed the case as bundling (of Google search results and Google Maps), the judge believed that 'Streetmap's contention is appropriately characterised as an allegation of discrimination.'[1133] The judge noted that the discrimination does not concern price 'as in the usual kind of discrimination case', but that the essence of discrimination – treating like products in an unlike way – was present:

> Google's display of a clickable thumbnail map on its SERP [search engine results page] exclusively from Google Maps, at the prime position at the top of the page [the Maps OneBox], involves a form of presentation of its online mapping product that is not given to other online maps; and this preference is alleged to place those competing online maps at a competitive disadvantage unrelated to their intrinsic merits.[1134]

The judge saw no reason why such intra-platform exclusion could not constitute an abuse but required proof of anticompetitive foreclosure.[1135] Such foreclosure was conceived as the use of 'market power to limit effective competitors' ability to compete by driving or hindering their necessary access to inputs or customers'.[1136] The judge thus focused on harm to competition as such (rather than to consumers directly), holding that the impugned conduct must be 'reasonably likely' to result in such harm.[1137] In the end, the judge concluded that Google's inclusion of Google Maps at the top of the search results page did not meet this threshold: 'on consideration of all the evidence', he found that 'the introduction of the new-style Maps OneBox ... did not in itself have an appreciable effect in taking custom away from Streetmap'.[1138] Even if there were an abuse, the judge held it could be objectively justified because the direct inclusion

1132 *Streetmap.eu v Google* (n 591) [4].

1133 ibid [51] and [54]. In its Re-Amended Particulars of the Claim, Streetmap also focused on discrimination (more favourable treatment of Google Maps in comparison with equivalent mapping services, resulting in a competitive disadvantage), see ibid [153].

1134 ibid [54].

1135 ibid [60] and [62].

1136 ibid [63].

1137 ibid [64]–[65], which include references to *GlaxoSmithKline* (n 463) and *Microsoft v Commission* (n 339) to support the view that the object of competition law is to prevent harm to the structure of competition in the market, and not simply direct harm to consumers.

1138 *Streetmap.eu v Google* (n 591) [139]. In coming to this conclusion, the judge relied on a wide range of evidence, including experiments by Google and search results data from comScore. On the one hand, Streetmap only drew a limited number of visitors from geographic queries on Google, who were now shown Google's own map on top of the search results (other visitors arrived on the Streetmap website directly or through navigational queries), so the effects were in any case limited. The OneBox introduction did not significantly affect visits to the blue links below either (moreover, because of changes to the 'trigger' of its maps, Google Maps itself was visited less after introducing the OneBox). On the other hand, the relative success of Google Maps versus Streetmap was explained by the superior quality of Google Maps (ie competition on the merits), not the introduction of the OneBox. Note how in *Google Search (Shopping)* (n 348), the EC took care to show how there was a significant drop in visits to non-Google CSSs and how this was not explained by Google's superior quality.

of Google Maps constituted a technical efficiency for which there was no less restrictive alternative.[1139]

In the *Funda* case, a Dutch court also had to rule on differentiated treatment by an online platform.[1140] Funda – a platform that connects real estate agents with potential buyers – is owned by NVM, the main federation of real estate agents in the Netherlands. The real estate agents of VBO, a competing real estate federation, complained that – in comparison to NVM agents – they were being discriminated against on Funda by being charged prices that were 640% higher, by consistently being ranked lower in search results (which led to 16% fewer contact requests), and by not having access to certain functionalities. The court tested such conduct against article 102(c) TFEU, accepting that Funda was applying dissimilar conditions to equivalent transactions but concluding that such discrimination did not lead to a competitive disadvantage: first, the prices charged did not differ significantly when accounting for indirect payments of NVM agents to Funda; second, despite a ranking disadvantage, the market share of VBO real estate agents had not declined over the last ten years or so.[1141]

On appeal, the *Funda Real Estate* judgment was confirmed. In particular, the appeals court relied on the ECJ's *MEO* judgment to test whether or not there was a competitive disadvantage in the downstream market for real estate services (the upstream market being that of the real estate platform).[1142] First, the court noted that the purchase of a house differs in importance (financial and otherwise) from the purchase of other consumer goods: as consumers will conduct their search diligently, a lower ranking does not necessarily lead to a competitive disadvantage. For that reason, it also found the analogy with *Google Shopping* unhelpful.[1143] Second, when it comes to the different prices charged, the court held – in line with *MEO* – that the existence of a direct disadvantage was not in itself sufficient for discrimination to amount to an abuse.[1144] The court did not find that there was a strategy to drive non-NVM real estate agents from the market underlying Funda's preferential treatment of NVM real estate agents; VBO real estate agents did not sufficiently prove that the differentiation constituted an illegal form of discrimination.[1145] In the end, it appears that VBO real estate agents lost their case because they could not point to enough concrete circumstances to support the competitive disadvantage they alleged to suffer.

NCAs have also been looking at cases of discrimination. The Austrian competition authority has examined preferential treatment by Amazon of its own products, but closed its investigation when Amazon modified its terms and conditions, which include the pledge

1139 *Streetmap.eu v Google* (n 591) [142]–[176].

1140 Rechtbank Amsterdam, Case C/13/528337, *VBO Makelaar v Funda Real Estate*, 21 March 2018.

1141 ibid, paras 2.16–17. It does not appear that the court considered the counterfactual (ie how the market share of VBO real estate agents would have evolved absent the discrimination).

1142 ibid, para 3.9.

1143 ibid, para 3.12. The court also nuances the 16% fewer contact requests, which may be due to other factors.

1144 ibid, para 3.18.

1145 ibid, paras 3.18–19. The court also nuances the 640% price difference and puts the listing fee into perspective by comparing it with a real estate agent's total costs.

to impose sales restrictions in a non-discriminatory manner.[1146] The Polish competition authority fined the e-commerce platform Allegro for favouring its own retail operation.[1147] The Dutch competition investigated the 'preferential treatment' Apple gives its own apps,[1148] but ended up conceiving the case as one of exploitation. The AdlC is examining App Tracking Transparency (ATT) – the Apple policy that limits how app developers can monitor users on third-party apps and websites.[1149] The investigation is meant

> to verify that the implementation by Apple of the ATT framework cannot be regarded as a form of discrimination or 'self-preferencing', which could in particular be the case if Apple applied without justification, more binding rules on third-party operators than those it applies to itself for similar operations.[1150]

The AGCM, finally, has fined Amazon for leveraging its marketplace dominance 'to favour the adoption of its own logistics service', FBA.[1151] The authority relied on the tying framework but also qualified the conduct as self-preferencing (with reference to *Google Shopping*) and discrimination.[1152]

9.1.3.2 EU Clarification

The diversity of intra-platform exclusion methods is matched by an almost equally large number of qualifications of that conduct (leveraging, favouring, self-preferencing, preferential treatment, discrimination, etc). Adding to the confusion is the fact that not

1146 BWB, *Amazon.de Marketplace* (Case Report), 11 September 2019, para 56. Tribunal de commerce de Paris, case 2017050625, *Ministre de l'Économie et des Finances v Amazon*, 2 September 2019, also concerned discrimination.

1147 Office of Competition and Consumer Protection, 'President of UOKiK issued two decisions concerning Allegro's practices' (press release, 29 December 2022) <https://uokik.gov.pl/news.php?news_id=19185>. In opening its investigation, the NCA referenced *Google Shopping*, see Office of Competition and Consumer Protection, 'Procedure against Allegro' (press release, 10 December 2019) <https://www.uokik.gov.pl/news.php?news_id=16014>.

1148 ACM, 'ACM launches investigation into abuse of dominance by Apple in its App Store' (press release, 11 April 2019) <https://www.acm.nl/en/publications/acm-launches-investigation-abuse-dominance-apple-its-app-store>. Interestingly, in an earlier report on video platforms, the ACM conceived the 'less prominent placement of third-party content' as a potential refusal to supply, requiring proof that (i) the input (platform) is essential; (ii) third-party content is actually placed less prominently on a consistent and systematic basis; (iii) there is no objective justification for such behaviour; (iv) this behaviour leads, or may lead, to publishers of this content being impeded in their ability to compete, see ACM, 'A Closer Look at Online video Platforms' (Report, 2018) 68.

1149 Such monitoring is important for the 'hub-and-spoke' digital advertising model that many developers rely on, see Eric Seufert, 'Lose-Lose' (*Mobile Dev Demo*, 30 November 2022) <https://mobiledevmemo.com/lose-lose/>.

1150 AdlC, 'Apple's implementation of the ATT framework: the Autorité does not issue urgent interim measures against Apple but continues to investigate into the merits of the case' (press release, 17 March 2021) <https://www.autoritedelaconcurrence.fr/en/communiques-de-presse/targeted-advertising-apples-implementation-att-framework-autorite-does-not>. For the full decision, see AdlC, Decision 21-D-07, *Interactive Advertising Bureau France et al v Apple*, 17 March 2021 (in which the AdlC preliminarily rejects allegations of tying and unfair T&Cs).

1151 AGCM, 'Amazon fined over €1,128 billion for abusing its dominant position' (press release, 9 December 2021) <https://en.agcm.it/en/media/press-releases/2021/12/A528>.

1152 See Francesco Tognato, Irene Picciano and Enzo Marasà, 'The Italian Competition Authority Fines an e-Commerce Company €1.128 Billion for Abuse of Dominance by Making Exclusive Advantages for Its Online Marketplace Conditional upon the Purchase of its Logistics Services (*Amazon*)' e-Competitions December 2021, art no 104177 <www.concurrences.com/104177>. The remedy was also one of non-discrimination.

every qualification corresponds neatly to a legal test. In some cases, there is no established legal test – a problem that is sometimes solved by relying on the legal test of a seemingly different abuse (eg tying). Clarification at the EU level would be most helpful. The GC judgment in *Google Shopping* offered such clarification, at least in part and for readers willing to squint.

First, the GC addressed the leveraging status as an allegedly well-established form of abuse.[1153] The GC held that the judgments the EC referenced to support that statement do not 'permit the inference that any use of a dominant position on one market to extend that dominant position to one or more adjacent markets constitutes a well-established form of abuse'.[1154] Leveraging *in itself* does not constitute proof of conduct that departs from normal competition – it is just a 'generic term' designating different types of conduct that can be abusive.[1155] In the hearing before the GC, however, the EC had already pre-empted such a correction by holding that the specific way in which Google favoured its own comparison shopping service 'constitutes a form of leveraging abuse', rather than leveraging itself being the form of abuse.[1156]

Second, the GC held that the form of abuse consisted in Google favouring its own comparison shopping service through prominent display and positioning under three specific circumstances identified in the EC decision: (i) the importance of Google traffic for CSSs; (ii) user behaviour when searching online (attention mostly for top results, thought to be the most relevant); and (iii) the fact that diverted traffic from Google's general results pages cannot be effectively replaced.[1157]

These clarifications – or corrections – are welcome. Leveraging, as a form of abuse, was underdefined ('extending a dominant position to an adjacent market'). The alternative form of abuse, favouring, has the opposite problem of being overdefined. Given the three specific circumstances under which it becomes abusive, favouring's utility is essentially limited to cases of prominent display and positioning in searches. In other words, a favouring abuse plugs the *Google Shopping* gap but not the broader platform leveraging gap. In sum, neither leveraging nor favouring offers an appropriate legal qualification/test for conduct by which online platforms exclude third-party services by treating them differently from their own, vertically integrated offering. In addition, neither theory has a solid basis in case law (reference is only made to other, specific leveraging abuses), which further limits any legal certainty.

Perhaps because of these reasons, the GC went a step further in conceptualizing the relevant form of abuse. While 'discrimination' is completely absent from the EC

1153 *Google Search (Shopping)* (n 348), para 649. See Section 5.3.2.

1154 *Google v Commission* (n 767), paras 609–10.

1155 ibid, paras 162–63.

1156 Case T–612/17 *Google v Commission* (Hearing Report), para 322.

1157 *Google v Commission* (n 767), paras 166–75. The anticompetitiveness threshold for the suggested leveraging and favouring abuses is the same, ie capability/likelihood of anticompetitive effects.

decision,[1158] the GC had no qualms about using the term. It described the EC decision as based on 'internal discrimination' between Google's own CSSs and competing CSSs, and the remedy as principled on 'non-discrimination'.[1159] More significantly, from a legal perspective, the GC grounded its analysis in the discrimination provision and doctrine.[1160] To corroborate its statement that 'abuse may take the form of an unjustified difference in treatment', for example, the GC referenced cases such as *GT-Link* and *Irish Sugar*.[1161]

One has to read closely, and sometimes even between the lines, but the GC judgment in *Google Shopping* is an important step towards recognizing intra-platform discrimination as an abuse under EU competition law. There are important arguments for doing so. Discrimination has a Treaty basis that has been fleshed out in the case law, benefitting its administrability and legal certainty. The form of abuse is neither overinclusive (as leveraging is) or underinclusive (as favouring is). The anticompetitiveness threshold of 'competitive disadvantage' has been brought in line with that of other forms of leveraging abuse, ie a capability/likelihood of anticompetitive effects. Cases before national courts illustrate how the risk of false positives is limited, at least as long as the anticompetitiveness threshold is taken seriously.

In its *Amazon Buy Box* case, the EC seems to be following the GC's lead.[1162] The conduct at issue was twofold: first, Amazon favours its own retail offering, in particular through selection for prominent placement (in the Buy Box, responsible for 90% of sales); second, Amazon provides third-party sellers that use its FBA service an artificial competitive advantage (via Buy Box placement and Prime eligibility) compared to sellers that fulfil their own orders.[1163] Throughout the decision, the EC denotes the first conduct as 'favouring' and the second as 'discrimination'.[1164] Its preliminary legal assessment, however, is fully centred around article 102(c) TFEU and references the GC's discrimination-focused paragraph in *Google Shopping*.[1165] The EC references *MEO* for its anticompetitiveness threshold, although it did not seem to apply it all too rigorously.[1166]

1158 The EC did include article 102(c) TFEU's definition of discrimination in *Google Search (Shopping)* (n 348), para 336, but only as part of an illustrative list of abusive practices.

1159 *Google v Commission* (n 767), paras 237 and 71.

1160 The GC referred to article 102(c) TFEU in distinguishing the legal qualification from refusal to supply, see ibid, para 239.

1161 ibid, para 155, referencing *GT-Link v De Danske Statsbaner* (n 1112), para 41 and *Irish Sugar v Commission* (n 561), para 140. The GC also referenced Case C–82/01 P *Aéroports de Paris v Commission* EU:C:2002:617, para 114, which is less relevant as it concerns discrimination between unaffiliated third parties.

1162 Earlier on the case, see Sections 2.3.1 and 8.3.3.

1163 *Amazon Marketplace* and *Amazon Buy Box* (n 369), para 5.

1164 ibid, ss 4.7.3.2 and 4.7.3.4.

1165 ibid, paras 162–64, referencing *Google v Commission* (n 767), para 155.

1166 ibid, para 164, referencing *MEO v Autoridade da Concorrência* (n 671), para 24. The lack of rigour may be explained in part by this being a commitment decision. Even then, the EC is vague in identifying the nature of the harm and the markets where it manifests itself. It does note, in a way reminiscent of tying cases, that consumers may be driven towards inferior offers.

9.2 Disruptive Discrimination

The discrimination abuse has an important role to play in assessing instances of intra-platform exclusion. That need not be a dominant role though. Rather, I suggest having recourse to discrimination in cases where other forms of leveraging abuse – margin squeeze, *de novo* refusal, and tying – are not applicable. This subsidiarity is justified because, despite strides in establishing and concretizing platform discrimination, those other forms of abuse continue to have a more structured legal test (administrability) and 'name recognition' (legal certainty).

Further, it is important to keep some limiting principles in mind. Discrimination shares some of these principles with other leveraging abuses. Obviously, conduct cannot infringe article 102 TFEU without dominance.[1167] And discrimination's anticompetitiveness threshold is the standard effects test that governs other leveraging abuses with the exception of *de novo* refusal. The as-efficient-competitor principle, if not test, provides the background for the effects analysis – as it does for other leveraging abuses, sometimes more explicitly (eg margin squeeze), other times more implicitly (eg refusal to supply).[1168]

One important factor is the role of disruption. I'm referring to disruption in the sense of a reversal in established commercial relations, not as in innovation, although the former certainly has an impact on the latter. Earlier, I argued a less stringent legal test should apply when there is a disruption of rather than a refusal to supply (such disruptions being one form of installed base opportunism).[1169] The same arguments justify being especially sensitive to situations where a platform introduces discrimination in established supplier relations, as opposed to maintaining discrimination from the start. On the supplier side, such discrimination frustrates the expectations of ecosystem partners, which is all the more harmful when they have made relation-specific investments. The effect goes beyond the suppliers directly affected by the discrimination: it also introduces uncertainty in the relations with other ecosystem partners, which can discourage them from investing in a platform where they might be expropriated. On the platform side, the prior, non-discriminatory conduct suggests that such dealing was efficient, ie the platform was receiving adequate compensation for its investment. In other words, there is little risk to the platform's incentives to invest when prohibiting such discrimination. In addition, prior dealing offers a benchmark for a potential non-discrimination remedy.

In *Google Shopping*, the GC was sensitive to the fact that Google started discriminating against CSSs *after* running an open search engine for years. Google went from showing the best results to showing its own results. According to the GC, this reversal 'of the

---

1167 See Section 4.1.

1168 On the as-efficient-competitor test, and how recent judgments may attribute too great a role to it, see Fernando Castillo de la Torre 'Is the Effects-Based Approach Too Cumbersome? Taking Stock of Recent Practice and Case Law on Article 102 TFEU' (2023) <https://ssrn.com/abstract=4395401>. On how the test is economically too lenient, see Salop, 'Economic Analysis of Exclusionary Vertical Conduct: Where Chicago Has Overshot the Mark' (n 573) 152–55.

1169 See Sections 7.1.2 and 7.2.2 (see also Section 5.3.2).

economic model underpinning the initial success of its search engine cannot but involve a certain form of abnormality.'[1170] Indeed, alienating suppliers on which it relies is generally not a rational strategy for a platform, but this can change when a platform becomes dominant and suppliers have few alternatives to turn to.[1171] The GC picked up on this when stating that

> for a search engine, limiting the scope of its results to its own entails an element of risk and is not necessarily rational, save in a situation, as in the present case, where the dominance and barriers to entry are such that no market entry within a sufficiently short period of time is possible in response to that limitation of internet users' choice.[1172]

Given the 'open early, closed late' scenario, the GC put the burden on Google to justify the discrimination.[1173] This reversal of the burden of proof, which normally rests on the EC, is a significant shift. As part of a more structured legal test, however, it can be justified. Under such a test, the platform that introduces discrimination first has to justify it, in the absence of which there is naked exclusion that can be condemned with little risk of false positives.[1174] If the platform plausibly argues a justification, the burden is put back on the authority to show anticompetitive effects. If it can prove such effects, the burden is on the platform once more. It can then further develop its justification, showing in particular how the procompetitive effects outweigh the anticompetitive ones.

9.3 *Bronner*'s Expansionism Revisited

I sketched how, according to the case law and sound economic logic, the *Bronner* test should be curtailed to *de novo* refusals.[1175] Tying, disruptions of supply and margin squeeze are properly assessed without reference to indispensability. In this section, I argue that discrimination need not be assessed according to *Bronner* either. In part, this is simply an extension of the previous argument. The prominent role that *Bronner* and its refusal to supply brethren played in the self-preferencing debate, however, offers an opportunity to expand and finetune the argument.

1170 *Google v Commission* (n 767), para 179.

1171 See Section 5.2.2.

1172 *Google v Commission* (n 767), para 178.

1173 ibid ('it is for the person responsible for that difference in treatment to justify it in the light of competition law'), referencing Case C–413/08 P *Lafarge v Commission* EU:C:2010:346, paras 29–30 ('Even if the burden of proof rests, according to those principles, on the Commission or on the undertaking or association concerned, the evidence on which a party relies may be of such a kind as to require the other party to provide an explanation or justification, failing which it is permissible to conclude that the rules on the burden of proof have been satisfied').

1174 I am assuming a preliminary step (the opening of the investigation) where the authority proves some exclusion, though it need not be of a general nature or of as-efficient competitors.

1175 See Sections 7.1.3 and 8.2.2.

9.3.1 Refusal Redux

Some argue that discrimination can only be abusive if the refusal to supply conditions are met. On one occasion, the EC itself even mingled the two forms of abuse:

> A dominant undertaking which both owns or controls and itself uses an essential facility, i.e., a facility or infrastructure without access to which competitors cannot provide services to their customers, and which refuses its competitors access to that facility or grants access to competitors only on terms less favourable than those which it gives its own services, thereby placing the competitors at a competitive disadvantage, infringes Article [102 TFEU], if the other conditions of that Article are met.[1176]

At issue is a vertically integrated undertaking favouring its own services (*in casu*, a port discriminating against a competitor of its ferry business). What appears to be an assessment of discriminatory conduct is, however, contaminated by the essential facilities doctrine. Further in the same paragraph, the EC is less ambiguous: 'A company in a dominant position may not discriminate in favour of its own activities in a related market.'[1177] In the end, the presence of an essential facility seems incidental: it appears to be included to strengthen the case, rather than as a requirement. Moreover, logic commands that, if it is unlawful for the operator of an essential facility to discriminate in favour of its activities in a related market, this does not imply that such discrimination is lawful absent an essential facility.[1178]

Voices that self-preferencing can only be abusive under the *Bronner* conditions reached a fever pitch in the run-up to *Google Shopping*.[1179] As covered extensively in this work, however, many leveraging abuses (eg tying and margin squeeze) come down to self-preferencing. Requiring indispensability in these cases goes against the letter of the Treaty (article 102(d) and (a), respectively) and against the case law. The same goes for discrimination by a vertically integrated firm in favour of its own downstream operations.[1180] *Bronner* itself does not support the position that its legal test applies widely: as AG Jacobs noted, the referring court in that case asked the ECJ to make abstraction of confounding factors such as discrimination and focus on refusal to supply, meaning the judgment is not dispositive on the choice between the two.[1181] Even AG Mazák, who in *TeliaSonera* argued for requiring indispensability for both refusal to supply *and* margin squeeze, nevertheless ruled out the indispensability

1176 *Sealink/B&I – Holyhead* (Case IV/34.174) Commission Decision, para 41. Note that the decision is one of interim measures, which limits the depth of the legal assessment.

1177 ibid. The EC also includes the condition of a 'competitive disadvantage', which corroborates its reliance on article 102(c) TFEU rather than 102(b) TFEU – the legal basis of refusal to supply decisions.

1178 Petit, 'Theories of Self-Preferencing Under Article 102 TFEU: A Reply to Bo Vesterdorf' (n 1113).

1179 See eg Bo Vesterdorf, 'Theories of Self-Preferencing and Duty to Deal – Two Sides of the Same Coin?' (2015) 1 Competition Law & Policy Debate 4 (note that the paper was commissioned by Google); with regard to *Google Search* specifically, see Renato Nazzini, 'Unequal Treatment by Online Platforms: A Structured Approach to the Abuse Test in *Google*' (2016) GCLC Annual Conference Series (note that the paper was commissioned by Google).

1180 See the half-dozen cases referenced in Section 9.1.1.

1181 *Oscar Bronner v Mediaprint*, Opinion of AG Jacobs (n 902), para 54.

requirement where 'the dominant undertaking may be discriminating between competitors and its own downstream operations under Article 102(c) TFEU'.[1182]

Put simply, there is more than *one* form of abuse of dominance, and not every form of abuse must mirror the conditions of the refusal to supply doctrine. Depending on the conduct in question, self-preferencing can qualify as tying, margin squeeze, refusal/disruption of supply, and discrimination. Granted, qualifying conduct can be something of a Platonic exercise, where one has to find the ethereal Form reflected by the conduct at issue. But that is not an impossible exercise. In *Microsoft I*, for example, the EC had no trouble distinguishing the tying and refusal to supply limbs of the case. The GC's judgment in *Google Shopping* was a bit less clear. It suggested qualifying the conduct as discrimination but also noted that 'Google's general results page has characteristics akin to those of an essential facility'.[1183] The GC added, however, that 'the practices at issue … can nevertheless be distinguished in their constituent elements from the refusal to supply at issue in … *Bronner*'.[1184]

It must be acknowledged that there are good arguments for having a single standard for the variety of conduct falling under the self-preferencing banner.[1185] If more than one standard applies 'for strategies that are essentially different manifestations of the same course of conduct', then 'stakeholders can be expected to exploit such formal frictions opportunistically'.[1186] They could, in other words, go 'label shopping': avoiding the stringent indispensability standard and opting instead for a laxer standard (eg discrimination). Finding one standard for every form of self-preferencing recalls the search for a 'theory of everything' – the scientific quest for an as-of-yet-undiscovered way to reconcile the contradictory theories of general relativity and quantum mechanics.[1187] The difference, of course, is that the theory of everything must correspond to an objective reality, while legal theories are constructs. This makes the search for a coherent legal framework an inherently normative exercise on which reasonable minds can disagree. One possible outcome of this exercise is to find unison in diversity: every form of self-preferencing constitutes a refusal to supply and should be assessed as such. Another possible outcome is to value the diversity: various legal tests can apply to various forms of self-preferencing; depending on the exact form, one should find the right qualification.

Apart from these (meta)physical considerations, there is a more practical issue with imposing a single standard: doing away with different qualifications requires its own

1182 *Konkurrensverket v TeliaSonera Sverige*, Opinion of AG Mazák (n 1042), para 32.

1183 *Google v Commission* (n 767), para 224 (the reason being that 'there is currently no actual or potential substitute available that would enable it to be replaced in an economically viable manner on the market').

1184 ibid, para 229. A refusal to supply in the sense of *Bronner* requires '(i) that it is express, that is to say, that there is a "request" or in any event a wish to be granted access and a consequential "refusal", and (ii) that the trigger of the exclusionary effect – the impugned conduct – lies principally in the refusal as such, and not in an extrinsic practice such as, in particular, another form of leveraging abuse' (para 232).

1185 See, in particular, Ibáñez Colomo, 'Exclusionary Discrimination Under Article 102 TFEU' (n 553).

1186 ibid 160.

1187 On the state of that research, see elegantly Carlo Rovelli, *Reality Is Not What It Seems: The Journey to Quantum Gravity* (Riverhead Books 2018).

qualifications. For example, does tying fall under self-preferencing? Depending on whether one wants to see it included, one has to start adapting the definition of the self-preferencing qualification, which is no easy feat. Even recourse to the economic concept of 'raising rivals' costs' does not help: both tying and refusal to supply by a vertically integrated undertaking (say, Microsoft) are covered by this concept.[1188] In fact, most cases of vertical foreclosure can be qualified as raising rivals' costs strategies. Before you know it, all exclusionary conduct (and thus virtually all EC enforcement of article 102 TFEU) must be assessed according to *Bronner*. All of this is not to say that qualifications are inherently problematic (indeed, I would argue the opposite); rather, it is to say that exercises in doing away with them may end up affirming them. Until we find the elusive theory of everything for exclusionary conduct, there will always be a dividing line between different kinds of conduct. And the theories of everything proposed thus far have not improved on the current system.[1189]

9.3.2 Remedy Reasoning

An alternative theory holds that the EC may have the power to choose the theory of harm (and corresponding form of abuse/legal test) that fits the conduct in question, but that its choice limits the remedies it can impose.[1190] Put differently, the remedies sought by the EC determine the theory of harm it must pursue. If it only seeks a *reactive* remedy (a negative obligation to bring certain conduct to a halt), the EC can get away with carrying out the standard effects test applicable to most leveraging abuses. However, if the EC wants to impose a *proactive* remedy (a positive obligation to adopt a certain conduct), an enhanced effects test is appropriate, which means the EC must prove indispensability in line with *Bronner*.

Again, the theory is not limited to scholarly writing but rears its head in decisional practice. In *Google Shopping*, the EC even appears to endorse it, holding that

> the *Bronner* criteria are irrelevant in a situation, such as that of the present case, where bringing to an end the infringement does not involve imposing a duty on the dominant undertaking to 'transfer an asset or enter into agreements with persons with whom it has not chosen to contract'. While the Decision requires Google to cease the Conduct, it does not require it either to transfer any asset or to enter into agreements with one or more competing comparison shopping services.[1191]

1188 Earlier on raising rivals' costs, see Sections 5.1.2 and 8.4. Discussing Microsoft's conduct as raising rivals' costs, see Tom and Wells (n 582).

1189 See eg Douglas Melamed, 'Exclusive Dealing and Other Exclusionary Conduct – Are There Unifying Principles? (2006) 73 Antitrust Law Journal 375, arguing in favour of the 'no economic sense test' for exclusionary conduct and discarding alternatives such as the equally-efficient-competitor test; arguing for a more tailored approach, see Popofsky (n 532); Baker, 'Taking the Error Out of "Error Cost" Analysis: What's Wrong with Antitrust's Right' (n 531); Salop, 'An Enquiry Meet for the Case: Decision Theory, Presumptions, and Evidentiary Burdens in Formulating Antitrust Legal Standards' (n 539).

1190 Ibáñez Colomo, 'Legal Tests in EU Competition Law: Taxonomy and Operation' (n 669) 435–36.

1191 *Google Search (Shopping)* (n 348), para 651.

The EC appears to accept that if it were to impose a positive obligation to deal with certain parties (a proactive remedy), the refusal to supply criteria would be relevant. This statement seems to be an extension of the paragraph before, in which the EC states that Google's conduct does not concern a 'passive refusal' to give competing CSSs access to its general search results pages but 'active behaviour' relating to the more favourable positioning and display of its own CSSs.[1192] One could read the full reasoning in two ways: either the EC is endorsing the theory that imposing a proactive remedy requires meeting the *Bronner* criterion of indispensability, or the EC is simply supporting its statement that Google's conduct does not constitute a refusal to supply by referring to the fact that the remedy does not consist in a duty to deal (ie the remedy supports the theory of harm but does not necessarily determine it).

The (case) law, while not always as crystal clear, does not offer strong support for the theory.[1193] Regulation 1/2003 holds that the EC 'may impose on [infringers of article 102 TFEU] any behavioural or structural remedies which are proportionate to the infringement committed and necessary to bring the infringement effectively to an end'.[1194] Case law only confirms that the existence of an abuse and the choice of remedy are two separate questions.[1195] The cases referenced by the EC do not challenge this.[1196] In *Van den Bergh Foods*, the ECJ merely explained that an exclusive dealing obligation does not constitute a refusal to supply; accordingly, it need not be tested against the *Bronner* criteria.[1197] In *AstraZeneca*, AG Mazák was more ambiguous, as he seemingly linked the refusal to supply conditions to the obligation 'to transfer an asset or enter into a contract'.[1198] However, both the ECJ (in its *AstraZeneca* judgment)[1199] and that same AG (in his *TeliaSonera* Opinion)[1200] did not subsequently confirm – and even

1192 ibid, para 650.

1193 Dunne, 'Dispensing with Indispensability' (n 869) 32–36.

1194 Council Regulation (EC) No 1/2003 of 16 December 2002 on the implementation of the rules on competition laid down in Articles 81 and 82 of the Treaty [2003] OJ L1/1, art 7 (see also consideration 12).

1195 See eg *Commercial Solvents v Commission* (n 862), paras 45–46.

1196 *Google Search (Shopping)* (n 348), para 651, referencing Case T–65/98 *Van den Bergh Foods v Commission* EU:T:2003:281, para 161 and Case C–457/10 P *AstraZeneca v Commission* EU:C:2012:293, Opinion of AG Mazák, paras 94–95.

1197 *Van den Bergh Foods v Commission* (n 1196), para 161 ('HB's reference to the Opinion of Advocate General Jacobs in the judgment in *Bronner*, is irrelevant in the present case because [the EC] did not claim … that HB's freezer cabinets were an essential facility, which is the issue examined in his Opinion, and it is not necessary for HB to transfer an asset or to conclude contracts with persons which it has not selected in complying with the contested decision').

1198 *AstraZeneca v Commission*, Opinion of AG Mazák (n 1196), paras 94–95 ('I consider that the *IMS Health* case-law is wholly inapplicable as the present case does not concern, inter alia, a refusal by a dominant undertaking to provide access to or licence information which is indispensable in order to allow a potential competitor to have access to the market in which the undertaking which owns the right occupies a dominant position. It is clear that the contested decision did not oblige AZ to transfer an asset or enter into a contract with persons with whom it has not chosen to contract.').

1199 Case C–457/10 P *AstraZeneca v Commission* EU:C:2012:770, paras 147–56. AstraZeneca abused regulatory procedures to block generic entry, *inter alia* by deregistering market authorizations. According to the ECJ, limiting this option is 'unlike a situation in which the unfettered exercise of an exclusive right awarded for the realisation of an investment or creation is limited' – in the latter case, the refusal to supply criteria do apply. Again, the distinction is between forms of abuse themselves, not between remedies subsequently imposed.

1200 *Konkurrensverket v TeliaSonera*, Opinion of AG Mazák (n 1042), para 15, listing the *Bronner* criteria to establish the existence of an abuse (rather than having their application determined by the chosen remedy).

implicitly rejected – such a link. It is no surprise then that the GC also rejected the EC's reasoning, holding that 'the obligation for an undertaking which is abusively exploiting a dominant position to transfer assets, enter into agreements or give access to its service under non-discriminatory conditions does not necessarily involve the application of the criteria laid down in *Bronner*'.[1201]

The 'remedy determines abuse' theory is not only legally but also practically challenging.[1202] First, there is the difficulty of distinguishing between proactive and reactive remedies: after all, every proactive remedy (give X access) can be rephrased as a reactive remedy (stop not giving X access).[1203] While this argument may look like a *reductio ad absurdum*, it is in fact realistic. Consider, for example, the *Google Shopping* decision: on the one hand, the EC obliges Google 'to bring the infringement ... effectively to an end'; on the other hand, it specifies that '[a]ny measure chosen by Google ... should ... ensure that Google treats competing comparison shopping services no less favourably than its own comparison shopping service within its general search results pages'.[1204] Bringing discrimination to an end seems reactive, but equal treatment appears proactive – it is a matter of perspective, and the lines are in any case blurred. Another difficulty is that the EC would have to start each investigation with an idea of whether it wants to impose a proactive remedy – only then can it determine the legal test and thus the shape of its investigation, after which it can impose the chosen remedy. In the words of others, the theory 'put[s] the horse before the cart'.[1205]

9.4 Conclusion

With a good understanding of the platform business model and taking advantage of one of competition law's greatest strengths – its flexibility – established leveraging abuses (tying, disruption of and refusal to supply, and margin squeeze) can find effective application in the digital economy. Even then, however, they cannot plug the leveraging gap that *Google Shopping* laid bare. Discrimination, sometimes overlooked as a leveraging abuse, can play an important role. It is more versatile than tying as it does not need the involvement of two distinct products. As *Bronner*'s indispensability test should be limited to cases of *de novo* refusal, the discrimination test can govern disruption of supply cases. And discrimination need not be price-based, which is an advantage compared to margin squeeze's price-centred test.

1201 *Google v Commission* (n 767), para 244. The GC does so based on a distinction between passive refusals (as in *Bronner*) and active exclusionary conduct (as in *Google Shopping*).

1202 A point also picked up on by the GC in *Google Shopping*, see ibid, para 246.

1203 See also Case T–612/17 *Google v Commission* (Hearing Report), para 333, where Google argues that the EC took issue with it 'for passively refraining from including' competing CSSs in specialized search results and ads.

1204 *Google Search (Shopping)* (n 348), paras 697 and 699.

1205 Jones, Sufrin and Dunne (n 655) 531–32.

Discrimination should not be relied on indiscriminately. In case more than one form of abuse fits the conduct in question, the non-discrimination form should take precedence for reasons of administrability and legal certainty. Concerns for false positives may linger, but cases at the national level should put those to rest. In addition, authorities should focus their efforts on cases of *disruptive* discrimination. These are easier cases with a lower risk of false positives. They can also proceed in accordance with a more sophisticated burden-shifting framework, under which the discriminating firm starts by justifying that discrimination to sift out cases of naked exclusion.

Discrimination is now slowly making it to the EU level, and hopefully developing in line with the principles set out above. Other paths of development, which centre around theories of everything ('each instance of self-preferencing is a refusal to supply'), are open. And having a single standard has its benefits. But such theories come with their own conceptual and practical difficulties. In the end, it is better to recognize the diversity of intra-platform exclusion and, in Platonic fashion, match its different manifestations with the appropriate form of abuse. Even then, the differences between different leveraging abuses are eroding as all of them with the exception of *de novo* refusals are subject to a standard effects test. And of course, courts must guard that plaintiffs (or, for that matter, defendants) do not opportunistically qualify conduct with a legal test in mind.

10

JUSTIFYING ANTICOMPETITIVE BEHAVIOUR: PLATFORM GOVERNANCE

The platform economy is a boon to consumers. There are plenty of experiments that show how consumers derive significant surplus from the digital economy[1206] (although most of them are vulnerable to the behavioural bias of loss aversion or the endowment effect).[1207] But competition law does not ask what the net benefit of a firm or a type of service is; it examines specific practices.[1208] Therefore, in order to justify prima facie anticompetitive conduct, the practice(s) in question must result in offsetting efficiencies. This section examines which justifications are particularly important in the platform economy, ie reducing transaction and search costs, ensuring financial viability (by preventing free riding), safeguarding the quality of users on the platforms, and protecting users' security and privacy.[1209] Before doing so, it starts with some general considerations on the topic.

10.1 Justifications for Prima Facie Anticompetitive Behaviour

The fact that (some) platforms are at the heart of an interrelated network of suppliers and complements has a flip side: not unlike biological ecosystems, platform ecosystems are fragile. Unless managed carefully, there is a risk that unwelcome elements disrupt

1206 See eg Erik Brynjolfsson and Avinash Collis, 'How Should We Measure the Digital Economy?' (2020) Hutchins Center Working Paper 57.

1207 These experiments generally ask how much a user would have to be paid to *give up* a digital service. However, the endowment effect is at play here, meaning that people often demand much more to give up an object than they would be willing to pay for it. The endowment effect is a manifestation of loss aversion, which means that the disutility of giving up an object is greater than the utility associated with acquiring it. See Kahneman, Knetsch and Thaler (n 690).

1208 At the remedy stage, it is, of course, recommended to consider whether no surplus is being destroyed.

1209 This section draws on Bostoen and Mândrescu (n 856) 476–84.

the ecosystem. While biological ecosystems need to be guarded against invasive species, platform ecosystems need to avoid the presence of too many low-quality or even dangerous users ('bad actors'). Such actors generate *negative* – rather than positive – indirect network effects; their presence makes the platform *less* attractive for users on the other side. In the presence of too many bad actors, users may start leaving the platform in droves as the positive feedback loop reverses into a death spiral.[1210] While carefully managing their audience, platforms also need to ensure their financial viability by making sure every user contributes its fair share rather than free riding.

Platform operators must therefore manage their ecosystem as 'private regulators', limiting access to new users and interactions between existing users.[1211] An analogy can be made with nightclubs, which need to maintain a door policy and collect entry fees; occasionally, they even need to kick drunken or rowdy guests out.[1212] In the same sense, platforms need to charge fees to at least some users and may sometimes need to refuse or remove low-quality or unsafe suppliers/complements. In keeping with the nightclub analogy, Evans terms this possibility – and sometimes necessity – for platforms to exclude bad actors a 'bouncer's right'.[1213]

Evidently, it is better to prevent bad actors from being present on the platform rather than having to remove them. The proactive process that platforms organize to filter out bad actors is referred to as 'curation'.[1214] Curation measures are manifold and include authenticating or approving users, restricting which conduct is (technically) possible on the platform, monitoring user activity, imposing transparency, and empowering users to control their interactions. Such curation measures are part of a broader platform governance mechanism that is implemented through filters, rules, signals and incentives:

> Filters ensure that users identify relevant information and interaction possibilities through (search) algorithms. Rules prevent undesirable (value distorting) behaviour on the platform, e.g., to protect consumers against providers of defective products and services … Signals may indicate scarcity, such as the dynamic pricing system of Uber which signals to drivers when is the best time for offering taxi services. Incentives aim to stimulate desirable (value creating) behaviour, e.g., credits for providing reviews of restaurants[.][1215]

1210 See Section 2.2.2.

1211 Kevin Boudreau and Andrei Hagiu, 'Platforms Rules: Multi-Sided Platforms as Regulators' in Annabelle Gawer (ed), *Platforms, Markets and Innovation* (Edward Elgar 2009) 163–91.

1212 See Kaiser (n 376) 98.

1213 David Evans, 'Governing Bad Behavior by Users of Multi-Sided Platforms' (2012) 27 Berkeley Technology Law Journal 1201.

1214 See Cusumano, Gawer and Yoffie (n 614) 185–86. See also Kevin Kelly, *The Inevitable: Understanding the 12 Technological Forces That Will Shape Our Future* (Viking Press 2016), ch 7 on filtering.

1215 van Gorp and de Bijl (n 410) 5.

An effective governance mechanism, including curation, should maximize value created on the platform. Measures taken in the context of such a mechanism, while apt to prompt abuse allegations, can be justified. Three justifications stand out: ensuring the platform's financial viability, guaranteeing the quality of users (and thus the platform's reputation), and safeguarding the security of users (which also affects the platform's reputation).[1216] More general efficiencies, such as the reduction of search and transaction costs, can also justify certain platform conduct.

Before we delve into each of these justifications, let me stress that they are no get-out-jail-free cards. Firstly, the burden of proof lies on the dominant undertaking relying on the justification.[1217] Secondly, the dominant undertaking can justify its prima facie anticompetitive conduct by demonstrating either its objective necessity or that it produces substantial efficiencies that outweigh any anticompetitive effects.[1218] While financial viability, quality of users and privacy fit better under the 'efficiency' heading, security can also be qualified as an objective necessity. Thirdly, justifications – particularly efficiency-based ones – must fulfil conditions that mirror those of article 101(3) TFEU, ie the efficiencies are conduct-specific, cannot be achieved by a less restrictive alternative (proportionality), and do not eliminate effective competition.[1219] Importantly, the ECJ has held in *Mastercard* that there is only limited scope for cross-platform efficiencies:

> [W]here, as in the present case, restrictive effects have been found on only one market of a two-sided system, the advantages flowing from the restrictive measure on a separate but connected market also associated with that system cannot, in themselves, be of such a character as to compensate for the disadvantages resulting from that measure in the absence of any proof of the existence of appreciable objective advantages attributable to that measure in the relevant market, in particular … where the consumers on those markets are not substantially the same.[1220]

In other words, harm on one side of the platform cannot be offset by efficiencies benefitting the other side of the platform. However, given the reference to markets,

---

1216 There is an analogy here with vertical restraints, which can also be used to structure healthy commercial relations upstream and downstream, see EC, 'Guidelines on vertical restraints' (Communication) [2022] OJ C248/1, para 107 (describing various justifications including free riding and quality/reputation concerns).

1217 *Post Danmark v Konkurrencerådet* (n 464), para 42. Evans, 'Governing Bad Behavior by Users of Multi-Sided Platforms' (n 1213) 1243–49 suggests shifting this burden of proof as follows: If the platform can show it has an established governance system, the burden of proof shifts to the complainant to show that 'that the governance system is not reasonably related to enforcement of the goals the governance mechanism is designed to achieve'. If the complainant cannot 'demonstrate that the practice is inconsistent with the mitigation of negative externalities', its claim should be rejected. If it can, the practice is analysed under the rule of reason.

1218 *Post Danmark v Konkurrencerådet* (n 464), para 41. See further Tjarda van der Vijver, 'Objective Justification and Article 102 TFEU' (2012) 35 World Competition 55, 65–69.

1219 Exclusionary Conduct Guidance Paper (n 461), para 30 and van der Vijver (n 1218) 69–75 (in particular on proportionality).

1220 Case C–382/12 P *Mastercard v Commission* EU:C:2014:2201, para 242. See similarly 'Guidelines on the application of Article 81(3) of the Treaty' (n 460), para 43.

this restriction appears to be tempered somewhat by the fact that two user groups are sometimes considered part of the same market.[1221]

Assessing the validity of a justification requires a fairly clear view of alternative business methods or even models (to check proportionality) and the magnitude of anticompetitive effects (to check whether they are outweighed). Rather than completing such a complex assessment, I present a framework for analysis. Some of the justifications discussed here have surfaced before while examining different forms of abuse, in particular when the justifications have played a central role in their legal test.[1222] This underlines AG Jacobs' observation that 'the two-stage analysis suggested by the distinction between abuse and its objective justification is … somewhat artificial'.[1223]

10.2 Reduced Transaction and Search Costs

Platforms bring together a large variety of suppliers and complements, filter them, and recommend them to consumers. As such, the fundamental role of platforms can be described as reducing transaction costs.[1224] To increase the quality of the platform, an operator may even want to *directly* provide consumers with complements by integrating them. Such integration was at the heart of the *Microsoft* and *Google Android* cases. Both Microsoft and Google argued that adding apps to their OS reduced transaction costs by providing an out-of-the-box experience: consumers would not have to download them separately.[1225] This argument is theoretically valid but failed practically given that OEMs were the ones responsible for the out-of-the-box experience; the preinstalled apps question simply constrained their choice (and thus the consumers') regarding the exact offering.

Platforms also want to minimize search costs (which can be considered a subset of transaction costs). Not surprisingly, search engines constitute the best example here. The *Shopping*, *Streetmap* and *Verband* cases all concerned situations in which Google started directly providing users with specialized (vertical) search results in response to queries (about products, places and the weather, respectively).[1226] The direct provision of search results may certainly constitute 'technical improvements in the quality of goods',[1227] so the assessment often turns on whether there was no less restrictive alternative to achieve this improvement. The judge in *Streetmap* seriously considered

1221 See Section 4.1.1.

1222 See in particular Section 6.6.

1223 *Syfait v GlaxoSmithKline*, Opinion of AG Jacobs (n 878), para 72.

1224 Evans and Schmalensee, 'The Industrial Organization of Markets with Two-Sided Platforms' (n 393) 158. See also Marshall Van Alstyne and Michael Schrage, 'The Best Platforms Are More than Matchmakers' (*HBR*, 2 August 2016) <https://hbr.org/2016/08/the-best-platforms-are-more-than-matchmakers> ('Where traditional business models sell products and/or services, matchmaking models sell reduced transaction costs').

1225 See Section 6.6.

1226 See Sections 5 and 6 on *Google Shopping*, 9.3.1.3 on *Google Streetmap* and 6.4 on *Verband*.

1227 Exclusionary Conduct Guidance Paper (n 461), para 30.

alternatives (including displaying links to competing map providers and letting users select their preferred map provider) but found they were either not effective or faced great (technical) complications.[1228] In its *Google* case, the FTC also concluded that Google's ranking policy was meant to improve the quality of its results by answering queries more quickly.[1229] The EC decided otherwise in *Google Shopping*: it did not disagree with the fact that answering search queries directly constitutes an efficient reduction of search costs, but took issue with the fact that this involved discrimination between Google's own and competing CCSs.[1230] The EC's analysis of the technical feasibility of effectively returning a diversity of results (not only Google's own) in response to shopping queries was, however, very limited.[1231]

10.3 Financial Viability of the Platform

Disputes concerning the fees levied by digital platforms on their participants inevitably raise questions regarding the freedom of platform owners to make strategic pricing decisions. Although complaints about the fees charged should be taken seriously, so should the notion that nothing can be both truly free *and* financially viable. The facilitation of interactions between separate user groups by platforms entails significant costs. Platforms need not only to cover those costs but also to ensure their pricing scheme brings and maintains on board all user groups, which often results in a heavily skewed price structure.[1232] Challenging the pricing scheme of platforms can be problematic, especially if it entails changes to that carefully balanced price *structure*. Those changes run the risk of alienating one or more user groups (imagine forcing Google to charge users for queries in order to lower the price for advertisers). Courts may not have the necessary expertise to mandate such changes (this also goes for competition authorities, although their expertise is slightly greater); platforms themselves are in the best position to determine their price structure. It is generally less problematic to intervene in the price *level* imposed by platforms.

The question becomes even more difficult when the platform subsidizes not only between user groups, but also between different products. In *Google Android*, Google argued that tying its search engine and browser to its app store was a legitimate way to monetize its investments in Android and its non-revenue-generating apps.[1233] The problem was that the tying product, the Play Store, was already the source of significant

1228 *Streetmap.eu v Google* (n 591) [142]–[176].

1229 FTC, File no 111-0163, *In the Matter of Google* (Statement regarding Google's search practices, 3 January 2013). The case was closed against the recommendation of the FTC staff, see Brody Mullins, Rolfe Winkler and Brent Kendall, 'Inside the U.S. Antitrust Probe of Google' (*WSJ*, 19 March 2015) <https://www.wsj.com/articles/inside-the-u-s-antitrust-probe-of-google-1426793274>.

1230 *Google Search (Shopping)* (n 348) para 662.

1231 The GC dives slightly deeper but from a legal rather than a technical point of view, see *Google v Commission* (n 767), paras 569–78.

1232 See Section 2.1.

1233 See Section 6.6.

revenue in the form of commission and advertising fees. In other words, distributing Android together with the Play Store already funded the OS; the necessity of an *additional* tie with its various apps had not been demonstrated.

Beyond these more general financial viability considerations, a specific issue affecting platforms is free riding, meaning that users benefit from the platform without paying (enough) to support its operation. The platform may have to adopt certain restrictions to prevent such free riding. For example, hotel booking platforms have argued that a concern for free riding justified imposing narrow most-favoured-nation clauses. Without those clauses, consumers would visit the platform to see what is on offer and make a selection, before visiting the hotels' own website to book at a cheaper price, thus avoiding the platform commission fee. Most competition authorities therefore considered it justified that platforms restricted hotels from charging lower prices on their website.[1234]

Apple also defended the allegedly abusive obligation of app developers to use IAP by reference to free riding. Specifically, Apple describes how it provides an app distribution platform, critical software development tools and a secure payment system, which requires significant investment. Apple therefore accuses Spotify, which seeks to use other payment systems than IAP, of wanting to free ride on its investment:

> After using the App Store for years to dramatically grow their business, Spotify seeks to keep all the benefits of the App Store ecosystem – including the substantial revenue that they draw from the App Store's customers – without making any contributions to that marketplace.[1235]

Spotify replied that it does not 'want a free ride, [just] a fair ride'.[1236] However, if all developers were able to use external payment systems, contributions to the App Store would dry up, which is not sustainable without a more fundamental rethinking of the fee structure (eg increasing developer subscription fees or charging a distribution fee separate from payment processing fees).

10.4 Quality of Users on the Platform

In its *Hilti* judgment, the GC held that a dominant firm 'may not argue that the allegedly dangerous nature or inferior quality of its competitors' products intended

1234 Konkurrensverket, Decision 596/2013, *Booking.com*, 15 April 2015, paras 28–30; AdlC, Decision 15-D-06, *Booking.com*, 21 April 2015, paras 170–98; AGCM, 'Commitments offered by Booking.com: closed the investigation in Italy, France and Sweden' (press release, 21 April 2015) <http://www.agcm.it/en/newsroom/press-releases/2207>. For a discussion, see Friso Bostoen, 'Most Favoured Nation Clauses: Towards an Assessment Framework Under EU Competition Law' (2017) 1 CoRe 223, 232.

1235 Apple, 'Addressing Spotify's claims' (press release, 14 March 2019) <www.apple.com/newsroom/2019/03/addressing-spotifys-claims/>.

1236 Spotify, 'Time to Play Fair – Frequently Asked Questions' <www.timetoplayfair.com/frequently-asked-questions/> (Spotify continues that it is not 'seeking special treatment, but the opportunity to compete on a level playing field' and turns the tables by holding that the 'App Store is the success it is today in large part because of third-party apps such as Spotify').

to be used with a tool manufactured and sold by it justify abusive practices which seek to eliminate those products from the market in order to protect its commercial position'.[1237] The 'tool' here was a nail gun, and Hilti – accused of using its power in the market for cartridge strips to exclude competitors in the adjacent nail market – justified its actions by referring to the inferior quality of competing nails. The GC did not accept this justification, as there are laws (eg on product liability) that solve this kind of issue.

Analogously, one could argue that platform operators should also not be the ones to decide whom to exclude from their platform. However, this analogy would be mistaken, as platforms differ in important respects from more traditional tools such as nail guns. Most importantly, one has to consider their multisided nature: platforms must get the 'right' kind of consumers and suppliers on board, prevent them from misbehaving, and balance their ratio. Inevitability, ensuring the platform's long-term health in this way requires refusing or later removing low-quality suppliers and complements. In the absence of such actions, the platform's reputation will suffer as *it* – rather than suppliers – may be blamed for subpar complements.[1238] Moreover, compared to nail gun manufacturers, platforms have a much greater ability to screen and filter users.

However, 'quality' is a very broad term, which can therefore be used to justify just about any exclusion. It is therefore important that the platform sets out the grounds for exclusion beforehand, and subsequently carries out removals in line with those grounds. The Platform-to-Business Regulation ('P2B Regulation') obliges platforms to 'ensure that their terms and conditions 'set out the grounds for decisions to suspend or terminate or impose any other kind of restriction upon, in whole or in part, the provision of their online intermediation services'.[1239] If the platform restricts or suspends a user, it must give reasons for doing so; in case of termination, the platform must also give the supplier 30 days' notice.[1240] The required statement of reasons must refer to specific facts or circumstances as well as the specific ground in its terms and conditions to which the decision relates.

There are easy cases of exclusion, such as those based on illegal or harmful practices by the supplier (eg IP violations, scams, spam, misinformation). At other times, the difference between anticompetitive and justified exclusion is less clear and must be sought in the underlying motive of such actions.[1241] Close scrutiny is warranted when the removal concerns suppliers that compete with the platform in an *adjacent* market.

1237 *Hilti v Commission* (n 715), para 6 of the introductory summary (quote) and paras 102–18, and similarly Case T–83/91 *Tetra Pak v Commission* (n 716), paras 83–84 and 136–40. See also Exclusionary Conduct Guidance Paper (n 461), para 29.

1238 See Todd, 'Digital Platforms and the Leverage Problem' (n 556) 518.

1239 Regulation (EU) 2019/1150 of the European Parliament and of the Council on promoting fairness and transparency for business users of online intermediation services [2019] OJ L186/57 (hereafter, 'P2B Regulation'), art 3. See eg the many grounds for removal in Apple's App Store Review Guidelines <https://developer.apple.com/app-store/review/guidelines/>.

1240 P2B Regulation, art 4.

1241 The concept of abuse is an objective concept, but intention does play a role, both in the assessment of the abuse and in its objective justification, see Jan Blockx, 'Revaluing the Role of Intent Evidence in EU Antitrust Law' (2019) 3 CoRe 354.

The removal of parental control apps by Apple provides an example.[1242] A guiding question should be whether the exclusion is 'reasonably related to enforcement of the goals the governance mechanism is designed to achieve'.[1243] If it is not (eg a clearly qualitative app that has been in the app store for years is suddenly excluded), an anticompetitive motive is not unlikely. In other cases, the quality justification demands a deeper assessment. For example, Amazon may argue it discriminates against sellers not using FBA because their shipments are less punctual.[1244] Assessing this justification requires examining whether shipments of competing logistics providers (eg DHL) are indeed more often delayed. Even if that is the case, however, a less restrictive alternative may be to impose shipping specifications that FBA does meet (eg 'packages must arrive within 48 hours') and exclude sellers from the Buy Box only when those are not met.

10.5 Security and Privacy of Users on the Platform

The final justification ground in this (non-exhaustive) list concerns the security and privacy of users on the platform. Guaranteeing the security of consumers is incredibly important for any platforms. That is why Amazon, for example, bans a large number of dangerous products (and their suppliers) from its Marketplace.[1245] Security is especially important for innovation platforms, which is why app stores have extensive approval processes to sift out apps containing malware (including adware) that affect the integrity of mobile devices.[1246] Most of these refusals (as well as later removals) on grounds of security are uncontroversial – indeed, strict standards in this regard should be applauded. Still, there are more difficult cases. For example, Apple denies wallet apps access to its near-field communication (NFC) chip, which allows for contactless mobile payments, while its own Apple Pay does make use of it.[1247] Google, on the other hand, does open up its NFC chip to developers, but doing so has been linked to security concerns.[1248] Apple can rely on such concerns to justify keeping its NFC chip to itself, although accepting the justification requires verifying those concerns, balancing them against any anticompetitive effects, and considering less restrictive alternatives.

1242 See Section 7.3.

1243 Evans, 'Governing Bad Behavior by Users of Multi-Sided Platforms' (n 1213) 1248.

1244 Discussing the case, see Sections 8.3.3 and 9.1.3.2. The EC did not analyse justifications as the case was settled with commitments, see *Amazon Marketplace* and *Amazon Buy Box* (n 369), paras 223–24.

1245 With varying degrees of success, see Alexandra Berzon, Shane Shifflett and Justin Scheck, 'Amazon Has Ceded Control of Its Site. The Result: Thousands of Banned, Unsafe or Mislabeled Products' (*WSJ*, 23 August 2019) <https://www.wsj.com/articles/amazon-has-ceded-control-of-its-site-the-result-thousands-of-banned-unsafe-or-mislabeled-products-11566564990>.

1246 Again, with varying degrees of success, see eg '172 Malicious Apps with 335M+ Installs Found on Google Play' (*The Next Web*, 1 October 2019) <https://thenextweb.com/apps/2019/10/01/google-play-android-malware-2/>.

1247 The EC is investigating this refusal, see EC, 'Commission sends Statement of Objections to Apple over practices regarding Apple Pay' (press release, 2 May 2022) IP/22/2764.

1248 ACM, 'Market Study into Mobile App Stores' (n 609) 81–83.

Platforms are also expected to protect the privacy of their users. While privacy is dealt with separately here, it can also be conceptualized as a quality parameter of competition.[1249] Of the main online platforms, Apple in particular has made a point of safeguarding user privacy.[1250] Accordingly, it has banned certain apps because of privacy concerns – a justification that is beyond reproach, as long as it does not become a cover for anticompetitive behaviour.[1251] When it removed several parental control apps from its store, for example, Apple stated it did so because these apps were using a 'highly invasive technology', namely MDM, which 'gives third parties control and access over a device and its most sensitive information', thus putting the users' privacy at risk.[1252] However, some of those apps claim to be removed because of functionalities that are essential for their operation – and that Apple's own Screen Time app does incorporate.[1253] As with other justifications, competition authorities are thus tasked with ascertaining the underlying motive of app stores' actions, and to balance any anticompetitive effects against privacy benefits.

1249 See eg Samson Esayas, 'Privacy-as-a-Quality Parameter of Competition' in Björn Lundqvist and Michal Gal (eds), *Competition Law for the Digital Economy* (Edward Elgar 2019) 126–72.

1250 See Apple, 'Privacy' <www.apple.com/privacy/> and Apple, 'App Store – Principles and Practices' <www.apple.com/ios/app-store/principles-practices/>.

1251 Facebook in particular has alleged so, see Jack Nicas and Mike Isaac, 'Facebook Takes the Gloves Off in Feud with Apple' (*NYT*, 16 December 2020) <https://www.nytimes.com/2020/12/16/technology/facebook-takes-the-gloves-off-in-feud-with-apple.html>.

1252 Apple, 'The Facts about Parental Control Apps' (n 992).

1253 See Section 7.3.

PART 3

REGULATING PLATFORMS BEYOND ARTICLE 102

11

INTRODUCTION TO PLATFORM REGULATION

Across the globe, policymakers have set their sights on regulating platforms. In Europe, from Germany[1254] to the United Kingdom,[1255] lawmakers have adopted or are set to adopt specific acts targeting abusive platform conduct. Bills have also been introduced in the US,[1256] although their adoption is a more distant prospect. The most consequential regulatory regime is likely to be the EU's DMA,[1257] a follow-up to the earlier P2B Regulation. These instruments are not limited to intra-platform exclusion, although a large part of their provisions relate to self-preferencing.

From Part 2's focus on intra-platform exclusion under article 102 TFEU, Part 3 broadens the scope in two ways.[1258] First, it moves beyond intra-platform competition to also include inter-platform competition. As explained, the two forms of competition are related: as a platform attains more power in its market, switching to other platforms becomes less of an option, which means suppliers become more dependent on the platform – a dependence that can then be abused.[1259] That is why most regulatory initiatives seek not only to prevent abusive (or unfair) platform practices but also to ensure that the positions of the incumbent platforms remain contestable. Second, the focus shifts from *ex post* to *ex ante* regulation. The goal is not to dissect specific

1254 Gesetz zur Änderung des Gesetzes gegen Wettbewerbsbeschränkungen für ein fokussiertes, proaktives und digitales Wettbewerbsrecht 4.0 (GWB-Digitalisierungsgesetz), 18 January 2021. For an English translation highlighting the new provisions, see 'German Competition Act 2021 – Unofficial Translation' (*D'Kart*) <https://www.d-kart.de/wp-content/uploads/2021/01/GWB-2021-01-14-engl.pdf>.

1255 See 'A New Pro-Competition Regime for Digital Markets' (July 2021) CP 489.

1256 See in particular HR3816 – American Choice and Innovation Online Act, 117th Congress (2021–22) and S2710 – Open App Markets Act, 117th Congress (2021–22).

1257 Regulation (EU) 2022/1925 of the European Parliament and of the Council on contestable and fair markets in the digital sector [2022] OJ L265/1 (hereafter, 'DMA').

1258 This part is adapted from the unpublished working paper Friso Bostoen, 'Regulating Online Platforms: Lessons from 100 years of Telecommunications Regulation' (2019), winner of the 2019 AdC Competition Policy Award.

1259 See Section 3.3.

instruments such as the DMA, although they will pop illustratively.[1260] Rather, the idea is to establish a more general taxonomy of potential interventions and to illuminate the trade-offs inherent in them.

Even though platform regulation might be new, there are antecedents that are relevant, even if only by analogy. The goal of contestability, for example, is reminiscent of the pluralism pursued by media regulation.[1261] And blacklists of banned practices find a predecessor in unfair commercial practices regulation.[1262] Platform regulation's closest genetic match, however, is telecom regulation. Telecom regulation provides *the* prototype for the interaction between *ex ante* and *ex post* interventions, and is therefore chosen as the comparative paradigm. To be clear, the idea is not to blindly subject platforms to utility-style regulation, but rather to examine whether telecom interventions can inspire or caution against different forms of platform regulation. US regulatory action is included to have a more comprehensive record to draw on – for both telecom precedents and contemporary platform interventions.

This introduction continues by taking a closer look at the analogy between telecom providers and online platforms (Section 11.1) and presenting a theoretical framework for regulation by examining its rationale and forms (Section 11.2). Next, we dive into platform regulation. In Part 2, the focus was on abuse – not dominance; in Part 3, the focus is on specific regulatory measures – not their scope. Still, Section 12 shortly surveys the addressees of *ex ante* platform regulation. Section 13, the heart of this part, is dedicated to the various potential interventions in the platform sphere, ie merger control, non-discrimination, data portability, interoperability, forced access and breakup.

11.1 From Providers to Platforms

The comparison between platform and telecom regulation is primarily explained by the fact that the latter constitutes the prototype for the interaction between *ex ante* and *ex post* regulation. There are, however, additional reasons that make the comparison worthwhile. For one, telecom providers and online platforms can be considered different layers of the same network – namely, the internet.[1263] The first layer is made up of open

1260 For a dissection, see Friso Bostoen, 'Understanding the Digital Markets Act' (2023) 68 Antitrust Bulletin 263. Insofar as this part relates to the DMA, it draws on this work.

1261 eg Directive 2010/13/EU of the European Parliament and of the Council on the coordination of certain provisions laid down by law, regulation or administrative action in Member States concerning the provision of audiovisual media services [2010] OJ L95/1, as amended by Directive (EU) 2018/1808 of the European Parliament and of the Council amending the Audiovisual Media Services Directive in view of changing market realities [2018] OJ L303/69.

1262 eg Directive 2005/29/EC of the European Parliament and of the Council concerning unfair business-to-consumer commercial practices in the internal market [2005] OJ L149/22.

1263 See Stuart Benjamin and James Speta, *Telecommunications Law and Policy* (Carolina Academic Press 2015), 537; Kevin Werbach, 'A Layered Model for Internet Policy' (2002) 1 Journal of Telecommunications & High Technology Law 37; Annemarie Bridy, 'Remediating Social Media: A Layer-Conscious Approach' (2018) 24 Boston University Journal of Science and Technology Law 193. See also Joel Monegro, 'Fat Protocols' (*Union Square Ventures*, 8 August 2016) <http://www.usv.com/blog/fat-protocols> and 'The

standards (such as the Transmission Control Protocol/Internet Protocol – TCP/IP) that technically facilitate the transport of information over the internet network. The second layer consists in the telecom infrastructure that makes this transport physically possible, either through wires (copper, cable, or fibre) or wireless (satellite or terrestrial). Thirdly, there is an application layer, ie the services that are offered over the internet. Over the past decade, this application lawyer has further segmented into a platform layer providing the digital infrastructure for the distribution of products (including content, services, etc) and a complements layer (or 'edge'), populated by the suppliers making use of those platforms.

Two of these layers are particularly prone to concentration and market power: the physical layer and the platform layer.[1264] The physical layer is dominated by telecom operators, in particular internet service providers (ISPs). While the commercial internet only dates back to the 1990s, most of these firms have been around since long before its advent, given that internet infrastructure largely overlaps with telephony and television infrastructure (all three services can be provided through the same wires). The platform layer, on the other hand, is increasingly dominated by online platforms, in particular GAFAM. As described above, the market power of telecom providers and online platforms is explained largely by the same economic characteristics.[1265] This means that, just like telecom providers, online platforms can exhibit natural monopoly features.[1266]

Some authors are taking the analogy between telecom providers and platforms further, up to the point that platforms are viewed as utilities.[1267] The implication is usually that they should be regulated as such.[1268] In my view, taking the analogy this far is not helpful.[1269] For example, while online platforms do offer infrastructure, said infrastructure does not show the same degree of necessity for everyday life (I, for one, would rather delete Facebook than give up sewage). Moreover, utility regulation is particularly heavy-handed, which is a poor fit for dynamic platform business models.[1270] Finally, the success of utility regulation has not always been exemplary.

Story of the Internet Is All about Layers' (*The Economist*, 28 June 2018) <https://www.economist.com/special-report/2018/06/28/the-story-of-the-internet-is-all-about-layers>.

1264 See similarly Gigi Sohn, 'A Policy Framework for an Open Internet Ecosystem' (2018) 2 Georgetown Law Technology Review 335, 335–40.

1265 See Section 4.1.2.

1266 See Section 7.3.

1267 See eg Sabeel Rahman, 'Regulating Informational Infrastructure: Internet Platforms as the New Public Utilities' (2018) 2 Georgetown Law Technology Review 234 and Mark Scott, 'Coronavirus Crisis Shows Big Tech for What It Is – A 21st Century Public Utility' (*Politico*, 25 March 2020) <https://www.politico.eu/article/coronavirus-big-tech-utility-google-facebook/>.

1268 See eg 'What If Large Tech Firms Were Regulated Like Sewage Companies?' (*The Economist*, 23 September 2017) <https://www.economist.com/business/2017/09/23/what-if-large-tech-firms-were-regulated-like-sewage-companies> and Tristan Harris, 'EU Should Regulate Facebook and Google as "Attention Utilities"' (*FT*, 1 March 2020) <https://www.ft.com/content/abd80d98-595e-11ea-abe5-8e03987b7b20>.

1269 See similarly Rosa Abrantes-Metz and Albert Metz, 'Regulating Multisided Platforms? The Case against Treating Platforms as Utilities' (2020) CPI Antitrust Chronicle August and Susan Crawford, 'Calling Facebook a Utility Would Only Make Things Worse' (*Wired*, 20 April 2018) <https://www.wired.com/story/calling-facebook-a-utility-would-only-make-things-worse/>.

1270 See Ioannis Lianos, 'General Conceptual Framework' in BRICS Competition Law and Policy Centre (ed), 'Digital Era Competition: A BRICS View' (Report, 2020) 355–57.

There are, however, undeniable similarities between the current *conduct* of online platforms and that of telecom providers at different points in time, eg when it comes to monopolistic acquisition strategies, the discrimination of downstream competitors, impeding portability and interoperability, and refusing access to (potential) competitors. Those practices are only possible because of the aforementioned market power, which makes certain providers 'bottlenecks' – an idea that has gained ground in the platform sphere under the epithet 'gatekeepers'.[1271]

To prevent excessive concentration, and the abusive practices that may result from it, the conduct of telecom providers has been regulated in the EU as well as in the US, which once played a leading role in this field. Regulators thus have ample experience in keeping this layer open *ex ante*. The same cannot be said with regard to online platforms, most of which have only become a significant force over the last decade or two. Therefore, there is something to be learned from telecom precedents.

11.2 Regulatory Framework

Regulation cannot be presumed necessary. That is why this section starts with an inquiry into the rationale for regulatory intervention in the economic sphere, ie market failure. It then examines the main types of intervention: *ex ante* vs *ex post*, and structural vs behavioural. This typology serves as a framework when examining specific interventions.

11.2.1 Rationale for Regulatory Intervention

Leaving aside value-based rationales for regulation (such as freedom of speech), market failure is the most important justification for regulatory intervention.[1272] Market power constitutes one such failure as it entails not only a deadweight loss but also 'x-inefficiency', meaning prices[1273] will be higher than in a competitive market.[1274] Of particular concern is natural monopoly, which exists when 'the entire demand within a relevant market can be satisfied at lowest cost by one firm rather than by two or more'.[1275] Situations of natural monopoly thus present the most extreme case of market

1271 Although the 'bottleneck' terminology has been more prevalent, telecom regulation has also been premised on the idea of 'gatekeepers', see eg FCC, Order 15-24, Protecting and Promoting the Open Internet, 12 March 2015, 8 ('broadband providers have both the incentive and the ability to act as gatekeepers standing between edge providers and consumers').

1272 Benjamin and Speta (n 1263) 5–11.

1273 Price effects are used as a shorthand for output, quality, choice and innovation effects.

1274 The concept of x-inefficiency was introduced in Harvey Leibenstein, 'Allocative Efficiency vs. "X-Efficiency"' (1966) 56 The American Economic Review 392. For an empirical illustration, see James Schmitz, 'What Determines Productivity? Lessons from the Dramatic Recovery of the U.S. and Canadian Iron Ore Industries Following Their Early 1980s Crisis' (2005) 113 Journal of Political Economy 582.

1275 Richard Posner, 'Natural Monopoly and Its Regulation' (1968) 21 Stanford Law Review 548, 548. Another important if not essential feature of natural monopolies is the existence of significant sunk costs.

power but are distinguished by the fact that monopoly is the more rather than less efficient market structure in this case.[1276]

Natural monopoly – and market power more generally – is traditionally explained by strong economies of scale/scope and network effects. As these barriers to entry become higher, monopoly becomes more likely. As discussed above, online platforms do enjoy strong economies of scale/scope and network effects, which may lead some platform markets to tip in favour of one firm (the 'winner takes all' dynamic).[1277] Tirole has gone as far as stating that 'by dint of network effects and economies of scale, the digital economy almost inexorably creates "natural monopolies."'[1278]

Tirole's statement is a little hyperbolic but directionally correct. Ducci has examined platforms more closely through the natural monopoly lens. He finds that modern platforms may be more prone to monopoly for several reasons: (i) economies of scale are compounded by negligible marginal costs; (ii) in addition, scale economies derive from data collection and analysis (for the purpose of algorithmic matching and prediction); (iii) network effects are not only direct but also indirect.[1279] At the same time, multihoming and the threat of disruption are likely stronger in platform markets (compared, eg to telecom providers), which may counteract the tendency towards natural monopoly.[1280]

As Joskow already stated in relation to traditional natural monopolies: 'It is important to recognize that in reality there is not likely to be a bright line between industries that are "natural monopolies" and those that are (imperfectly) "competitive."'[1281] Ducci takes an in-depth look at three case studies and finds that general search has the features of natural monopoly, online marketplaces do not, and ride-hailing platforms are situated between those two on the spectrum of natural monopoly.[1282] Relying on five factors to test for natural monopoly in digital markets, Hovenkamp concludes that few platforms qualify as such.[1283] He considers Google Search to come closest to constituting a natural

1276 Francesco Ducci, *Natural Monopolies in Digital Platform Markets* (CUP 2020) 37 ('The distinguishing feature of a natural monopoly is that the most efficient way to serve the market is to have a single firm serving the entire demand').

1277 See Sections 2.2.1–2 and 4.1.2.

1278 Jean Tirole, 'Regulating the Disruptors' (*Project Syndicate*, 9 January 2019) <https://www.project-syndicate.org/onpoint/regulating-the-disrupters-by-jean-tirole-2019-01>.

1279 Ducci (n 1276) 40–41. See similarly Lianos (n 1270) 354.

1280 Ducci (n 1276) 42–43.

1281 Paul Joskow, 'Regulation of Natural Monopolies' in Mitchell Polinsky and Steven Shavell (eds), *Handbook of Law and Economics* (Elsevier 2007) 1248.

1282 Ducci (n 1276) 47–125.

1283 Herbert Hovenkamp, 'Antitrust and Platform Monopoly' (2021) 130 Yale Law Journal 1952, 1972–2001. The factors are:

1. lack of stable competition or multi-homing among incumbent firms;
2. durability of a dominant position and the ability to accommodate or resist technological change;
3. declining costs or network effects and structure requiring single-firm control;
4. lack of significant product differentiation; and
5. lack of interoperability or data sharing.

monopoly, but finally concludes that it likely does not, based in particular on its payments for default status.[1284]

While only some platforms are situated on the (natural) monopoly end of the spectrum, the main ones have at least crossed the threshold of market power. Even then, Petit shows that platforms do not behave like textbook monopolists: due to increasing returns to scale (network effects), they seek to expand rather than limit output.[1285] Network effects also engender uncertainty, which operates as a competitive constraint on platforms. These findings caution against regulating online platforms *like* (natural) monopolists, but do not rule out targeted intervention. The following section sets out a framework for such intervention.

11.2.2 Types of Regulatory Intervention

When a need for regulation has been established, one has to determine which type of intervention would meet this need in the most effective way. In terms of scope of application, there is a choice between *ex post* competition law, which applies horizontally but requires anticompetitive effects, and *ex ante* regulation, which applies only to the firms within its scope (generally those operating within a certain sector, but potentially an even narrower set) without necessarily requiring proof of anticompetitive effects. This dichotomy is not strict.[1286] For example, merger control intervenes *before* a merger takes place, rather than once the merger results in anticompetitive effects.[1287] Conversely, *ex ante* regulation may incorporate competition law formulations, thus limiting its application to situations where anticompetitive effects are established.[1288] When it comes to the regulation itself, there is a distinction between *structural* rules, which concern the organization of a firm (eg prohibiting the combination of different activities within it), and *behavioural* rules, which govern the conduct a firm can engage in (eg prohibiting cross-subsidization between those different activities).

11.2.2.1 *Ex Ante* vs *Ex Post*

Competition law is the baseline: it will apply in any case, disregarding an increasingly limited set of exceptions.[1289] As *ex ante* rules are a more intrusive tool to protect – or even promote – competition, their adoption should be properly justified. Regulators

1284 ibid. Due to its durable high market share, Microsoft's Windows is another good candidate for natural-monopoly status, although Hovenkamp again concludes that the qualification is doubtful.

1285 Nicolas Petit, *Big Tech & the Digital Economy: The Moligopoly Scenario* (OUP 2020) 64–92.

1286 In fact, the dichotomy is even inaccurate, see Kevin Coates, 'Ex-Post and Ex-Ante Rules' (*21st Century Competition*, 6 August 2020) <https://www.twentyfirstcenturycompetition.com/2020/08/ex-ante-and-ex-post/>. Borrowing from George Box ('all models are wrong, but some are useful'), I rely on the *ex ante–ex post* distinction as wrong but useful.

1287 Even under article 102 TFEU, proving *potential* anticompetitive effects suffices, so that competition authorities can intervene before those effects *actually* take place.

1288 *Ex ante* regulation may also require further specification by the authority, or enforcement on a case-by-case basis, thus resembling *ex post* competition law.

1289 See Einer Elhauge and Damien Geradin, *Global Antitrust Law and Economics* (Foundation Press 2018) 43–51 (US) and 76–77 (EU).

often engage in this exercise on a case-by-case basis, without reference to an overarching framework. In the telecom sector, however, the EU provides some guidance. It established the so-called three-criterion test to determine under which conditions a market may require *ex ante* regulation to safeguard competition:

(a) high and non-transitory structural, legal or regulatory barriers to entry are present;

(b) there is a market structure which does not tend towards effective competition within the relevant time horizon, having regard to the state of infrastructure-based and other sources of competition behind the barriers to entry;

(c) competition law alone is insufficient to adequately address the identified market failure(s).[1290]

Under conditions (a) and (b), the EC is essentially tasked with carrying out a market power assessment, but rather than focusing on a *specific* firm, it focuses on the *overall* market.[1291] US policymaking is also based on the premise that market-wide market power justifies *ex ante* regulation.[1292] Natural monopolies, of which the market power is by definition market-wide, therefore qualify for *ex ante* regulation. And certain platform markets, certainly those on the monopoly end of the spectrum, do operate in the presence of high and non-transitory barriers to entry. Disruptive competition is said to always loom around the corner, but the current equilibrium has held for quite some time.

Under (c), however, it must also be established competition law is insufficient to address the market failures. Is this the case in platform markets? EU lawmakers believe so, as evident from the DMA's recitals:

> [M]arket processes are often incapable of ensuring fair economic outcomes with regard to core platform services. Although Articles 101 and 102 [TFEU] apply to the conduct of gatekeepers, the scope of those provisions is limited to certain instances of market power, for example dominance on specific markets and of anti-competitive behaviour, and enforcement occurs *ex post* and requires an extensive investigation of often very complex facts on a [case-by-case] basis.[1293]

1290 Directive (EU) 2018/1972 of the European Parliament and of the Council establishing the European Electronic Communications Code [2018] OJ L321/36, art 67.

1291 See 'Explanatory Note accompanying the document 'Commission Recommendation on relevant product and service markets within the electronic communications sector susceptible to *ex ante* regulation in accordance with Directive (EU) 2018/1972' (Staff Working Document) SWD(2020)337, 15–16.

1292 See eg the Cable Television Consumer Protection and Competition Act of 1992, 106 Stat 1460, s 2(a)(2) (citing 'undue market power for the cable operator as compared to that of consumers and video programmers' to justify regulation) and *Turner Broadcasting System v FCC* 512 US 622, 633–35 (1994) (confirming that Congress adopted the 1992 Cable Act because 'the overwhelming majority of cable operators exercise a monopoly over cable service').

1293 DMA, recital 5.

I am more optimistic. When it comes to intra-platform exclusion, my analysis of the various leveraging abuses has shown that the scope of article 102 TFEU is sufficiently wide to effectively capture many anticompetitive manifestations. This view is bolstered by the fact that many of the DMA's obligations are modelled on cases the EC has pursued.[1294] Substantively, competition law is largely up to the task.

Procedurally, the situation is different. Experts are unanimous in identifying the speed of intervention as a pain point of competition law enforcement.[1295] Complex, case-by-case investigations take years, and by the time there is a decision, the foreclosure of competition can have cemented a dominant position (either in the platform's core market or in the target market). Remedies have not been adept at *restoring* competition. Speed is therefore a better reason for *ex ante* platform regulation.[1296] Under such a regime, clear(er) obligations are fixed beforehand so that competition is not distorted in the first place.

In my view, article 102 TFEU remains the best tool to tackle exclusionary abuses of platform power. There does appear to be some room for *ex ante* regulation, not in the form of traditional utility-style regulation, but in the form of specific obligations targeting the most harmful practices, where the potential for harm and the need for speed are the greatest. In addition to obligations aimed at protecting intra-platform competition, it can be worth promoting inter-platform competition by keeping markets contestable.[1297] That way, the associated uncertainty and threat of displacement can help keep platforms acting *as if* they were operating in competitive markets.

11.2.2.2 Structural vs Behavioural

A second regulatory choice is between structural and behavioural interventions. This choice must be made when adopting *ex ante* regulation, but also when imposing remedies after finding an abuse of dominance or accepting them in the context of merger control. The same competitive issue can usually be solved through either type of rule. Consider a vertically integrated firm involved in both production (upstream) and distribution (downstream). This 'dual role' may give the firm an incentive to discriminate against competing distributors by withholding its product.[1298] A regulator could solve this issue

1294 See Part 2: The *Microsoft I*, *Google Shopping*, and *Google Android* cases have largely been confirmed by the GC; other cases, such as *Microsoft II* and *Amazon*, ended with commitments.

1295 Jacques Crémer, Yves-Alexandre de Montjoye and Heike Schweitzer, 'Competition Policy for the Digital Era' (Special Advisers' Report, 2019) (hereafter, 'Crémer Report'), 45 and 52–53, Jason Furman, Diane Coyle, Amelia Fletcher, Derek McAuley and Philip Marsden, 'Unlocking Digital Competition' (Digital Competition Expert Panel's Report, 2019) (hereafter, 'Furman Report') 104–5; Commission 'Competition Law 4.0', 'A New Competition Framework for the Digital Economy' (Report for the Federal Ministry for Economic Affairs and Energy, 2019) 23–24; Stigler Committee, 'Digital Platforms' (Final Report, 2019) (hereafter, 'Stigler Report') 119.

1296 Looking at its procedural setup, including strict time limits, speed appears to be the main driver of the DMA.

1297 The idea of contestability goes back to William Baumol, John Panzar and Robert Willig, *Contestable Markets and the Theory of Industry Structure* (Harcourt Brace 1982). For a modern revision, see James Bessen, *The New Goliaths: How Corporations Use Software to Dominate Industries, Kill Innovation, and Undermine Regulation* (Yale University Press 2022) 94–95.

1298 Alternatively, the firm could discriminate against competing producers by refusing to distribute their products.

either by mandating access to the firm's product (behavioural), or by mandating ownership separation between production and distribution (structural), in which case the independent producer would lose any incentive to withhold its product from distributors.[1299]

As the above examples make clear, structural regulation (separation) is very intrusive.[1300] In particular, it can eliminate the efficiencies brought about by (vertical) integration and negatively impact investment.[1301] At the same time, structural regulation is also more effective as it eliminates the *incentive* itself to engage in anticompetitive conduct. By contrast, behavioural regulation only prohibits firms from *acting* upon those incentives. This means the competent authority needs to constantly monitor compliance by the addressees, which can be costly and ineffective.[1302]

What should guide the choice for one form of regulation over the other? The OECD has issued a recommendation on structural separation in regulated industries. In that context (but presumably also beyond it), it instructs the regulator to 'carefully balance the benefits and costs of structural measures against the benefits and costs of behavioural measures'.[1303] Of course, *any* government policy should be subject to a cost-benefit analysis, which limits the practical relevance of this recommendation. An accompanying report concludes that structural separation remains a relevant remedy to liberalize markets and notes it could also play a role in vertically integrated industries where only some activities are subject to competitive constraints.[1304]

Additional guidance on the choice between behavioural and structural measures can be found in the context of merger control. As a general matter, the EC must ensure that the chosen remedy is necessary, effective, and proportionate.[1305] With a view to proportionality, the EU Merger Regulation states that '[s]tructural remedies should only be imposed ... where there is no equally effective behavioural remedy'.[1306] With

---

1299 Similarly, faced with a merger between firms engaged in production and distribution, an authority could pursue access obligations (behavioural) or the divestment of the production/distribution business (structural).

1300 Note that several kinds of separation exist, which vary in how significantly they interfere with business conduct (ownership separation being the most intrusive form), see Martin Cave, 'Six Degrees of Separation: Operational Separation as a Remedy in European Telecommunications Regulation' (2006) 64 Communications and Strategies 89.

1301 OECD, 'Structural Separation in Regulated Industries: Implementing the OECD Recommendation' (Report, 2016) 9.

1302 ibid.

1303 OECD, Structural Separation in Regulated Industries (Recommendation) C(2016)11–C/M(2016)3, 3 (adding: 'The benefits and costs to be balanced include the effects on competition, effects on the quality and cost of regulation, effects on corporate incentives to invest, the transition costs of structural modifications and the economic and public benefits of vertical integration, based on the economic characteristics of the industry in the country under review.').

1304 OECD, 'Structural Separation in Regulated Industries: Implementing the OECD Recommendation' (n 1301) 3.

1305 Council Regulation (EC) 139/2004 on the control of concentrations between undertakings [2004] OJ L24/1, art 7. On the application of these principles, see Frank Maier-Rigaud, 'Behavioural versus Structural Remedies in EU Competition Law' in Philip Lowe, Mel Marquis and Giorgio Monti (eds), *European Competition Law Annual 2013: Effective and Legitimate Enforcement of Competition Law* (Hart 2016) 207–24. Similarly in the US, see DOJ, 'Merger Remedies' (Policy Guide, 2011) 2–4.

1306 Council Regulation 139/2004, recital 12.

a view to effectiveness, however, the EC has a stated preference for structural remedies.[1307] In particular, the EC notes that behavioural remedies are not suitable for horizontal concentrations and only rarely in situations of vertical integration.[1308]

The bar for structural measures thus is lower under competition law than under *ex ante* regulation. This is not surprising as, firstly, competition law remedies are imposed on a specific firm rather than a set of firms (making them less intrusive), and secondly, the remedies are imposed on the artificial acquisition of market power (while organic monopolization is almost always curtailed by behavioural remedies). When behavioural interventions prove ineffective (eg in case of serial infringements), structural solutions are nevertheless advised.

1307 'Commission Notice on remedies acceptable under Council Regulation (EC) No 139/2004' [2008] OJ C267/1, para 15 ('commitments which are structural in nature … are, as a rule, preferable … inasmuch as such commitments prevent, durably, the competition concerns which would be raised by the merger as notified, and do not, moreover, require medium or long-term monitoring measures').

1308 ibid, para 17.

12

SCOPE OF PLATFORM REGULATION

While competition law applies horizontally, the scope of *ex ante* regulation must be determined precisely. On the one hand, it must be wide enough to cover those firms that cause the (competitive) harm that motivates its adoption. On the other hand, it must be narrow enough so as not to burden a wide array of firms with compliance costs. As we know from the banking sector, compliance costs give larger firms a cost advantage over smaller ones, thus raising barriers to entry.[1309] The GDPR too is said to entrench the market power of already larger players, thus further concentrating markets.[1310] However, the wide scope of financial and privacy regulation may be justified because the concerns they seek to address are not limited to large players. By contrast, the competitive concerns regarding online platforms are mostly limited to larger – or rather, dominant – players. The question is how and where to draw the line.

In telecommunications, the line is drawn first by the EC, which carries out the three-criterion test discussed above to come up with a list of markets susceptible to *ex ante* regulation.[1311] National regulatory authorities then assess whether adopting *ex*

1309 Drew Dahl, Andrew Meyer and Michelle Neely, 'Scale Matters: Community Banks and Compliance Costs' (2016) The Regional Economist July 1 ('banks with assets of $1 billion to $10 billion reported total compliance costs averaging 2.9 percent of their noninterest expenses, while banks with less than $100 million in assets reported costs averaging 8.7 percent of their noninterest expenses'); 'Regulation is Good for Goldman' (*WSJ*, 11 February 2015) <https://www.wsj.com/articles/regulation-is-good-for-goldman-1423700859> (quoting the Goldman Sachs CEO: 'More intense regulatory and technology requirements have raised the barriers to entry higher than at any other time in modern history … This is an expensive business to be in, if you don't have the market share in scale.').

1310 Michal Gal and Oshrit Aviv, 'The Competitive Effects of the GDPR' (2020) 16 JCLE 349. For data, see Chinchih Chen, Carl Benedikt Frey and Giorgio Presidente, 'Privacy Regulation and Firm Performance: Estimating the GDPR Effect Globally' (2022) Oxford Martin Working Paper Series on Technological and Economic Change no 2022-1 (finding an especially large decline in profits and reduction in sales for small tech companies, while large tech companies appear relatively unaffected). See also Björn Greiff, 'Study: Google Is the Biggest Beneficiary of the GDPR' (*Cliqz*, 10 October 2018) <https://cliqz.com/en/magazine/study-google-is-the-biggest-beneficiary-of-the-gdpr>.

1311 Directive 2018/1972, art 67. The list has grown smaller over the years; the 2020 version only includes two markets (down from four in 2014), namely, 'wholesale local access provided at a fixed location' and 'wholesale dedicated capacity', see 'Commission Recommendation on relevant product and service markets within the electronic communications sector susceptible to *ex ante* regulation in accordance with Directive (EU) 2018/1972', C(2020)8750 and its Annex.

ante regulation in said markets is indeed justified. If so, they identify those undertakings with 'significant market power' (in accordance with specific EC Guidelines)[1312] and impose tailored regulatory obligations on them.

When it comes to *ex ante* regulation of online platforms, determining its scope is no easy feat. A preliminary difficulty concerns the definition of 'online platform', given the considerable disagreement on this point.[1313] This difficulty is apparent in the P2B Regulation, which does not refer to platforms, but rather to 'online intermediation services'.[1314] The 'online' part is defined by reference to the InfoSoc Directive, which applies to 'any service normally provided for remuneration, at a distance, by electronic means and at the individual request of a recipient of services'.[1315] More challenging is the 'intermediation service' part, which is defined as

> services which … allow business users to offer goods or services to consumers, with a view to facilitating the initiating of direct transactions between those business users and consumers, irrespective of where those transactions are ultimately concluded [and] are provided to business users on the basis of contractual relationships between the provider of those services and business users which offer goods or services to consumers[.][1316]

While the reference to 'direct transactions' is an effective way of distinguishing platforms from other businesses, the reference to 'contractual relationships' is restrictive: those are present in the case of online marketplaces, app stores and social networks, but not in the case of search engines. The P2B therefore has to explicitly add 'online search engines' to its scope.[1317]

The P2B Regulation's scope is wide (there are thousands of platforms), which is justifiable for an instrument with relatively minor obligations (transparency). When adopting more intrusive (and thus expensive) *ex ante* regulation, the net cannot be cast as wide. Moreover, the scope must be in line with the concerns the regulation seeks to address. While the designations vary, the underlying idea is the same: to target those platforms that pose the greatest risks for competition. There is, however, diversity in the methods to establish which platforms those are.[1318] Two main methods stand out:

1312 EC, 'Guidelines on market analysis and the assessment of significant market power under the EU regulatory framework for electronic communications networks and services' (Communication) C(2018)2374.

1313 See Section 1.1.

1314 P2B Regulation, art 1.

1315 P2B Regulation, art 2(2)(a), referring to Directive (EU) 2015/1535 of the European Parliament and of the Council laying down a procedure for the provision of information in the field of technical regulations and of rules on Information Society services [2015] OJ L241/1, art 1(1)(b).

1316 P2B Regulation, art 2(2)(b)–(c).

1317 P2B Regulation, art 1.

1318 For insightful opinions on which platforms should be subject to *ex ante* regulation, see Damien Geradin, 'What Is a Digital Gatekeeper? Which Platforms Should Be Captured by the EC Proposal for a Digital Market Act?' (2021) <https://ssrn.com/abstract=3788152>.

either *ex ante* regulation sticks close competition law, as telecom regulation did, and relies on market power (or a platform-specific variety of it), or *ex ante* regulation leaves competition law's market power trigger behind in favour of a more quantitative, size-related threshold. Platform regulation can also combine the two methods in a more hybrid way.

The 10th Amendment to the German Competition Act relies on the first method. Under the new section 19(a), the Bundeskartellamt can declare a platform 'of paramount significance for competition across markets'.[1319] In that assessment, the first factor to account for is the platform's dominant position in one or several markets, although a number of other factors come into play as well.[1320] Thus, the declaration rests on a market power test, but once 'paramount significance' has been established, the Bundeskartellamt can prohibit a range of specific conduct (eg self-preferencing and impeding interoperability).

A similar approach is taken in the UK.[1321] According to the latest proposal, the Digital Markets Unit (DMU) can designate platforms with 'strategic market status', which is the case for firms with 'substantial and entrenched market power in at least one activity, providing it with a strategic position'.[1322] The focus is on market power because a large size or number of users does not in itself indicate a competition problem.[1323] But it goes further: the market power must result in a strategic position, ie 'a position where the effects of its market power are likely to be particularly widespread or significant'.[1324] In assessing whether the platform is in a strategic position, the DMU must take into account different criteria, including whether the platform has achieved a very significant size or scale in an activity.[1325] The DMU therefore needs to prioritize the designation of firms with large revenue.[1326] Such revenue serves as a proxy for the harm that can result from the platform's market power and gives clarity to firms (in particular smaller ones) on whether they risk being designated. In short, the UK regime

1319 Competition Act in the version published on 26 June 2013 (Federal Law Gazette I, p 1750), as last amended by art 2 of the Act of 19 July 2022 (Federal Law Gazette I, p 1214) (hereafter, 'German Competition Act'), s 19(a).

1320 The factors are (i) financial strength or access to other resources; (ii) vertical integration and activities in otherwise related markets; (iii) access to data relevant for competition; and (iv) relevance of its activities for third-party access to supply and sales markets and its related influence on the business activities of third parties. Note that a market power assessment would generally account for those factors, although the last one is platform-specific.

1321 See 'A New Pro-Competition Regime for Digital Markets' (n 1255). The proposal is informed by the Furman Report (n 1295) and Digital Markets Taskforce, 'A New Pro-Competition Regime for Digital Markets' (Advice, 2020). The government meanwhile consulted on the proposal, see 'Government Response to the Consultation on a New Pro-Competition Regime for Digital Markets' (May 2022) CP 657.

1322 'A New Pro-Competition Regime for Digital Markets' (n 1255), para 50.

1323 ibid, para 62.

1324 ibid, para 66.

1325 ibid, para 68. The other three criteria are: (i) whether the firm is an important access point to consumers; (ii) whether the platform can use the activity to further entrench or protect its market power in that activity, or to extend its market power into a range of other activities; and (iii) whether the firm can use the activity to determine the 'rules of the game' for the users of its ecosystem and also set practice for businesses in the wider market.

1326 ibid, para 77.

is based on an enhanced market power test, although a more quantitative focus also emerges.

The DMA takes this quantitative focus further. It does not rely on market power at all but on the broader concept of 'economic power', which is further concretized as 'gatekeeper power'.[1327] The reason for this shift is that EU law does not effectively address 'the conduct of gatekeepers that are not necessarily dominant in competition-law terms'.[1328] Conceptually, gatekeeper power derives from the same characteristics as market power, namely, extreme scale economies, very strong network effects, lock-in effects, a lack of multihoming, and vertical integration.[1329] In practice, however, gatekeeper designation rests on quantitative thresholds (which correspond to qualitative criteria), namely:

(a) Achieving annual EU turnover ≥€7.5 billion in each of the last three financial years or having an average market cap ≥€75 billion in the last financial year, and providing the same core platform service (CPS) in at least three Member States (showing the platform has 'significant impact on the internal market');

(b) In the last financial year, providing a CPS with ≥45 million monthly active end users established or located in the EU and ≥10,000 yearly active business users established in the EU (showing the platform is 'an important gateway for business users to reach end users'); and

(c) Meeting the thresholds in (b) in each of the last three financial years (showing the platform's position is 'entrenched and durable').[1330]

All of the above proposals seek to limit their scope to platforms that serve as a crucial gateway for suppliers. A straightforward way of doing so is combining the platform concept with the market power concept. But importing the market power concept into *ex ante* instruments increases the overlap between the two forms of regulation, while complementarity should be sought. Moreover, establishing market power requires a complex, time-consuming analysis, while one of the main drivers of *ex ante* platform regulation is the need for speed. There are therefore benefits to relying on more quantitative measurements of gatekeeper power. While decision costs are lower and legal certainty higher, however, there is a greater risk of including large platforms (in terms of revenue, users, or other measures) that do not actually have the kind of power that concerns policymakers and, though less likely, missing smaller platforms that do

1327 DMA, recital 3.

1328 ibid, recital 5.

1329 ibid, recital 13.

1330 ibid, art 3. For its CPS concept, the DMA works with a closed list of ten types of platforms, see art 2(2). Two of the most important types, online intermediation services and search engines, are defined by reference to the P2B Regulation.

have such power. To some extent, this risk of over- and underinclusiveness can be mitigated through qualitative backstop provisions such as those found in the DMA.[1331] In the end, all instruments are calibrated to apply to platforms with market power, although the accuracy of that calibration can differ.[1332] Few instruments have been put into practice, so any estimate of their eventual scope is preliminary, but the final differences seem likely to be small.[1333]

1331 ibid, arts 3 and 17. Based on the quantitative thresholds, the platform is subject to a gatekeeper presumption, which it can rebut (preventing overinclusiveness). EC may also identify gatekeepers that do not meet the quantitative thresholds but only on the basis of a market investigation (preventing underinclusiveness). In such a market investigation, the EC is essentially carrying out a market power assessment.

1332 See Friso Bostoen, 'Understanding the Digital Markets Act' (n 1260) 272–79 on how the DMA's thresholds are likely to capture GAFAM and not many other firms, thus serving as a reasonably accurate proxy for market power in GAFAM's core markets (not so much in adjacent markets).

1333 The Bundeskartellamt has been designating GAFAM as of paramount significance across markets and is poised to go through the complete acronym, see eg Bundeskartellamt, Case B2-55/21, *Amazon*, 26 October 2022.

13

POTENTIAL REGULATORY INTERVENTIONS

As there are many different kinds of platforms and many types of anticompetitive conduct, there is no one regulatory instrument that can remedy the ills currently associated with platform power. Therefore, the main goal is to build a taxonomy of potential regulatory interventions, elucidate the interaction between them, and clarify the trade-offs inherent in each. The potential interventions under examination can be organized among different lines. The typology of regulatory interventions established above is a good start:[1334]

- Some measures fit better under the *competition law* umbrella (merger control, breakup), while others better qualify as *ex ante regulation* (structural non-discrimination or separation, portability), but many can be imposed through both regimes (behavioural non-discrimination, interoperability, forced access);
- Some measures are rather *structural* (merger control, structural non-discrimination or separation, breakup), while others are rather *behavioural* (behavioural non-discrimination, portability, interoperability, forced access).

1334 See Section 11.2.2.

Visually, the categorization looks as follows:

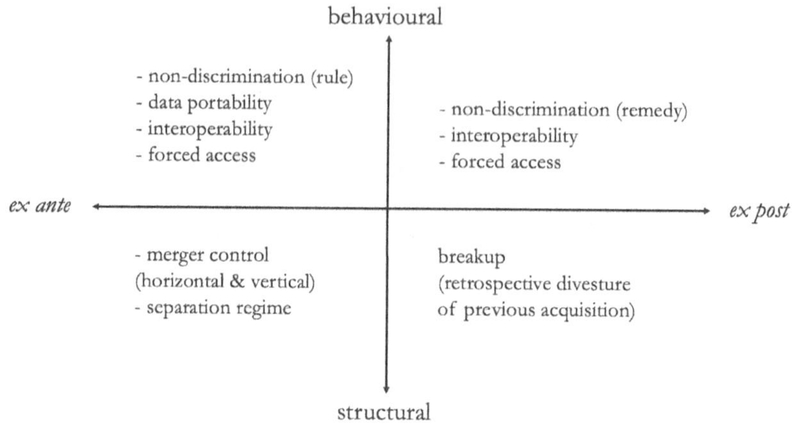

Figure 7 Regulatory matrix

As will become clear, another distinction is as – if not more – important. Some measures promote competition or contestability in the *upstream* platform market (horizontal merger control, portability), while others primarily protect competition in the *downstream* market (vertical merger control, non-discrimination). Certain measures can have effects on both upstream and downstream competition (interoperability, forced access, breakup), depending on their exact form. I return to this categorization in the conclusion but let's start by examining the distinct regulatory interventions (remembering that non-competition law interventions apply only to the platforms within their specific scope).

13.1 Merger Control

Online platforms have seen immense growth over the past years. Most of this growth has been organic, fuelled by network effects and platforms' ease of entry in adjacent markets.[1335] A not inconsiderable part of it, however, was artificial – realized through the acquisition of competitors or firms offering complementary services.[1336] Google leads the pack with over 250 acquisitions, some of which bolstered its core advertising business (DoubleClick and AdMob), while others allowed it to kickstart its entry into new markets (YouTube and Android). As the youngest of the GAFAM, Facebook also has a strong acquisition record (around 100): the purchases of Instagram and WhatsApp are (in)famous but acquisitions have also targeted smaller social networks (tbh) and virtual reality (Oculus).

1335 See Section 2.2.2.

1336 An overview of GAFA acquisitions is appended to US House of Representatives – Judiciary Subcommittee on Antitrust, 'Investigation of Competition in Digital Markets' (Majority Staff Report and Recommendations, 2020) (hereafter, 'House Judiciary Report') 405–51. See also FTC, 'Non-HSR Reported Acquisitions by Select Technology Platforms, 2010–2019' (Study, 2021).

Some argue that these acquisitions are used as anticompetitive tools to snuff out competition and sap innovation. Rather than outperforming competitors, the argument goes, tech giants use their outsized war chests to buy them out through horizontal acquisitions.[1337] When a platform acquires a company in a vertical relationship (ie integrates vertically), on the other hand, it has incentives to exclude similar companies that use its platform. In the two following sections, I look at how regulators have dealt with merger waves in the telecom industry, and whether it can inspire today's regulation.

13.1.1 Horizontal Merger Control

Although there is ongoing disagreement about who invented the first telephone, Bell was undeniably the first to be granted US patents for it. Many lawsuits followed, but the patent was never invalidated. At some point, however, the patents started expiring, leading to new firms challenging Bell's AT&T in local telephone markets. They did so successfully: between 1894 and 1907, AT&T's market share fell from 95 to 49%.[1338] To turn things around, AT&T started a campaign of aggressively acquiring local networks. In order to protect competition, which was delivering lower prices and greater availability of phone services, the DOJ filed suit against AT&T. The case was settled quickly with the 1913 Kingsbury Commitment (named after AT&T Vice President Kingsbury, who proposed it in a letter to the attorney general).[1339] Under this commitment, AT&T agreed to stop acquiring independent local telephone companies.[1340]

Today's online platforms also shop liberally, buying out firms that (potentially) compete with them. Outsized academic attention has been commanded by 'killer acquisitions', in which incumbent firms acquire innovative targets solely to discontinue the target's innovation projects and pre-empt future competition.[1341] Around 5–7% of acquisitions in the pharmaceutical industry qualify as such. In theory, killer acquisitions can also occur in the digital economy. Facebook, for example, has shut down almost half of the companies it acquired. In practice, however, it is difficult to establish which, if any, of

1337 When the acquired competitor is not an *actual* but rather a *potential* competitor, these acquisitions are considered 'conglomerate mergers'. However, as the principles of horizontal merger control apply to such acquisitions, they are discussed under that heading.

1338 Ajit Pai, 'Remarks on the 100th Anniversary of the Kingsbury Commitment' (TechFreedom Forum, Washington, DC, 19 December 2013). This shift in market share was due not only to head-to-head competition between AT&T and local telephone companies but also to an expansion of the market by the latter.

1339 The Kingsbury Commitment thus consists primarily of two letters: (i) a letter from AT&T Vice Present Nathan Kingsbury to US Attorney General George McReynolds; and (ii) a reply letter from US Attorney General George McReynolds to AT&T Vice President Nathan Kingsbury. President Woodrow Wilson also replied. The three letters are available via <http://vcxc.org/kingsbury100/>. See further Milton Mueller, *Universal Service: Competition, Interconnection and Monopoly in the Making of the American Telephone System* (MIT/AEI Press 1997) 127–31.

1340 The Kingsbury Commitment was only effective for a couple of years. In 1917, the commitment was interpreted as allowing AT&T to acquire new lines as long as it sold an equal amount of them. As a result, AT&T and local telephone companies started exchanging lines to divide markets rather than compete. See Peter Decherney, Nathan Ensmenger and Christopher Yoo, 'Are Those Who Ignore History Doomed to Repeat It? (Reviewing *The Master Switch: The Rise and Fall of Information Empires* by Tim Wu)' (2011) 78 The University of Chicago Law Review 1627, 1633–37.

1341 Colleen Cunningham, Florian Ederer and Song Ma, 'Killer Acquisitions' (2021) 129 Journal of Political Economy 649.

those acquisitions were killer acquisitions.[1342] Rather than killing off the startups they acquire, platforms tend to integrate them into their ecosystems.[1343] This is not necessarily harmless from an innovation perspective: integration can lead platforms to discontinue their competing innovation project (a 'reverse' killer acquisition).[1344] In addition, it is worth noting that platforms can identify potential targets more effectively than traditional businesses by using the data gathered through their services. Facebook offers an example again: it bought Onavo, an app that tracks data usage on smartphones, and has used the aggregated data of its millions of users to guide its acquisition strategy.[1345]

Startups – especially VC-backed ones – already have strong incentives to sell to the incumbent.[1346] And even when founders refuse to sell to the platform, that is not the end of it. First, the incumbent platform may pressure the startup into selling by relying on its vast amounts of capital. When Amazon took an interest in Quidsi (a startup providing recurring orders of diapers), for example, its owners were not immediately ready to sell. In response, Amazon started a price war with the startup, systematically undercutting it and then introducing a new service similar to Quidsi's with further discounts and free shipping.[1347] Unable to withstand the below-cost (and potentially predatory) prices, the startup founders saw no other option than to sell. Second, the incumbent platform may decide to simply copy the features of the new product and subsequently rely on its established user base to win out against the entrant.[1348] Facebook in particular is notorious for doing so.[1349] After Snapchat refused Facebook's acquisition offer, for

1342 Tim Wu and Stuart Thompson, 'The Roots of Big Tech Run Disturbingly Deep' (*NYT*, 7 June 2019) <https://www.nytimes.com/interactive/2019/06/07/opinion/google-facebook-mergers-acquisitions-antitrust.html>.

1343 Axel Gautier and Joe Lamesch, 'Mergers in the Digital Economy' (2020) CESifo Working Paper 8056 find that in 60% of GAFAM acquisitions, the acquired products were discontinued (the discontinuation policy is more systemic for Apple and Facebook). Most of the acquisitions are undertaken either to reinforce the platforms' innovation efforts by purchasing R&D and talent ('acqui-hires') or to add functionalities to their core products. They argue there are incentives against discontinuing the acquired target when its value is based on its users, and single out only one potential killer acquisition (based on a rather restrictive definition of the term): Facebook's acquisition of Masquerade.

1344 Cristina Caffarra, Gregory Crawford and Tommaso Valletti, '"How Tech Rolls": Potential Competition and "Reverse" Killer Acquisitions' (2020) CPI Antitrust Chronicle May.

1345 Deepa Seetharaman and Betsy Morris, 'Facebook's Onavo Gives Social-Media Firm Inside Peek at Rivals' Users' (*WSJ*, 13 August 2017) <https://www.wsj.com/articles/facebooks-onavo-gives-social-media-firm-inside-peek-at-rivals-users-1502622003>; Josh Constine, 'Facebook Will Shut Down Its Spyware VPN App Onavo' (*TechCrunch*, 22 February 2019) <https://techcrunch.com/2019/02/21/facebook-removes-onavo/>. See also Margrethe Vestager, 'A digital future that works for Europeans' (Business Forum of the German Ambassadors' Conference, Berlin, 27 August 2019) (discussing Onavo).

1346 Selling to the incumbent means that the startup strengthens the incumbent's market power and can share in the resulting rents. Beyond paying for the startup's future profits, incumbents will pay for their own avoided losses, which may be larger than future profits given the incumbent's market power is at risk. See Mark Lemley and Andrew McCreary, 'Exit Strategy' (2020) Stanford Law and Economics Olin Working Paper 542, 32–39.

1347 Brad Stone, *The Everything Store* (Corgi 2014) 361–67 describes how, based on shipping rates and wholesale prices, executives of Quidsi calculated that Amazon was on track to lose $100 million over three months in the diaper category. From the Antitrust Subcommittee investigation, we learned that Amazon was willing to lose $200 million in one month alone, see House Judiciary Report (n 1336), 264–65 and 301–2. After Amazon bought Quidsi, it hiked prices. In 2017, Amazon shut down the Quidsi service Diapers.com.

1348 For a legal analysis of such conduct, see John Obear, 'Move Last and Take Things: Facebook and Predatory Copying' (2018) 3 Columbia Business Law Review 994.

1349 For a collection of examples and discussion, see Friso Bostoen, '"We Have Reached 'Peak Cloning' in Silicon Valley": When Does Copying Your Competitor's Product Become Anticompetitive?' (*CoRe Blog*, 26 September 2019) <https://coreblog.lexxion.eu/anticompetitive-copying/>.

example, Facebook copied Snapchat's popular 'Stories' feature on its three major platforms (Facebook, Instagram, WhatsApp). Shortly thereafter, Snapchat's user growth slowed considerably.[1350]

This acquisition and copying process is said to result in a 'kill zone'[1351] around the incumbent platforms, where startups challenging them receive less and less VC funding, which stymies innovation.[1352] As one VC firm partner put it: 'We don't touch anything that comes too close to Facebook, Google or Amazon.'[1353] The evidence is not just anecdotal; there is also a growing body of empirical research based on VC investment data.[1354] Focusing on the 2015–17 period, Hathaway finds that 'the number of companies entering the venture-backed pipeline in industries that are in direct competition with core FGA [Facebook, Google, Amazon] activities have been on a steady and persistent decline [25–40%] that exceeds comparable groups'.[1355] Kamepalli et al have formally modelled the effects of startup acquisition by digital platforms. They also empirically find that VC investment in startups in the same space as a company acquired by Google or Facebook drops by over 40% in the three years after acquisition.[1356] More recent data (2018–20) paints a rosier funding picture but has not been expertly parsed.[1357]

The evidence is not conclusive, but it seems that the conduct of today's platforms makes it more difficult for entrants to get funded, which could prevent them from emerging as serious competitors to the incumbents tomorrow. Is it time to restrict monopolization through acquisition by online platforms, as the Kingsbury Commitment

1350 Josh Constine, 'Snapchat Growth Slowed 82% After Instagram Stories Launched' (*TechCrunch*, 2 February 2017) <https://techcrunch.com/2017/02/02/slowchat/>; Prachi Bhardwaj, 'As Snapchat Growth Stalls Out, Facebook Stories Hits 150 Million Daily Active Users' (*Business Insider*, 18 May 2018) <https://www.businessinsider.com/facebook-stories-versus-snapchat-users-2018-5>.

1351 See eg Asher Schechter, 'Google and Facebook's "Kill Zone": "We've Taken the Focus Off of Rewarding Genius and Innovation to Rewarding Capital and Scale"' (*ProMarket*, 25 May 2018) <https://promarket.org/google-facebooks-kill-zone-weve-taken-focus-off-rewarding-genius-innovation-rewarding-capital-scale/> and 'American Tech Giants Are Making Life Tough for Startups' (*The Economist*, 2 June 2018) <https://www.economist.com/business/2018/06/02/american-tech-giants-are-making-life-tough-for-startups>.

1352 For a deeper discussion of the anecdotal and empirical evidence presented here, see Friso Bostoen, 'Venture Capital and Antitrust: On Exit Strategies, Killer Acquisitions, and Innovation Harms' (*CoRe Blog*, 23 April 2020) <https://www.lexxion.eu/coreblogpost/venture-capital-and-antitrust/>. See also DOJ and Stanford University, 'Venture Capital and Antitrust' (Transcript of Public Workshop, 12 February 2020).

1353 Elizabeth Dwoskin, 'Facebook's Willingness to Copy Rivals' Apps Seen as Hurting Innovation' (*WaPo*, 10 August 2017) <https://www.washingtonpost.com/business/economy/facebooks-willingness-to-copy-rivals-apps-seen-as-hurting-innovation/2017/08/10/ea7188ea-7df6-11e7-a669-b400c5c7e1cc_story.html>.

1354 In particular data from Pitchbook and CrunchBase, as parsed, eg by Kevin Caves and Hal Singer, 'When the Econometrician Shrugged: Identifying and Plugging Gaps in the Consumer Welfare Standard' (2018) 26 George Mason Law Review 395, 403–4 and Oliver Wyman, 'Assessing the Impact of Big Tech on Venture Investment' (Report commissioned by Facebook, 2018).

1355 Ian Hathaway, 'Platform Giants and Venture-Backed Startups' (personal blog, 12 October 2018) <http://www.ianhathaway.org/blog/2018/10/12/platform-giants-and-venture-backed-startups>.

1356 Sai Krishna Kamepalli, Raghuram Rajan and Luigi Zingales, 'Kill Zone' (2020) NBER Working Paper 27146.

1357 There has been an uptick in both VC deal value and deal count, but most of that funding went to later-stage companies – not early-stage startups. See eg James Thorne and Priyamvada Mathur, 'The Year in Charts: VC Defies 2020 Expectations Despite the Pandemic' (*Pitchbook*, 21 December 2020) <https://pitchbook.com/news/articles/2020-vc-in-charts>.

once did (or tried to do) for AT&T? An important caveat is that competition authorities no longer turn to their monopolization provisions to challenge mergers, but now operate within detailed merger control regimes. Under these regimes, companies are obliged to notify any acquisition to competition authorities when it reaches certain thresholds. The thresholds of the EU Merger Regulation (EUMR) are based on the merging parties' turnover. Crucially, a merger only has to be notified when both the acquirer *and target* reach a large enough turnover *within the EU.*[1358] By contrast, in the US, the thresholds are based on the transaction value of the merger or acquisition.[1359]

Two of Facebook's acquisitions are emblematic of the governing regimes. In 2012, Facebook acquired Instagram, the photo-based social network. In the EU, the EC did not even have jurisdiction to scrutinize it. The CMA, whose jurisdiction is based not only on turnover (which Instagram had not generated by that point) but also on the firms' 'share of supply', did examine the transaction. Given that there were plenty of other photo apps and Instagram did not appear particularly well placed to compete against Facebook in advertising, the CMA did not refer the transaction to the Competition Commission.[1360] The FTC also examined the transaction but closed its investigation into the merger with a 5–0 vote, holding that no further action was warranted.[1361]

In 2014, Facebook acquired the messaging app WhatsApp in a $19 billion transaction. The merger went completely unchallenged (or even examined) by the FTC.[1362] Again, the transaction did not have to be notified to the EC as WhatsApp did not generate significant turnover in the EU (or anywhere, for that matter). The case only made it to the EC after three different Member States with jurisdiction to review the merger agreed to transfer it under the EUMR's referral mechanism.[1363] After an investigation, the EC did not oppose the merger.

Authorities have been concerned about potential gaps in the current EU merger control regime. The EC organized a public consultation on the effectiveness of turnover-based thresholds to identify potentially anticompetitive merges in the tech sector, 'where the acquired company, while having generated little turnover as yet, may play a competitive role, hold commercially valuable data, or have a considerable market potential

1358 Council Regulation 139/2004, art 1. One set of criteria requires a turnover of €250 million per company; an alternative set requires a turnover of only €100 million, but this lower requirement is compensated with stricter accompanying requirements.

1359 Hart-Scott-Rodino Antitrust Improvements Act of 1976, 15 USC s 18a (s 7a of the Clayton Act).

1360 OFT, Case ME/5525/12 *Facebook/Instagram*, 14 August 2012.

1361 FTC, 'FTC closes its investigation into Facebook's proposed acquisition of Instagram photo sharing program' (press release, 22 August 2012) <https://www.ftc.gov/news-events/press-releases/2012/08/ftc-closes-its-investigation-facebooks-proposed-acquisition>.

1362 The Bureau of Competition did not issue any statement on *Facebook/WhatsApp*. Only the Bureau of Consumer Protection sent a letter to the companies highlighting their promises on privacy, see FTC, 'FTC notifies Facebook, WhatsApp of privacy obligations in light of proposed acquisition' (press release, 10 April 2014) <https://www.ftc.gov/news-events/press-releases/2014/04/ftc-notifies-facebook-whatsapp-privacy-obligations-light-proposed>.

1363 *Facebook/ WhatsApp* (Case M.7217) Commission Decision C(2014)7239, paras 9–12. The referral was based on Council Regulation 139/2004, art 4(5).

for other reasons'.[1364] But the EC did not pursue a shift towards EUMR thresholds based on transaction value rather than turnover.[1365] Commissioner Vestager set out the EC's reasoning:

> [I]t's not easy to set [a value-based threshold] at the right level. If it's too high, it doesn't really help – you still end up missing a lot of the cases that matter. On the other hand, if you set it low enough to make sure that you see all those mergers, you risk making companies file a lot of cases that simply aren't relevant.[1366]

Instead, the EC opted for new guidance on merger referrals. Article 22 EUMR always allowed Member States to refer transactions that do not meet the EU thresholds to the EC.[1367] The EC had previously discouraged referrals from Member States that did not have original jurisdiction over the transaction (based on their thresholds, turnover-based or otherwise). In its new guidance, however, the EC clarified that the referral mechanism also applies to transactions that do *not* meet the jurisdictional criteria of referring Member States.[1368] The EC encourages referrals of transactions where the turnover of the target does not reflect its actual or future competitive potential.[1369] Value-based thresholds are brought in through the backdoor as the EC 'may also take into account whether the value of the consideration received by the seller is particularly high compared to the current turnover of the target'.[1370] It is no surprise that the referral mechanism has been used for digital economy transactions such as *Facebook/Kustomer*, which was cleared with commitments.[1371]

The referral mechanism is strengthened by the DMA, which obliges gatekeepers to inform the EC of all transactions.[1372] This does not give the EC jurisdiction to scrutinize those transactions, but it can subsequently encourage Member States to refer them. In addition, some Member States such as Germany and Austria have complemented their turnover-based thresholds with value-based thresholds.[1373] Their NCAs are now able

1364 EC, 'Evaluation of procedural and jurisdictional aspects of EU merger control' (Consultation, 2016).

1365 Crémer Report (n 1295) 113–16 also counsels against such a shift.

1366 Margrethe Vestager, 'The Future of EU Merger Control' (International Bar Association 24th Annual Competition Conference, 11 September 2020).

1367 Council Regulation 139/2004, art 22 ('One or more Member States may request the Commission to examine any concentration … that does not have a Community dimension … but affects trade between Member States and threatens to significantly affect competition within the territory of the Member State or States making the request.').

1368 EC, 'Commission Guidance on the application of the referral mechanism set out in Article 22 of the Merger Regulation to certain categories of cases' (Communication) C(2021)1959. Illumina pleaded the new guidance was illegal, but its action was dismissed by the GC, see Case T–227/21 *Illumina v Commission* EU:T:2022:447.

1369 EC, 'Commission Guidance on the application of the referral mechanism set out in Article 22 of the Merger Regulation to certain categories of cases' (n 1368), para 19.

1370 ibid.

1371 *Meta/Kustomer* (Case M.10262) Commission Decision C(2022)409.

1372 DMA, art 14.

1373 German Competition Act, s 35(1a); Federal Act against Cartels and other Restrictions of Competition originally published in 2005 (Federal Law Gazette I No. 61/2005), as last amended in 2021 (Federal Law Gazette I No. 176/2021), s 9(4).

to scrutinize acquisitions with a transaction value exceeding €400 and €200 million, respectively.[1374] The value-based thresholds thus empower the NCAs to scrutinize acquisitions of valuable firms that do not yet realize significant turnover.[1375]

One wonders, however, whether the jurisdictional thresholds are really the issue. Indeed, even the WhatsApp acquisition finally made it to the EC, while the CMA scrutinized *Facebook/Instagram*. But all of those mergers were then approved, which many commentators consider a mistake.[1376] To prevent such mistakes, substantive changes to merger control may be required.

The EUMR prohibits mergers that 'significantly impede effective competition' (the 'SIEC test').[1377] The burden of proving an SIEC lies on the EC.[1378] The standard of proof has been one of 'balance of probabilities', although this has been called into question by the GC judgment in *CK Telecoms*:

> [T]he Commission is required to produce sufficient evidence to demonstrate with a strong probability the existence of significant impediments following the concentration. Thus, the standard of proof applicable in the present case is therefore stricter than that under which a significant impediment to effective competition is 'more likely than not', on the basis of a 'balance of probabilities' ... By contrast, it is less strict than a standard of proof based on 'being beyond all reasonable doubt'[.][1379]

Different amendments are possible. First, one could change the *standard of proof*. While the acquisition of a startup by an incumbent platform has a low probability of harm (given that the startup is statistically unlikely to replace the incumbent), the size of the harm is potentially large (the loss of the potential competitor that would succeed). The Furman Report describes how, under the current 'balance of probabilities' standard, the CMA may not have been able to block Facebook's acquisition of Instagram even if it wanted to.[1380] It therefore proposes a 'balance of harms' approach, which would allow the CMA to intervene where it expects, on average, for the harm of the merger to be substantially greater than the benefits.[1381] The authority could thus intervene, for example, where there was a 20% chance of serious harm to consumers arising from a

1374 To prevent covering an unduly large number of transactions that lack effects on the national market ('local nexus'), the provisions require that the acquired undertaking 'has substantial operations in Germany'/'is active to a large extent on the [Austrian] market'.

1375 The agencies have digital transactions firmly in mind, as is clear from guidelines they published: Bundeskartellamt and BWB, 'Transaction Value Thresholds for Mandatory Pre-merger Notification (Guidance, 2018) 24–25 (using the acquisition of a free smartphone communication app with many users but no significant turnover as an example of new transactions covered by the merger).

1376 See Section 13.5.

1377 Council Regulation 139/2004, art 2(3).

1378 Case T–342/07 *Ryanair v Commission* EU:T:2010:280, para 23.

1379 Case T–399/16 *CK Telecoms v Commission* EU:T:2020:217, para 118. The judgment is under appeal.

1380 Furman Report (n 1295), paras 3.85–87.

1381 ibid, paras 3.88–100.

proposed merger, set against an 80% chance of relatively small benefits occurring.[1382] Others seek to lower the burden of proof more subtly, eg by replacing the 'more likely than not' with a 'realistic prospect' standard.[1383]

Second, one could shift the *burden of proof* in specific circumstances. Based on extensive empirical research on error rates, Kwoka has long recommended adopting presumptions against mergers resulting in few competitors.[1384] Focusing specifically on online platforms, the Stigler Report proposes a rebuttable presumption against mergers between a dominant firm and any substantial competitor or uniquely likely future competitor.[1385] Going one step further, Petit suggests that 'antitrust might subject horizontal mergers on a tipped market to a non-rebuttable presumption of consumer harm'.[1386]

Third, one could develop more accurate *theories of harm* under the SIEC test. The Crémer Report recommends focusing not (only) on product markets but on 'users' spaces', asking whether the platform and the target compete for the same users.[1387] This could have better captured the dynamics in *Facebook/Instagram*: while they appeared to be in separate product markets at the time (social networking vs photo editing and sharing), they did compete for the same users. Still, such acquisitions would only meet the SIEC test if in the counterfactual – ie without the merger – the target could have succeeded as a stand-alone company or would realistically have been bought by another competitor.[1388]

The *potential* nature of competition is not the only difficulty. Arguably, merger control is not well prepared for strategies whereby platforms *systematically* buy out those future rivals. In isolation, many of these acquisitions may appear harmless, but taken together, they can significantly limit innovation, choice and quality. Therefore, a German expert report proposes to amend the substantive merger provision so as to allow the authority to consider, before approving or blocking a merger, 'the existence of an overall strategy of a dominant company to systematically acquire fast-growing companies with a recognizable and considerable potential to become competitors in the dominated market in the future'.[1389]

1382 ibid, para 4.17.

1383 Digital Markets Taskforce (n 1321), paras 4.149–55 (and rejecting the 'balance of harms' approach).

1384 John Kwoka, *Controlling Mergers and Market Power: A Program for Reviving Antitrust in America* (CPI 2020) 56–63 (the presumption should be 'nearly irrebuttable' in case of mergers resulting in three or less competitors, and 'still formidable' against those resulting in four or five competitors).

1385 Stigler Report (n 1295) 98 ('This presumption would be valuable, not because it would identify anticompetitive mergers with precision, but because it would shift the burden to the party with the best access to relevant information on issues of competitive effects and efficiencies from the merger.').

1386 Petit (n 1285) 201–5.

1387 Crémer Report (n 1295) 121–23.

1388 ibid.

1389 Heike Schweitzer et al, 'Modernising the Law on Abuse of Market Power – Summary of the Report's Recommendations' (Report for the Federal Ministry for Economic Affairs, 2018) para 8. The report adds:

> It may be an indication for such future competition that the company to be acquired – while only being a niche competitor to the dominant firm – is active in a market that addresses the same basic needs as the acquirer. Instead of looking at relatively narrowly defined markets, the [Bundeskartellamt] could

Changes to merger control regimes so far have been on the jurisdictional, not the substantive, front. It is too early, and in any case difficult, to assess their effectiveness – let alone weigh any benefits against the increased administrative burden and compliance costs new measures necessarily come with. But it will be interesting to track the work of NCAs with greater jurisdiction such as the CMA (with its share-of-supply test) and the Bundeskartellamt (with its value-based thresholds). The CMA in particular appears to be taking a more aggressive stance. It prohibited Facebook's acquisition of Giphy (a repository of GIFs used in online communication) based in part on the theory that Giphy could potentially compete with Facebook in the display advertising market.[1390] The theory seemed far-fetched, but theories of potential competition are wont to do so. Looking at error rates more generally, there is certainly room for a more interventionist approach. As the Furman Report puts it:

> To date, there have been no false positives in mergers involving the major digital platforms, for the simple reason that all of them have been permitted. Meanwhile, it is likely that some false negatives will have occurred during this time.[1391]

While acquisitions by platforms can be beneficial, in particular where they allow for the further development and wide distribution of edge innovation, the current approach seems overly permissive. Indeed, a wealth of research has shown that acquisitions of (potential) competitors by incumbent platforms can be harmful to innovation, corroborating the finding that false negatives have likely occurred.[1392]

This section has examined *ex ante* control of horizontal mergers. Exceptionally, mergers can also be reconsidered *ex post*, which is discussed under Section 13.5.

13.1.2 Vertical Merger Control

Contrary to horizontal mergers, the main concern with vertical mergers is not the accumulation of market power but foreclosure. Once a company not only owns the distribution channels for a good or service, but also produces goods or services

therefore look at a broader category of competitive relationships which may better capture the reality of fast-changing markets in the presence of potentially disruptive activities.

For the full study in German, see Heike Schweitzer et al, 'Modernisierung der Missbrauchsaufsicht für marktmächtige Unternehmen' (Report for the Federal Ministry for Economic Affairs, 2018). For a discussion, see Rupprecht Podszun, 'How to Reform the Law on Abusive Practices: The Study That Will Serve as a Basis for the Reform of Abusive Practices in Germany (and Europe?)' (2018) CPI Europe Column September.

1390 CMA, *Meta/Giphy* (Final Report), 30 November 2021, confirmed by *Meta v CMA* [2022] CAT 26. The CMA also relied on a more traditional theory of vertical foreclosure.

1391 Furman Report (n 1295), para 3.43. See similarly Kevin Bryan and Erik Hovenkamp, 'Startup Acquisitions, Error Costs, and Antitrust Policy' (2020) 87 The University of Chicago Law Review 331, 331 ('it is unlikely that society is best served by a policy of near-universal inaction … We therefore argue for expanded antitrust intervention (that is, more than zero)').

1392 Lear, 'Ex-Post Assessment of Merger Control Decisions in Digital Markets' (Final Report, 2019); Carl Shapiro, 'Antitrust in a Time of Populism' (2018) 61 Journal of Industrial Organization 714, 741; Kevin Bryan and Erik Hovenkamp, 'Antitrust Limits on Startup Acquisitions' (2020) 56 Review of Industrial Organization 615; Michael Katz, 'Big Tech Mergers: Innovation, Competition for the Market, and the Acquisition of Emerging Competitors' (2020) 54 Information Economics and Policy.

itself, it has an incentive to (i) deny rival producers access to its distribution network (customer foreclosure); and/or (ii) refuse to supply rival distributors with products (input foreclosure). As a result, the competitiveness of those rivals can be impaired.[1393] Such effects depend, however, on the market power of the vertically integrated entity over distribution/inputs. At the same time, as vertical mergers allow for the integration of complementary products or services, they provide substantial scope for efficiencies – more so than horizontal mergers.[1394]

The last few years have seen a wave of telecom operators integrating vertically (especially in the US), expanding from the distribution of content into its production. This process of vertical integration was usually not organic but artificial, ie merger-driven. Two mergers – Comcast with NBC Universal (NBCU) and AT&T with Time Warner (TW) – stand out and may be useful to inform our approach to vertical integration by online platforms.[1395]

The *Comcast/NBCU* merger brought together the largest US cable operator and ISP (ie distributor of content) with a significant player in the market for video programming (ie content). The DOJ and FCC were concerned that Comcast–NBCU would (i) withhold programming from rival distributors (input foreclosure) and (ii) refuse access to its distribution systems to rival programmers (customer foreclosure). The agencies therefore imposed conditions on the merger in order to safeguard access to both programming and distribution.[1396] When it comes to programming, these conditions took the form of a specific arbitration process to resolve any disputes that would arise about licensing terms. When it comes to distribution, the conditions prohibited discrimination in programming on the basis of affiliation or non-affiliation with Comcast–NBCU.[1397]

AT&T and TW followed suit in a merger bringing together a telecom giant with one of the world's largest media organizations – another distribution–content combination. This time, however, the DOJ sued to block the merger (its first vertical merger litigation in forty years). Its theory of harm relied mainly on the combined AT&T–TW entity's ability to negotiate a higher price for its 'must-have content' (such as CNN and HBO) with rival distributors. It would be empowered to do so: if rival distributors walked

1393 In the extreme, competitors would have to be active at both levels (eg production and distribution) in order to compete effectively, see Guidelines on the assessment of non-horizontal mergers under the Council Regulation on the control of concentrations between undertakings [2008] OJ C265/6, paras 29–77.

1394 In particular, vertical mergers may decrease transaction costs, allow for better coordination, and eliminate double marginalization (ie the charging of markups at each level of the supply chain), see Guidelines on the assessment of non-horizontal mergers under the Council Regulation on the control of concentrations between undertakings (n 1393), paras 13–14.

1395 For a broader overview that also includes EU cases, see Cristina Caffarra, Gregory Crawford and Helen Weeds, 'Kabuki Dances or Rube Goldberg Machines? Vertical Analyses of Media Mergers' (2018) CPI Antitrust Chronicle August.

1396 *United States v Comcast*, no 1:11-cv-00106 (DDC, 1 September 2011) and FCC, MB Docket no 10-56, Comcast Memorandum Opinion and Order, 18 January 2011. For insight into the merger process and its aftermath, see Susan Crawford, *Captive Audience* (Yale University Press 2013) 123–40.

1397 Comcast was also prohibited from discriminating against unaffiliated online video distributors when transmitting their traffic to Comcast broadband customers (a net neutrality obligation).

away without an agreement and TW content became unavailable on their channels (a 'blackout'), their customers might switch to DirecTV (AT&T's main distribution channel). A vertically integrated AT&T–TW could thus only win, either through higher prices or more customers. While the district judge ruled against the DOJ[1398] (and was confirmed by the court of appeals),[1399] post-merger developments including blackouts[1400] and price hikes[1401] support the DOJ's theory.

Online platforms are also busy integrating vertically. More often than not, they enter adjacent markets organically, leveraging their strong position at the platform level.[1402] But artificial entry is no rarity. Amazon, for example, made headlines when it bought the grocery chain Whole Foods in a $13.7 billion deal that was quickly approved by the FTC.[1403] Whether organic or artificial, the result of vertical integration is the same: the platform offers not only the digital infrastructure for the distribution of products or services (upstream), but also some of those products or services themselves (downstream). Given that online platforms are most likely to have market power in the upstream market, customer foreclosure is the main concern.

In particular, the platform infrastructure can be used to discriminate against downstream providers in favour of its own offering. Amazon could, for example, start limiting its grocery delivery programme to products from Whole Foods, rather than offering multiple supermarkets or producers the opportunity to sell their wares online. Such concerns are not purely speculative. After all, Amazon did stop distributing Nest's smart home products through its Marketplace after it acquired the competing manufacturer Ring.[1404] Then again, the anticompetitive effects of such discrimination depend on Amazon's market power.

There are reasons to think online platforms may be more effective at foreclosing rivals than distributors of programming. First, the media market is more differentiated, with strong consumer preferences for various content. Comcast may want to stop showing HBO's *Game of Thrones* to draw viewers to an NBCU alternative, but customers passionate about that series will not easily forgive Comcast. Smart doorbells, by contrast, do not incite the same kind of passion in consumers. Second, platforms have more effective (and more concealed) ways to exclude competing downstream products

1398 *United States v AT&T*, no 17-2511 (DDC, 12 June 2018). For a critique of the judgment, see Steven Salop, 'The AT&T/Time Warner Merger: How Judge Leon Garbled Professor Nash' (2018) 6 JAE 459.

1399 *United States v AT&T*, no 18-5214 (DC Cir, 26 February 2019).

1400 Elizabeth Winkler, 'How HBO's Blackout on Dish Could Affect AT&T' (*WSJ*, 26 November 2018) <https://www.wsj.com/articles/how-hbos-blackout-on-dish-could-affect-at-t-1543235401>.

1401 Todd Shields, 'DirecTV to Hike Prices After Owner AT&T Promised Cheaper Bills' (*Bloomberg*, 14 March 2019) <https://www.bloomberg.com/news/articles/2019-03-14/directv-to-hike-prices-after-owner-at-t-promised-cheaper-bills>.

1402 See Section 2.2.2.

1403 FTC, 'Statement of Acting Director of the Bureau of Competition on the Agency's review of Amazon.com's acquisition of Whole Foods Market' (press release, 23 August 2017) <https://www.ftc.gov/news-events/press-releases/2017/08/statement-federal-trade-commissions-acting-director-bureau>.

1404 Chris Welch, 'Amazon Will Soon Stop Selling All Nest Products' (*The Verge*, 3 March 2018) <https://www.theverge.com/2018/3/3/17074844/>.

or services. On top of increasing their distribution fee for those products, they can push competitors down the ranking of search results (whether on a search engine or online marketplace) and impose various kinds of technical restrictions limiting free distribution.

On both sides of the Atlantic, we are seeing a reappreciation of the potential harms of vertical mergers. This is explained at least in part by competition authorities recognizing that the validity of Chicago School theories about vertical mergers, in particular the SMP theory, is limited to specific circumstances.[1405] In the US, the FTC went as far as withdrawing its Vertical Merger Guidelines.[1406] In the EU, Google's acquisition of Fitbit offers a good example. The transaction was finally cleared, but only after a 'phase II' investigation.[1407] As is common in the digital economy, the merging firms showed both overlap (in data, particularly health data) and complementarity (between Fitbit's wearables and Android). To prevent discrimination of competing wearables suppliers, Google committed to keeping licensing for free to Android OEMs, those public APIs covering core functionalities that wrist-worn devices need to interoperate with an Android smartphone. The commitment thus prevents platform foreclosure to safeguard competition.

Most of the proposals discussed in the context of horizontal merger control also apply to vertical merger control. This goes for the proposals for jurisdictional changes (thresholds) as well as those for more substantive changes (the SIEC test, its standard and burden of proof, and theories of harm). Other proposals are specific to vertical mergers. In particular, four prominent academics are calling for the adoption of a 'dominant platform presumption'.[1408] According to this presumption, the acquisition by a dominant platform of a firm in an adjacent market would be prima facie illegal, given that the platform's market power enables it to exclude competitors of that firm from the downstream market. In addition, firms in vertically adjacent or complementary markets are often potential entrants, so the presumption also helps prevent the elimination of future rivals. Before acquiring the downstream firm, the platform would therefore have to rebut the presumption.

A new, evidence-based focus on vertical merger enforcement is to be welcomed, as it was unduly weakened by meanwhile disproven Chicago School economics. To reduce exclusionary practices by online platforms, however, vertical merger enforcement's

1405 See Section 5.1.2.

1406 FTC, 'Federal Trade Commission withdraws Vertical Merger Guidelines and Commentary' (press release, 15September2021)<https://www.ftc.gov/news-events/news/press-releases/2021/09/federal-trade-commission-withdraws-vertical-merger-guidelines-commentary> ('the guidelines adopted a particularly flawed economic theory regarding purported pro-competitive benefits of mergers, despite having no basis of support in the law or market reality').

1407 *Google/Fitbit* (Case M.9660) Commission Decision C(2020) 9105.

1408 Jonathan Baker, Nancy Rose, Steven Salop and Fiona Scott Morton, 'Five Principles for Vertical Merger Enforcement Policy' (2019) 33 Antitrust 12, 17. See Petit (n 1285) 199 ('merger assessment could also be strengthened, to limit platform's opportunities to vertically integrate into products sold by competing suppliers').

impact will be limited, as platforms' vertical integration often happens through internal rather than external expansion.

Further, while stricter scrutiny of (vertical) mergers may spur VC investment and innovation in the startup sphere, it could also have a negative impact on the startup ecosystem. As many startup founders and VCs now consider acquisition rather than IPO their most likely liquidity event (or 'exit'), erecting roadblocks on this route may dampen entrepreneurial investment and innovation.[1409] In this sense, a DOJ official warned that we need to be careful about making it too difficult for startups to be acquired: 'If we remove one of the important "exit strategies" for entrepreneurs, we may unintentionally reduce incentives to invest in the first place.'[1410]

There are, however, good reasons to question this intuition. First of all, the transactions that commentators usually worry about, ie those by GAFAM firms, account for only a small share of all startup acquisitions.[1411] Accordingly, the incentive effect of more closely scrutinizing dominant platform acquisitions should be rather small. Moreover, economic research provides a more complex picture than simple intuition. Katz finds that a permissive merger policy may indeed increase innovation incentives by facilitating 'entry for buyout', though only weakly. On the other hand, a permissive merger policy can also lower entrants' innovation incentives either because marginal product improvements reduce merger gains or by facilitating 'incumbency for buyout'.[1412] Other research shows that the prospect of acquisition suppresses the novelty of innovation as the entrant seeks to maximize its value to the incumbent.[1413]

Finally, the necessity of blocking/conditioning vertical mergers depends not only on the possibility and ubiquity of post-merger exclusionary conduct, but also on other rules to remedy such conduct (under competition law and beyond). If effective rules exist to police intra-platform exclusion, this weakens the case for proactive enforcement against vertical mergers (which can produce efficiencies). Before passing final judgment, we must therefore examine non-discrimination rules.

1409 Daniel Sokol, 'Vertical Mergers and Entrepreneurial Exit' (2018) 70 Florida Law Review 1357.

1410 Andrew Finch, 'Concentrating on Competition: An Antitrust Perspective on Platforms and Industry Consolidation' (Capitol Forum's Fifth Annual Tech, Media & Telecom Competition Conference, Washington, DC, 14 December 2018), adding:

> And it's important to remember in this regard that a start-up's success as an independent firm may not be inevitable. Entrepreneurs often can't take their creations to market successfully on their own, and may not even be interested in running a company long-term. Acquisitions enable firms with the necessary capital and skill set to bring innovative products and services to consumers that might not have reached them otherwise.

1411 Ben Evans, 'When Big Tech Buys Small Tech' (*Benedict Evans*, 12 November 2021) <https://www.ben-evans.com/benedictevans/2021/11/12/when-big-tech-buys-small-tech> ('Selling to those five companies was 4% of decent-sized exits'). Evans relies on data from FTC, 'Non-HSR Reported Acquisitions by Select Technology Platforms, 2010–2019' (n 1336).

1412 Katz (n 1392) ('incumbency for buyout' implies that incumbent invests in strengthening its competitive position solely to induce the entrant to merge on more favourable terms). For more intuition, see Lemley and McCreary (n 1346) 59 ('we doubt that making incumbent acquisitions more difficult will dampen VC investment to a concerning degree').

1413 Steven Callander and Niko Matouschek, 'The Novelty of Innovation: Competition, Disruption, and Antitrust Policy' (2022) 68 Management Science 37.

13.1.3 Conclusion

In the platform economy, the dividing line between horizontal and vertical mergers is blurry. One can refer to most of these mergers as conglomerate, but this terminology does not clarify matters much, given that conglomerate concerns too are either more horizontal (relating to *potential* competition) or more vertical (relating to complements). In the case of online platforms, the line can also shift over time, given that suppliers of complements are often best placed to challenge the platform in the future.

Whatever the type of merger, the primary concern is the same, namely, that intense acquisition activity by online platforms impedes innovation. Killer acquisitions are likely rare, but the idea of a 'kill zone' finds more empirical support. In addition, vertical acquisitions can give the platform an incentive to foreclose the target's competitors. Competition authorities have so far been erring on the side of false negatives rather than on the side of false positives. Therefore, increased intervention is warranted (although it is also important not to overcorrect for past mistakes).

Intervention can be spurred in various ways. Firstly, one could increase authorities' jurisdiction over startup acquisitions by introducing transaction value in addition to turnover thresholds. Some Member States have done so, but the EC chose to expand its referral mechanism instead. In concert with the DMA's information obligation, the most important acquisitions are now likely to make it up to the EC. Secondly, and more importantly, one could focus on the substantive SIEC test. It is certainly a good idea to ensure that theories of harm reflect the competitive reality of platforms more closely, eg by looking at user spaces rather than strictly delineated product markets. More fundamentally, one can intervene in the way an SIEC is proven. A good case can be made for a targeted shift of both the burden and standard of proof.

13.2 Non-Discrimination

Vertical integration changes a firm's incentives and thereby opens the door for discrimination – a dynamic that is prevalent in the telecom industry. Many firms started by owning the infrastructure (upstream) that allows for the conduit of content of other firms (downstream): ISPs offer the conduit for online content, while cable television providers offer the conduit for programming. However, telecom firms have shown a tendency to integrate vertically, meaning they also start producing the downstream content itself (the Comcast–NBCU and AT&T–TW mergers are two prominent examples). Once a firm provides both conduit and content, it may have an incentive to favour its own content, or in other words, to discriminate against the content of competing providers. Of course, the competitive harm of such discrimination will depend on the market power of the discriminating firm; if there are enough other ways to get content to consumers, being foreclosed from one conduit will not significantly hamper a firm's ability to compete. Moreover, discrimination can take various forms, from the more obvious (flatly refusing to carry the content of competitors) to the more subtle (hindering consumers' access to competitors' content, eg by slowing it down or making it difficult to find).

A similar process of vertical integration has been taking place in digital markets.[1414] Increasingly, platforms provide not only the online infrastructure (eg an app store, online marketplace or search engine), but also the products distributed through that infrastructure (eg apps, goods or more specialized search services). This can give the platforms an *incentive* to exclude, through discriminatory conduct, downstream competitors.[1415] If platforms also have that *ability*, on account of their dominance, such exclusion may result in anticompetitive *effects*.[1416] Then again, discrimination does not inevitably result in anticompetitive effects, and may even be accompanied by efficiencies. Competition law, in particular through the various forms of leveraging, already has rules in place to tackle anticompetitive discrimination. The question is therefore whether adding an extra *ex ante* rule is desirable.

The following subsections discuss how discrimination has been regulated *ex ante* in the telecom sector, and whether and how it can inspire modern platform regulation. The regulation of discrimination generally involves some kind of separation between conduit (upstream) and content (downstream), and such separation can be mandated either behaviourally or structurally. Below, both forms of regulatory intervention are assessed and weighed against each other.

13.2.1 Non-Discrimination Rules and Remedies

Non-discrimination rules have formed an essential part of telecom regulation for decades. In the EU, the telecom sector was progressively liberalized during the 1990s.[1417] Member States were obliged to abolish exclusive or special rights for the provision of telecom services, which were generally provided by former state monopolies, and the telecom network was opened up to entrants who could compete with the incumbent in providing those services.[1418] In this situation, the incumbent would regularly end up both providing network access to entrants (upstream) and competing with them in offering services to end users (downstream). To ensure effective competition, Member States had to 'ensure that vertically integrated public undertakings which provide electronic communications networks and which are in a dominant position do not discriminate in favour of their own activities'.[1419]

1414 See Section 2.2.2.

1415 See Section 5.2.2.

1416 See Sections 4.1.2 on market power and 5.2.3 on effects.

1417 Liberalization proceeded through a series of 'telecom packages', starting around 1990 and achieving liberalization by the 2000s. The current regulatory framework was adopted in 2002, updated in 2009, and recast in 2018, see Directive 2018/1972.

1418 Commission Directive 90/388/EEC on competition in the markets for telecommunications services [1990] OJ L192/10.

1419 Commission Directive 2002/77/EC on competition in the markets for electronic communications, networks and services [2002] OJ L249/21, art 3; see also Directive 2002/19/EC of the European Parliament

More recently, the policy of net neutrality expanded non-discrimination obligations from the telecom network itself to the internet traffic passing through the network.[1420] Once more, the concern – at least in part – is vertical integration and the incentives that come with it: ISPs could be tempted to discriminate against online services that compete with their own downstream offering. They could, for example, slow down the service of YouTube and Netflix to draw users to their own video service.[1421] Such conduct is prohibited by the Net Neutrality Regulation:

> Providers of internet access services shall treat all traffic equally, when providing internet access services, without discrimination, restriction or interference, and irrespective of the sender and receiver, the content accessed or distributed, the applications or services used or provided, or the terminal equipment used.[1422]

A net neutrality policy was also adopted in the US,[1423] but then abandoned by the next administration.[1424] However, the US also has a longer history of non-discrimination in telecommunications. In the 1990s, the Congress was concerned with the 'bottleneck monopoly power' of cable television distributors: as they served as the conduit between content providers (programmers) and consumers while possessing market power in many geographical markets, they could essentially decide which content reached consumers.[1425] Moreover, many cable television distributors were vertically integrated and offered their own (affiliated) content, giving them an incentive to discriminate against competing (unaffiliated) content. Congress therefore adopted section 616 of the 1992 Cable Act, mandating the FCC to adopt regulations preventing cable television distributors from discriminating against unaffiliated content in distribution decisions, at least when such discrimination 'unreasonably restrain[s] the ability of an unaffiliated [provider] to compete fairly'.[1426] The FCC obliged and created a specific complaint mechanism for content providers believing they were subject to such discrimination.[1427] The regulatory intervention thus had two components: a substantive one (the prohibition of anticompetitive discrimination) and an

---

and of the Council on access to, and interconnection of, electronic communications networks and associated facilities [2002] OJ L108/7, art 10 (currently, see Directive 2018/1972, art 70).

1420 The term 'net neutrality' was coined by Wu, see Tim Wu, 'Network Neutrality, Broadband Discrimination' (2003) 2 Journal on Telecommunications & High Technology Law 141.

1421 The ACM has warned ISPs not to alter video traffic, see ACM, 'ACM warns telecom companies about net neutrality' (press release, 12 July 2016) <https://www.acm.nl/en/publications/publication/16037/ACM-warns-telecom-companies-about-net-neutrality>. This concern was also at the heart of the net neutrality condition imposed on the Comcast–NBCU merger, see DOJ, 'Justice Department allows Comcast–NBCU joint venture to proceed with conditions' (press release, 18 January 2018) <https://www.justice.gov/opa/pr/justice-department-allows-comcast-nbcu-joint-venture-proceed-conditions>.

1422 Regulation (EU) 2015/2120 of the European Parliament and of the Council laying down measures concerning open internet access [2015] OJ L310/1, art 3(3). There are, however, exceptions, most notably for zero rating (art 3(2)), reasonable traffic management (art 3(3)) and optimized services (art 3(5)).

1423 FCC, Order 15-24, Protecting and Promoting the Open Internet, 13 April 2015.

1424 FCC, Order 17-108, Restoring Internet Freedom Order, 4 January 2018.

1425 See *Comcast v FCC*, no 12-1337 (DC Cir, 28 May 2013) (Kavanaugh, concurring) 3.

1426 Cable Television Consumer Protection and Competition Act of 1992, s 616.

1427 47 CFR s 76.1302 Carriage agreement proceedings.

institutional one (the administrative rather than judicial procedure for aggrieved parties).

In the EU, lawmakers started addressing platform discrimination through the P2B Regulation. The instrument does not prohibit platforms from treating business users differently than their own downstream operations, but it does require them to include a description of such practices in their terms and conditions.[1428] The EC subsequently adopted guidelines clarifying the transparency obligation in case of discriminatory ranking.[1429] The underlying idea appears to be that obliging platforms to spell out discriminatory practices in their terms and conditions might make them think twice about adopting them in the first place. However, while transparency is valuable, its conditioning effects could be rather limited, especially in the presence of market power.

In addition, competition law cases pursued by the EC should deter the most harmful forms of discrimination. To facilitate those kinds of cases, the Crémer Report proposes shifting the burden of proof from the EC to the platform:

> In cases of vertically integrated dominant digital platforms in markets with particularly high barriers to entry, and where the platform serves as an intermediation infrastructure of particular relevance, we propose that … it should bear the burden of proving that self-preferencing has no long-run exclusionary effects on product markets.[1430]

Certainly, this reversal of the burden of proof would make discrimination cases easier for the EC. However, the platform's burden would be high or even impossible to meet, as it would have to prove a negative (the absence of effects). Alternatively, one could burden the platform with providing a justification at the beginning of a discrimination case. In the absence of a justification, the discrimination is considered abusive; if the platform can offer a justification, the burden of proving anticompetitive effects shifts to the EC. This burden-shifting framework could filter out cases of naked exclusion, although it may not significantly shorten the runtime of most investigations.[1431]

Rather than working with competition law presumptions, the DMA institutes a number of *ex ante* non-discrimination rules. For example, assuming gatekeeper designation of the respective firms, the DMA obliges Apple to give developers non-discriminatory access to its App Store.[1432] It must also give developers equal access to iOS software

1428 P2B Regulation, art 7. In France, the law on 'platform fairness' already imposed more limited transparency obligations, see Law no 2016-1321 for a Digital Republic [2016] JORF no 0235, art 49.

1429 'Commission Notice Guidelines on ranking transparency pursuant to Regulation (EU) 2019/1150' [2020] OJ C424/1.

1430 Crémer Report (n 1295) 66–67. In addition, it would be required that the platform perform a regulatory function (see the discussion of platforms as 'private regulators' in Section 10.1).

1431 To safeguard the rights of defence, the platform would have to be given more time to meet its burden of proof. And it is to be expected that platforms would be able, in most cases, to plead an at least prime facie plausible justification.

1432 DMA, art 6(4) and (12).

and hardware features.[1433] Amazon and Google can no longer discriminate in favour of their own goods and services in rankings.[1434] These cases closely track competition law enforcement by the EC.[1435] Thus, *ex post* remedies and *ex ante* rules impose non-discrimination in a substantively similar way, although the latter have the procedural advantage of speed.

Whether shifting the burden of proof or adopting non-discrimination rules, the intervention is behavioural. Even non-discrimination rules are not self-executing but require specification, monitoring and, in case of non-compliance, enforcement.[1436] At best, a non-discrimination remedy or rule can thus limit the occurrence of discrimination and shorten its duration. By contrast, structural separation could prevent discrimination altogether.

13.2.2 Non-Discrimination through Structural Separation

The most obvious solution in this category is inspired, once more, by telecom regulation.[1437] In 1982, the Bell Company entered into a consent decree with the DOJ, which determined that the telecom incumbent would be broken up into seven Regional Bell Operating Companies (RBOCs) and one long-distance company (AT&T).[1438] The RBOCs were local monopolists, while AT&T and its competitors provided the complementary infrastructure for long-distance phone calls. The consent decree prohibited RBOCs from entering the long-distance market in their regions – a so-called line of business restriction. The idea was that RBOCs, if so allowed, would have the incentive to leverage their monopoly power from the local to the long-distance market, thus foreclosing competition. They would have the power to do so: as long-distance carriers relied on RBOCs for local network access, the RBOCs could discriminate against those carriers in favour of their own long-distance operations.[1439] The line of business restrictions in the consent decree prevented the RBOCs from monopolizing the long-distance market and successfully fostered competition,[1440] after which the restrictions

1433 ibid, art 6(7).

1434 ibid, art 6(5). Amazon can also not rely on business-user data to decide which goods to start offering, see art 6(2).

1435 They follow the *Apple App Store*, *Apple Pay*, *Google Shopping* and *Amazon* cases (all discussed above, Part 2).

1436 All of the DMA's non-discrimination obligations discussed here are 'susceptible of being further specified' according to art 6 (the specification procedure is found in art 8).

1437 For a discussion of other structural separation regimes (in railroads, banking, television networks), see Lina Khan, 'The Separation of Platforms and Commerce' (2019) 119 Columbia Law Review 973, 1037–49.

1438 *United States v AT&T* 552 F Supp 131 (DDC 1982).

1439 The RBOCs would be able to do so as they set the 'originating fee' for long-distance phone calls. By increasing this fee to long-distance carriers (or by decreasing their own long-distance rates, after entry), RBOCs could 'squeeze' them out of the market. See Nicholas Economides, 'Telecommunications Regulation: An Introduction' in Richard Nelson, *The Limits of Market Organization* (Russel Sage Foundation 2005) 56–58.

1440 ibid; Kenneth Arrow, Dennis Carlton and Hal Sider, 'The Competitive Effects of Line-of-Business Restrictions in Telecommunications' (1995) 16 Managerial and Decision Economics 301 and Daniel Spulber, 'Deregulating Telecommunications' (1995) 12 Yale Journal of Regulation 25.

were eased by the 1996 Telecommunications Act.[1441] Note that the Bell regime constitutes one of two (or more) forms of structural separation: apart from fully prohibiting entry into distinct lines of business, one can also allow such entry but only through structurally separate affiliates.

The above description of the Bell regime focused on long-distance calls, but the RBOCs were also prohibited from entering into other markets, such as those for telephone equipment and information services. In *The Master Switch*, Wu argues that 'it is no coincidence that the period thereafter marked one of the greatest and longest booms in the history of information industries'.[1442] He therefore argues regulating communications industries through a 'Separations Principle', ie 'a salutary distance between differing functions in the information economy'.[1443] In practice, this would mean that those who develop information, those who own the network infrastructure on which it travels, and those who control the tools or venues of access must be kept apart from one another. The goal is to prevent a situation 'where a single firm takes ownership of a fully integrated information monopoly that crosses multiple markets'.[1444]

Wu was focused on media markets, where information is the primary commodity. According to his Separations Principle, a combination of a media company with an ISP would be particularly problematic. While such concerns remain relevant today, vertical integration by online platforms – and the consequent potential for exclusion – has taken centre stage. Khan has specified Wu's Separation Principle for the platform economy.[1445] She seeks to remedy the problem that 'a platform's involvement across multiple related lines of business can give rise to conflicts of interest by creating circumstances in which a platform has an incentive to privilege its own business and disadvantage other companies'.[1446] Rather than policing these conflicts of interest, Khan wants to prevent them in the first place by 'banning a dominant firm from entering any market that it already serves as a platform – in other words, from competing directly with the businesses that depend on it.'[1447]

While the structural separation of platforms appears – and *is* – drastic, a version of it has been adopted in India, which prohibits foreign online retailers from selling products through vendors they hold an equity stake in. As a result, Amazon had to pull its own products from its Marketplace.[1448]

1441 Telecommunications Act of 1996, 110 Stat 56, s 271.

1442 Tim Wu, *The Master Switch: The Rise and Fall of Information Empires* (Vintage 2011) 313.

1443 ibid 304 (and 311–13 for precedents).

1444 ibid 305.

1445 Lina Khan, 'Amazon's Antitrust Paradox' (2017) 126 Yale Law Journal 710, 793–97; Lina Khan, 'Sources of Tech Platform Power' (2018) 2 Georgetown Law Technology Review 325, 332–33; Khan, 'The Separation of Platforms and Commerce' (n 1437).

1446 Khan, 'Amazon's Antitrust Paradox' (n 1445) 793.

1447 ibid.

1448 James Vincent, 'Amazon and Walmart Hit Hard After New e-Commerce Rules in India Restrict Sales' (*The Verge*, 1 February 2019) <https://www.theverge.com/2019/2/1/18206538/>.

To devise their own policy, policymakers can learn from the OECD recommendation on structural separation in regulated industries. The recommendation holds that there is room for such intervention when a firm operates simultaneously in a non-competitive activity and a complementary competitive activity. Even then, however, the benefits and costs must be weighed against those of behavioural measures:

> The principal benefits of vertical separation [are that] separation limits the need for regulation that is difficult and costly to devise and implement, and may be only partly effective; it improves information; and it eliminates the risk of cross-subsidies by the incumbent from its non-competitive to its competitive segments. Conversely, separation may involve the loss of (potentially very significant) cost economies that arise from integration. Moreover, … separation may – but does not *necessarily* – have a negative impact on incentives to invest for network owners and operators.[1449]

In the EU, structural separation has been imposed in various utility sectors, but there has been no appetite for such intervention in platform markets.[1450] Cognisant of previous instances of structural separation, the Crémer Report holds that it is not clear that 'the balance of costs and benefits argues for some version of unbundling of vertically integrated platforms'.[1451] The European Parliament does occasionally call on the EC 'to consider proposals aimed at unbundling search engines from other commercial services'.[1452]

In the US, Senator Warren advocated for 'legislation that requires large tech platforms to be designated as "Platform Utilities" and broken apart from any participant on that platform'.[1453] They would also be required to meet a standard of fair, reasonable, and nondiscriminatory dealing with users.[1454] The consequences of putting this proposal into practice cannot be overstated: Amazon Marketplace would be split from Amazon Basics (as in India), Google Search from its vertical search services, and the App Store from Apple's apps.

1449 OECD, 'Structural Separation in Regulated Industries: Implementing the OECD Recommendation' (n 1301) 9–10.

1450 Structural separation has been implemented in rail and energy networks, for example, but not in telecommunications, see ibid. Note that structural separation can also be attained through competition law, see eg *Deutsche Post* (Case COMP/35.141) Commission Decision [2001] OJ L125/27, paras 18–22.

1451 Crémer Report (n 1295) 67–68 (the Report is short on reasons, noting only that 'platforms differ [from traditional infrastructure] as aspects of infrastructure provisions and service provision may be mixed').

1452 EP, 'Supporting consumer rights in the digital single market' (Resolution) 2014/2973(RSP), para 15 (quote); EP, 'On the Annual Report on Competition Policy' (Report) A8-0049/2018, para 42 ('without a full-blown structural separation between the company's general and specialised search services, an auction-based approach might not deliver equal treatment').

1453 Elizabeth Warren, 'Here's How We Can Break Up Big Tech' (*Medium*, 8 March 2019) <https://medium.com/@teamwarren/heres-how-we-can-break-up-big-tech-9ad9e0da324c> (defining platform utilities as firms with an annual global revenue ≥$25 billion that offer to the public an online marketplace, an exchange, or a platform for connecting third parties).

1454 ibid. Smaller platforms (with annual global revenue between $90 million and $25 billion) would also have to abide by this standard, but would not be required to structurally separate. Violating these requirements would result in a fine of 5% of annual revenue.

Warren's proposal was immediately met with criticism that is not without merit. Thompson takes a nuanced view. On the one hand, he does recognize the underlying problem, noting for example that 'Apple has quite clearly leveraged the fact it owns the platform to compete with Spotify'.[1455] On the other hand, he seriously worries about the implications for consumers: Would iPhones be shipped without apps at all, given that iOS/the App Store would have to be separated from Apple's app business? An independent iOS/App Store could, of course, preinstall apps from independent app companies, but this would probably decrease security/privacy as well as the user-friendly nature of the ecosystem, which are some of Apple's biggest selling points.[1456] Hovenkamp, for his part, worries about the effects on consumer prices.[1457] Because, while vertical integration may lead to the exclusion of downstream competitors, it can also lead to lower prices and thus increased competitive pressure on those competitors.[1458] Amazon, for example, cut prices at Whole Foods after acquiring the grocery chain,[1459] while its Amazon Basics batteries perform as well as those of competing brands at a fraction of the price.[1460] Finally, as under vertical merger control, the concern for restricting acquisition as an exit strategy applies.[1461] Acquisition has become such a dominant exit strategy that startups may not even have a stand-alone path to profitability; rather, their utility can only be truly realized by integration into the ecosystem of one of the established platforms. A separation regime would prevent such vertical acquisitions, and therefore has the potential to prevent the consumer-friendly integration of complementary products in addition to dampening investment in startups.[1462] However, any resulting decrease in innovation would have to be weighed against an increase in innovation from startups that start bringing their products to market rather than being bought out.

1455 Ben Thompson, 'Where Warren's Wrong' (*Stratechery*, 12 March 2019) <https://stratechery.com/2019/where-warrens-wrong/>.

1456 Apple would still be able to control the installation of apps through the App Store approval process, given that Warren only appears to propose a separation between the App Store/apps, not between iOS/the App Store (contrary to what Thompson suggests)

1457 Herbert Hovenkamp, 'The Warren Campaign's Antitrust Proposals' (*The Regulatory Review*, 25 March 2019) <https://www.theregreview.org/2019/03/25/hovenkamp-warren-campaigns-antitrust-proposals/>.

1458 These lower prices are explained by (i) the elimination of double marginalization: since Amazon does not have to pay its own Marketplace commission fees, there is effectively no retail/distribution markup (although this can be seen, in itself, as an unfair competitive advantage); and (ii) private labels' lack of price premiums that result from trademarks or entrenched brands.

1459 Jennifer Kaplan and Matthew Boyle, 'Amazon Cuts Whole Foods Prices as Much as 43% on First Day' (*Bloomberg*, 28 August 2017) <https://www.bloomberg.com/news/articles/2017-08-28/amazon-cuts-prices-at-whole-foods-as-much-as-50-on-first-day>; Craig Giammona, 'Amazon's Whole Foods Price Cuts Brought 25% Jump in Shoppers' (*Bloomberg*, 11 September 2017) <https://www.bloomberg.com/news/articles/2017-09-11/amazon-s-whole-foods-price-cuts-brought-25-jump-in-customers>.

1460 Amy Livingston, 'Best Batteries' (*consumersearch*, 17 July 2017) <https://www.consumersearch.com/batteries>.

1461 See Section 13.1.2.

1462 A handful of reactions by VCs to Warren's proposal anecdotally support the investment effect, see Jonathan Shieber, 'Venture Investors and Startup Execs Say They Don't Need Elizabeth Warren to Defend Them from Big Tech' (*TechCrunch*, 8 March 2019) <https://techcrunch.com/2019/03/08/venture-investors-and-startup-execs-say-they-dont-need-elizabeth-warren-to-defend-them-from-big-tech/> ('If big companies like Google, Facebook, and Amazon are prevented from acquiring startups, that actually reduces competition. The reason is that if there is less M&A due to legal uncertainty, there is a reduced incentive for angels & VCs to fund those startups in the first place.').

13.2.3 Conclusion

The instances of platforms entering markets they serve and then using their digital infrastructure to exclude competitors are more than numerous enough to cause legitimate concern. While specific cases have shown how discrimination *can* lead to anticompetitive foreclosure, it is difficult to say *generally* whether its anti- or procompetitive effects dominate. This alone is reason enough to reject a structural separation regime, especially as such a regime prevents not only discrimination but also vertical integration as such. However, while there are potential efficiencies from vertical integration, these are certainly not likely to win out in most cases involving dominant platforms. Therefore, the argument for a behavioural rule is stronger: it can preserve efficiencies while also providing a basis for intervention whenever the anticompetitive effects take the upper hand. The question is which form this rule should take. Competition law precedent, confirmed by European courts, amounts to something of a rule in itself. It may even be opportune to reverse the burden of proof when crystallizing this rule, as platforms are in the best position to point out the (procompetitive) effects of their conduct. Even a more structured competition law rule, however, is enforced on an *ex post* basis, which means its implementation can take years. This is especially problematic when the conduct is systematic, and the harm potentially large and difficult to remedy (eg because markets have tipped). Such arguments support the adoption of a targeted *ex ante* rule (or set of rules).

13.3 Portability and Interoperability

Even when a competitor with a superior platform enters the market, its odds of success are rather slim. The reason is that users can be locked into the incumbent platform ecosystem, inter alia due to network effects.[1463] Users would therefore not easily make the switch to the superior entrant (eg one more protective of user privacy) because all of their friends are already on Facebook. Users could, in theory, all make the switch at the same time, but a collective action problem prevents them from doing so.[1464] This is why the #DeleteFacebook movement following the Cambridge Analytica scandal quickly ran out of steam.[1465] There is a related, equally important impediment to switching from one platform to another: all of a user's data is siloed on that platform, and the user cannot take it anywhere else. Moving social networks thus means losing all your pictures, posts, likes, conversations, etc. And an Uber driver switching to Lyft loses their hard-earned reputation score – the standard for trust online. Taken together, network effects and data centralization thus create high switching costs for users, cementing the market power of the incumbent platforms, which in turn increases the risk that platforms will abuse it.

1463 See Sections 2.2.2 and 4.1.

1464 Garth Saloner, Andrea Shepard and Joel Podolny, *Strategic Management* (Wiley 2001) 313.

1465 See Tiffany Hsu, 'For Many Facebook Users, a "Last Straw" That Led Them to Quit' (*NYT*, 21 March 2018) <https://www.nytimes.com/2018/03/21/technology/users-abandon-facebook.html>.

Two related interventions can decrease user lock-in, namely, data portability and interoperability. Simply put, data portability means that users can take their data with them when switching platforms. Interoperability comes in two forms.[1466] First, 'data interoperability' constitutes a stronger form of portability, meaning that users can *directly* port their data from one platform to the other (as opposed to separately downloading and then uploading it, for example). Second, 'protocol interoperability' (or simply 'interoperability') ensures the access of suppliers (in particular developers) to the platform's functionalities (generally through APIs). This section starts by discussing data portability and data interoperability, and then moves on to protocol interoperability.

13.3.1 Data Portability and Data Interoperability

User lock-in used to impede competition in the telephone industry. In the past, when users wanted to switch telecom providers, they could not keep their old number but would be given a new one. The cost of switching prevented many consumers from doing so and thus insulated carriers from a healthy dose of competition. This changed when regulators in the EU and US introduced number portability, ie the right to retain your phone number when switching providers.[1467] This policy change spurred greater competition between telecom providers, which led to a decrease in prices and an increase in consumer welfare.[1468]

While the data users have ceded to platforms is greater than the eight or ten digits of a phone number, one could extend the principle of portability to the digital economy. The EU first did so by enshrining a right to data portability in the GDPR.[1469] It then strengthened that right in the DMA:

> The gatekeeper shall provide end users and third parties authorised by an end user, at their request and free of charge, with effective portability of data provided by the end user or generated through the activity of the end user in the context of the use of the relevant core platform service, including by providing, free of charge, tools to facilitate the effective

1466 See Crémer Report (n 1295) 83–85.

1467 In the EU, see Directive 2018/1972, recitals 278–81, art 106 and Annex VI, Part C (and before that, Directive 2002/22/EC of the European Parliament and of the Council on universal service and users' rights relating to electronic communications networks and services [2002] OJ L108/51, art 30). In the US, see Telecommunications Act of 1996, s 251(b)(2) (and further FCC, 'Porting: Keeping Your Phone Number When You Change Providers' <https://www.fcc.gov/consumers/guides/porting-keeping-your-phone-number-when-you-change-providers>).

1468 Daegon Cho, Pedro Ferreira and Rahul Telang, 'The Impact of Mobile Number Portability on Price, Competition and Consumer Welfare' (2016) <https://ssrn.com/abstract=2265104>.

1469 Regulation (EU) 2016/679 of the European Parliament and of the Council on the protection of natural persons with regard to the processing of personal data and on the free movement of such data [2016] OJ L119/1, art 20(1) ('The data subject shall have the right to receive the personal data concerning him or her, which he or she has provided to a controller, in a structured, commonly used and machine-readable format and have the right to transmit those data to another controller without hindrance from the controller to which the personal data have been provided'). For a discussion, see Paul De Hert et al, 'The Right to Data Portability in the GDPR: Towards User-Centric Interoperability of Digital Services' (2018) 34 CLSR 193.

> exercise of such data portability, and including by the provision of continuous and real-time access to such data.[1470]

Data portability comes with challenges. Firstly, there is a question of scope: To which data does the right apply? A popular classification distinguishes between volunteered, observed and inferred data: volunteered data is intentionally contributed by the user (eg name, email address, posts and photos); observed data is obtained automatically from a user's activity (eg click, location and search history); inferred data is derived from volunteered and observed data (eg music taste, interests, likeliness to buy certain products).[1471] Both the GDPR and the DMA seem to cover only volunteered and observed data.[1472]

A greater difficulty relates to its effective implementation. Some forms of portability should pose no significant difficulty. For example, it should be relatively easy to download your Apple Music playlists and port them to Spotify. However, it is much more difficult to see how you could download all your Facebook data and use this huge file as input for a competing social network. Firstly, there is a practical impediment to doing so: if users still face high costs (effort) in porting their data from one platform to another, we are back at square one. Secondly, there is a technical problem: porting data from one platform to another requires common standards, and such standards either do not exist or are only nascent.[1473]

The data portability provisions engage with this implementation difficulty. The GDPR mandates that 'the data subject shall have the right to have the personal data transmitted *directly* from one controller to another, *where technically feasible*'.[1474] The DMA goes a step further and assumes the technical feasibility of continuous and real-time access. Making that assumption a reality requires APIs that are externally accessible not only by the user but also by competing services authorized by the user. Such strong portability (or data interoperability) could effectively lower the cost of switching but requires standards.[1475] The question is who should be in charge of establishing them. The Data Protection Working Party encourages industry stakeholders and trade associations to work together on standards for data interoperability, which appears prudent given the complexity of the undertaking.[1476]

1470 DMA, art 6(9).

1471 Crémer Report (n 1295) 24–25.

1472 On the GDPR, see Article 29 Data Protection Working Party, 'Right to data portability' (Guidelines, 2016) 9–11.

1473 Helena Ursic, 'Unfolding the New-Born Right to Data Portability: Four Gateways to Data Subject Control' (2018) 15 Scripted 42, 67–68 ('The success of data portability as a right will be correlated with the success of standardisation initiatives'); Oscar Borgogno and Giuseppe Colangelo, 'Data Sharing and Interoperability: Fostering Innovation and Competition Through APIs' (2019) 35 CLSR 1, 13–15.

1474 Regulation 2016/679, art 20(2) (emphasis added). However, see also recital 68 ('The data subject's right to transmit or receive personal data concerning him or her should not create an obligation for the controllers to adopt or maintain processing systems which are technically compatible.').

1475 On this topic, see extensively Michal Gal and Daniel Rubinfeld, 'Data Standardization' (2019) 94 New York University Law Review 737.

1476 Article 29 Data Protection Working Party (n 1472) 17–18.

Industry cooperation has already commenced. Facebook is teaming up with Apple, Google, Microsoft and Twitter on the 'Data Transfer Project' – a project with the ambition to create 'an open-source, service-to-service data portability platform so that all individuals across the web could easily move their data between online service providers whenever they want'.[1477] The plan is to build a common framework that can connect any two online service providers, enabling seamless, direct, and user-initiated data portability between the two platforms. A first achievement consisted in enabling data interoperability between Facebook and Google Photos, allowing for direct transfer between the two services.[1478] Still, it remains to be seen whether the Data Transfer Project is a good faith push for portability or an effort by incumbents to delay or capture the process.[1479]

The benefits of effective portability can be substantial. A successful example is offered by the Payment Services Directive 2 (PSD 2). One of its objectives is to level the playing field between financial services (eg incumbent banks and fintech entrants), which it sought to achieve in part through banking data interoperability.[1480] Among others, third-party access to such data would allow the creation of innovative money management, lending and payment services. The European Banking Authority published a series of guidelines on standards, APIs, security, etc,[1481] while Member States were tasked with transposing the Directive into national law.[1482] The UK Open Banking initiative has been lauded as particularly successful.[1483]

Finally, in addition to technical implementation questions and potential benefits, there are potential risks. First, there are privacy and security risks when users initiate data transfer. Remember that the Cambridge Analytica affair originated from an app that Facebook users authorized to access their data.[1484] And 'personal data' cannot be interpreted too narrowly for portability to be effective, which means it necessarily

1477 See <https://datatransferproject.dev/> and the white paper 'Data Transfer Project Overview and Fundamentals' uploaded there. Facebook appears to be the driving force behind the project, see Mark Zuckerberg, 'Four Ideas to Regulate the Internet' (*Facebook Newsroom*, 30 March 2019) <https://newsroom.fb.com/news/2019/03/four-ideas-regulate-internet/> and Erin Egan, 'Data Portability and Privacy. Charting a Way Forward' (Facebook White Paper) 2019.

1478 William Morland, 'Data Transfer Project: Enabling Portability of Photos and Videos Between Services' (*Facebook Engineering*, 2 December 2019) <https://engineering.fb.com/2019/12/02/security/data-transfer-project/>.

1479 The dedicated website does not inspire confidence. It appears barely updated since its launch in 2018 (at the time of writing, the 'updates' tab directs you to a white webpage). A GitHub page shows more recent activity but no significant progress either.

1480 Directive (EU) 2015/2366 of the European Parliament and of the Council of 25 November 2015 on payment services in the internal market [2015] OJ L337/35, art 66ff.

1481 For an overview, see <https://eba.europa.eu/regulation-and-policy/payment-services-and-electronic-money>.

1482 For an overview, see <https://eur-lex.europa.eu/legal-content/EN/NIM/?uri=CELEX:32015L2366>.

1483 See <https://www.openbanking.org.uk/>. On its success and outstanding challenges, see Nadja Bennett, 'Charting the Rise of Open Banking Payments' (*TrueLayer blog*, 3 November 2022) <https://truelayer.com/blog/product/charting-the-rise-of-open-banking-payments/>. Note that the UK regime builds not only on PSD 2 but also on the CMA's work in this area, see CMA, 'Retail Banking Market Investigation' (Order) 2017.

1484 However, due to Facebook's negligence, the app could also access the app user's friends' data, which greatly exacerbated the breach.

includes data on third parties with whom the user interacted, making the privacy question more acute.[1485] Second, the GDPR applies to all processing of personal data, not only that by large players.[1486] It thus comes with the risk of benefitting incumbents by entrenching their market power, inter alia due to economies of scale in dealing with compliance.[1487] The DMA does better in this regard, by restricting its strengthened data portability right to the incumbents. Third, there is concern that data portability can dampen incentives to invest, thus stymying innovation.[1488] Of course, such concern only tells half of the story: while it is true that the incentives of incumbents – which have to share certain data they collected – may decrease, the incentives of entrants – who now have a greater chance of success – should increase.[1489]

13.3.2 Protocol Interoperability

Protocol interoperability (as opposed to data interoperability) ensures suppliers' – in particular developers' – access to the platform's functionalities (through APIs). Protocol interoperability too comes in different forms.[1490] The first form, 'regular' protocol operability, ensures access so that developers can provide *complements* to the platform. Consider, for example, the *Microsoft I* case, in which Sun Microsystems sought interoperability with Windows OS in order to provide complementary work group server OSs.[1491] An interoperability obligation of this sort thus prevents platforms from discriminating against suppliers. The second form, 'full' protocol interoperability, ensures that two or more *substitute* services can work together. It could, for example, allow users with different messaging apps to communicate across services. This sort of interoperability thus promotes contestability.

Both forms of interoperability have been implemented in the telecom sector. In both the EU[1492] and the US,[1493] sector-specific regulation imposes interconnection obligations so that network operators cannot refuse to connect their network to that of competitors. In the EU, such interconnection allows for cross-border service and even the gradual duplication (and improvement) of facilities: entrants can start providing service to a more limited area based on their own facilities while interconnection ensures wider

1485 See Article 29 Data Protection Working Party (n 1472) 9 (recommending against interpreting 'personal data' too narrowly).

1486 This is only natural given that the GDPR takes a rights-based rather than a market failure perspective.

1487 See Section 12.

1488 Jian Jia, Ginger Jin and Liad Wagman, 'The Short-Run Effects of GDPR on Technology Venture Investment' (*Vox – CEPR Policy Portal*, 7 January 2019) <https://voxeu.org/article/short-run-effects-gdpr-technology-venture-investment> (at best, this study examines the impact of GDPR *as a whole* – it remains unclear which role the data portability obligation plays).

1489 One could still argue that even these entrants have less of an incentive to invest, because – if they ever become the incumbent – they will have to abide by data portability obligations.

1490 Crémer Report (n 1295) 83–85.

1491 See Section 7.

1492 Directive 2018/1972, arts 59–61 (before, see Directive 2002/19/EC).

1493 Telecommunications Act of 1996, s 251(a)(1) ('Each telecommunications carrier has the duty to interconnect directly or indirectly with the facilities and equipment of other telecommunications carriers') and s 251(c)(2) (specifically targeted at incumbent local exchange carriers).

coverage. The importance of interconnection cannot be overstated: without it, subscribers to different telecom providers would not even be able to communicate with each other. In the US, interconnection was particularly important given the Bell consent decree. Remember that after the breakup, RBOCs had local monopolies while AT&T provided long-distance service.[1494] To spur competition in the long-distance market, RBOCs had to interconnect with competitors of AT&T.[1495] Even before the consent decree was in place, interconnection between networks had been imposed through a combination of sector-specific regulation and competition law (in particular, the essential facilities doctrine).[1496]

Interconnection obligations concerned not only competing networks but also complements. On this point, the *Hush-A-Phone* case is instructive.[1497] In the first half of the 20th century, Hush-A-Phone sold 'a cup-like device of the same name, which snaps on to a telephone instrument and makes for privacy of conversation [and] office quiet'.[1498] However, AT&T prohibited the connection of such devices to its network because it allegedly impaired telephone service. The FCC agreed: after all, when using a Hush-A-Phone, there could be a loss of intelligibility due to the decreased volume. The circuit court rejected this absurd reasoning, especially given that the alternative offered by the FCC was cupping your own hand around the receiver, which results in a similar sound distortion. The path was thus cleared to attach *mechanical* complements to the telephone network. The FCC's subsequent *Carterfone* decision further cleared the path for *electrical* complements.[1499]

These telecom precedents highlight the difference between the two forms of interoperability. Regular protocol interoperability (eg between a telephone network and add-ons) prevents an incumbent in one market from leveraging its market power to a complementary market. It solves an issue of *intra-platform* competition. In many if not most cases, regular protocol interoperability equates to a behavioural prohibition of discrimination. The *Apple Pay* case illustrates this dynamic.[1500] The EC is investigating how Apple denies wallet apps access to iOS's NFC functionality, thus preventing them

---

1494 See Section 13.2.2.

1495 *United States v AT&T* (n 1438) 225–26 ('whenever, as permitted by the decree, a separated BOC fails to offer exchange access to an interexchange carrier that is equal in type and quality to that provided for the interexchange traffic of AT&T, the tariffs filed for such less-than-equal access shall reflect the lesser cost, if any, of such access as compared to the exchange access provided AT&T'). See further Philip Weiser, 'Regulating Interoperability: Lessons from *AT&T*, *Microsoft*, and Beyond' (2009) 76 Antitrust Law Journal 271, 274–79.

1496 See the long-running *MCI Communications v AT&T* 708 F2d 1081 (7th Cir 1983), which intersected with the FCC interconnection regime established by its Specialized Common Carriers decision ('hardly a model of clarity', according to judgment in *MCI*). For a discussion, see Spencer Weber Waller, 'The "New" Law of Monopolization: An Examination of *MCI Communications Corp. v American Telephone & Telegraph Co*' (1983) 32 DePaul Law Review 595, 610–13.

1497 *Hush-A-Phone v United States*, 238 F2d 266 (DC Cir 1956). For a discussion, see Wu, *The Master Switch: The Rise and Fall of Information Empires* (n 1442) 101–14.

1498 *Hush-A-Phone v United States* (n 1497) 267. While perhaps difficult to imagine today, more than 125,000 Hush-A-Phones went into use between 1921 and the date of the judgment.

1499 *Carterfone v AT&T* 13 FCC2d 420 (1968).

1500 As does the parental control app saga, see Section 7.3.

from offering mobile payment services on par with Apple Pay, which uses NFC.[1501] One can assess this case both from a non-discrimination and an interoperability perspective: to stop discriminating against third-party wallet apps, Apple would have to grant those competitors of Apple Pay interoperability with iOS's NFC functionality.

By contrast, full protocol interoperability (eg between different telephone networks) promotes entry, given that smaller players can benefit from interconnection with larger players while they build their network. It solves an issue of *inter-platform* competition. For example, it could allow users to find friends, publish posts and send messages across different social networks. This facilitates multihoming by users, from which social networks could benefit while they build their user base, perhaps up to the point that they displace the incumbent network. Full interoperability thus decreases lock-in, thereby increasing the contestability of platform markets.

The regular and full versions of protocol interoperability differ not only as to their goals, but also as to their methods. Both rely on access to APIs, either by suppliers of complements or by providers of substitutes, but full interoperability requires a much greater level of standardization. Such standardization is not impossible: Facebook, for example, is making its various properties (Facebook, Instagram, WhatsApp) interoperable.[1502] But it took years just to realize cross-app messaging – and this is an internal integration; interoperability with external apps adds difficulty.[1503] Less far-reaching forms of interoperability (eg cross-network access to friends and cross-posting) are easier: these features have long been available.

As in the telecom sector, platform interoperability is being pursued through both competition law and *ex ante* regulation. One option is the refusal to supply doctrine, as in *Microsoft I*.[1504] The *Apple Pay* investigation may provide a contemporary interpretation of its principles, although justification questions linger.[1505] But the most interesting intervention comes from the other side of the Atlantic, where the FTC is suing Facebook for implementing an 'open early, closed late' strategy.[1506] Initially, Facebook opened up its platform to developers to spur its growth. Of particular value was the 'Find Friends' API, which allowed developers of third-party apps to enable

---

1501 EC, 'Commission sends Statement of Objections to Apple over practices regarding Apple Pay' (press release, 2 May 2022) IP/22/2764.

1502 Mike Isaac, 'Zuckerberg Plans to Integrate WhatsApp, Instagram and Facebook Messenger' (*NYT*, 25 January 2019) <https://www.nytimes.com/2019/01/25/technology/facebook-instagram-whatsapp-messenger.html>.

1503 That difficulty does not prevent firms from building those protocols. See eg Paul Sawers, 'Inside Matrix, the Protocol That Might Finally Make Messaging Apps Interoperable' (*TechCrunch*, 30 December 2022) <https://techcrunch.com/2022/12/30/inside-matrix-the-protocol-that-might-finally-make-messaging-apps-interoperable>.

1504 Merger decisions have included commitments on API access as well, see, inter alia, *Google/Fitbit* (n 1407) and *Meta/Kustomer* (n 1371).

1505 See Section 10.5.

1506 *FTC v Facebook*, no 1:20-cv-03590-JEB (DDC, 19 August 2021) (Amended Complaint), Section B. This complaint survived the motion-to-dismiss stage; a previous one did not due to unclarity about the market power metrics and methods used.

users to find their Facebook friends who also used the third-party app and to invite those friends that did not yet. Later, when some third-party apps appeared to present a nascent competitive threat to Facebook, it closed the APIs on which they relied.[1507] Promising apps that fell victim to the change in policy include Path, Circle and Vine.

While the *Microsoft I* decision and *Apple Pay* investigation clearly concern *complements* (against which the platform competed in the downstream market), the target of the interoperability restriction in the Facebook case is more difficult to pinpoint. The fact that API access was conditioned on not competing against Facebook indicates that the third-party apps were *substitutes* for Facebook. More precisely, they probably constituted *potential* substitutes that might one day challenge Facebook's supremacy.[1508] In a technical sense, the access in this case aligns more closely with regular than with full interoperability, given that no deep standardization is required.

Policymakers are also pursuing interoperability interventions beyond competition law. The Furman Report ambitiously envisages a system with open standards modelled on those underlying the internet.[1509] In the context of its digital advertising market study, the CMA also recommended mandating increased interoperability, seeing particular potential in APIs that allow social media users to access friends and publish posts across networks.[1510] The DMA includes both regular and full protocol interoperability obligations. First, a gatekeeper must provide third parties effective interoperability with the OS-mediated hardware and software features that are available to its own services.[1511] This regular protocol interoperability aligns with competition law, as it seeks to protect competition between developers and the gatekeeper's downstream operation. Going further, the DMA obliges gatekeeper providers of number-independent interpersonal communications services (NIICS) to enable cross-service messaging and, after some time, voice and video calls.[1512] This full protocol interoperability seeks to promote the contestability of messenger markets, thus leaving the realm of competition law.

How far should interoperability obligations reach? There is a case for regular protocol interoperability: it greatly increases the opportunities to innovate in complementary markets, while the platform's incentives to invest should not be

1507 Facebook rationalized its API policy as open to developers of apps that did not compete with it (phrased as 'replicating core functionality' of a Facebook product). This policy was in place from 2011 onwards. It was removed in 2018, one day before a member of the UK Parliament published a cache of documents obtained from litigation between Facebook and the app Six4Three, making the policy public.

1508 This is certainly true for Vine, which relied on seven-second videos. Path offered a more personal social network (initially limited to 50 contacts) and relied heavily on photos. Circle was a more local social network with a strong focus on what was happening nearby.

1509 Furman Report (n 1295), paras 2.68–2.78.

1510 CMA, 'Online Platforms and Digital Advertising Market Study' (Final Report, 2020), paras 8.54–68.

1511 DMA, art 6(7). Also relating to interoperability, see arts 5(7) and 6(4).

1512 DMA, art 7. To start, gatekeeper NIICS must make it possible for two individual end users to text messages and share images, voice messages, videos, and other files; after two years, they must enable these functionalities within groups; after four years, they must enable voice and video calls.

significantly affected (it is already rewarded for its core platform service and does not require an additional monopoly). The case for full protocol interoperability is weaker, as the effect on the platform's incentives to invest will be significantly greater. There are other arguments against full protocol interoperability. First, the degree of standardization required for such interoperability risks reducing innovation rather than promoting it. The concern is that the interoperability of a selected set of features will limit the variety between services. The CEO of Signal came out against interoperable protocols for a related reason: once standards are adopted, it becomes very difficult to make changes, which is a poor fit for dynamic, consumer-facing markets such as messaging.[1513] Email, which is based on the open Single Mail Transfer Protocol (SMTP), is not exactly a hotbed of innovation. Second, there are significant privacy and security risks.[1514] Full protocol interoperability requires users to trust not only their own messenger service but also that of their communication partners. Experts are largely in agreement that end-to-end encryption, the standard for messenger security, becomes difficult, if not impossible.[1515] Despite these strong counterarguments, there may still be room for targeted forms of interoperability, in particular to facilitate cross-platform access to friend lists as well as cross-platform posting, which require less standardization and engender fewer privacy and security risks.

13.3.3 Conclusion

Data portability and interoperability come in many forms, which complicates the discussion. It is useful to distinguish data portability, data interoperability and full protocol interoperability, all of which *promote inter-platform* competition, from regular protocol interoperability, which *protects intra-platform* competition. Regular protocol interoperability thus overlaps with non-discrimination obligations (and, as the next section shows, with forced platform infrastructure access).

The case for empowering users through data portability is strong. One-off portability of the 'download your data' kind is a dead end; effective portability is continuous, platform-to-platform (ie data interoperability). The DMA's portability obligation gets these preconditions right, but even an effective data portability regime may have only limited effects. While users could switch networks more easily, a collective action problem can still prevent them from actually doing so. This is where full protocol interoperability comes in. If users of the entrant network can easily find their friends

1513 Moxie Marlinspike, 'Reflections: The Ecosystem Is Moving' (*Signal blog*, 10 May 2016) <https://signal.org/blog/the-ecosystem-is-moving/>. For a good discussion of that blog post, see Matthew Wild, 'Products vs Protocols: What Signal Got Right' (*Snikket blog*, 9 February 2021) <https://snikket.org/blog/products-vs-protocols/>.

1514 Mikołaj Barczentewicz, 'Privacy and Security Implications of Regulation of Digital Services in the EU and in the US' (2022) Stanford-Vienna TTLF Working Paper no 84, 3–17.

1515 Corin Faife, 'Security Experts Say New EU Rules Will Damage WhatsApp Encryption' (*The Verge*, 28 May 2022) <https://www.theverge.com/2022/3/28/23000148/>. Other experts are more optimistic, suggesting messenger services switch to the same cryptographic standard as a solution, see Matthew Hodgson, 'Interoperability Without Sacrificing Privacy: Matrix and the DMA' (*Matrix blog*, 25 March 2022) <https://matrix.org/blog/2022/03/25/interoperability-without-sacrificing-privacy-matrix-and-the-dma>.

of the incumbent network who are also using the new network, and even invite those who are not yet using it, switching becomes more feasible. While switching occurs, users can multihome, which would be facilitated by cross-posting. More far-reaching forms of full protocol interoperability are not recommended.

Regular protocol interoperability can help solve issues of platform discrimination. While *ex ante* regulation can play a complementary role in specific cases, competition law is the preferred instrument. The applicable legal test depends on the competitive situation: (i) the strict refusal to supply test (*Bronner*) for *de novo* refusals of interoperability (as in *Apple Pay*); (ii) the less stringent refusal to supply or discrimination test for disruptions of interoperability, in particular in 'open early, close late' scenarios (as in *Microsoft I*).[1516] The following section examines forced platform access, of which one version overlaps with regular protocol interoperability.

13.4 Forced Access

Lawmakers in both the US and the EU have sought to liberalize their telecom sector by forcing incumbents to give entrants access to their network. In the EU, telecom providers (with significant market power) have been forced to grant entrants access to their local networks.[1517] Those entrants could thus compete in providing services to end users and gradually climb the 'ladder of investment' by progressively establishing their own network (while benefitting from interconnection with that of the incumbent). When sector-specific provisions, as enforced by national regulators, fell short, the EC would complement them with competition law enforcement, in particular of margin squeezes and refusals to supply. In the US, the 1996 Telecommunications Act imposed on network operators:

> The duty to provide, to any requesting telecommunications carrier …, nondiscriminatory access to network elements on an unbundled basis at any technically feasible point on rates, terms, and conditions that are just, reasonable, and nondiscriminatory [and] in a manner that allows requesting carriers to combine such elements in order to provide such telecommunications service.[1518]

1516 The underdeveloped disruption of supply test is more appropriate in cases where the platform does not have a competing downstream operation (likely a minority of cases, as there is no incentive to exclude in that scenario); the discrimination test is more appropriate where the platform does operate downstream. The difference between the two tests is, in any case, not very significant.

1517 Directive 2018/1972, arts 59–61 (before, see Directive 2002/19/EC and 'Notice on the application of the competition rules to access agreements in the telecommunications sector – framework, relevant markets and principles' [1998] OJ C265/2).

1518 Telecommunications Act of 1996, s 251(c)(3); see s 251(b)(1) on the access duty for all telecom carriers. US courts have been more reluctant to burden regulated firms with additional antitrust enforcement, at least when it comes to refusals to supply, but their complementary has nevertheless been confirmed, see *Verizon Communications v Law Offices of Curtis V Trinko* 540 US 398, 404 (2004) ('the 1996 Act preserves claims that satisfy existing antitrust standards').

As pointed out above, non-discrimination and interconnection/interoperability are closely related.[1519] Forced access is related to both of these regulatory interventions, as is clear from EU provisions such as: 'A national regulatory authority may … impose obligations of non-discrimination, in relation to interconnection or access.'[1520] It is also clear from the terms on which access to telecom networks must be granted, namely, 'fair, reasonable and nondiscriminatory' ones. In addition to solving issues of downstream discrimination, forced access can promote contestability: once an entrant has established its own network, it can keep expanding that network while relying on access to the incumbent's network for those areas it does not cover yet.

When considering forced access in a platform context, a similar distinction must be made. On the one hand, one can mandate access to platform *infrastructure* (on FRAND terms), which solves a discrimination issue. An authority could, for example, force an app store to grant access to apps that compete with its own offering. The *Microsoft I* case also concerned platform infrastructure access, via interoperability information, highlighting once more the close connection between the two. On the other hand, one can mandate access to the *data* held by the platform, which promotes contestability. An authority could, for example, force a search engine to provide clickstream data to entrants, which would allow them to improve their search algorithms. Put differently, access to platform infrastructure is generally a matter of *intra*-platform competition, while access to data generally affects *inter*-platform competition.[1521]

On a preliminary note, it is worth mentioning a continental drift in the treatment of refusals to supply: in the US, it has become increasingly difficult to prove a refusal to supply; in the EU, courts are more open to recognizing refusal to supply claims.[1522] This drift may hint at a more fundamental difference in antitrust traditions: the EU, in contrast to the US, has always shied away from the nuclear option of breakups, but it has not been afraid to deal with monopoly through forced access – a point made by Commissioner Vestager.[1523]

I previously discussed under which conditions platform *infrastructure* can (and should) be qualified as an essential facility, including the trade-offs relevant for that assessment. I refer to the relevant section rather than repeating myself here.[1524] The treatment of platform *data* as an essential facility has been discussed at length in the literature, so

1519 See Section 13.3.2.

1520 Directive 2018/1972, art 70. Before, using the exact same wording, see Directive 2002/19/EC, art 10.

1521 The dichotomy is not strict: access for app stores to an OS (platform infrastructure) would nevertheless be a matter of inter-platform competition (because app stores are themselves platforms).

1522 See eg Andrea Renda, 'Competition–Regulation Interface in Telecommunications: What's Left of the Essential Facility Doctrine' (2010) 34 Telecommunications Policy 23, 24 ('while the essential facilities doctrine is spreading, some advanced countries started to significantly depart from its application, either reneging completely (like the US) or expanding its interpretation (the EU)').

1523 Natasha Lomas, 'Don't Break Up Big Tech – Regulate Data Access, Says EU Antitrust Chief' (*TechCrunch*, 11 March 2019) <https://techcrunch.com/2019/03/11/dont-break-up-big-tech-regulate-data-access-says-eu-antitrust-chief/>.

1524 See Section 7.

I limit myself to a short review. In the EU, the discussion took off through the work of Graef, who established a strong framework for the assessment of data as an essential facility.[1525] The German and French competition authorities have also weighed in, observing in a joint report that data can meet the standards of the EU case law if it is 'truly unique and … there is no possibility for the competitor to obtain the data that it needs to perform its services'.[1526] But critics argue that data is non-rivalrous (the same data can be given to and used by many different firms) and widely available, meaning it will never be unique.[1527] Others argue that access to data misses the point: it is not data *collection* but rather data *processing* that gives certain firms a competitive edge.[1528] In other words, the success of Google's search engine is not a result of the more than 100,000 search queries per second that it learns from but is rather due to its superior search algorithm. Accordingly, the effects of mandating access to data will be limited. Finally, if data is considered an essential facility, the remedy would consist in granting competitors access to that data. However, as much of this data is personal, privacy laws (in particular the GDPR) complicate implementing an access remedy.[1529] While the academic debate on this issue is rich, the theory of data as an essential facility has gone largely untested in practice.[1530]

Various expert reports have called for a revision of access regimes relating to platform infrastructure and data.[1531] Some find that the refusal to supply doctrine can already be used effectively. The threshold for finding a refusal to supply data may be lower, in particular when such a refusal relates to data generated virtually incidentally and without special investment.[1532] Others confirm that the refusal to supply doctrine can play a role, but also has limits, in particular when it comes to the speed of intervention, the determination of remuneration and the guarantee of continuous (rather than one-off) access.[1533] An *ex ante* regime may thus be called for.[1534] These reports give more

---

1525 Inge Graef, *EU Competition Law, Data Protection and Online Platforms: Data as Essential Facility* (Kluwer 2016). For a US perspective, see Zachary Abrahamson, 'Essential Data' (2014) 124 Yale Law Journal 867.

1526 AdlC and Bundeskartellamt, 'Competition Law and Data' (Joint Report, 2016) 18.

1527 Catherine Tucker, 'Digital Data, Platforms and the Usual [Antitrust] Suspects: Network Effects, Switching Costs, Essential Facility' (2019) 54 Review of Industrial Organization 683 (note that Tucker received research funding from Google and CCIA and consulted for Facebook).

1528 Giuseppe Colangelo and Mariateresa Maggiolino, 'Big Data as Misleading Facilities' (2017) 13 European Competition Journal 249, 251 ('the economic utility of big data does not depend on the data as such but on the material and intellectual resources that a firm invests in developing the analytics necessary to draw reliable and grounded inferences out of those data').

1529 See Rok Dacar, 'Is the Essential Facilities Doctrine Fit for Access to Data Cases? The Data Protection Aspect' (2022) 18 Croatian Yearbook of European Law and Policy 61.

1530 For two examples from the energy sector, see AdlC, Decision 14-MC-02, *GDF Suez*, 9 September 2014 and CMA, 'Energy Market Investigation' (Final Report, 2016), paras 11.64–66. An EC investigation has also prompted Reuters to commit to providing certain firms with access to its data feed, see *Reuters Instrument Codes* (Case AT.39654) Commission Decision C(2012) 9635.

1531 In addition to the reports cited in the following footnotes, see Stigler Report (n 1295) 96–97 and 117.

1532 Schweitzer et al (n 1389), paras 9–13.

1533 Crémer Report (n 1295) 98–109; Furman Report (n 1295), paras 2.79–99; Rupprecht Podszun, 'Innovation, Variety & Fair Choice – New Rules for the Digital Economy' (Expert Opinion for Finanzplatz München Initiative, 2017) 40–44.

1534 Some have gone one step further and proposed a 'progressive data-sharing mandate', according to which every company above a certain size (eg 10% of the market) that systematically collects and analyses

attention to data access than infrastructure access, although that is only true of *explicit* attention: non-discrimination rules and interoperability obligations that imply platform access have been discussed at length.[1535]

The DMA contains provisions relating both to data and infrastructure access. In terms of infrastructure access, the DMA focuses on innovation platforms, in particular gatekeeper OSs and app stores, to which developers can be guaranteed access.[1536] When it comes to data access, the DMA focuses on search engines, which may be obliged to

> provide to any third-party undertaking providing online search engines, at its request, with access on fair, reasonable and non-discriminatory terms to ranking, query, click and view data in relation to free and paid search generated by end users on its online search engines. Any such query, click and view data that constitutes personal data shall be anonymised.[1537]

The focus of the DMA provisions is sensible. Innovation platforms, including OS and app stores, offer the foundation for complementary innovation (they are 'market makers', not just 'matchmakers') and are therefore most effective at foreclosing suppliers.[1538] However, the security risks are also the greatest for innovation platforms, so it is recommended to duly weigh them when specifying any access obligation.[1539] Given that learning effects play a crucial role for search engines,[1540] limiting the data sharing mandate to this type of platform also makes sense. Potential privacy issues arise, given the private nature of search queries, but anonymization appears feasible.

In cases of forced access, the trade-off between the different parties' incentives to invest or innovate is particularly salient.[1541] Mandating access can benefit both allocative and dynamic efficiency as entrants make use of the facility to provide competing or alternative products downstream, but can also decrease incentives to innovate upstream, both for the incumbent (which profits less from its innovation when it has to be shared) and of entrants (which are not motivated to develop their own facilities). This effect may be even greater when an upstream facility has to be shared to promote competition in that *same* upstream market (eg Google having to share search data). To prevent entrants from

---

data would have to let other companies in the same market access a subset of its data, see Viktor Mayer-Schönberger and Thomas Ramge, *Reinventing Capitalism in the Age of Big Data* (Basic Books 2018).

1535 See Sections 13.2.1 and 13.3.2.

1536 DMA, art 6(4) and (12), see also art 6(7) (discussed above, Section 13.3.2).

1537 DMA, art 6(11). Art 6(2) and (10) also concern data access, but with a view to levelling the playing field between platform and supplier, not with a view to increasing the contestability of the platform market.

1538 See Section 7.

1539 See Section 10.5. The DMA acknowledges this, see art 6(4) ('The gatekeeper shall not be prevented from taking, to the extent that they are strictly necessary and proportionate, measures to ensure that third-party software applications or software application stores do not endanger the integrity of the hardware or operating system provided by the gatekeeper').

1540 See Section 4.1.2.

1541 See Section 7.1.

simply free riding on the investment of incumbents, a fair price for access has to be determined – a task more suited to sectoral regulators than competition authorities.

When relying on *ex ante* regulation for access questions, the legal and economic considerations of the refusal to supply doctrine should continue to inform the answers. When it comes to platform infrastructure, a strong case can be made in cases involving innovation platforms, especially when they granted access in the first place (ie cases where access was subsequently refused or degraded). When it comes to platform data, however, it is more difficult to build a strong competition law case, in part due to the nature of data and in part due to the fact that contestability fits awkwardly with the objectives of competition law. If Google Search is in fact a natural monopoly, pursuing contestability is a fool's errand.[1542] But even accepting contestability as a goal, questions of feasibility and effectiveness remain. For example, access to Google's query and click data may allow competing search engines to improve their algorithm, but Google's competitive advantage also derives from its index, which is much larger than that of competitors.[1543] The reason is twofold: on the webpage side, virtually every owner allows Google's crawler 'Googlebot' while some block others because of the increase in running costs; on the search engine side, crawling and indexing represent a significant cost (subject to scale economies). As a result, Google's index contains 500–600 billion pages, while Bing's only contains 100–200 billion pages even after a multibillion-dollar investment (those of other search engines lag far behind). And then there is the fact that Google is the default search engine on the great majority of desktop and mobile web browsers (in terms of market share).[1544] Access to search data can thus contribute to contestability, but definitely does not guarantee it.

13.5 Breakup

The final intervention discussed here is the most aggressive one: breakup. Unlike the EU, the US has a history of breaking up monopolies. After the Sherman Anti-Trust Act was adopted in 1890, it was used – as its name suggests – to prevent and dismantle a number of trusts.[1545] In 1911, for example, the Supreme Court found that Standard Oil had taken control of more than 90% of the oil industry and was using this monopoly position anticompetitively to fix prices and exclude competitors. Therefore, the Court

1542 See Sections 7.2 and 11.2.1. Whether Google Search is a natural monopoly depends on at which point the value of the dataset flattens out, see Kevin Coates, 'Data: The Uniqueness of the Dataset and the Slope of the Value Curve' (*21st Century Competition*, 1 November 2020) <https://www.twentyfirstcenturycompetition.com/2020/11/data-the-uniqueness-of-the-dataset-and-the-slope-of-the-value-curve/> ('If a dataset covering 51% of the market is more valuable (in terms of improving the product for which the dataset is an input), then the market is perhaps a natural monopoly'). If Google Search is indeed a natural monopoly, FRAND access to the search engine itself should be regulated, which the DMA also does in art 6(12).

1543 CMA, 'Online Platforms and Digital Advertising Market Study' (n 1510) paras 3.52–63 and House Judiciary Report (n 1336) 77–84.

1544 The DMA also targets this default status, see arts 5(7), and 6(3) and (6).

1545 See eg *Northern Securities v United States* 193 US 197 (1904); *The Standard Oil Company of New Jersey v United States* 221 US 1 (1911); *United States v American Tobacco* 221 US 106 (1911).

ordered its dissolution into 34 separate companies.[1546] After an initial wave of trust-busting, the enthusiasm for breakups ebbed away but never disappeared. In 1961, the Supreme Court held in *DuPont*: 'Divestiture has been called the most important of antitrust remedies. It is simple, relatively easy to administer, and sure.'[1547] As the FTC rightly noted, this simplicity, administrability and certainty 'appl[y] most clearly to a clean separation of two ongoing businesses – essentially, undoing the merger or acquisition', as was the case in *DuPont*.[1548] In 1982, the Bell consent decree offered an (at that point rare) example of a breakup of a business that had grown organically, at least in part.[1549] Much like in the case of Standard Oil, however, a wave of consolidation followed: the seven Baby Bells merged into two, namely, AT&T and Verizon.[1550] The last subject of a breakup order was Microsoft. The DOJ had filed suit against the company for anticompetitively maintaining its monopoly in the OS market by destroying middleware threats.[1551] The district court validated this theory of harm and ordered a divestiture, namely:

> The separation of the Operating Systems Business from the Applications Business, and the transfer of the assets of one of them (the 'Separated Business') to a separate entity along with (a) all personnel, systems, and other tangible and intangible assets (including Intellectual Property) used to develop, produce, distribute, market, promote, sell, license and support the products and services of the Separated Business, and (b) such other assets as are necessary to operate the Separated Business as an independent and economically viable entity.[1552]

On appeal, however, the circuit court upheld only part of the claim and vacated the breakup remedy. Citing *DuPont*, the court confirmed that 'divestiture is a common form of relief in successful antitrust prosecutions: it is indeed "the most important of antitrust remedies."'[1553] It also, however, noted that divestiture is particularly apt for the 'dissolution of entities formed by mergers and acquisitions', which Microsoft was not.[1554] The primary reason is one of logistics:

> A corporation that has expanded by acquiring its competitors often has preexisting internal lines of division along which it may more easily be

1546 *The Standard Oil Company of New Jersey v United States* (n 1545).

1547 *United States v EI du Pont de Nemours* 366 US 316, 330–31 (1961).

1548 David Balto and Richard Parker, 'The Evolving Approach to Merger Remedies' (Public Statement, as published in Antitrust Report, 2000). See also FTC, 'The Commission's Divestiture Process' (Study, 1999).

1549 *United States v AT&T* (n 1438).

1550 For a detailed graph illustrating the trajectory of consolidation, see Thomas Gryta, Keach Hagey, Dana Cimilluca and Amol Sharma, 'AT&T Reaches Deal to Buy Time Warner for $85.4 Billion' (*WSJ*, 22 October 2016) <https://www.wsj.com/articles/at-t-reaches-deal-to-buy-time-warner-for-more-than-80-billion-1477157084>.

1551 See Section 6.

1552 *United States v Microsoft* 97 F Supp 2d 59, 65 (DDC 2000).

1553 *United States v Microsoft* 253 F3d 34, 105 (DC Cir 2001).

1554 ibid.

> split than a corporation that has expanded from natural growth. Although time and corporate modifications and developments may eventually fade those lines, at least the identifiable entities preexisted to create a template for such division as the court might later decree.[1555]

Given the appeals judgment (and a change of administration), the DOJ ended up settling with Microsoft.[1556] The last breakup order thus dates back to the start of the 20th century; the last successful breakup to the 1980s. Nevertheless, calls to break up the large tech platforms again pervade public discourse.[1557] To evaluate this discourse, it is useful to distinguish between three kinds of breakups: horizontal breakups, vertical breakups, and breakups of past acquisitions (ie undoing them).[1558]

The idea underlying *horizontal breakups* is simple: market power/lack of competition is the source of many ills, including anticompetitive conduct; if we break up a dominant company, its different divisions will have to compete against each other, which will incentivize good behaviour. While this theory is generally valid, horizontal breakups of platforms such as Facebook and Amazon are not a good idea. Remember that platforms benefit from significant economies of scale both on the supply side and the demand side (ie network effects). This means that a breakup could decrease allocative efficiency, thus harming consumers (that can either only access some connections or sellers, or have to split their time across networks). Moreover, such a breakup would probably not be very durable, as network effects would naturally draw users to the most popular platform until a winner takes all or most.[1559] Note also that a breakup would not necessarily solve some of the issues that motivate calls for breakup because they are not *competition* issues. As Haucap remarked, for example, 'there is little evidence that would suggest that larger firms violate data protection and privacy standards in a more systematic fashion than smaller firms'.[1560] In other words, three Facebabies would not be more protective of privacy than the current Facebook. However, that claim is not undebated: in her work, Srinivasan has established a link

1555 ibid 106.

1556 Civil Action no 98-1232 (CKK) (DDC 2003), Civil Action no 98-1233 (CKK) (DDC 2002).

1557 See eg Zephyr Teachout, *Break 'Em Up: Recovering Our Freedom from Big Ag, Big Tech, and Big Money* (St Martin's Press 2020); Jonathan Taplin, 'Is It Time to Break Up Google?' (*NYT*, 22 April 2017) <https://www.nytimes.com/2017/04/22/opinion/sunday/is-it-time-to-break-up-google.html>; Tim Harford, 'The Case for Ending Amazon's Dominance' (*FT*, 19 January 2018) <https://www.ft.com/content/aba8d444-fb94-11e7-a492-2c9be7f3120a>; Chris Hughes, 'It's Time to Break Up Facebook' (*NYT*, 9 May 2019) <https://www.nytimes.com/2019/05/09/opinion/sunday/chris-hughes-facebook-zuckerberg.html>.

1558 For an overview of the arguments against breaking up online platforms, some of which I discuss below, see Robert Crandall, 'The Dubious Antitrust Argument for Breaking Up the Internet Giants' (2019) 54 Review of Industrial Organization 627 (note that the author works for the Technology Policy Institute, which is funded mainly by those 'internet giants') and Stephen Houck, 'Breaking Up Is Hard to Do' (2020) <https://ssrn.com/abstract=3457348> (note that the paper was commissioned by CCIA, a tech industry association).

1559 Shapiro (n 1392) 744.

1560 Justus Haucap, 'The Facebook Decision: First Thoughts' (*D'Kart*, 7 February 2019) <https://www.d-kart.de/the-facebook-decision-first-thoughts-by-haucap/>. See further Shoshana Zuboff, *The Age of Surveillance Capitalism* (PublicAffairs 2019) 23 ('calls to break up Google or Facebook on monopoly grounds could easily result in establishing multiple surveillance capitalist firms, though at a diminished scale, and thus clear the way for more surveillance capitalist competitors') and Petit (n 1285) 241–46.

between the withering of Facebook's competitors (such as Google+) and its privacy degradation.[1561] Finally, these platforms have initially acquired success by offering a superior product (at least in their core market); punishing them for this feat could chill incentives to invest in the future.

A *vertical breakup*, then, is essentially equivalent to a structural separation regime – both the merits and pitfalls of such an intervention are thus similar.[1562] The platform, once broken off from its downstream operations, would have no incentive to exclude downstream competitors; rather, it would be focused on optimizing participation on its platform. For example, Amazon Marketplace would have no reason to favour the products of the independent company Amazon Basics in its product rankings. At the same time, such a breakup would eliminate the efficiencies derived from vertical integration. Finally, incentives to innovate could be dampened. In contrast to a horizontal breakup, however, platforms' incentives to invest remain equal. Rather, incentives to invest in the startup scene could be dampened when the risk of breakups makes acquisition by a large platform a less attractive proposition both for the platform and the startup.

A final form of breakup consists in the *divestiture of an acquisition*. This can be achieved in two ways. First, such divestiture can be the remedy of a monopolization suit.[1563] However, such suits have become less prevalent since the adoption of specific merger control regimes. Second, the FTC can conduct a retrospective merger analysis and, if it finds substantial anticompetitive effects, impose remedies, including a divestiture.[1564] But while retrospective analyses and especially divestitures are rare, substantial post-merger price increases are common.[1565] Authorities on both sides of the Atlantic are starting to invest more in retrospective analyses, which can inform future merger decisions.[1566]

Facebook/Instagram – the acquisition that is really driving the conversation – was reported to the FTC.[1567] Wu has been particularly vocal about the need to split Instagram (as well as WhatsApp) from Facebook.[1568] He argues that the FTC's non-opposition to the acquisition was a big mistake driven by a fundamental misunderstanding of digital competition – a statement corroborated by Lear's *ex post* assessment of the

1561 Dina Srinivasan, 'The Antitrust Case against Facebook' (2019) 16 Berkeley Business Law Journal 39.

1562 See Section 13.2.2.

1563 Before the EU merger control regime was in place, the EC also relied on its abuse of dominance provision to challenge mergers, see Case 6–72 *Continental Can v Commission* EU:C:1973:22.

1564 See eg Joseph Farrell, Paul Pautler and Michael Vita, 'Economics at the FTC: Retrospective Merger Analysis with a Focus on Hospitals' (2009) 35 Review of Industrial Organization 369.

1565 John Kwoka, *Mergers, Merger Control, and Remedies* (MIT Press 2014); Matthew Weinberg, 'The Price Effects of Horizontal Mergers' (2008) 4 JCLE 433; Orley Ashenfelter, Daniel Hosken and Matthew Weinberg, 'Did Robert Bork Understate the Competitive Impact of Mergers? Evidence from Consummated Mergers' (2014) 57 The Journal of Law and Economics 67.

1566 In the US, see FTC, 'Merger Retrospective Program' <https://www.ftc.gov/policy/studies/merger-retrospective-program>. In the EU, there has been a tender for the 'collection of key qualitative and quantitative information from past European Commission's Merger decisions' (COMP/2022/OP/0006).

1567 See Section 13.1.1.

1568 See Tim Wu, *The Curse of Bigness* (Columbia Global Reports 2018) 132–33 and Tim Wu, 'The Case for Breaking Up Instagram and Facebook' (*WaPo*, 28 September 2018) <https://www.washingtonpost.com/outlook/2018/09/28/case-breaking-up-facebook-instagram/>.

CMA's *Facebook/Instagram* decision.[1569] Wu has therefore been calling on the FTC and DOJ to recognize that the acquisition was anticompetitive and illegal when it happened, and to file a suit in federal court asking for a divestiture. The idea is that, should Facebook have a serious competitor like Instagram, it would have an incentive to 'do better' in terms of product innovation and quality, including privacy – if not, it could actually lose users as they would have somewhere else to go.

Wu's proposal has been subject to various critiques, some more convincing than others.[1570] First, critics argue that the FTC should not be allowed to go back on its approval of the deal. Technically, this critique does not hold up. When it approved the deal, the FTC was very clear that no further action was warranted 'at this time':

> Accordingly, the investigation has been closed. This action is not to be construed as a determination that a violation may not have occurred, just as the pendency of an investigation should not be construed as a determination that a violation has occurred. The Commission reserves the right to take such further action as the public interest may require.[1571]

A broader argument can be constructed around legal certainty, but challenging one consummated acquisition every few decades is unlikely to have a big impact. Moreover, new evidence has surfaced since then, including internal emails and third-party testimony.[1572] And the strategy that Facebook is accused of – namely, *serial* anticompetitive acquisition – can, by its very nature, only become apparent after some time. Reassessing a case in light of new evidence seems like a good enforcement practice rather than a reason for criticism.

Second, some critics argue that, to unwind the merger, the FTC 'would have to prove that the but-for world – that is, the world that would exist today had the government blocked the merger before consummation – would likely be more competitive than the actual world in which the merger has occurred.'[1573] In other words, the question is whether Instagram would have grown into a serious competitor *on its own*; if not, then Facebook did not eliminate a competitor but rather nurtured one into being. Facebook, of course, argues it is responsible for Instagram's success: 'Facebook has built Instagram from a niche photo-sharing app with no monetization plans into the phenomenal success story that it is today – and which it never would have become without Facebook's

1569 Lear (n 1392) 51–71. Lear finds 'a number of gaps in the way the Authorities have assessed the *Facebook/Instagram* merger': inter alia, the CMA should not have used downloads as a proxy for market shares, erred in finding that Instagram did not generate significant user engagement, and – most importantly – was wrong in concluding that Instagram was not well placed to compete against Facebook in the provision of social networking services.

1570 Addressing some criticism, see Scott Hemphill and Tim Wu, 'Nascent Competitors' (2020) 168 University of Pennsylvania Law Review 1879.

1571 FTC, File no 121-0121, *Facebook/Instagram* (Closing Letter, 2012).

1572 See House Judiciary Report (n 1336) 152–54.

1573 Timothy Muris and Jonathan Nuechterlein, 'First Principles for Review of Long-Consummated Mergers' (2020) 5 The Criterion Journal on Innovation 29, 30.

investment of time, resources, and know-how.'[1574] The truth of that statement can be debated.[1575] At a more fundamental level, however, the standard of proof proposed here may not be the right one. In *Microsoft*, the circuit court held that conditioning liability on the 'ability to reconstruct the hypothetical marketplace absent a defendant's anticompetitive conduct would only encourage monopolists to take more and earlier anticompetitive action'.[1576] It is virtually impossible to 'confidently reconstruct a product's hypothetical technological development in a world absent the defendant's exclusionary conduct'.[1577] Therefore, the proof required is rather

> (1) whether as a general matter the exclusion of nascent threats is the type of conduct that is reasonably capable of contributing significantly to a defendant's continued monopoly power and (2) whether [the excluded companies] reasonably constituted nascent threats at the time [of] the anticompetitive conduct at issue.[1578]

The third and final major critique is one that applies to every breakup, namely, that it is difficult if not impossible to 'unscramble the eggs'; in other words, the task of disentangling a company is too complex.[1579] As a general matter, this argument is doubtful.[1580] However, as recognized by courts and authorities, it is particularly doubtful in case of breakups of past acquisitions (as opposed to internal expansions); in that case, the lines of the divestiture do not have to be determined *de novo* but are already drawn. Facebook is in the process of blurring those lines by integrating Facebook and Instagram,[1581] but as a former Instagram employee put it: 'If you can put them together, you can pull them apart.'[1582]

Currently, the FTC is – not without difficulty – trying to unwind Facebook acquisitions.[1583] The agency is arguing that Facebook unlawfully maintained its monopoly during a crucial period of transition (from web to mobile) by neutralizing the competitive threats posed by Instagram and WhatsApp via acquisition. This is said to

1574 Sarah Frier, 'The Number Facebook Won't Say' (*Bloomberg*, 6 October 2020) <https://www.bloomberg.com/news/newsletters/2020-10-06/the-number-facebook-won-t-say>. For a more elaborate overview of the ways in which the acquisition helped Instagram's development (according to representatives of Facebook), see Lear (n 1392) 58–59.

1575 See House Judiciary Report (n 1336) 155–56.

1576 *United States v Microsoft* (n 1553) 79.

1577 ibid.

1578 ibid.

1579 On this point, see Christopher Mims, '"Too Complex to Break Up" Is the New "Too Big to Fail"' (*WSJ*, 10 October 2020) <https://www.wsj.com/articles/too-complex-to-break-up-is-the-new-too-big-to-fail-11602302406>. Even Tirole, who is not a priori opposed to big tech breakups, states he has yet to see a well-formulated proposal, see Matt Richards, 'Big Tech Platforms Could Be Broken Up, Says Nobel-Winning Economist' (*Global Competition Review*, 18 January 2019) <https://globalcompetitionreview.com/big-tech-platforms-could-be-broken-says-nobel-winning-economist>.

1580 See John Kwoka and Tommaso Valletti, 'Scrambled Eggs and Paralyzed Policy: Breaking Up Consummated Mergers and Dominant Firms' (2021) 30 Industrial and Corporate Change 1286.

1581 Isaac (n 1502).

1582 House Judiciary Report (n 1336) 152.

1583 *FTC v Facebook* (Amended Complaint) (n 1506). This amended complaint survived the motion-to-dismiss stage; a similar one brought by almost every state attorney general was dismissed because they waited too long after acquisition to bring their case.

reflect Facebook's deeply rooted strategy that it is 'better to buy than to compete' (a quote from Zuckerberg). After the acquisition of Instagram, Facebook halted the development of its own photo-sharing product (code-named 'Snap') and limited the promotion of Instagram to prevent cannibalization, to the frustration of its founders.[1584] As relief, the FTC is requesting divestiture of the acquired apps.

In his dissent in the first breakup case in the US, Justice Oliver Wendell Holmes wrote that '[g]reat cases, like hard cases, make bad law'.[1585] While great cases do require great care, their greatness should not disqualify them (just like a firm's bigness should not automatically lead to condemnation). One major issue facing breakups is the practicality of it. This is true mostly of breakups of platforms that have reached their current size organically (and even then, it must be noted that firms routinely break themselves up).[1586] When it comes to acquisitions, the case for divestiture becomes stronger. There are fewer practical difficulties, as the breakup lines are drawn already, and the negative effect on incentives to innovative is more limited.[1587] However, one still has to consider a breakup's effect on the efficiencies that were generated through the acquisition. These will generally be greater in case of a vertical acquisition that allows for the integration of complementary products, rather than a horizontal acquisition that primarily adds to the platform's market coverage. Given all of the above, the argument for undoing Facebook's past acquisitions is certainly the strongest.

1584 For a deeper look at this dynamic and the associated founder frustration, see Sarah Frier, *No Filter: The Inside Story of Instagram* (Simon & Schuster 2020).

1585 *Northern Securities v United States* (n 1545) 400 (Holmes, dissenting).

1586 See eg Rajesh Kumar Singh and Abhijith Ganapavaram, 'GE, an Industrial Conglomerate Pioneer, to Break Up' (*Reuters*, 10 November 2021) <https://www.reuters.com/business/ge-form-three-public-companies-2021-11-09/>; Jonathan Rockoff and Peter Loftus, 'Johnson & Johnson's Breakup: What to Know' (*WSJ*, 12 November 2021) <https://www.wsj.com/articles/johnson-johnsons-breakup-what-to-know-11636715701>; Jane Zhang, 'Alibaba Shares Soar After Historic Overhaul Heralds IPO Wave' (*Bloomberg*, 28 March 2023) <https://www.bloomberg.com/news/articles/2023-03-28/alibaba-splits-into-six-units-that-may-pursue-individual-ipos>.

1587 Rather than negatively affecting the platform's incentives to innovate, the divestiture of an acquisition mainly affects incentives to innovate in the startup market – a less direct and thus presumably smaller effect.

14

CONCLUSION ON PLATFORM REGULATION

This is something that I'm having a hard time comprehending.
You learned from a mistake and you made an improvement in the law?
That's so Europe.[1588]

It should be clear at this point that the competitive issues that result from the market power held by platforms are not new. Indeed, regulators have dealt with similar issues in the telecom industry over the past 100 years. One benefit of looking at this variety of precedents is being able to put together a comprehensive taxonomy of potential regulatory interventions. In addition, the benefit of hindsight allows for the evaluation of such interventions. Of course, the regulation of old technologies cannot and should not simply be transposed to the platforms that dominate the online landscape, but past experience can certainly help inform modern platform regulation.

The question of platform regulation has not been answered definitively. Nevertheless, many regulators have decided to act anyway, which they can hardly be blamed for. After all, the question of *when* to regulate technology presents an exceedingly difficult dilemma: 'Regulate too early and you risk stymieing innovators; wait too long and you risk losing the opportunity to regulate a technology or service before it becomes widespread, potentially harming consumers or markets in the interim.'[1589] This Part also examined the available instruments of platform regulation, in particular in the DMA.

The methodology of this Part consisted in categorizing the regulatory interventions in the platform sphere based on a clear framework. The trade-offs inherent in each

1588 Michael Kosta, 'Switzerland: So Many Guns, No Mass Shootings' (*The Daily Show*, 9 December 2018) <https://www.youtube.com/watch?v=KjlT4BME2aE>.

1589 Shrupti Shah, Rachel Brody and Nick Olson, 'The Regulator of Tomorrow: Rulemaking and Enforcement in an Era of Exponential Change' (Report, 2015) 3. See also Mark Fenwick, Wulf Kaal and Erik Vermeulen, 'Regulation Tomorrow: What Happens When Technology Is Faster than the Law?' (2017) 6 American University Business Law Review 561, 571–72.

intervention were exposed, not only on a conceptual level, but also with a sensitivity to questions of implementation, which do not always receive the attention they deserve. However, the fact that these trade-offs generally do not concern price/output effects but rather effects on innovation, as well as quality and choice, makes quantifying the trade-off significantly more difficult. Still, based on the available evidence, I have tried to at least point policymakers in the right direction.

One important (but perhaps facile) conclusion is that the heterogeneity of platforms and problems requires a multifaceted response. There are too many types of platforms, with differing degrees of market power, which engage in a wide variety of potentially abusive practices, to solve the perceived issues with one instrument. This Part has shown that some regulatory interventions overlap, while others are complementary (sometimes up to the point that adopting one without the other would result in its ineffectiveness). A useful distinction exists between measures that promote contestability of the platform market and measures that protect competition in the complementary markets where suppliers are active (often in competition with the platform):

- Promoting contestability: horizontal (conglomerate) merger control, data portability and data interoperability, full protocol interoperability, platform data access, horizontal breakup
- Protecting competition: vertical (conglomerate) merger control, non-discrimination (rule or remedy), structural separation, protocol interoperability, platform infrastructure access, vertical breakup.

Do not let this distinction obscure the fact that the measures in these two categories are intimately related. By promoting contestability of platform markets – in other words, by increasing the threat of displacement – platforms can be made to act *as if* they were operating in competitive markets, at least to some extent. This can decrease the incidence of anticompetitive practices in complementary markets, thus protecting competition. The relation also goes the other way. Challengers to the core platform often start in a niche market related to the platform (think of a photo app becoming the next incumbent social network). Therefore, protecting competition in complementary markets can increase the contestability of the platform market.

While it is unnecessary to repeat the conclusions on every single regulatory intervention, a short overview is presented here.

To promote contestability, stricter horizontal merger control is an excellent place to start. An immediate, worthwhile change is to rely more on theories of harm centred on the *serial* acquisition of *potential* competitors. So far, the error has definitely been on the side of false negatives. While extreme caution is warranted when considering the unwinding of past acquisitions of (potential) competitors, *Facebook/Instagram* presents an unusually strong case for doing so. Another way of promoting contestability is to force platforms to give competitors access to their data. Such a measure is only helpful where learning effects are considerable, ie in the case of search engines, but even then, there are serious questions of effectiveness (the competitive advantage of Google relies on more than the amount of training data for its algorithm). A more general and promising intervention is data portability. One-off portability is doomed to fail, but a regime mandating direct and continuous portability (ie interoperability) has a chance. A narrow form of full protocol interoperability (finding friends and cross-posting) should complement data interoperability so as to spur multihoming, thus decreasing collective action problems in switching.

To protect competition, the abuse of dominance prohibition should take centre stage. Part 2 has specified the application of article 102 TFEU to platforms, with a focus on the choice of legal test and the related theories of harm. With regard to the most concerning tendency of online platforms, ie self-preferencing (or discrimination), we are starting to see a body of precedent, which is slowly bringing us from competition law standard to something closer to a rule against discrimination.

The question is whether *additional* rules are necessary to protect competition between the platform and its suppliers. A non-discrimination rule, (regular) protocol interoperability and platform infrastructure access all limit self-preferencing by online platforms. Putting aside platform infrastructure access, which has been discussed in the previous Part, leaves us with a non-discrimination rule or protocol interoperability. The latter is narrower (it generally concerns APIs) and can thus be considered a specification of the former. They can coexist, just like *Google Shopping* (on discrimination) and *Microsoft I* (on interoperability) coexist. A case can be made for crystallizing the competition law experience on specific points in *ex ante* rules, in particular to make up for institutional/procedural shortcomings.

Going one step further and structurally separating platforms is not justified. While the conceptually similar policy of breaking up previous vertical acquisitions is not justified either, policing those acquisitions more closely through *ex ante* merger control is recommended. After all, vertical integration, which regularly happens through acquisition, brings with it the conflict of interest that leads to the discrimination of competing suppliers. When such acquisitions are waved through anyway, eg because of the significant synergies they can produce, competition authorities should demand binding non-discrimination commitments from the acquiring platform.

CONCLUSION

The centre cannot hold.[1590]

Competition policy is becoming increasingly polarized. This polarization is particularly strong when it comes to the power of online platforms. According to the president of the AdlC, for example: 'The debate about antitrust and big tech is an example where we hear very extreme views.'[1591] Ibáñez Colomo speaks of the 'footballization' of competition policy, noting that '[t]here is always a strong temptation to simplify debates and to look for simple and definitive answers to complex problems. The ubiquity of this temptation goes a long way to explain polarisation as a phenomenon.'[1592] This polarization is not helped by the fact that more and more of the research into competition law in the platform economy is funded, directly or indirectly, by incumbent platforms or their challengers.[1593]

The 'extreme views', along with the not-so-extreme views, are increasingly divided into camps: left vs right, progressive vs conservative, hipster antitrust vs reactionary antitrust. Even within these camps, there can be infighting, eg when progressive idealists turn on progressive pragmatists. In the end, however, groupthink is harmful. It may lead scholars to announce they (or their camp) have *the* answers, which is unlikely in complex matters such as online platforms and abuse of dominance. Indeed, as Philippon notes, 'there is often a negative correlation between outward certainty and factual information.'[1594]

In this work, I have tried to modestly contribute to the debate on anticompetitive platform conduct, with a bias for factual information and against outward certainty. The unsatisfactory summation is that matters are complex. This does not invite paralysis but does mean that there is no panacea. Rather, the key is to intelligently adapt the variety of existing competition law doctrines to the economic and technological features of platforms, with a keen understanding of how the doctrines fit together. Where substantive doctrines, or institutional and procedural structures, cannot be stretched to suit the exigencies of the platform economy, additional rules may be called for. I must, however, disappoint those readers flipping to the conclusion to get a bite-sized version of these doctrinal and regulatory changes. They are described throughout the work, often enough in interim conclusions, and there is no use repeating them here. May this be an incentive to dive into the chapters,[1595] rather than to put the book back on the shelf.

1590 From the poem 'The Second Coming' by WB Yeats, first published in 1920.

1591 Isabelle de Silva, 'The Future of Competition Law: Time to Change or Time to Adapt?' (46th Annual Conference on International Antitrust Law and Policy, New York, 12 September 2019).

1592 Pablo Ibáñez Colomo, 'Against the Footballisation of Competition Policy: How to Advance the General Interest and Avoid Polarisation' (*Chillin' Competition*, 18 September 2019) <https://chillingcompetition.com/2019/09/18/>.

1593 The disclosure of such funding is an absolute minimum requirement. I have 'imported' these disclosures into my footnotes, so that the readers can make up their own mind.

1594 Thomas Philippon, *The Great Reversal: How America Gave Up on Free Markets* (HUP 2019) viii.

1595 Time-constrained readers may want to start with Section 2.2.2, pick up some essentials from Section 5, take time to disagree with Section 9, and then read a summary of the third act in Section 14.

TABLE OF LEGISLATION

AUSTRIA

Federal Act against Cartels and other Restrictions of Competition originally published in 2005 (Federal Law Gazette I No. 61/2005), as last amended in 2021 (Federal Law Gazette I No. 176/2021)

EUROPEAN UNION

Treaty establishing the European Coal and Steel Community (1951)

Commission Directive 90/388/EEC on competition in the markets for telecommunications services [1990] OJ L192/10

Treaty establishing the European Community [2002] OJ C325/33

Directive 2002/19/EC of the European Parliament and of the Council on access to, and interconnection of, electronic communications networks and associated facilities [2002] OJ L108/7

Directive 2002/22/EC of the European Parliament and of the Council on universal service and users' rights relating to electronic communications networks and services [2002] OJ L108/51

Commission Directive 2002/77/EC on competition in the markets for electronic communications, networks and services [2002] OJ L249/21

Council Regulation (EC) 1/2003 of 16 December 2002 on the implementation of the rules on competition laid down in Articles 81 and 82 of the Treaty [2003] OJ L1/1

Council Regulation (EC) 139/2004 on the control of concentrations between undertakings [2004] OJ L24/1

Directive 2005/29/EC of the European Parliament and of the Council concerning unfair business-to-consumer commercial practices in the internal market [2005] OJ L149/22

Consolidated version of the Treaty on European Union – Protocol (no 27) on the internal market and competition [2008] OJ C115/309

Directive 2010/13/EU of the European Parliament and of the Council on the coordination of certain provisions laid down by law, regulation or administrative action in Member States concerning the provision of audiovisual media services [2010] OJ L95/1

Directive (EU) 2015/1535 of the European Parliament and of the Council laying down a procedure for the provision of information in the field of technical regulations and of rules on Information Society services [2015] OJ L241/1

Regulation (EU) 2015/2120 of the European Parliament and of the Council laying down measures concerning open internet access [2015] OJ L310/1

Directive (EU) 2015/2366 of the European Parliament and of the Council of 25 November 2015 on payment services in the internal market [2015] OJ L337/35

Regulation (EU) 2016/679 of the European Parliament and of the Council on the protection of natural persons with regard to the processing of personal data and on the free movement of such data [2016] OJ L119/1

Directive (EU) 2018/1808 of the European Parliament and of the Council amending the Audiovisual Media Services Directive in view of changing market realities [2018] OJ L303/69

Directive (EU) 2018/1972 of the European Parliament and of the Council establishing the European Electronic Communications Code [2018] OJ L321/36

Directive (EU) 2019/633 of the European Parliament and of the Council on unfair trading practices in business-to-business relationships in the agricultural and food supply chain [2019] OJ L111/59

Regulation (EU) 2019/1150 of the European Parliament and of the Council on promoting fairness and transparency for business users of online intermediation services [2019] OJ L186/57

Regulation (EU) 2022/1925 of the European Parliament and of the Council on contestable and fair markets in the digital sector [2022] OJ L265/1

FRANCE

Law no 2016-1321 for a Digital Republic [2016] JORF no 0235

GERMANY

Competition Act in the version published on 26 June 2013 (Federal Law Gazette I, p 1750), as last amended by article 2 of the Act of 19 July 2022 (Federal Law Gazette I, p 1214)

UNITED STATES

National Industrial Recovery Act of 1933 (NIRA), 48 Stat 195

Hart-Scott-Rodino Antitrust Improvements Act of 1976, 15 USC § 18a

Cable Television Consumer Protection and Competition Act of 1992, 106 Stat 1460

HR3816 – American Choice and Innovation Online Act, 117th Congress (2021–22)

S2710 – Open App Markets Act, 117th Congress (2021–22)

TABLE OF CASES

AUSTRIA

2019, BWB, *Amazon.de Marketplace* (Case Report), 11 September 2019

EUROPEAN UNION

European Court of Justice

1973, Case 6–72 *Continental Can v Commission* EU:C:1973:22

1974, Joined Cases 6 and 7–73 *Commercial Solvents v Commission* EU:C:1974:18

1975, Case 109/75 R *National Carbonising v Commission* EU:C:1975:133

1978, Case 27/76 *United Brands v Commission* EU:C:1978:22

1979, Case 22/78 *Hugin v Commission* EU:C:1979:138

1979, Case 85/76 *Hoffmann-La Roche v Commission* EU:C:1979:36

1981, Case 60/81 *IBM v Commission* EU:C:1981:264

1983, Case 322/81 *Michelin v Commission* EU:C:1983:313

1985, Case 311/84 *CBEM v CLT and IPB ('Télémarketing')* EU:C:1985:394

1988, Case 53/87 *Renault* EU:C:1988:472

1988, Case 238/87 *Volvo v Veng* EU:C:1988:477

1991, Case C–62/86 *AKZO Chemie v Commission* EU:C:1991:286

1995, Joined Cases C–241/91 P and C–242/91 P *RTE and ITP v Commission* ('*Magill*') EU:C:1995:98

1996, Case C–333/94 P *Tetra Pak v Commission* EU:C:1996:436

1997, Case C–242/95 *GT-Link v De Danske Statsbaner* EU:C:1997:376

1998, Case C–7/97 *Oscar Bronner v Mediaprint* EU:C:1998:569

2002, Case C–82/01 P *Aéroports de Paris v Commission* EU:C:2002:617

2004, Case C–418/01 *IMS Health v NDC Health* EU:C:2004:257

2007, Case C–95/04 P *British Airways v Commission* EU:C:2007:166

2008, Case C–413/06 P *Bertelsmann and Sony v Independent Music Publishers and Labels Association (Impala)* EU:C:2008:392

2008, Joined Cases C–468/06 to C–478/06 *Sot. Lélos v GlaxoSmithKline* EU:C:2008:504

2009, Case C–501/06 P *GlaxoSmithKline* EU:C:2009:610

2010, Case C–280/08 P *Deutsche Telekom v Commission* EU:C:2010:603

2010, Case C–413/08 P *Lafarge v Commission* EU:C:2010:346

2011, Case C–52/09 *Konkurrensverket v TeliaSonera Sverige* EU:C:2011:83

2012, Case C–457/10 P *AstraZeneca v Commission* EU:C:2012:770

2012, Case C–209/10 *Post Danmark v Konkurrencerådet* EU:C:2012:172

2012, Case C–549/10 P *Tomra Systems v Commission* EU:C:2012:221

2014, Case C–382/12 P *Mastercard v Commission* EU:C:2014:2201

2014, Case C–295/12 P *Telefónica v Commission* EU:C:2014:2062

2015, Case C–23/14 *Post Danmark v Konkurrencerådet* EU:C:2015:651

2017, Case C–413/14 P *Intel v Commission* EU:C:2017:632

2017, Case C–434/15 *Asociación Profesional Élite Taxi v Uber Systems Spain* EU:C:2017:981

2018, Case C–525/16 *MEO v Autoridade da Concorrência* EU:C:2018:270

2021, Case C–165/19 P *Slovak Telekom v Commission* EU:C:2021:239

2022, Case C–377/20 *Servizio Elettrico Nazionale* EU:C:2022:379

General Court (Court of First Instance)

1991, Case T–30/89 *Hilti v Commission* EU:T:1991:70

1994, Case T–83/91 *Tetra Pak v Commission* EU:T:1994:246

1997, Case T–229/94 *Deutsche Bahn v Commission* EU:T:1997:155

1999, Case T–228/97 *Irish Sugar v Commission* EU:T:1999:246

2000, Case T–5/97 *IPS v Commission* EU:T:2000:278

2003, Case T–65/98 *Van den Bergh Foods v Commission* EU:T:2003:281

2006, Case T–168/01 *GlaxoSmithKline Services Unlimited v Commission* EU:T:2006:265

2006, Joined Cases T–213/01 and T–214/01 *Österreichische Postsparkasse v Commission* EU:T:2006:151

2007, Case T–201/04 *Microsoft v Commission* EU:T:2007:289

2008, Case T–271/03 *Deutsche Telekom v Commission* EU:T:2008:101

2009, Case T–301/04 *Clearstream v Commission* EU:T:2009:317

2010, Case T–427/08 *Confédération européenne des associations d'horlogers-réparateurs v Commission* EU:T:2010:517

2010, Case T–342/07 *Ryanair v Commission* EU:T:2010:280

2012, Case T–336/07 *Telefónica v Commission* EU:T:2012:172

2013, Case T–79/12 *Cisco v Commission* EU:T:2013:635

2018, Case T–851/14 *Slovak Telekom v Commission* EU:T:2018:929

2020, Case T–399/16 *CK Telecoms v Commission* EU:T:2020:217

2021, Case T–612/17 *Google v Commission* EU:T:2021:763

2022, Case T–604/18 *Google v Commission* EU:T:2022:541

2022, Case T–227/21 *Illumina v Commission* EU:T:2022:447

Advocate General Opinions

1998, Case C–7/97 *Oscar Bronner v Mediaprint* EU:C:1998:264, Opinion of AG Jacobs

2004, Case C–53/03 *Syfait v GlaxoSmithKline* EU:C:2004:673, Opinion of AG Jacobs

2010, Case C–52/09 *Konkurrensverket v TeliaSonera* EU:C:2010:483, Opinion of AG Mazák

2012, Case C–457/10 P *AstraZeneca v Commission* EU:C:2012:293, Opinion of AG Mazák

2015, Case C–23/14 *Post Danmark v Konkurrencerådet* EU:C:2015:343, Opinion of AG Kokott

2016, Case C–413/14 P *Intel v Commission* EU:C:2016:788, Opinion of AG Wahl

2017, Case C–177/16 *AKKA/LAA v Konkurences padome* EU:C:2017:286, Opinion of AG Wahl

2020, Cases C–152/19 P and C–165/19 P *Slovak Telekom v Commission* EU:C:2020:678, Opinion of AG Saugmandsgaard Øe

European Commission

1979, *Vaessen/Moris* (Case IV/C-29.290) Commission Decision 79/86/EEC [1979] OJ L19/32

1987, *Eurofix-Bauco v Hilti* (Cases IV/30.787 and 31.488) Commission Decision 88/138/EEC [1988] OJ L65/19

1988, *Napier Brown – British Sugar* (Case IV/30.178) Commission Decision 88/518/EEC [1988] OJ L284/4

1991, *Tetra Pak II* (IV/31043) Commission Decision 92/163/EEC [1992] OJ L72/1

1992, *Sealink/B&I – Holyhead* (Case IV/34.174) Commission Decision

2001, *British Post/Deutsche Post* (Case COMP/C-1/36.915) Commission Decision [2001] OJ L331/40

2001, *Deutsche Post* (Case COMP/35.141) Commission Decision [2001] OJ L125/27

2003, *Deutsche Telekom* (Cases COMP/C-1/37.451, 37.578, 37.579) Commission Decision 2003/707/EC [2003] OJ L263/9

2004, *GIMD/Socpresse* (Case COMP/M.3420) Commission Decision [2004] OJ C265/3

2004, *Microsoft* (Case COMP/C-3/37.792) Commission Decision C(2004)900

2004, *BdKEP/Deutsche Post* (Case COMP/38.745) Commission Decision

2005, *Microsoft* (Case COMP/C-3/37.792) Commission Decision C(2005)4420

2007, *Travelport/Worldspan* (Case COMP/M.4523) Commission Decision C(2007)3938

2007, *Wanadoo España v Telefónica* (Case COMP/38.784) Commission Decision

2008, *German Electricity Wholesale Market and German Electricity Balancing Market* (Case COMP/39.388-389) Commission Decision C(2008)7367

2008, *Google/DoubleClick* (Case COMP/M.4731) Commission Decision C(2008)927

2009, *Microsoft (tying)* (Case COMP/C-3/39.530) Commission Decision [2010] OJ C36/7

2009, *RWE Gas Foreclosure* (Case COMP/39.402) Commission Decision

2010, *Microsoft/Yahoo! Search Business* (Case COMP/M.5727) Commission Decision C(2010)1077

2011, *IBM Maintenance Services* (Case COMP/C-3/39692) Commission Decision C(2011)9245

2011, *Microsoft/Skype* (Case COMP/M.6281) Commission Decision C(2011)7279

2012, *Reuters Instrument Codes* (Case AT.39654) Commission Decision C(2012)9635

2012, *Rio Tinto Alcan* (Case AT.39230) Commission Decision C(2012)9439

2013, *Deutsche Bahn I and II* (Cases AT.39678 and AT.39731) Commission Decision [2014] OJ C86/4

2013, *Microsoft/Nokia* (Case COMP/M.7047) Commission Decision C(2013)8873

2013, *Microsoft (tying)* (Case AT.39530) Commission Decision C(2013)1210

2014, *Facebook/ WhatsApp* (Case M.7217) Commission Decision C(2014)7239

2014, *Slovak Telekom* (Case AT.39523) Commission Decision C(2014)7465

2014, *Watch Repair* (Case AT.39097) Commission Decision C(2014)5462

2016, *Microsoft/LinkedIn* (Case M.8124) Commission Decision C(2016)8404

2017, *Google Search (Shopping)* (Case AT.39740) Commission Decision C(2017)4444

2018, *Google Android* (Case AT.40099) Commission Decision C(2018)4761

2019, *Google Search (AdSense)* (Case AT.40411) Commission Decision C(2019)2173

2020, *Google/Fitbit* (Case M.9660) Commission Decision C(2020)9105

2022, *Amazon Marketplace* and *Amazon Buy Box* (Cases AT.40462 and AT.40703) Commission Decision C(2022) 9442

2022, *Meta/Kustomer* (Case M.10262) Commission Decision C(2022)409

—*Apple – App Store Practices* (Case AT.40716)

—*Apple – App Store Practices (e-books/audiobooks)* (Case AT.40652)

—*Apple – App Store Practices (music streaming)* (Case AT.40437)

—*Google Jobs* (Case AT.40592)

—*Google Local* (Case AT.40585)

LUXEMBOURG

2017, Conseil de la concurrence, Decision 2017-C-02, *Amazon Services Europe*, 21 June 2017

FRANCE

Court

2019, Tribunal de commerce de Paris, case 2017050625, *Ministre de l'Économie et des Finances v Amazon*, 2 September 2019

Competition Authority

2014, AdlC, Decision 14-MC-02, *GDF Suez,* 9 September 2014

2015, AdlC, Decision 15-D-06, *Booking.com*, 21 April 2015

2021, AdlC, Decision 21-D-07, *Interactive Advertising Bureau France et al v Apple*, 17 March 2021

GERMANY

Court

2013, Court of Hamburg, Case 408 HKO 36/13 *Verband Deutscher Wetterdienstleister v Google*, 11 April 2013

Competition Authority

2013, Bundeskartellamt, Case B6-46/12, *Amazon removes price parity obligation for retailers on its Marketplace platform*, 26 November 2013

2019, Bundeskartellamt, Case B2-88/18, *Amazon*, 17 July 2019

2019, Bundeskartellamt, Case B6-22/16, *Facebook*, 7 February 2019

2022, Bundeskartellamt, Case B2-55/21, *Amazon*, 26 October 2022

2022, Bundeskartellamt, Case B6–55/20, *Linkage of Meta Quest (formerly Oculus) with the Facebook network*, 23 November 2022

ITALY

2021, AGCM, Case A528, *Amazon*, 9 December 2021

2021, AGCM, Case A529, *Google (Android Auto)*, 13 May 2021

NETHERLANDS

Court

2018, Rechtbank Amsterdam, Case C/13/528337, *VBO Makelaar v Funda Real Estate*, 21 March 2018

Competition Authority

2007, NMa, Case 5901 *Bloemenveiling Aalsmeer/FloraHolland*, NMa, 21 August 2007

2021, ACM, Case ACM/19/035630, *Apple*, 24 August 2021

SWEDEN

2015, Konkurrensverket, Decision 596/2013, *Booking.com*, 15 April 2015

UNITED KINGDOM

Court

2016, *Streetmap.eu v Google* [2016] EWHC 253 (Ch)

2022, *Meta v CMA* [2022] CAT 26

Competition Authority

2012, OFT, Case ME/5525/12 *Facebook/Instagram*, 14 August 2012

2017, CMA, 'Retail Banking Market Investigation' (Order) 2017

2021, CMA, *Meta/Giphy* (Final Report), 30 November 2021

UNITED STATES

Courts

1904, *Northern Securities v United States* 193 US 197 (1904)

1911, *The Standard Oil Company of New Jersey v United States* 221 US 1 (1911)

1911, *United States v American Tobacco* 221 US 106 (1911)

1921, *American Column & Lumber v United States* 257 US 37 (1921)

1935, *ALA Schechter Poultry v United States* 295 US 495 (1935)

1949, *Standard Oil v United States* 337 US 293 (1949)

1951, *Lorain Journal v United States* 342 US 143 (1951)

1953, *Times-Picayune v United States* 345 US 594 (1953)

1956, *Hush-A-Phone v United States*, 238 F2d 266 (DC Cir 1956)

1958, *Northern Pacific Railway v United States* 356 US 1 (1958)

1961, *United States v EI du Pont de Nemours* 366 US 316 (1961)

1962, *Brown Shoe v United States* 370 US 294 (1962)

1966, *United States v Von's Grocery* 384 US 270 (1966)

1968, *Carterfone v AT&T* 13 FCC2d 420 (1968)

1972, *United States v Topco Associates* 405 US 596 (1972)

1979, *Reiter v Sonotone* 442 US 33 (1979)

1982, *United States v AT&T* 552 F Supp 131 (DDC 1982)

1983, *MCI Communications v AT&T* 708 F2d 1081 (7th Cir 1983)

1984, *Jefferson Parish Hosp v Hyde* 466 US 2 (1984)

1992, *Eastman Kodak v Image Technical Servs* 504 US 451 (1992)

1994, *Turner Broadcasting System v FCC* 512 US 622 (1994)

2000, *United States v Microsoft* 87 F Supp 2d 30 (DDC 2000)

2000, *United States v Microsoft* 97 F Supp 2d 59 (DDC 2000)

2001, *United States v Microsoft* 253 F3d 34 (DC Cir 2001)

2002, Civil Action no 98-1233 (CKK) (DDC 2002)

2003, Civil Action no 98-1232 (CKK) (DDC 2003)

2004, *Verizon Communications v Law Offices of Curtis V Trinko* 540 US 398 (2004)

2007, *Leegin Creative Leather Products v PSKS* 551 US 877 (2007)

2009, *Pacific Bell Telephone v linkLine Communications* 555 US 438 (2009)

2011, *United States v Comcast*, no 1:11-cv-00l06 (DDC, 1 September 2011)

2013, *Comcast v FCC*, no 12-1337 (DC Cir, 28 May 2013)

2018, *Ohio v American Express* 585 US ____ (2018)

2018, *United States v AT&T*, no 17-2511 (DDC, 12 June 2018)

2018, *Williams-Sonoma v Amazon*, no 18-cv-07548 (ND Cal, 14 December 2018) (Complaint)

2019, *Genius v Google and LyricFind*, no 526241/2019 (NY, 3 December 2019) (Complaint)

2019, *United States v AT&T*, no 18-5214 (DC Cir, 26 February 2019)

2020, *Genius v Google and LyricFind*, no 19-cv-7279 (EDNY, 20 August 2020)

2020, *United States and 11 States v Google*, no 1:20-cv-03010 (DDC, 20 October 2020) (Complaint)

2021, *Epic Games v Apple*, no 4:20-cv-05640-YGR (ND Cal, 10 September 2021)

2021, *FTC v Facebook*, no 1:20-cv-03590-JEB (DDC, 19 August 2021) (Amended Complaint)

Competition Authority

2012, FTC, File no 121-0121, *Facebook/Instagram* (Closing Letter, 2012)

2013, FTC, File no 111-0163, *In the Matter of Google* (Statement regarding Google's search practices, 3 January 2013)

BIBLIOGRAPHY

Books and Chapters in Edited Collections

Arrow K, 'Economic Welfare and the Allocation of Resources for Invention' in *The Rate and Direction of Inventive Activity: Economic and Social Factors* (Princeton University Press, 1962)

Baker J, *The Antitrust Paradigm: Restoring a Competitive Economy* (HUP 2019)

Baumol W, Panzar J and Willig R, *Contestable Markets and the Theory of Industry Structure* (Harcourt Brace 1982)

Belleflamme P and Peitz M, *The Economics of Platforms* (CUP 2021)

Benjamin S and Speta J, *Telecommunications Law and Policy* (Carolina Academic Press 2015)

Bessen J, *The New Goliaths: How Corporations Use Software to Dominate Industries, Kill Innovation, and Undermine Regulation* (Yale University Press 2022)

Bork R, *The Antitrust Paradox* (Basic Books 1978)

Bostoen F, 'Competition Law in the Peer-to-Peer Economy' in Bram Devolder (ed), *The Platform Economy: Unravelling the Legal Status of Online Intermediaries* (Intersentia 2019)

Boudreau K and Hagiu A, 'Platforms Rules: Multi-Sided Platforms as Regulators' in Annabelle Gawer, *Platforms, Markets and Innovation* (Edward Elgar 2009)

Bradford A, *The Brussels Effect: How the European Union Rules the World* (OUP 2020)

Christensen C, *The Innovator's Dilemma: When New Technologies Cause Great Firms to Fail* (HBR Press 1997)

Crawford S, *Captive Audience* (Yale University Press 2013)

Cusumano M, Gawer A and Yoffie D, *The Business of Platforms* (Harper Business 2019)

Dayen D, *Monopolized: Life in the Age of Corporate Power* (The New Press 2020)

de Streel A, 'The Antitrust Activism of the European Commission in the Telecommunications Sector' in Philip Lowe and Mel Marquis (eds), *European Competition Law Annual 2012* (Hart 2014)

Ducci F, *Natural Monopolies in Digital Platform Markets* (CUP 2020)

Dunne N, 'Competition Law (and Its Limits) in the Sharing Economy' in Nestor Davidson, Michèle Finck and John Infranca (eds), *Cambridge Handbook on Law and Regulation of the Sharing Economy* (CUP 2018)

Economides N, 'Telecommunications Regulation: An Introduction' in Richard Nelson, *The Limits of Market Organization* (Russel Sage Foundation 2005)

Elhauge E and Geradin D, *Global Antitrust Law and Economics* (Foundation Press 2018)

Ellis J, *Founding Brothers* (Knopf 2003)

Eriksson M, Fleischer R, Johansson A, Snickars P and Vonderau P, *Spotify Teardown: Inside the Black Box of Streaming Music* (MIT Press 2019)

Esayas S, 'Privacy-as-a-Quality Parameter of Competition' in Björn Lundqvist and Michal Gal (eds), *Competition Law for the Digital Economy* (Edward Elgar 2019)

Evans D and Schmalensee R, *Matchmakers: The New Economics of Multi-Sided Platforms* (*HBR* Press 2016)

Ezrachi A and Bernitz U (eds), *Private Labels, Brands and Competition Policy* (OUP 2009)

—— and Stucke M, *Virtual Competition: The Promise and Perils of the Algorithm-Driven Economy* (HUP 2016)

Farrell J and Klemperer P, 'Coordination and Lock-In: Competition with Switching Costs and Network Effects' in Mark Armstrong and Robert Porter, *Handbook of Industrial Organization* (Elsevier 2007)

Frier S, *No Filter: The Inside Story of Instagram* (Simon & Schuster 2020)

Fumagalli C, Motta M and Calcagno C, *Exclusionary Practices: The Economics of Monopolization and Abuse of Dominance* (CUP 2018)

Galloway S, *The Four: The Hidden DNA of Amazon, Apple, Facebook, and Google* (Portfolio 2017)

García Martínez A, *Chaos Monkeys: Obscene Fortune and Random Failure in Silicon Valley* (Harper 2016)

Gavil A, 'Burden of Proof in U.S. Antitrust Law' in *Issues in Competition Law and Policy* (ABA Section of Antitrust Law 2008)

—— and First H, *The Microsoft Antitrust Cases: Competition Policy for the Twenty-First Century* (MIT Press 2014)

Gore D and van Rooijen A, '*Ex Post* Assessment of European Competition Policy: The *Microsoft* Cases' in Assimakis Komninos and Nicolas Petit (eds), *Ex Post Evaluation of Competition Cases* (Kluwer 2021)

Graef I, *EU Competition Law, Data Protection and Online Platforms: Data as Essential Facility* (Kluwer 2016)

Hovenkamp H, *The Antitrust Enterprise: Principle and Execution* (HUP 2005)

Ibáñez Colomo P, *The Shaping of Competition Law* (CUP 2018)

Isaacson W, *The Innovators: How a Group of Hackers, Geniuses, and Geeks Created the Digital Revolution* (Simon & Schuster 2014)

—— *Steve Jobs* (Abacus 2015)

Jones A, Sufrin B and Dunne N, *EU Competition Law: Text, Cases, and Materials* (OUP 2019)

Joskow P, 'Regulation of Natural Monopolies' in Mitchell Polinsky and Steven Shavell (eds), *Handbook of Law and Economics* (Elsevier 2007)

Kalintiri A, *Evidence Standards in EU Competition Enforcement* (Hart 2019)

Katz M and Shapiro C, 'Antitrust in Software Markets' in Jeffrey Eisenach and Thomas Lenard (eds), *Competition, Innovation and the Microsoft Monopoly: Antitrust in the Digital Marketplace* (Springer 1999)

Kelly K, *The Inevitable: Understanding the 12 Technological Forces That Will Shape Our Future* (Viking Press 2016)

Kovacic W, 'Two Views of Exclusion: Why the European Union and the United States Diverged on Google' in Guy Rolnik (ed), *Digital Platforms and Concentration* (ProMarket e-book 2018)

Kwoka J, *Mergers, Merger Control, and Remedies* (MIT Press 2014)

—— *Controlling Mergers and Market Power: A Program for Reviving Antitrust in America* (CPI 2020)

Lambert T, *How to Regulate: A Guide for Policymakers* (CUP 2017)

Maier-Rigaud F, 'Behavioural versus Structural Remedies in EU Competition Law' in Philip Lowe, Mel Marquis and Giorgio Monti (eds), *European Competition Law Annual 2013: Effective and Legitimate Enforcement of Competition Law* (Hart 2016)

Mayer-Schönberger V and Ramge T, *Reinventing Capitalism in the Age of Big Data* (Basic Books 2018)

McCullough B, *How the Internet Happened: From Netscape to the iPhone* (Liveright 2018)

Miller C, *Chip War: The Fight for the World's Most Critical Technology* (Scribner 2022)

Monti G, *EC Competition Law* (CUP 2007)

Mueller M, *Universal Service: Competition, Interconnection and Monopoly in the Making of the American Telephone System* (MIT/AEI Press 1997)

O'Donoghue R and Padilla J, *The Law and Economics of Article 102 TFEU* (Hart 2020)

O'Mara M, *The Code: Silicon Valley and the Remaking of America* (Penguin 2019)

Page W and Lopatka J, *The Microsoft Case: Antitrust, High Technology, and Consumer Welfare* (The University of Chicago Press 2007)

Parker G, Van Alstyne M and Choudary S, *Platform Revolution* (Norton 2016)

Petit N, *Big Tech & the Digital Economy: The Moligopoly Scenario* (OUP 2020)

Philippon T, *The Great Reversal: How America Gave Up on Free Markets* (HUP 2019)

Robertson V, *Competition Law's Innovation Factor: The Relevant Market in Dynamic Contexts in the EU and the US* (Hart 2020)

Rovelli C, *Reality Is Not What It Seems: The Journey to Quantum Gravity* (Riverhead Books 2018)

Sagers C, *United States v Apple: Competition in America* (HUP 2019)

Saloner G, Shepard A and Podolny J, *Strategic Management* (Wiley 2001)

Salop S, 'Economic Analysis of Exclusionary Vertical Conduct: Where Chicago Has Overshot the Mark' in Robert Pitofsky (ed), *How the Chicago School Overshot the Mark: The Effect of Conservative Economic Analysis on U.S. Antitrust* (OUP 2008)

Schmidt E and Rosenberg J, *How Google Works* (John Murray 2014)

Schumpeter J, *Capitalism, Socialism and Democracy* (Harper & Brothers 1942)

Shapiro C, 'Competition and Innovation: Did Arrow Hit the Bull's Eye?' in Josh Lerner and Scott Stern (eds), *The Rate and Direction of Inventive Activity Revisited* (University of Chicago Press 2012)

Srnicek N, *Platform Capitalism* (Polity 2017)

Stone B, *The Everything Store* (Corgi 2014)

—— *Amazon Unbound* (Simon & Schuster 2021)

Strowel A and Vergote W, 'Digital Platforms: To Regulate or Not to Regulate?' in Bram Devolder (ed), *The Platform Economy: Unravelling the Legal Status of Online Intermediaries* (Intersentia 2019)

Sunstein C, *The Cost-Benefit Revolution* (MIT Press 2018)

Taplin J, *Move Fast and Break Things: How Facebook, Google and Amazon Have Cornered Culture and What It Means for All of Us* (Macmillan 2017)

Thiel P, *From Zero to One: Notes on Startups, or How to Build the Future* (Crown Business 2014)

Tzoulia E, 'Competition Law Issues' in Ioannis Iglezakis (ed), *Legal Issues of Mobile Apps: A Practical Guide* (Kluwer 2020)

Van den Bergh R, *Comparative Competition Law and Economics* (Edward Elgar 2017)

van Schewick B, *Internet Architecture and Innovation* (MIT Press 2010)

Webb A, *The Big Nine: How the Tech Titans and Their Thinking Machines Could Warp Humanity* (PublicAffairs 2019)

Whish R and Bailey D, *Competition Law* (OUP 2018)

Witt A, *The More Economic Approach to EU Antitrust Law* (Hart 2016)

Wu T, *The Master Switch: The Rise and Fall of Information Empires* (Vintage 2011)

—— *The Attention Merchants: The Epic Scramble to Get Inside our Heads* (Knopf 2016)

—— *The Curse of Bigness* (Columbia Global Reports 2018)

Zittrain J, *The Future of the Internet – And How to Stop It* (Yale University Press 2008)

Zuboff S, *The Age of Surveillance Capitalism* (PublicAffairs 2019)

Journal Articles, Working Papers, Speeches

—— 'Mr. Justice Brandeis, Competition and Smallness: A Dilemma Re-Examined' (1956) 66 The Yale Law Journal 69

Abrahamson Z, 'Essential Data' (2014) 124 Yale Law Journal 867

Abrantes-Metz R and Metz A, 'Regulating Multisided Platforms? The Case against Treating Platforms as Utilities' (2020) CPI Antitrust Chronicle August

Adner R, Chen J and Zhu F, 'Frenemies in Platform Markets: Heterogeneous Profit Foci as Drivers of Compatibility Decisions' (2019) 66 Management Science 2432

Akman P, 'Searching for the Long-Lost Soul of Article 82 EC' (2009) 29 Oxford Journal of Legal Studies 267

—— 'The Theory of Abuse in *Google Search*: A Positive and Normative Assessment Under EU Competition Law' (2017) Journal of Law, Technology & Policy 302

Albors-Llorens A, 'Refusal to Deal and Objective Justification in EC Competition Law' (2006) 65 The Cambridge Law Journal 24

Alexiadis P and de Streel A, 'Designing an EU Intervention Standard for Digital Platforms' (2020) EUI Working Paper RSCAS 2020/14

Allendesalazar Corcho R, 'Can We Finally Say Farewell to the "Special Responsibility" of Dominant Companies?' (2007) EUI Robert Schuman Centre EU Competition Law and Policy Workshop/Proceedings

Allensworth R, 'The Commensurability Myth in Antitrust' (2016) 69 Vanderbilt Law Review 1

Amelio A and Jullien B, 'Tying and Freebies in Two-Sided Markets' (2012) 30 International Journal of Industrial Organization 436

Anderson S and Bedre-Defolie Ö, 'Hybrid Platform Model' (2022) CEPR Discussion Paper no DP16243 <https://ssrn.com/abstract=3886686>

Argenton C and Prüfer J, 'Search Engine Competition with Network Externalities' (2012) 8 JCLE 73

Armstrong M, 'Competition in Two-Sided Markets' (2006) 37 RAND Journal of Economics 668

Arrow K, 'The Economic Implications of Learning by Doing' (1962) 29 The Review of Economic Studies 155

—— Carlton D and Sider H, 'The Competitive Effects of Line-of-Business Restrictions in Telecommunications' (1995) 16 Managerial and Decision Economics 301

Ashenfelter O, Hosken D and Weinberg M, 'Did Robert Bork Understate the Competitive Impact of Mergers? Evidence from Consummated Mergers' (2014) 57 The Journal of Law and Economics 67

Auer D, 'Appropriability and the European Commission's Android Investigation' (2017) 23 Columbia Journal of European Law 647

—— and Petit N, 'Two-Sided Markets and the Challenge of Turning Economic Theory into Antitrust Policy' (2015) 60 The Antitrust Bulletin 426

Auf'mkolk H, 'The "Feedback Effect" of Applying EU Competition Law to Regulated Industries: Doctrinal Contamination in the Case of Margin Squeeze' (2012) 3 JECLAP 149

Bailey D, 'Presumptions in EU Competition Law' (2010) 31 ECLR 20

Baker J, 'Taking the Error Out of "Error Cost" Analysis: What's Wrong with Antitrust's Right' (2015) 80 Antitrust Law Journal 1

—— Rose N, Salop S and Scott Morton F, 'Five Principles for Vertical Merger Enforcement Policy' (2019) 33 Antitrust 12

Balto D and Parker R, 'The Evolving Approach to Merger Remedies' (Public Statement, as published in Antitrust Report, 2000)

Bamberger K and Lobel O, 'Platform Market Power' (2017) 32 Berkeley Technology Law Journal 1051

Barczentewicz M, 'Privacy and Security Implications of Regulation of Digital Services in the EU and in the US' (2022) Stanford-Vienna TTLF Working Paper no 84

Baumol W, 'On the Theory of Expansion of the Firm' (1962) 52 The American Economic Review 1078

Binet C, 'Buyer Power in EU Competition Law: A Boon or Impediment to Consumer Welfare?' (2015) unpublished PhD thesis, available at <https://dial.uclouvain.be/pr/boreal/object/boreal:156352>

Biro Z, Houpis G and Hunt M, 'Applying Margin Squeeze in Telecommunications: Some Economic Insights' (2011) 2 JECLAP 588

Bitton D, Dolmans M, Mostyn H and Pearl D, 'Competition in Display Ad Technology: A Retrospective Look at Google/DoubleClick and Google/Admob' (2019) CPI Antitrust Chronicle April

Blockx J, 'Revaluing the Role of Intent Evidence in EU Antitrust Law' (2019) 3 CoRe 354

Bok D, 'Section 7 of the Clayton Act and the Merging of Law and Economics' (1960) 74 Harvard Law Review 226

Bonanno A and Lopez R, 'Private Label Expansion and Supermarket Milk Prices' (2005) 3 Journal of Agricultural & Food Industrial Organization 1

Bontemps C, Orozco V, Réquillart V and Trévisiol A, 'Price Effects of Private Label Development (2005) 3 Journal of Agricultural & Food Industrial Organization 1

Borgogno O and Colangelo G, 'Data Sharing and Interoperability: Fostering Innovation and Competition Through APIs' (2019) 35 CLSR 1

Bork R, 'Legislative Intent and the Policy of the Sherman Act' (1966) 9 The Journal of Law & Economics 7

—— and Bowman W, 'The Crisis in Antitrust' (1965) 65 Columbia Law Review 363

Bostoen F, 'Margin Squeeze: Where Competition Law and Sector Regulation Compete' (2017) 53 Jura Falconis 3

—— 'Most Favoured Nation Clauses: Towards an Assessment Framework Under EU Competition Law' (2017) 1 CoRe 223

—— 'Online Platforms and Vertical Integration: The Return of Margin Squeeze?' (2018) 6 JAE 355

—— 'Regulating Online Platforms: Lessons from 100 years of Telecommunications Regulation' (2019)

—— 'The General Court's *Google Shopping* Judgment: Finetuning the Legal Qualifications and Tests for Platform Abuse' (2022) 13 JECLAP 75

—— 'Understanding the Digital Markets Act' (2023) 68 Antitrust Bulletin 263

—— and Mândrescu D, 'Assessing Abuse of Dominance in the Platform Economy: A Case Study of App Stores' (2020) 16 European Competition Journal 431

Bowman W, 'Tying Arrangements and the Leverage Problem' (1957) 67 The Yale Law Journal 19

Bridy A, 'Remediating Social Media: A Layer-Conscious Approach' (2018) 24 Boston University Journal of Science and Technology Law 193

Brin S and Page L, 'The PageRank Citation Ranking: Bringing Order to the Web' (1998) Working Paper <http://ilpubs.stanford.edu:8090/422/1/1999-66.pdf>

Bryan K and Hovenkamp E, 'Antitrust Limits on Startup Acquisitions' (2020) 56 Review of Industrial Organization 615

—— and Hovenkamp E, 'Startup Acquisitions, Error Costs, and Antitrust Policy' (2020) 87 The University of Chicago Law Review 331

Brynjolfsson E and Collis A, 'How Should We Measure the Digital Economy?' (2020) Hutchins Center Working Paper 57

—— 'Innovations – Challenges for Competition Law Practice' (Series of papers on 'Competition and Consumer Protection in the Digital Economy', 2017)

Caffarra C, Crawford G and Valletti T, '"How Tech Rolls": Potential Competition and "Reverse" Killer Acquisitions' (2020) CPI Antitrust Chronicle May

—— Crawford G and Weeds H, 'Kabuki Dances or Rube Goldberg Machines? Vertical Analyses of Media Mergers' (2018) CPI Antitrust Chronicle August

Caillaud B and Jullien B, 'Chicken & Egg: Competition Among Intermediation Service Providers' (2003) 34 RAND Journal of Economics 309

Callander S and Matouschek N, 'The Novelty of Innovation: Competition, Disruption, and Antitrust Policy' (2022) 68 Management Science 37

Carlton D and Waldman M, 'The Strategic Use of Tying to Preserve and Create Market Power in Evolving Industries' (2002) 33 The RAND Journal of Economics 194

Carrier M, 'Only "Scraping" the Surface: The Copyright Hole in the FTC's Google Settlement' (2013) 46 UBC Law Review 759

Castillo de la Torre F, 'Is the Effects-Based Approach Too Cumbersome? Taking Stock of Recent Practice and Case Law on Article 102 TFEU' (2023) <https://ssrn.com/abstract=4395401>

Cave M, 'Six Degrees of Separation: Operational Separation as a Remedy in European Telecommunications Regulation' (2006) 64 Communications and Strategies 89

Caves K and Singer H, 'When the Econometrician Shrugged: Identifying and Plugging Gaps in the Consumer Welfare Standard' (2018) 26 George Mason Law Review 395

Cennamo C and Santaló J, 'Generativity tension and value creation in platform ecosystems' (2019) 30 Organization Science 617

Chen C, Frey CB and Presidente G, 'Privacy Regulation and Firm Performance: Estimating the GDPR Effect Globally' (2022) Oxford Martin Working Paper Series on Technological and Economic Change no 2022-1

Chirita A, 'Google's Anti-Competitive and Unfair Practices in Digital Leisure Markets' (2015) 11 The Competition Law Review 109

Cho D, Ferreira P and Telang R, 'The Impact of Mobile Number Portability on Price, Competition and Consumer Welfare' (2016) <https://ssrn.com/abstract=2265104>

Choi JP, 'Tying in Two-Sided Markets with Multi-Homing' (2010) 58 The Journal of Industrial Economics 607

—— and Jeon D-S, 'A Leverage Theory of Tying in Two-Sided Markets' (2016) TSE Working Paper 16–689

—— and Stefanadis C, 'Tying, Investment, and the Dynamic Leverage Theory' (2001) 32 The RAND Journal of Economics 52

Coase R, 'The Problem of Social Cost' (1960) 3 The Journal of Law & Economics 1

Colangelo G and Maggiolino M, 'Big Data as Misleading Facilities' (2017) 13 European Competition Journal 249

Colangelo M, 'The Interface Between Competition Rules and Sector-Specific Regulation in the Telecommunications Sector: Evidence from Recent EU Margin Squeeze Cases' (2013) 14 Competition and Regulation in Network Industries 214

Competition Bureau of Canada, 'Big Data and Innovation: Implications for Competition Policy in Canada' (Draft Discussion Paper, 2017)

Condorelli D and Padilla J, 'Harnessing Platform Envelopment in the Digital World' (2020) 16 JCLE 143

Crandall R, 'The Dubious Antitrust Argument for Breaking Up the Internet Giants' (2019) 54 Review of Industrial Organization 627

Crocioni P, 'Leveraging of Market Power in Emerging Markets: A Review of Cases, Literature, and a Suggested Framework' (2007) 4 JCLE 449

Cseres K, 'The Controversies of the Consumer Welfare Standard' (2007) 3 The Competition Law Review 121

Cunningham C, Ederer F and Ma S, 'Killer Acquisitions' (2021) 129 Journal of Political Economy 649

Dacar R, 'Is the Essential Facilities Doctrine Fit for Access to Data Cases? The Data Protection Aspect' (2022) 18 Croatian Yearbook of European Law and Policy 61

Dahl D, Meyer A and Neely M, 'Scale Matters: Community Banks and Compliance Costs' (2016) The Regional Economist July

De Hert P et al, 'The Right to Data Portability in the GDPR: Towards User-Centric Interoperability of Digital Services' (2018) 34 CLSR 193

de Silva I, 'The Future of Competition Law: Time to Change or Time to Adapt?' (46th Annual Conference on International Antitrust Law and Policy, New York, 12 September 2019)

de Streel A, 'Should Digital Antitrust Be Ordoliberal?' Concurrences no 1-2020, art no 92610 <www.concurrences.com/92610>

Decherney P, Ensmenger N and Yoo C, 'Are Those Who Ignore History Doomed to Repeat It?' (2011) 78 The University of Chicago Law Review 1627

Delrahim M, 'All Roads Lead to Rome: Enforcing the Consumer Welfare Standard in Digital Media Markets' (Jevons Institute Colloquium, Rome, 22 May 2018)

Deng Y et al, 'Friend or Foe: When a Platform Enters the Market to Compete with its Third-Party Sellers' (2021) <https://ssrn.com/abstract=3979173>

Dina Srinivasan D, 'The Antitrust Case against Facebook' (2019) 16 Berkeley Business Law Journal 39

Ducci F, 'Procedural Implications of Market Definition in Platform Cases' (2019) 7 JAE 419

Dunne N, 'Margin Squeeze: Theory, Practice, Policy – Part 1' (2012) 33 ECLR 29

—— 'Margin Squeeze: Theory, Practice, Policy – Part 2' (2012) 33 ECLR 61

—— 'Dispensing with Indispensability' (2019) LSE Law, Society and Economy Working Paper 15/2019

Easterbrook F, 'The Limits of Antitrust' (1984) 63 Texas Law Review 1

Eben M, 'Fining Google: A Missed Opportunity for Legal Certainty?' (2018) 14 European Competition Journal 129

Economides N, 'Vertical Leverage and the Sacrifice Principle: Why the Supreme Court Got *Trinko* Wrong' (2005) 61 New York University Annual Survey of American Law 379

Edelman B, 'Does Google Leverage Market Power Through Tying and Bundling?' (2015) 11 JCLE 365

Egan E, 'Data Portability and Privacy: Charting a Way Forward' (Facebook White Paper) 2019

Eisenmann T, Parker G and Van Alstyne M, 'Platform Envelopment' (2011) 32 Strategic Management Journal 1270

Elhauge E, 'Tying, Bundled Discounts, and the Death of the Single Monopoly Profit Theory' (2009) 123 Harvard Law Review 397

—— and Nalebuff B, 'The Welfare Effects of Metering Ties' (2017) 33 The Journal of Law, Economics, and Organization 68

Etro F and Caffarra C, 'On the Economics of the Android Case' (2017) 13 European Competition Journal 282

Eurich M and Burtscher M, 'The Business-to-Consumer Lock-In Effect' (2014) Cambridge Service Alliance Working Paper 1

Evans D, 'The Antitrust Economics of Multi-Sided Platform Markets' (2003) 20 Yale Journal on Regulation 325

—— 'Governing Bad Behavior by Users of Multi-Sided Platforms' (2012) 27 Berkeley Technology Law Journal 1201

—— 'Why the Dynamics of Competition for Online Platforms Leads to Sleepless Nights but not Sleepy Monopolies' (2017) <https://ssrn.com/abstract=3009438>

—— and Schmalensee R, 'The Industrial Organization of Markets with Two-Sided Platforms' (2007) 3 CPI 151

—— and Schmalensee R, 'Failure to Launch: Critical Mass in Platform Businesses' (2010) 9 Review of Network Economics 1

—— and Schmalensee R, 'The Antitrust Analysis of Multi-Sided Platform Businesses' (2012) Coase-Sandor Institute for Law and Economics Working Paper 623

Evans P and Gawer A, 'The Rise of the Platform Enterprise: A Global Survey' (2016) The Emerging Platform Economy Series 1

Ezrachi A, 'Unchallenged Market Power? The Tale of Supermarkets, Private Labels, and Competition Law' (2010) 33 World Competition 257

—— 'EU Competition Law Goals and the Digital Economy' (BEUC Discussion Paper 2019)

—— and Stucke M, 'The Fight over Antitrust's Soul' (2018) 9 JECLAP 1

Faella G and Pardolesi R, 'Squeezing Price Squeeze Under EC Antitrust Law' (2010) 6 European Competition Journal 255

Farrell J and Katz M, 'Innovation, Rent Extraction, and Integration in Systems Markets' (2000) 48 The Journal of Industrial Economics 413

—— Pautler P and Vita M, 'Economics at the FTC: Retrospective Merger Analysis with a Focus on Hospitals' (2009) 35 Review of Industrial Organization 369

—— and Weiser P, 'Modularity, Vertical Integration, and Open Access Policies: Towards a Convergence of Antitrust and Regulation in the Internet Age' (2003) 17 Harvard Journal of Law & Technology 85

Feldman R, 'Defensive Leveraging in Antitrust' (1999) 87 The Georgetown Law Journal 2079

Fenwick M, Kaal W and Vermeulen E, 'Regulation Tomorrow: What Happens When Technology Is Faster than the Law?' (2017) 6 American University Business Law Review 561

Filistrucchi L, Geradin D, van Damme E and Affeldt P, 'Market Definition in Two-Sided Markets: Theory and Practice' (2014) 10 JCLE 293

Filistrucchi L, Geradin D and van Damme E, 'Identifying Two-Sided Markets' (2013) 36 World Competition 33

Finch A, 'Concentrating on Competition: An Antitrust Perspective on Platforms and Industry Consolidation' (Capitol Forum's Fifth Annual Tech, Media & Telecom Competition Conference, Washington, DC, 14 December 2018)

Flynn J, 'The Reagan Administration's Antitrust Policy, "Original Intent" and the Legislative History of the Sherman Act' (1988) 33 The Antitrust Bulletin 259

Fox E, 'The Battle for the Soul of Antitrust' (1987) 75 California Law Review 917

Fumagalli C and Motta M, 'Tying in Evolving Industries, when Future Entry Cannot Be Deterred' (2020) 73 International Journal of Industrial Organization 1

Gal M and Aviv O, 'The Competitive Effects of the GDPR' (2020) 16 JCLE 349

—— and Rubinfeld D, 'Data Standardization' (2019) 94 New York University Law Review 737

Gautier A and Lamesch J, 'Mergers in the Digital Economy' (2020) CESifo Working Paper 8056

George D, 'Trends in Retail Competition: Private Labels, Brands and Competition Policy' (Report on the Eleventh Annual Symposium on Competition Amongst Retailers and Suppliers, 22 May 2015)

Gerard D, 'Fairness in EU Competition Policy: Significance and Implications' (2018) 9 JECLAP 211

Geradin D, 'Refusal to Supply and Margin Squeeze: A Discussion of Why the "Telefónica Exceptions" Are Wrong' (2011) TILEC Discussion Paper Series 2011–51

—— 'What Is a Digital Gatekeeper? Which Platforms Should Be Captured by the EC Proposal for a Digital Market Act?' (2021) <https://ssrn.com/abstract=3788152>

—— and Katsifis D, 'The Antitrust Case against the Apple App Store' (2020) 17 JCLE 503

—— and O'Donoghue R, 'The Concurrent Application of Competition Law and Regulation: The Cases of Margin Squeeze Abuses in the Telecommunications Sector' (2005) 1 JCLE 355

—— and Petit N, 'Price Discrimination Under EC Competition Law: The Need for a Case-by-Case Approach' (2005) GCLC Working Paper 07/05

Gerber D, 'The Transformation of European Community Competition Law?' (1994) 35 Harvard International Law Journal 97

Graef I, 'Differentiated Treatment in Platform-to-Business Relations' (2019) 38 YEL 448

Grimmelman J and Ohm P, 'Dr. Generative, or: How I Learned to Stop Worrying and Love the iPhone' (2010) 69 Maryland Law Review 910

Grullon G, Larkin Y and Michaely R, 'Are US Industries Becoming More Concentrated?' (2019) 23 Review of Finance 697

Grunes A, 'Is "Fake News" a Competition Problem?' (2017) CPI Antitrust Chronicle December 1

Gürkaynak G, Inanılır Ö, Diniz S and Gizem Yasar A, 'Multi-Sided Markets and the Challenge of Incorporating Multi-Sided Considerations into Competition Law Analysis' (2017) 5 JAE 100

Hagiu A, The T-H and Wright J, 'Should Platforms Be Allowed to Sell on Their Own Marketplaces?' (2022) 53 The RAND Journal of Economics 297

—— and Wright J, 'Marketplace or Reseller?' (2015) 61 Management Science 184

—— and Wright J, 'Multi-Sided Platforms' (2015) 43 International Journal of Industrial Organization 162

Hand J, 'Evidence on the Winner-Takes-All Business Model: The Profitability Returns-to-Scale of Expenditures on Intangibles Made by U.S. Internet Firms, 1995–2001' (2001) <https://ssrn.com/abstract=292099>

Haucap J and Heimeshoff U, 'Google, Facebook, Amazon, eBay: Is the Internet Driving Competition or Market Monopolization?' (2014) 11 International Economics and Economic Policy 49

Heinzerling L, 'How Not to Regulate' (2018) 85 The University of Chicago Law Review 2015

Hemphill S and Wu T, 'Nascent Competitors' (2020) 168 University of Pennsylvania Law Review 1879

Höppner T, 'Google's (Non-)Compliance with the EU Shopping Decision: A Study Based upon Empirical Data of 25 Comparison Shopping Services' (2020) <https://ssrn.com/abstract=3700748>

Houck S, 'Breaking Up Is Hard to Do' (2020) <https://ssrn.com/abstract=3457348>

Hovenkamp H, 'Platforms and the Rule of Reason: The *American Express* Case' (2019) Columbia Business Law Review 35

—— 'Whatever *Did* Happen to the Antitrust Movement?' (2019) 94 Notre Dame Law Review 583

—— 'Antitrust and Platform Monopoly' (2021) 130 Yale Law Journal 1952

—— and Scott Morton F, 'Framing the Chicago School of Antitrust Analysis' (2019) 168 University of Pennsylvania Law Review 1843

Iacobucci E and Ducci F, 'The Google Search Case in Europe: Tying and the Single Monopoly Profit Theorem in Two-Sided Markets' (2019) 47 European Journal of Law and Economics 15

Ibáñez Colomo P, 'Exclusionary Discrimination Under Article 102 TFEU' (2014) 51 Common Market Law Review 141

—— 'Legal Tests in EU Competition Law: Taxonomy and Operation' (2019) 10 JECLAP 424

—— 'Anticompetitive Effects in EU Competition Law' (2021) 17 JCLE 309

Italianer A, 'Competition Policy in the Digital Age' (47th Innsbruck Symposium, Innsbruck, 7 March 2014)

Joskow P and Klevorick A, 'A Framework for Analyzing Predatory Pricing Policy' (1979) 89 The Yale Law Journal 213

Kadar M, 'European Union Competition Law in the Digital Era' (2015) <https://ssrn.com/abstract=2703062>

Kahneman D, Knetsch J and Thaler R, 'Anomalies: The Endowment Effect, Loss Aversion, and Status Quo Bias' (1991) 5 Journal of Economic Perspectives 193

Kaiser H, 'Are "Closed Systems" an Antitrust Problem?' (2011) 7 CPI 91

Kamepalli SK, Rajan R and Zingales L, 'Kill Zone' (2020) NBER Working Paper 27146

Kang H, 'Intra-Platform Envelopment: The Coopetitive Dynamics Between the Platform Owner and Complementors' (2017) <https://doi.org/10.5465/AMBPP.2017.11205abstract>

Kaplow L, 'Extension of Monopoly Power through Leverage' (1985) 85 Columbia Law Review 515

—— 'Why (Ever) Define Markets?' (2010) 124 Harvard Law Review 437

Katz M, 'Big Tech Mergers: Innovation, Competition for the Market, and the Acquisition of Emerging Competitors' (2020) 54 Information Economics and Policy

—— and Sallet J, 'Multisided Platforms and Antitrust Enforcement' (2018) 127 The Yale Law Journal 2142

—— and Shapiro C, 'Network Externalities, Competition, and Compatibility' (1985) 75 The American Economic Review 424

—— and Shapiro C, 'Systems Competition and Network Effects' (1994) 8 Journal of Economic Perspectives 93

Kenney M and Zysman J, 'The Rise of the Platform Economy' (2016) 33 Issues in Science and Technology 61

Khan L, 'Amazon's Antitrust Paradox' (2017) 126 Yale Law Journal 710

—— 'Sources of Tech Platform Power' (2018) 2 Georgetown Law Tech Review 325

—— 'The Ideological Roots of America's Market Power Problem' (2018) The Yale Law Journal Forum 960

—— 'The New Brandeis Movement: America's Antimonopoly Debate' (2018) 9 JECLAP 131

—— 'The Separation of Platforms and Commerce' (2019) 119 Columbia Law Review 973

Kim H and Luca M, 'Product Quality and Entering Through Tying: Experimental Evidence' (2019) 65 Management Science 596

King S, 'Sharing Economy: What Challenges for Competition Law?' (2015) 6 JECLAP 729

Kotapati B, Mutungi S, Newham M, Schroeder J, Shao S and Wang M, 'The Antitrust Case against Apple' (2020) Digital Platform Theories of Harm Paper Series: Paper 2

Kovacic W, 'The Intellectual DNA of Modern U.S. Competition Law for Dominant Firm Conduct: The Chicago/Harvard Double Helix (2007) Columbia Business Law Review 1

Krattenmaker T and Salop S, 'Anticompetitive Exclusion: Raising Rivals' Costs to Achieve Power over Price' (1986) 92 The Yale Law Journal 209

Kuenzler A, 'Advancing Quality Competition in Big Data Markets' (2020) 15 JCLE 500

Kwoka J and Valletti T, 'Scrambled Eggs and Paralyzed Policy: Breaking Up Consummated Mergers and Dominant Firms' (2021) 30 Industrial and Corporate Change 1286

Laitenberger J, 'EU Competition Law in Innovation and Digital Markets: Fairness and the Consumer Welfare Perspective' (MLex/Hogan Lovells event, Brussels, 10 October 2017)

—— 'Fairness in Unilateral Practice Cases' (GCLC Conference, Brussels, 26 January 2018)

—— 'Fairness in EU Competition Law Enforcement' (British Chambers of Commerce EU & Belgium, Brussels, 20 June 2018)

Lamadrid de Pablo A, 'Competition Law as Fairness' (2017) 8 JECLAP 147

—— 'Shortcuts and Courts in the Era of Digitization' (2019) CPI Antitrust Chronicle October 7

Lande R, 'Consumer Choice as the Ultimate Goal of Antitrust' (2001) 62 University of Pittsburgh Law Review 503

Larouche P and Schinkel MP, 'Continental Drift in the Treatment of Dominant Firms: Article 102 TFEU in Contrast to § 2 Sherman Act' (2013) TILEC Discussion Paper 2013-20

Leibenstein H, 'Allocative Efficiency vs. "X-Efficiency"' (1966) 56 The American Economic Review 392

Lemley M and McCreary A, 'Exit Strategy' (2020) Stanford Law and Economics Olin Working Paper 542

Li J, 'Is Online Media a Two-Sided Market?' (2015) 31 CLSR 99

Liikanen E, 'The European Union Telecommunications Policy' (Telecommunications Seminar, Sarajevo, 16 July 2001)

Lobel O and Bamberger K, 'Platform Market Power' (2017) 32 Berkeley Technology Law Journal 1051

Madsen E and Vellodi N, 'Insider Imitation' (2022) <https://fass.nus.edu.sg/ecs/wp-content/uploads/sites/4/2022/05/Insider-Imitation.pdf>

Mândrescu D, 'Applying (EU) Competition Law to Online Platforms, Reflections on the Definition of the Relevant Market(s)' (2018) 41 World Competition 453

—— 'Tying and Bundling by Online Platforms: Distinguishing Between Lawful Expansion Strategies and Anti-Competitive Practices' (2021) 40 CLSR 1

Marco Colino S, 'The Antitrust F Word: Fairness Considerations in Competition Law' (2019) The Chinese University of Hong Kong Faculty of Law Research Paper 2018–19

Martens B, 'An Economic Policy Perspective on Online Platforms' (2016) JRC Digital Economy Working Paper 2016/05

Mays L, 'The Consequences of Search Bias: How Application of the Essential Facilities Doctrine Remedies Google's Unrestricted Monopoly on Search in the United States and Europe' (2015) 83 George Washington Law Review 721

Medvedovsky K (ed), 'Hipster Antitrust' (2018) Antitrust Chronicle April

Mehra S, 'Paradise Is a Walled Garden? Trust, Antitrust, and User Dynamism' (2011) 18 George Mason Law Review 889

Melamed D, 'Exclusive Dealing and Other Exclusionary Conduct—Are There Unifying Principles? (2006) 73 Antitrust Law Journal 375

Metcalfe B, 'Metcalfe's Law After 40 Years of Ethernet' (2013) 46 Computer Society 26

Mishel L, 'Uber and the Labor Market: Uber Drivers' Compensation, Wages, and the Scale of Uber and the Gig Economy' (2018) Economic Policy Institute Working Paper

Moore G, 'Cramming More Components onto Integrated Circuits' (1965) 38 Electronics 114

Muris T and Nuechterlein J, 'First Principles for Review of Long-Consummated Mergers' (2020) 5 The Criterion Journal on Innovation 29

Nalebuff B, 'Bundling as an Entry Barrier' (2004) 119 The Quarterly Journal of Economics 159

Nazzini R, '*Google* and the (Ever-stretching) Boundaries of Article 102 TFEU' (2015) 6 JECLAP 301

—— 'Unequal Treatment by Online Platforms: A Structured Approach to the Abuse Test in *Google*' (2016) GCLC Annual Conference Series

—— 'The Evolution of the Law and Policy on Tying: A European Perspective from Classic Leveraging to the Challenges of Online Platforms' (2017) 27 Journal of Transnational Law and Policy 1

Nevo H and Van den Bergh R, 'Private Labels: Challenges for Competition Law and Economics' (2017) 40 World Competition 271

Newman J, 'Antitrust in Zero-Price Markets: Applications' (2016) 94 Washington University Law Review 49

—— 'Antitrust in Digital Markets' (2019) 72 Vanderbilt Law Review 1497

—— 'Reactionary Antitrust' Concurrences no 4-2019, art no 92005 <www.concurrences.com/92005>

Newman P, 'Revenge: John Sherman, Russell Alger and the Origins of the Sherman Act' (2018) 174 Public Choice 257

Obear J, 'Move Last and Take Things: Facebook and Predatory Copying' (2018) 3 Columbia Business Law Review 994

Olbrich R and Grewe G, 'Consequences of Competition Between National Brands and Private Labels: Empirical Results from Different German Outlet Formats' (2009) 37 International Journal of Retail & Distribution Management 933

Orbach B, 'The Present New Antitrust Era' (2019) 60 William & Mary Law Review 1439

Padilla J, Perkins J and Piccolo S, 'Self-Preferencing in Markets with Vertically-Integrated Gatekeeper Platforms' (2020) <https://ssrn.com/abstract=3701250>

Pai A, 'Remarks on the 100th Anniversary of the Kingsbury Commitment' (TechFreedom Forum, Washington, DC, 19 December 2013)

Panzar J and Willig R, 'Economies of Scale in Multi-Output Production' (1977) 91 The Quarterly Journal of Economics 481

Panzar J and Willig R, 'Economies of Scope' (1981) 71 The American Economic Review 268

Parker G and Van Alstyne M, 'Two-Sided Network Effects: A Theory of Information Product Design' (2005) 51 Management Science 1494

Petit N, 'Theories of Self-Preferencing Under Article 102 TFEU: A Reply to Bo Vesterdorf' (2015) <https://ssrn.com/abstract=2592253>

—— 'Technology Giants, the "Moligopoly" Hypothesis and Holistic Competition: A Primer' (2016) <https://ssrn.com/abstract=2856502>

—— and Neyrinck N, 'Behavioral Economics and Abuse of Dominance: A Fresh Look at the Article 102 TFEU Case-Law' (2010) 6 ÖZK 203

—— and Neyrinck N, 'Back to Microsoft I and II: Tying and the Art of Secret Magic' (2011) 2 JECLAP 117

Petzold D, 'It Is All Predatory Pricing: Margin Squeeze Abuse and the Concept of Opportunity Costs in EU Competition Law' (2015) 6 JECLAP 346

Picker R, 'The Arc of Monopoly: A Case Study in Computing' (2020) 87 The University of Chicago Law Review 523

Podszun R, 'Innovation, Variety & Fair Choice – New Rules for the Digital Economy' (Expert Opinion for Finanzplatz München Initiative, 2017)

—— 'How to Reform the Law on Abusive Practices: The Study That Will Serve as a Basis for the Reform of Abusive Practices in Germany (and Europe?)' (2018) CPI Europe Column September

—— 'Digital Ecosystems, Decision-Making, Competition and Consumers – On the Value of Autonomy for Competition' (2019) <https://ssrn.com/abstract=3420692>

—— and Kreifels S, 'Digital Platforms and Competition Law' (2016) 5 Journal of European Consumer and Market Law 33

Popofsky M, 'Defining Exclusionary Conduct' (2006) 73 Antitrust Law Journal 435

Porter M, 'How Competitive Forces Shape Strategy' (1979) HBR March–April 137

Posner R, 'Natural Monopoly and Its Regulation' (1968) 21 Stanford Law Review 548

Prüfer J and Schottmüller C, 'Competing with Big Data' (2017) TILEC Discussion Paper 2017-6

Rahman S, 'Regulating Informational Infrastructure: Internet Platforms as the New Public Utilities' (2018) 2 Georgetown Law Technology Review 234

Rasmussen E, Ramseyer M and Wiley J, 'Naked Exclusion' (1991) 81 The American Economic Review 1137

Rato M and Petit N, 'Abuse of Dominance in Technology-Enabled Markets: Established Standards Reconsidered' (2013) 9 European Competition Journal 1

Renda A, 'Competition-Regulation Interface in Telecommunications: What's Left of the Essential Facility Doctrine' (2010) 34 Telecommunications Policy 23

Rietveld J, Schilling M and Bellavitis C, 'Platform Strategy: Managing Ecosystem Value Through Selective Promotion of Complements' (2019) 30 Organization Science 1232

Rochet J-C and Tirole J, 'Platform Competition in Two-Sided Markets' (2003) 1 Journal of the European Economic Association 990

—— and Tirole J, 'Two-Sided Markets: A Progress Report' (2006) 37 RAND Journal of Economics 645

Rysman M, 'The Economics of Two-Sided Markets' (2009) 23 Journal of Economic Perspectives 125

Sagers C, 'The Worst Opinion in Living Memory: AT&T/Time Warner and America's Broken Merger Law' (2019) <https://ssrn.com/abstract=3346431>

Salop S, 'An Enquiry Meet for the Case: Decision Theory, Presumptions, and Evidentiary Burdens in Formulating Antitrust Legal Standards' (2017) <https://ssrn.com/abstract=3068157>

—— 'The Raising Rivals' Cost Foreclosure Paradigm, Conditional Pricing Practices, and the Flawed Incremental Price-Cost Test' (2017) 81 Antitrust Law Journal 371

—— 'The AT&T/Time Warner Merger: How Judge Leon Garbled Professor Nash' (2018) 6 JAE 459

—— and Scheffman D, 'Raising Rivals' Costs' (1983) 73 American Economic Review 267

Schilling M, 'Towards Dynamic Efficiency: Innovation and Its Implications for Antitrust' (2015) 60 The Antitrust Bulletin 191

Schmitz J, 'What Determines Productivity? Lessons from the Dramatic Recovery of the U.S. and Canadian Iron Ore Industries Following Their Early 1980s Crisis' (2005) 113 Journal of Political Economy 582

Schrepel T, 'Antitrust Without Romance' (2019) <https://ssrn.com/abstract=3395001>

Schweitzer H, 'Parallels and Differences in the Attitudes Towards Single-Firm Conduct: What Are the Reasons? The History, Interpretation and Underlying Principles of Sec. 2 Sherman Act and Art. 82 EC' (2007) EUI Working Paper Law 2007/32

Shapiro C, 'Exclusionary Conduct' (Testimony before the Antitrust Modernization Commission, 2005)

—— 'Antitrust in a Time of Populism' (2018) 61 Journal of Industrial Organization 714

Shelanski H, 'Information, Innovation, and Competition Policy for the Internet' (2013) 161 University of Pennsylvania Law Review 1663

Sng Y, 'Tying Conduct Under Article 102 TFEU: Can Intervention against Google Be Justified?' (2016) 37 ECLR 406

Sohn G, 'A Policy Framework for an Open Internet Ecosystem' (2018) 2 Georgetown Law Technology Review 335

Sokol D, 'Vertical Mergers and Entrepreneurial Exit' (2018) 70 Florida Law Review 1357

Sousa Ferro M, 'De Gratis Non Curat Lex: Abuse of Dominance in Online Free Services' (2017) 12 Competition Law Review 153

Spulber D, 'Deregulating Telecommunications' (1995) 12 Yale Journal of Regulation 25

Srinivasan D, 'The Antitrust Case against Facebook' (2019) 16 Berkeley Business Law Journal 39

Stallibrass D and Pang S, 'Clash of Titans: How China Disciplines Internet Markets' (2015) 6 JECLAP 418

Steinbaum M and Stucke M, 'The Effective Competition Standard: A New Standard for Antitrust' (2018) Roosevelt Institute Issue Brief

Stephen Zoepf, 'The Economics of Ride Hailing, Revisited' (Statement, 2018)

Stucke M and Ezrachi A, 'How Digital Assistants Can Harm Our Economy, Privacy, and Democracy' (2017) 32 Berkeley Technology Law Journal 1239

Sussman S, 'Prime Predator: Amazon and the Rationale of Below Average Variable Cost Pricing Strategies Among Negative-Cash Flow Firms' (2019) 7 JAE 203

Taylor G, 'Search Quality and Revenue Cannibalization by Competing Search Engines' (2013) 22 Journal of Economics & Management Strategy 445

Todd P, 'Out of the Box: Illegal Tying and Google's Suite of Apps for the Android OS' (2017) 13 European Competition Journal 62

—— 'Digital Platforms and the Leverage Problem' (2019) 98 Nebraska Law Review 486

Tognato F, Picciano I and Marasà E, 'The Italian Competition Authority Fines an e-Commerce Company €1.128 Billion for Abuse of Dominance by Making Exclusive Advantages for its Online Marketplace Conditional upon the Purchase if Its Logistics Services (*Amazon*)' e-Competitions December 2021, art no 104177 <www.concurrences.com/104177>

Tom W and Wells, G 'Raising Rivals' Costs: The Problem of Remedies' (2003) 12 George Mason Law Review 389

Tucker C, 'Digital Data, Platforms and the Usual [Antitrust] Suspects: Network Effects, Switching Costs, Essential Facility' (2019) 54 Review of Industrial Organization 683

Ursic H, 'Unfolding the New-Born Right to Data Portability: Four Gateways to Data Subject Control' (2018) 15 Scripted 42

Vaheesan S, 'The Profound Nonsense of Consumer Welfare Antitrust' (2019) 64 The Antitrust Bulletin 479

van der Vijver T, 'Objective Justification and Article 102 TFEU' (2012) 35 World Competition 55

Varian H, 'Use and Abuse of Network Effects' (2017) <https://ssrn.com/abstract=3215488>

Vásquez Duque O, 'Active Choice vs. Inertia? An Exploratory Analysis of Choice Screens Applied in the European Microsoft Antitrust Case' (2021) <https://ssrn.com/abstract=3766468>

Vestager M, 'Clearing the Path for Innovation' (Web Summit, Lisbon, 7 November 2017)

—— 'Fairness and Competition' (GCLC Annual Conference, Brussels, 25 January 2018)

—— 'A Digital Future That Works for Europeans' (Business Forum of the German Ambassadors' Conference, Berlin, 27 August 2019)

—— 'Defining Markets in a New Age' (Chillin' Competition Conference, Brussels, 9 December 2019)

—— The Future of EU Merger Control' (International Bar Association 24th Annual Competition Conference, 11 September 2020)

Vesterdorf B, 'Theories of Self-Preferencing and Duty to Deal – Two Sides of the Same Coin?' (2015) 1 Competition Law & Policy Debate 4

—— and Fountoukakos K, 'An Appraisal of the Remedy in the Commission's *Google Search (Shopping)* Decision and a Guide to its Interpretation in Light of an Analytical Reading of the Case Law' (2018) 9 JECLAP 3

Waller SW, 'The "New" Law of Monopolization: An Examination of *MCI Communications Corp. v American Telephone & Telegraph Co*' (1983) 32 DePaul Law Review 595

Walton N, 'New Conglomerates and the Ecosystem Advantage' (2014) 13 China-USA Business Review 431

Weinberg M, 'The Price Effects of Horizontal Mergers' (2008) 4 JCLE 433

Weiser P, 'Regulating Interoperability: Lessons from *AT&T*, *Microsoft*, and Beyond' (2009) 76 Antitrust Law Journal 271

Wen W and Zhu F, 'Threat of Platform-Owner Entry and Complementor Responses? Evidence from the Mobile App Market' (2019) Strategic Management Journal 1336

Werbach K, 'A Layered Model for Internet Policy' (2002) 1 Journal of Telecommunications & High Technology Law 37

Werden G, 'The Law and Economics of the Essential Facility Doctrine' (1987) 32 Saint Louis University Law Journal 433

Weyl G, 'A Price Theory of Multi-Sided Platforms' (2010) 100 American Economic Review 1642

Whinston M, 'Tying, Foreclosure, and Exclusion' (1990) 80 The American Economic Review 837

—— 'Exclusivity and Tying in U.S. v. Microsoft: What We Know, and Don't Know' (2001) 15 Journal of Economic Perspectives 2001

Wils W, 'The Judgment of the EU General Court in *Intel* and the So-Called More Economic Approach to Abuse of Dominance' (2014) 37 World Competition 405

Winerman M, 'The Origins of the FTC: Concentration, Cooperation, Control, and Competition' (2003) 71 Antitrust Law Journal 1

Wright J, 'One-Sided Logic in Two-Sided Markets' (2004) 3 Review of Network Economics 44

—— Dorsey E, Klick J and Rybnicek J, 'Requiem for a Paradox: The Dubious Rise and Inevitable Fall of Hipster Antitrust' (2019) 51 Arizona State Law Journal 293

Wu T, 'Network Neutrality, Broadband Discrimination' (2003) 2 Journal on Telecommunications & High Technology Law 141

—— 'After Consumer Welfare, Now What? The "Protection of Competition" Standard in Practice' (2018) CPI Antitrust Chronicle April

—— 'Tech Dominance and the Policeman at the Elbow' (2019) Columbia Public Law Research Paper 14-623

—— 'The *American Express* Opinion, the Rule of Reason, and Tech Platforms' (2019) 7 JAE 117

Wyman O, 'Assessing the Impact of Big Tech on Venture Investment' (Report commissioned by Facebook, 2018)

Yoo Y, Boland R, Lyytinen K and Majchrzak A, 'Organizing for Innovation in the Digital World' (2012) 23 Organization Science 1398

Zhang V, contribution to 'The First Antitrust Decision by the Chinese Supreme People's Court: Qihoo 360 vs. Tencent' (transcript of CPI webinar, 16 December 2014)

Zhu F, 'Friends or Foes? Examining Platform Owners' Entry into Complementors' Spaces' (2019) 28 Journal of Economics & Management Strategy 23

—— and Liu Q, 'Competing with Complementors: An Empirical Look at Amazon.com' (2018) 39 Strategic Management Journal 2618

Zittrain J, 'The Generative Internet' (2006) Harvard Law Review 1974

Zoepf S, Chen S, Adu P and Pozo G, 'The Economics of Ride-Hailing: Driver Revenue, Expenses and Taxes' (2018) MIT CEEPR Working Paper 2018-5

Online Reviews, Blogs, Newspapers and Other Websites

—— '172 Malicious Apps with 335M+ Installs Found on Google Play' (*The Next Web*, 1 October 2019) <https://thenextweb.com/apps/2019/10/01/google-play-android-malware-2/>

—— 'Amazon's Share of US eCommerce Sales Hits All-Time High of 56.7% in 2021' (*PYMNTS*, 14 March 2022) <https://www.pymnts.com/news/retail/2022/amazons-share-of-us-ecommerce-sales-hits-all-time-high-of-56-7-in-2021/>

—— 'American Tech Giants Are Making Life Tough for Startups' (*The Economist*, 2 June 2018) <https://www.economist.com/business/2018/06/02/american-tech-giants-are-making-life-tough-for-startups>

—— 'Apple's Move to Services' (*Digital Innovation and Transformation*, 22 April 2018) <https://digital.hbs.edu/platform-digit/submission/the-app-store-apples-move-to-services/>

—— 'Data Transfer Project Overview and Fundamentals' <https://datatransferproject.dev/>

—— 'Fortnite Reluctantly Comes to Google Play Store' (*BBC*, 22 April 2020) <www.bbc.com/news/technology-52383286>

—— 'How to Make Sense of the Latest Tech Surge' (*The Economist*, 20 February 2020) <https://www.economist.com/leaders/2020/02/20/how-to-make-sense-of-the-latest-tech-surge>

—— 'LyricFind Offers Corrections to Inaccuracies in Wall Street Journal Reporting' (*LyricFind*, 17 June 2019) <https://celebrityaccess.com/2019/06/18/lyricfind-disputes-genius-lyric-theft-claim-challenges-wsj-reporting/>

—— 'The *New* Four Horsemen of Tech' (*CNN Money*) <https://money.cnn.com/technology/storysupplement/four-horsemen-of-tech/>

—— 'Qustodio & Kidslox File a Complaint against Apple with the European Commission over Abuse of Dominant Position' (*Globenewswire*, 30 April 2019) <https://www.globenewswire.com/news-release/2019/04/30/1812192/0/en/Qustodio-Kidslox-File-a-Complaint-Against-Apple-with-the-European-Commission-over-Abuse-of-Dominant-Position.html>

—— 'Regulation is Good for Goldman' (*WSJ*, 11 February 2015) <https://www.wsj.com/articles/regulation-is-good-for-goldman-1423700859>

—— 'Russian Regulator Says Apple in Breach of Mobile Apps Market Regulations' (*Interfax*, 10 August 2020) <https://interfax.com/newsroom/top-stories/69512/>

—— 'The Story of the Internet Is All About Layers' (*The Economist*, 28 June 2018) <https://www.economist.com/special-report/2018/06/28/the-story-of-the-internet-is-all-about-layers>

—— 'The Tech Giants Are Still in Rude Health' (*The Economist*, 4 August 2018) <www.economist.com/business/2018/08/04/the-tech-giants-are-still-in-rude-health>

—— 'What If Large Tech Firms Were Regulated Like Sewage Companies?' (*The Economist*, 23 September 2017) <https://www.economist.com/business/2017/09/23/what-if-large-tech-firms-were-regulated-like-sewage-companies>

—— 'You've Been Sherlocked' (*The Economist*, 13 July 2012) <https://www.economist.com/babbage/2012/07/13/youve-been-sherlocked>

Albergotti R, 'How Apple Uses Its App Store to Copy the Best Ideas' (*WaPo*, 5 September 2019) <https://www.washingtonpost.com/technology/2019/09/05/how-apple-uses-its-app-store-copy-best-ideas/>

Amadeo R, 'Google's Iron Grip on Android: Controlling Open Source by any Means Necessary' (*Ars Technica*, 21 October 2013) <https://arstechnica.com/gadgets/2018/07/googles-iron-grip-on-android-controlling-open-source-by-any-means-necessary/>

Amazon, 'Fulfilment by Amazon – benefits' <https://sell.amazon.de/en/versand-durch-amazon> and <https://services.amazon.co.uk/services/fulfilment-by-amazon/features-benefits.html>

—— 'What is Prime Music?' <https://www.amazon.com/primeinsider/music/set-up-music.html>

Angwin J and Mattu S, 'Amazon Says It Puts Customers First. But Its Pricing Algorithm Doesn't' (*ProPublica*, 20 September 2016) <https://www.propublica.org/article/amazon-says-it-puts-customers-first-but-its-pricing-algorithm-doesnt>

Apple, 'App Store – Principles and Practices' <www.apple.com/ios/app-store/principles-practices/>

—— App Store Review Guidelines <https://developer.apple.com/app-store/review/guidelines/>

—— 'Move from Android to iPhone, iPad, or iPod touch' <https://support.apple.com/en-us/HT201196>

—— 'Privacy' <www.apple.com/privacy/>

—— 'Addressing Spotify's claims' (press release, 14 March 2019) <www.apple.com/newsroom/2019/03/addressing-spotifys-claims/>

—— 'The facts about parental control apps' (press release, 28 April 2019) <www.apple.com/mg/newsroom/2019/04/the-facts-about-parental-control-apps/>

Bennett N, 'Charting the Rise of Open Banking Payments' (*TrueLayer blog*, 3 November 2022) <https://truelayer.com/blog/product/charting-the-rise-of-open-banking-payments/>

Berzon A, Shifflett S and Scheck J, 'Amazon Has Ceded Control of Its Site. The Result: Thousands of Banned, Unsafe or Mislabeled Products' (*WSJ*, 23 August 2019) <https://www.wsj.com/articles/amazon-has-ceded-control-of-its-site-the-result-thousands-of-banned-unsafe-or-mislabeled-products-11566564990>

Bessarabova E, 'To Android and Back: How to Port your iOS App to Android and Vice Versa?' (*Mind Studios*, 12 May 2018) <https://themindstudios.com/blog/port-ios-app-to-android-and-vice-versa/>

Bezos J, '2018 Letter to Shareholders' (*Day One – the Amazon blog*, 11 April 2019) <https://blog.aboutamazon.com/company-news/2018-letter-to-shareholders>

Bhardwaj P, 'As Snapchat Growth Stalls Out, Facebook Stories Hits 150 Million Daily Active Users' (*Business Insider*, 18 May 2018) <https://www.businessinsider.com/facebook-stories-versus-snapchat-users-2018-5>

Bork R, 'What Antitrust Is All About' (*NYT*, 4 May 1998) <https://www.nytimes.com/1998/05/04/opinion/what-antitrust-is-all-about.html>

Bostoen F, 'Venture Capital and Antitrust: On Exit Strategies, Killer Acquisitions, and Innovation Harms' (*CoRe Blog*, 23 April 2000) <https://www.lexxion.eu/coreblogpost/venture-capital-and-antitrust/>

—— '"We Have Reached 'Peak Cloning' in Silicon Valley": When Does Copying Your Competitor's Product Become Anticompetitive?' (*CoRe Blog*, 26 September 2019) <https://coreblog.lexxion.eu/anticompetitive-copying/>

—— 'Abuse of Relative Dominance in the Platform Economy: A French Court Finds Amazon's Contracts with Third-Party Sellers Significantly Imbalanced' (*CoRe Blog*, 12 November 2019) <https://coreblog.lexxion.eu/amazon-case-france/>

—— 'Disruptions vs Refusals of Supply: A Guide to the Case Law' (*CoRe Blog*, 4 May 2022) <https://www.lexxion.eu/coreblogpost/disruptions-vs-refusals-of-supply/>

—— 'Requiem for an Objection: The Commission Drops Half of Its App Store Case' (*CoRe Blog*, 8 March 2023) <https://www.lexxion.eu/coreblogpost/requiem-for-an-objection/>

Capital Forum, 'Amazon: By Prioritizing Its Own Fashion Label Brands in Product Placement on Its Increasingly Dominant Platform, Amazon Risks Antitrust Enforcement by a Trump Administration' (Brief, 2016)

Chee Y and Dave P, 'Google's Jobs Search Draws Antitrust Complaints from Rivals' (*Reuters*, 13 August 2019) <https://www.reuters.com/article/us-eu-google-antitrust-exclusive/exclusive-googles-jobs-search-draws-antitrust-complaints-from-rivals-idUSKCN1V30IX>

Clover J, 'App Developers Claim Apple's iOS 13 Location Tracking Changes Are Anti-Competitive' (*MacRumors*, 16 August 2019) <https://www.macrumors.com/2019/08/16/app-developers-tracking-restrictions-ios-13/>

Coates K, 'Ex-Post and Ex-Ante Rules' (*21st Century Competition*, 6 August 2020) <https://www.twentyfirstcenturycompetition.com/2020/08/ex-ante-and-ex-post/>

—— 'Data: The Uniqueness of the Dataset and the Slope of the Value Curve' (*21st Century Competition*, 1 November 2020) <https://www.twentyfirstcenturycompetition.com/2020/11/data-the-uniqueness-of-the-dataset-and-the-slope-of-the-value-curve/>

Constine J, 'Snapchat Growth Slowed 82% After Instagram Stories Launched' (*TechCrunch*, 2 February 2017) <https://techcrunch.com/2017/02/02/slowchat/>

—— 'Instagram Stories Hits 200M Users, Surpassing Snapchat as It Copies Its AR Stickers' (*TechCrunch*, 13 April 2017) <https://techcrunch.com/2017/04/13/instagram-stories-bigger-than-snapchat/>

—— 'Facebook Will Shut Down Its Spyware VPN App Onavo' (*TechCrunch*, 22 February 2019) <https://techcrunch.com/2019/02/21/facebook-removes-onavo/>

Crawford S, 'Calling Facebook a Utility Would Only Make Things Worse' (*Wired*, 20 April 2018) <https://www.wired.com/story/calling-facebook-a-utility-would-only-make-things-worse/>

Creswell J, 'How Amazon Steers Shoppers to Its Own Products' (*NYT*, 23 June 2018) <https://www.nytimes.com/2018/06/23/business/amazon-the-brand-buster.html>

Dougherty C, 'Inside Yelp's Six-Year Grudge against Google' (*NYT*, 1 July 2017) <https://www.nytimes.com/2017/07/01/technology/yelp-google-european-union-antitrust.html> and a supporting website 'Focus on the user' set up by Yelp, TripAdvisor and others <http://focusontheuser.eu/>

Dredge S, 'ERA Says Apple's HMV App Ban Raises "Serious Issues of Competition"' (*Musically*, 22 October 2013) <http://musically.com/2013/10/22/era-says-apples-hmv-app-ban-raises-serious-issues-of-competition/>

Dwoskin E, 'Facebook's Willingness to Copy Rivals' Apps Seen as Hurting Innovation' (*WaPo*, 10 August 2017) <https://www.washingtonpost.com/business/economy/facebooks-

willingness-to-copy-rivals-apps-seen-as-hurting-innovation/2017/08/10/ea7188ea-7df6-11e7-a669-b400c5c7e1cc_story.html>

Dzieza J, 'Prime and Punishment: Dirty Dealing in the $175 Billion Amazon Marketplace' (*The Verge*, 19 December 2018) <https://www.theverge.com/2018/12/19/18140799/>

EC, 'Telecommunications' (overview, 18 December 2019) <https://ec.europa.eu/competition/sectors/telecommunications/overview_en.html>

Eikelboom J and Maalderink J, 'Mens gebruikte 20 duizend jaar geleden al geen Yahoo' (*De Speld*, 19 June 2017) <https://speld.nl/2017/06/19/mens-gebruikte-20-duizend-jaar-geleden-al-geen-yahoo/>

Elstrom P and Chen L, 'Alibaba's New Chairman Says He Has to Reinvent Retail Before Someone Else Does' (*Bloomberg*, 9 September 2019) <https://www.bloomberg.com/news/articles/2019-09-09/alibaba-s-new-chair-says-he-ll-find-the-way-to-kill-his-business>

Evans B, 'Apple, Services and Moats' (*Benedict Evans*, 13 September 2019) <https://www.ben-evans.com/benedictevans/2019/9/13/Apple-services-moats>

—— 'How to Lose a Monopoly' (*Benedict Evans*, 1 January 2020) <https://www.ben-evans.com/benedictevans/2020/01/01/microsoft-monopoly-and-dominance>

—— 'When Big Tech Buys Small Tech' (*Benedict Evans*, 12 November 2021) <https://www.ben-evans.com/benedictevans/2021/11/12/when-big-tech-buys-small-tech>

Evans D and Schmalensee R, 'What Platforms Do Differently than Traditional Businesses' (*HBR*, 11 May 2016) <https://hbr.org/2016/05/what-platforms-do-differently-than-traditional-businesses>

Faife C, 'Security Experts Say New EU Rules Will Damage WhatsApp Encryption' (*The Verge*, 28 May 2022) <https://www.theverge.com/2022/3/28/23000148/>

Fishkin R, 'Less Than Half of Google Searches Now Result in a Click' (*SparkToro*, 17 June 2019) <https://sparktoro.com/blog/less-than-half-of-google-searches-now-result-in-a-click/>

Fried I and McCabe D, 'DOJ Antitrust Official: Supreme Court Ruling Won't Shield Big Tech' (*Axios*, 26 June 2018) <https://www.axios.com/makan-delrahim-in-aspen-1530038874-a289ad1a-012b-4ccb-9cb7-69658ee78c33.html>

Frier S, 'The Number Facebook Won't Say' (*Bloomberg*, 6 October 2020) <https://www.bloomberg.com/news/newsletters/2020-10-06/the-number-facebook-won-t-say>

Gallagher B, 'Copycat: How Facebook Tried to Squash Snapchat' (*Wired*, 16 February 2018) <https://www.wired.com/story/copycat-how-facebook-tried-to-squash-snapchat/>

Gennai P, 'Presenting Search App and Browser Options to Android Users in Europe' (*The Keyword – Google Blog*, 18 April 2019) <https://www.blog.google/around-the-globe/google-europe/presenting-search-app-and-browser-options-android-users-europe/>

Geuss M, 'Which Browser Should You Use?' (*PCWorld*, 26 February 2012) <https://www.pcworld.com/article/250566/which_browser_should_you_use_.html>

Giammona C, 'Amazon's Whole Foods Price Cuts Brought 25% Jump in Shoppers' (*Bloomberg*, 11 September 2017) <https://www.bloomberg.com/news/articles/2017-09-11/amazon-s-whole-foods-price-cuts-brought-25-jump-in-customers>

Google, 'About Us' <https://www.google.com/about/our-company/>

—— 'Design for Android' Quality Guidelines <https://developer.android.com/design>

—— 'Search Quality Evaluator Guidelines' <https://static.googleusercontent.com/media/guidelines.raterhub.com/en//searchqualityevaluatorguidelines.pdf>

Gordon A and Mehrotra D, 'Uber and Lyft Take a Lot More from Drivers than They Say' (*Jalopnik*, 26 August 2019) <https://jalopnik.com/uber-and-lyft-take-a-lot-more-from-drivers-than-they-sa-1837450373>

Greene J, 'Amazon Tests Pop-Up Feature Touting Its Lower-Priced Products' (*WSJ*, 15 March 2019) <https://www.wsj.com/articles/amazon-tests-pop-up-feature-touting-its-lower-priced-products-11552655614>

—— 'Aggressive Amazon Tactic Pushes You to Consider Its Own Brand Before You Click "Buy"' (*WaPo*, 28 August 2019) <https://www.washingtonpost.com/technology/2019/08/27/aggressive-amazon-tactic-pushes-you-consider-its-own-brand-before-you-click-buy/>

Greiff B, 'Study: Google Is the Biggest Beneficiary of the GDPR' (*Cliqz*, 10 October 2018) <https://cliqz.com/en/magazine/study-google-is-the-biggest-beneficiary-of-the-gdpr>

Griffith E, 'Will Facebook Kill All Future Facebooks?' (*Wired*, 25 October 2017) <https://www.wired.com/story/facebooks-aggressive-moves-on-startups-threaten-innovation/>

Gryta T, Hagey K, Cimilluca D and Sharma A, 'AT&T Reaches Deal to Buy Time Warner for $85.4 Billion' (*WSJ*, 22 October 2016) <https://www.wsj.com/articles/at-t-reaches-deal-to-buy-time-warner-for-more-than-80-billion-1477157084>

Hagey K and Ngo V, 'How Google Edged Out Rivals and Built the World's Dominant Ad Machine: A Visual Guide' (*WSJ*, 7 November 2019) <https://www.wsj.com/articles/how-google-edged-out-rivals-and-built-the-worlds-dominant-ad-machine-a-visual-guide-11573142071>

Hagiu A and Wright J, 'Do You Really Want to Be an eBay?' (*HBR*, March 2013) <https://hbr.org/2013/03/do-you-really-want-to-be-an-ebay>

Halpern S, 'The search for anti-conservative bias on Google' (*The New Yorker*, 19 December 2018) <https://www.newyorker.com/tech/annals-of-technology/the-search-for-anti-conservative-bias-on-google>

Harford T, 'The Case for Ending Amazon's Dominance' (*FT*, 19 January 2018) <https://www.ft.com/content/aba8d444-fb94-11e7-a492-2c9be7f3120a>

Harris T, 'EU Should Regulate Facebook and Google as "Attention Utilities"' (*FT*, 1 March 2020) <https://www.ft.com/content/abd80d98-595e-11ea-abe5-8e03987b7b20>

Hathaway I, 'Platform Giants and Venture-Backed Startups' (personal blog, 12 October 2018) <http://www.ianhathaway.org/blog/2018/10/12/platform-giants-and-venture-backed-startups>

Haucap J, 'The Facebook Decision: First Thoughts' (*D'Kart*, 7 February 2019) <https://www.d-kart.de/the-facebook-decision-first-thoughts-by-haucap/>

Heckmann O, 'Changes to Google Shopping in Europe' (*Ads & Commerce – Google Blog*, 27 September 2017) <https://www.blog.google/products/ads/changes-to-google-shopping-in-europe>

Hodgson M, 'Interoperability Without Sacrificing Privacy: Matrix and the DMA' (*Matrix blog*, 25 March 2022) <https://matrix.org/blog/2022/03/25/interoperability-without-sacrificing-privacy-matrix-and-the-dma>

Hollister S, 'With Edge, Microsoft's Forced Windows Updates Just Sank to a New Low' (*The Verge*, 2 July 2020) <https://www.theverge.com/21310611/>

Hovenkamp H, 'The Warren Campaign's Antitrust Proposals' (*The Regulatory Review*, 25 March 2019) <https://www.theregreview.org/2019/03/25/hovenkamp-warren-campaigns-antitrust-proposals/>

Hsu T, 'For Many Facebook Users, a "Last Straw" That Led Them to Quit' (*NYT*, 21 March 2018) <https://www.nytimes.com/2018/03/21/technology/users-abandon-facebook.html>

Hughes C, 'It's Time to Break Up Facebook' (*NYT*, 9 May 2019) <https://www.nytimes.com/2019/05/09/opinion/sunday/chris-hughes-facebook-zuckerberg.html>

Ibáñez Colomo P, 'How to Distinguish Between Tying and Refusal to Deal Cases (Hint: It's Not Just Words)' (*Chillin' Competition*, 24 April 2015) <https://chillingcompetition.com/2015/04/24/>

—— 'Against the Footballisation of Competition Policy: How to Advance the General Interest and Avoid Polarisation' (*Chillin' Competition*, 18 September 2019) <https://chillingcompetition.com/2019/09/18/>

—— 'Is It an Abuse for Apple to Embed a Camera in Its iPhones? What Is Special and Different about Digital Cases' (*Chillin' Competition*, 21 July 2020) <https://chillingcompetition.com/2020/07/21/>

Isaac M, 'Zuckerberg Plans to Integrate WhatsApp, Instagram and Facebook Messenger' (*NYT*, 25 January 2019) <https://www.nytimes.com/2019/01/25/technology/facebook-instagram-whatsapp-messenger.html>

Jeffries A, 'How Google Eats a Business Whole' (*The Outline*, 17 April 2017) <https://theoutline.com/post/1399/how-google-ate-celebritynetworth-com?zd=1&zi=6sl4cz6sW>

Jia J, Jin G and Wagman L, 'The Short-Run Effects of GDPR on Technology Venture Investment' (*Vox – CEPR Policy Portal*, 7 January 2019) <https://voxeu.org/article/short-run-effects-gdpr-technology-venture-investment>

Kalra A and Stecklow S, 'Amazon Copied Products and Rigged Search Results to Promote Its Own Brands, Documents Show' (*Reuters*, 13 October 2021) <https://www.reuters.com/investigates/special-report/amazon-india-rigging/>

Kanter J, 'Google Offers Concessions to Europe After Record Antitrust Fine' (*NYT*, 27 September 2017) <https://www.nytimes.com/2017/09/27/business/google-eu-antitrust.html>

Kaplan J and Boyle M, 'Amazon Cuts Whole Foods Prices as Much as 43% on First Day' (*Bloomberg*, 28 August 2017) <https://www.bloomberg.com/news/articles/2017-08-28/amazon-cuts-prices-at-whole-foods-as-much-as-50-on-first-day>

Kaspersky Team, 'Kaspersky's Antitrust Complaint against Apple in Russia' (*Kaspersky Daily*, 19 March 2019) <www.kaspersky.com/blog/apple-fas-complaint/26017/>

—— 'Kaspersky Statement on the FAS ruling in the Antimonopoly Investigation against Apple' (Kaspersky, 10 August 2020) <https://www.kaspersky.com/about/press-releases/2020_kaspersky-statement-on-the-fas-ruling-in-the-antimonopoly-investigation-against-apple>

Kastrenakes J, 'Facebook is Shutting Down a Teen App It Bought Eight Months Ago' (*The Verge*, 2 July 2018) <https://www.theverge.com/2018/7/2/17528896/>

Kaziukėnas J, 'Amazon Takes a 50% Cut of Seller's Revenue' (*Marketplace Pulse*, 23 February 2023) <https://www.marketplacepulse.com/articles/amazon-takes-a-50-cut-of-sellers-revenue>

Kim E, 'Amazon Quietly Removes Promotional Spots That Gave Special Treatment to its Own Products as Scrutiny of Tech Giants Grows' (*CNBC*, 3 April 2019) <https://www.cnbc.com/2019/04/03/amazon-removes-special-promo-spots-for-private-label-products.html>

King A, 'Apple Officially Unveils TV+ – Get Ready for Some Serious Bundling' (*Digital Music News*, 1 November 2019) <https://www.digitalmusicnews.com/2019/11/01/apple-tv-plus-launch/>

Kornblum J, 'Netscape Sets Source Code Free' (*CNET*, 31 March 1998) <https://www.cnet.com/news/netscape-sets-source-code-free/>

Kosta M, 'Switzerland: So Many Guns, No Mass Shootings' (*The Daily Show*, 9 December 2018) <https://www.youtube.com/watch?v=KjlT4BME2aE>

Kumar Singh R and Ganapavaram A, 'GE, an Industrial Conglomerate Pioneer, to Break Up' (*Reuters*, 10 November 2021) <https://www.reuters.com/business/ge-form-three-public-companies-2021-11-09/>

Lai E, 'IE Still Top Dog Over Firefox in Corporate Browser Kennel' (*Computerworld*, 11 January 2008) <https://www.computerworld.com/article/2538552/>

Lamadrid de Pablo A, 'Google Shopping Decision – First Urgent Comments' (*Chillin' Competition*, 27 June 2017) <https://chillingcompetition.com/2017/06/27/>

Lepore J, 'The Disruption Machine: What the Gospel of Innovation Gets Wrong' (*The New Yorker*, 16 June 2014) <https://www.newyorker.com/magazine/2014/06/23/the-disruption-machine#>

Levy S, 'Inside Chrome: The Secret Project to Crush IE and Remake the Web' (*Wired*, 2 September 2008) <https://www.wired.com/2008/09/mf-chrome/>

Livingston A, 'Best Batteries' (*consumersearch*, 17 July 2017) <https://www.consumersearch.com/batteries>

Lockheimer H, 'Complying with the EC's Android Decision' (*The Keyword – Google Blog*, 16 October 2018) <https://www.blog.google/around-the-globe/google-europe/complying-ecs-android-decision/>

Lomas N, 'Don't Break Up Big Tech – Regulate Data Access, Says EU Antitrust Chief' (*TechCrunch*, 11 March 2019) <https://techcrunch.com/2019/03/11/dont-break-up-big-tech-regulate-data-access-says-eu-antitrust-chief/>

—— 'Aptoide, a Play Store Rival, Cries Antitrust Foul over Google Hiding Its App' (*TechCrunch*, 4 June 2019) <https://techcrunch.com/2019/06/04/aptoide-a-playstore-rival-cries-antitrust-foul-over-google-hiding-its-app/>

Mândrescu D, 'Lessons and Questions from *Google Android* – Part 1: The Market Definition' (*CoRe Blog*, 29 October 2019) <https://coreblog.lexxion.eu/lessons-and-questions-from-google-android-part-1-the-market-definition/

—— '*Slack v. Microsoft* – More Than Just Another Tying Case' (*CoRe Blog*, 27 August 2020) <https://www.lexxion.eu/coreblogpost/slack-v-microsoft-more-than-just-another-tying-case/>

Manjoo F, 'Why Facebook Keeps Beating Every Rival: It's the Network, of Course' (*NYT*, 19 April 2017) <https://www.nytimes.com/2017/04/19/technology/facebook-snapchat-instagram-innovation.html>

Marlinspike M, 'Reflections: The Ecosystem Is Moving' (*Signal blog*, 10 May 2016) <https://signal.org/blog/the-ecosystem-is-moving/>

Marson I, 'Still "No Demand" for Media-Player-Free Windows' (*CNET*, 18 November 2005) <https://www.cnet.com/news/still-no-demand-for-media-player-free-windows/>

Matsakis L, 'Facebook Dating Looks a Whole Lot Like Hinge' (*Wired*, 3 May 2018) <https://www.wired.com/story/facebook-dating-hinge-app/>

Mattioli D, 'Amazon Changed Search Algorithm in Ways That Boost its Own Products' (*WSJ*, 16 September 2019) <https://www.wsj.com/articles/amazon-changed-search-algorithm-in-ways-that-boost-its-own-products-11568645345>

—— 'Amazon Scooped Up Data from Its Own Sellers to Launch Competing Products' (*WSJ*, 23 April 2020) <https://www.wsj.com/articles/amazon-scooped-up-data-from-its-own-sellers-to-launch-competing-products-11587650015>

McMillan R, 'Lyrics Site Accuses Google of Lifting Its Content' (*WSJ*, 16 June 2019) <https://www.wsj.com/articles/lyrics-site-genius-com-accuses-google-of-lifting-its-content-11560677400>

Meyers P, 'Google's Walled Garden: Are We Being Pushed Out of Our Own Digital Backyards?' (*Moz Blog*, 27 February 2018) <https://moz.com/blog/googles-walled-garden>

Mickle T, 'Apple Dominates App Store Search Results, Thwarting Competitors' (*WSJ*, 23 July 2019) <https://www.wsj.com/articles/apple-dominates-app-store-search-results-thwarting-competitors-11563897221>

Microsoft, 'Fact Sheet: Windows XP N Sales' (*Microsoft*, April 2006) <https://regmedia.co.uk/2009/06/12/microsoft_windows_xp_n_fact_sheet.pdf>

Mims C, '"Too Complex to Break Up" Is the New "Too Big to Fail"' (*WSJ*, 10 October 2020) <https://www.wsj.com/articles/too-complex-to-break-up-is-the-new-too-big-to-fail-11602302406>

Miranda L, 'Amazon Sellers Say the Tech Giant Is Crushing Them with Competitive Pricing' (*BuzzFeedNews*, 7 June 2018) <https://www.buzzfeednews.com/article/leticiamiranda/amazon-sellers-say-the-tech-giant-is-crushing-them-with#.jdyrW1KZj>

Molla R, 'Amazon's Tiny Profits, Explained' (*Recode*, 24 October 2019) <https://www.vox.com/recode/2019/8/21/20826405/amazons-profits-revenue-free-cash-flow-explained-charts>

Monegro J, 'Fat Protocols' (*Union Square Ventures*, 8 August 2016) <http://www.usv.com/blog/fat-protocols>

Moore J, 'Predators and Prey: A New Ecology of Competition' (*HBR*, May–June 1993) <https://hbr.org/1993/05/predators-and-prey-a-new-ecology-of-competition>

Morland W, 'Data Transfer Project: Enabling Portability of Photos and Videos Between Services' (*Facebook Engineering*, 2 December 2019) <https://engineering.fb.com/2019/12/02/security/data-transfer-project/>

Morris B and Seetharaman D, 'The New Copycats: How Facebook Squashes Competition from Startups' (*WSJ*, 9 August 2017) <https://www.wsj.com/articles/the-new-copycats-how-facebook-squashes-competition-from-startups-1502293444>

Mullins B, Winkler R and Kendall B, 'Inside the U.S. Antitrust Probe of Google' (*WSJ*, 19 March 2015) <https://www.wsj.com/articles/inside-the-u-s-antitrust-probe-of-google-1426793274

Nicas J, 'Apple Cracks Down on Apps That Fight iPhone Addiction' (*NYT*, 27 April 2019) <https://www.nytimes.com/2019/04/27/technology/apple-screen-time-trackers.html>

—— 'Apple Backs Off Crackdown on Parental-Control Apps' (*NYT*, 3 June 2019) <https://www.nytimes.com/2019/06/03/technology/apple-parental-control-apps.html>

—— and Collins K, 'How Apple's Apps Topped Rivals In the App Store It Controls' (*NYT*, 9 September 2019) <https://www.nytimes.com/interactive/2019/09/09/technology/apple-app-store-competition.html>

—— and Isaac M, 'Facebook Takes the Gloves Off in Feud with Apple' (*NYT*, 16 December 2020) <https://www.nytimes.com/2020/12/16/technology/facebook-takes-the-gloves-off-in-feud-with-apple.html>

Niu E, 'Apple Music Is Boosting Services Revenue, but Not Profits' (*The Motley Fool*, 17 April 2018) <https://www.fool.com/investing/2018/04/17/apple-music-is-boosting-services-revenue-but-not-p.aspx>

Oliver J, 'Net Neutrality II' (*Last Week Tonight*, 7 May 2017) <https://www.youtube.com/watch?v=92vuuZt7wak>

Pasquale F, 'From Territorial to Functional Sovereignty: The Case of Amazon' (*Law and Political Economy Blog*, 6 December 2017) <https://lpeblog.org/2017/12/06/from-territorial-to-functional-sovereignty-the-case-of-amazon/#more-442>

Peters J, 'Apple Acquires Popular Weather App Dark Sky and Will Shut Down the Android Version' (*The Verge*, 31 March 2020) <https://www.theverge.com/2020/3/31/21201666/>

Philips J, 'The "Frightful Five" Aren't So Scary, as Long as They're Competing' (*The NYT*, 8 May 2017) <https://www.nytimes.com/2017/05/08/business/dealbook/the-frightful-five-arent-so-scary-as-long-as-theyre-competing.html>

Picker R, 'Breaking up Amazon? Platforms, Private Labels and Entry' (*Truth on the Market*, 17 July 2019) <https://truthonthemarket.com/2019/07/17/breaking-up-amazon-platforms-private-labels-and-entry/>

Porter J, 'You Can Now Waste $139 on a Wooden Case for Your Precious Apple Card' (*The Verge*, 2 September 2019) <https://www.theverge.com/tldr/2019/9/2/20844377/>

Rankin J, 'Third-Party Sellers and Amazon – A Double-Edged Sword in e-Commerce' (*The Guardian*, 23 June 2015) <https://www.theguardian.com/technology/2015/jun/23/amazon-marketplace-third-party-seller-faustian-pact>

Reece M, 'Micro.blog Moving iOS App to React Native' (*Michael Tsai Blog*, 10 February 2020) <https://mjtsai.com/blog/2022/02/10/micro-blog-moving-ios-app-to-react-native/>

Richards M, 'Big Tech Platforms Could Be Broken Up, Says Nobel-Winning Economist' (*Global Competition Review*, 18 January 2019) <https://globalcompetitionreview.com/big-tech-platforms-could-be-broken-says-nobel-winning-economist>

Rockoff J and Loftus P, 'Johnson & Johnson's Breakup: What to Know' (*WSJ*, 12 November 2021) <https://www.wsj.com/articles/johnson-johnsons-breakup-what-to-know-11636715701>

Rubin B, 'Amazon "Probably Copied Us" on Echo Show, Startup CEO Says' (*CNET*, 10 May 2017) <https://www.cnet.com/news/amazon-echo-show-alexa-probably-copied-us-nucleus-intercom-startup-ceo-says/>

Salgar S, 'How We Help You Find Lyrics in Google Search' (*The Keyword – Google Blog*, 18 June 2019) <https://blog.google/products/search/how-we-help-you-find-lyrics-google-search/>

Samat S, 'Building a Better Shopping Experience' (*Google Commerce Blog*, 31 May 2012) <https://commerce.googleblog.com/2012/05/building-better-shopping-experience.html>

Sawers P, 'Inside Matrix, the Protocol That Might Finally Make Messaging Apps Interoperable' (*TechCrunch*, 30 December 2022) <https://techcrunch.com/2022/12/30/inside-matrix-the-protocol-that-might-finally-make-messaging-apps-interoperable>

Schechter A, 'Richard Posner: "The Real Corruption Is the Ownership of Congress by the Rich"' (*ProMarket*, 28 March 2017) <https://promarket.org/richard-posner-real-corruption-ownership-congress-rich/>

—— 'Google and Facebook's "Kill Zone": "We've Taken the Focus Off of Rewarding Genius and Innovation to Rewarding Capital and Scale"' (*ProMarket*, 25 May 2018) <https://promarket.org/google-facebooks-kill-zone-weve-taken-focus-off-rewarding-genius-innovation-rewarding-capital-scale/>

Schonfeld E, 'Eric Schmidt's Gang of Four: Google, Apple, Amazon, and Facebook' (*TechCrunch,* 1 June 2011) <https://techcrunch.com/2011/05/31/schmidt-gang-four-google-apple-amazon-facebook/>

Scott M, 'Coronavirus Crisis Shows Big Tech for What It Is – A 21st Century Public Utility' (*Politico*, 25 March 2020) <https://www.politico.eu/article/coronavirus-big-tech-utility-google-facebook/>

Seetharaman D and Morris B, 'Facebook's Onavo Gives Social-Media Firm Inside Peek at Rivals' Users' (*WSJ*, 13 August 2017) <https://www.wsj.com/articles/facebooks-onavo-gives-social-media-firm-inside-peek-at-rivals-users-1502622003>

Seufert E, 'Lose-Lose' (*Mobile Dev Demo*, 30 November 2022) <https://mobiledevmemo.com/lose-lose/>

Shady S, 'Understanding How Amazon's Use of Capital Leases Overstates Its Cash Flow Metrics' (*Seeking Alpha*, 9 December 2014) <https://seekingalpha.com/article/2743335-understanding-how-amazons-use-of-capital-leases-overstates-its-cash-flow-metrics>

Shieber J, 'Venture Investors and Startup Execs Say They Don't Need Elizabeth Warren to Defend Them from Big Tech' (*TechCrunch*, 8 March 2019) <https://techcrunch.com/2019/03/08/venture-investors-and-startup-execs-say-they-dont-need-elizabeth-warren-to-defend-them-from-big-tech/>

Shields T, 'DirecTV to Hike Prices After Owner AT&T Promised Cheaper Bills' (*Bloomberg*, 14 March 2019) <https://www.bloomberg.com/news/articles/2019-03-14/directv-to-hike-prices-after-owner-at-t-promised-cheaper-bills>

Singer H and Sussman S, 'Can It. Amazon Is *Not* Your Typical Grocery Store' (*Wired*, 4 May 2020) <https://www.wired.com/story/opinion-can-it-amazon-is-not-your-typical-grocery-store/>

Singhal A, 'Introducing the Knowledge Graph: things, not strings' (*Inside Search – Google Blog*, 16 May 2012) <https://search.googleblog.com/2012/05/introducing-knowledge-graph-things-not.html>

Smith A, 'How to Port your iOS App to Android' (*Marino Software*, 30 January 2018) <https://www.marinosoftware.com/insights/so-you-want-to-port-to-android>

Smith N, 'Amazon's Winner-Take-All Approach to Small Business' (*Bloomberg*, 19 February 2019) <https://www.bloomberg.com/opinion/articles/2019-02-19/amazon-uses-search-to-undercut-small-businesses-on-its-site>

Solon O and Wong JC, 'Jeff Bezos v the World: Why All Companies Fear "Death by Amazon"' (*The Guardian*, 24 April 2018) <https://www.theguardian.com/technology/2018/apr/24/amazon-jeff-bezos-customer-data-industries>

Soper S, 'Got a Hot Seller on Amazon? Prepare for E-Tailer to Make One Too' (*Bloomberg*, 20 April 2016) <https://www.bloomberg.com/news/articles/2016-04-20/got-a-hot-seller-on-amazon-prepare-for-e-tailer-to-make-one-too>

Spotify, 'Time to Play Fair' <https://www.timetoplayfair.com/>

—— 'Time to Play Fair – Frequently Asked Questions' <www.timetoplayfair.com/frequently-asked-questions/>

Stapp A, 'Amazon, Antitrust, and Private Label Goods' (*Progressive Policy Institute*, 24 April 2020) <https://www.progressivepolicy.org/pressrelease/amazon-antitrust-and-private-label-goods/>

Statt N, 'Facebook May Copy Your App, but Amazon Will Copy Your Shoe' (*The Verge*, 19 September 2019) <https://www.theverge.com/tldr/2019/9/19/20874818/>

Steele A and Mickle T, 'Apple Music Overtakes Spotify in Paid U.S. Subscribers' (*WSJ*, 5 April 2019) <https://www.wsj.com/articles/apple-music-overtakes-spotify-in-u-s-subscribers-11554475924>

Sterling G, 'Google Wins Vertical Search Antitrust Case in Germany' (*Search Engine Land*, 7 May 2013) <https://searchengineland.com/google-wins-vertical-search-antitrust-case-in-germany-158544>

Stone B, 'What's in Amazon's Box? Instant Gratification' (*Bloomberg*, 24 November 2010) <https://www.bloomberg.com/news/articles/2010-11-24/whats-in-amazons-box-instant-gratification>

Streitfeld D, 'Amazon's Antitrust Antagonist Has a Breakthrough Idea' (*NYT*, 7 September 2018) <https://www.nytimes.com/2018/09/07/technology/monopoly-antitrust-lina-khan-amazon.html>

Stucke M and Ezrachi A, 'The Rise, Fall and Rebirth of the U.S. Antitrust Movement' (*HBR*, 15 December 2017) <https://hbr.org/2017/12/the-rise-fall-and-rebirth-of-the-u-s-antitrust-movement>

Sweney M, 'Spotify UK Revenues Surge to Almost £190M as Mobile Subscriptions Take Off' (*The Guardian*, 14 October 2016) <https://www.theguardian.com/media/2016/oct/14/spotify-uk-revenues-surge-to-almost-190m-as-mobile-subscriptions-take-off>

Teachout Z, *Break 'Em Up: Recovering Our Freedom from Big Ag, Big Tech, and Big Money* (St Martin's Press 2020); Jonathan Taplin, 'Is It Time to Break Up Google?' (*NYT*, 22 April 2017) <https://www.nytimes.com/2017/04/22/opinion/sunday/is-it-time-to-break-up-google.html>

Thompson B, 'Apple's Middle Age' (*Stratechery*, 5 February 2018) <https://stratechery.com/2018/apples-middle-age/>

—— 'Where Warren's Wrong' (*Stratechery*, 12 March 2019) <https://stratechery.com/2019/where-warrens-wrong/>

—— 'Day Two to One Day' (*Stratechery*, 17 September 2019) <https://stratechery.com/2019/day-two-to-one-day/>

—— 'A Framework for Regulating Competition on the Internet' (*Stratechery*, 9 December 2019) <https://stratechery.com/2019/a-framework-for-regulating-competition-on-the-internet/>

—— 'The End of the Beginning' (*Stratechery*, 7 January 2020) <https://stratechery.com/2020/the-end-of-the-beginning/>

Thorne J and Mathur P, 'The Year in Charts: VC Defies 2020 Expectations Despite the Pandemic' (*Pitchbook*, 21 December 2020) <https://pitchbook.com/news/articles/2020-vc-in-charts>

Tiku N, 'Do Not Mistake Orrin Hatch for #HipsterAntitrust' (*Wired*, 3 August 2017) <https://www.wired.com/story/orrin-hatch-antitrust-hipster-antitrust/>

Tirole J, 'Regulating the Disruptors' (*Project Syndicate*, 9 January 2019) <https://www.project-syndicate.org/onpoint/regulating-the-disrupters-by-jean-tirole-2019-01>

Tynan D, 'The 25 Worst Tech Products of All Time' (*PCWorld*, 26 May 2006) <https://www.pcworld.com/article/125772/>

Vaheesan S, 'How Robert Bork Fathered the New Gilded Age' (*ProMarket*, 5 September 2019) <https://promarket.org/how-robert-bork-fathered-the-new-gilded-age/>

Van Alstyne M, Parker G and Choudary S, 'Pipelines, Platforms, and the New Rules of Strategy' (*HBR*, April 2016) <https://hbr.org/2016/04/pipelines-platforms-and-the-new-rules-of-strategy>

—— and Schrage M, 'The Best Platforms Are More than Matchmakers' (*HBR*, 2 August 2016) <https://hbr.org/2016/08/the-best-platforms-are-more-than-matchmakers>

Vincent J, 'Amazon and Walmart Hit Hard After New e-Commerce Rules in India Restrict Sales' (*The Verge*, 1 February 2019) <https://www.theverge.com/2019/2/1/18206538/>

Viswanathan P, 'iOS App Store vs. Google Play Store for App Developers' (*Lifewire*, 24 January 2019) <https://www.lifewire.com/ios-app-store-vs-google-play-store-for-app-developers-2373130>

Warner B, 'How Google Uses Content Theft and Algorithm Updates to Maintain Its Search Monopoly' (*Medium*, 16 October 2019) <https://medium.com/@brianwarner/how-google-uses-content-theft-and-algorithm-updates-to-maintain-its-search-monopoly-a5aeed4a53e4>

Warren E, 'Here's How We Can Break Up Big Tech' (*Medium*, 8 March 2019) <https://medium.com/@teamwarren/heres-how-we-can-break-up-big-tech-9ad9e0da324c>

—— 'Bill Gates Thinks Windows Mobile Would Have Beaten Android Without Microsoft's Antitrust Woes' (*The Verge*, 6 November 2019) <https://www.theverge.com/2019/11/6/20952370/>

—— 'Microsoft's New Edge Chromium Browser Launches on Windows and MacOS' (*The Verge*, 15 January 2020) <https://www.theverge.com/2020/1/15/21066767/>

Weise K, 'Prime Power: How Amazon Squeezes the Businesses Behind Its Store' (*NYT*, 19 December 2019) <https://www.nytimes.com/2019/12/19/technology/amazon-sellers.html>

Welch C, 'Amazon Will Soon Stop Selling All Nest Products' (*The Verge*, 3 March 2018) <https://www.theverge.com/2018/3/3/17074844/>

Wild M, 'Products vs Protocols: What Signal Got Right' (*Snikket blog*, 9 February 2021) <https://snikket.org/blog/products-vs-protocols/>

Winkler E, 'How HBO's Blackout on Dish Could Affect AT&T' (*WSJ*, 26 November 2018) <https://www.wsj.com/articles/how-hbos-blackout-on-dish-could-affect-at-t-1543235401>

Woodcock R, 'The Time's Elastic Concept of Monopoly' (*What Am I Missing?*, 16 December 2019) <https://zephyranth.pw/2019/12/16/the-times-elastic-conception-of-monopoly/>

Wu T, 'The Case for Breaking Up Instagram and Facebook' (*WaPo*, 28 September 2018) <https://www.washingtonpost.com/outlook/2018/09/28/case-breaking-up-facebook-instagram/>

—— 'Antitrust Revival, a Reading List' (*Medium*, 18 November 2019) <https://medium.com/@superwuster/antitrust-revival-a-reading-list-8ff8bcca0d67>

—— 'The Utah Statement: Reviving Antimonopoly Traditions for the Era of Big Tech' (*Medium*, 18 November 2019) <https://onezero.medium.com/the-utah-statement-reviving-antimonopoly-traditions-for-the-era-of-big-tech-e6be198012d7>

—— 'Ben Thompson's "Stratechery": Smart, but a Little Too Much Kool-Aid' (*Medium*, 29 October 2020) <https://superwuster.medium.com/reviewing-ben-thompsons-stratechery-45b545dd959>

—— and Thompson S, 'The Roots of Big Tech Run Disturbingly Deep' (*NYT*, 7 June 2019) <https://www.nytimes.com/interactive/2019/06/07/opinion/google-facebook-mergers-acquisitions-antitrust.html>

Zhang J, 'Alibaba Shares Soar After Historic Overhaul Heralds IPO Wave' (*Bloomberg*, 28 March 2023) <https://www.bloomberg.com/news/articles/2023-03-28/alibaba-splits-into-six-units-that-may-pursue-individual-ipos>

Zhu F and Iansiti M, 'Why Some Platforms Thrive and Others Don't' (*HBR*, January–February 2019) <https://hbr.org/2019/01/why-some-platforms-thrive-and-others-dont>

Zuckerberg M, 'Four Ideas to Regulate the Internet' (*Facebook Newsroom*, 30 March 2019) <https://newsroom.fb.com/news/2019/03/four-ideas-regulate-internet/>

Policy Papers and Reports, Guidelines, Press Releases

ACM, 'ACM warns telecom companies about net neutrality' (press release, 12 July 2016) <https://www.acm.nl/en/publications/publication/16037/ACM-warns-telecom-companies-about-net-neutrality>

—— 'A Closer Look at Online Video Platforms' (Report, 2018)

—— 'ACM launches investigation into abuse of dominance by Apple in its App Store' (press release, 11 April 2019) <https://www.acm.nl/en/publications/acm-launches-investigation-abuse-dominance-apple-its-app-store>

—— 'Market Study into Mobile App Stores' (Report, 2019) ACM/18/032693

AdlC, 'Apple's implementation of the ATT framework: the Autorité does not issue urgent interim measures against Apple but continues to investigate into the merits of the case' (press release, 17 March 2021) <https://www.autoritedelaconcurrence.fr/en/communiques-de-presse/targeted-advertising-apples-implementation-att-framework-autorite-does-not>

—— 'Targeted advertising/Apple's implementation of the ATT framework' (press release, 17March2021)<https://www.autoritedelaconcurrence.fr/en/press-release/targeted-advertising-apples-implementation-att-framework-autorite-does-not-issue>

—— and Bundeskartellamt, 'Competition Law and Data' (Joint Report, 2016)

—— and CMA, 'The Economics of Open and Closed Systems' (Report, 2014)

AGCM, 'Commitments offered by Booking.com: closed the investigation in Italy, France and Sweden' (press release, 21 April 2015) <http://www.agcm.it/en/newsroom/press-releases/2207>

—— 'Amazon: investigation launched on possible abuse of a dominant position in online marketplaces and logistic services' (press release, 16 April 2019) <https://en.agcm.it/en/media/press-releases/2019/4/A528>

—— 'Amazon fined over €1,128 billion for abusing its dominant position' (press release, 9 December 2021) <https://en.agcm.it/en/media/press-releases/2021/12/A528>

—— 'Japan Fair Trade commission closes App Store investigation' (press release, 1 September 2021) <https://www.apple.com/newsroom/2021/09/japan-fair-trade-commission-closes-app-store-investigation/>

Article 29 Data Protection Working Party, 'Right to data portability' (Guidelines, 2016)

Belgische Mededingingsautoriteit, 'Prijsniveau in supermarkten' (Study, 2012)

Bourreau M and de Streel A, 'Digital Conglomerates and EU Competition Policy' (CERRE Report, 2019)

Bundeskartellamt, 'The Market Power of Platforms and Networks' (Working Paper, 2016)

—— 'The Market Power of Platforms and Networks' (Working Paper – English summary, 2016)

—— and BWB, 'Transaction Value Thresholds for Mandatory Pre-merger Notification (Guidance, 2018)

CMA, 'Energy Market Investigation' (Final Report, 2016)

—— 'Mobile Ecosystems' (Market Study Interim Report, 2021)

—— 'Online Platforms and Digital Advertising Market Study' (Final Report, 2020)

—— 'Online Choice Architecture: How Digital Design Can Harm Competition and Consumers' (Discussion Paper, 2022)

Commission 'Competition Law 4.0', 'A New Competition Framework for the Digital Economy' (Report for the Federal Ministry for Economic Affairs and Energy, 2019)

Crémer J, de Montjoye Y-A and Schweitzer H, 'Competition Policy for the Digital Era' (Special Advisers' Report, 2019)

Digital Markets Taskforce, 'A New Pro-Competition Regime for Digital Markets' (Advice, 2020)

DOJ, 'Merger Remedies' (Policy Guide, 2011)

—— 'Justice Department allows Comcast–NBCU joint venture to proceed with conditions' (press release, 18 January 2018) <https://www.justice.gov/opa/pr/justice-department-allows-comcast-nbcu-joint-venture-proceed-conditions>

—— and Stanford University, 'Venture Capital and Antitrust' (Transcript of Public Workshop, 12 February 2020)

EC, 'Competition Policy' (XIVth report, 1985)

—— 'Competition Policy' (XXVIIth Report, 1997)

—— 'Commission Notice on the definition of relevant market for the purposes of Community competition law' [1997] OJ C372/5, para 7

—— 'Settlement reached with Belgacom on the publication of telephone directories – ITT withdraws complaint' (press release, 11 April 1997) IP/97/292

—— 'Notice on the application of the competition rules to access agreements in the telecommunications sector – framework, relevant markets and principles' [1998] OJ C265/2

—— 'Guidelines on the assessment of horizontal mergers under the Council Regulation on the control of concentrations between undertakings' [2004] OJ C31/5

—— 'The Application of Article 82 of the Treaty to Exclusionary Abuses' (Discussion Paper, 2005)

—— 'Commission Notice on remedies acceptable under Council Regulation (EC) No 139/2004' [2008] OJ C267/1

—— 'Guidelines on the assessment of non-horizontal mergers under the Council Regulation on the control of concentrations between undertakings' [2008] OJ C265/6

—— 'Guidance on the Commission's enforcement priorities in applying Article 82 of the EC Treaty to abusive exclusionary conduct by dominant undertakings' [2009] OJ C 45/7

—— 'Commission fines Microsoft for non-compliance with browser choice commitments' (press release, 6 March 2013) IP/13/196

—— 'Regulatory environment for platforms, online intermediaries, data and cloud computing and the collaborative economy' (Public Consultation, 2015)

—— 'Evaluation of procedural and jurisdictional aspects of EU merger control' (Consultation, 2016)

—— 'Online Platforms' (Staff Working Document) SWD(2016)172

—— 'Public consultation on the regulatory environment for platforms, online intermediaries and the collaborative economy' (Synopsis Report, 2016)

—— 'Mid-Term Review on the implementation of the Digital Single Market Strategy' (Communication) SWD(2017)155

—— 'Commission fines Google €2.42 billion for abusing dominance as search engine by giving illegal advantage to own comparison shopping service' (Factsheet, 27 June 2017) MEMO/17/1785

—— 'Commission fines Google €2.42 billion for abusing dominance as search engine by giving illegal advantage to own comparison shopping service' (press release, 27 June 2017) IP/17/1784

—— 'Guidelines on market analysis and the assessment of significant market power under the EU regulatory framework for electronic communications networks and services' (Communication) C(2018)2374

—— 'Commission Recommendation on relevant product and service markets within the electronic communications sector susceptible to *ex ante* regulation in accordance with Directive (EU) 2018/1972', C(2020)8750

—— 'Commission opens investigations into Apple's App Store rules' (press release, 16 June 2020) IP/20/1073

—— 'Commission Notice Guidelines on ranking transparency pursuant to Regulation (EU) 2019/1150' [2020] OJ C424/1

—— 'Commission sends Statement of Objections to Amazon for the use of non-public independent seller data and opens second investigation into its e-commerce business practices' (press release, 10 November 2020) IP/20/2077

—— 'Explanatory Note accompanying the document Commission Recommendation on relevant product and service markets within the electronic communications sector susceptible to *ex ante* regulation in accordance with Directive (EU) 2018/1972' (Staff Working Document) SWD(2020)337

—— 'Commission Guidance on the application of the referral mechanism set out in Article 22 of the Merger Regulation to certain categories of cases' (Communication) C(2021)1959

—— 'Commission sends Statement of Objections to Apple on App Store rules for music streaming providers' (press release, 30 April 2021) IP/21/2061

—— 'Commission sends Statement of Objections to Apple over practices regarding Apple Pay' (press release, 2 May 2022) IP/22/2764

—— 'Guidelines on vertical restraints' (Communication) [2022] OJ C248/1

—— 'Guidelines on the application of Article 81(3) of the Treaty' [2004] OJ C101/97

—— 'Commission sends Statement of Objections to Apple clarifying concerns over App Store rules for music streaming providers' (press release, 28 February 2023) IP/23/1217

EP, 'Supporting consumer rights in the digital single market' (Resolution) 2014/2973(RSP)

—— 'Online Platforms and the Digital Single Market' (Report) A8-0204/2017

—— 'On the Annual Report on Competition Policy' (Report) A8-0049/2018

FAS, 'FAS recognized Apple as abusing its dominant position in the application distribution market' [translation] (press release, 10 August 2020) <https://fas.gov.ru/news/30275>

FCC, 'Porting: Keeping Your Phone Number When You Change Providers' <https://www.fcc.gov/consumers/guides/porting-keeping-your-phone-number-when-you-change-providers>

Franck J-U and Peitz M, 'Market Definition and Market Power in the Platform Economy' (CERRE Report, 2019)

FTC, 'The Commission's Divestiture Process' (Study, 1999)

—— 'FTC closes its investigation into Facebook's proposed acquisition of Instagram photo sharing program' (press release, 22 August 2012) <https://www.ftc.gov/news-events/press-releases/2012/08/ftc-closes-its-investigation-facebooks-proposed-acquisition>

—— 'Google agrees to change its business practices to resolve FTC competition concerns in the markets for devices like smart phones, games and tablets, and in online search' (press release, 3 January 2013) <https://www.ftc.gov/news-events/press-releases/2013/01/google-agrees-change-its-business-practices-resolve-ftc>

—— 'FTC notifies Facebook, WhatsApp of privacy obligations in light of proposed acquisition' (press release, 10 April 2014) <https://www.ftc.gov/news-events/press-releases/2014/04/ftc-notifies-facebook-whatsapp-privacy-obligations-light-proposed>

—— 'Statement of Acting Director of the Bureau of Competition on the Agency's review of Amazon.com's Acquisition of Whole Foods Market' (press release, 23 August 2017) <https://www.ftc.gov/news-events/press-releases/2017/08/statement-federal-trade-commissions-acting-director-bureau>

—— 'Federal Trade Commission withdraws Vertical Merger Guidelines and Commentary' (press release, 15 September 2021) <https://www.ftc.gov/news-events/news/press-releases/2021/09/federal-trade-commission-withdraws-vertical-merger-guidelines-commentary>

—— 'Non-HSR Reported Acquisitions by Select Technology Platforms, 2010–2019' (Study, 2021)

—— 'Merger Retrospective Program' <https://www.ftc.gov/policy/studies/merger-retrospective-program

Furman J, Coyle D, Fletcher A, McAuley D and Marsden P, 'Unlocking Digital Competition' (Digital Competition Expert Panel's Report, 2019)

GMC, 'Competition Policy: The Challenge of Digital Markets (Special Report, 2015)

Heike Schweitzer H et al, 'Modernising the Law on Abuse of Market Power – Summary of the Report's Recommendations' (Report for the Federal Ministry for Economic Affairs, 2018)

Hellenic Competition Commission, 'Basic Consumer Goods' (Sector Inquiry, 2020) <https://www.epant.gr/en/enimerosi/sector-inquiry-into-basic-consumer-goods.html>

House Democrats, 'Crack Down on Corporate Monopolies & the Abuse of Economic and Political Power' (A Better Deal) <https://abetterdeal.democraticleader.gov/the-proposals/crack-down-on-abuse-of-power/>

House of Lords Select Committee on European Union, 'Online platforms and the Digital Single Market' (Report of Session, 2016)

ICN, 'Survey on Dominance/Substantial Market Power in Digital Markets' (Report on the Results, 2020)

Information Service High Authority of the European Community for Coal and Steel, 'The General Common Market' (Spaak Report, 1956)

Lear, 'Ex-Post Assessment of Merger Control Decisions in Digital Markets' (Final Report, 2019)

Lianos I, 'General Conceptual Framework' in BRICS Competition Law and Policy Centre (ed), 'Digital Era Competition: A BRICS View' (Report, 2020)

OECD, 'Margin Squeeze' (Roundtable) DAF/COMP(2009)36

—— Structural Separation in Regulated Industries (Recommendation) C(2016)11-C/M(2016)3

—— 'Structural Separation in Regulated Industries: Implementing the OECD Recommendation' (Report, 2016)

—— 'Competition Issues in Aftermarkets' (Background Note) DAF/COMP(2017)2

—— 'Competition Issues in Aftermarkets' (Note from the European Union) DAF/COMP/WD(2017)3

—— 'Implications of e-Commerce for Competition Policy' (Background Note) DAF/COMP(2018)3

—— 'Abuse of Dominance in Digital Markets' (Background Note, 2020)

—— 'Line of Business Restrictions' (Background Note) DAF/COMP/WP2(2020)1

Office of Competition and Consumer Protection, 'Procedure against Allegro' (press release, 10 December 2019) <https://www.uokik.gov.pl/news.php?news_id=16014>

Office of Competition and Consumer Protection, 'President of UOKiK issued two decisions concerning Allegro's practices' (press release, 29 December 2022) <https://uokik.gov.pl/news.php?news_id=19185>

Schweitzer H et al, 'Modernisierung der Missbrauchsaufsicht für marktmächtige Unternehmen' (Report for the Federal Ministry for Economic Affairs, 2018)

Schweitzer H et al, 'Modernising the Law on Abuse of Market Power – Summary of the Report's Recommendations' (Report for the Federal Ministry for Economic Affairs, 2018)

Shah S, Brody R and Olson N, 'The Regulator of Tomorrow: Rulemaking and Enforcement in an Era of Exponential Change' (Report, 2015)

Stigler Committee, 'Digital Platforms' (Final Report, 2019)

UK Government, 'A New Pro-Competition Regime for Digital Markets' (July 2021) CP 489

—— 'Government Response to the Consultation on a New Pro-Competition Regime for Digital Markets' (May 2022) CP 657

UNCTAD, 'Enforcement of Competition Policy in the Retail Sector: Competition Issues in the Food Retail Chain' (Note by the Secretariat) TD/B/C.I/CLP/38

US House of Representatives – Judiciary Subcommittee on Antitrust, 'Investigation of Competition in Digital Markets' (Majority Staff Report and Recommendations, 2020)

US Senate (62nd Congress), Hearing before the Committee on Interstate Commerce S Res 98, vol 1

van Gorp N and de Bijl P, 'Digital Gatekeepers: Assessing Exclusionary Conduct' (Discussion Paper commissioned by the Dutch Ministry of Economic Affairs, 2019)

Wismer S and Rasek A, 'Market Definition in Multi-Sided Markets' in OECD (ed), 'Rethinking Antitrust Tools for Multi-Sided Platforms' (Report, 2018)

INDEX

D

E

F

G

I

S

T

U

INSTITUTE of
Competition Law
Antitrust databases and resources

The Institute of Competition Law

The Institute of Competition Law is a publishing company, founded in 2004 by Dr. Nicolas Charbit, based in Paris, London and NewYork. The Institute cultivates scholarship and discussion about antitrust issues though publications and conferences. Each publication and event is supervised by editorial boards and scientific or steering committees to ensure independence, objectivity, and academic rigor. Thanks to this management, the Institute has become one of the few think tanks in Europe to have significant influence on antitrust policies.

Aim

The Institute focuses government, business and academic attention on a broad range of subjects which concern competition laws, regulations and related economics.

Boards

To maintain its unique focus, the Institute relies upon highly distinguished editors, all leading experts in national or international antitrust: Bill Kovacic, Mario Monti, Eleanor Fox, Laurence Idot, Frédéric Jenny, Ioannis Lianos, Richard Whish, etc.

Authors

4,000 authors, from 85 jurisdictions.

Partners

- Universities: University College London, King's College London, Queen Mary University, Paris Sorbonne Panthéon-Assas, etc.
- Law firms: Allen & Overy, Cleary Gottlieb Steen & Hamilton, Baker McKenzie, Hogan Lovells, Jones Day, Norton Rose Fulbright, Skadden Arps, White & Case, etc.

Events

Brussels, Dusseldorf, Hong Kong, London, Milan, New York, Paris, Singapore, Warsaw and Washington, DC.

Online version

Concurrences website provides all articles published since its inception.

Publications

The Institute publishes Concurrences Review, a print and online quarterly peer-reviewed journal dedicated to EU and national competitions laws. e-Competitions is a bi-monthly antitrust news bulletin covering 85 countries. The e-Competitions database contains over 23,000 case summaries from 4,000 authors.

www.ingramcontent.com/pod-product-compliance
Lightning Source LLC
Chambersburg PA
CBHW071415230926
51846CB00001B/96
9781954750111